AF594028

FROM ABOVE

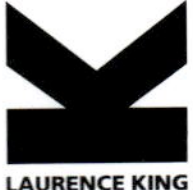

Published in 2019 by
Laurence King Publishing Ltd
361–373 City Road
London, EC1V 1LR
United Kingdom
T + 44 (0)20 7841 6900
F + 44 (0)20 7841 6910
enquiries@laurenceking.com
www.laurenceking.com

Texts compiled by Gemma Padley.

A catalogue record for this book is available from the British Library

ISBN: 978-1-78627-521-9

Printed in China

Commissioning editor: John Parton
Editor: Blanche Craig
Designer: Alexandre Coco
Picture researcher: Louise Thomas

FROM ABOVE

The Story of Aerial Photography

Eamonn McCabe & Gemma Padley

Laurence King Publishing

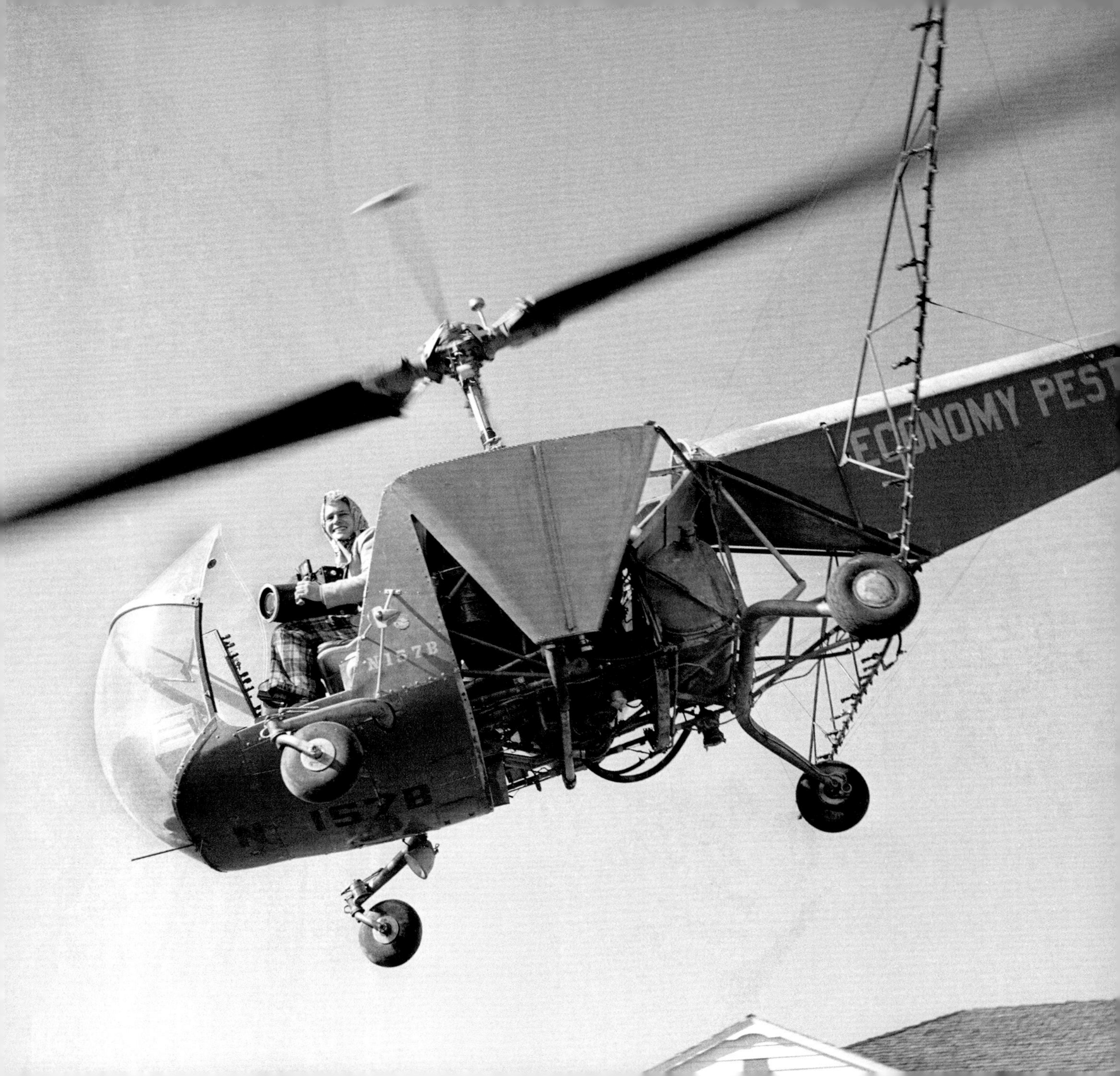

ECONOMY PEST
N157B
N 157B

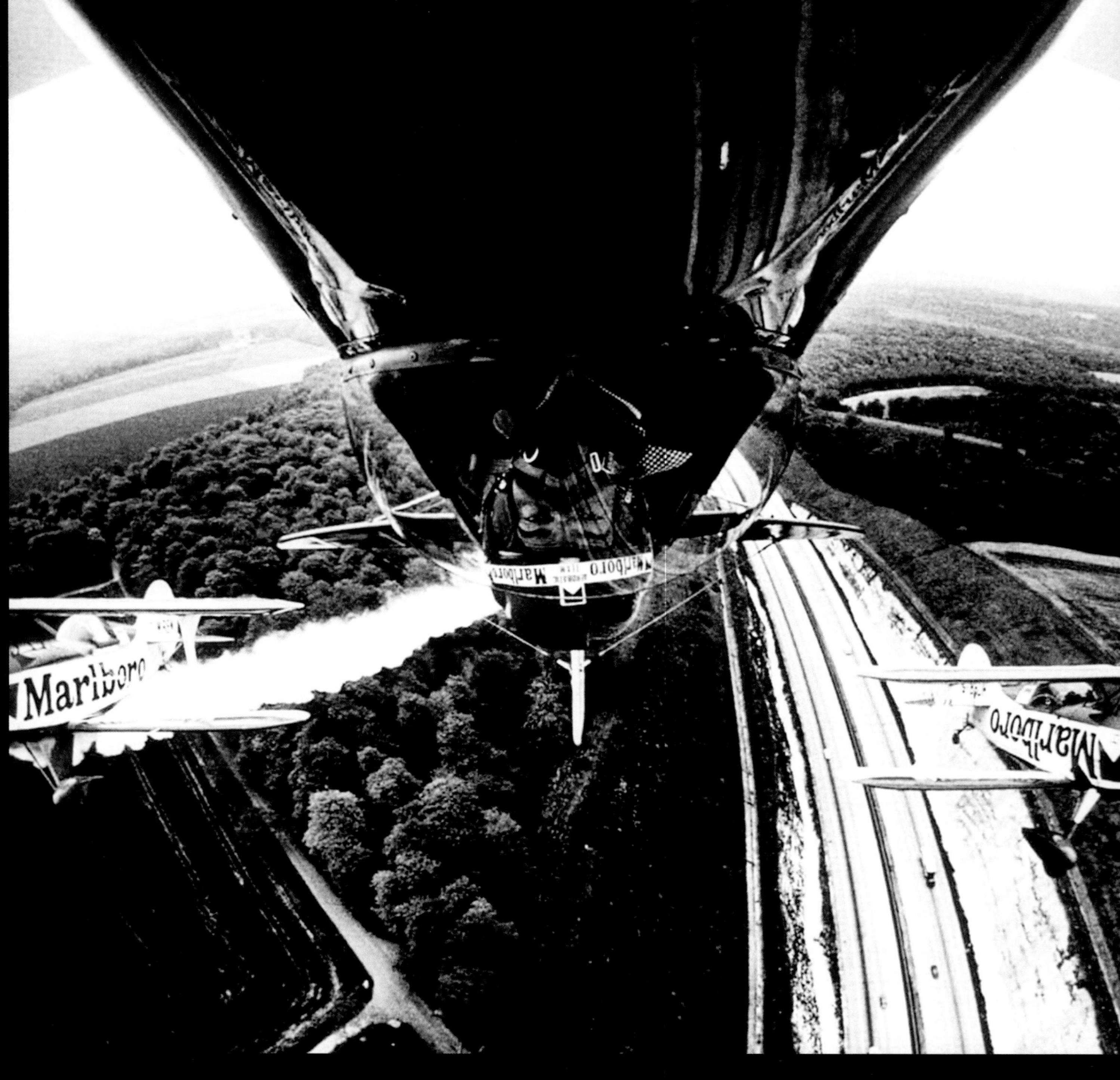
Marlboro
Marlboro
Marlboro

Eamonn McCabe
Phil Meeson participating in the Aerobatics World Championships, London, England, 1982.

The history of aerial photography has mirrored the history of photography itself. Without those early pioneers who had to solve the problem of how to take an image from high above the Earth while often flying a balloon or aircraft at the same time, we may never have had the invention of the digital camera or now ubiquitous mobile-phone camera.

From the moment that Nadar flew high above Paris in the 1850s, photographers were inspired to invent new ways of capturing the beauty of our world from the sky – and indeed, without their efforts, the manufacturer Hasselblad would never have been asked to adapt their famous camera so that it could record the mysterious landscape of the moon a century later. Hasselblad's famous lenses are now being used in their thousands on drones produced in China – a technological development that has allowed us to photograph places we would never have been able to reach before, some wonderful examples of which appear in this book.

I have taken photographs from helicopters from high above transatlantic yacht races. The unique view you get is stunning, if a little scary when your seat breaks and you realize the door is missing! But the craziest job I ever did was to photograph an aerobatics team sitting – or should that be, hanging – upside down in an open biplane.

The first thing Phil Meeson, the leader of the Marlboro Aerobatic Team, said to me when I arrived at the small aerodrome hidden away in the Surrey countryside was: 'Have you had breakfast?'

I am not a great flyer at the best of times, let alone with the prospect of taking photographs upside down from an open plane.

'No, I'm fine,' I insisted. 'I've had some tea and I'm a bit twitchy about what we are about to get up to, but I'll be fine.'

But Phil insisted, so I joined his small team of ex-colonial flyers in the canteen and nervously tucked into bacon, eggs and fried bread ... and even more tea.

'Right,' he said. 'Now what do you want to do?'

The night before I had drawn up a rough plan of action. I thought if we could fly upside down in the lead plane and get his two mates to fly close behind us in a sort of Red Arrows formation I would have my picture to show to *The Observer*, the newspaper I was working for at the time.

'Easy,' he said. 'That's level one!'

I began by sitting in the front of a two-seater biplane with Phil a few feet behind me. Practising, I put my camera over my head looking back at him, then taped the focus ring of the camera so that it wouldn't move when we turned upside down. All pretty easy so far, but we were still on the ground.

We soon bumped our way across the grassy airfield and my adrenaline kicked in. But deep down I was wondering what on earth I had agreed to. We took off into a bright, cloudless sky and I relaxed a little; after all, Phil was one of the world's best. We were both kitted out in Biggles-style helmets and goggles and looked the part. So far, so good.

Once airborne we soon flipped upside down. Immediately, both my seatbelts slipped off the shoulders of the trendy photographer's leather jacket I was wearing. My heart was in my mouth. What was keeping me in this tiny capsule with no roof and a flimsy piece of plastic barely sufficient to block out the wind on a Lambretta?

I soon realized I wasn't going to fall out because the belt around my waist was keeping me in. Regaining some composure I drew my camera over my head and over the plastic shield, but the G-force then hit me so hard that the camera kept coming back over my head. This was nothing like being on the ground. But I forced my arms back again, then spotted Phil's two colleagues in perfect formation. 'Brilliant,' I thought. 'I've got it.' I took a few extra shots, just to be on the safe side.

To my relief, Phil then turned the plane the right way up. He tapped me on the shoulder, and I turned and gave him the thumbs up – just as I'd seen it done in war movies. But Phil took it to mean that my stomach was alright and proceeded to go through the whole routine for the forthcoming World

Championships, for which he was the favourite. It seemed to last forever; several series of loop the loops just like in the cartoons, often narrowly avoiding a collision with his two teammates. It must have looked impressive from the ground but it frightened the life out of me.

And then for his party piece. Phil flew straight up to heaven, turned around at St Peter's Gate and then flew straight down towards the ground at what seemed like hundreds of miles an hour. And, don't forget, I was in the front seat. Then, with the motorway fast approaching, the engine cut out. My first thought was that Phil was dead. Meanwhile the joystick was spinning out of control between my legs. Should I grab it? Was this some sort of initiative test?

I tried to remain calm by reminding myself that Phil was in the running for World Champion. And if I pulled the joystick, I could kill us both. Then, suddenly, the engine started up again; Phil had bump-started it like some old banger. I have never in my life since been so relieved to hear the sound of an engine.

Afterwards I sat in the tiny car park, unable to drive for hours. I had been looking at the world through a 16mm-wide lens, upside down. I had seen the world looking like a tiny Woolworths snow globe to me, curving away at the sides, so how could I drive on it? But at least I was now the right way up … and *The Observer* loved the picture.

It has been a real pleasure to research this book, and to discover the work of so many great photographers – some of whom, such as the legendary Edward Steichen and Margaret Bourke-White, I had no idea had worked as aerial photographers. And in addition, to have discovered the contributions of those guys who worked in small aerodromes all around the world, coming up with ideas and solving problems in order to show us the beauty of the world from high above. Respect.

– Eamonn McCabe

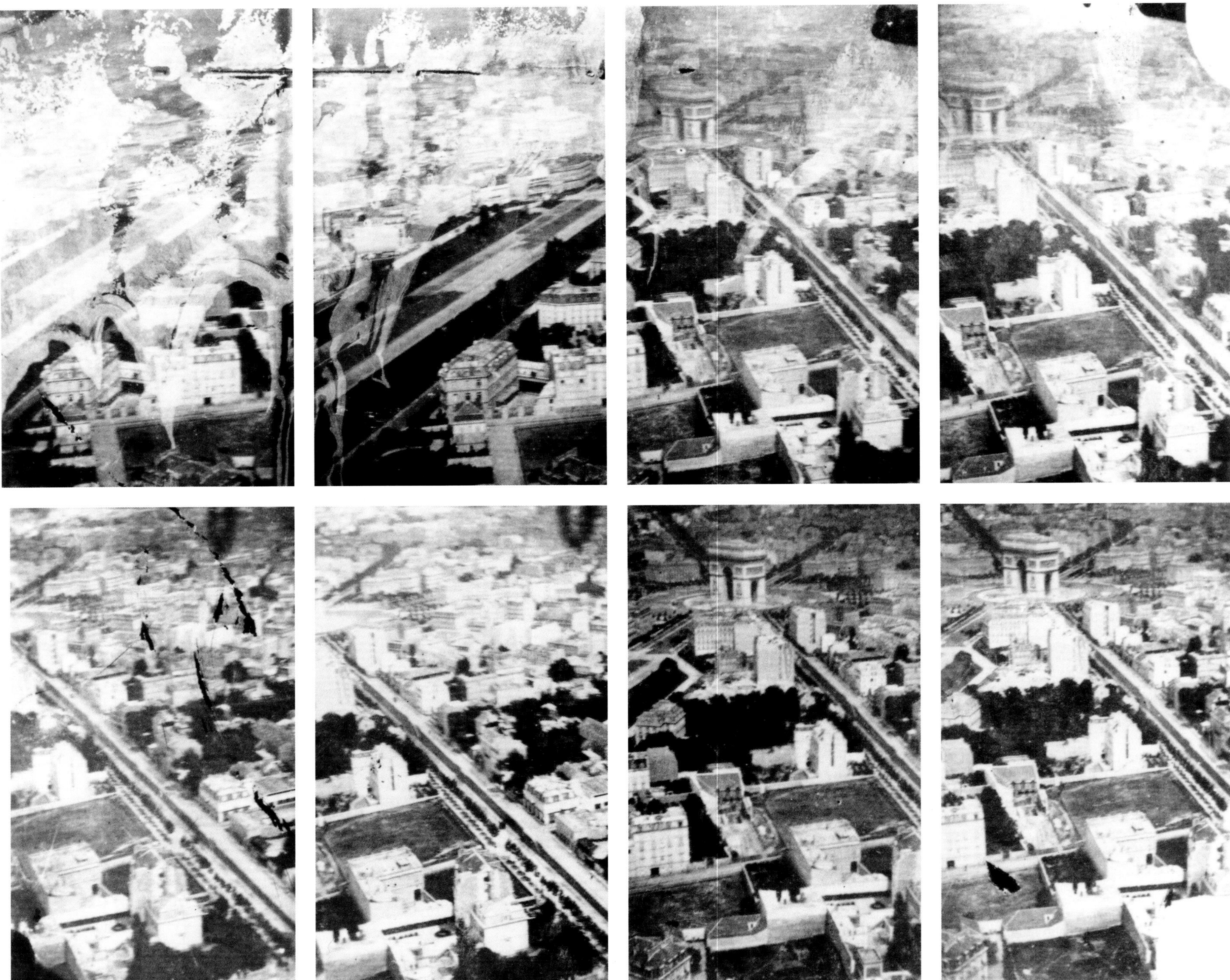

A flamboyant showman with an enquiring mind, Frenchman Gaspard-Félix Tournachon – or Nadar, as he was known – captured the world's first photographs from the air. A journalist and caricaturist by trade, as well as an acclaimed portrait photographer, Nadar achieved great renown for his efforts to elevate photography to the realm of art, so much so that he became something of a caricature himself, as Honoré-Victorin Daumier's illustration (pictured opposite) suggests. In 1858, Nadar captured his home city of Paris from a tethered balloon at an altitude of 520 metres. Challenges included finding a way to keep the balloon steady enough to make a photograph, a problem Nadar tackled by going up on still days and ensuring the cables were as tight as could be. Although his early photographs have been lost, others of Paris from the 1860s and 1880s have survived.

Nadar
Eight views of the Arc de Triomphe, Paris, France, *c.* 1858.

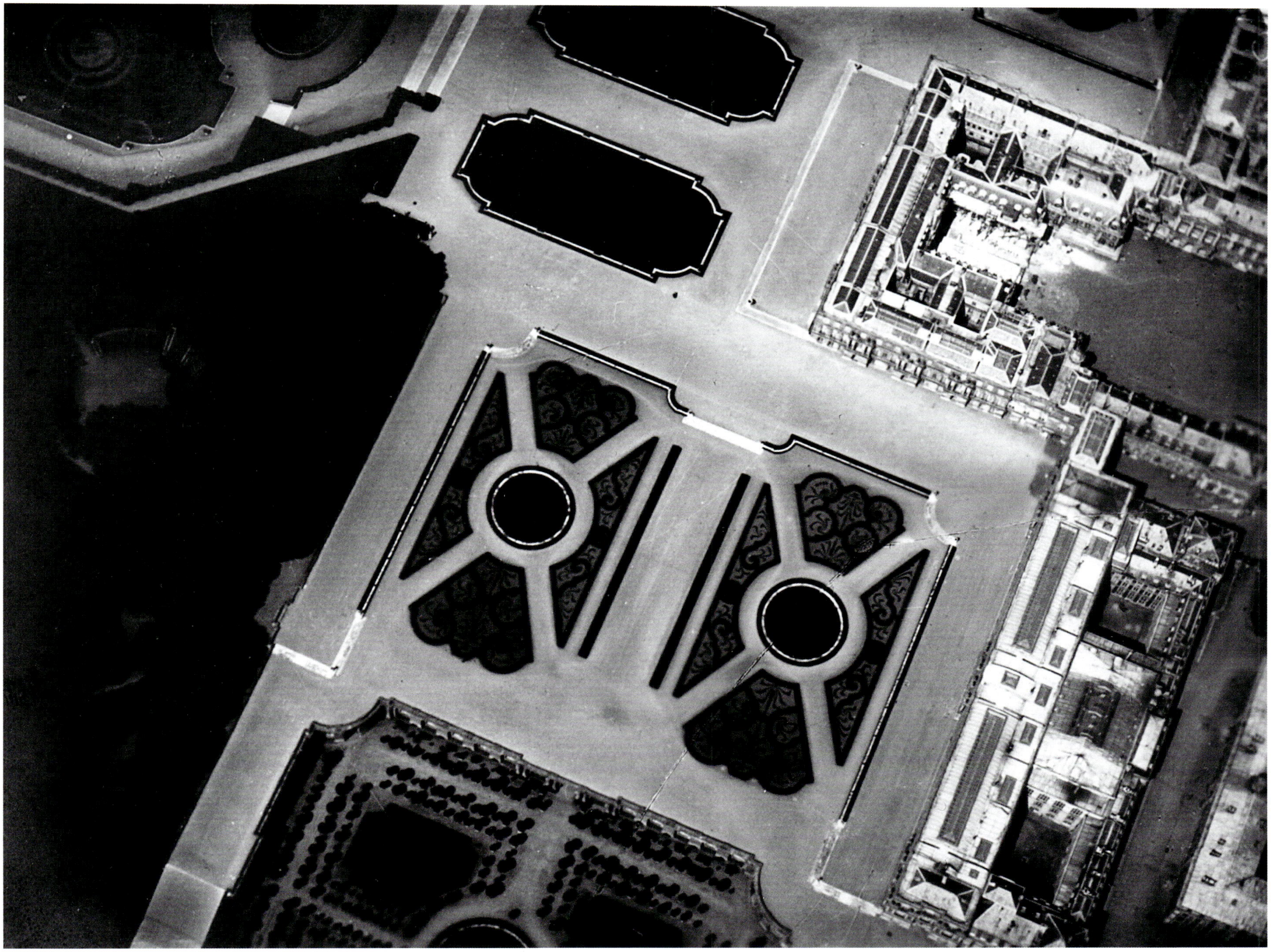

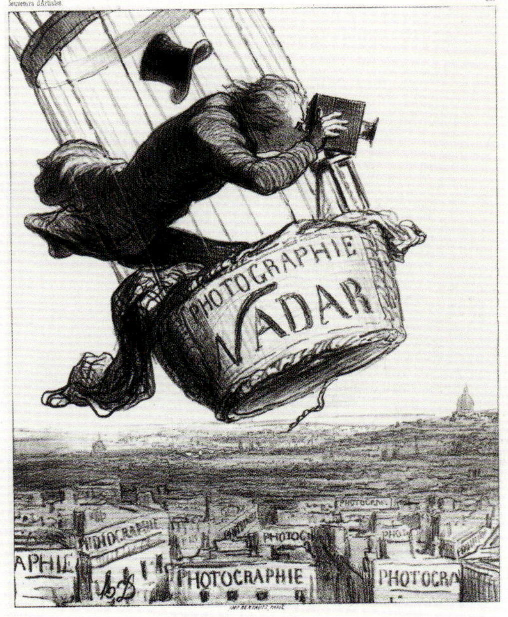

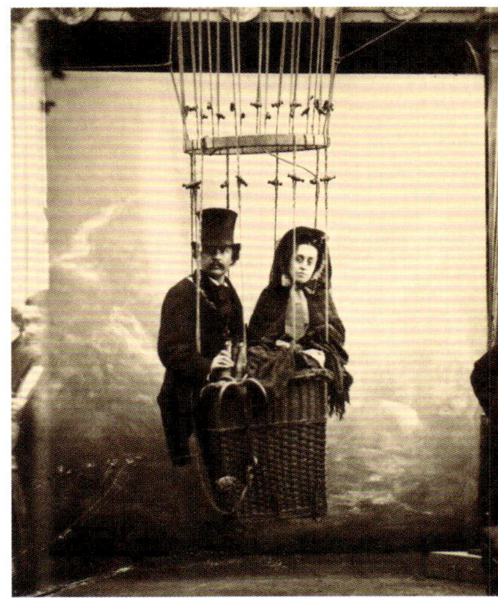

Far left
Honoré-Victorin Daumier
Caricature of Nadar 'raising photography to the height of art', *c.* 1860.

Left
Nadar
Self-portrait, with wife Ernestine, simulating a balloon flight in his Paris studio, France, 1865.

Above
Nadar
The palace and gardens of Versailles, Paris, France, 1886.

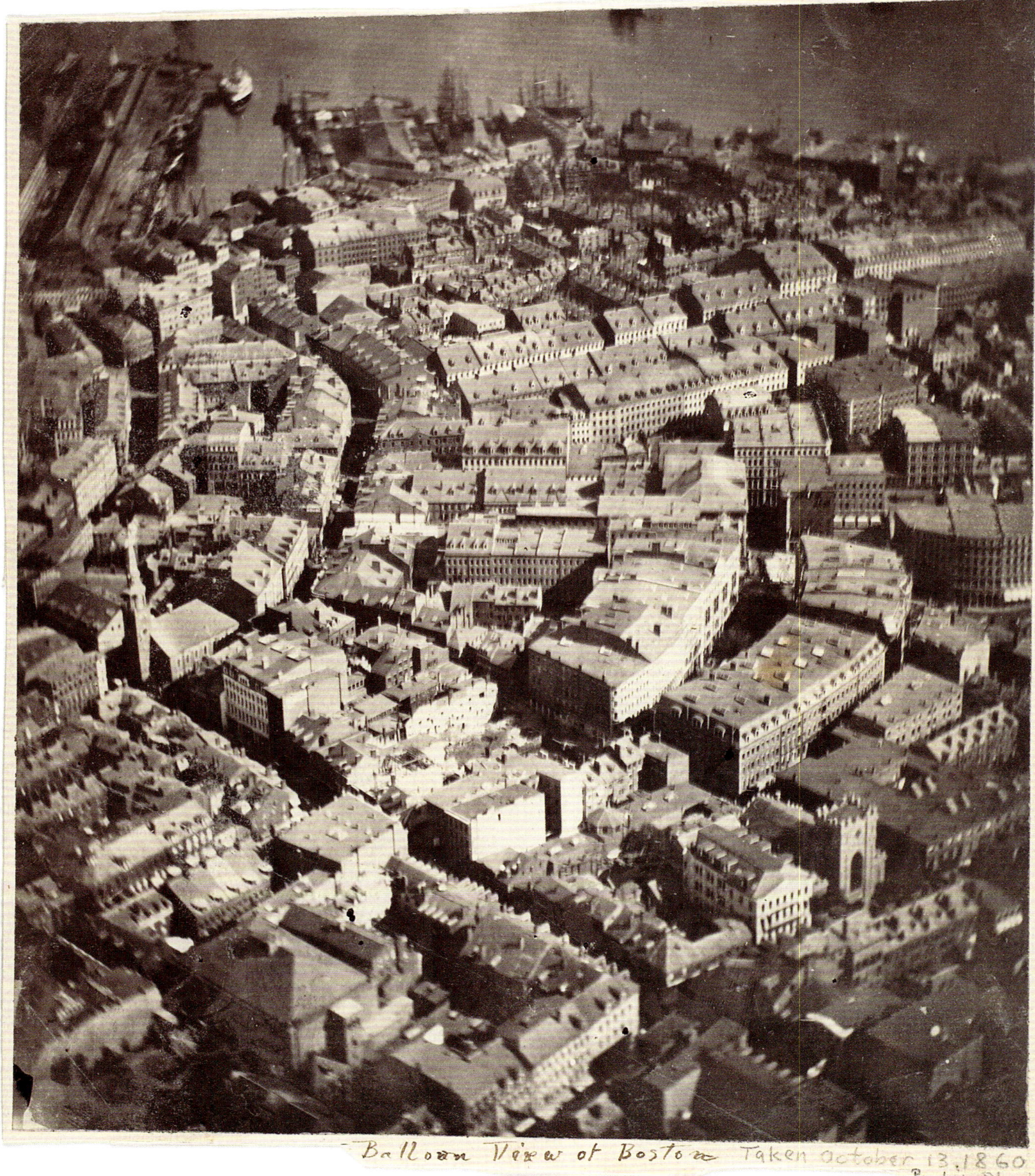

James Wallace Black
Boston, as the Eagle and the Wild Goose See It, Boston, USA, 1860.

While Nadar was experimenting with aerial photography in France, James Wallace (J. W.) Black was making photographs from the air in the United States. In 1860, Black created a series of photographs from a hot-air balloon that included a view of Boston, Massachusetts (pictured). Widely believed to be the first picture of the US from above, the image is also the world's oldest surviving aerial photograph. Poet and Harvard University professor Oliver Wendell Holmes was so taken with Black's image that he wrote a passage about it, praising its merits. The photograph's rather elaborate title – *Boston, as the Eagle and Wild Goose See It* – comes from that text.

Balloonist and photographer Cecil Victor Shadbolt made history by taking what have been described as the earliest known aerial photographs of the UK. Between 1882 and 1892, Shadbolt made balloon trips mainly over London, during which he photographed Blackheath, Crystal Palace, Dartford and other locations from around 300 metres or more. Shadbolt, who was killed in 1892 in a balloon accident, amassed an impressive collection of Victorian glass lantern slides, which have been carefully conserved, digitized and catalogued by Historic England. An aerial view of Stamford Hill taken by Shadbolt has been declared the world's first successful vertical photograph, and his 1889 shot of the Eiffel Tower was published in the same year as the tower opened.

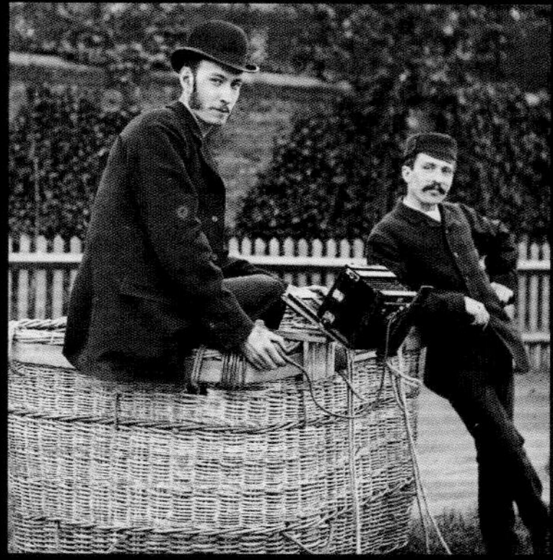

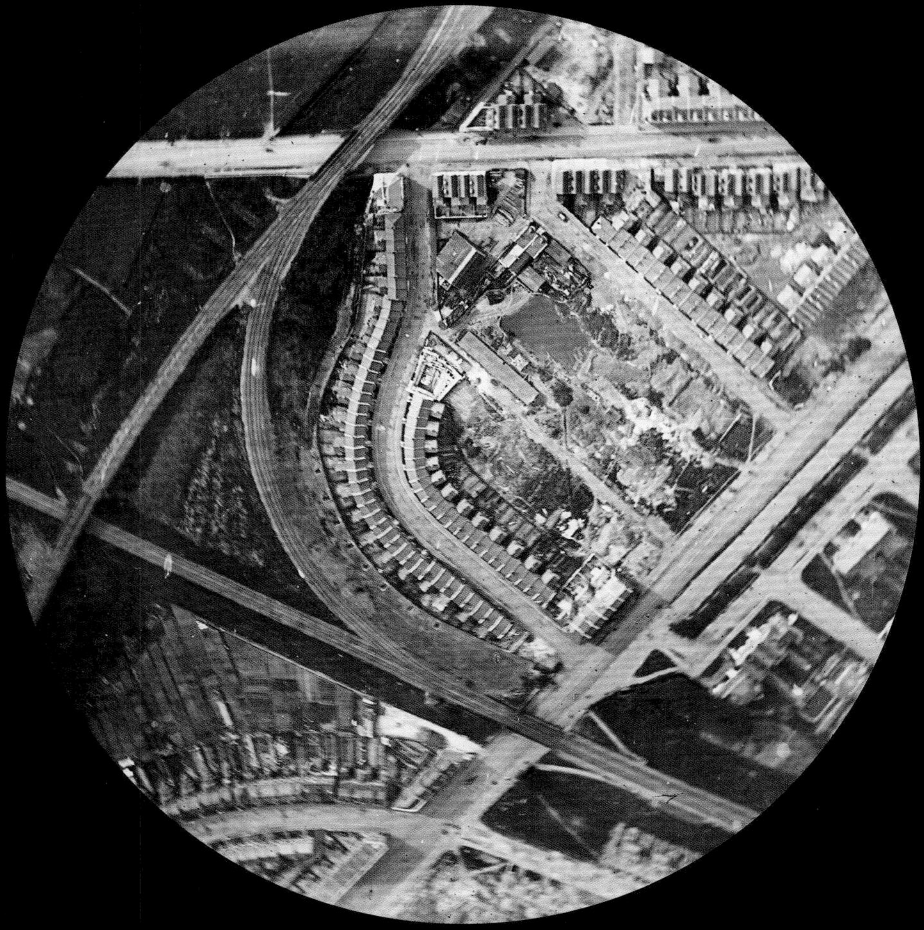

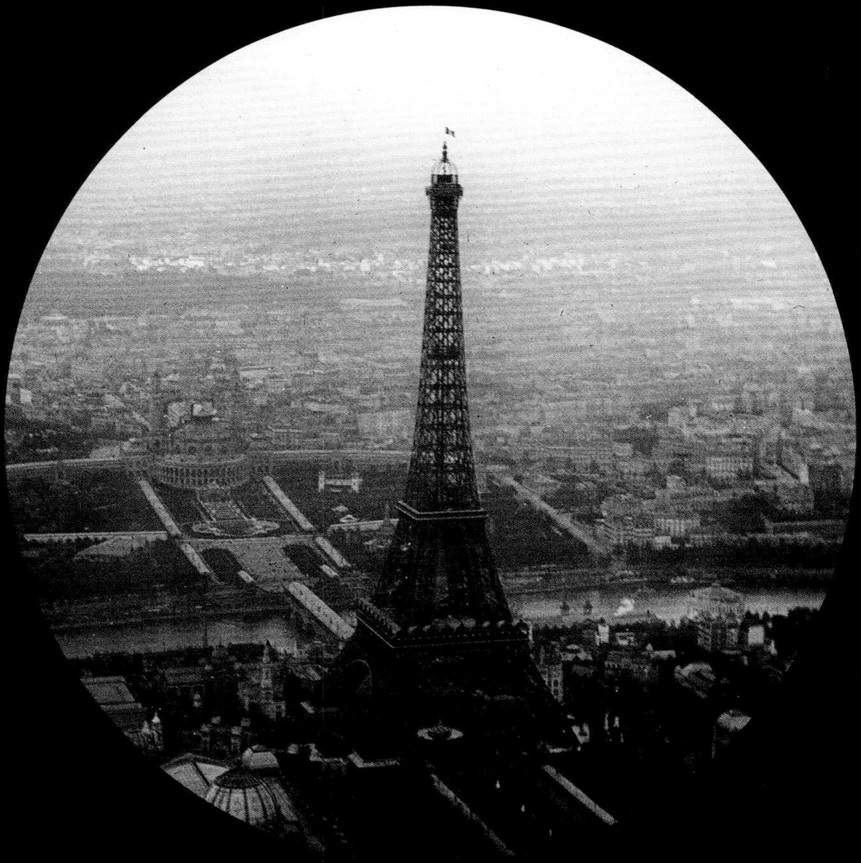

Above
Photographer unknown
Cecil Shadbolt (left) and 'Captain' William Dale (right) posed in the basket of a balloon. Shadbolt's camera can be seen, attached to the side of the basket, *c.* 1882.

Top right
Cecil Victor Shadbolt
Stonebridge Road, Stamford Hill, and Seven Sisters Curve, part of the Tottenham and Hampstead Junction Railway, taken from 600 metres, London, England, 1882.

Right
Cecil Victor Shadbolt
The Eiffel Tower, Paris, France, taken from a tethered balloon, 1889.

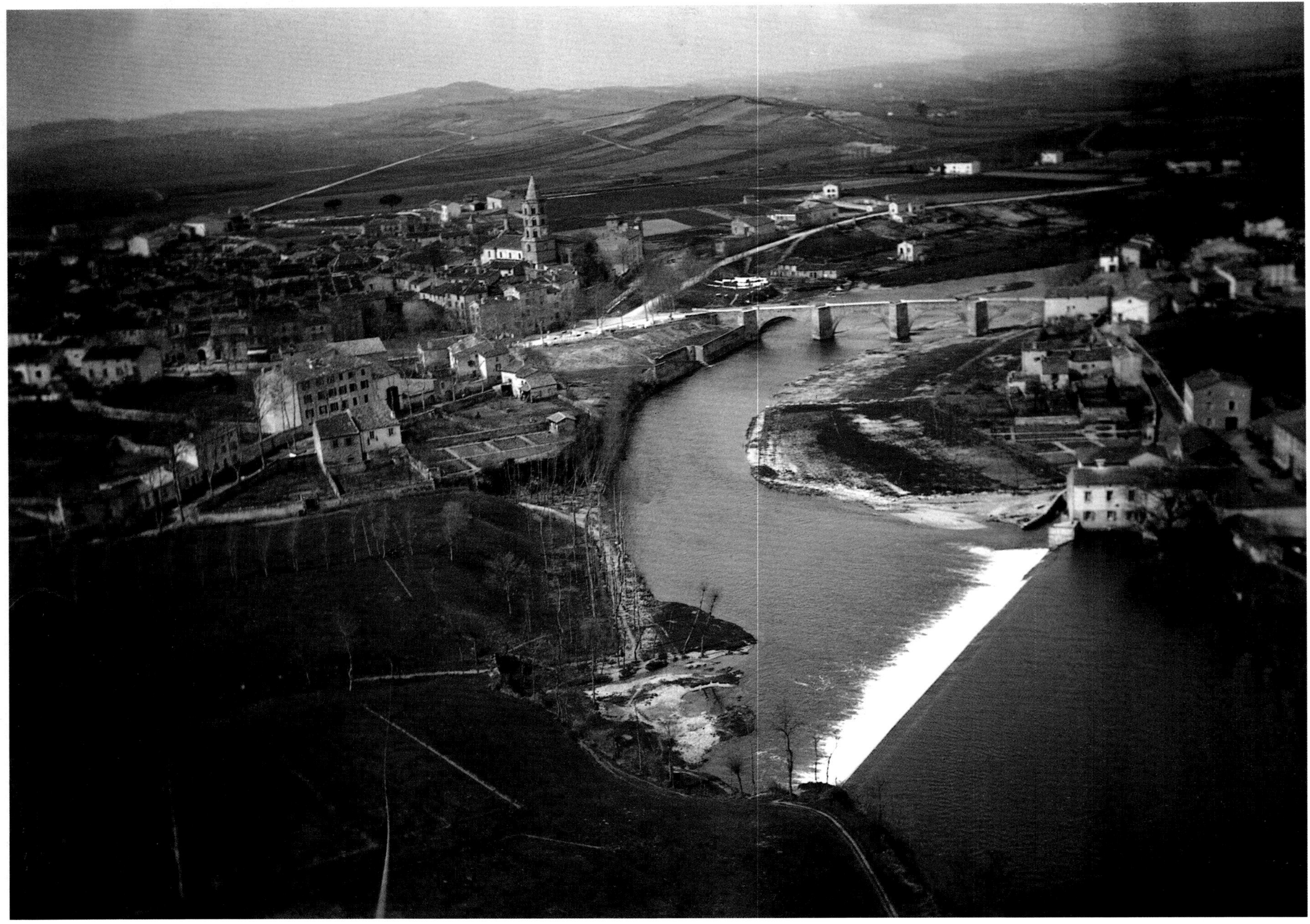

Born into a middle-class French family in 1846, Arthur Batut is thought to have been the first person to take photographs using a kite in flight. A man with many interests, including photography, Batut spent most of his life in the town of Labruguière in southern France, over which he made aerial photographs. His camera-kite set-up comprised a kite made from a wooden frame and paper, and a lightweight camera built from wood and cardboard. A slow-burning fuse activated the shutter. Batut wrote about his escapades in *La Photographie aérienne par cerf-volant*, published in 1890 and believed to be the earliest publication on aerial photography by kite.

Arthur Batut
The town of Labruguière, southern France, 1889.

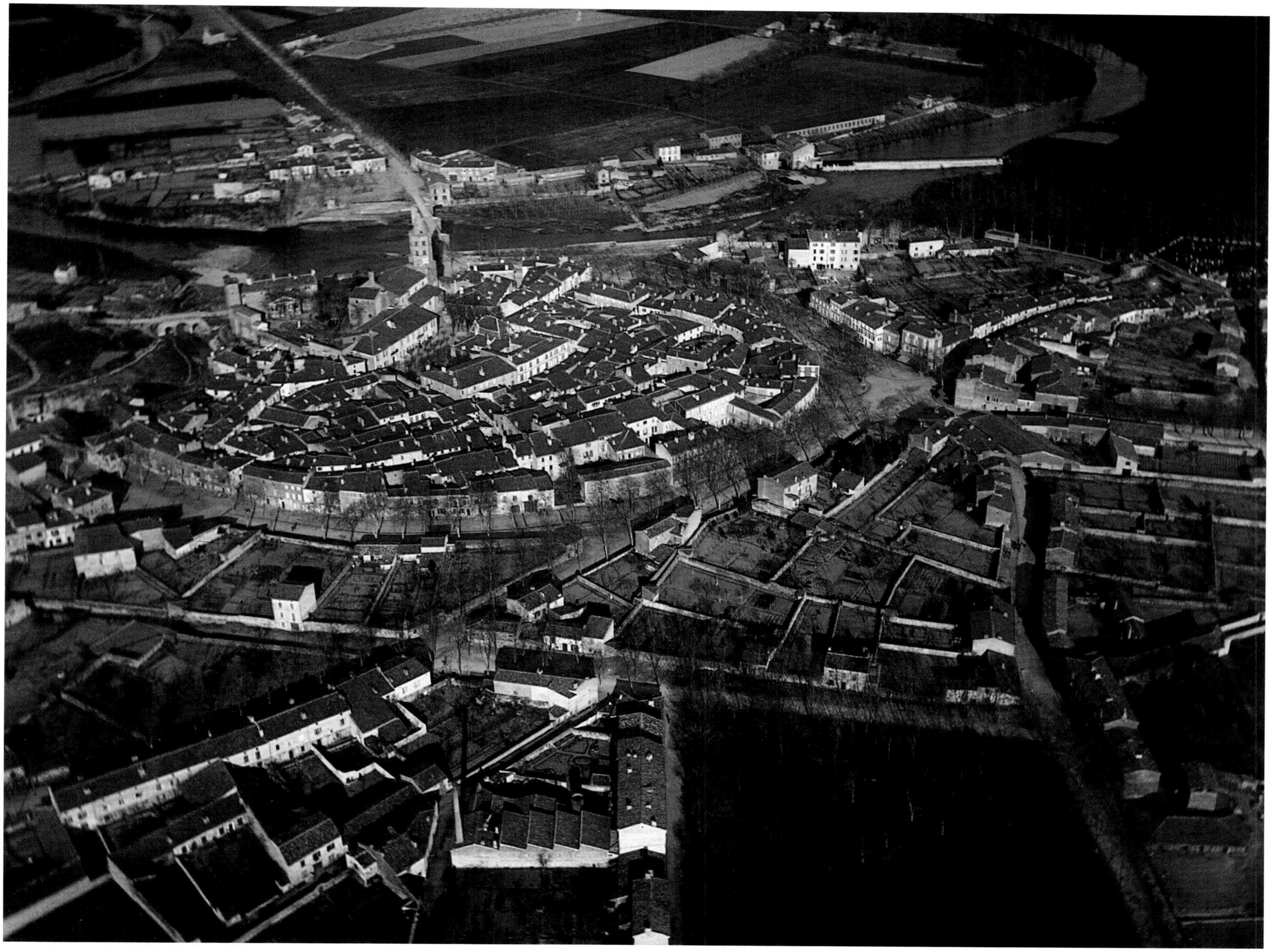

Above
Batut
Labruguière, southern France, 1889.

Right
Photographer unknown
Batut's camera-kite, 1889.

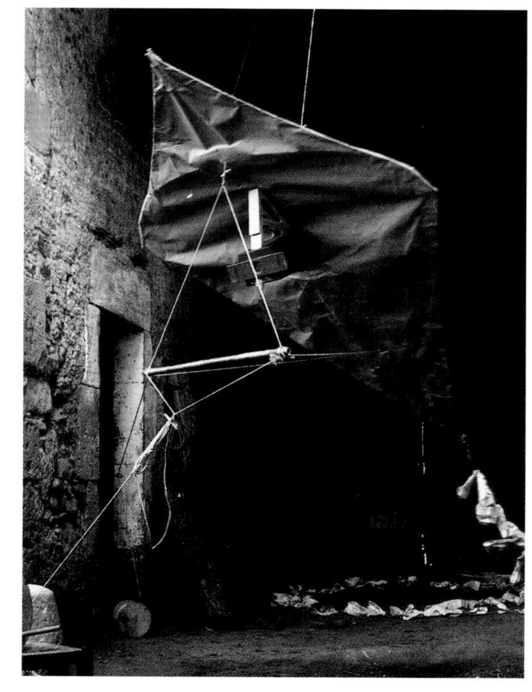

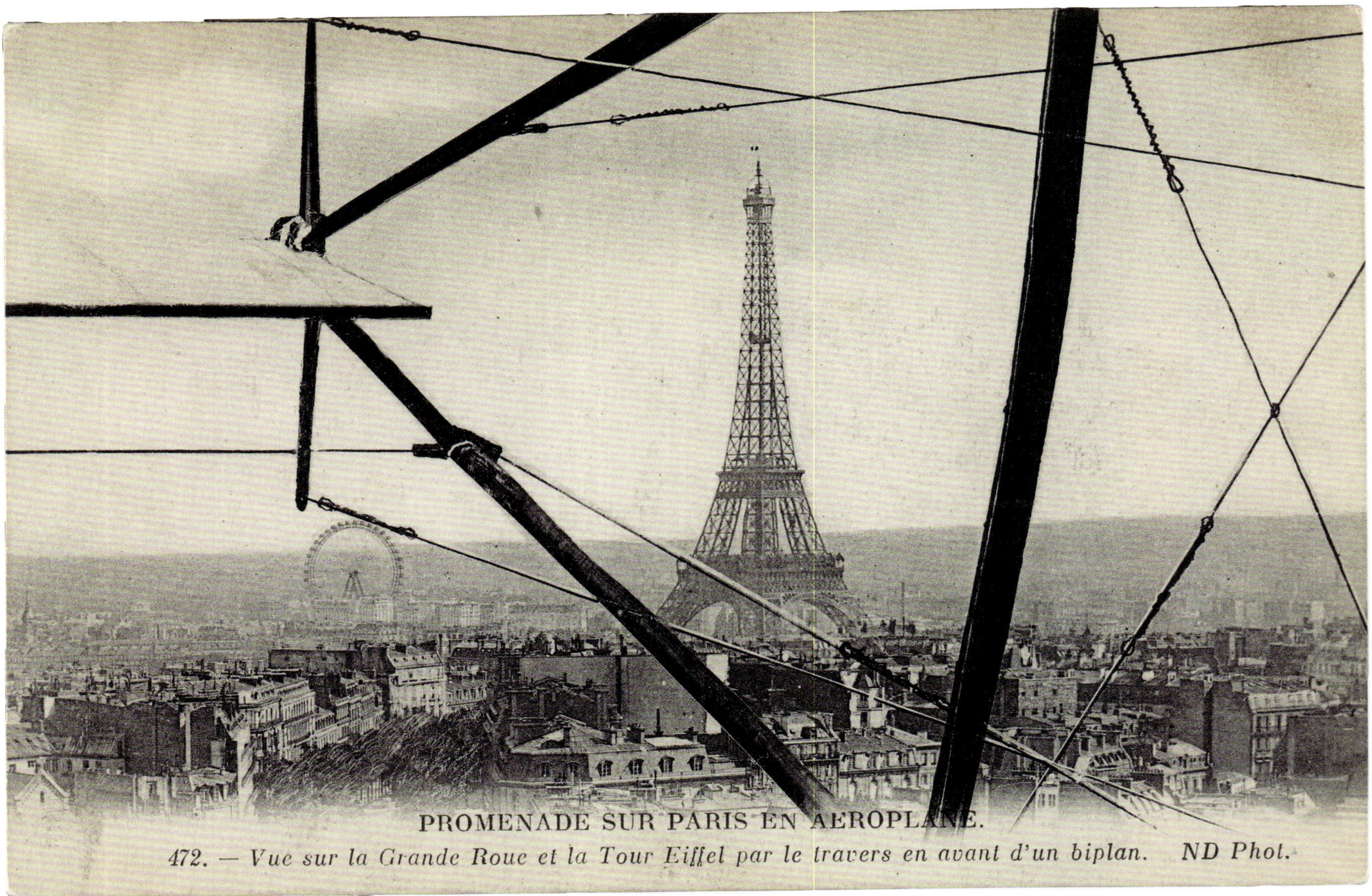

Many photographs exist that show the construction of the Eiffel Tower in the late nineteenth century, but considerably fewer show the famous Paris landmark like this. What is striking about the picture, attributed to the prolific French photography studio run by the Neurdein brothers, is the attention paid to the composition. The photographer, Étienne Neurdein, deliberately positioned his camera so that the biplane structure perfectly framed the tower, creating the impression of a frame within a frame. Gone were the days when a hastily captured view from the air was sufficient; now it was possible (and when it came to postcards, necessary) to present cityscapes and landscapes in artistic new ways.

Étienne Neurdein
Photomechanical print showing an aerial view of the Eiffel Tower in Paris, France; seen through the framework of a biplane, *c.* 1904.

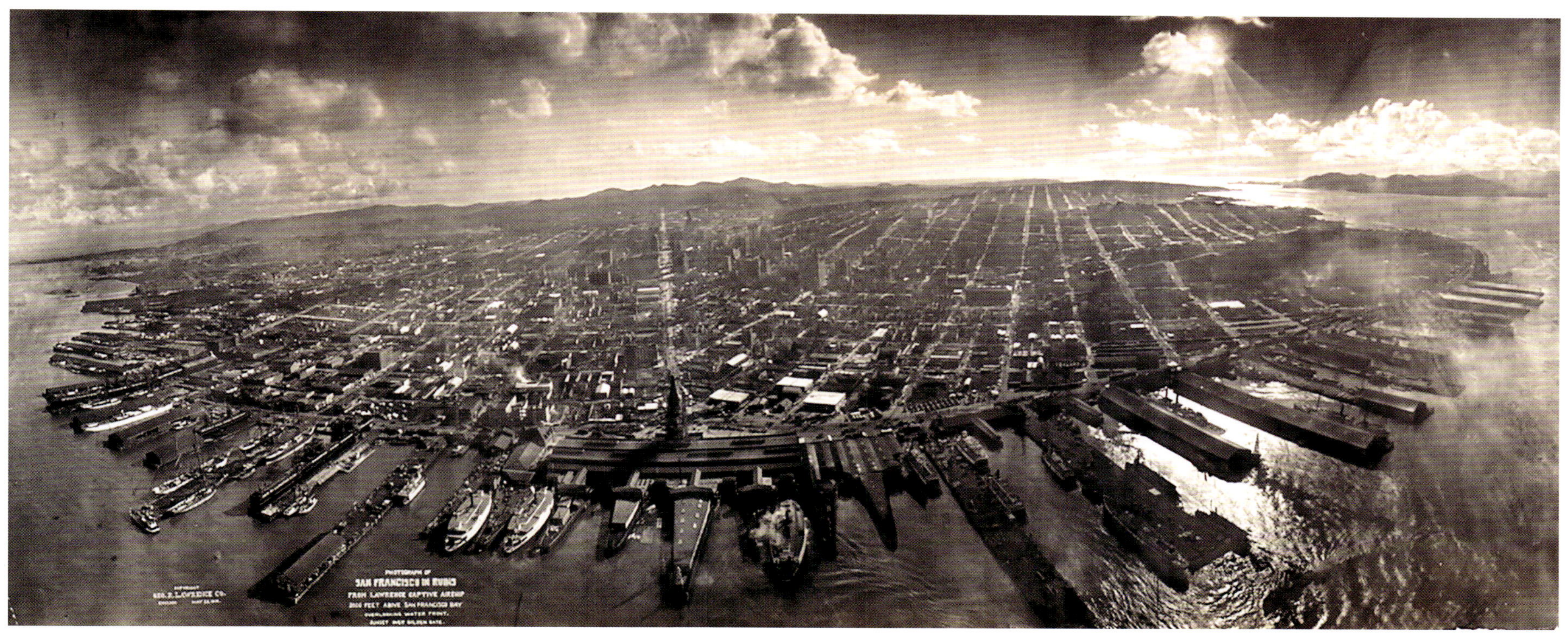

George R. Lawrence
Bird's-eye view of ruins of the waterfront from the *Captive Airship*, 180 metres above Folsom Street between Fifth and Sixth Streets, San Francisco, USA, 1906.

American George R. Lawrence began by photographing the world from ladders and high towers, but inevitably he looked to other methods, which included attaching a cage to a balloon from which he could shoot. He carried on using balloons until the creation of his famous Captive Airship – a network of kites from which a camera was suspended. Lawrence used his device, which some have called the world's first drone, to make detailed photographs of Ohio, New York City, Chicago and, most famously, San Francisco, in a picture that captured the aftermath of the deadly 1906 Californian earthquake that claimed the lives of 3,000 people.

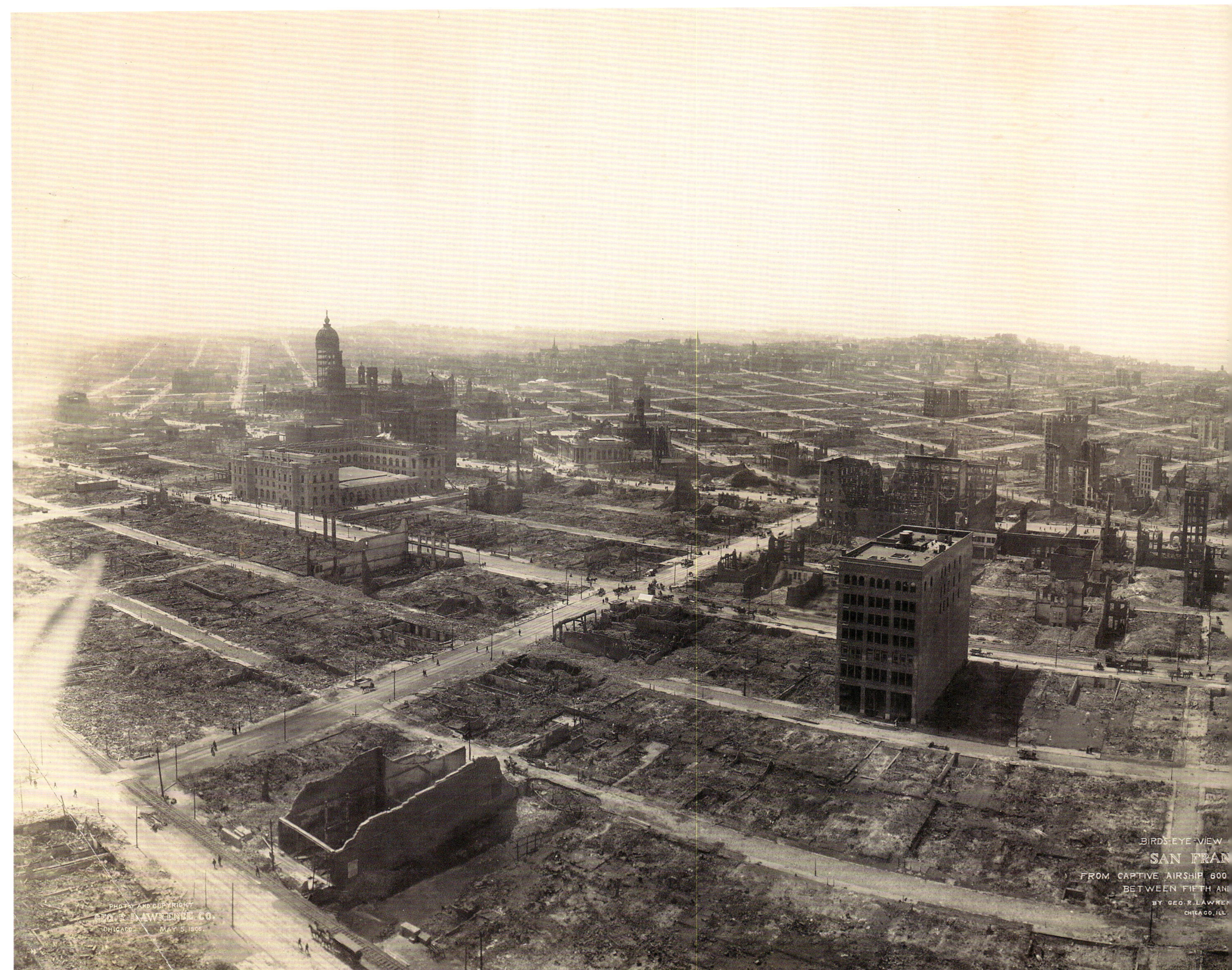

George R. Lawrence
Photograph of San Francisco in ruins from the *Captive Airship*, 600 metres above San Francisco Bay, USA, overlooking the waterfront, 1906.

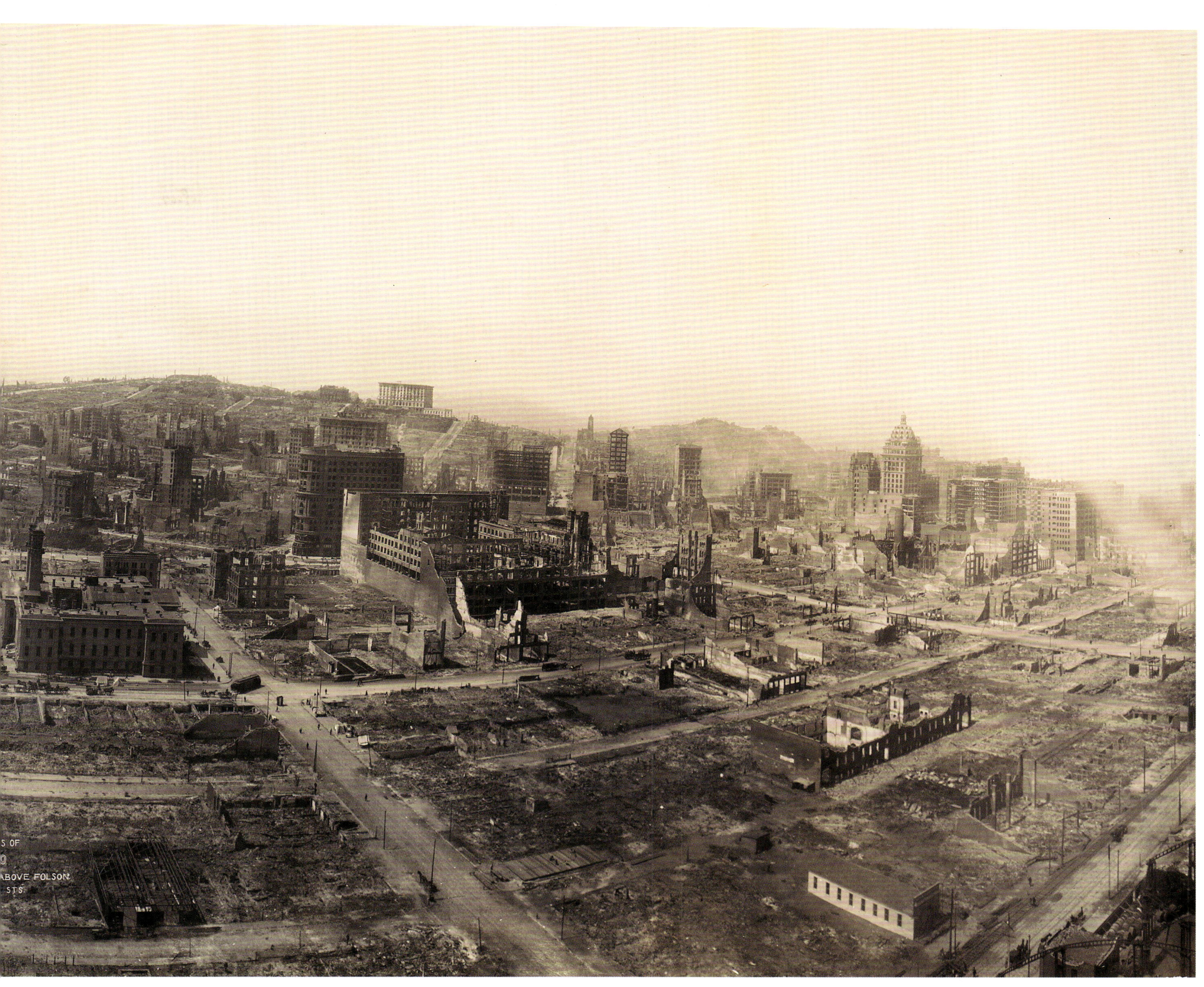
S OF
ABOVE FOLSOM
STS.

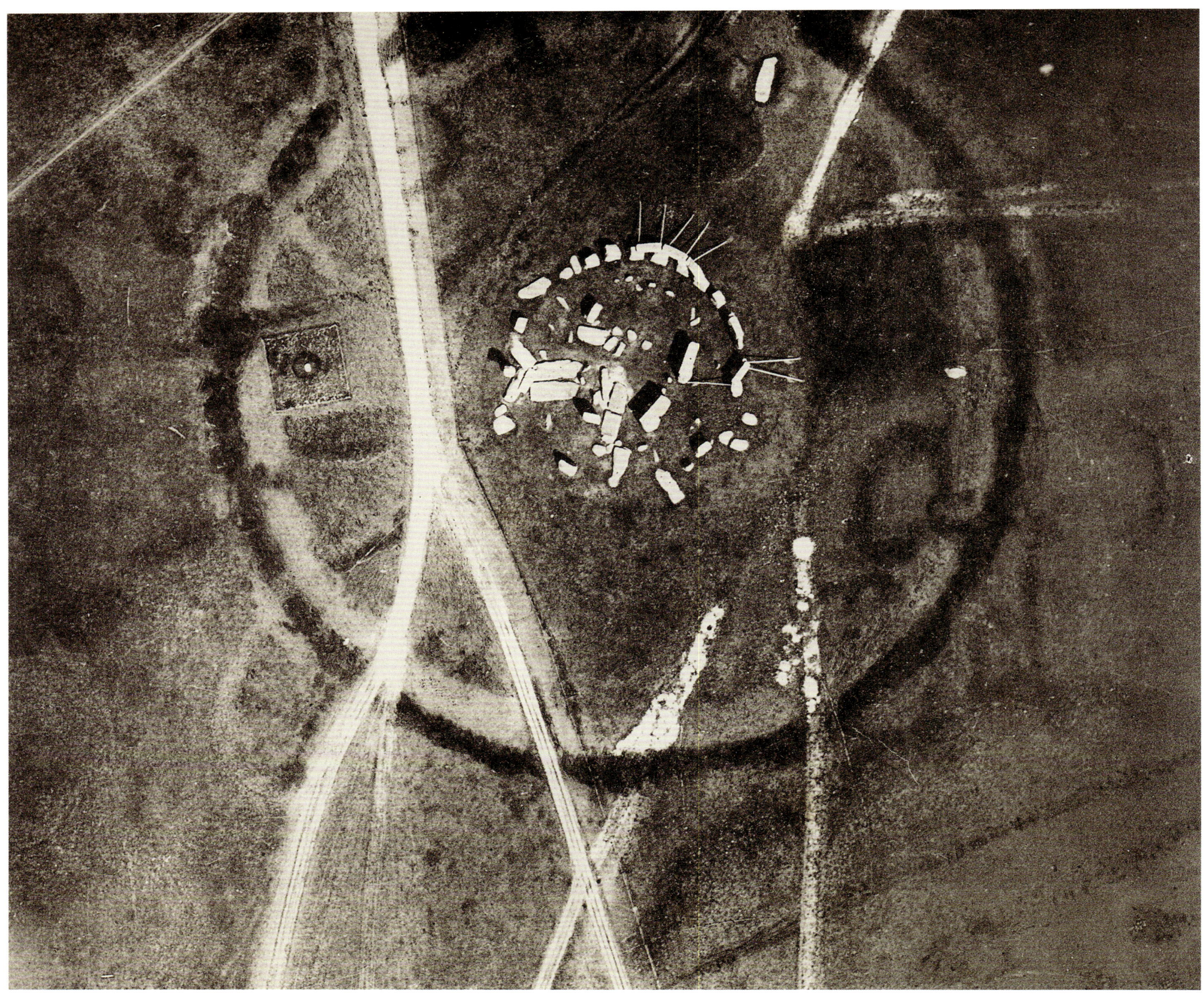

In 1906, Philip Henry Sharpe, a lieutenant with the Royal Engineers' Balloon Section (which later became the Royal Flying Corps, and then the Royal Air Force, or RAF), made history with this photograph of 5,000-year-old Stonehenge in Wiltshire, England. Until then, the ancient stone circle had never been photographed from the air. Sharpe's photograph, shot from a tethered hot-air balloon and one of three he took, is famous for being the first aerial image of an archaeological site anywhere in Britain, and because it set a precedent by neatly illustrating how aerial photography could be used in the study of ancient sites.

Philip Henry Sharpe
First aerial photo of the archaeological site of Stonehenge, Wiltshire, England, taken from a balloon, 1906.

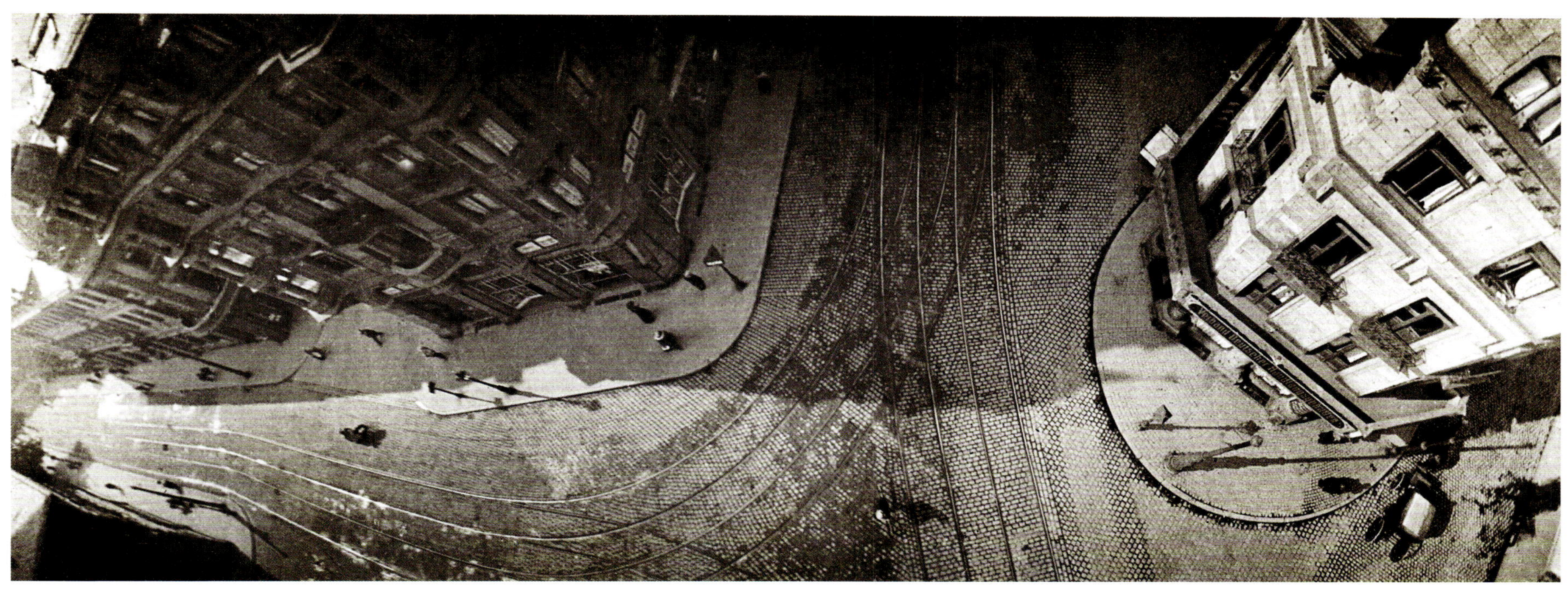

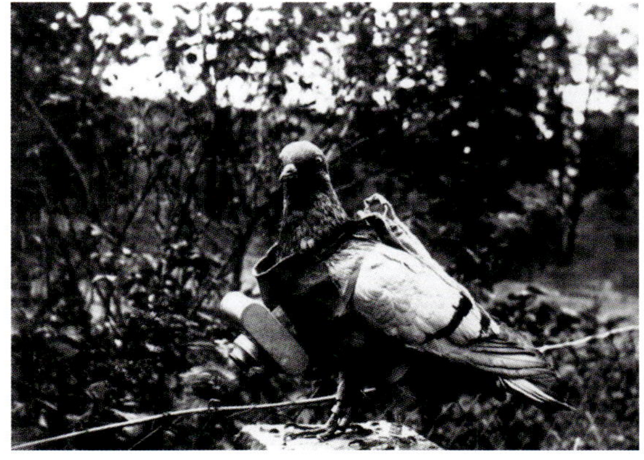

Above
Julius G. Neubronner
Aerial view of Frankfurt am Main, Germany, *c.* 1907.

Right
Julius G. Neubronner
One of Neubronner's homing pigeons wearing a miniature, self-timed camera, *c.* 1907.

In 1907, German apothecary Julius G. Neubronner designed and patented a camera that could be attached to pigeons to capture photographs from the air. Neubronner, who had taken over his father's pharmacy, had been using the birds to send medication across Germany when he had his groundbreaking idea. The miniature cameras were fitted using a harness and aluminium cuirass (breast- and backplate), and a timing mechanism was used to activate them. The birds captured aerial views of Frankfurt and surrounding areas as they flew between 50 and 100 metres in the air. Photographs were made into postcards and sold, and the technology was adapted for use in military air surveillance. His invention had a short lifespan, but Neubronner has gone down in history as an early pioneer of aerial photography.

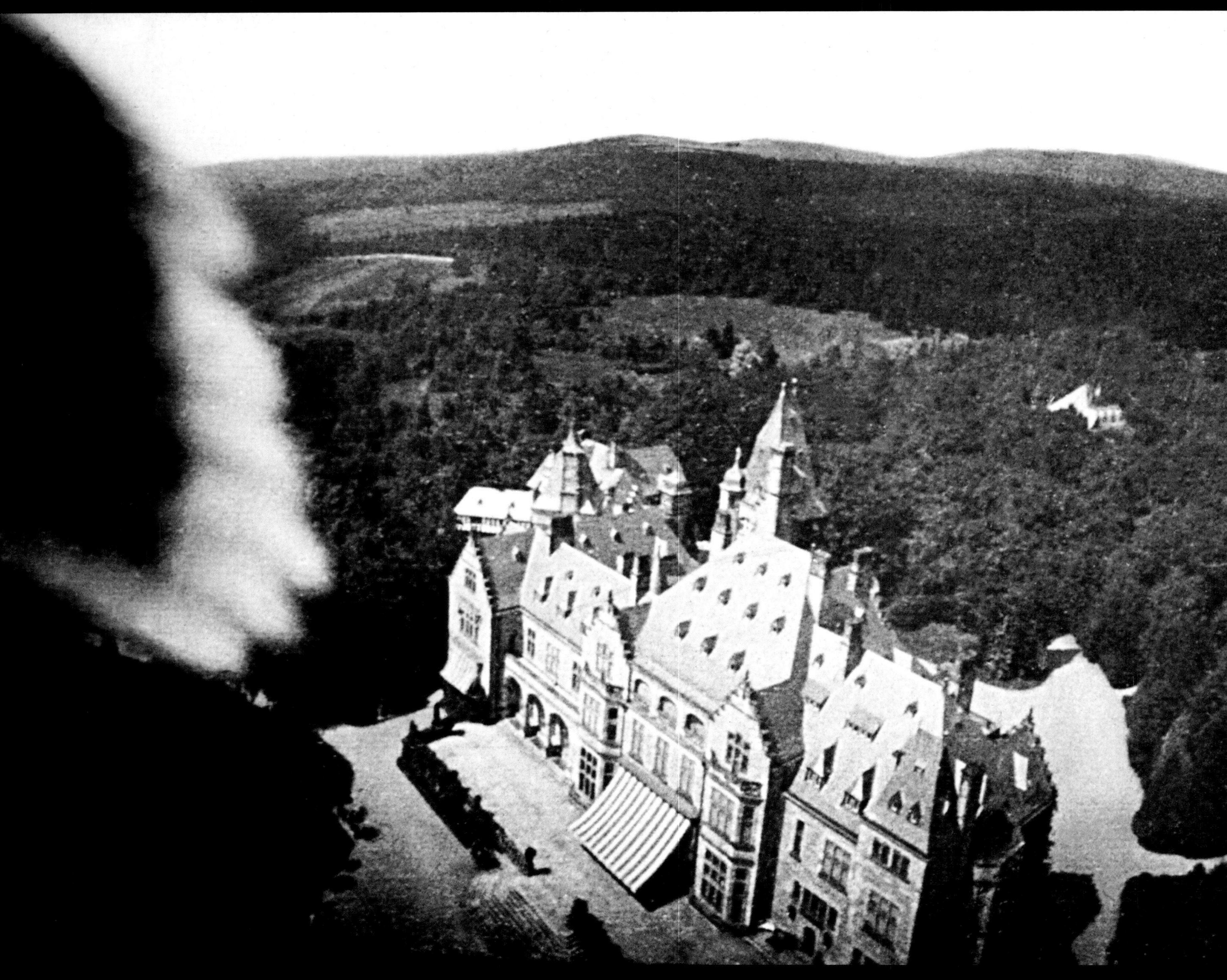

Julius G. Neubronner
Aerial view of Kronberg, Germany, *c*. 1907.

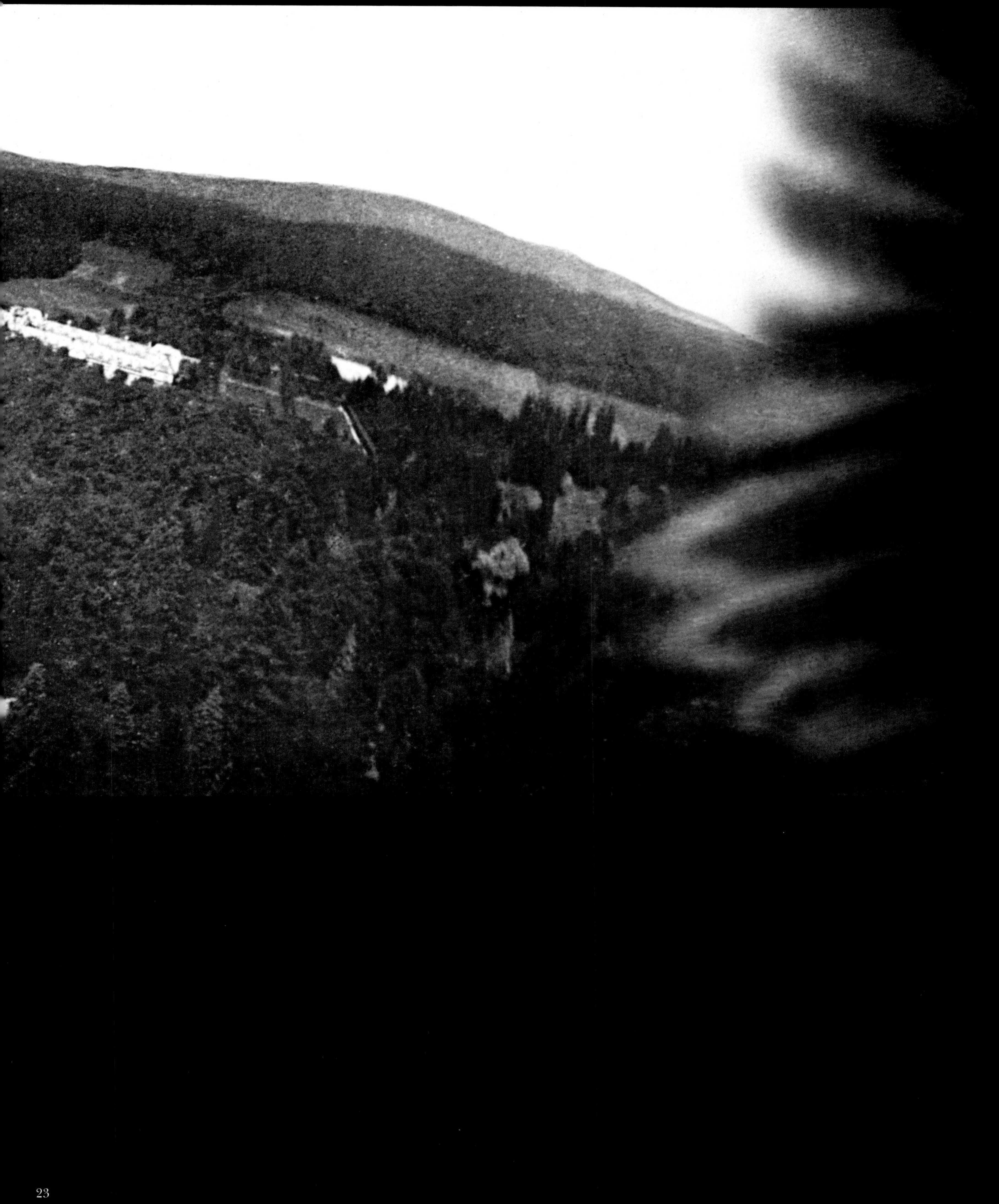

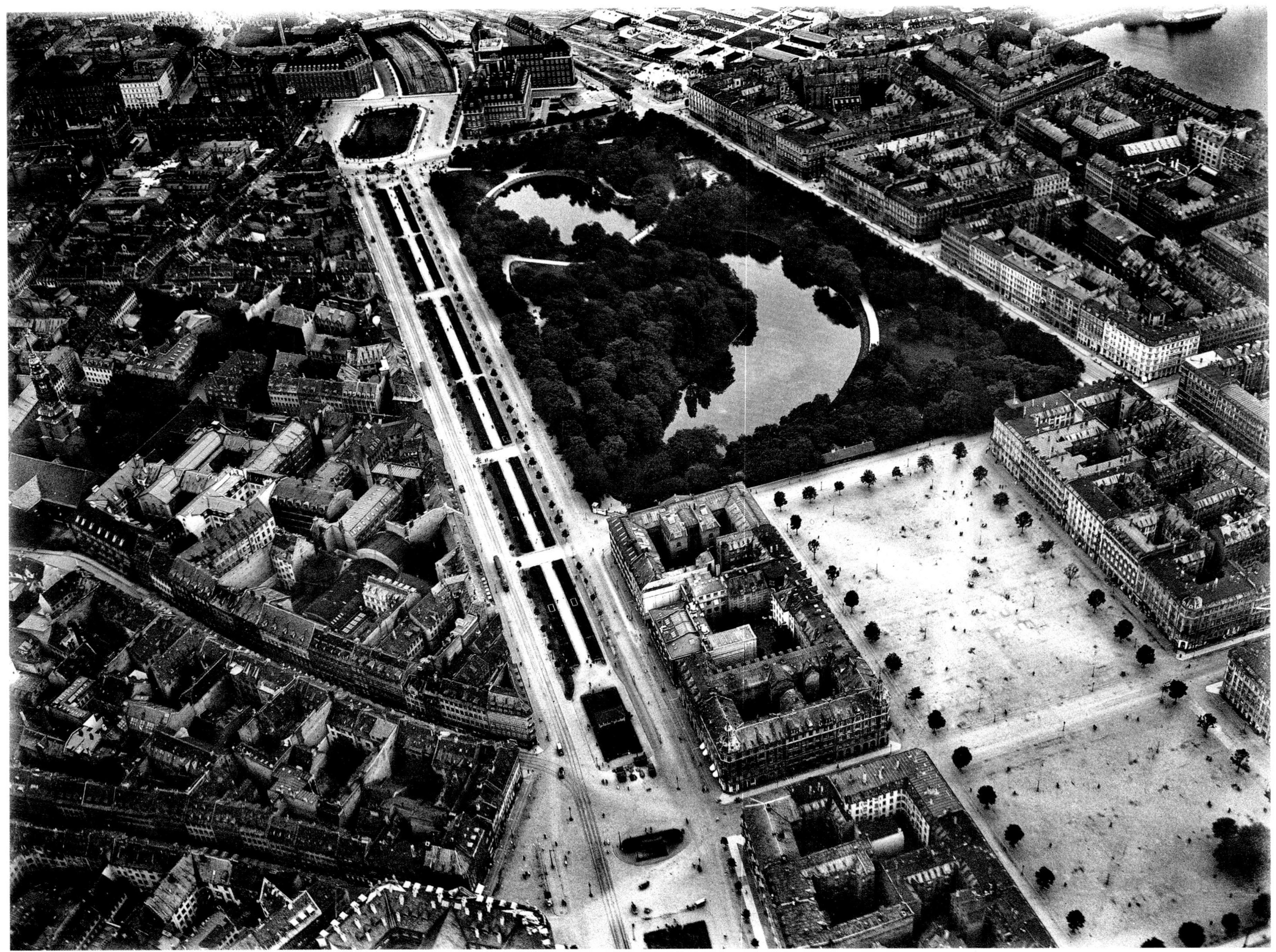

'Pioneer balloonist' Eduard Spelterini made countless glass-plate images from the air during flights across Cairo, Zurich, Johannesburg and elsewhere. The so-called 'King of the Air' began his illustrious career by flying royalty and aristocrats across Europe, but from 1893 he concentrated his efforts on photographing from the sky. For the next 30 years the Swiss adventurer created an astonishing body of work comprising never-seen-before views of landscapes and architecture. Most famous of all are the images taken on a hazardous journey over the Swiss Alps (the first time such a crossing had been successful), during which he created photographs of the sprawling glaciers below. Environmentalists are using those images today to map the impact of climate change across the Mer de Glace glacier.

Eduard Spelterini
Ørstedsparken, Copenhagen, Denmark, *c.* 1908.

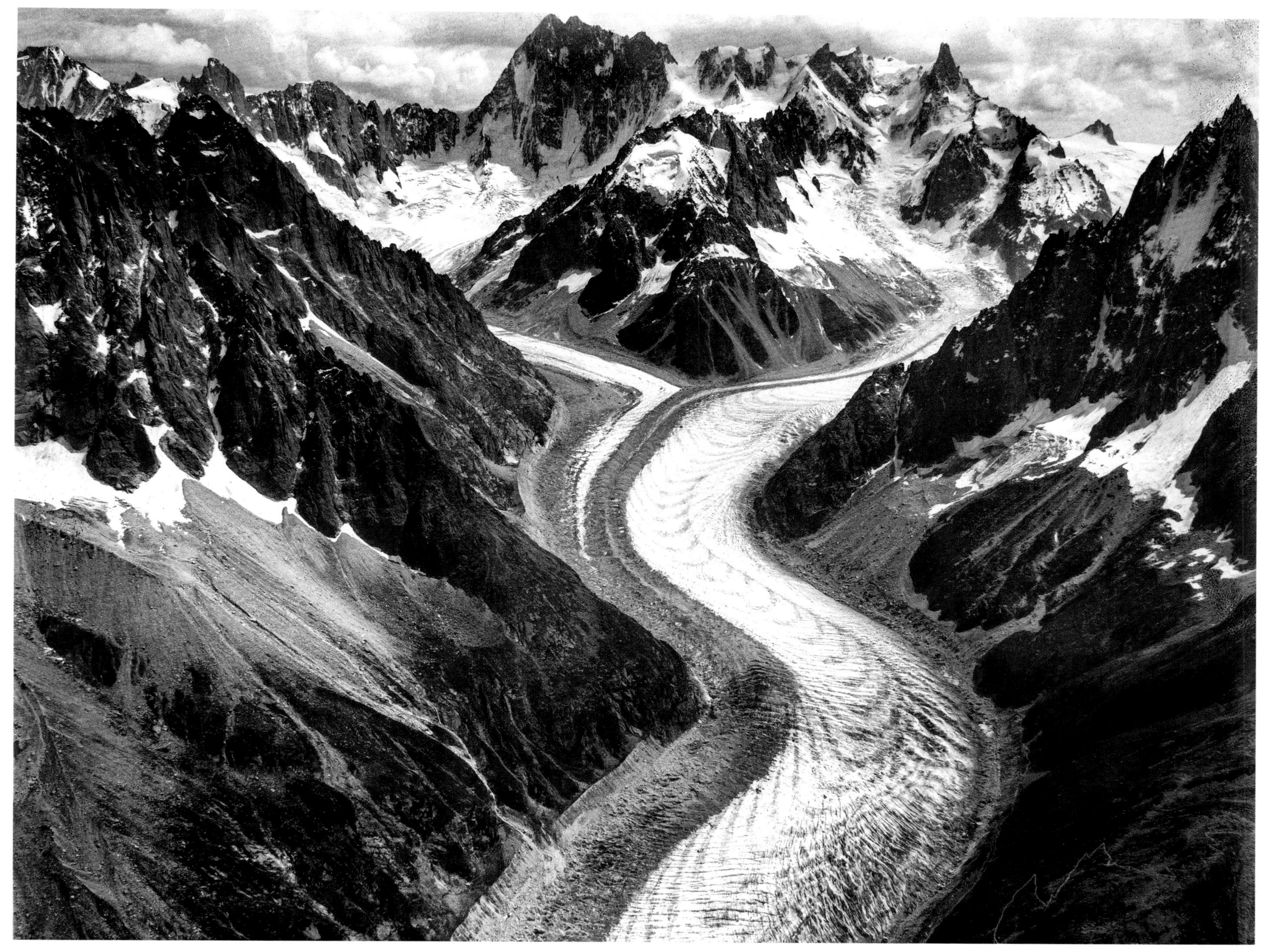

Above
Eduard Spelterini
Mer de Glace, Chamonix Valley, France, 1909.

Overleaf
Eduard Spelterini
Blüemlisalp, Switzerland, *c.* 1910.

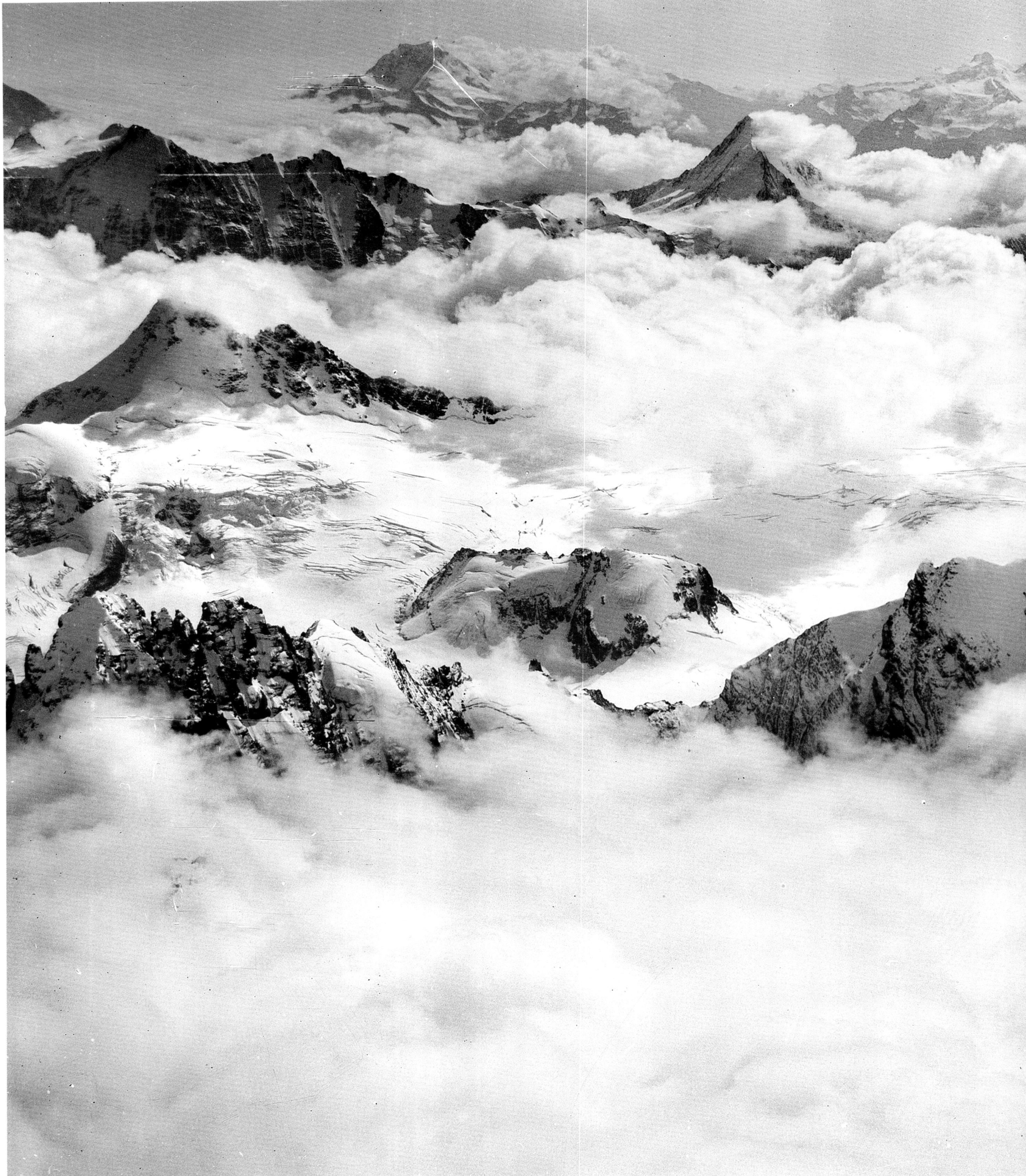

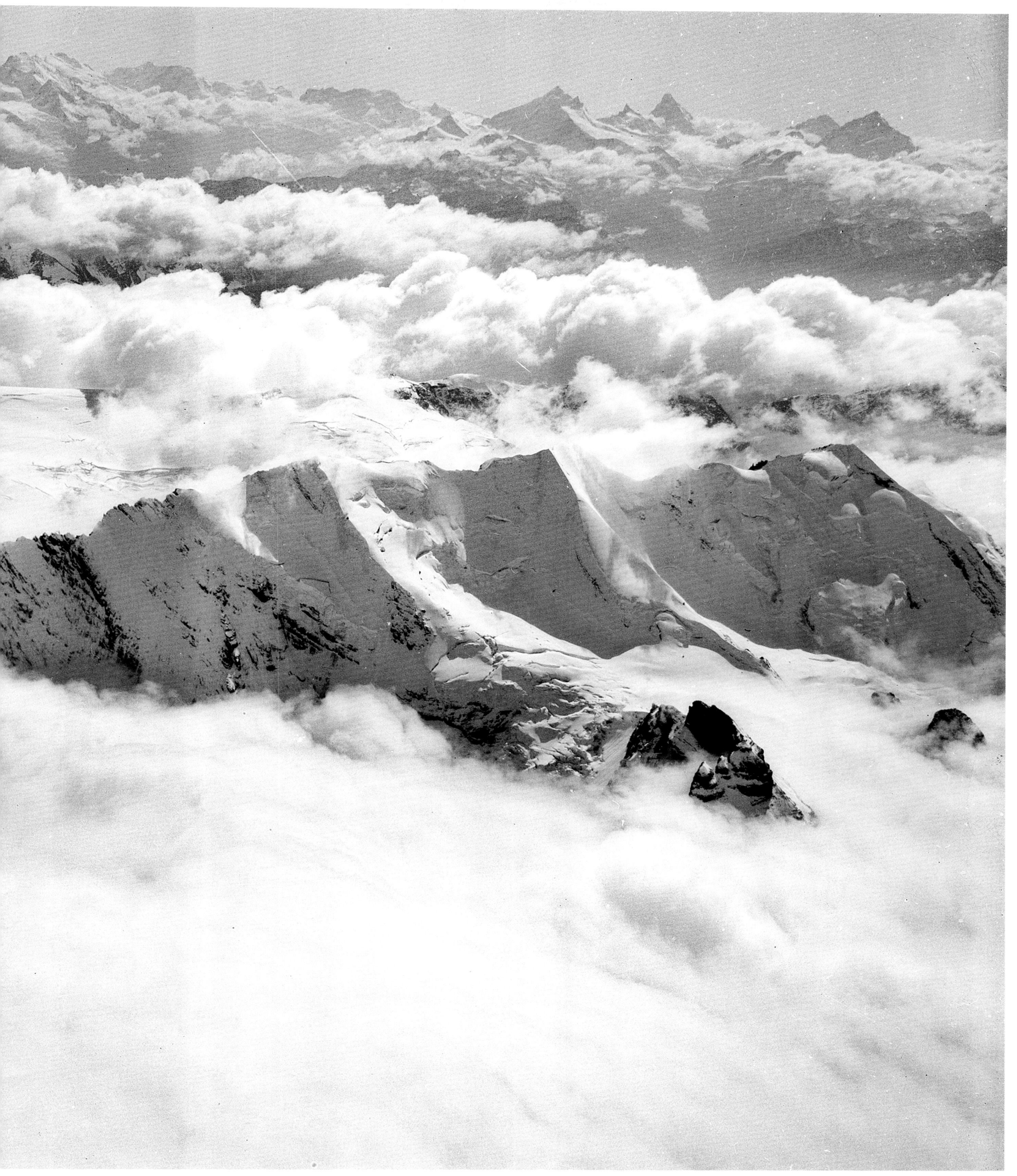

1909

Opposite
John Moore-Brabazon
St. Paul's Cathedral, London, England, 1909.

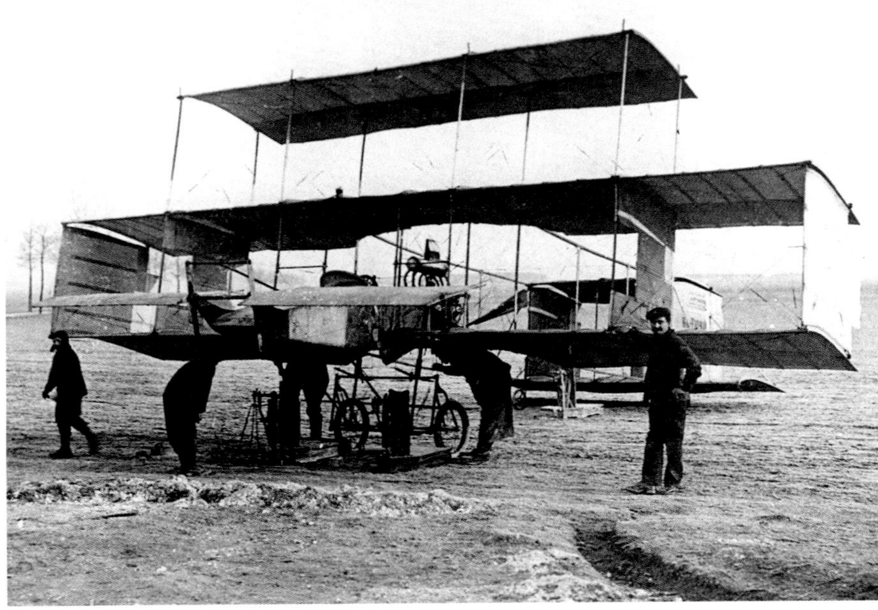

Left
Photographer unknown
Moore-Brabazon preparing to fly a Voisin-Farmen I-bis, 1910.

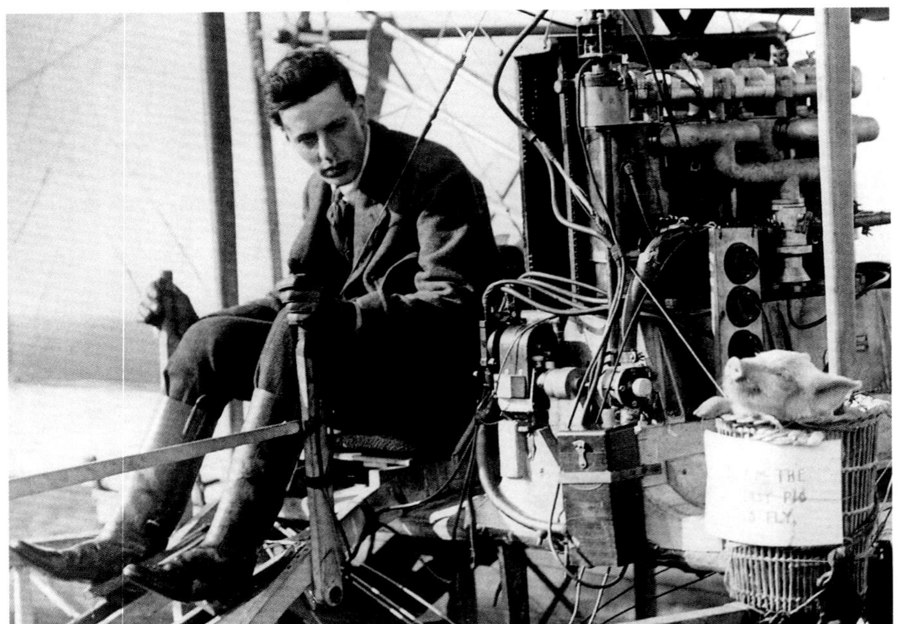

Below
Photographer unknown
Moore-Brabazon taking a pig in a basket for a flight in his aircraft, 1909.

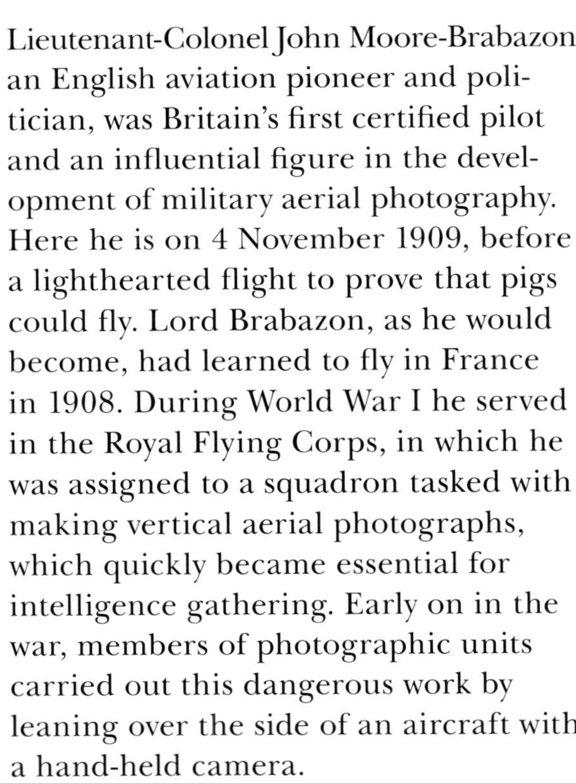

Lieutenant-Colonel John Moore-Brabazon, an English aviation pioneer and politician, was Britain's first certified pilot and an influential figure in the development of military aerial photography. Here he is on 4 November 1909, before a lighthearted flight to prove that pigs could fly. Lord Brabazon, as he would become, had learned to fly in France in 1908. During World War I he served in the Royal Flying Corps, in which he was assigned to a squadron tasked with making vertical aerial photographs, which quickly became essential for intelligence gathering. Early on in the war, members of photographic units carried out this dangerous work by leaning over the side of an aircraft with a hand-held camera.

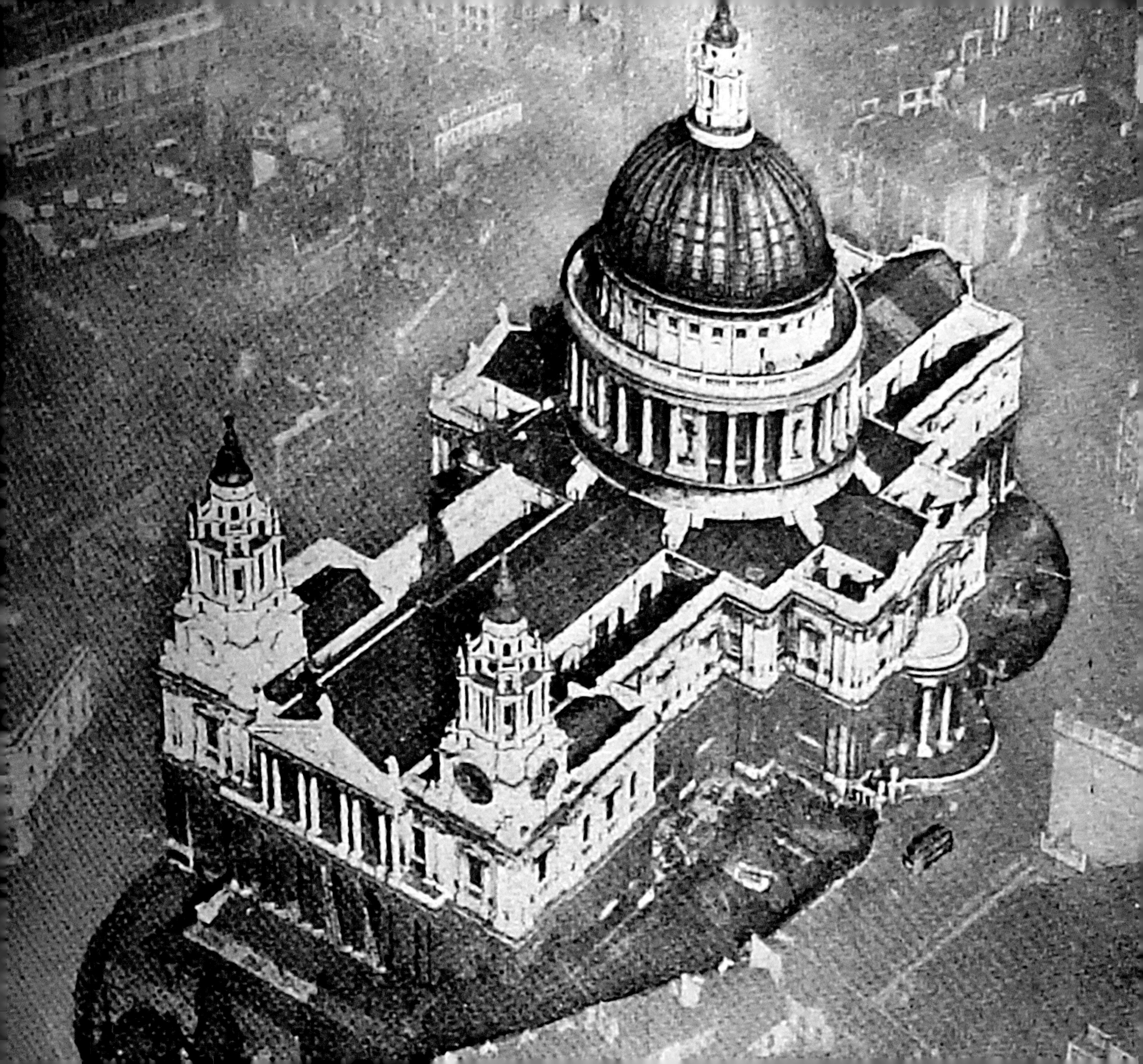

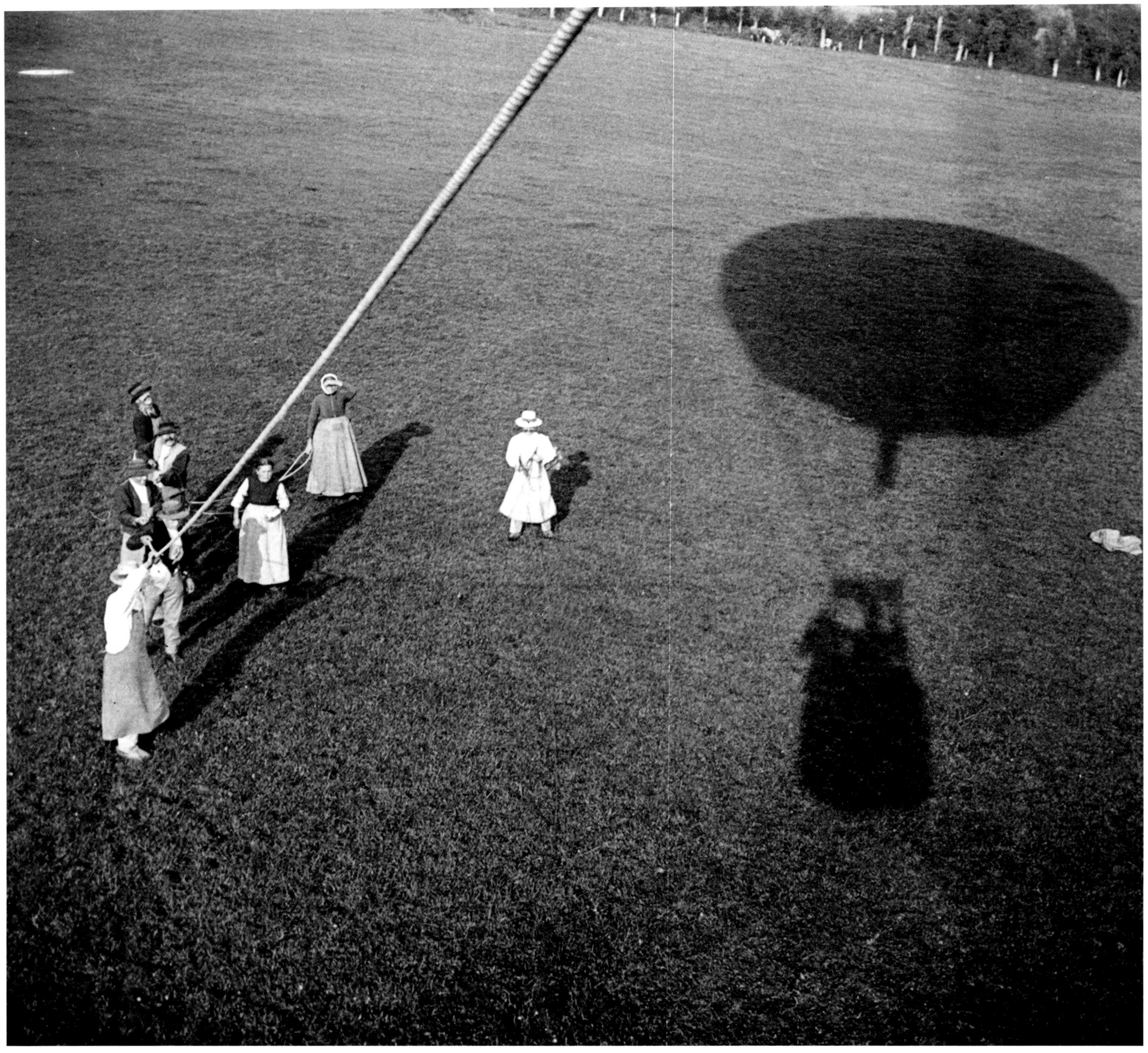

By 1910, when this photograph was taken, more than 50 years had passed since Nadar captured the first aerial photograph from a balloon. The Wright brothers had made history by successfully flying a powered aircraft and attention was focused on new ways of getting up into the air. And yet, despite rapid strides forward in air travel, this photograph suggests that ordinary people were still using hot-air balloons for recreation. What makes the image so remarkable is not just its clarity, but also the imaginative and deliberate composition. In fact, it's possible to view the picture as an early example of aerial photography's considerable creative potential.

Photographer unknown
Hot-air balloon leaving the ground, France, 1910.

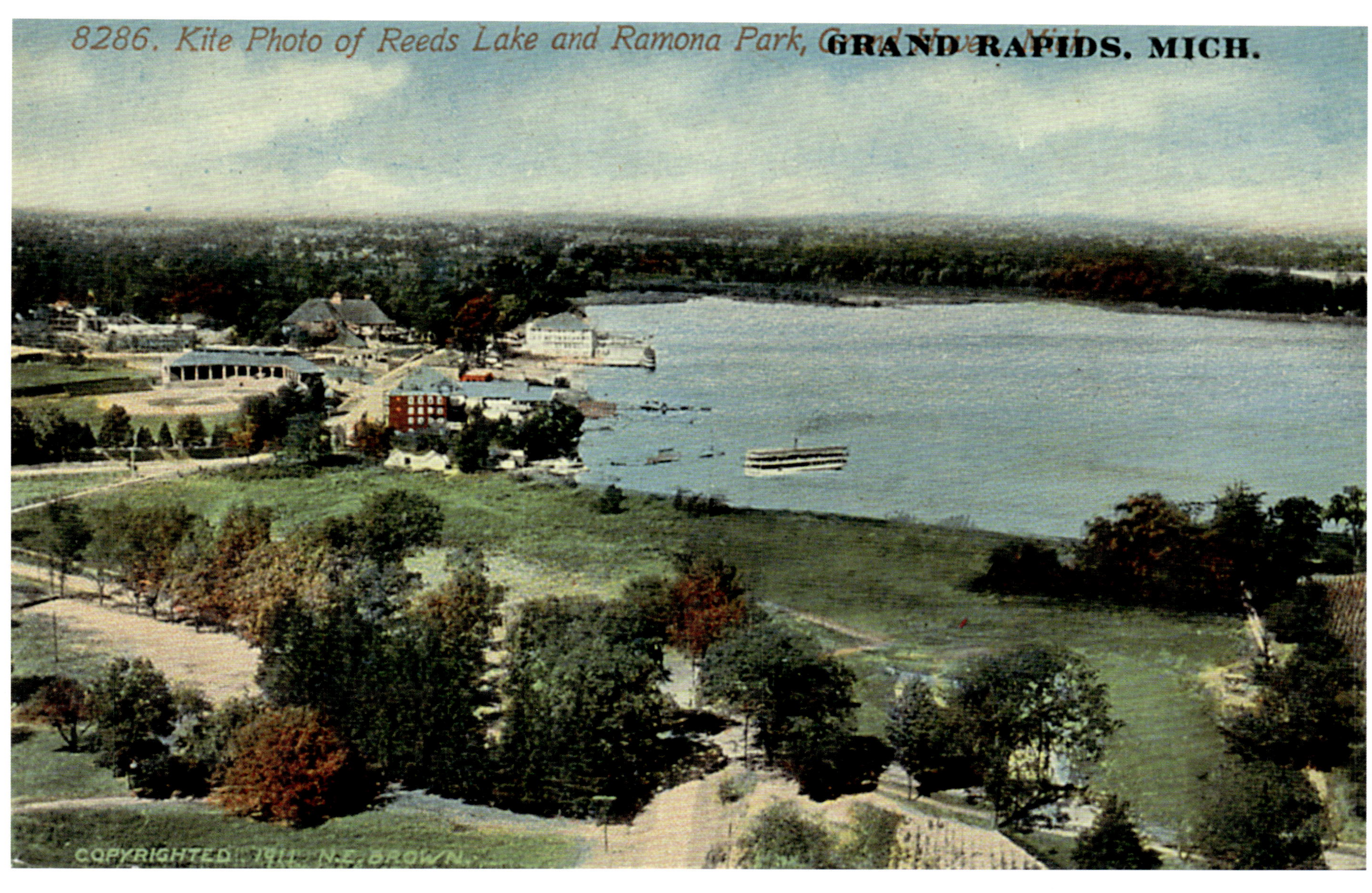

N. E. Brown
Reeds Lake and Ramona Park, East Grand Rapids, Michigan, USA, taken from a kite, *c.* 1911.

This idyllic scene is Reeds Lake and Ramona Park in East Grand Rapids, Michigan, captured here in 1911 or 1912 and attributed to N. E. Brown. People would come to this area to picnic. To create the image, which was based on a black-and-white photograph and then coloured, a camera was mounted on a kite and flown above the scene. The photographer tripped the shutter from the ground. Brown's photograph, like many others at the time, ended up as a postcard. These 'real photo' postcards were very popular during what has been called the 'Golden Age of Postcards' – the decade between 1905 and 1915, when millions of postcards were printed and mailed in the US.

British entrepreneur Sir Henry Wellcome is famous for his pioneering pharmaceutical work, but less well known are his considerable achievements in aerial photography. In 1900, Wellcome visited Sudan to set up what would become the Wellcome Tropical Research Laboratories in Khartoum. While there, he also had the idea of carrying out archaeological excavations, which took place between 1910 and 1914 in Jebel Moya in the south Sudan. Inevitably, there was talk of seeing the sites from above, and records suggest that Wellcome used a large box-kite, which could be manoeuvred using pulleys and fired remotely. British archaeologist O. G. S Crawford, who went on to become an authority on aerial photography, assisted Wellcome and recorded the exercise as the first time that aerial photography had been used for topographic purposes in the context of archaeological excavations. Archaeologists use kite cameras to this day.

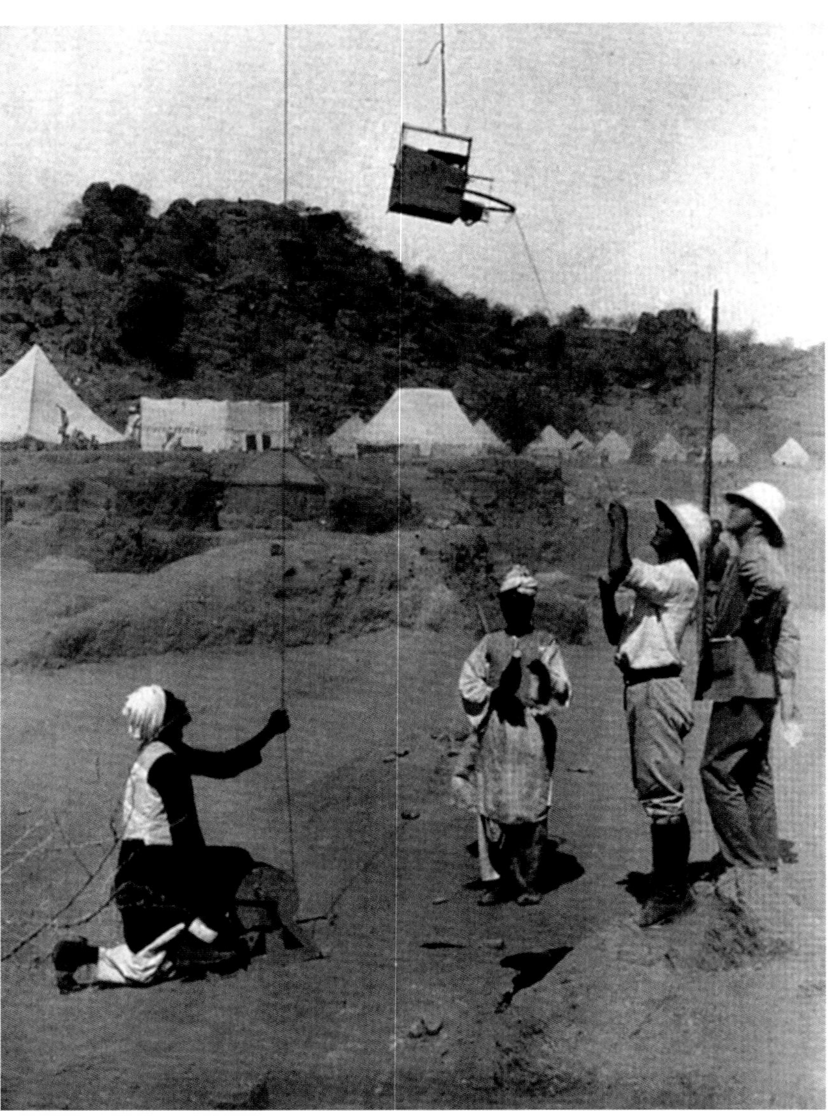

Left and below
Photographer unknown
The large box-kite that Sir Henry Wellcome used in his aerial photography of archaeological sites, 1913.

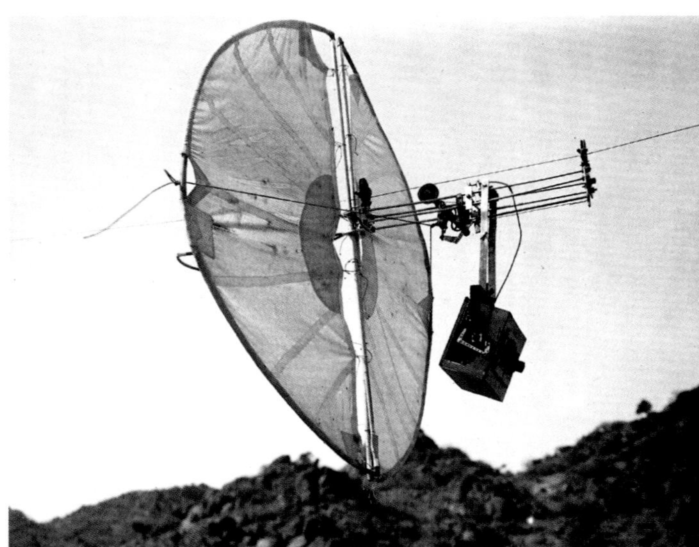

Below
Sir Henry Wellcome
Seqadi, Jebel Moya,
Sudan, 1913.

Overleaf
Sir Henry Wellcome
Excavation camp at Seqadi,
Jebel Moya, Sudan, 1913.

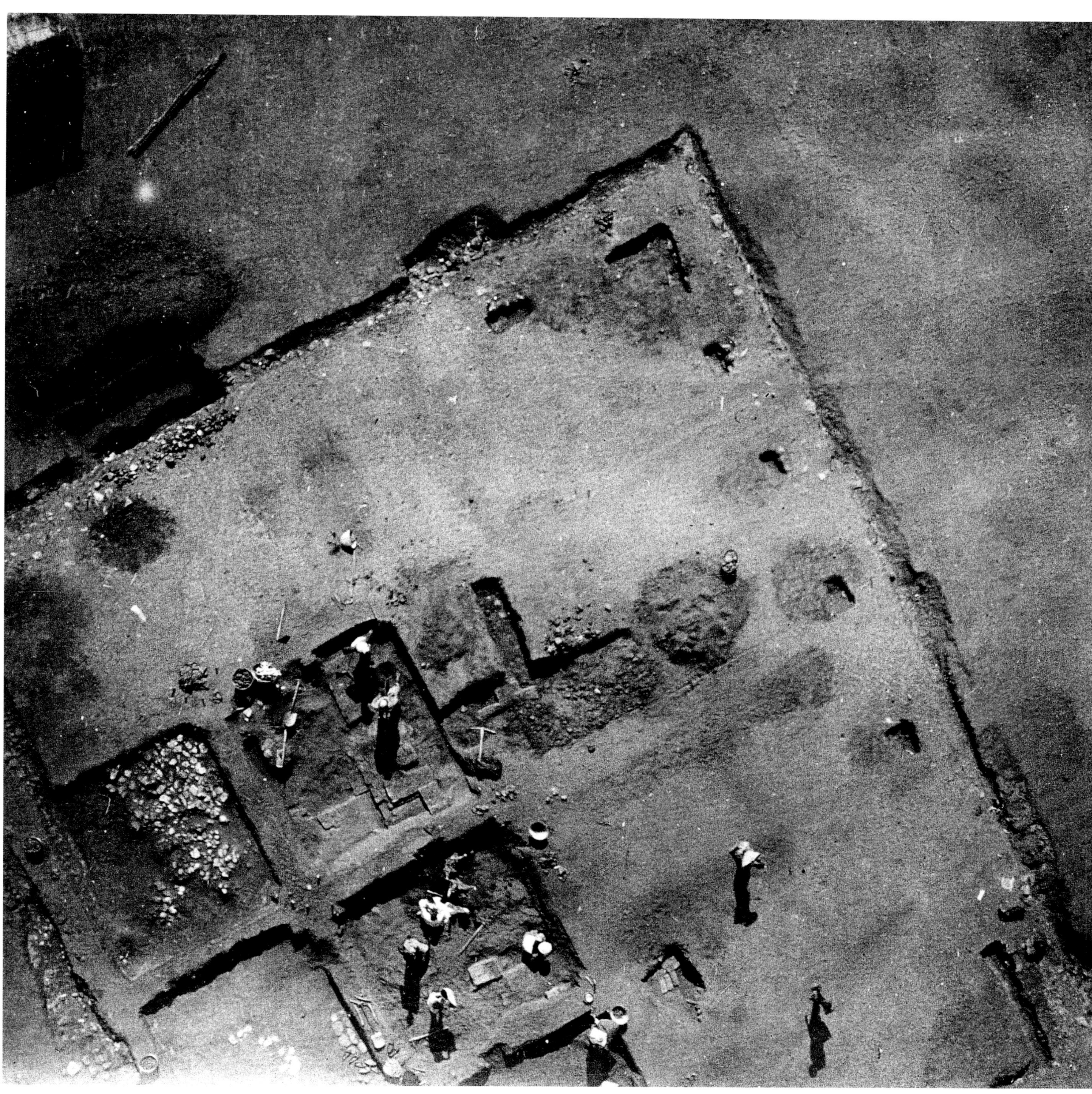

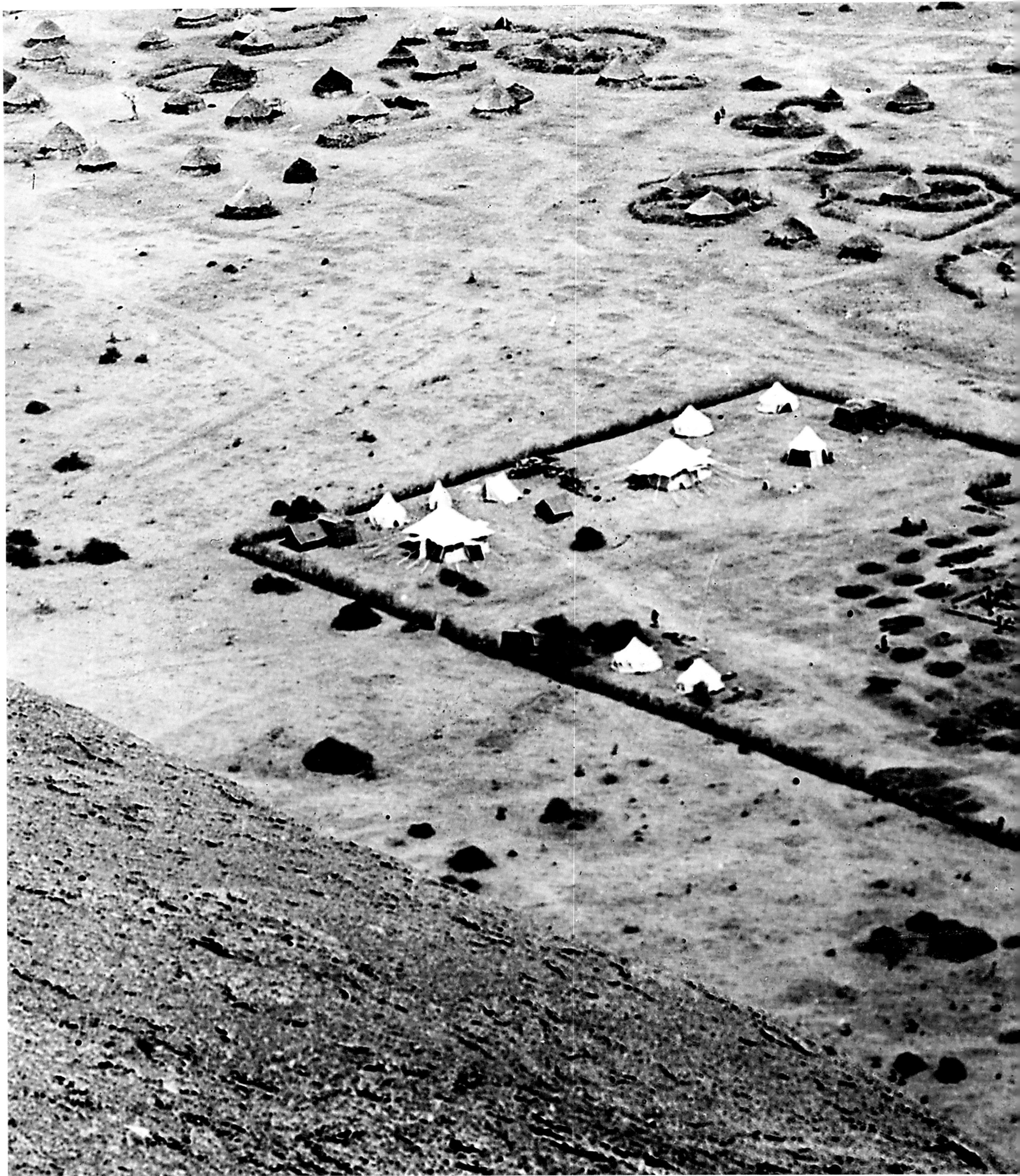

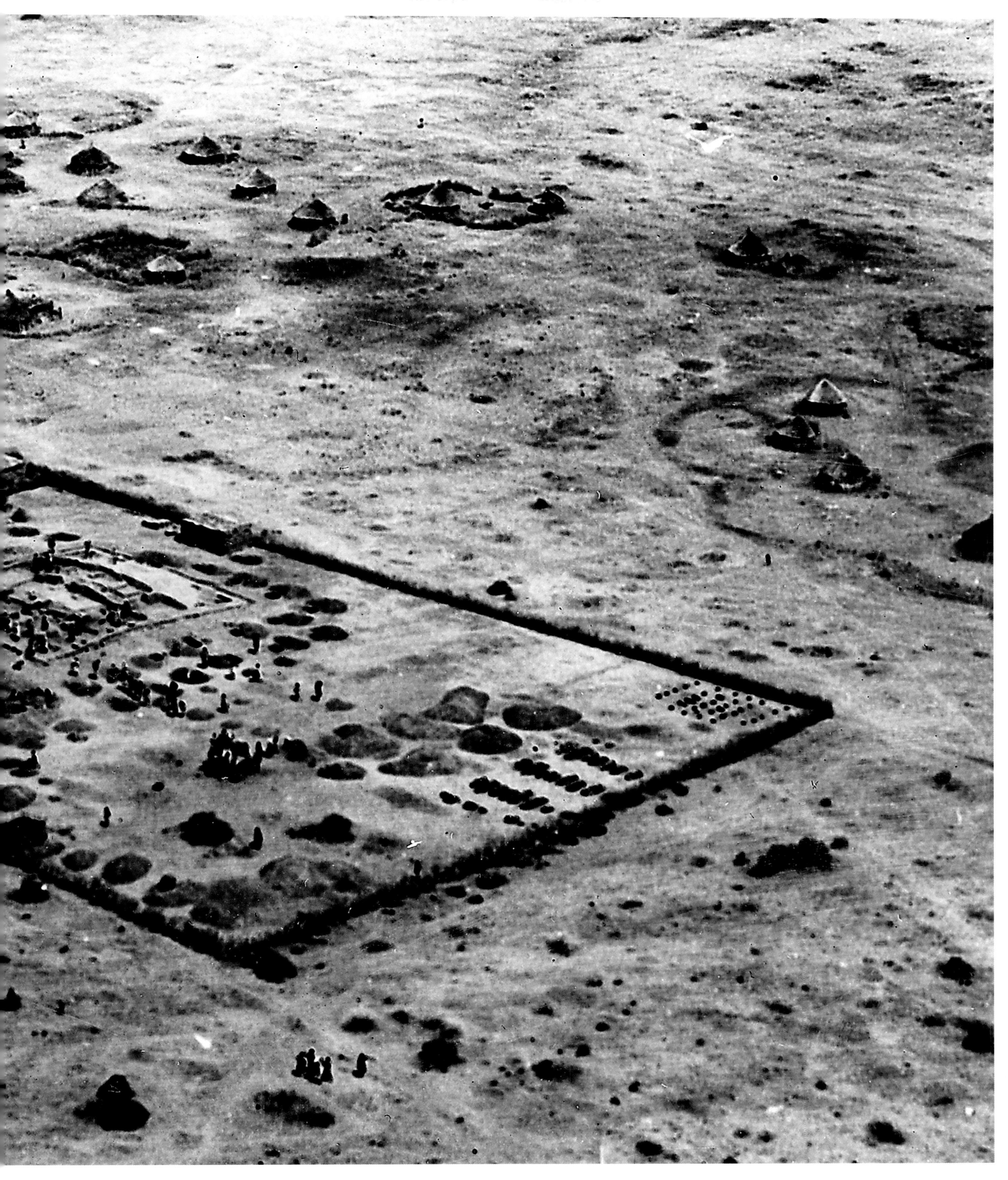

When World War I broke out in 1914, aerial reconnaissance by balloon was already an established part of modern warfare. But the use of aerial *photography* to gather military intelligence was still a fairly new phenomenon. Both German and Allied forces made aerial photographs to detect the movement of troops and better understand enemy intentions (opposite), including on the Western Front. Indeed, by the autumn of 1914, the French had set up specialist aerial photographic sections to collate and study intelligence from such photographs.

Aerial photography also took on new significance in that it could be used to record and reveal the scale of devastation caused by bombing raids. The city of Ypres in Belgium (pictured below), the site of three major battles during World War I and an important strategic landmark, was all but destroyed by bombing. It was here that the Allies crucially prevented German forces from advancing into France, but at a huge cost to both sides. Despite heavy losses, the Allies stood firm and Ypres never fell into German hands.

Photographer unknown
The ruins of central Ypres, Belgium, 1915.

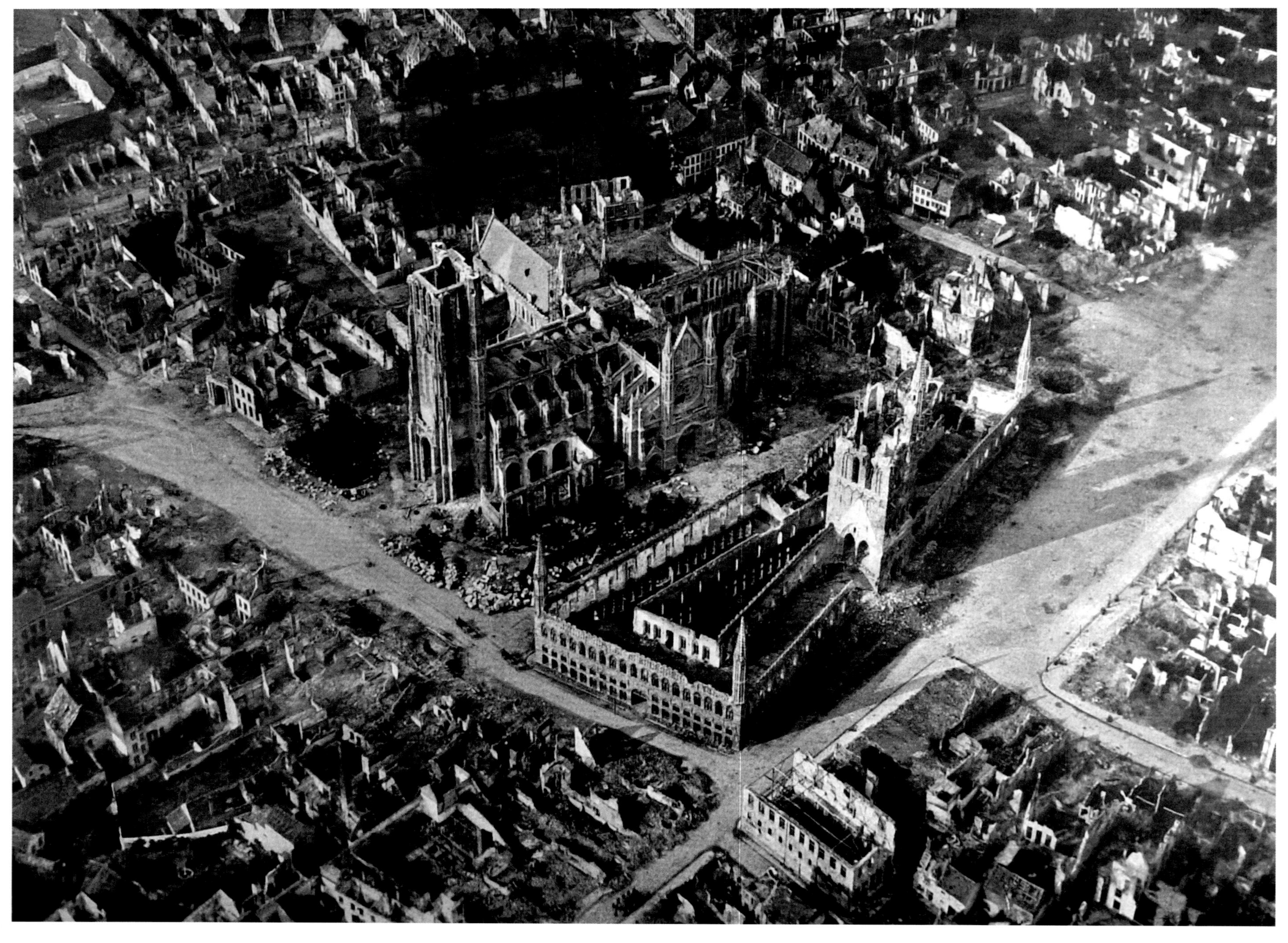

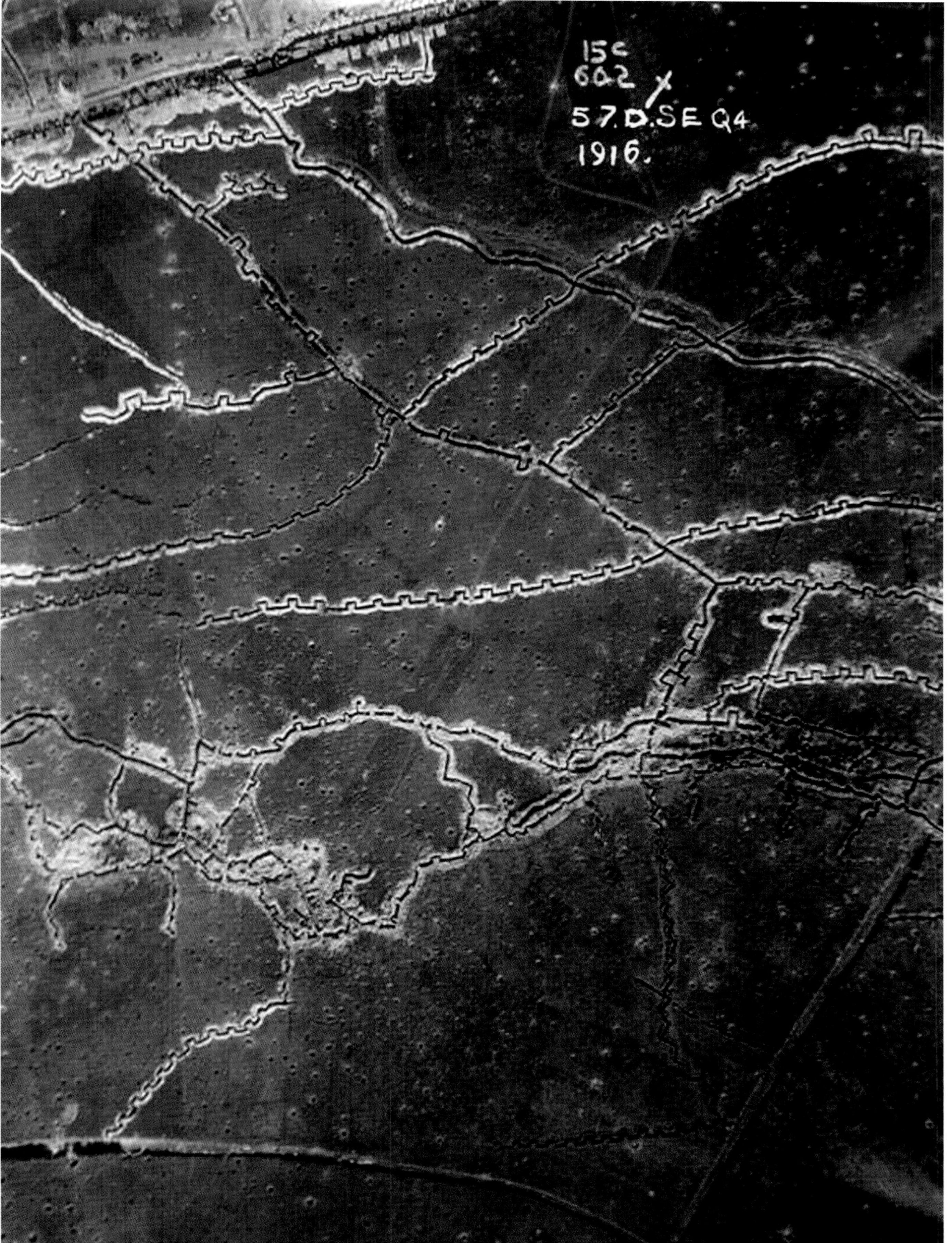

Photographer unknown
British and German frontlines, southwest of the village of Beaumont-Hamel, the Somme, France, *c.* 1916.

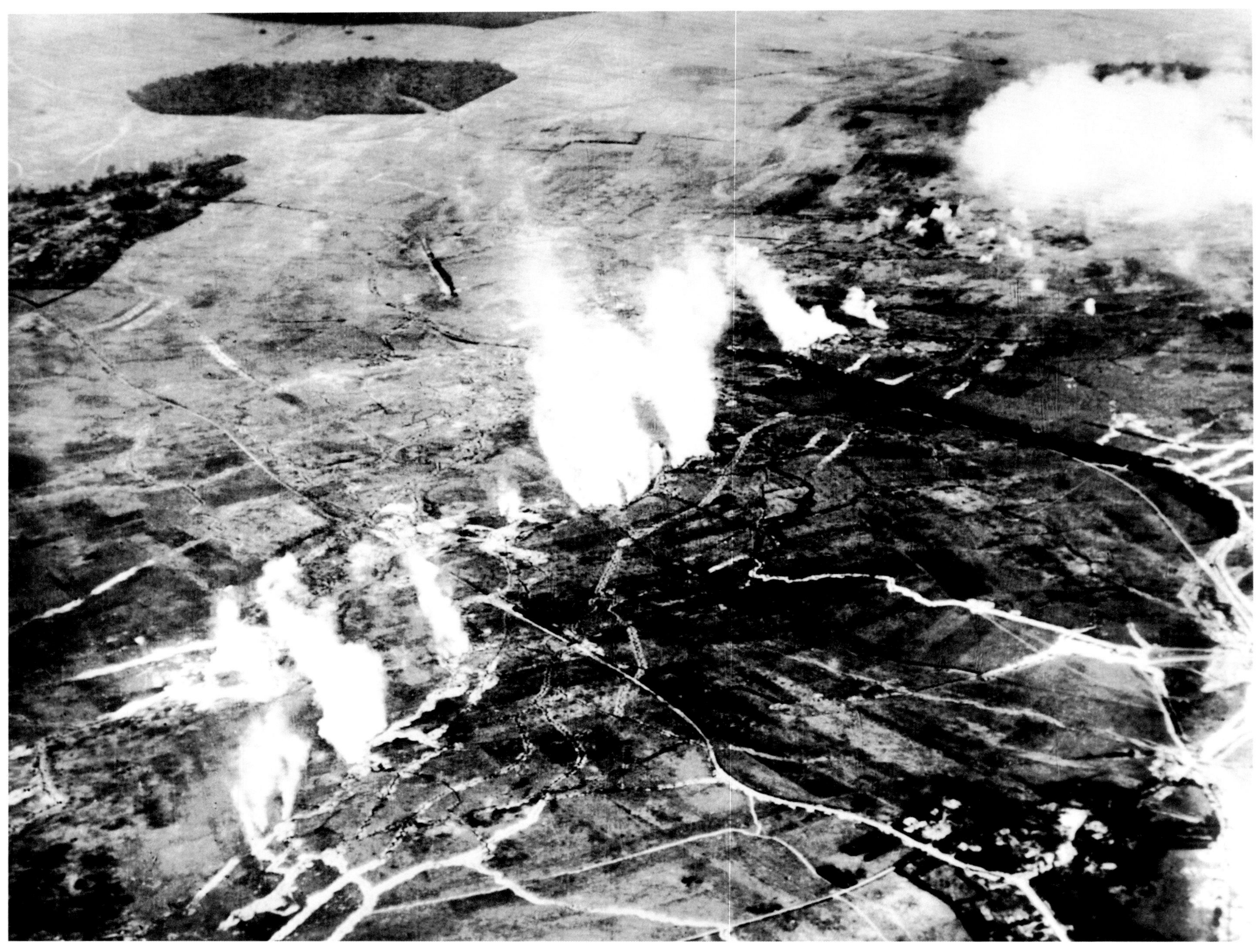

Photographer unknown
Gas attack by British forces on German trenches, the Somme front, France, 1916.

At a glance, this crater-filled scene (pictured below) could be mistaken for the moon's surface, but it is in fact an aerial view of a battlefield on the Somme front in France during World War I. The caption on verso tells us that a French aviator took the photograph from a height of 590 feet (180 metres). Look closely towards the bottom of the frame and you'll see barely visible French troops moving through trenches and shell craters into an area formerly held by the German army. The Battle of the Somme began on 1 July 1916 and lasted 141 days, with a great loss of life on both sides. More than 1 million soldiers fell during the battle. Britain's Royal Flying Corps squadrons made more than 19,000 aerial photographs of the German trenches during the battle itself, as well as before it officially began. The picture opposite depicts a gas attack by British forces on German trenches a month before the start of the battle.

Photographer unknown
A battlefield on the Somme front, France, 1916.

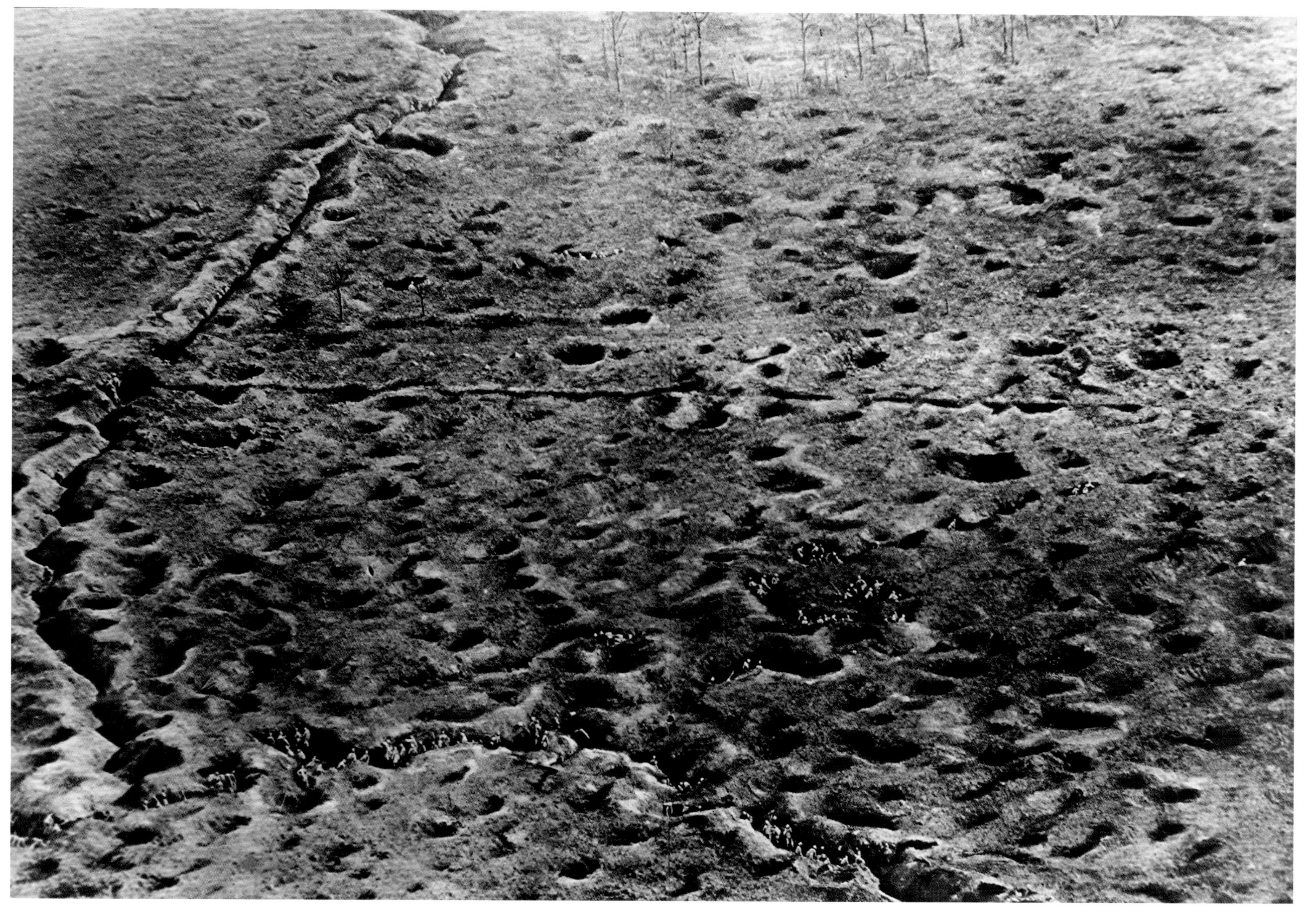

17

During World War I, photographer and adventurer Frank Hurley served as an official photographer with the Australian Imperial Force (AIF). Already a respected photographer, having accompanied explorers Douglas Mawson and Ernest Shackleton on expeditions to Antarctica just a couple of years earlier, Hurley was known for his willingness to take risks when making photographs. He made many photographs during the Third Battle of Ypres, including this eerie picture of the destroyed Belgian city of Ieper (Ypres), to use its Flemish name. Hurley, who was also active as a photographer during World War II, is remembered for his creative and bold approach to photography, which included the use of composites, and his commitment to showing the realities of war through photography.

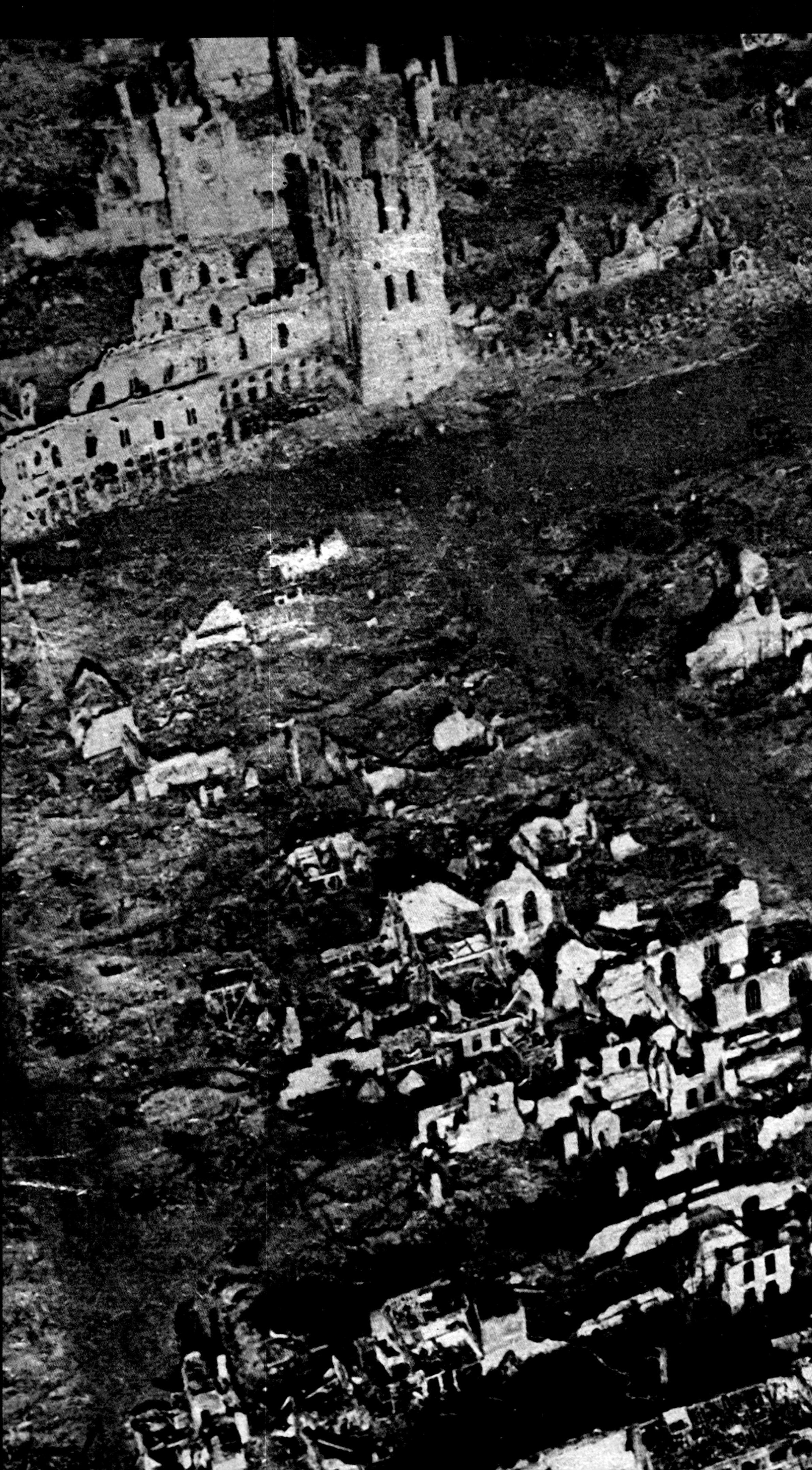

Frank Hurley
The ruins of Ypres, Belgium, from an observation balloon, 1917.

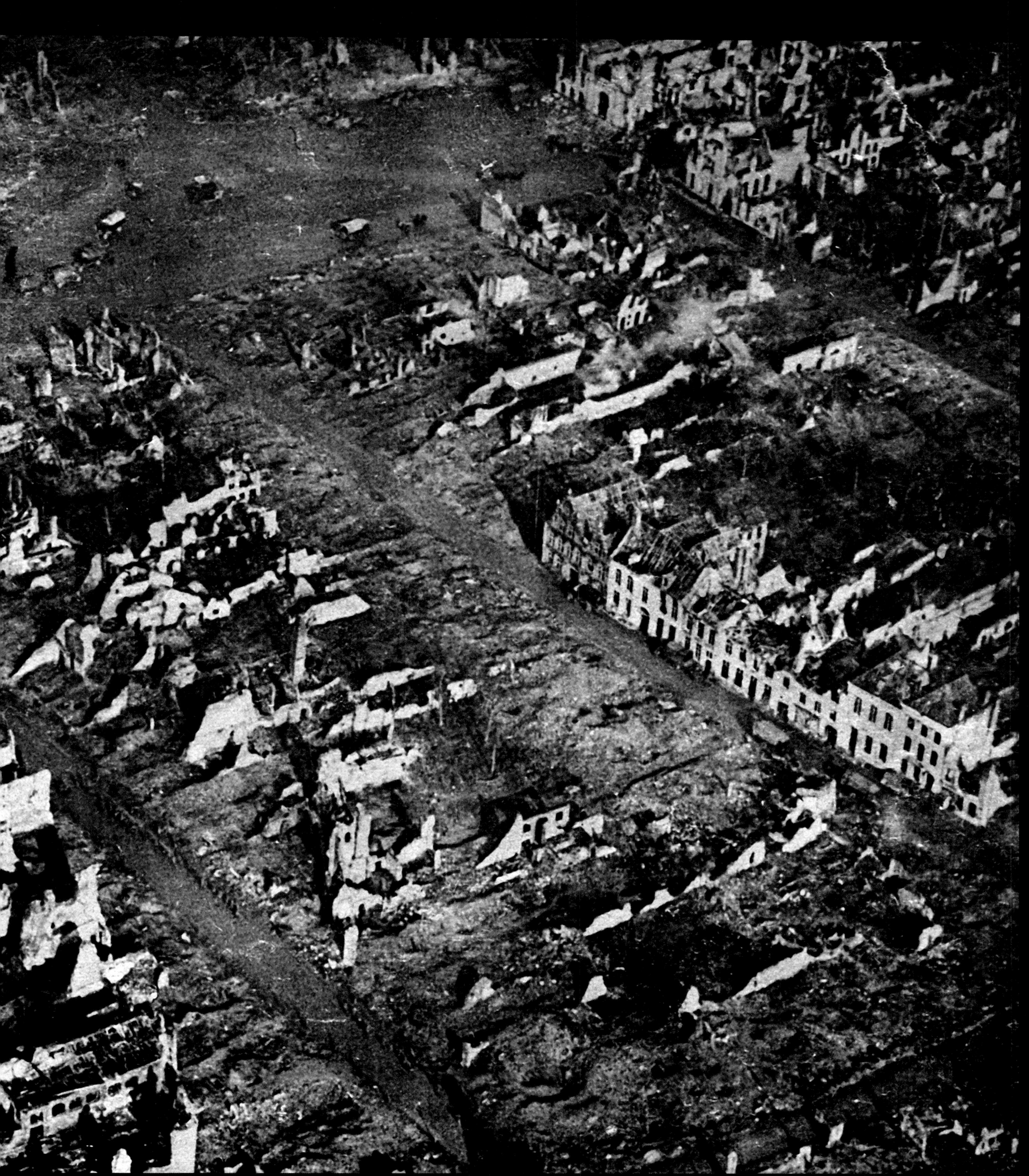

A keen amateur photographer before he joined the Royal Flying Corps during World War I, Walden Hammond became the RFC's photographic expert. Always experimenting with new ideas, Hammond attempted to find ways to tackle aircraft vibration so that clearer photographs could be made. He is also known to have trialled ways of making shots at an oblique angle that could be used for aerial reconnaissance purposes (the army favoured shots taken vertically overhead for intelligence gathering), although his approach was not officially adopted by the military until 1941. He also captured the wreckage of Zeppelin L48, which was shot down and crashed at Theberton in Suffolk on 17 June 1917, and pioneered a method of night photography that involved dropping a flare.

Walden Hammond
Wreck of Zeppelin L48, Theberton, England, 1917.

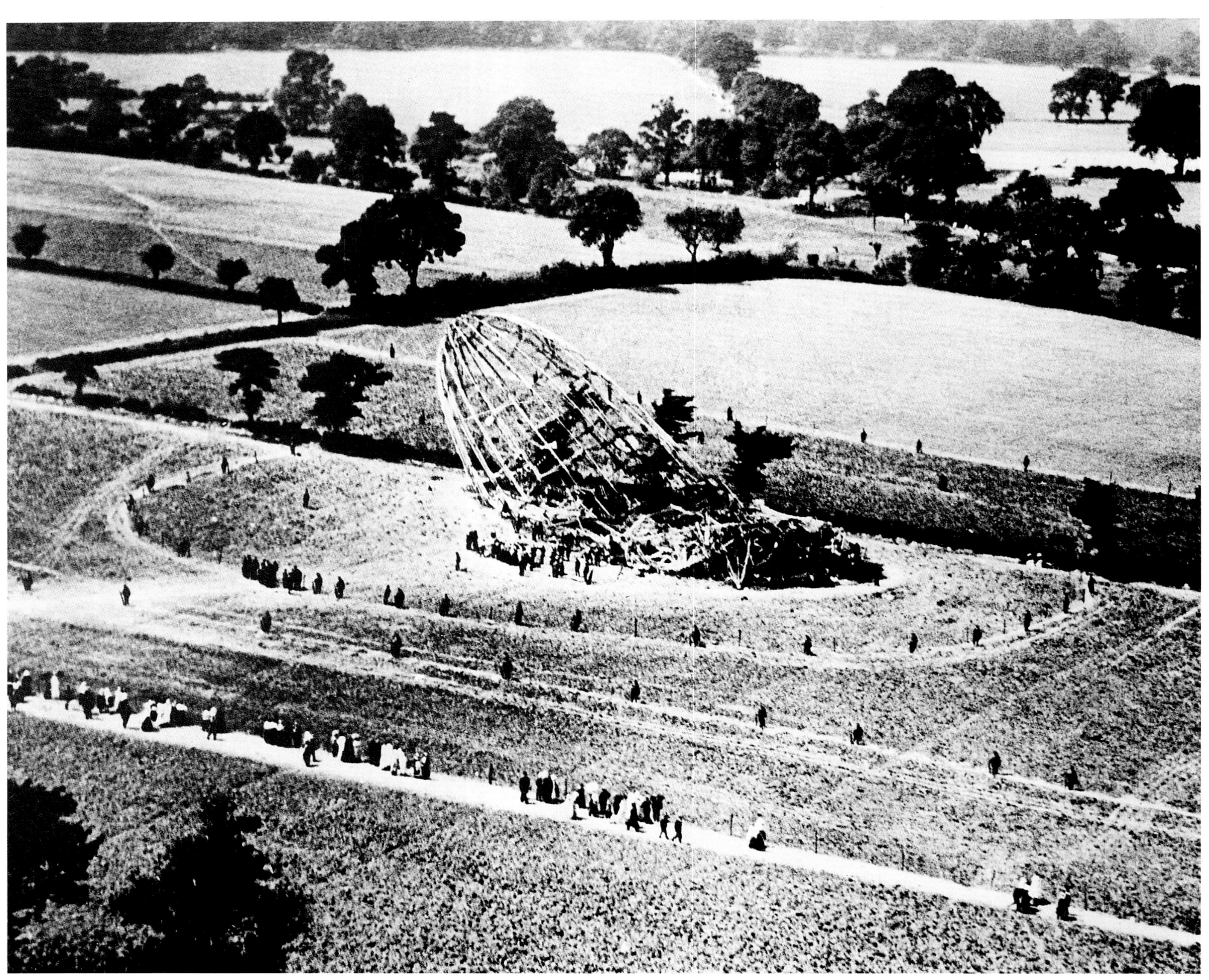

Right and below
Photographers unknown
The aftermath of the Battle of Passchendaele, Belgium, 1917.

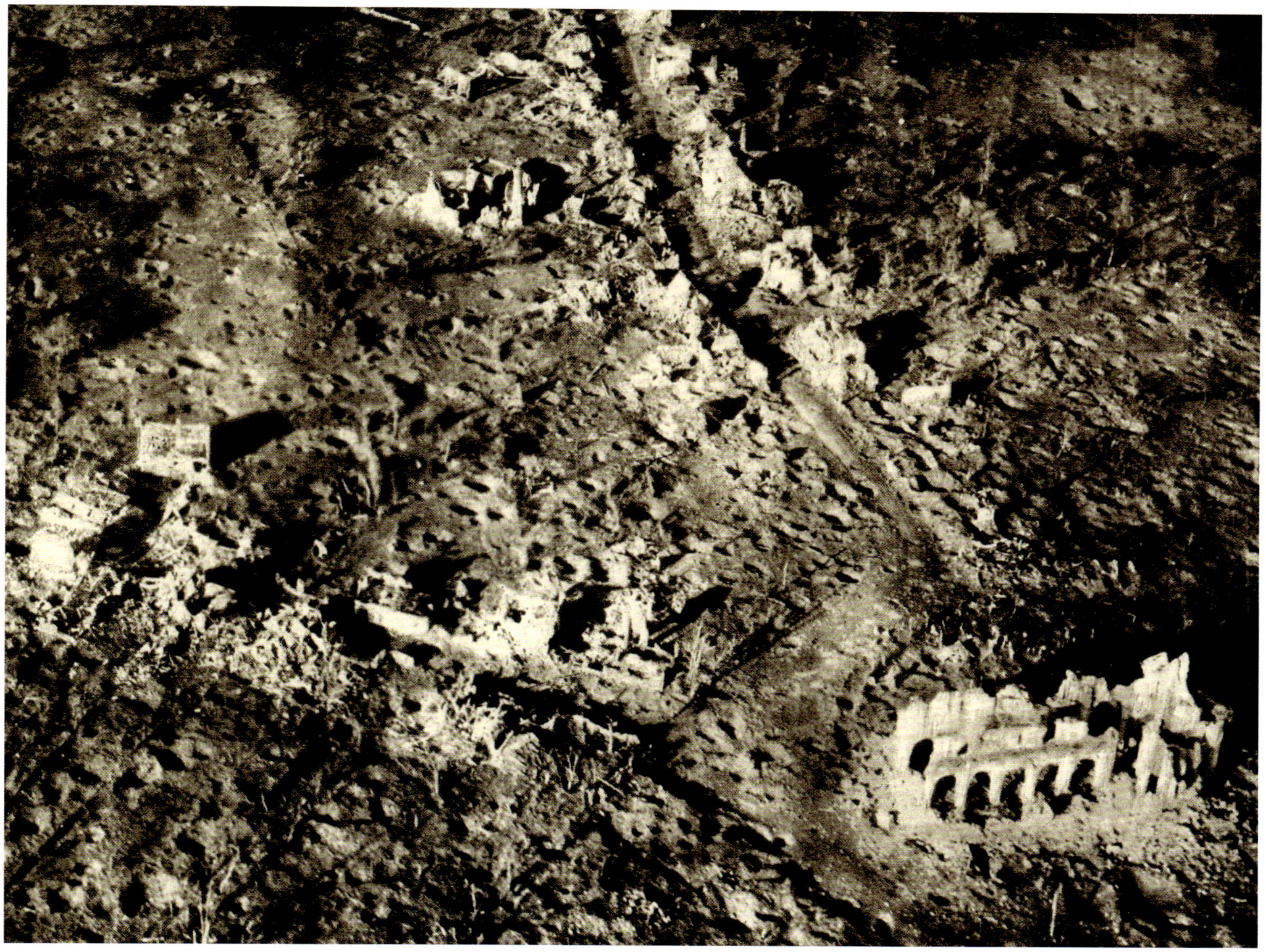

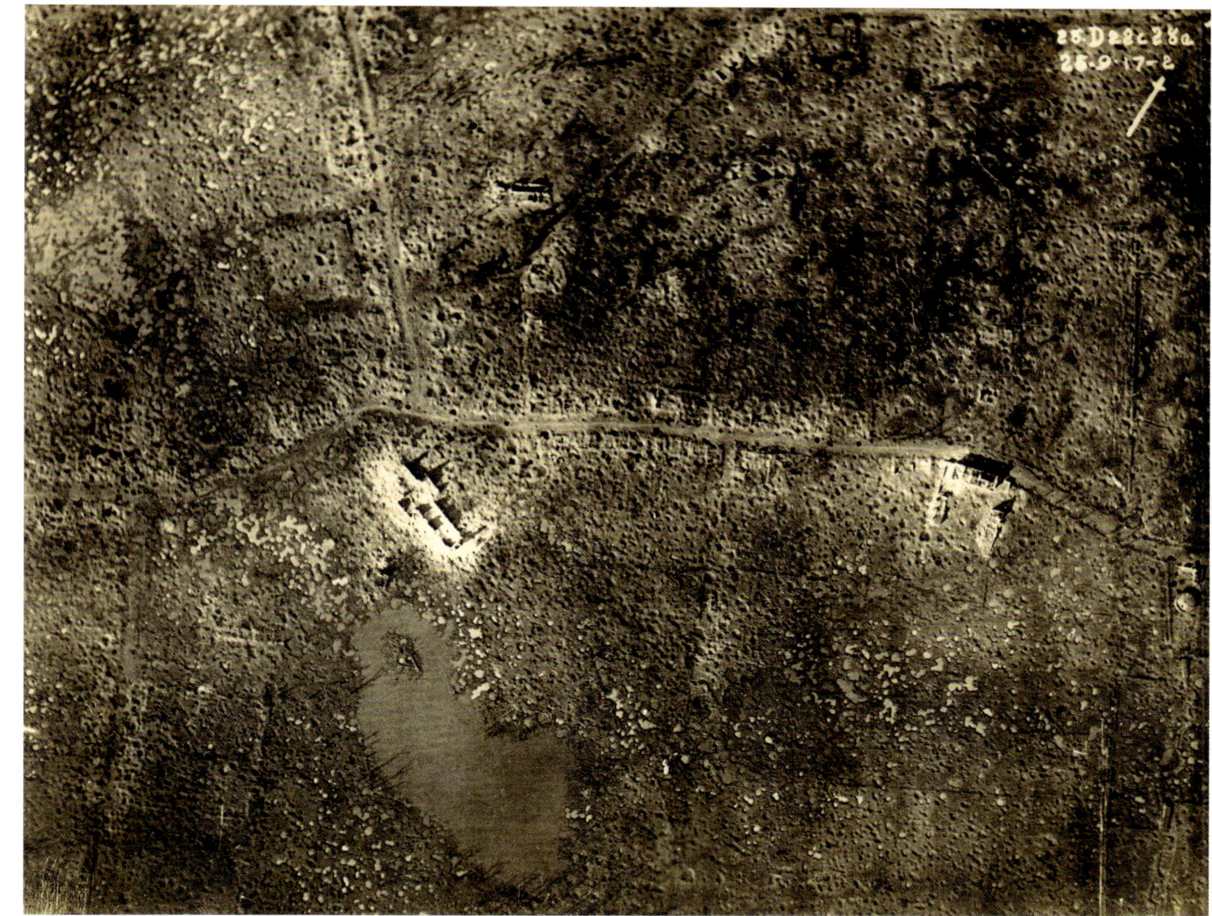

Before the infamous Third Battle of Ypres, the Belgian village of Passchendaele, located northeast of Ypres (pictured above and right) on 16 June 1917, was an ordinary rural community. But the bloody fighting that took place between the start of the battle on 31 July and its conclusion on 6 November 1917 obliterated the village and surrounding fields. Torrential rain turned the ground to mud and more than 325,000 Allied soldiers lost their lives. The extent of the destruction, as these aerial photographs show, was astounding. The landscape is barely recognizable. In the bottom image, only the roads leading into what was once the centre of the village are discernible.

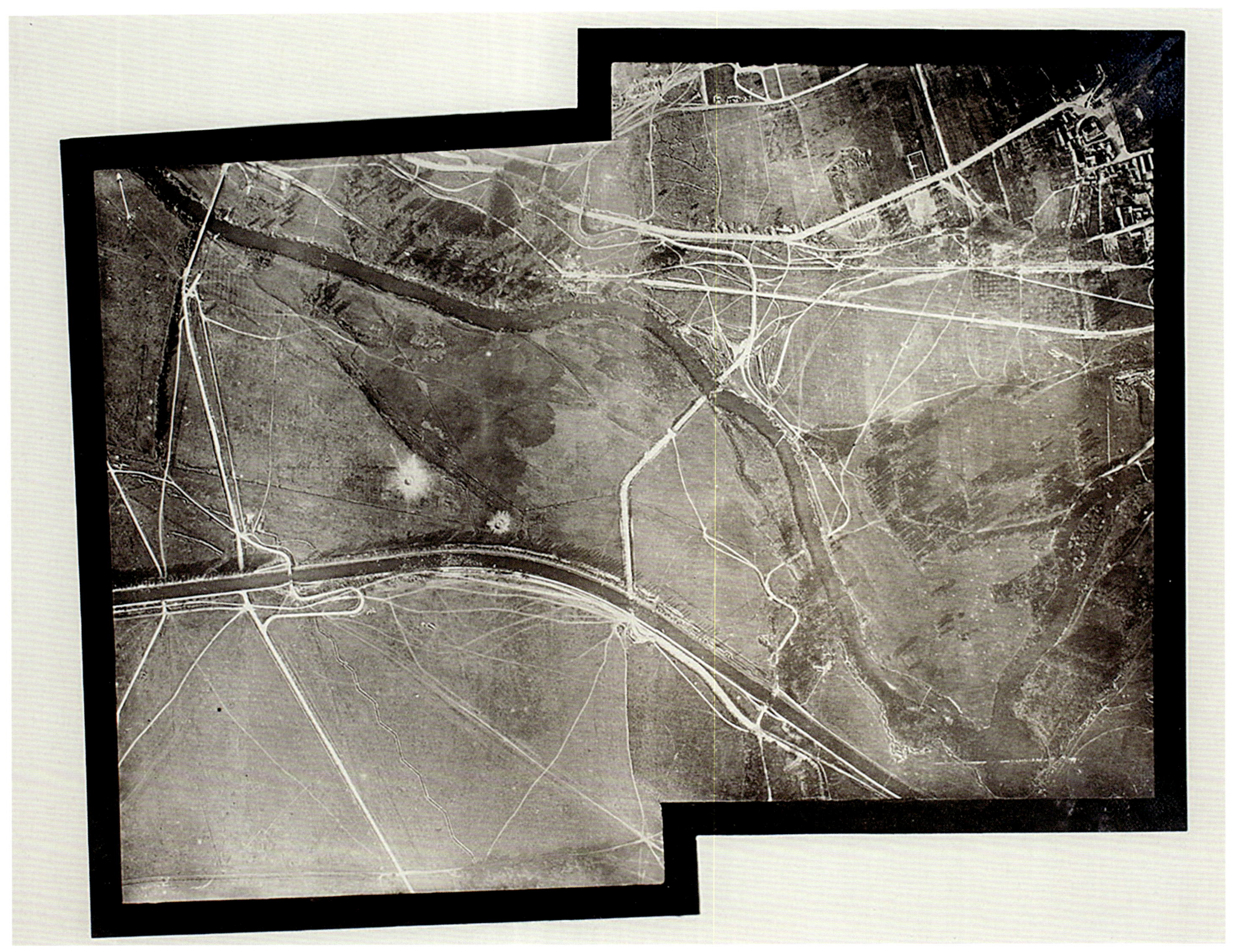

He had already made his name as a champion of pictorialist photography, but from 1917 to 1919 Edward Steichen was employed as chief of the Photographic Section of the American Expeditionary Forces. Responsible for the military's aerial photography, Steichen was instrumental in adapting this type of photography for intelligence and surveillance purposes. Inspired by the challenge of making sharp, clear pictures from a vibrating aircraft travelling at speed, hundreds of metres in the air, he commented that his experiences had brought him 'a new kind of technical interest in photography'. A folio assembled by Steichen and now in the care of the Art Institute of Chicago contains many oblique and vertical photographs showing the aftermath of battles, bridges being destroyed by retreating enemy forces, and even a bomb being dropped from a plane. In 1941, Steichen, then 62, attempted to enlist in the Army Air Corps, but he was turned away. Although he wasn't eligible for active service, Steichen accepted a commission that involved organizing a team of photographers whose job it was to record naval air activity.

Edward Steichen
Villers-en-Prayères, Aisne, northern France, 1918.

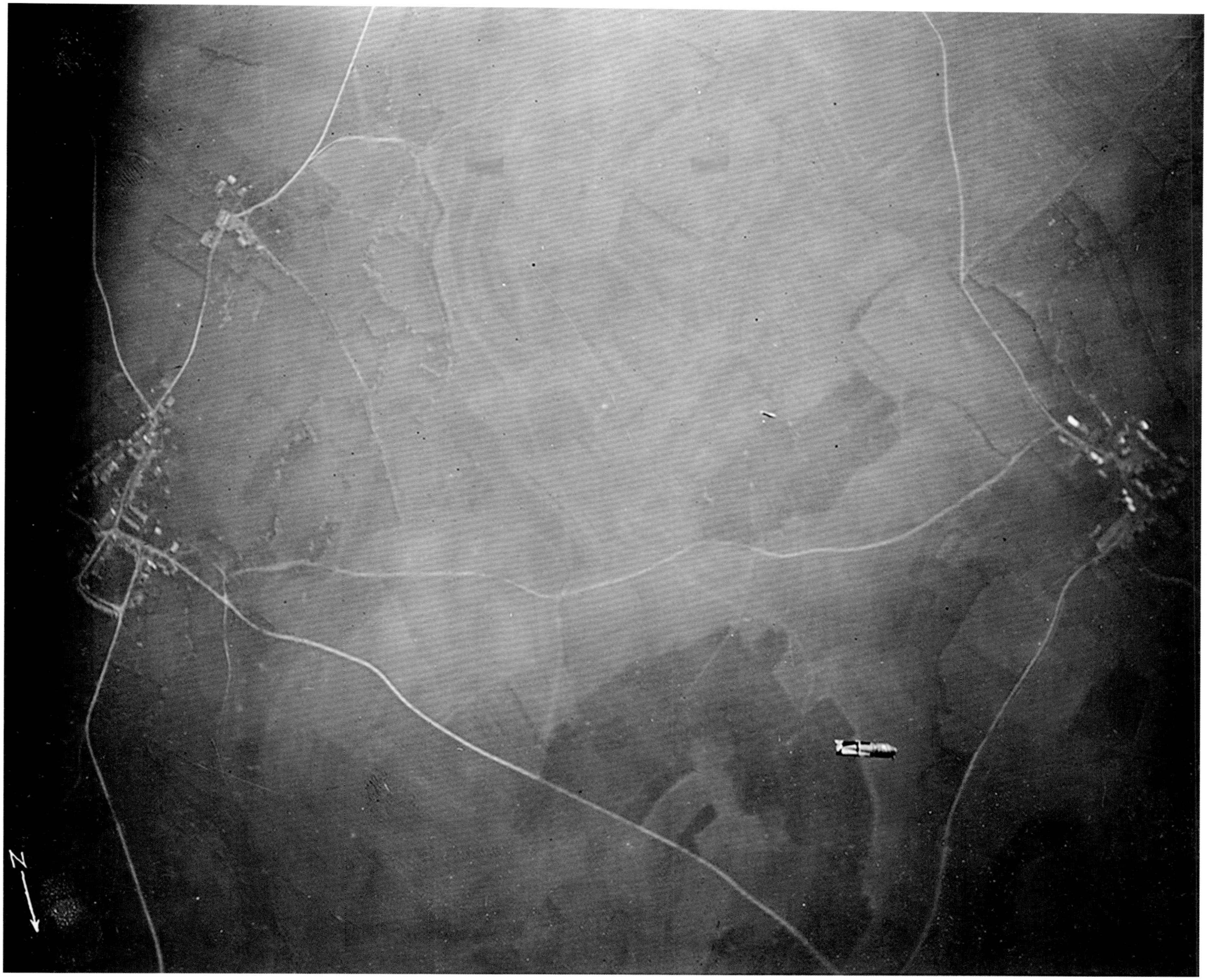

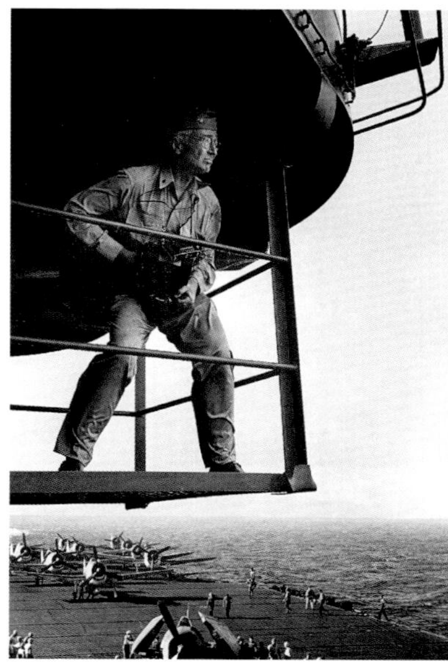

Above
Edward Steichen
Bombs being dropped on Montmédy, France, 1918.

Left
Photographer unknown
Edward Steichen aboard the USS *Lexington* aircraft carrier, 1943. This picture was taken while Steichen was on commission to organize the documentation of naval air activity during World War II.

Having originally wanted to be a painter, in 1905 Londoner Alfred Buckham took up photography and he went on to capture some of the most remarkable aerial photographs of his day. The peaceful beauty of his images depicting London, Edinburgh and South America is in stark contrast to the destruction and loss of life shown during the war. Buckham's images are impressive, not just because of the views they afforded, but also because of the manner in which they were taken. Buckham, who was head of aerial investigations for the Royal Navy during World War I, would lean out of his aeroplane with a heavy plate camera. Standing up allowed the necessary freedom of movement to make good photographs, he claimed, because vibration from the engine was reduced. Buckham's daring approach to picture-making may have led to breathtaking photographs such as this image (opposite) taken over the landscape around Rosyth, on the Firth of Forth in Scotland, where we can see just how close another biplane was to Buckham's aircraft, but it also got him in trouble on occasion. In 1918, Buckham crashed for the ninth time, close to where this photograph was made, and sustained serious injuries. His images are important because they reveal how aerial photography was beginning to be used not just for reconnaissance purposes, but instead to show and celebrate the beauty of the world below.

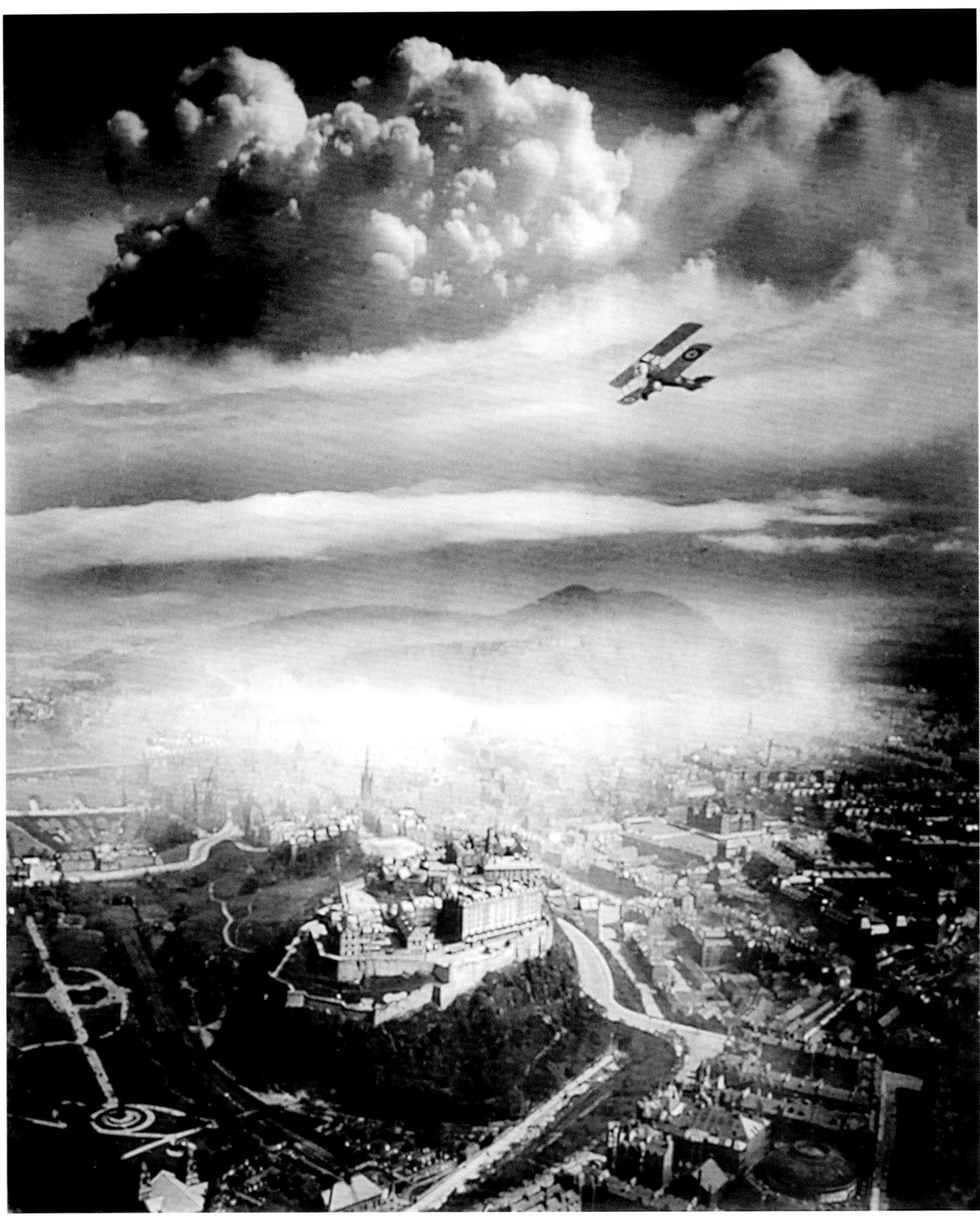

Left
Alfred Buckham
Edinburgh, Scotland, *c.* 1920.

Opposite
Alfred Buckham
Sunshine and Showers, view of Rosyth, Scotland, *c.* 1920.

Overleaf
Alfred Buckham
R100 airship, location unknown, *c.* 1920.

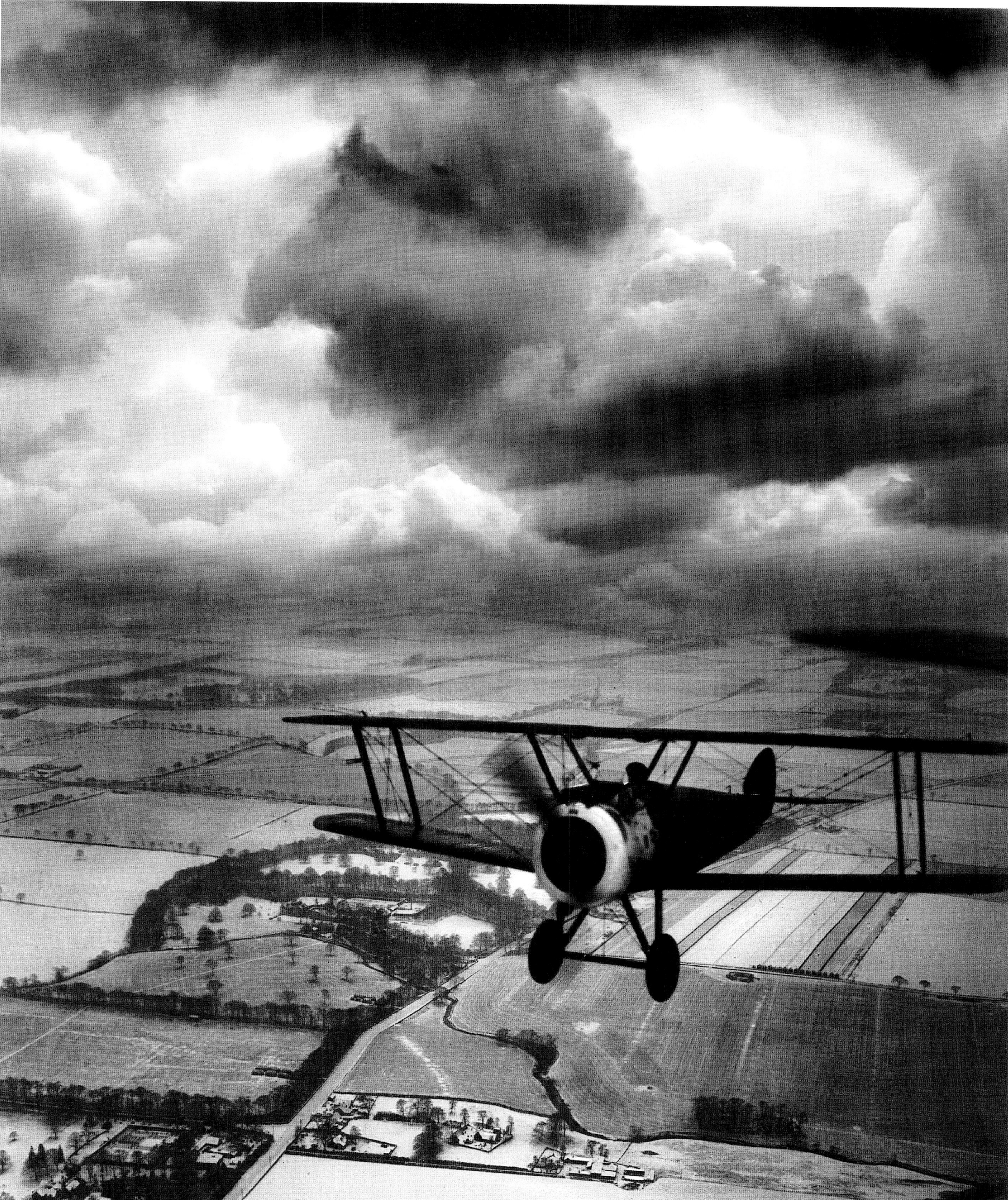

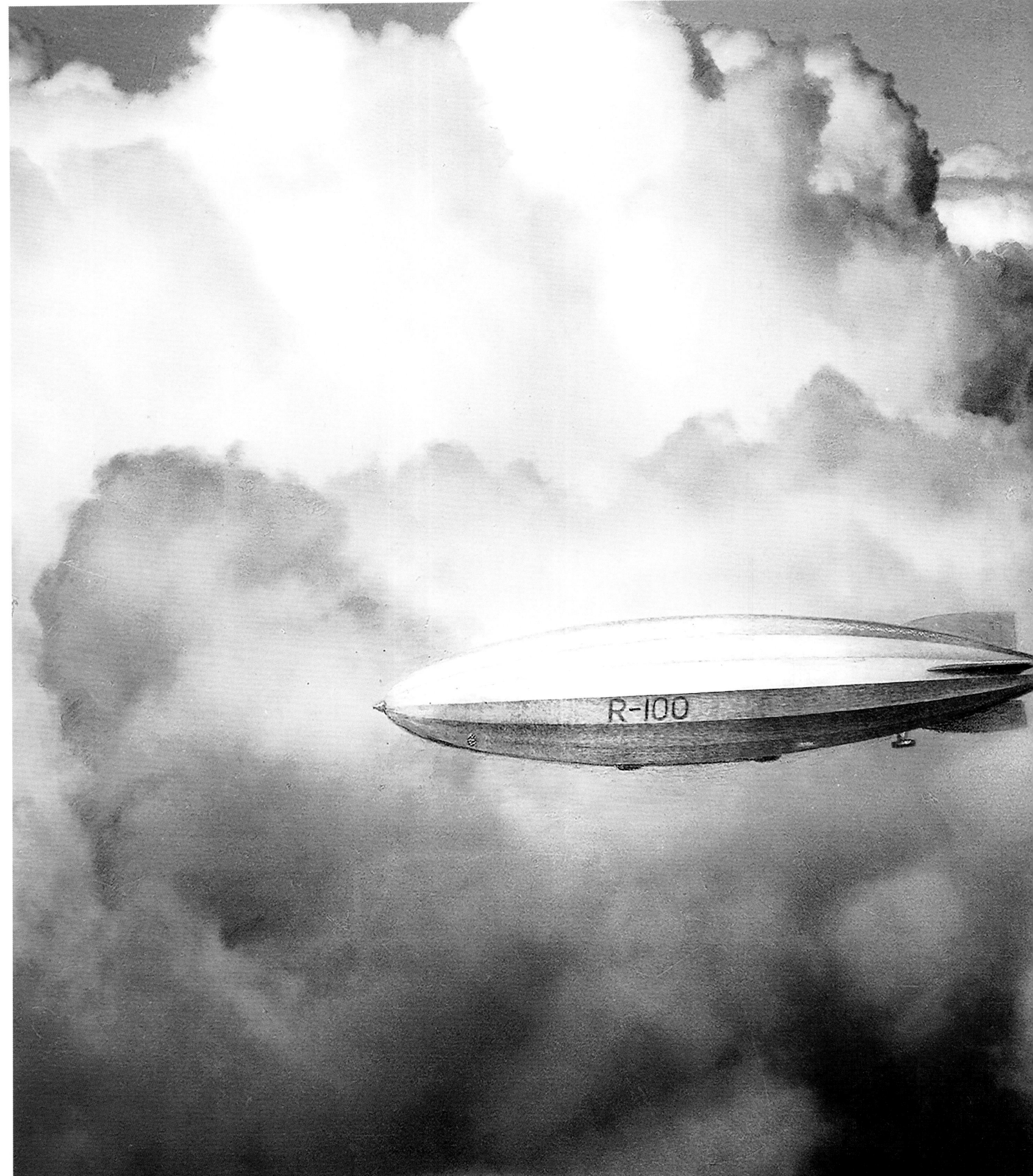
R-100

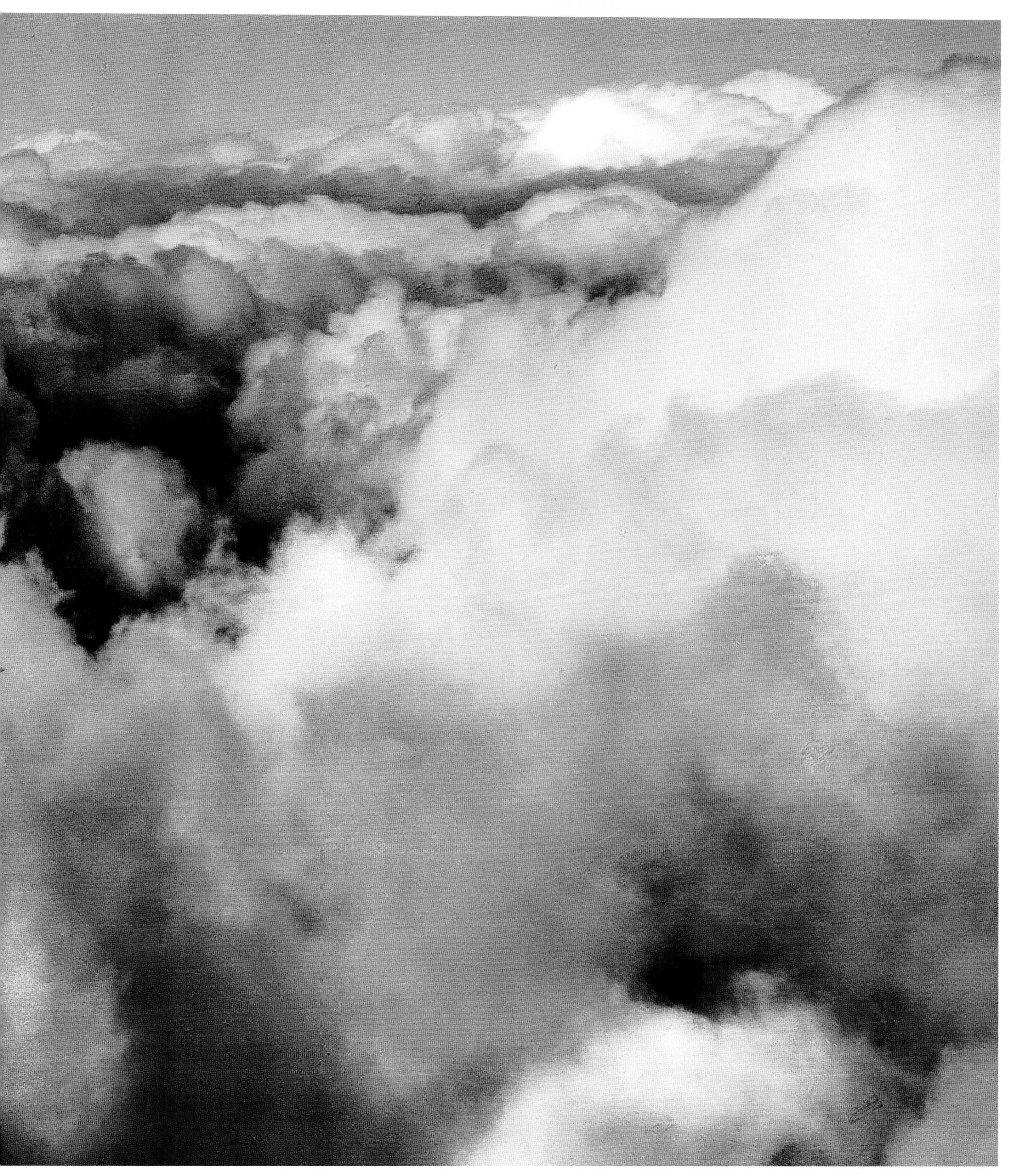

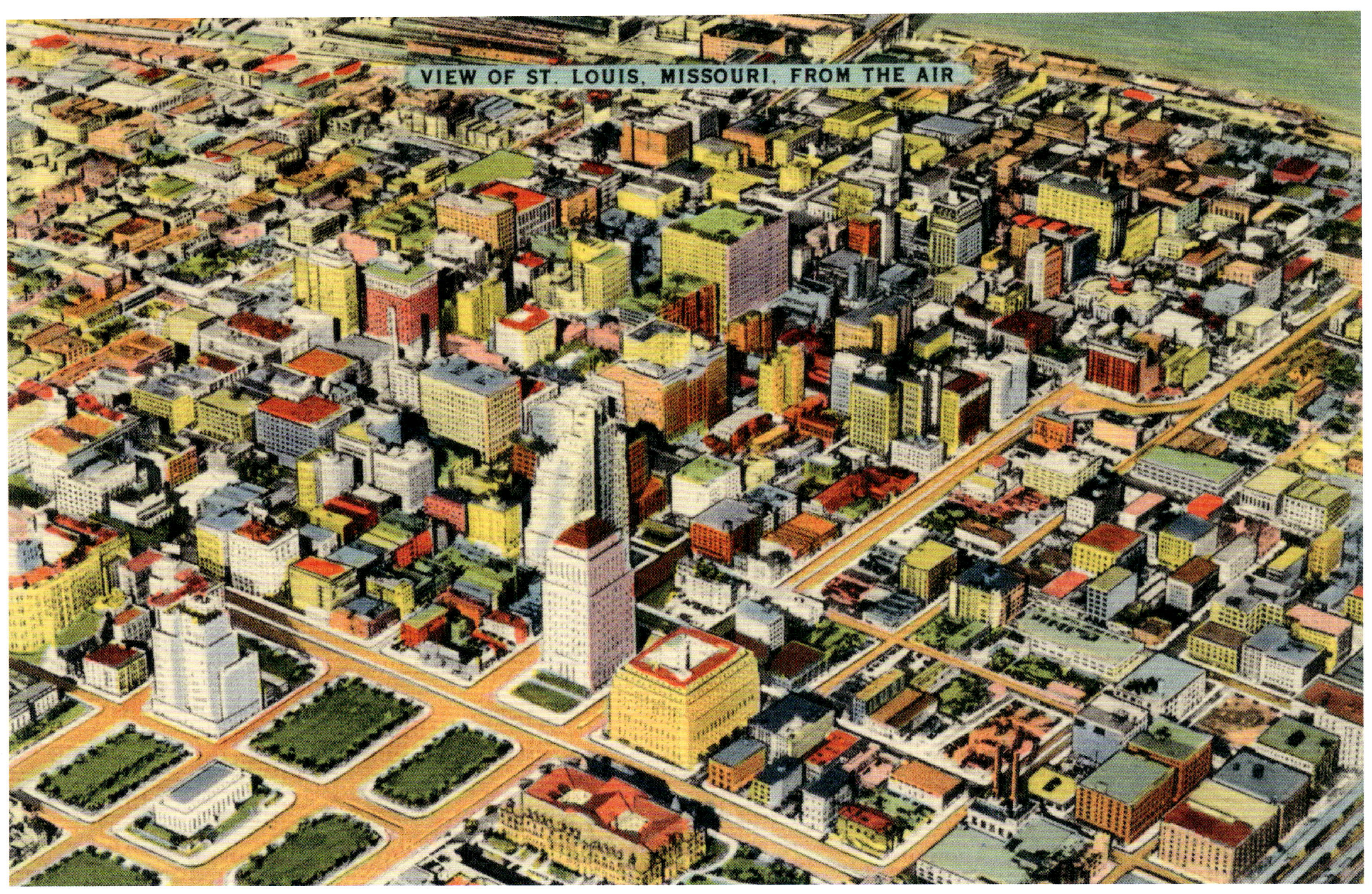

By 1920, the 'Golden Age of Postcards' had come to an end, but postcards were still part of everyday life. Postcards, or 'view cards', such as this one with the title *View of St. Louis, Missouri, from the Air,* depicted every kind of scene you could imagine, from America's main streets and civic buildings to factories, railroads, amusement parks and even cemeteries. Postcards also carried pastoral views of lakes, rivers and mountains – indeed, all manner of pastimes and settings.

Photographer unknown
View of St. Louis, Missouri, from the Air, USA, 1920.

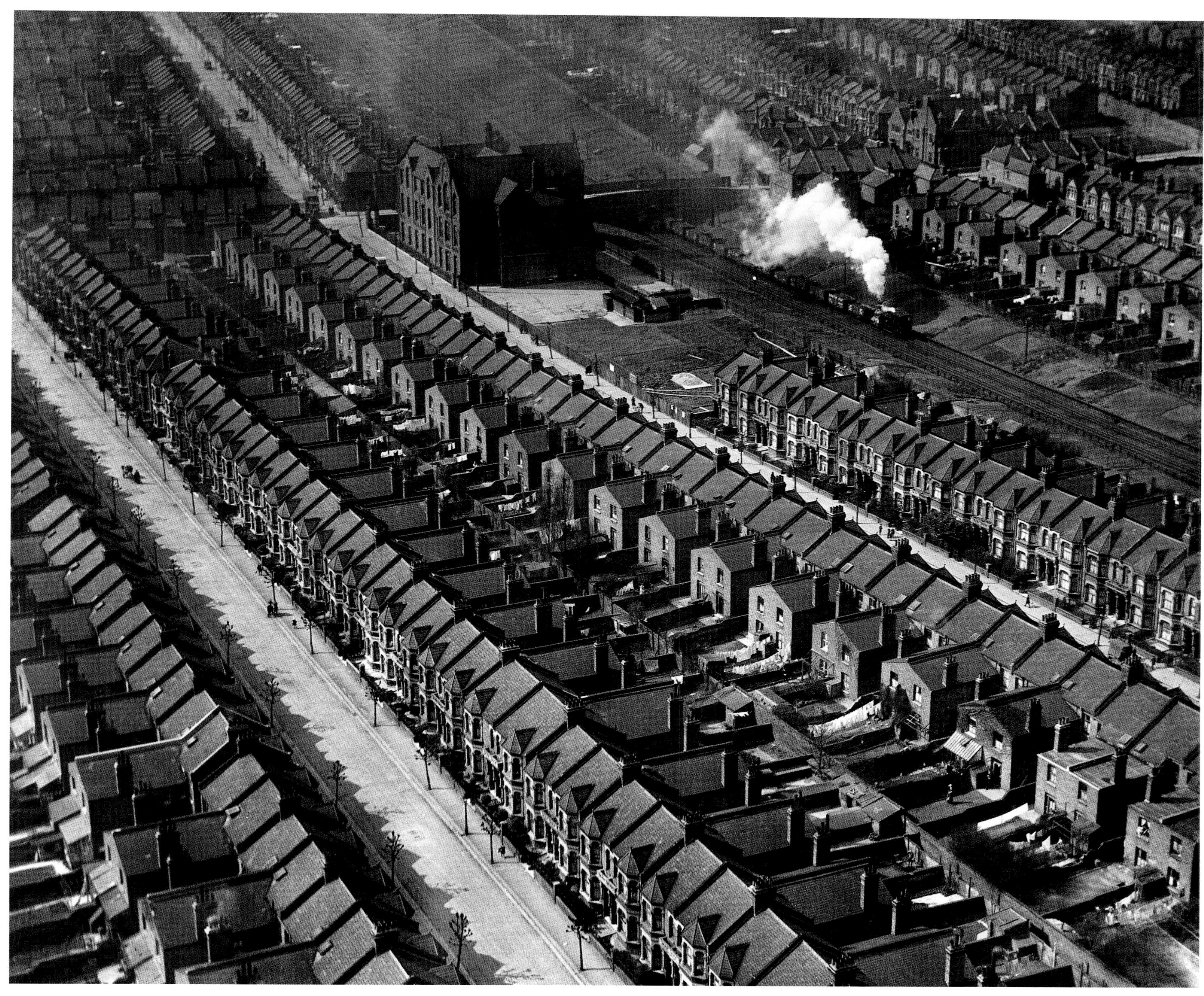

Aerofilms Ltd
Kensal Rise, London, England, 1921.

This is Kensal Rise, West London, as it would have looked in March 1921. A chugging steam train is visible towards the top of the picture, amid rows of densely packed houses. The image is one of hundreds of thousands of aerial photographs that belong to the Aerofilms collection. Co-founded in 1919 by English aviation pioneer and pilot Claude Grahame-White and Francis Lewis Wills, an architect who had flown with the Royal Naval Air Service during World War I, Aerofilms Ltd was the world's first aerial photography company. Together, Grahame-White and Wills did what no one had done before: created a successful business from what had until then been a practice primarily confined to the military. The image is now part of the Britain from Above archive and website, an initiative to conserve and make available to the public more than 95,000 photographs from the Aerofilms collection (see also pages 52, 86–7, 96).

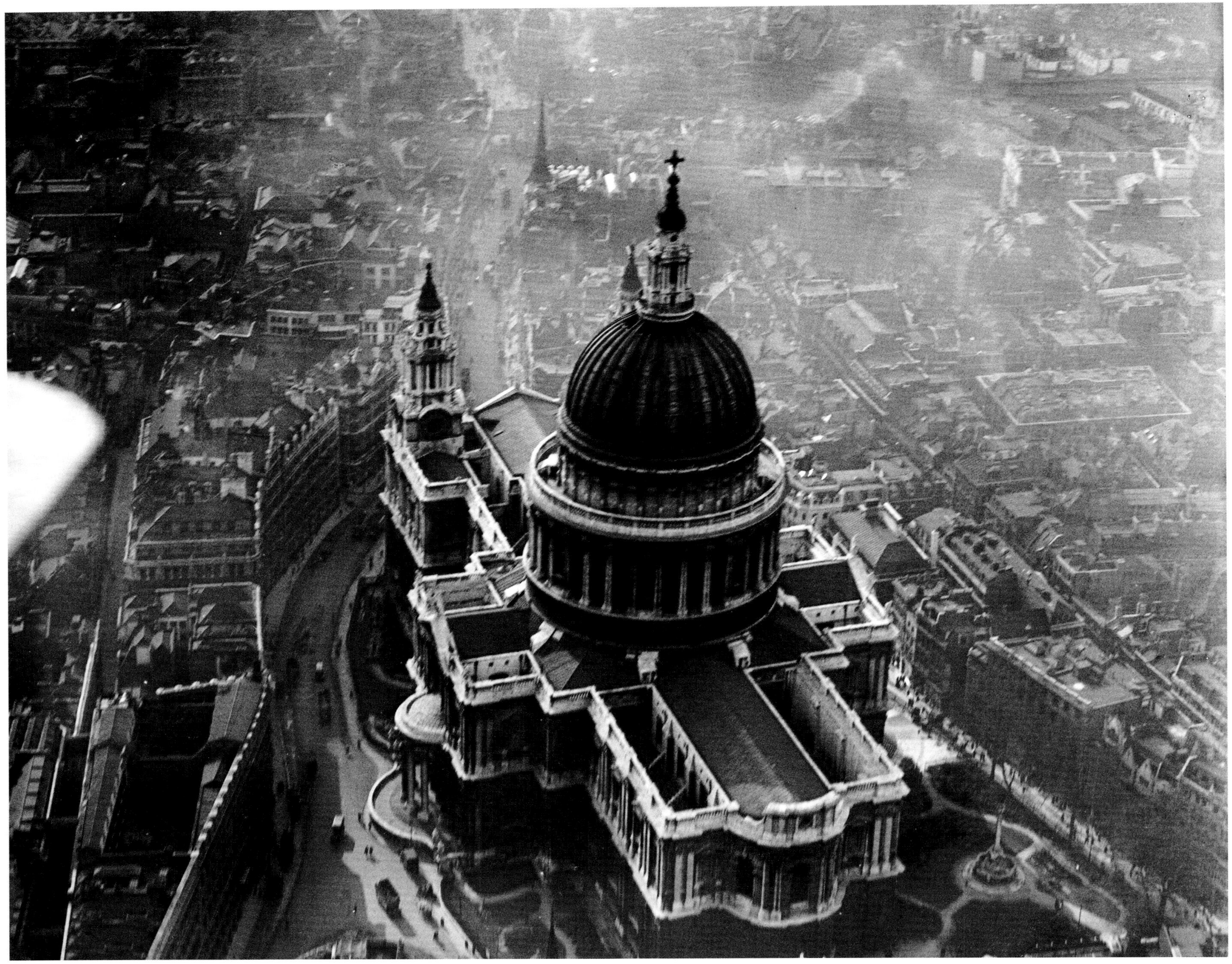

Here is St. Paul's Cathedral, also from the Aerofilms collection (see pages 51, 86–7, 96). In its day, the aerial photography work that the company was doing was nothing short of pioneering. Aerofilms Ltd made aerial photographs across London and all over Great Britain and Ireland, producing many thousands of photographs each year. Even before he co-founded the company in 1919, Claude Grahame-White, who had taken aerial photographs during World War I, had spotted the lucrative potential of aerial photography, and in the years that followed, continued to commercialize aerial photography successfully for the mass market. The company's work was instrumental in making everything from urban and suburban views to rural, coastal and industrial scenes visible from the air on a scale not seen before in peacetime. In doing so, they created a phenomenal archive of photographic evidence that not only aided the understanding and management of both built and natural environments at the time, but also remains an important historical record today.

Aerofilms Ltd
St. Paul's Cathedral from above, London, England, 1921.

A gift from France to America in 1885 and erected the following year, the Statue of Liberty needs little introduction. While a considerable number of photographs of the famous New York landmark dating back to the late nineteenth and early twentieth century can be found online, less commonplace are photographs of the statue shot from the air around this time. Thanks to weekly journals such as *Flight*, founded in 1909, audiences would have seen aerial views of famous landmarks, but even so, an image like this was still fairly unusual. The fact that we are clearly able to see the statue in her surroundings makes the photograph an especially useful historical visual document.

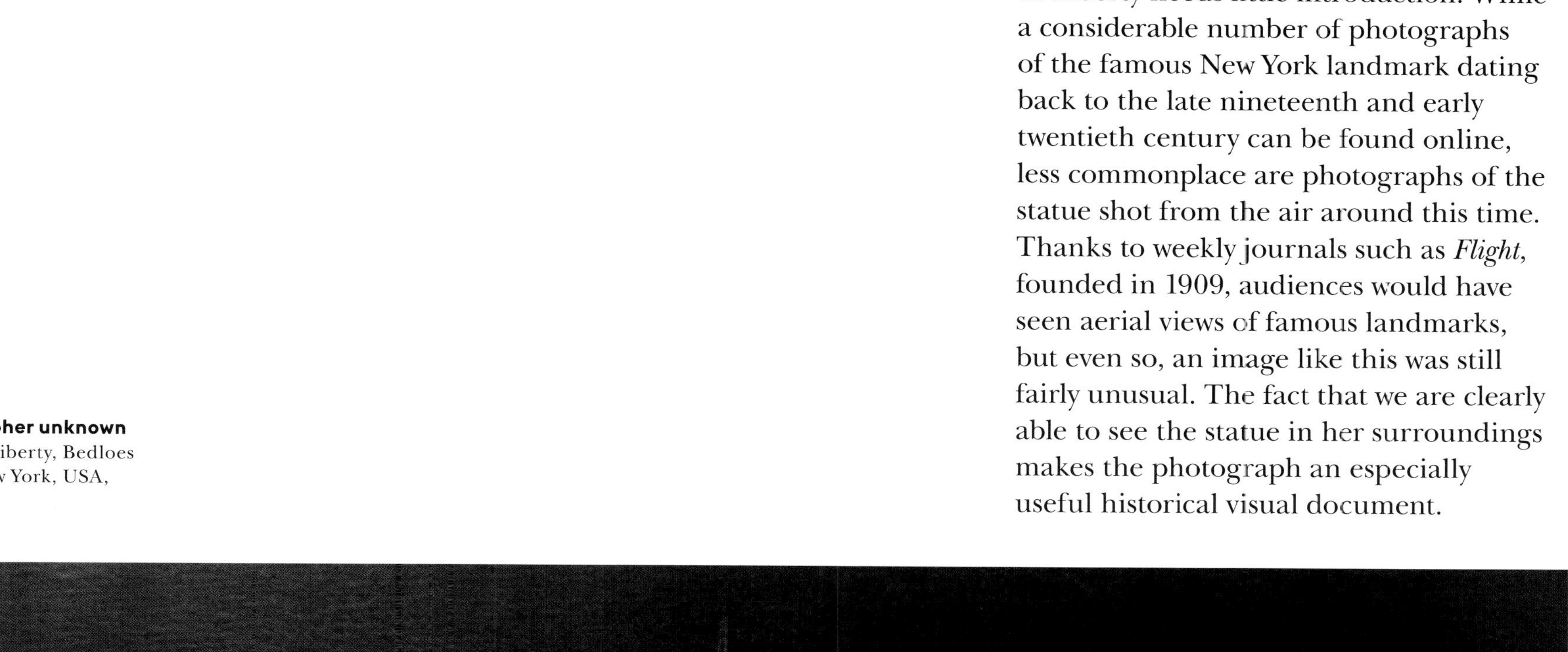

Photographer unknown
Statue of Liberty, Bedloes Island, New York, USA, *c.* 1922.

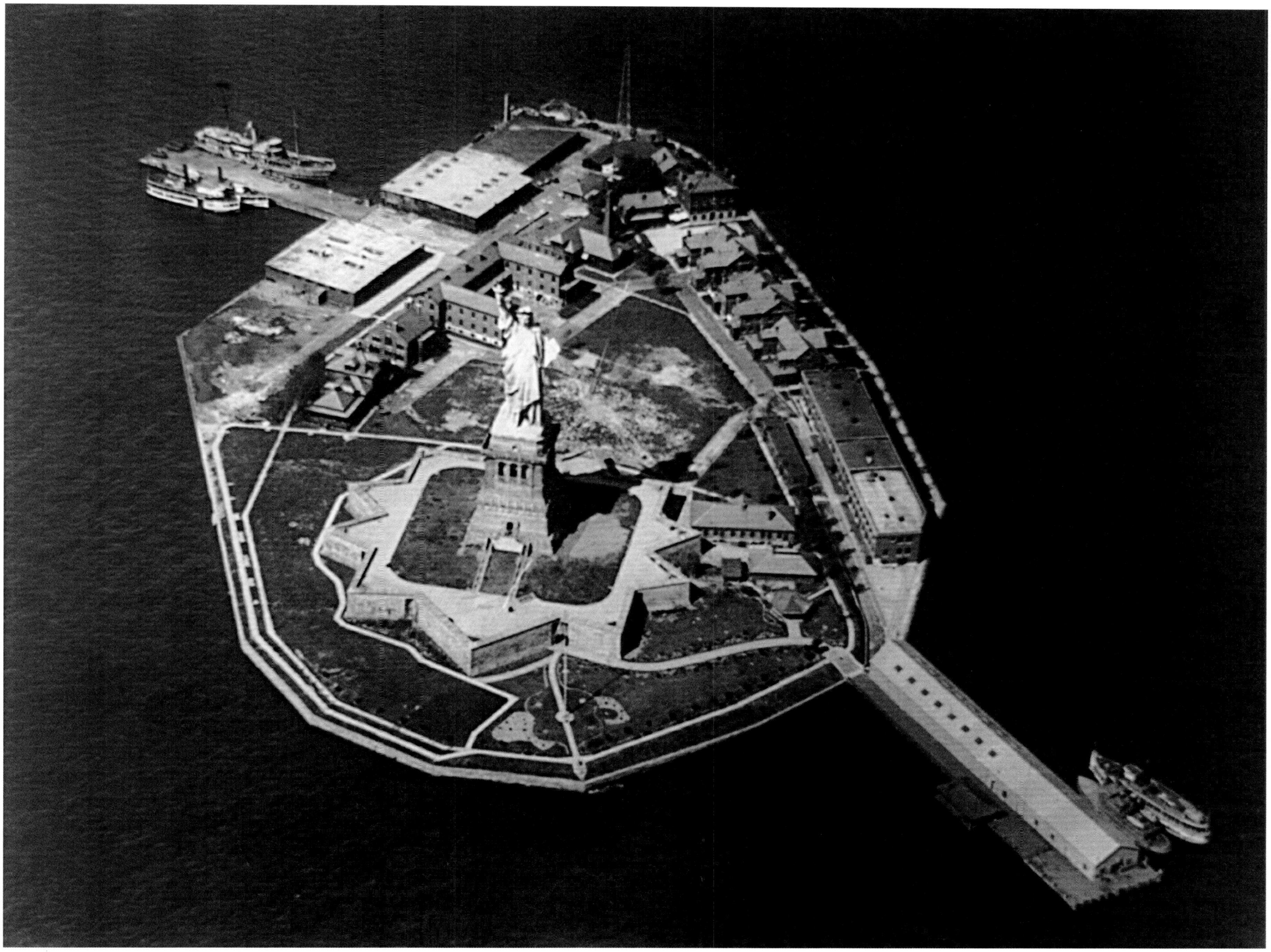

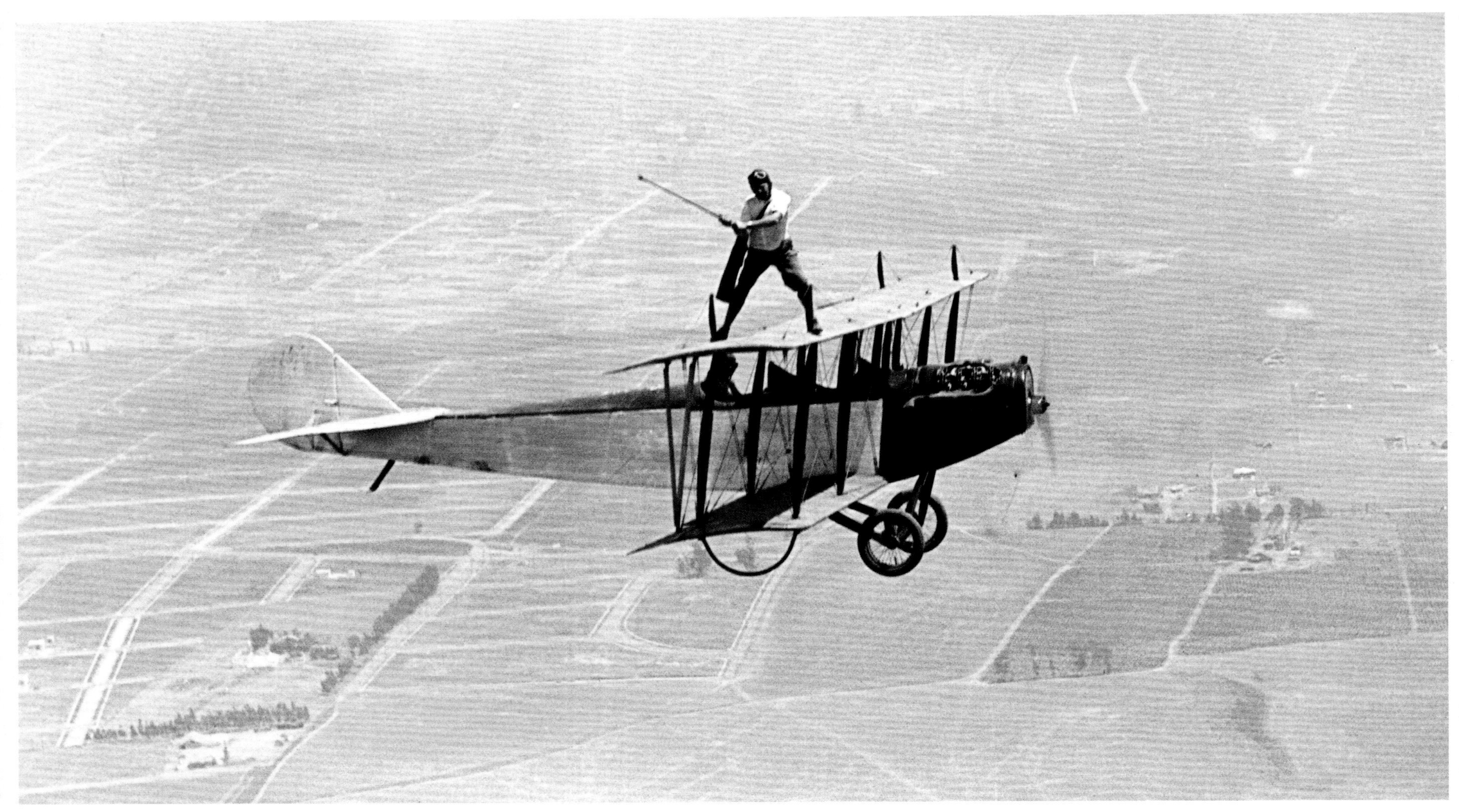

He was a Hollywood stuntman with a passion for flying. Al Wilson, seen here driving a golf ball off a plane's wing – the first time anyone had done such a thing – embraced danger and, seemingly, had no fear. Born in Kentucky towards the end of the nineteenth century, Wilson was a pilot who learned the art of flying stunts during his aviation training. He had hoped to fly and fight in World War I, but the war ended before the young pilot had qualified. Wilson, who died in 1932 in an air crash, aged 36, is remembered for his death-defying wing-walking acrobatics. The practice of performing aerial stunts was popular in 1920s America and sometimes images capturing airborne antics were made into postcards. As air travel continued to expand and improve, travel literature featuring aerial photographs grew in popularity. Gradually, thanks to advancements in aerial photography and the proliferation of travelogues and guidebooks that used this imagery, the world continued to open up.

Photographer unknown
Daredevil stuntman Al Wilson golfing on a biplane, 1924.

Among the thousands of photographs taken by pioneering aviator and photographer Walter Mittelholzer are many gems that offer unique views over the Middle East and Africa in the 1920s and '30s. The co-founder of Ad Astra Aero, which later became Swissair, Mittelholzer was an entrepreneur who took up photography at a young age. Ever enterprising, when he later learned to fly, the Swiss aviator found he was able to combine his two interests very well indeed. He even made a successful business of selling his aerial photography services. Mittelholzer made history in 1926 after completing the first flight across Africa from north to south, and in 1929 he was the first person to fly over Mount Kilimanjaro. His life and career have not escaped censure, however, critics have pointed out the troubling 'colonial gaze' with which he photographed.

Below and overleaf
Walter Mittelholzer
Kano, Nigeria, *c.* 1930.

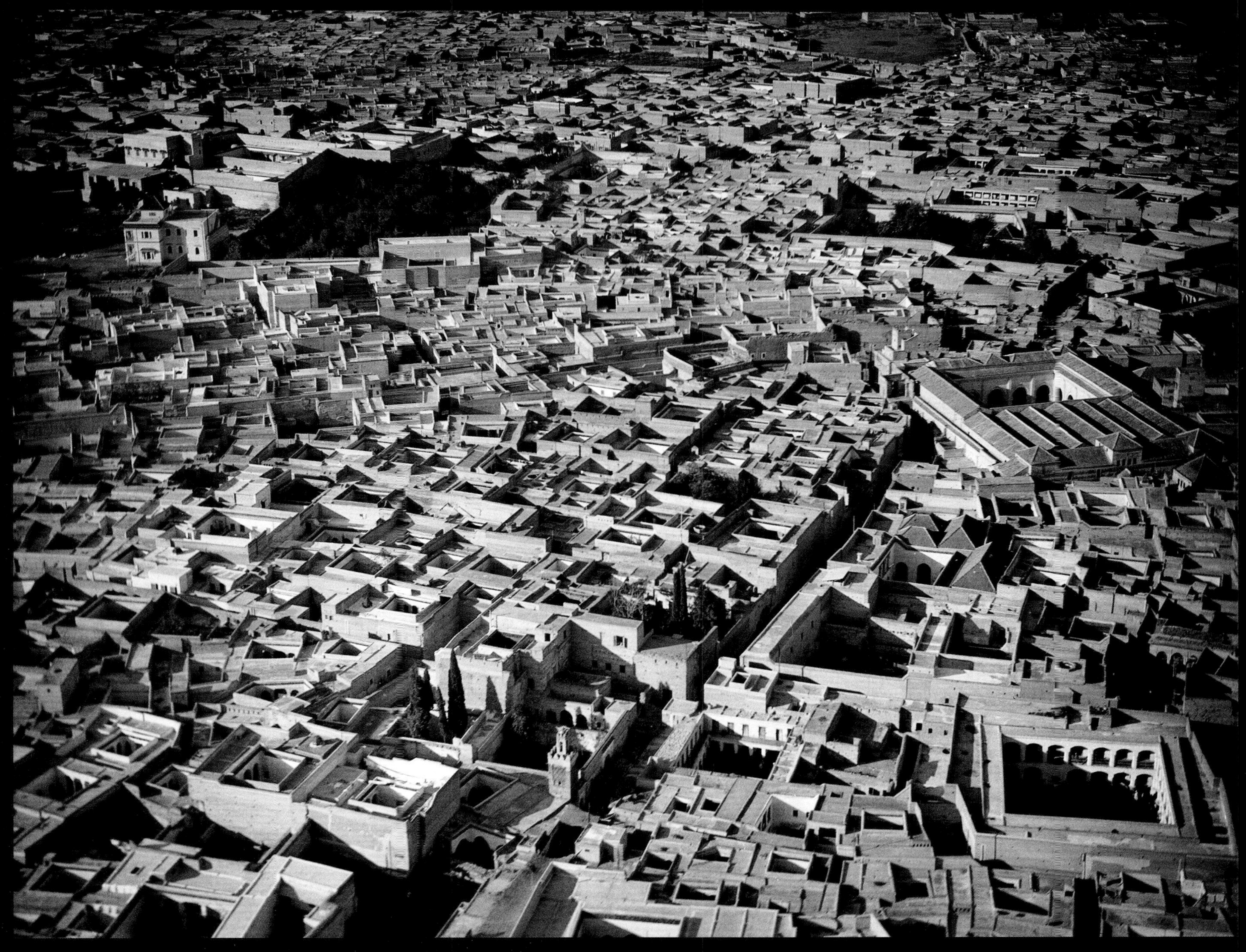

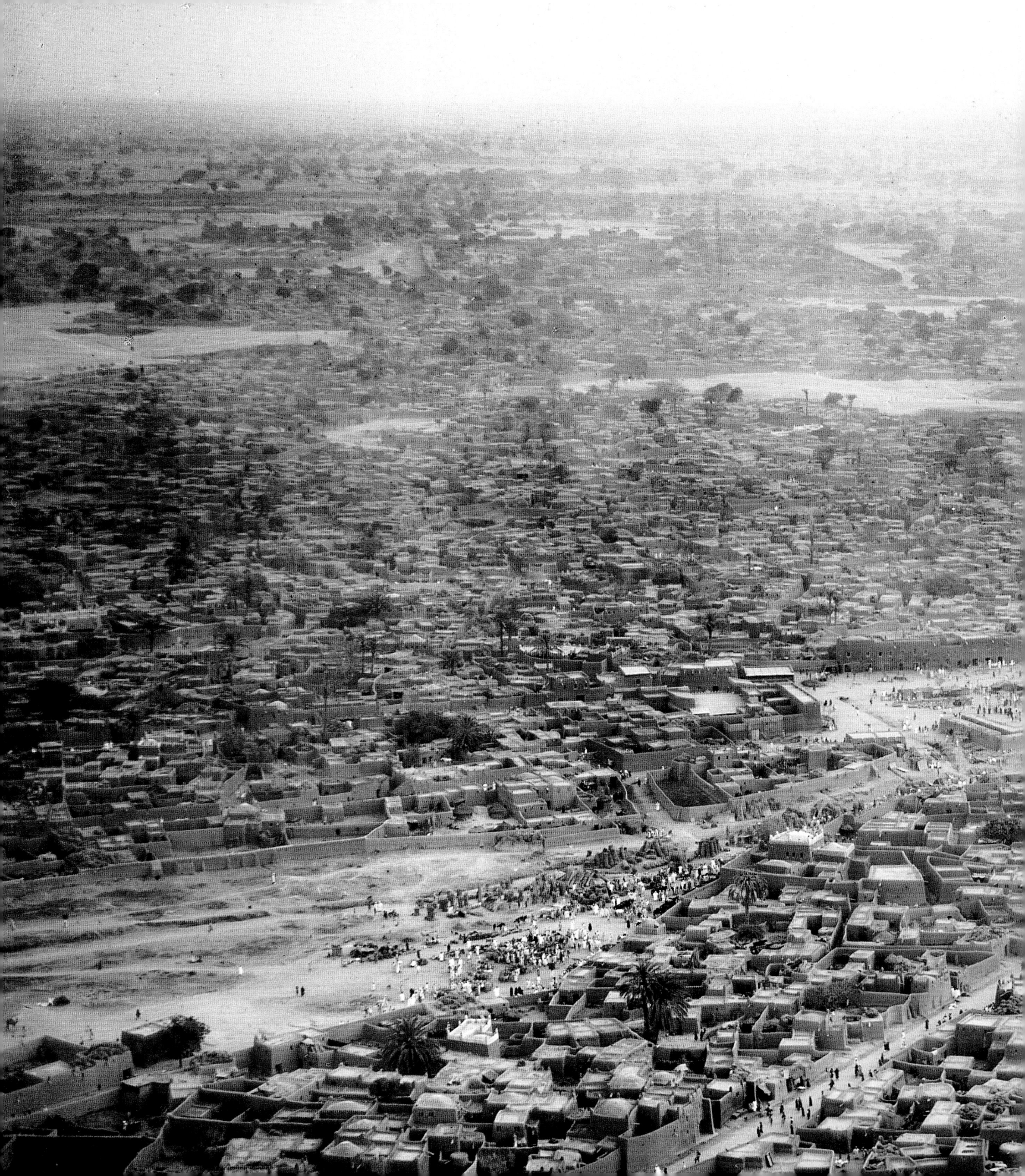

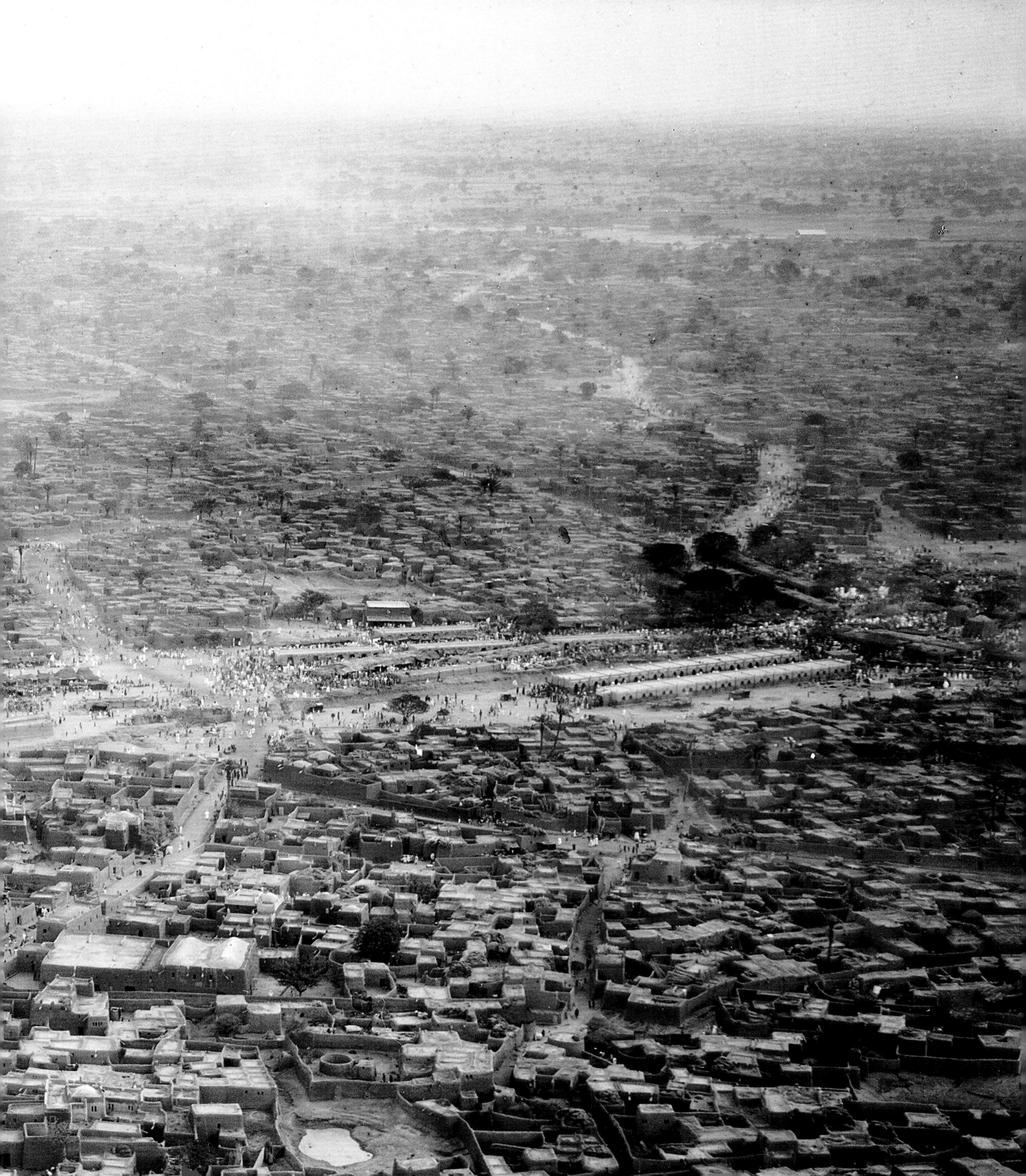

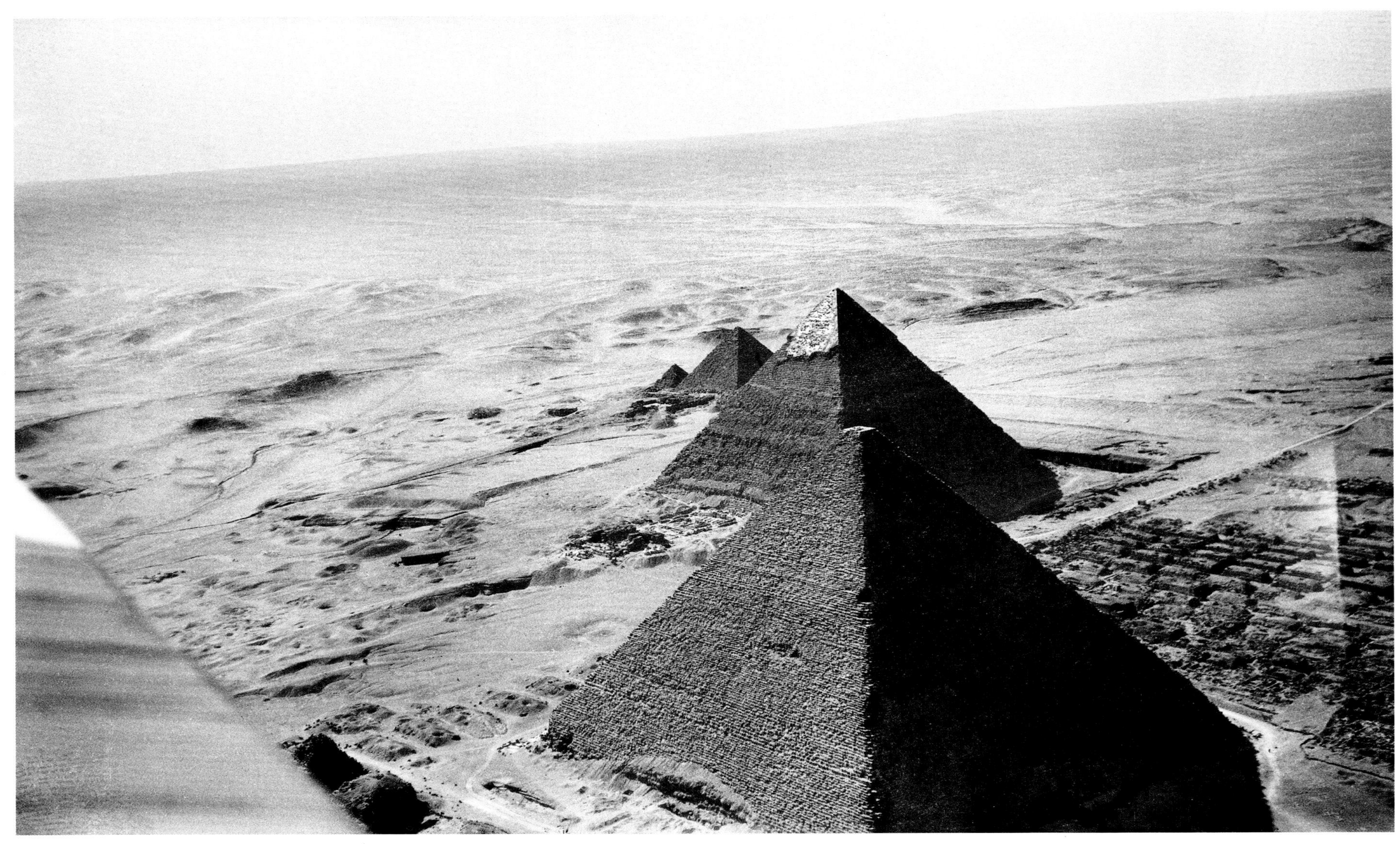

Egypt's mighty Pyramids of Giza, situated on the outskirts of Cairo, were built some 4,500 years ago, but little is known about how these magnificent tombs came to be. Though they have been photographed from every angle many times over, there is nothing quite like seeing these ancient monuments from the air. Shot at an oblique angle, with part of the aircraft visible to the left of the frame, this image gives a sense of what it would be like to fly towards and over these beguiling structures, which protrude from the desert landscape in such a way as to look almost unreal, or as though rendered in miniature. Images such as this are significant in that they show how aerial photography was being used in the early 1930s as a tool to aid and expand human understanding of the ancient world. By this point, aerial archaeology – the practice of examining archaeological sites from above – was fairly well established, championed by the likes of O. G. S. Crawford and Sir Henry Wellcome.

Photographer unknown
Pyramids of Giza, Egypt, 1931.

Photographer unknown
Brighton, England, 1933.

In the interwar period, aerial photography continued to be used for intelligence-gathering purposes by the RAF, but it was also being used commercially. Enterprising survey companies such as Aerofilms Ltd took on all kinds of commissions, creating aerial images of everything from seaside resorts (similar to this photograph of Brighton beach, below) to factories, agricultural sites and cityscapes. But while aerial photographs became an increasingly familiar sight, thanks in part to tourism and architecture magazines, the production of such photos between the world wars was limited by costs and technology. Aerial photography was still a long way from becoming ubiquitous but those who had the means made great leaps forward in terms of the volume of images being produced, their photographic quality and aesthetic merit.

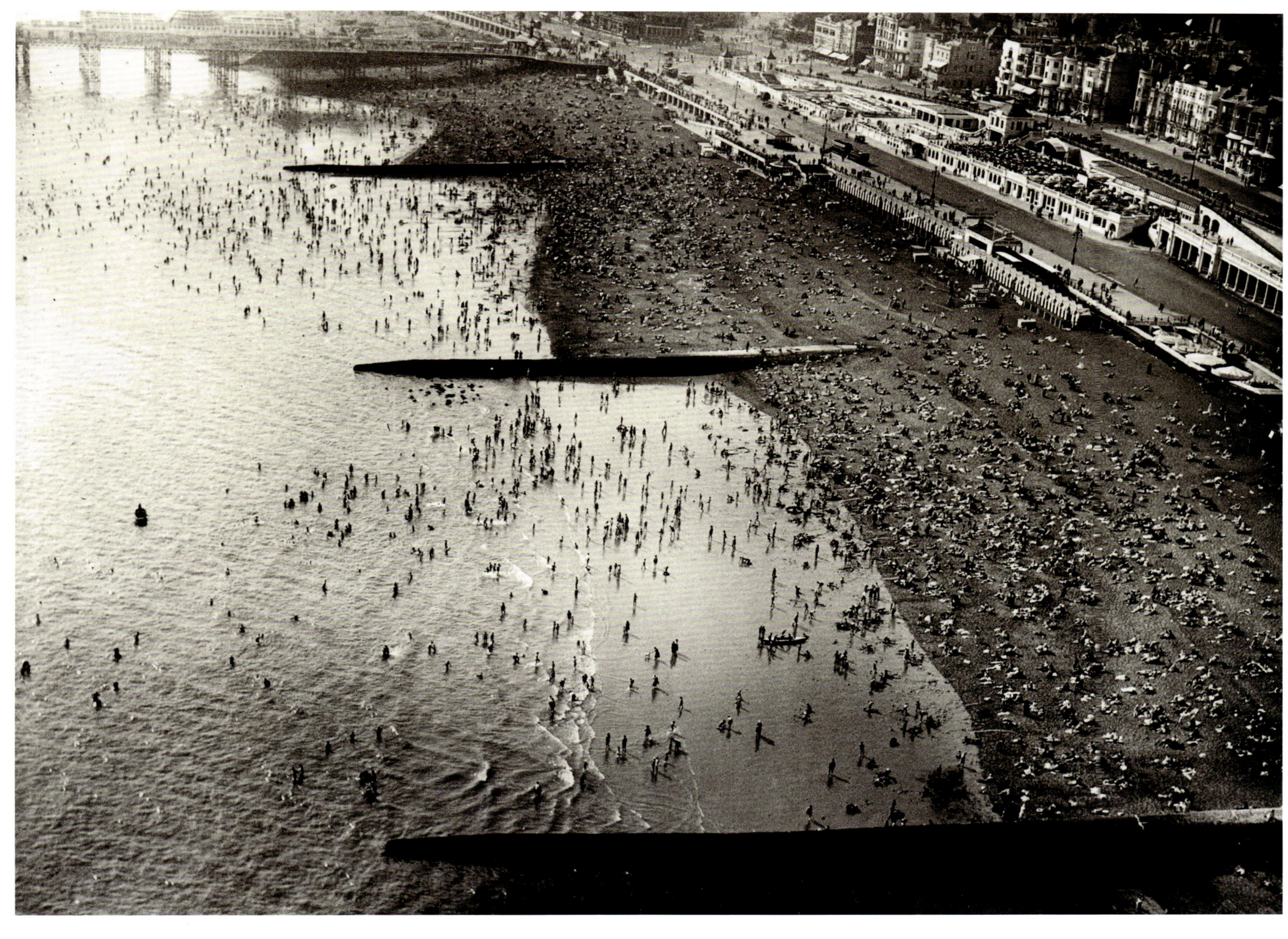

1935

Albert W. Stevens was an acclaimed aerial photographer and balloonist. After studying electrical engineering and learning the craft of photography, he worked as an engineer before enlisting in the US Army Air Corps. As the commanding officer of the Sixth Photographic Squadron, Stevens perfected the art of oblique aerial photography and was highly respected for his photographic pursuits during, and long after, World War I. On 11 November 1935, Stevens, along with commander Orvil A. Anderson, made history when they set a new altitude record for manned balloons. The image below shows the high-altitude balloon in which the men travelled as it returned to Earth. Vehicles can be seen trailing the balloon on the road beneath, creating clouds of dust behind them. The balloon landed safely after the successful mission that resulted in this image (pictured right) showing the curvature of the Earth – a powerful example of aerial photography's considerable ability to contribute to our scientific understanding of the world.

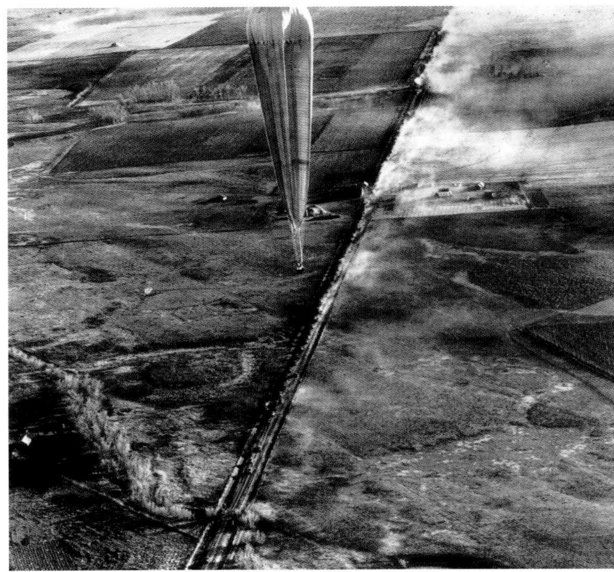

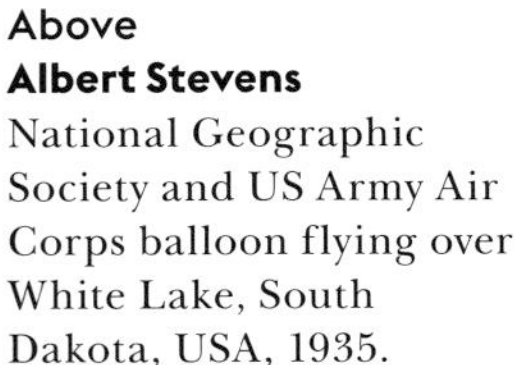

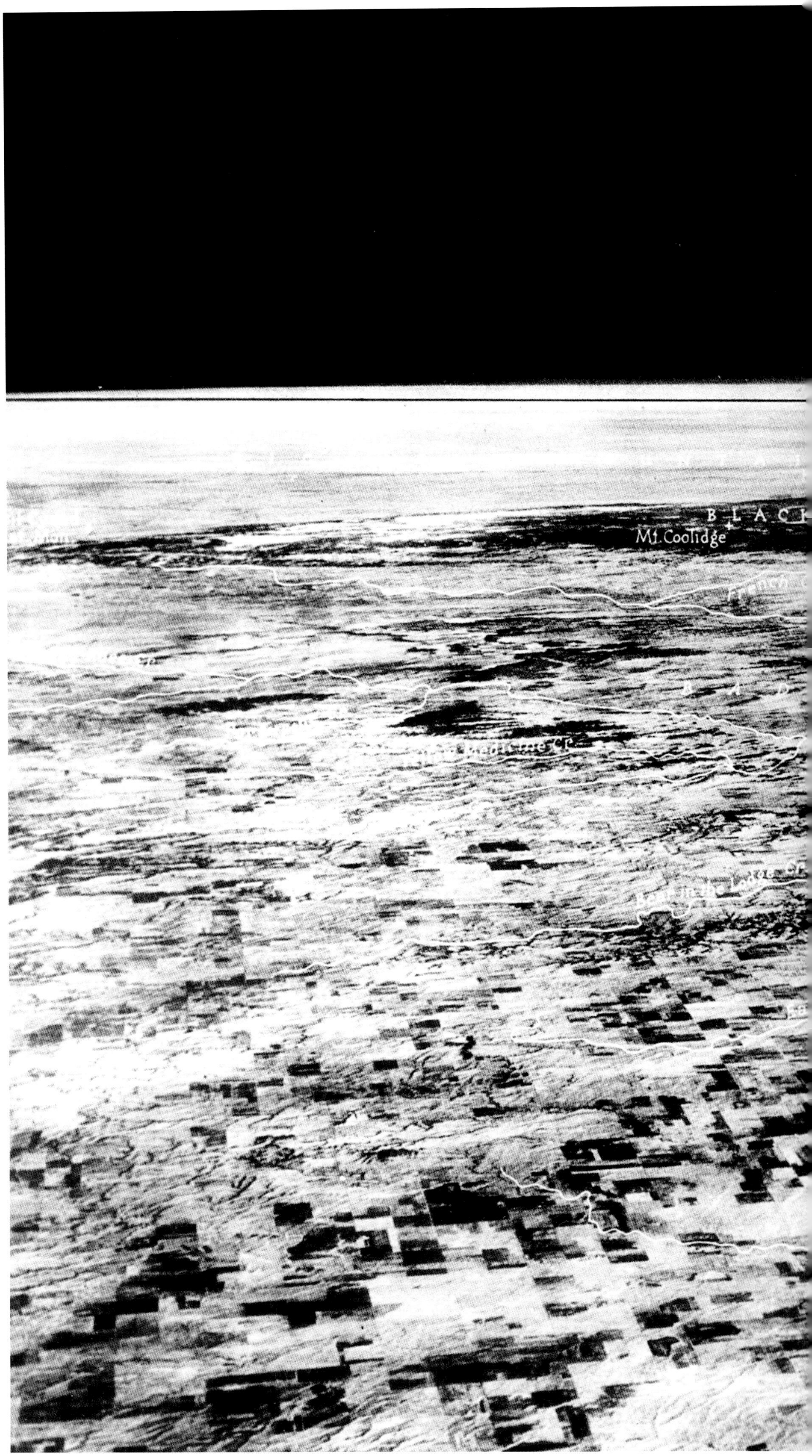

Above
Albert Stevens
National Geographic Society and US Army Air Corps balloon flying over White Lake, South Dakota, USA, 1935.

Right
Albert Stevens
Stratobowl, near Rapid City, South Dakota, USA, 1935.

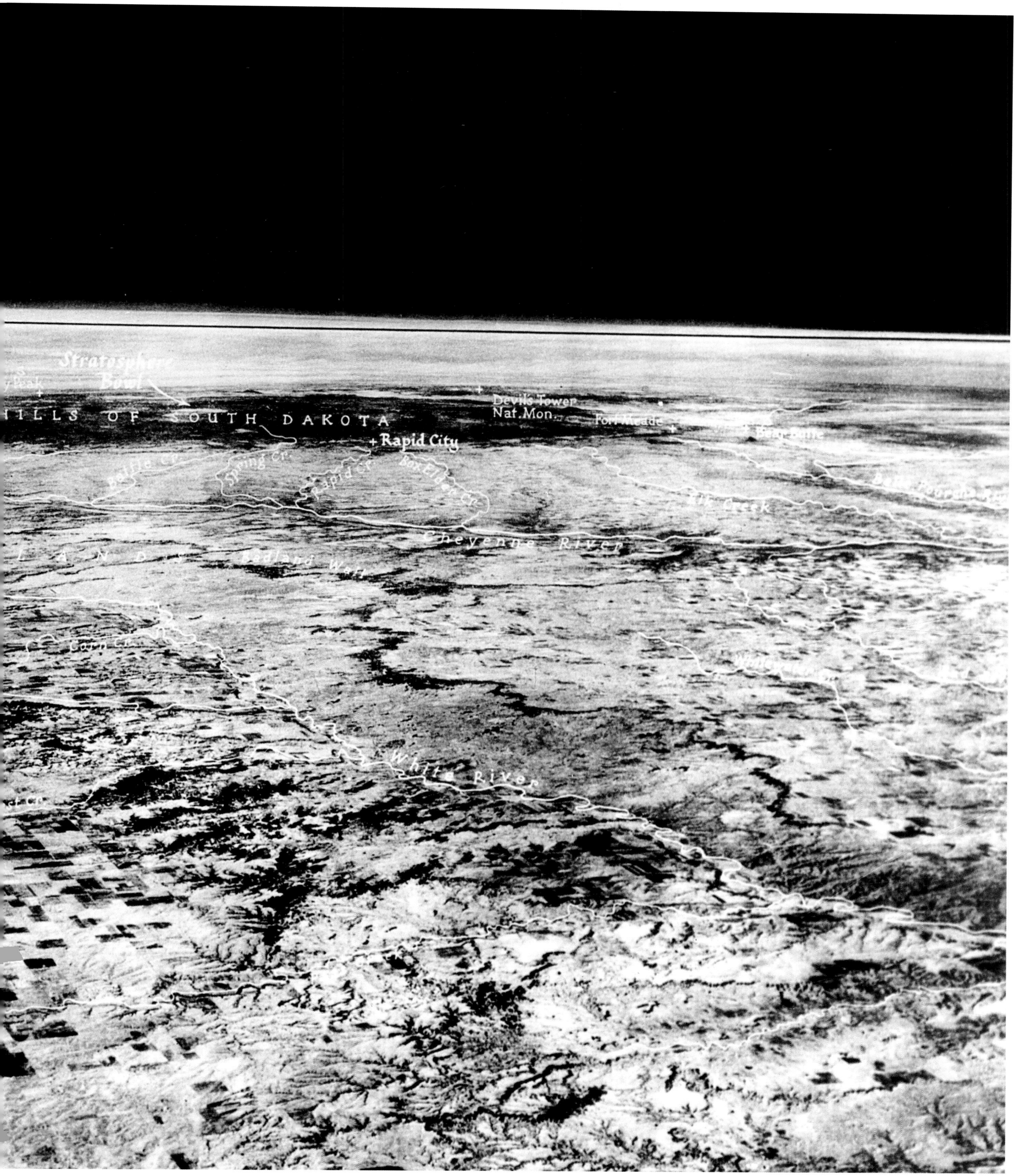

Stratosphere Bowl
SOUTH DAKOTA
Devil's Tower Nat. Mon.
Fort Meade
Rapid City
Battle Cr.
Spring Cr.
Rapid Cr.
Box Elder Cr.
Elk Creek
Cheyenne River
Badland Wall
Corn Cr.
White River

1935

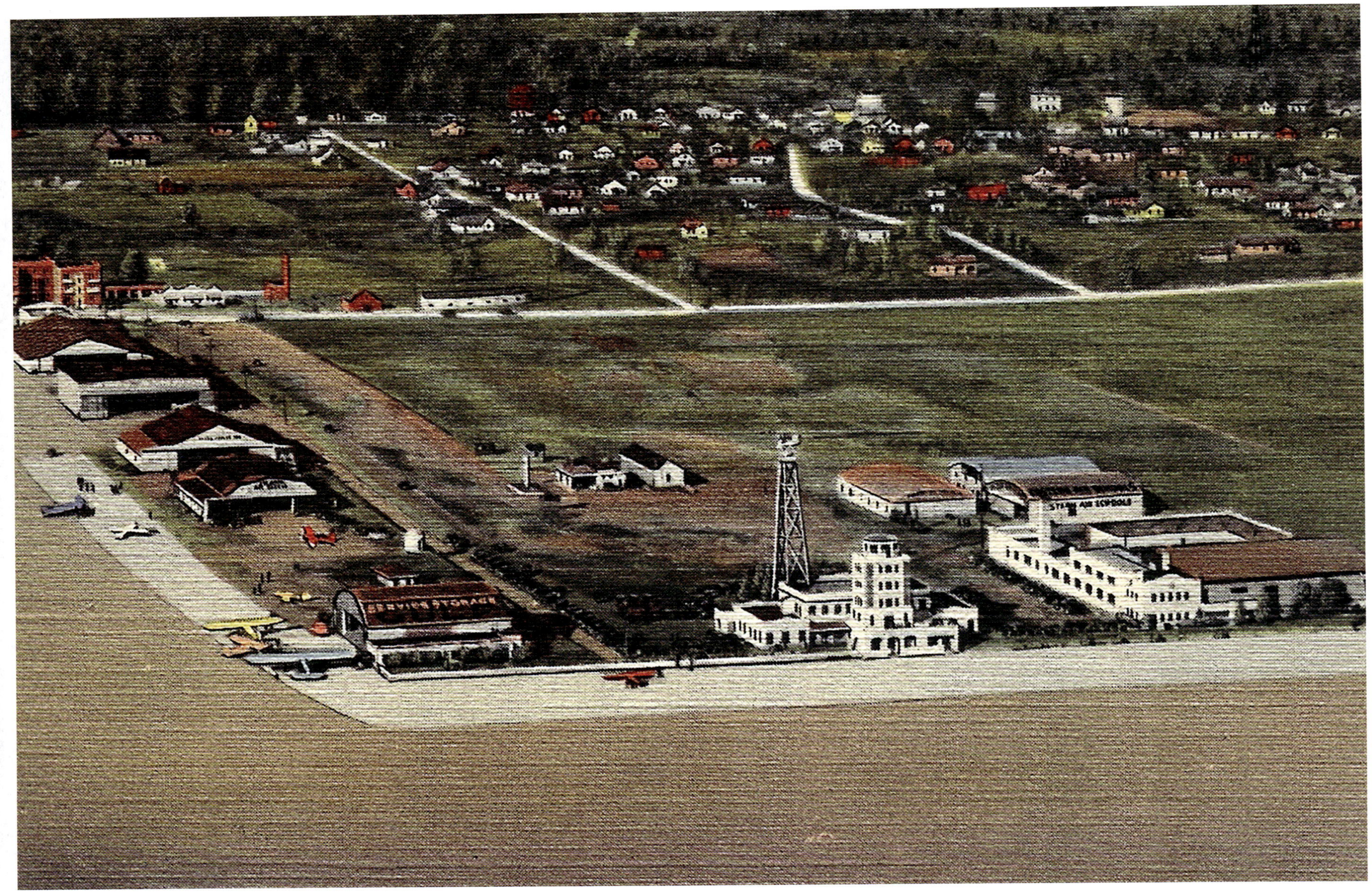

Edgar Orr
Atlanta Municipal Airport, USA, *c.* 1935.

Throughout the 1930s (and into the 1940s), photographs, including aerial photographs of landscapes and cityscapes, continued to be made into postcards. Dyes were used to colour images, and white borders – originally added to postcards between 1915 and 1930 to save ink – were frequently retained. The American photographer Edgar Orr, who took this image of Atlanta Municipal Airport, worked for a printing business called Atlanta Blue Print and Graphics Company, which employed commercial photographers to make photographs of rural and urban areas as a way of demonstrating their services.

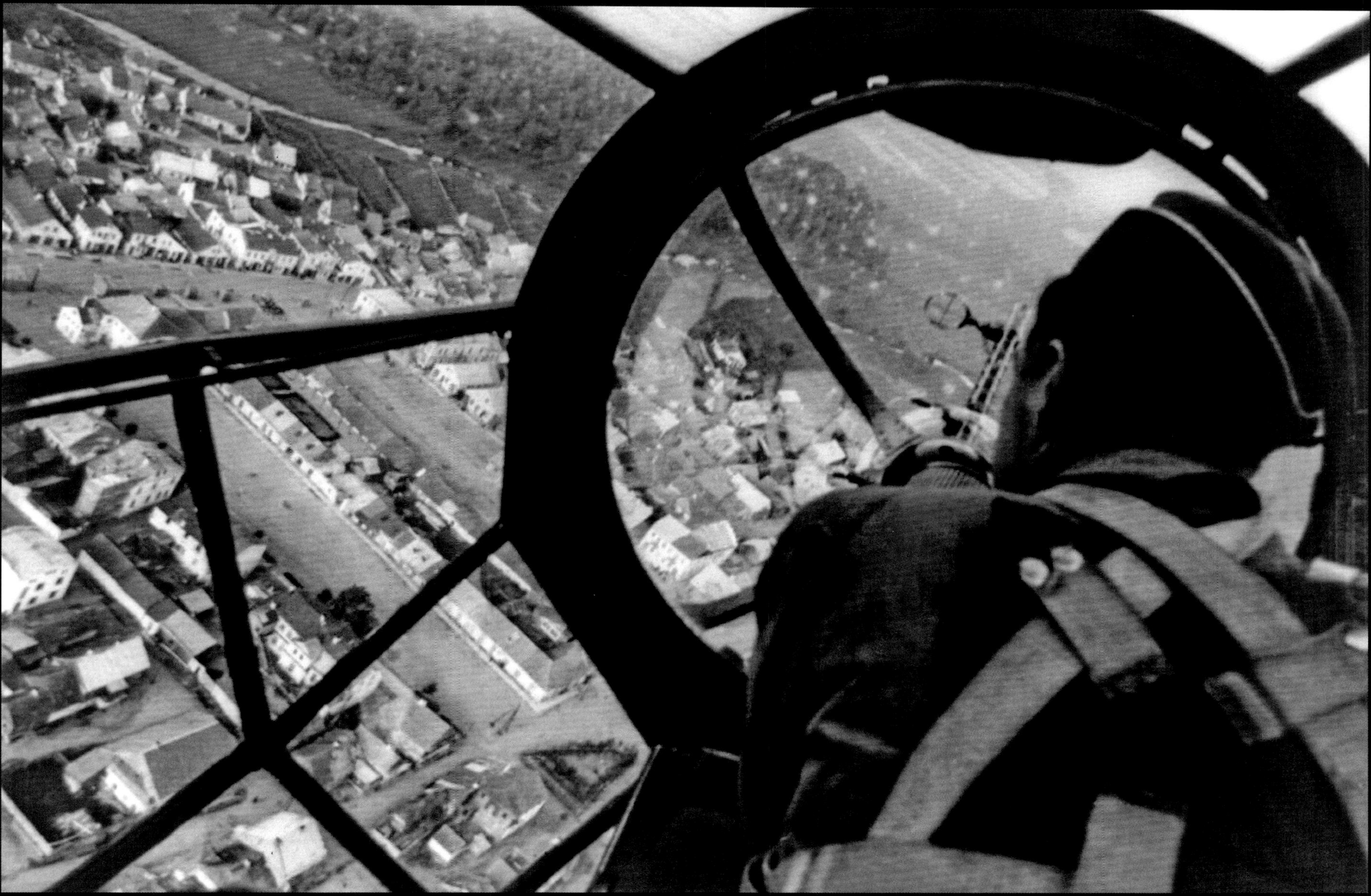

Above
Photographer unknown
Luftwaffe Heinkel III bomber over England, *c.* 1940.

Right
Photographer unknown
Luftwaffe technician preparing camera for Messerschmitt Bf 109 converted for reconnaissance use, Dinard, Brittany, France, *c.* 1940.

On 1 September 1939, Germany invaded Poland, heralding the start of World War II. In July the following year the Nazis started dropping bombs over parts of Britain, and in September focused their attacks on London, in what became known as The Blitz (see page 64). It is impossible not to feel close to the action in this revealing photograph (pictured above) taken from inside a Luftwaffe bomber during the campaign. German fighter aircraft such as the Messerschmitt Bf 109 (pictured right) were loaded with cameras specially designed for use in reconnaissance. Here, a Luftwaffe technician prepares a camera.

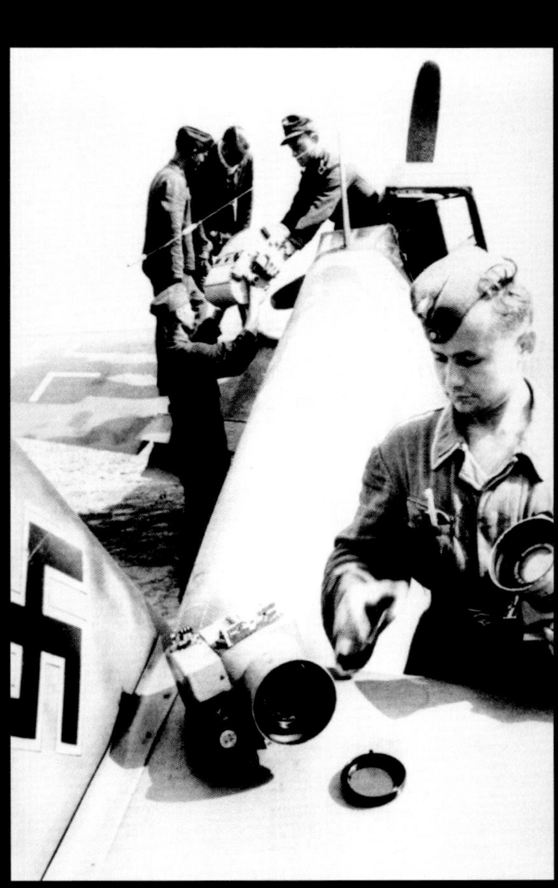

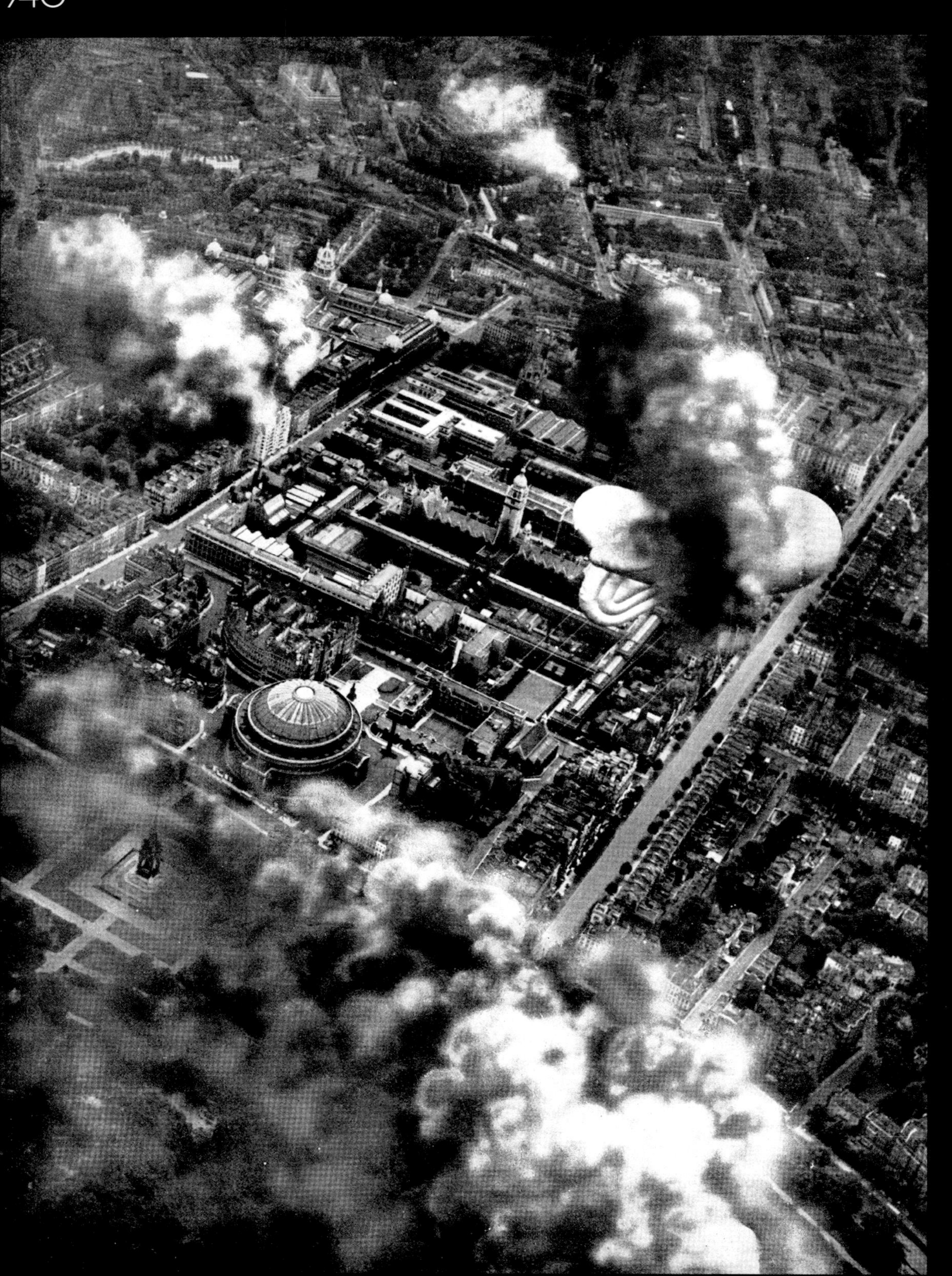

On 7 September 1940 the Luftwaffe launched a bombing campaign over London on a scale that had not been seen before. London's Royal Docks were the original target, but swathes of East and Southeast London were also badly hit. This was in fact the beginning of The Blitz, and air strikes would continue for the next 76 nights across the capital. Heavy raids on industrial and civilian targets in London and other major British cities lasted for eight months, killing more than 40,000 civilians.

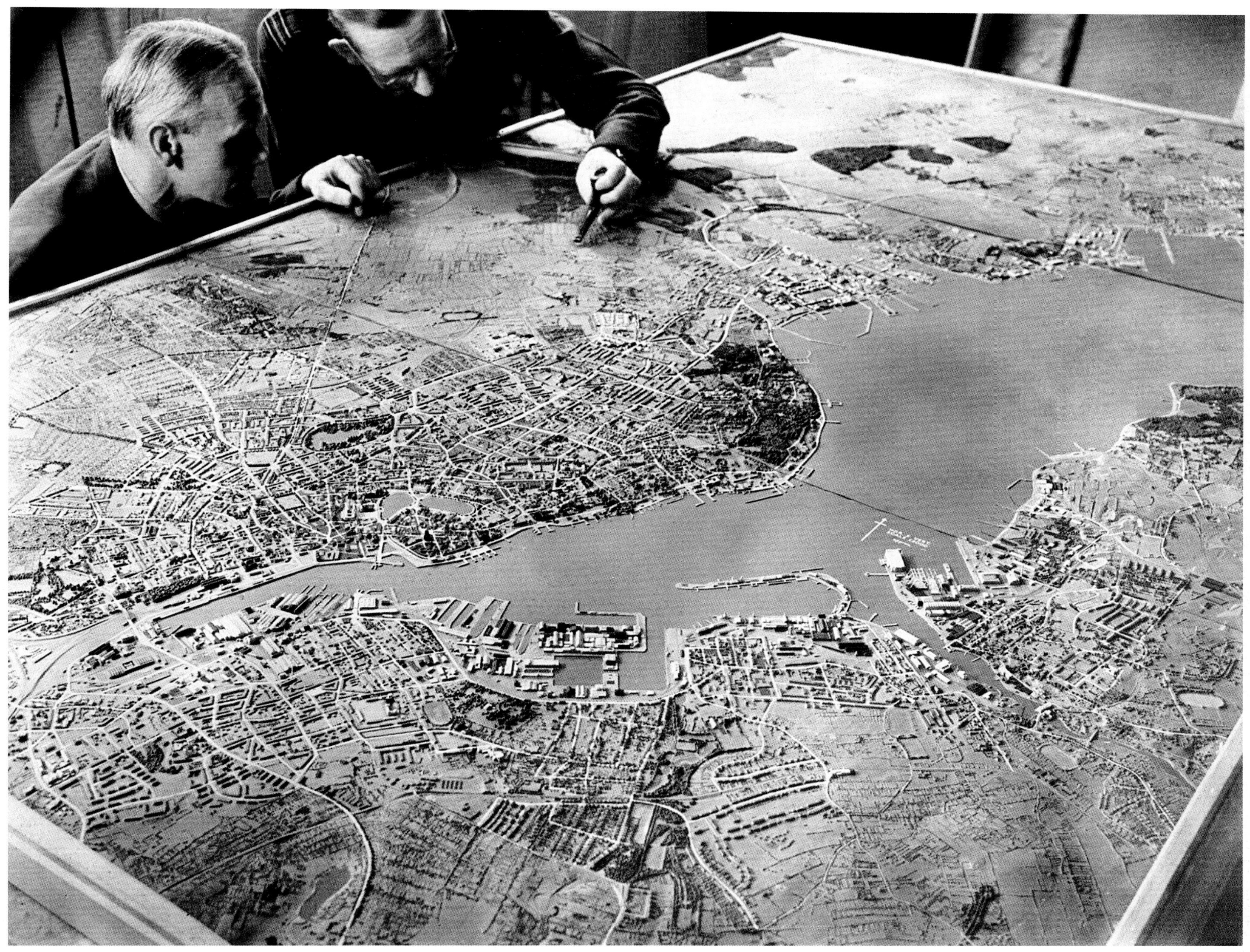

Photographer unknown
3D terrain model being built for military use during World War II, 1940.

Three-dimensional terrain models were used in military operations during both world wars, although it is thought that scale models had been used in Europe as early as the sixteenth century. In 1940, the British military created a model-making division, and a year later formed the Central Interpretation Unit (CIU), which assisted in the planning of wartime operations by analysing and interpreting images taken by photographic reconnaissance aircraft. In 1944, the CIU, comprising Allied photographic interpreters, was renamed the Allied Central Interpretation Unit (ACIU), and by the end of the war it had amassed 36 million aerial reconnaissance images from all over the world.

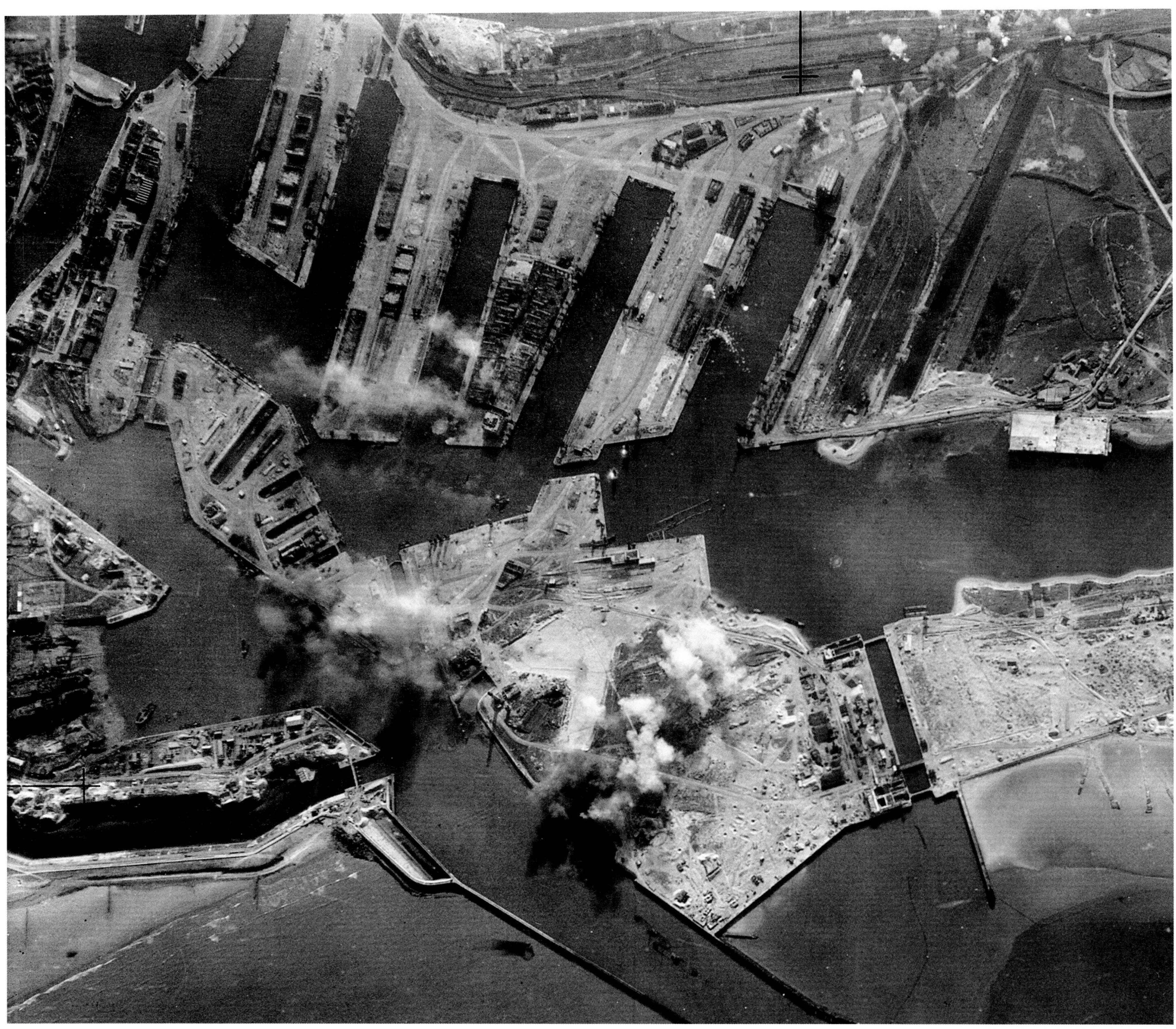

In this vertical aerial photograph we look down on the French port of Dunkirk (Dunkerque) during a daylight attack by Allied forces. Thick, choking smoke billows up from the ground following bombing by the RAF No. 2 Group. The famous evacuation of more than 300,000 soldiers from the beaches of Dunkirk took place between 26 May and 4 June 1940, but after the rescue – code-named Operation Dynamo – the German-occupied port was bombed and largely destroyed by the Allies. The US Army liberated Dunkirk on 9 May 1945, after which time the town and port were gradually rebuilt.

Photographer unknown
Dunkirk, France, during a daylight attack by Lockheed Venturas of RAF No. 2 Group, *c.* 1942.

The Dutch city of Zutphen, pictured here, suffered extensive damage during World War II. Occupied by German forces, the city was bombed by the Allies, who made strategic attacks on targets including airports, harbours, railway stations, factories and bridges, as seen in this vertical aerial photograph. The photograph, which would most likely have been used for surveillance purposes by the military, depicts a road and rail bridge across the River IJssel being bombed by the RAF's No. 2 Group. The picture has been 'cropped' using tape to clearly indicate the point of impact.

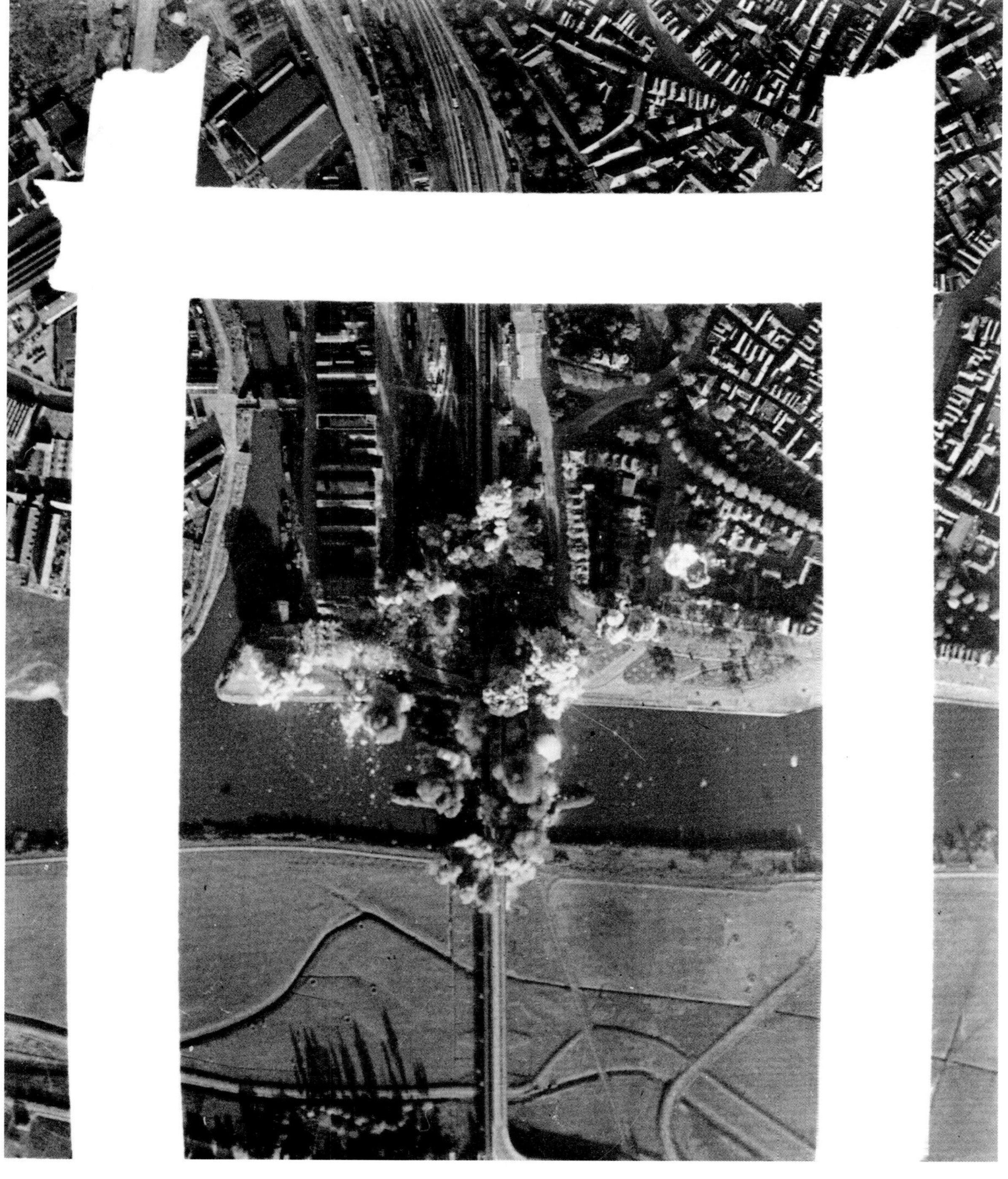

Photographer unknown
Zutphen, Holland, suffering blanket bombing during a daylight attack by medium bombers of RAF No. 2 Group, *c.* 1942.

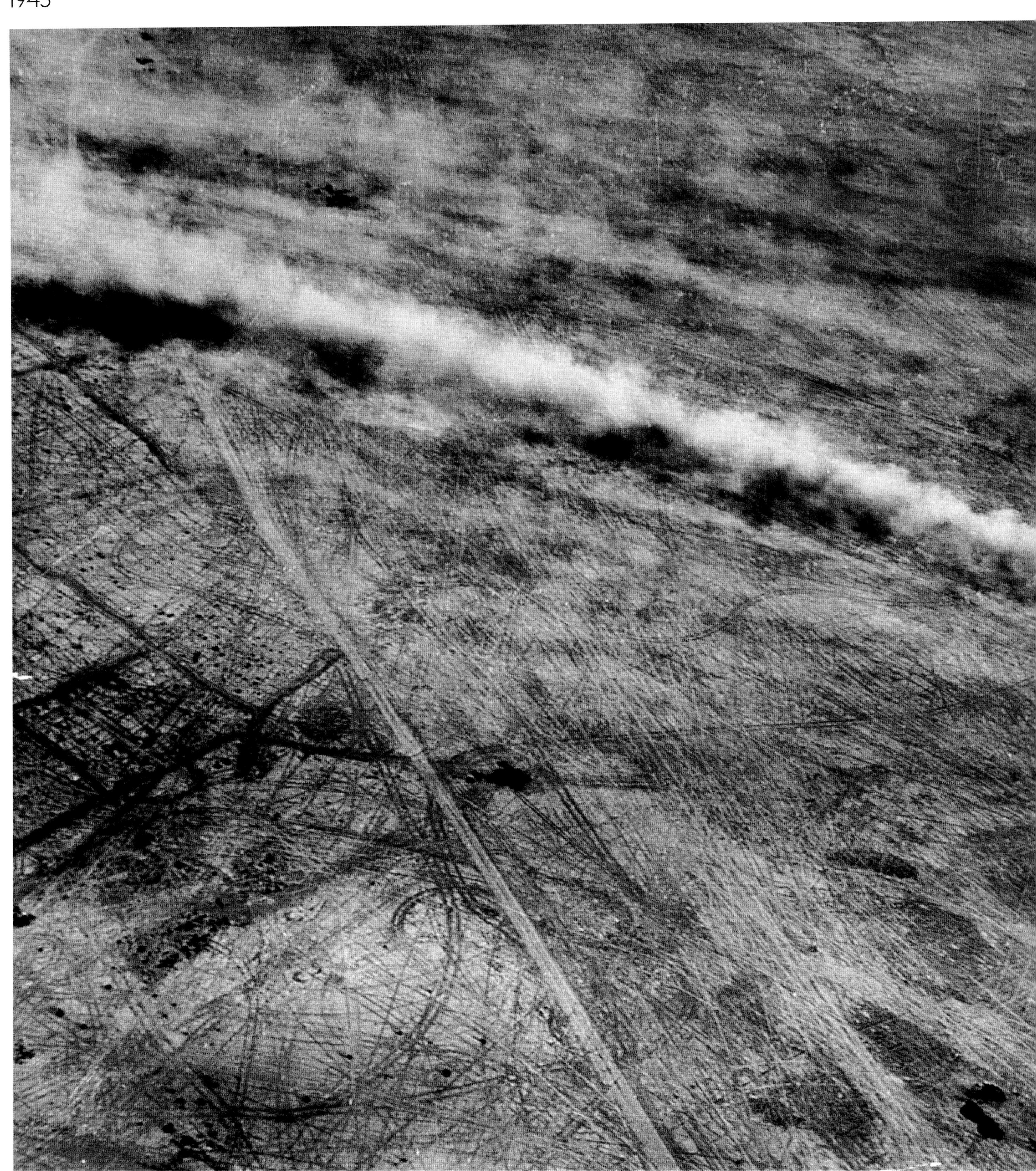

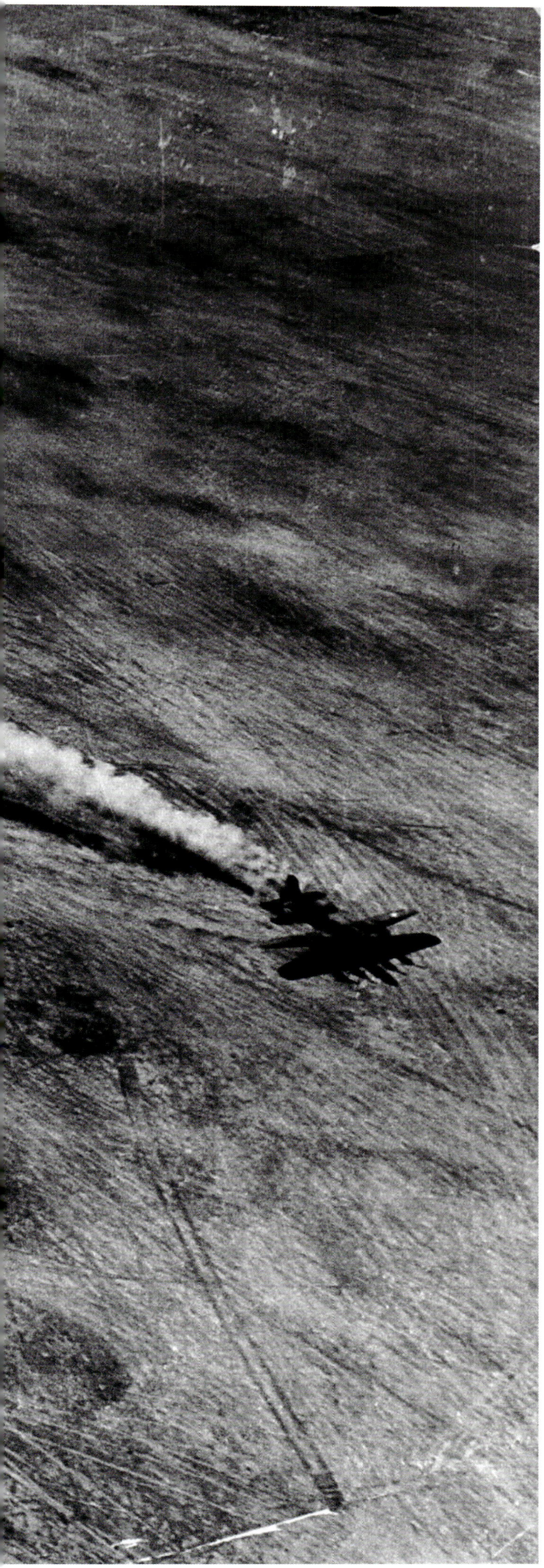

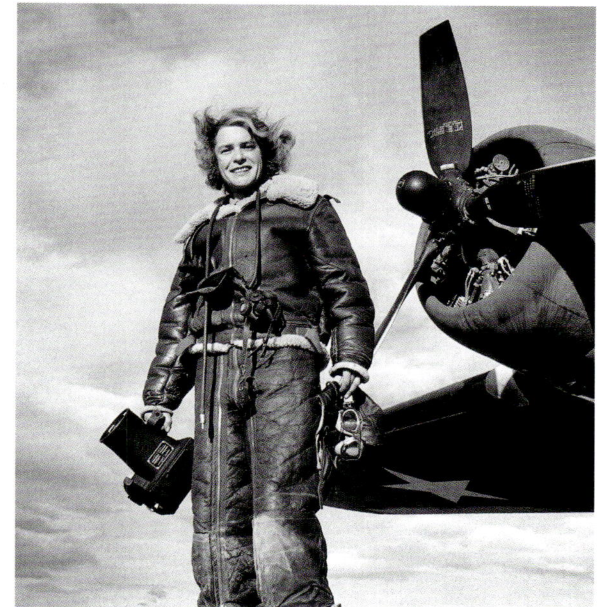

Fearless and tenacious, Margaret Bourke-White was the first female photographer authorized to photograph in combat zones during World War II. In the summer of 1942, she was accredited to the US Army Air forces, and in January 1943 climbed into a Flying Fortress bomber bound for Tunisia. There, she covered the US attack on the country, as *Life* magazine reported in its 1 March 1943 issue. Towards the end of the war, Bourke-White made aerial views of water-filled bomb craters in Nuremberg, and recorded the extensive damage caused by Allied forces in Cologne and other bombed German cities. After the war, and into the 1950s, she continued to photograph from the air when the opportunity arose (see pages 98–103).

Left
Margaret Bourke-White
American B-17 Flying Fortress taking off from a Sahara desert base on a bombing mission on targets in Ferryville, Tunisa and the country's captial, Tunis, 1943.

Above
Margaret Bourke-White
Standing in front of the Flying Fortress bomber in which she made combat mission photographs of the US attack on Tunis, 1943.

During World War I, mosaic maps, made by aligning vertical aerial photographs to create a view of enemy territory, were an important military tool. By the start of World War II, the usefulness of aerial photographs for topographic surveying was in no doubt. Germany was already systematically collecting geographical data from the air, and it wasn't long before Britain began using aerial photography to pinpoint potential targets and plan campaigns. In fact, aerial photography was integral to the success of the Allies' D-Day landings in June 1944 – photo interpreters had been carefully surveying and mapping the shoreline in northern France for some time and consequently knew every part of it.

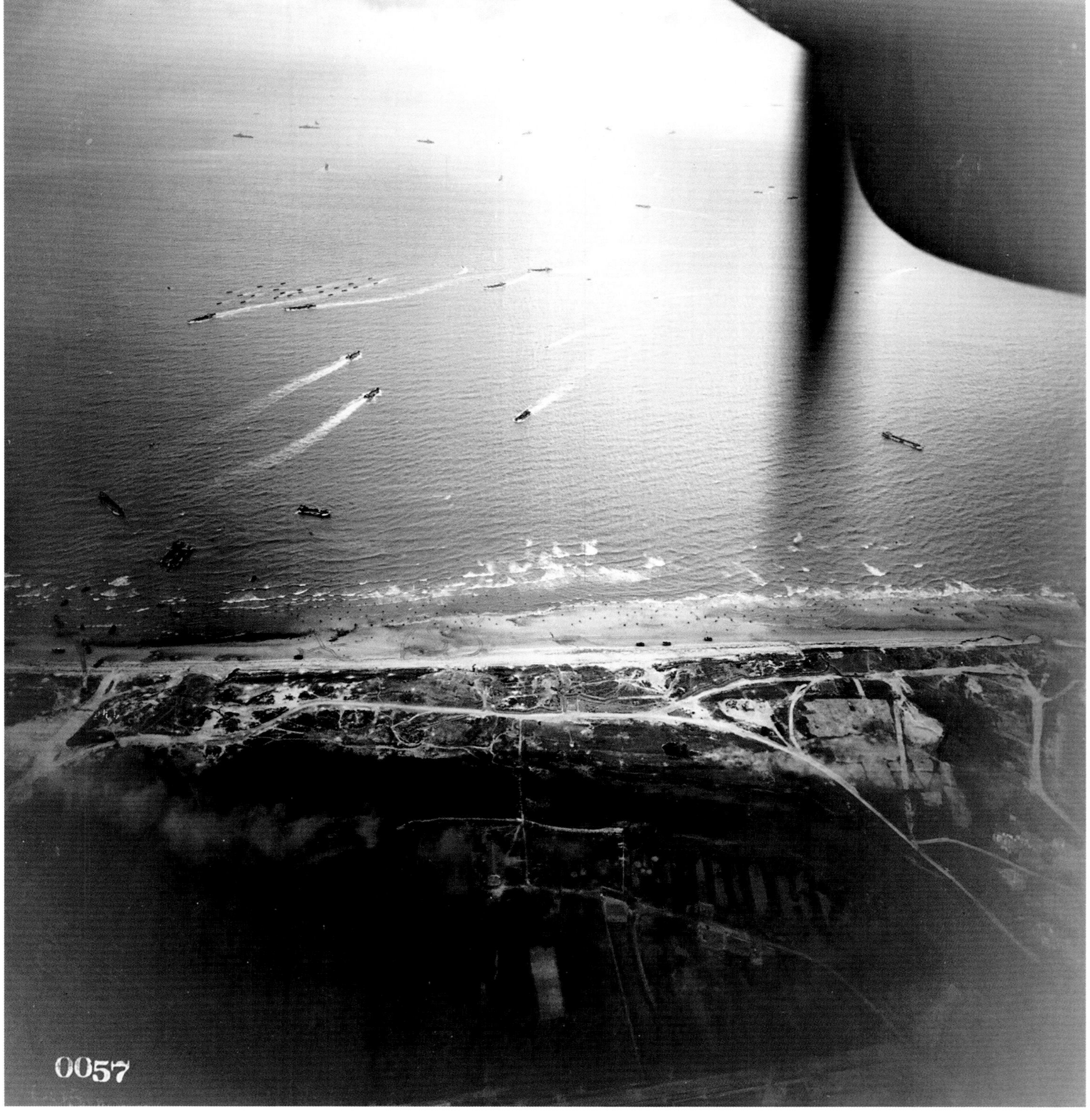

Photographer unknown
D-Day landings at Utah beach, Normandy, France, 1944.

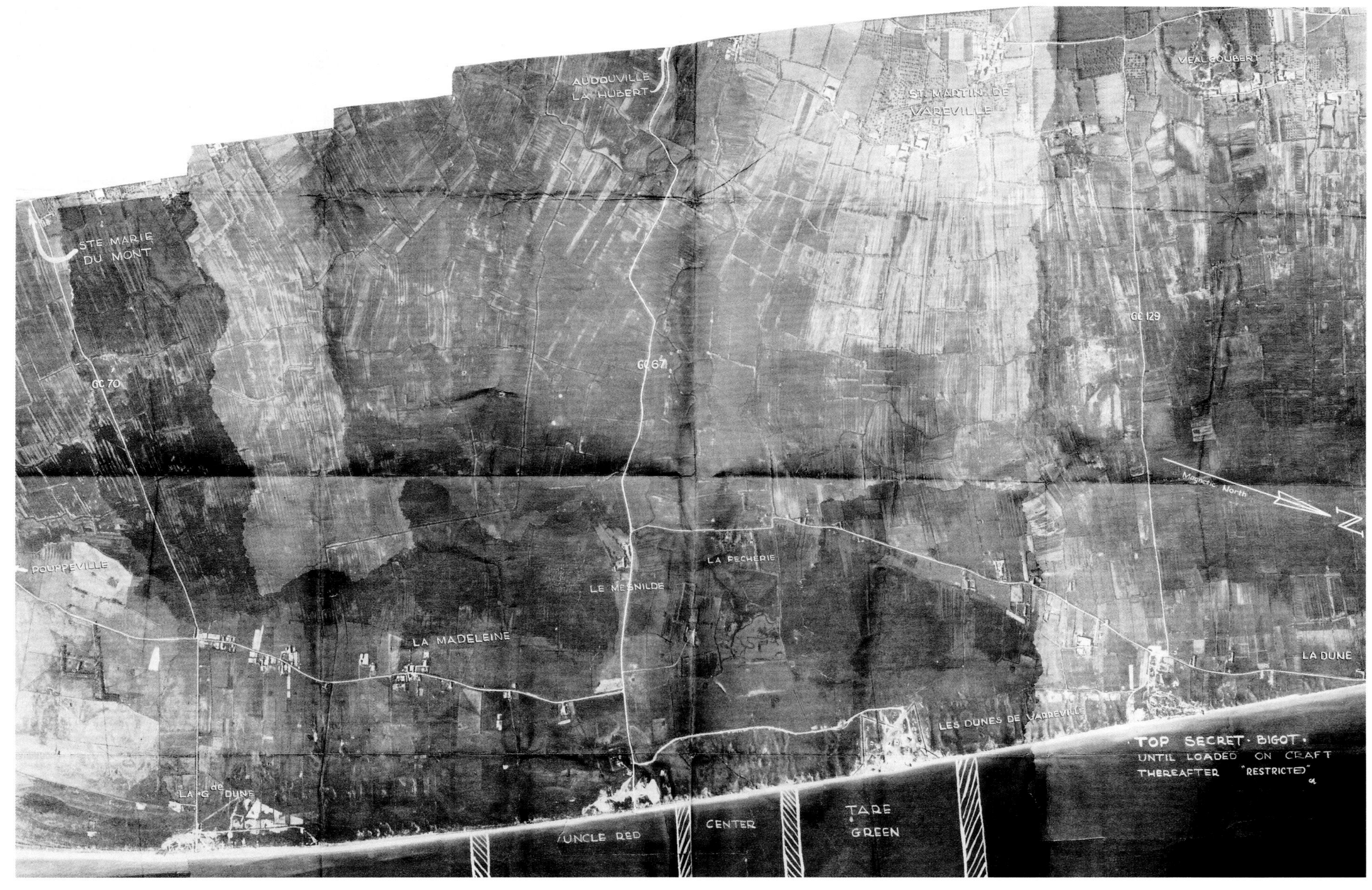

Photographer unknown
Utah beach, Normandy, France, prior to the D-Day Landings, 1944.

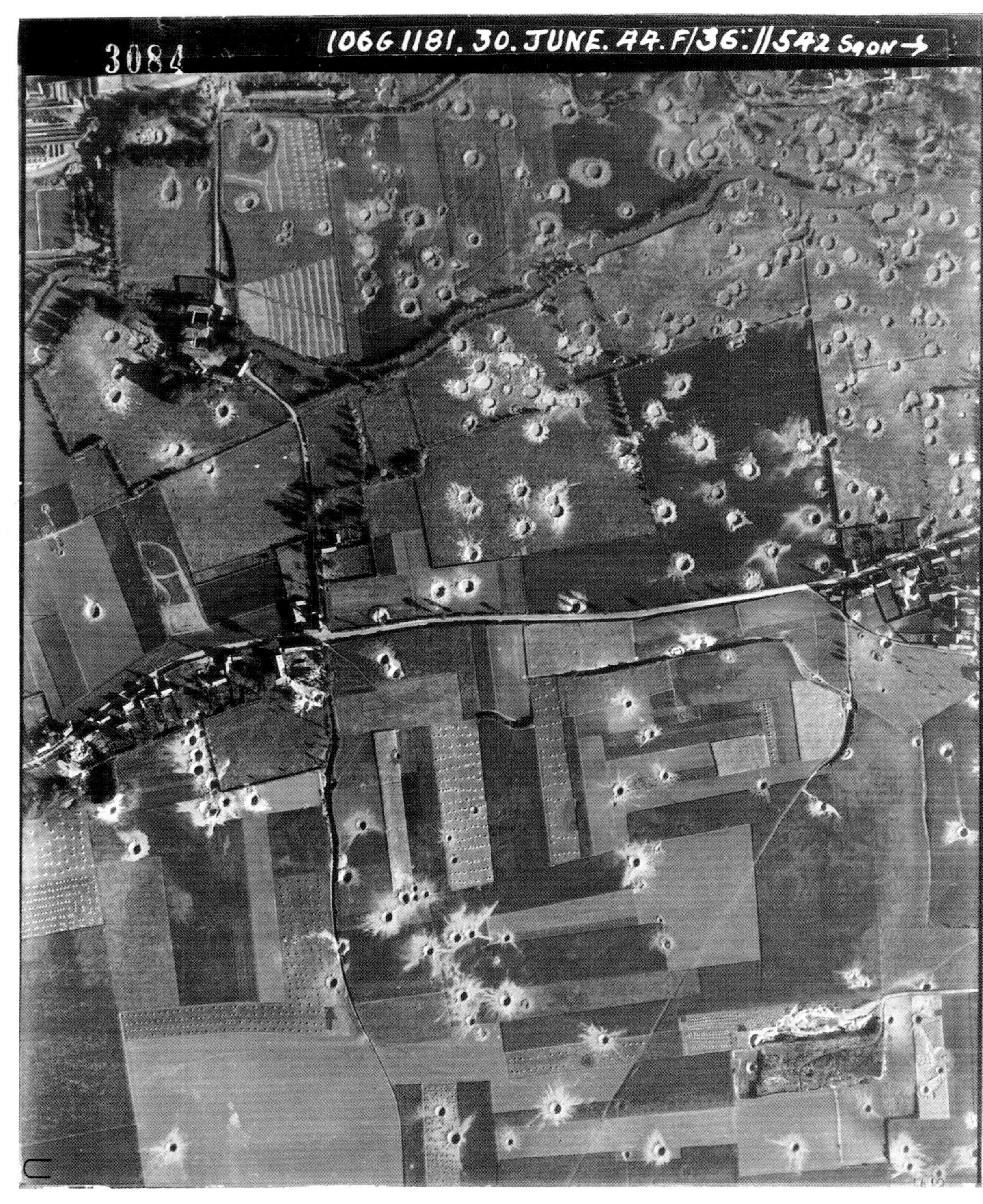

Photographer unknown
Wizernes, Nord-Pas-de-Calais, France, 1944.

Few would dispute how vital the work of reconnaissance pilots and photo interpreters (PIs) was to the war effort. In fact, it is estimated that as much as 80 per cent of Allied intelligence on the Nazis came from photo reconnaissance. Photographs taken over enemy territory, such as this image of Wizernes in northern France after a bombing raid, were made by Spitfire pilots and fed back to PIs at RAF Medmenham in Buckinghamshire, where Britain's Photographic Reconnaissance Unit was based. Wizernes and the surrounding area were caught up in heavy Allied bombing because of the nearby German V-2 rocket base and bunker complex, La Coupole, from where the Nazis had intended to launch missiles on an industrial scale.

This striking image shows the Nazi research site at Peenemünde, on the Baltic sea, in September 1944, after it had been attacked in an Allied bombing raid. The vertical angle presents a stark view of the devastated site where V-1 and V-2 weapons had been designed and tested. As the photograph shows, the area around the research centre was covered in craters. The image is part of the National Collection of Aerial Photography, which comprises millions of images taken by the RAF and used for intelligence purposes during World War II. By the end of the war, photographic equipment and techniques had improved so much that it was clear that aerial surveying had huge potential for use in mapping beyond a military context.

Photographer unknown
Craters at Peenemünde in Mecklenburg-Vorpommem, Germany, 1944.

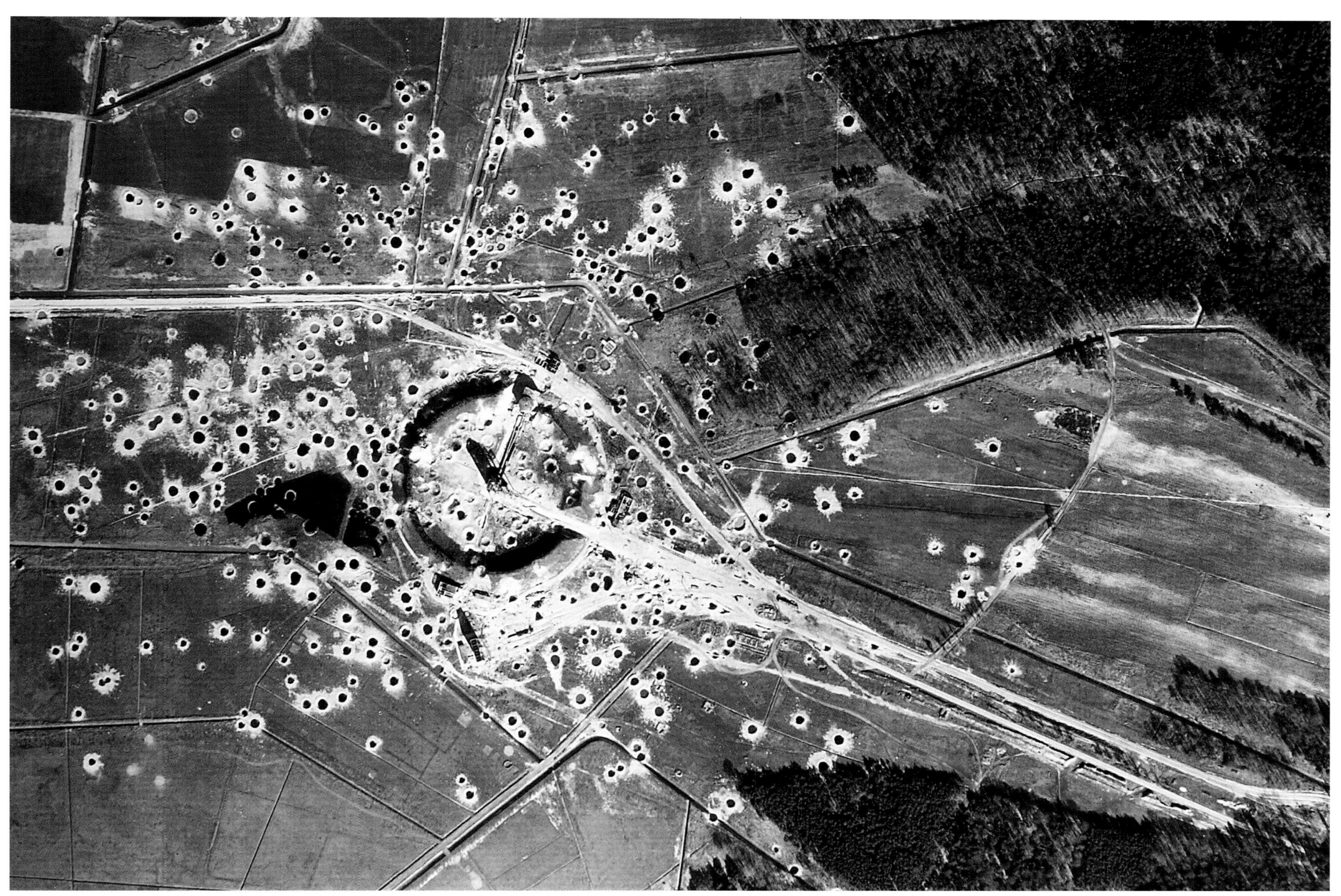

Amid the debris shown in this photograph, Cologne Cathedral stands tall. It did not survive World War II completely unscathed – indeed, the cathedral was hit many times by Allied bombers – but, remarkably, it was not destroyed, possibly because attacking aircraft relied on the cathedral's spires as a landmark for navigation purposes, or perhaps it was spared because of its heritage value. It would also have been very difficult to target the cathedral using the technology available at the time. Aerial reconnaissance photographs similar to this one were used to assess and verify the scale of devastation, and today these images serve as a startling reminder of the damage caused through aerial bombardment. At the time, the photograph put paid to the Nazi propaganda claim that the cathedral had been destroyed in air raids.

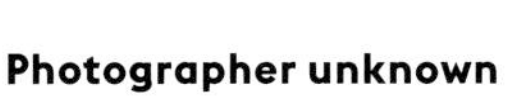

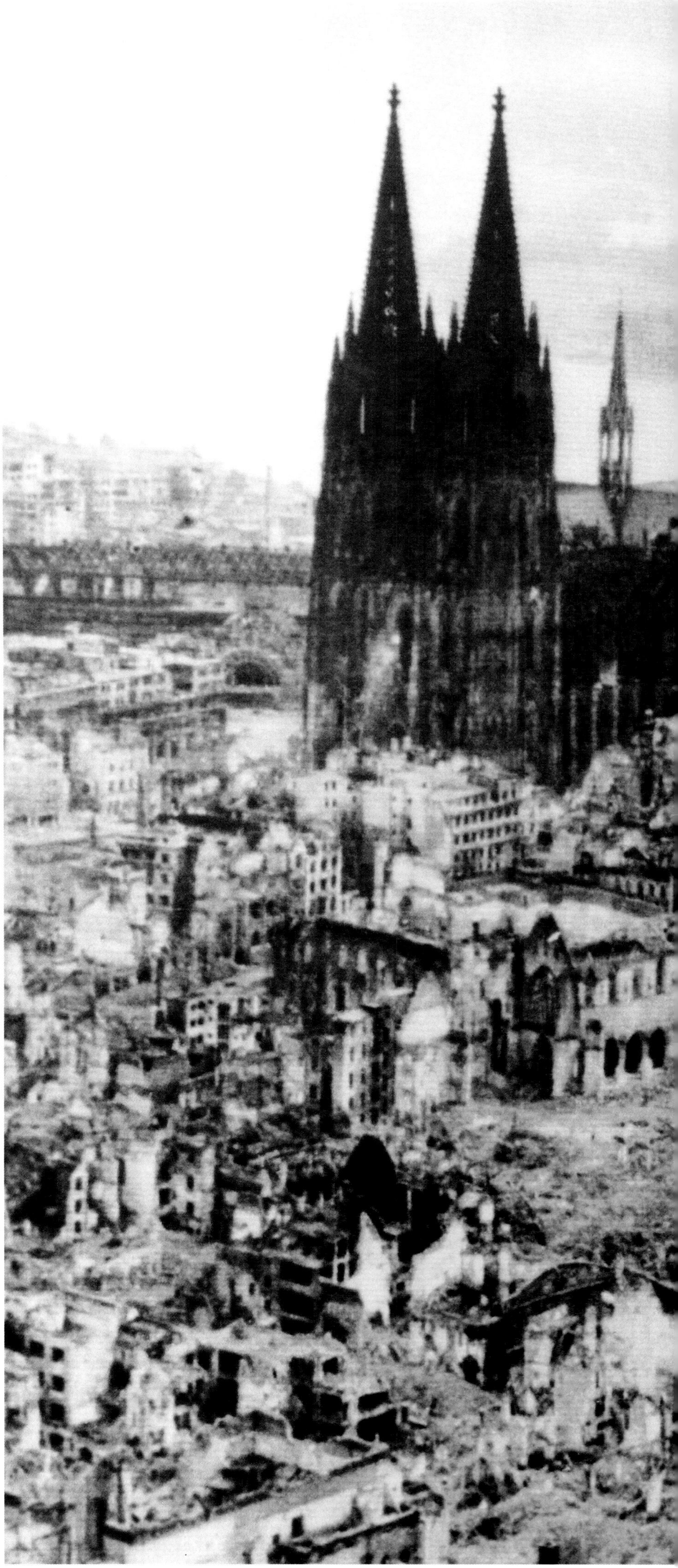

Photographer unknown
View of Cologne, Germany, showing the devastation from Allied air raids; the Cathedral and Rhine River visible in background, 1945.

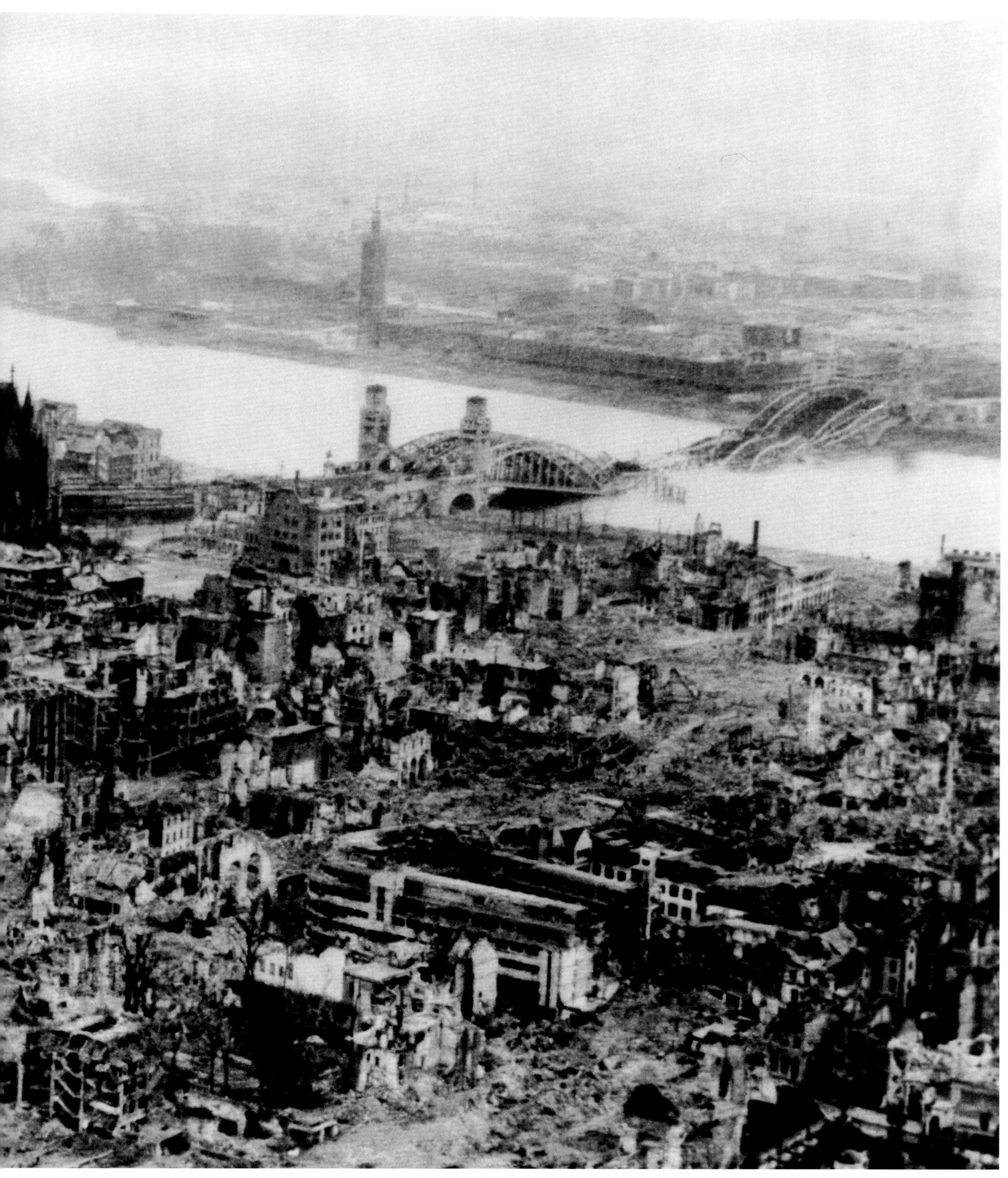

Credited with developing the editorial photo essay, American photojournalist W. Eugene Smith is remembered for his unwavering commitment to the stories he told. During his tenure as a war correspondent for *Life* magazine in the early 1940s, Smith famously documented the horrors of the battles in the Pacific. At this time he also photographed for the aviation magazine *Flying*, until he was badly wounded in 1945. This aerial view of ships in Pearl Harbor Naval Shipyard is from a series of images Smith made at the site in 1945, published in *Life*. The exquisite and precise composition could only be the work of a true master.

W. Eugene Smith
Ships in Pearl Harbor Naval Shipyard, Hawaii, 1945.

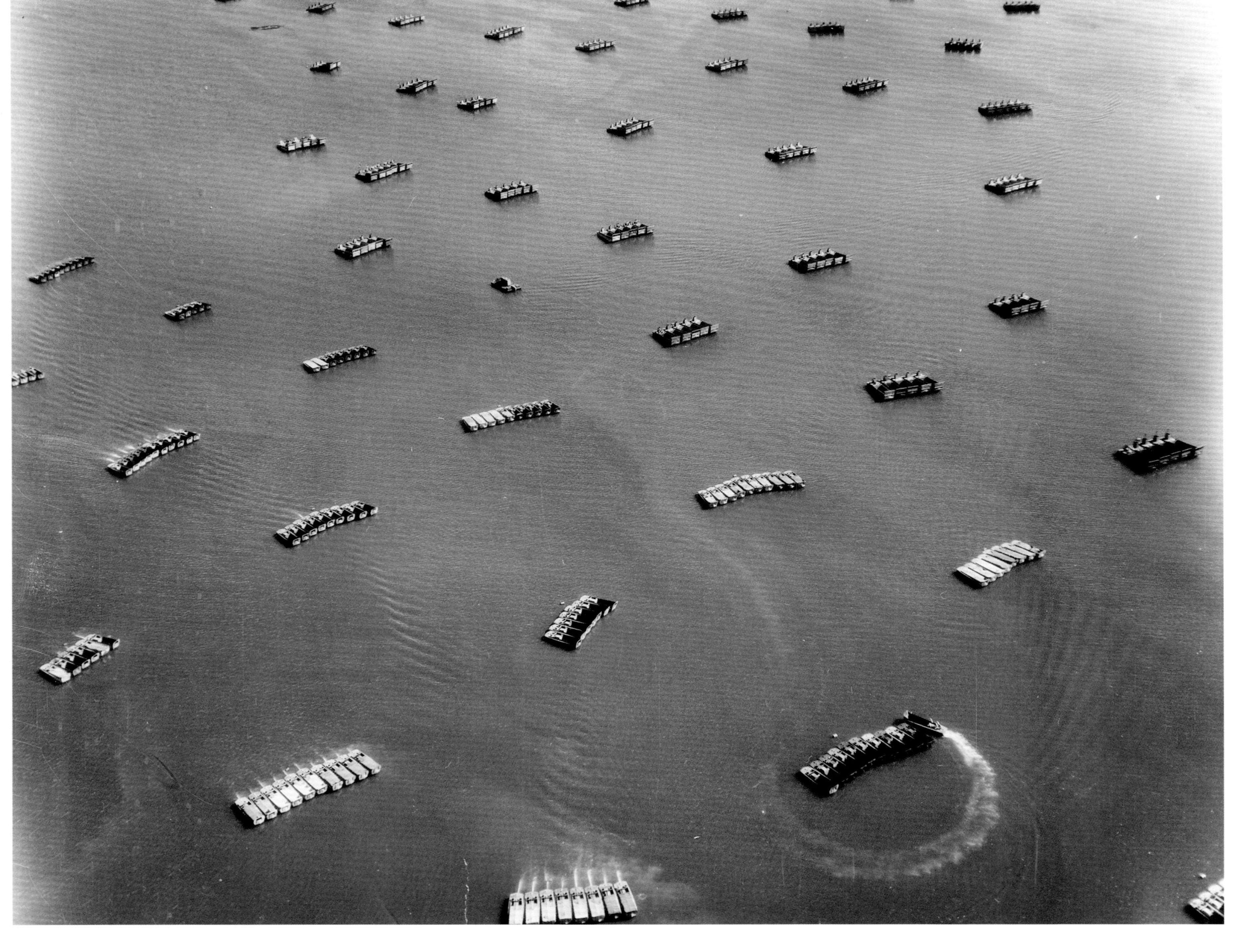

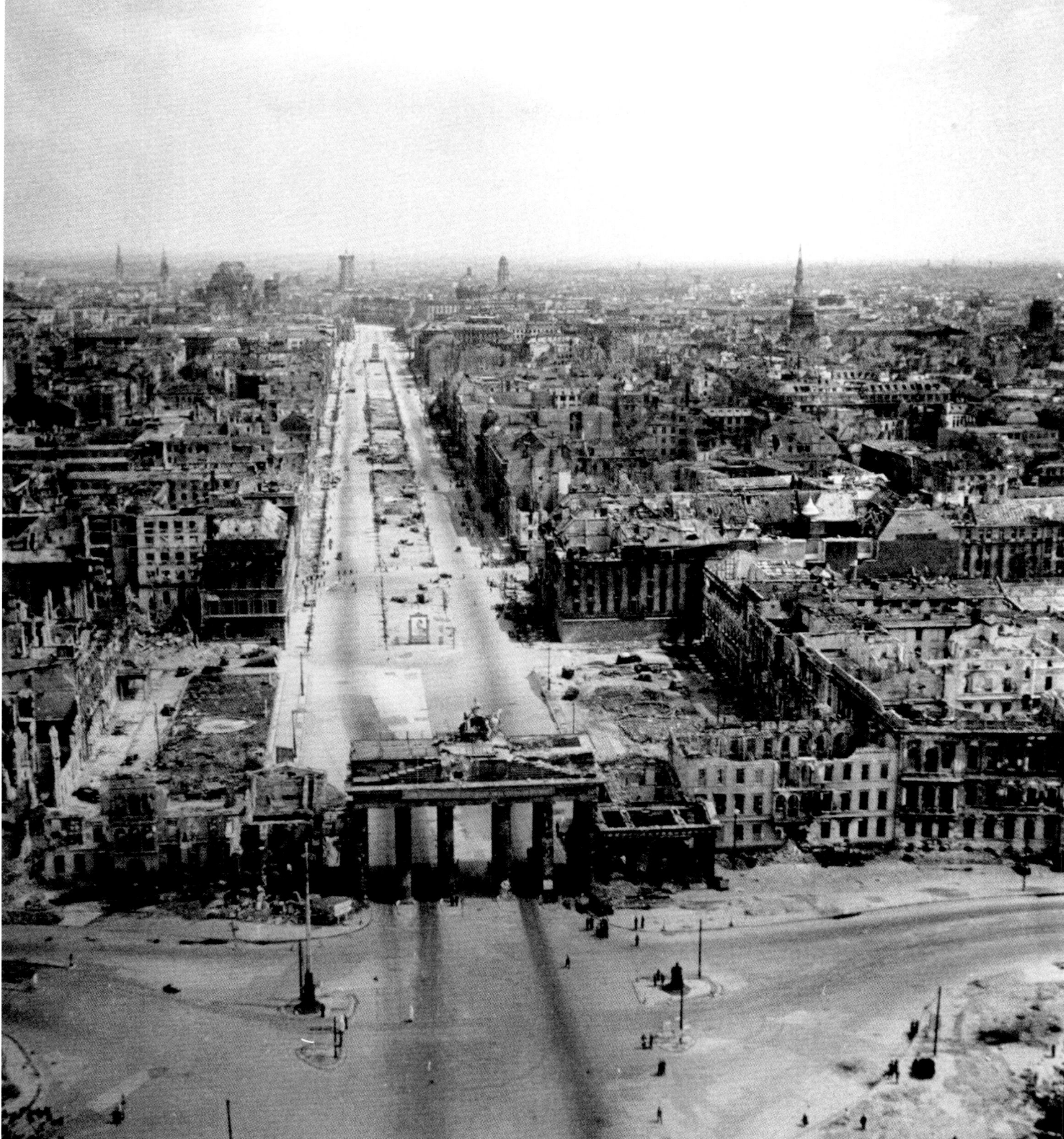

William Vandivert
Berlin, Germany, extending east beyond its border, the Brandenburg Gate, following Allied Forces' capture of the city, 1945.

In a similar way to the remarkable survival of St. Paul's Cathedral during The Blitz, it is something of a miracle that the Brandenburg Gate wasn't completely destroyed by Allied bombing in World War II. The eighteenth-century gate did undergo much-needed repair in the 1950s, but, as this photograph taken at the end of the war shows, the rest of Berlin came off far worse. Many buildings were skeletons, and the once bustling streets were filled with rubble, leaving a ghost town. It would take until the 1980s for the city to be rebuilt. The photograph is by American photographer William Vandivert, who was a staff photographer for *Life* magazine. A founding member of photography agency Magnum Photos, Vandivert had photographed London during The Blitz and flown in an RAF Blenheim bomber while on assignment in spring 1940, capturing shots of Spitfires doing mock dive attacks. Following the Allied capture of Berlin, Vandivert was the first Western photojournalist to photograph the bombed-out city.

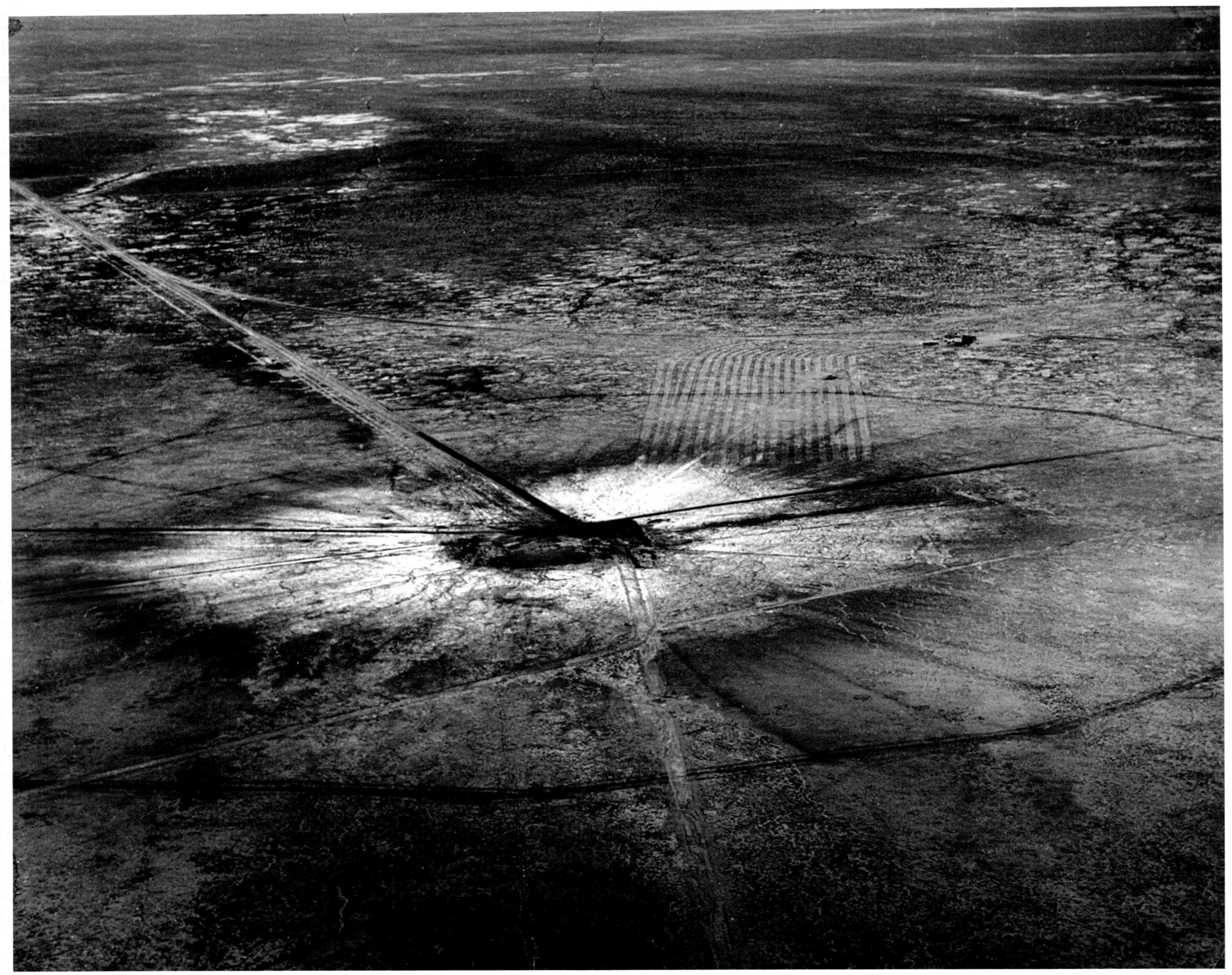

American-German science photographer Fritz Goro worked for *Life* magazine from the 1930s to the 1960s, during which time he covered many important scientific breakthroughs for the magazine. As well as photographing all manner of weird and wonderful experiments, Goro took this image of the burnt-out crater at the infamous nuclear-testing site (named Trinity Site) near Alamogordo, New Mexico, after the detonation of the world's first atomic bomb on 16 July 1945. Goro's image is celebrated as the first aerial photograph of the point of explosion, marking what many have called the dawn of the Atomic Age.

Fritz Goro
First atomic bomb crater, near Alamogordo, New Mexico, USA, 1945.

Photographer unknown
Atomic bombing of
Nagasaki, Japan, 1945.

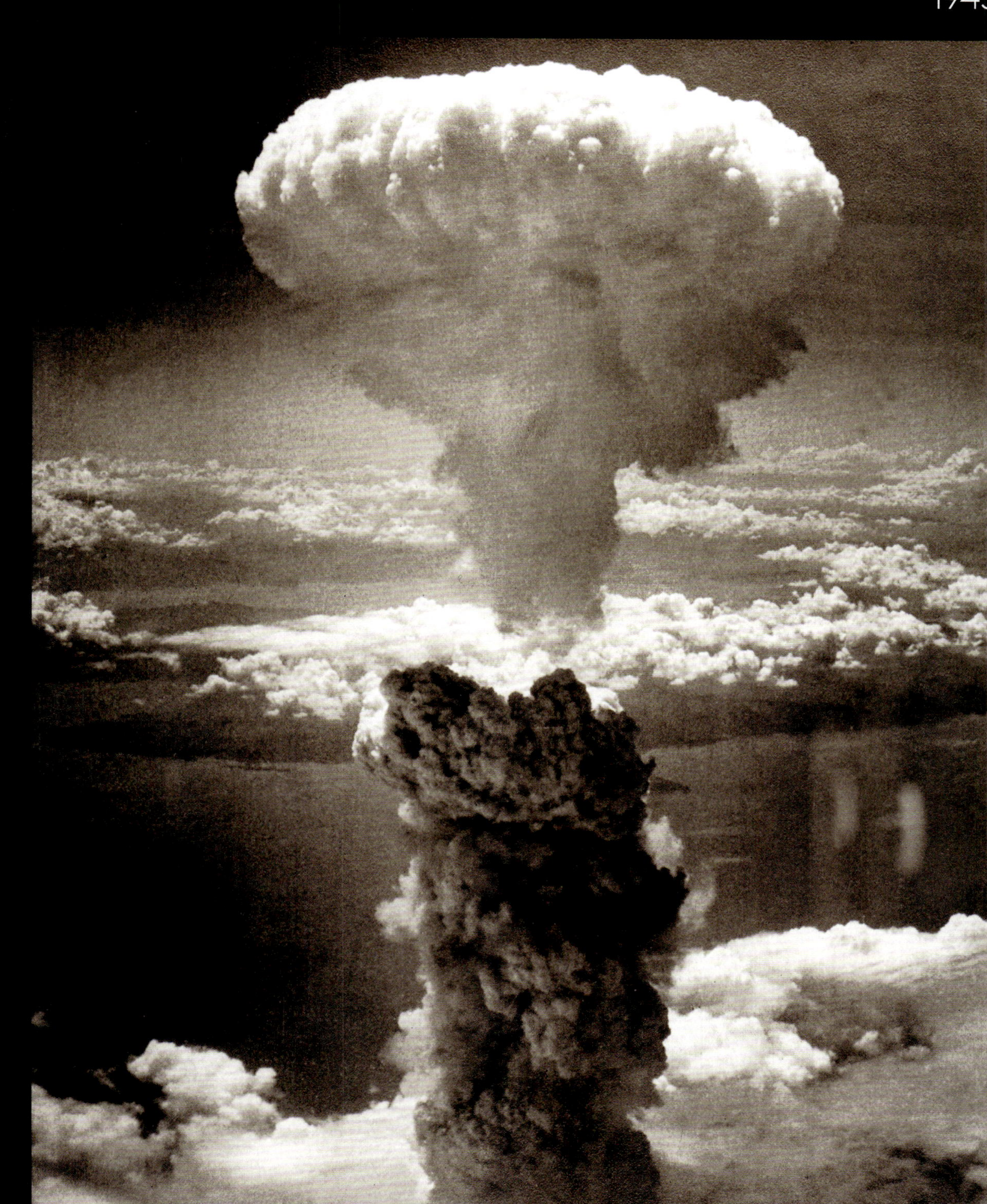

Two of the most devastating wartime attacks in world history occurred on 6 and 9 August 1945, when American forces dropped an atomic bomb on Hiroshima (see page 78) and another even larger bomb on Nagasaki just three days later. Reports suggest that between 60,000 and 80,000 Japanese were killed in the first attack, while around 40,000 perished at Nagasaki, but tens of thousands more died from radiation poisoning in the decades that followed.

Below
Photographer unknown
Aftermath of the atomic bomb, Hiroshima, Japan, 1945.

Right
John van Hasselt
Prefectural Industrial Promotion Hall, one of the only buildings left standing after the atomic bomb, Hiroshima, 1945.

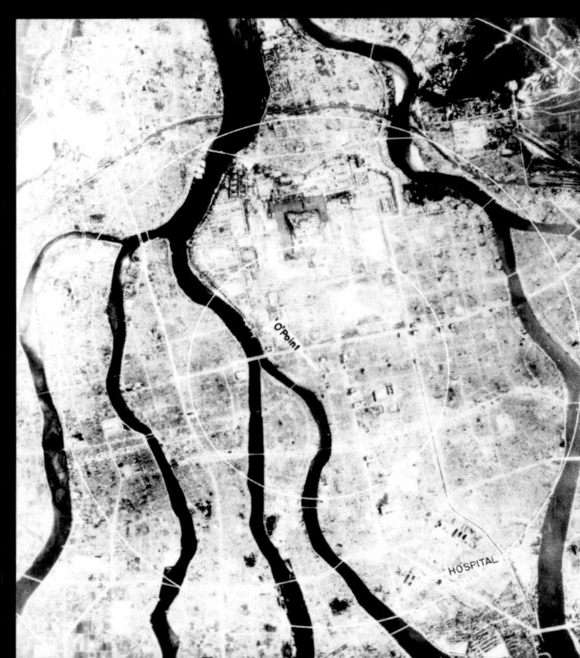

The atomic bomb that was dropped on Hiroshima all but wiped out the city. The only building left standing close to the bomb's hypocentre was the Hiroshima Prefectural Industrial Promotion Hall (pictured right), its distinctive dome damaged but not completely destroyed. The Genbaku Dome has been preserved and is now officially known as the Hiroshima Peace Memorial, around which a memorial park has been established. In the aftermath of the strike, the United States Strategic Bombing Survey, which had been studying the effects of US aerial attacks in Europe since its establishment in November 1944, was extended to cover events in Japan. Aerial images similar to this (pictured above) were made to assess the impact of the atomic bombings.

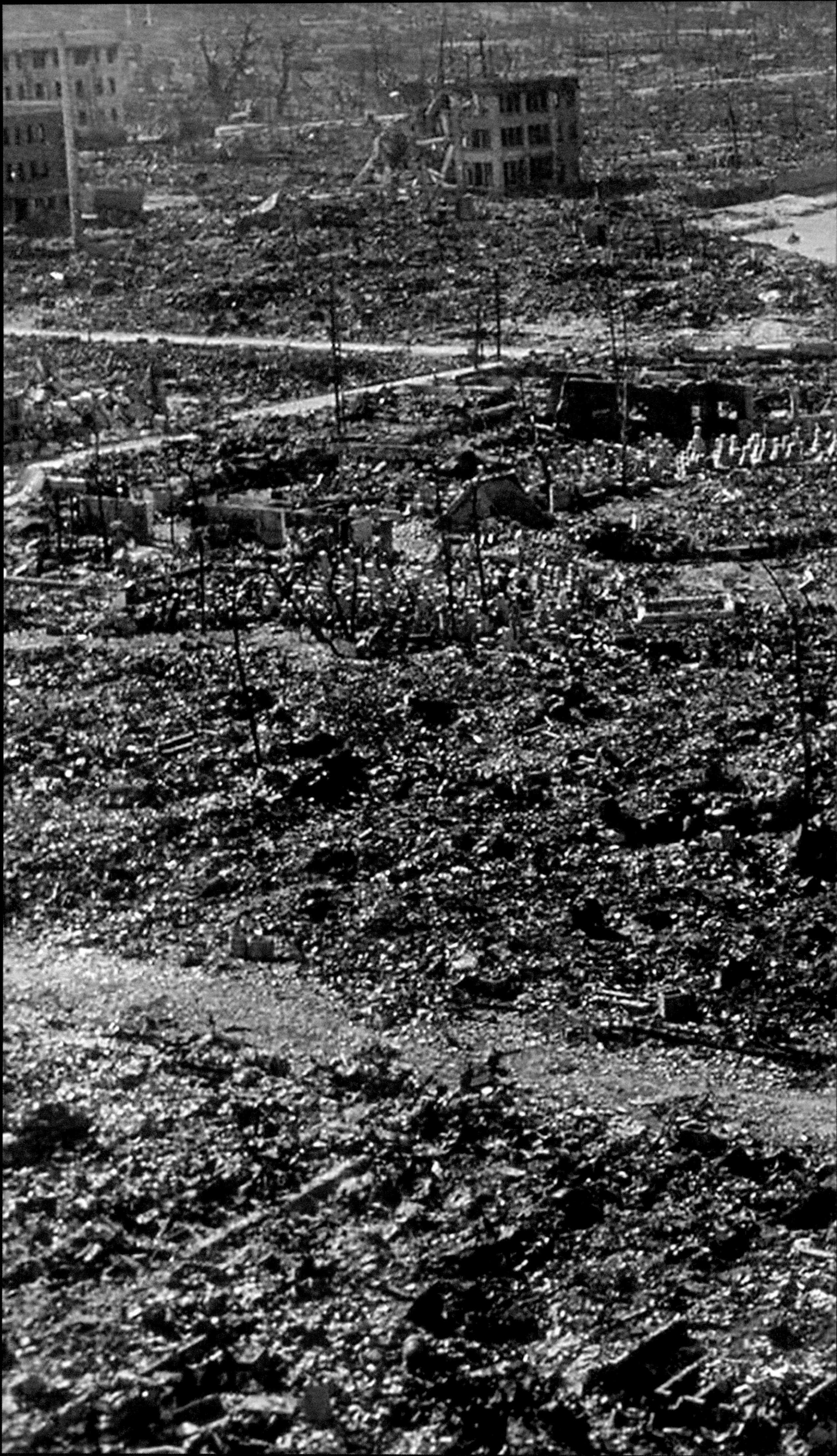

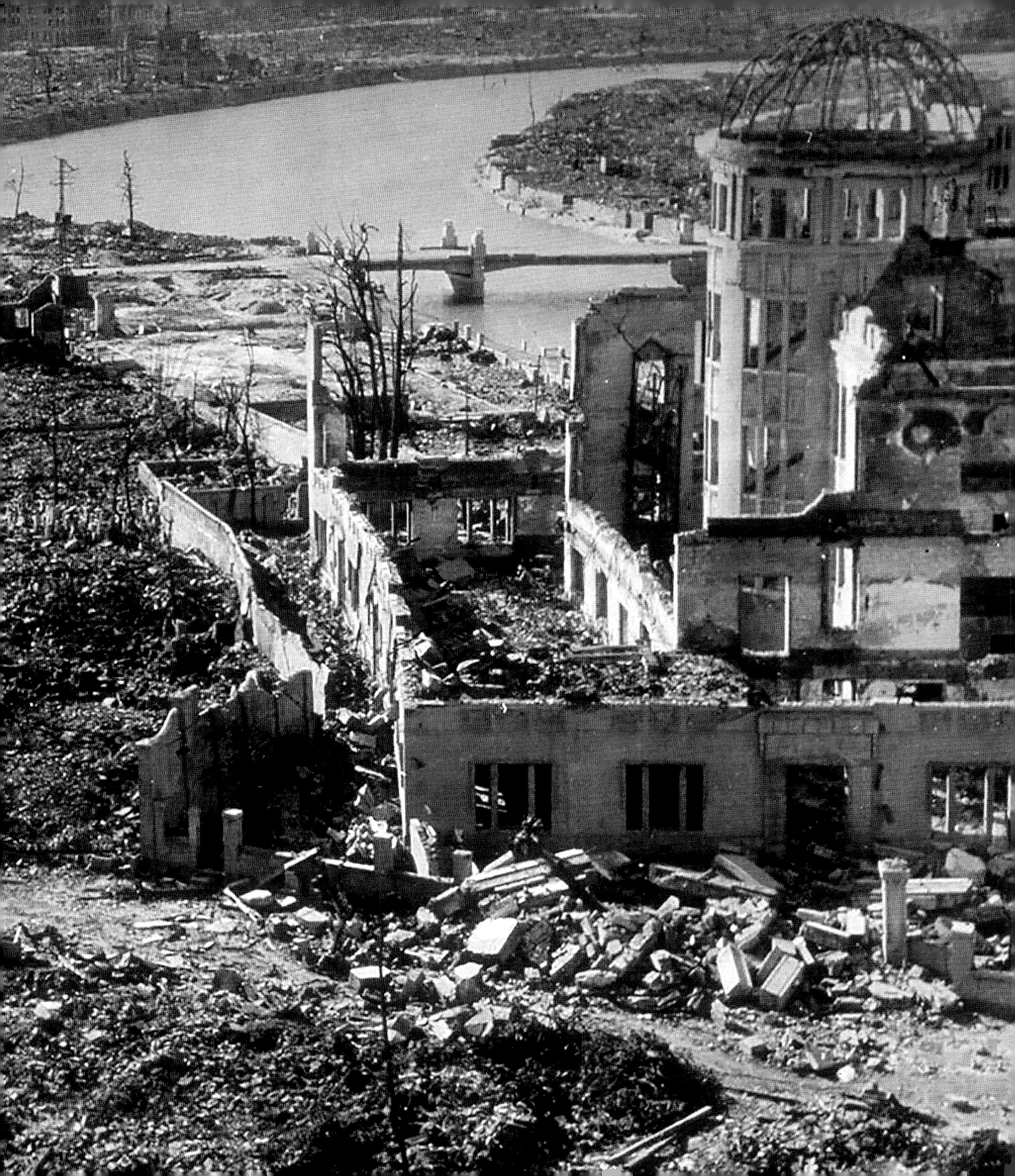

1945

The RAF had spent years gathering intelligence from the air during World War II, but this aerial assignment was far lighter in tone than most undertaken previously. The photograph shows crowds of jubilant people celebrating VE (Victory in Europe) Day in Piccadilly Circus, London, on 8 May 1945. Taken from a low-flying aircraft, it gives a surprisingly detailed view of the surrounding buildings, rooftops and activity below. In the centre, the Shaftesbury Memorial Fountain (also known mistakingly as Eros) is visible. It had been boarded up during the war to protect it during air strikes.

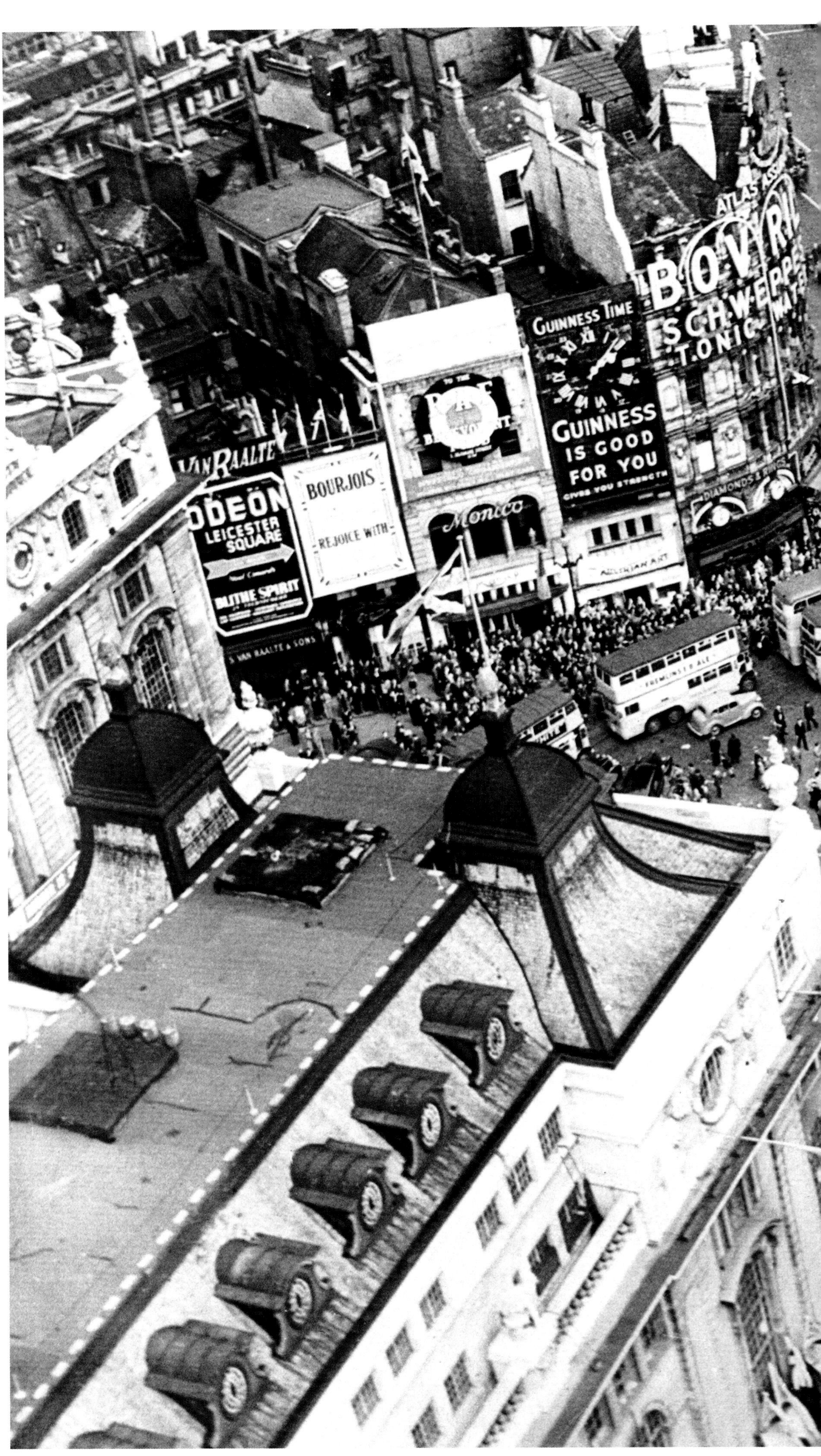

Photographer unknown
Piccadilly Circus, London, England, on VE Day, 8 May 1945.

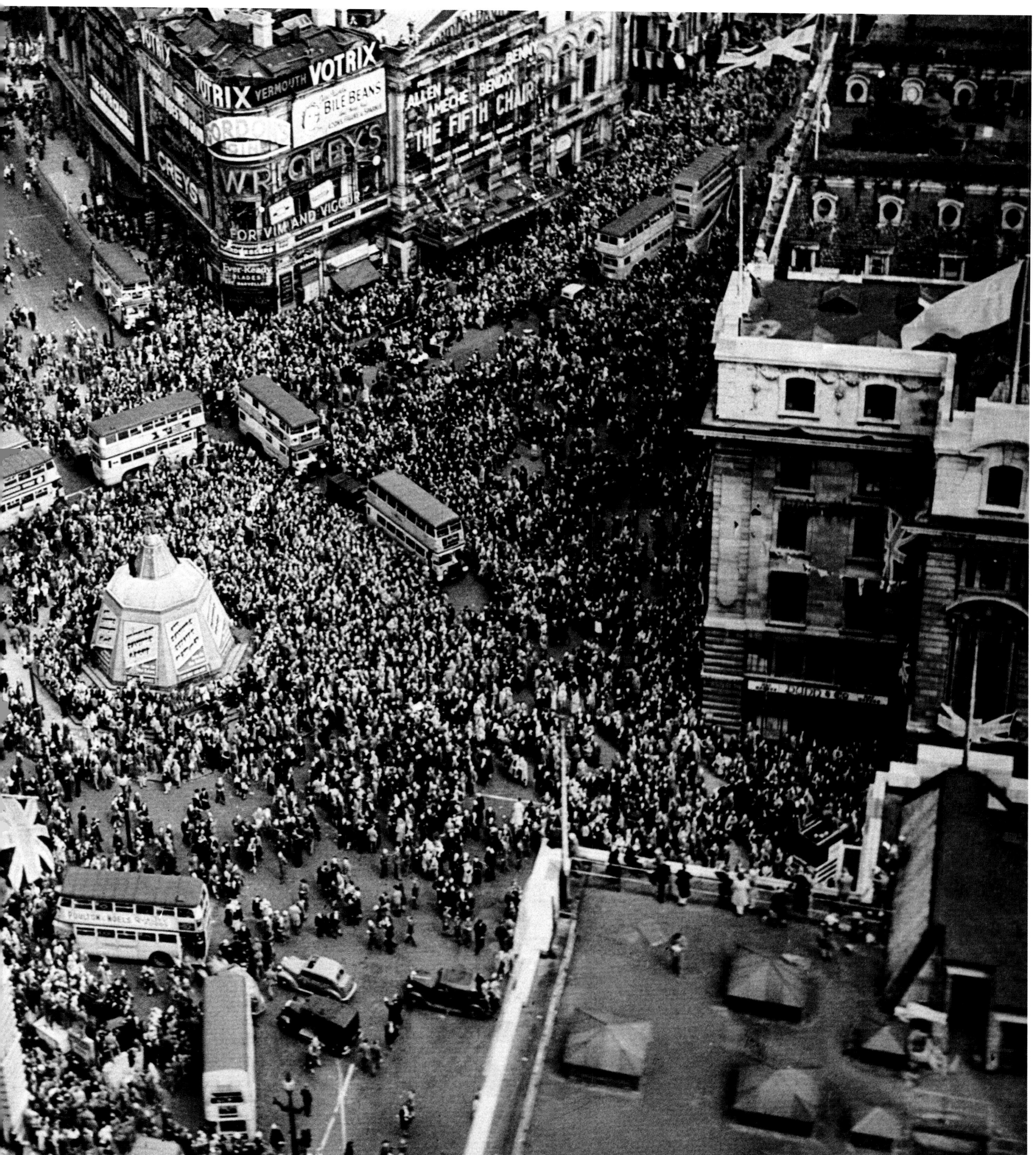
VOTRIX
VOTRIX VERMOUTH VOTRIX
BILE BEANS
WRIGLEY'S
FOR VIM AND VIGOUR
GREYS
Ever-Ready
BLADES
ALLEN
AMECHE
BENDIX
BENNY
THE FIFTH CHAIR

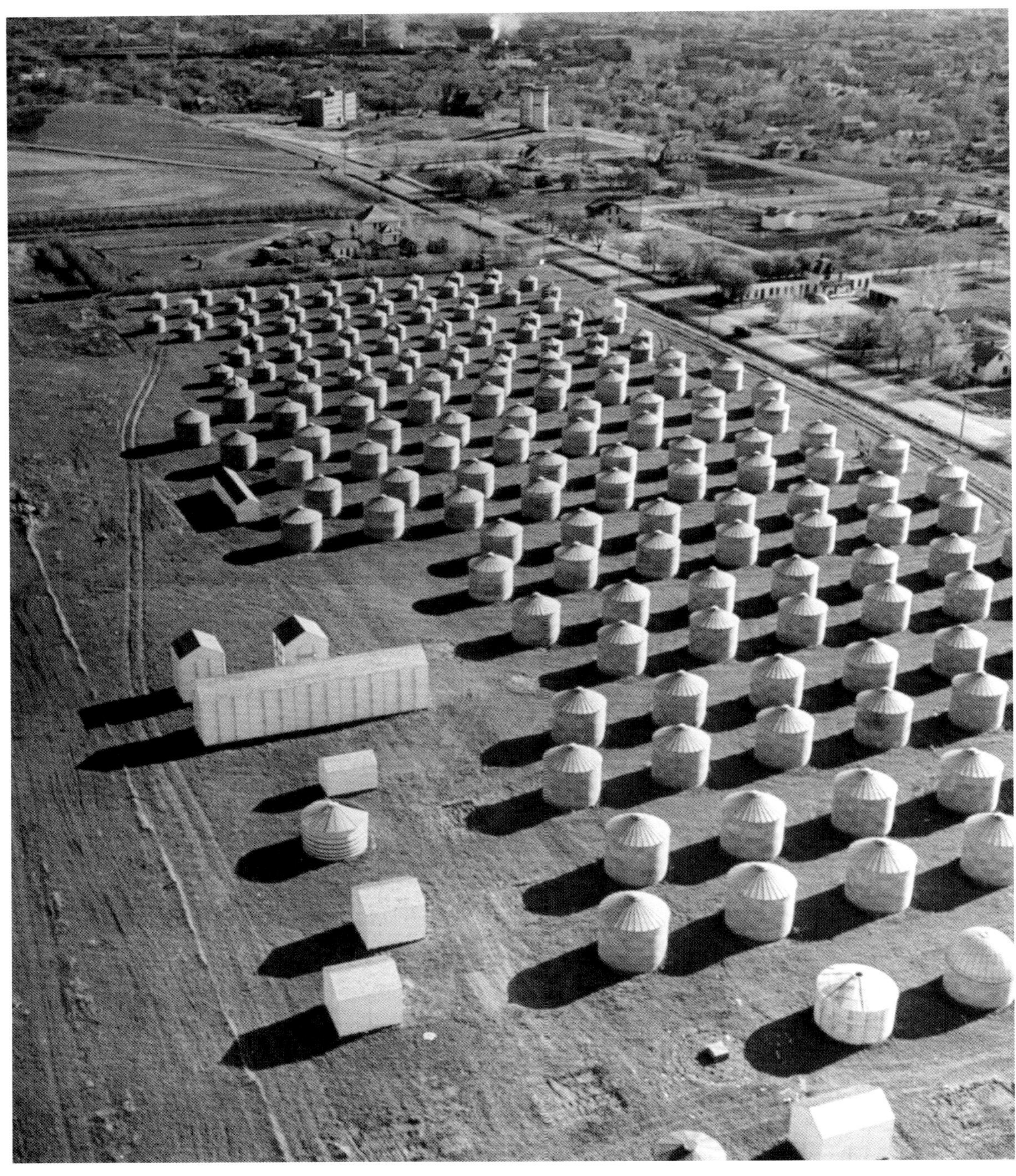

When Jamaican-born photographer Wallace Kirkland took this oblique aerial photograph of an American agricultural landscape in April 1946, it wasn't the first time the *Life* magazine photographer had taken pictures from the air. His first taste of aerial photography came while he was on assignment for the magazine in Iowa in the mid- to late 1930s. The three-dimensionality of this image, with its neat rows of conical granaries and shadows, creates an almost sculptural quality.

Wallace Kirkland
Small conical granaries dotting the ground, casting long shadows, USA, 1946.

On 1 July 1946, the US dropped a hydrogen bomb on Bikini Atoll in the Marshall Islands. It may have only been a nuclear test (residents were relocated), but the event marked the beginning of a series of 23 atomic and hydrogen bomb blasts that would be carried out on the atoll by the US government during the 1940s and '50s. This startling aerial photograph, shot from above the cloud and looking directly down, gives an indication of the vast and almost unimaginable scale of the blast. The first two detonations – code-named Operation Crossroads – were the first to take place after the bombings of Hiroshima and Nagasaki a year earlier. In 1954, a second series of tests (Operation Castle) began with the bomb Bravo, which was a thousand times more powerful than the Hiroshima and Nagasaki bombs.

Photographer unknown
Hydrogen-bomb explosion, Bikini Atoll, Marshall Islands, Pacific Ocean, 1946.

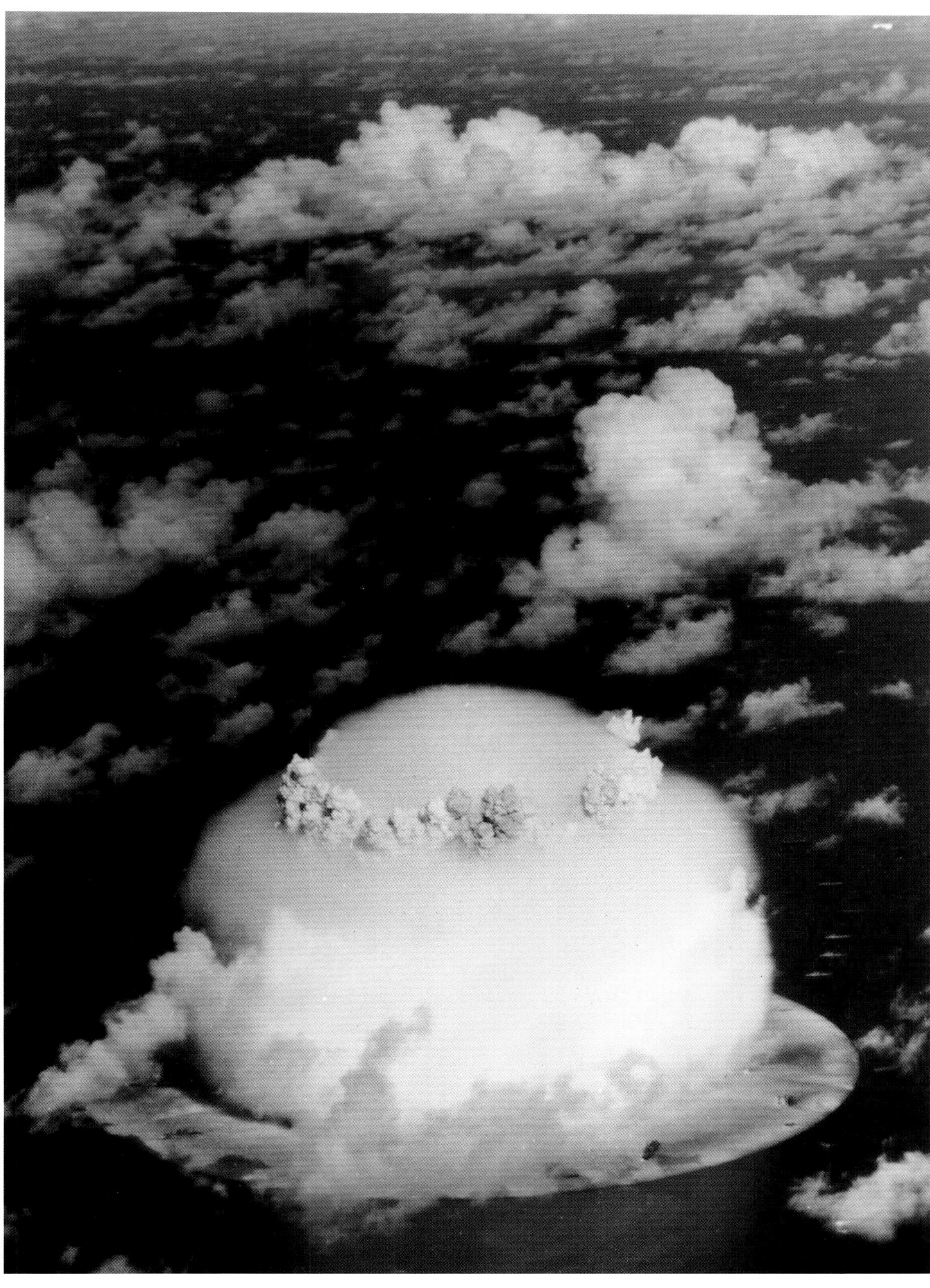

1946

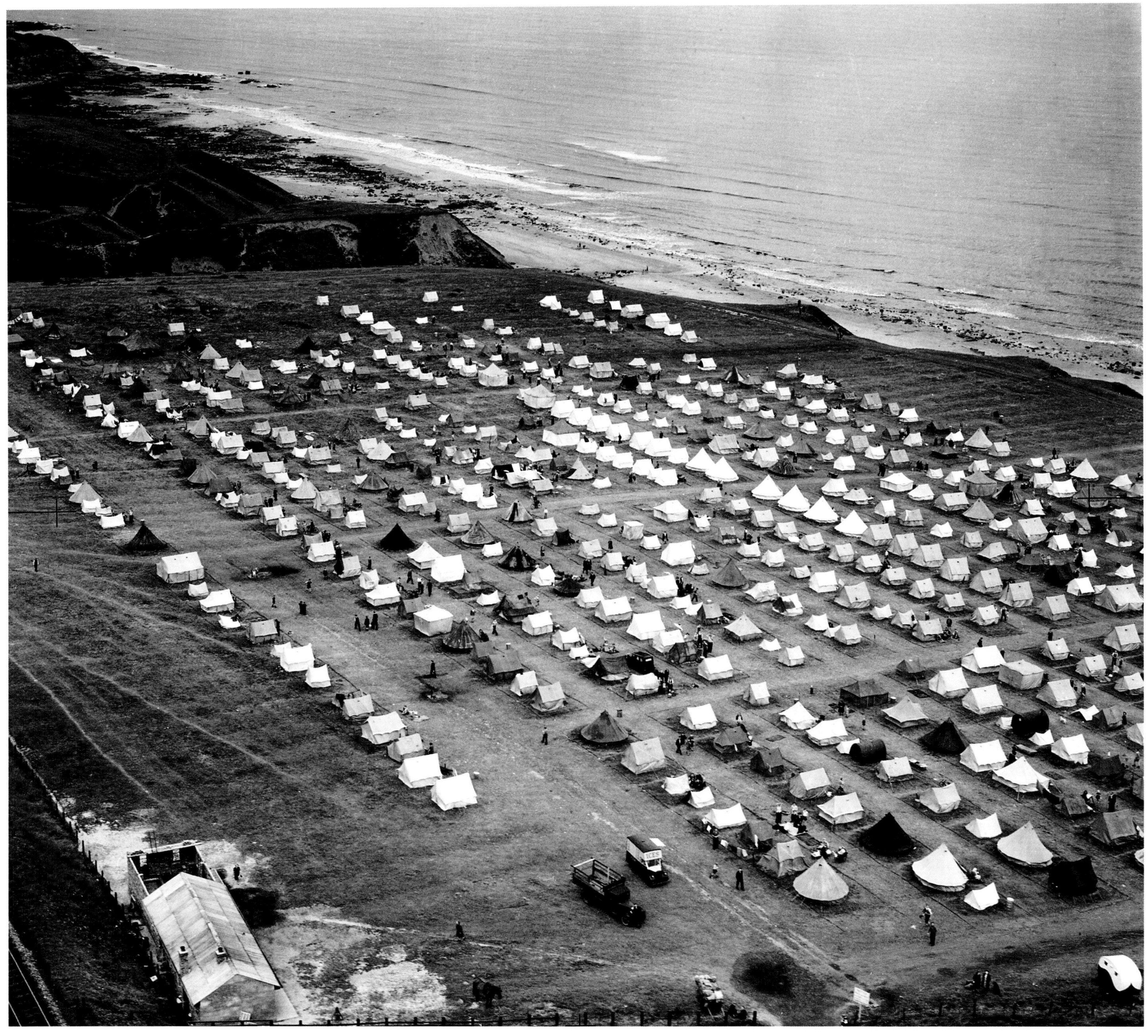

As the 1940s gave way to the ’50s, Aerofilms Ltd (see also pages 51, 52, 87, 96) continued to make oblique photographs of Britain from the skies. A leader in the field of commercial aerial photography, the company had survived the Great Depression of the 1930s and during World War II had assisted the war effort. Gradually, the firm was creating what is today a unique archive that shows the changing face of Britain in the twentieth century – from the transformation of the built environment to the British countryside and people at work and play. The breadth of subject matter is impressive. One image (pictured above) of a campsite in Crimdon Park, County Durham, in 1946 shows how ordinary Britons holidayed after World War II, while another (pictured opposite) from around 1947 depicts miners at a gala.

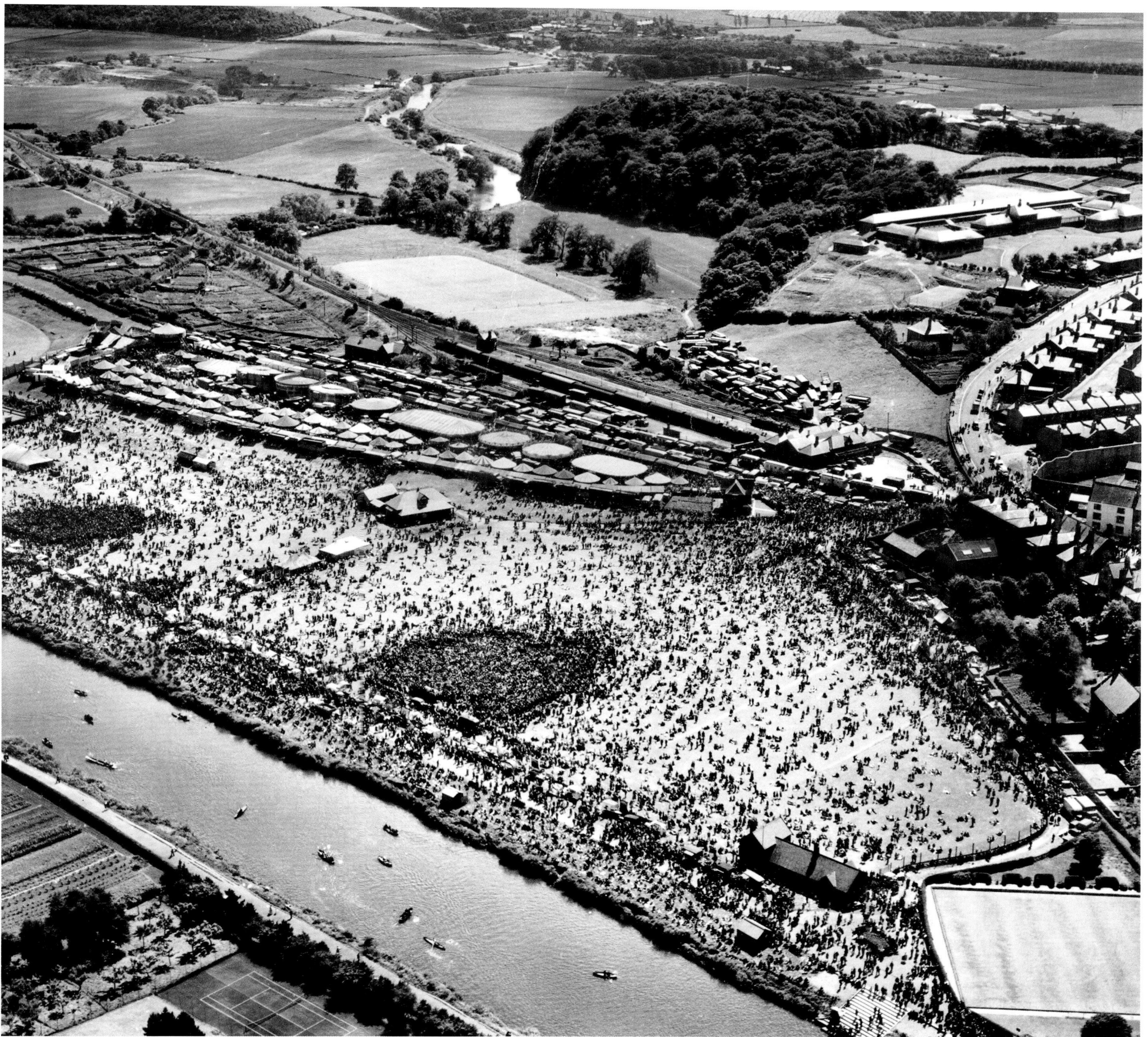

Opposite
Aerofilms Ltd
A clifftop campsite in Crimdon Park, County Durham, England, 1946.

Above
Aerofilms Ltd
Durham Miners' Gala at The Racecourse, Durham, England, *c.* 1947.

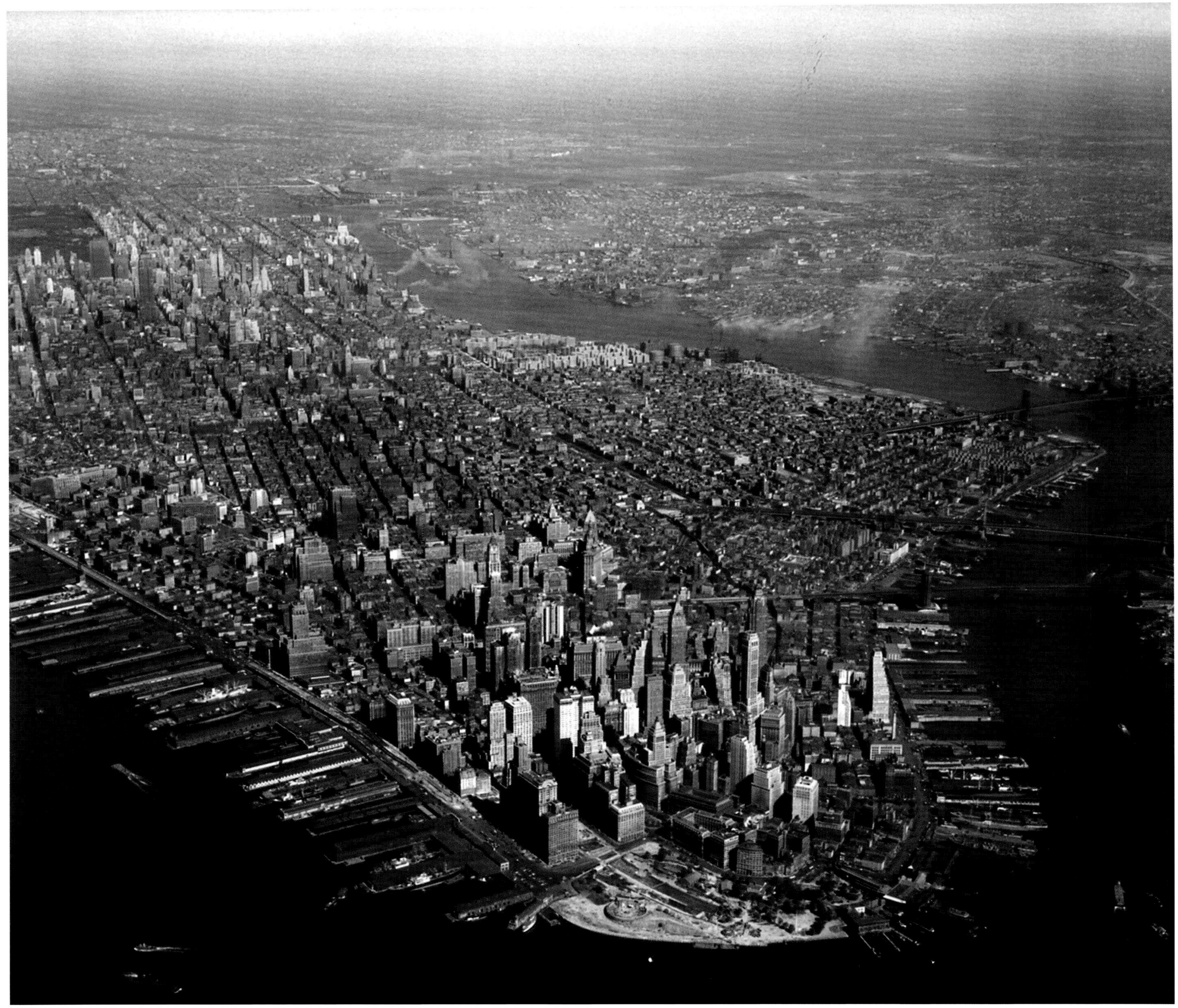

From the late 1940s into the 1950s and beyond, aerial-survey companies in the United States continued to produce photographs (such as the ones pictured above and opposite) of urban and rural landscapes, which provided reference material for map-making, land-use studies, urban planning and social scientific research, among other applications. Unwittingly, perhaps, these companies have created a valuable archive of aerial imagery that researchers and the public can look at today to see how the landscapes of yesteryear looked.

Above
Photographer unknown
Manhattan Island, New York, USA, 1947.

Opposite
Photographer unknown
Top of the Empire State Building in New York, USA, 1947.

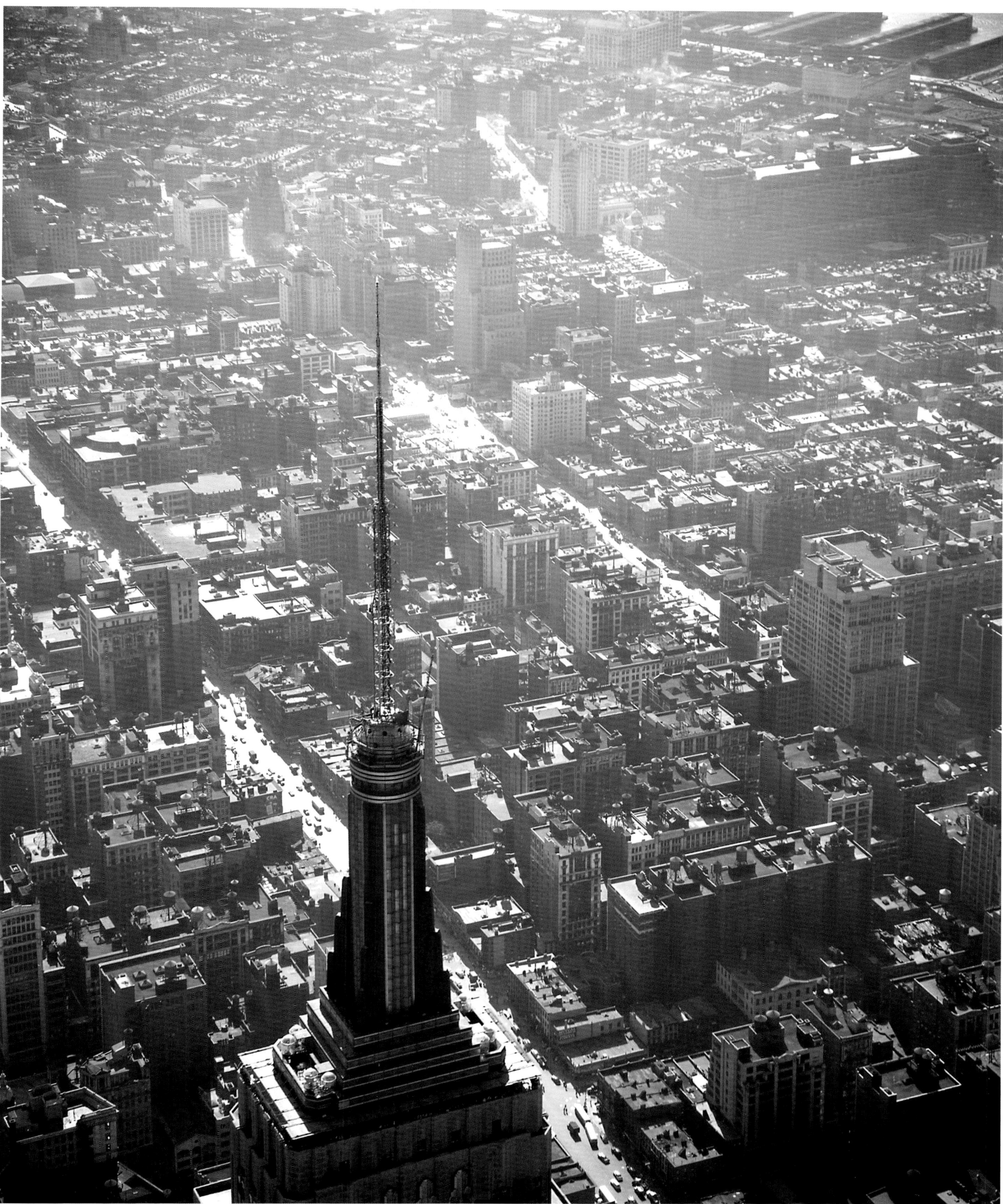

1949

The wealthy city of Los Alamos in New Mexico is now home to millionaires, but it was once shrouded in secrecy. The remote 'atomic city' was the site of production of atomic bombs by the US government during World War II, and occupied by scientists and engineers and their families, who were all sworn to secrecy. This photograph from 1949 is the first aerial photograph to be taken of the city. The image, credited to the *Denver Post* and the Los Alamos Scientific Laboratory, shows rows of houses hidden away by trees, and glimpses of the aircraft from which the photograph was taken are just visible.

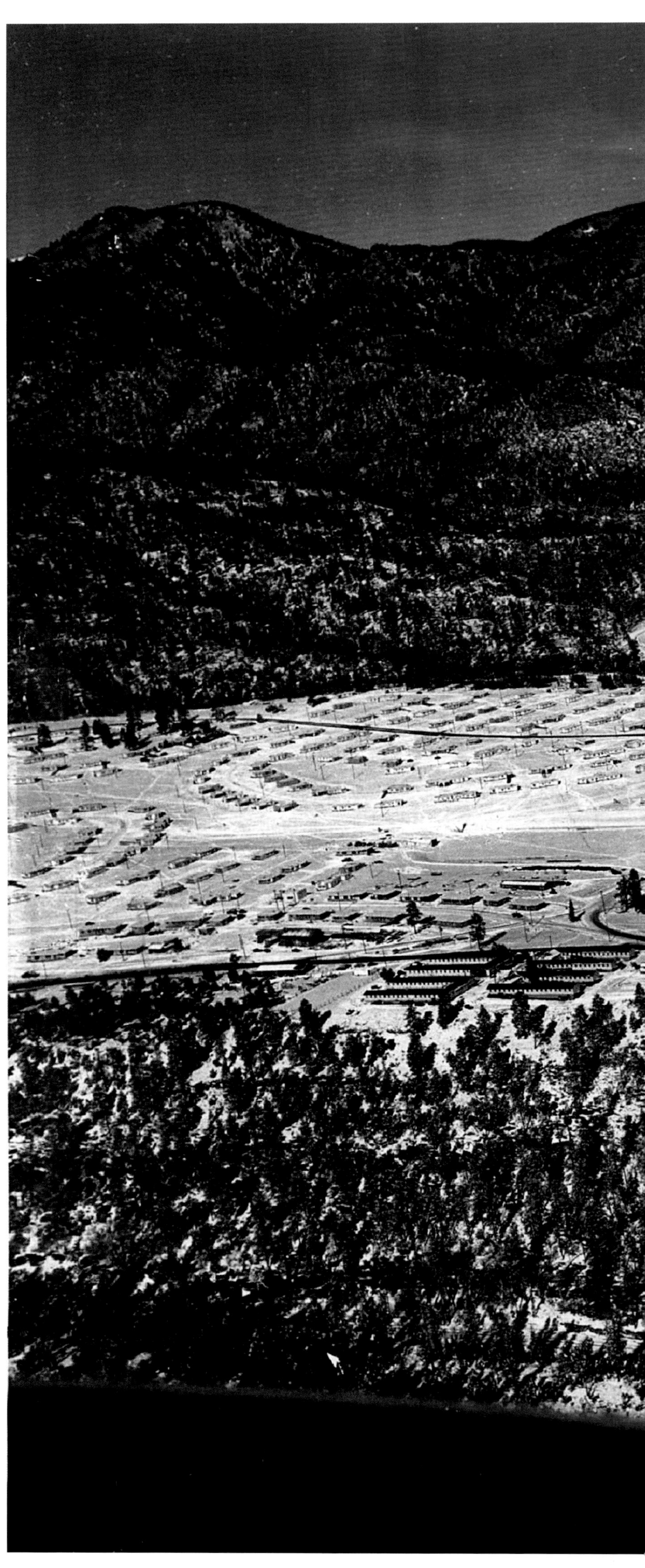

Photographer unknown
First aerial photograph of Los Alamos, New Mexico, USA, 1949.

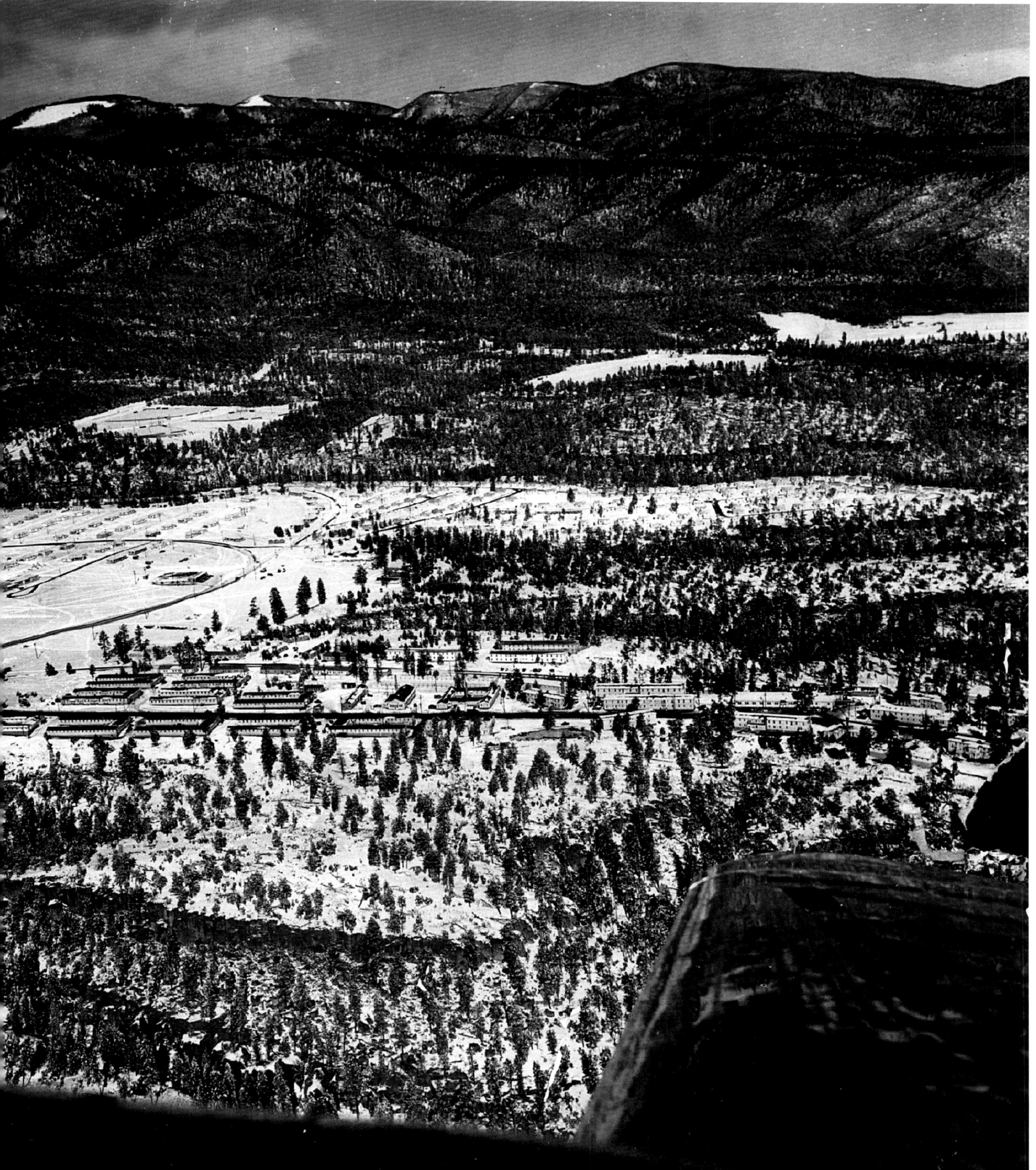

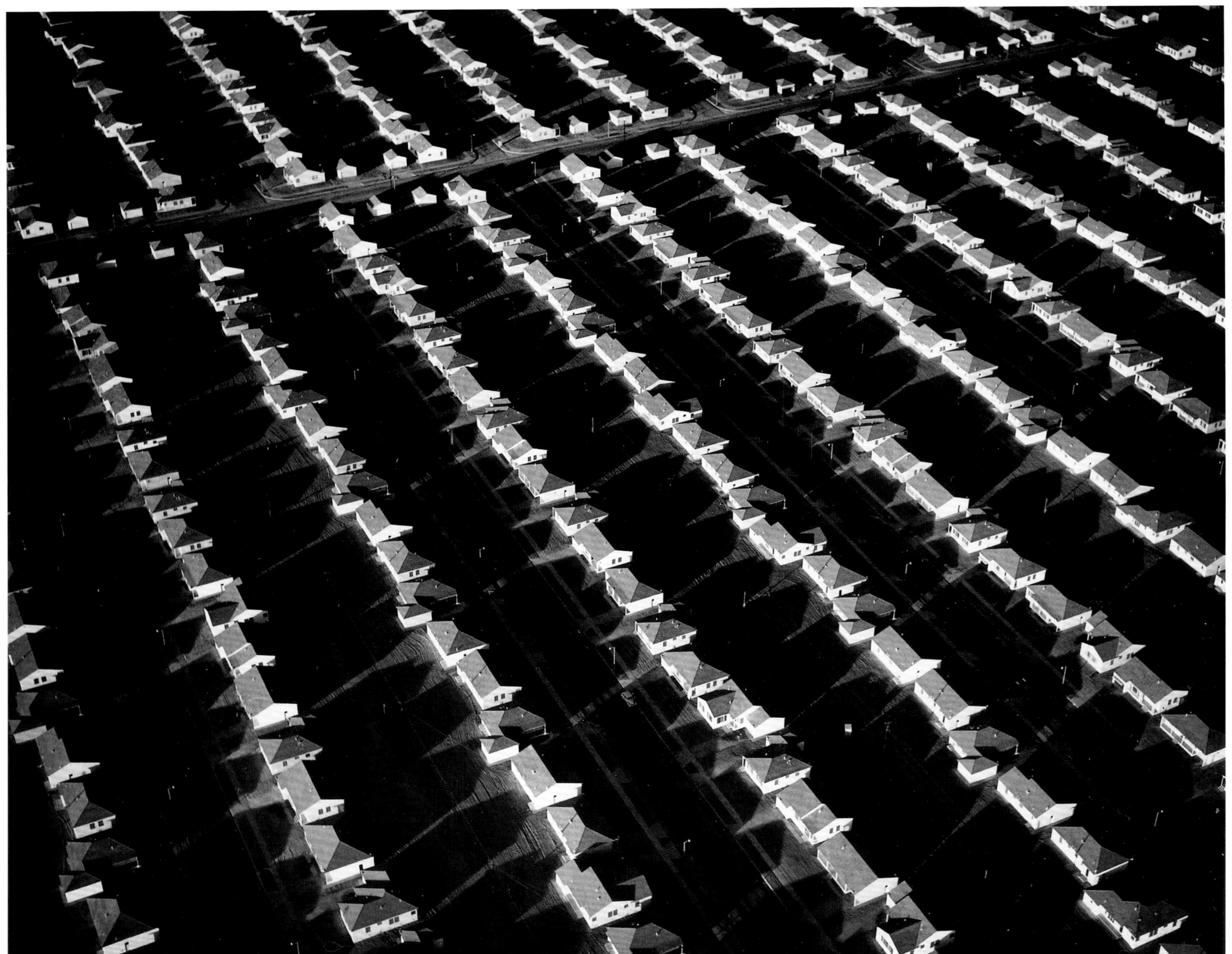

William A. Garnett was an early pioneer of aerial photography who helped to elevate it to an art form. He began making aerial photographs in the late 1940s, and in the mid-1950s bought a Cessna 170B plane, which he used to photograph rural and urban landscapes across America, sometimes for commercial commissions. Garnett often used two 35mm cameras and shot in black and white and colour, creating images that possess a unique visual poetry, the likes of which had not been seen before. Garnett's photographs, shot both directly down and at an oblique angle, tell us something of how humans live on planet Earth while at the same time presenting startlingly beautiful views of the world from the air.

Above
William A. Garnett,
Finished Housing, Lakewood, California, USA, 1950.

Opposite
William A. Garnett
Walnut Grove Standing, California, USA, 1953.

Overleaf left
William A. Garnett
Walnut Grove Saw Cut, California, USA, 1953.

Overleaf right
William A. Garnett
Walnut Groves Uprooted by Bulldozers, California, USA, 1953.

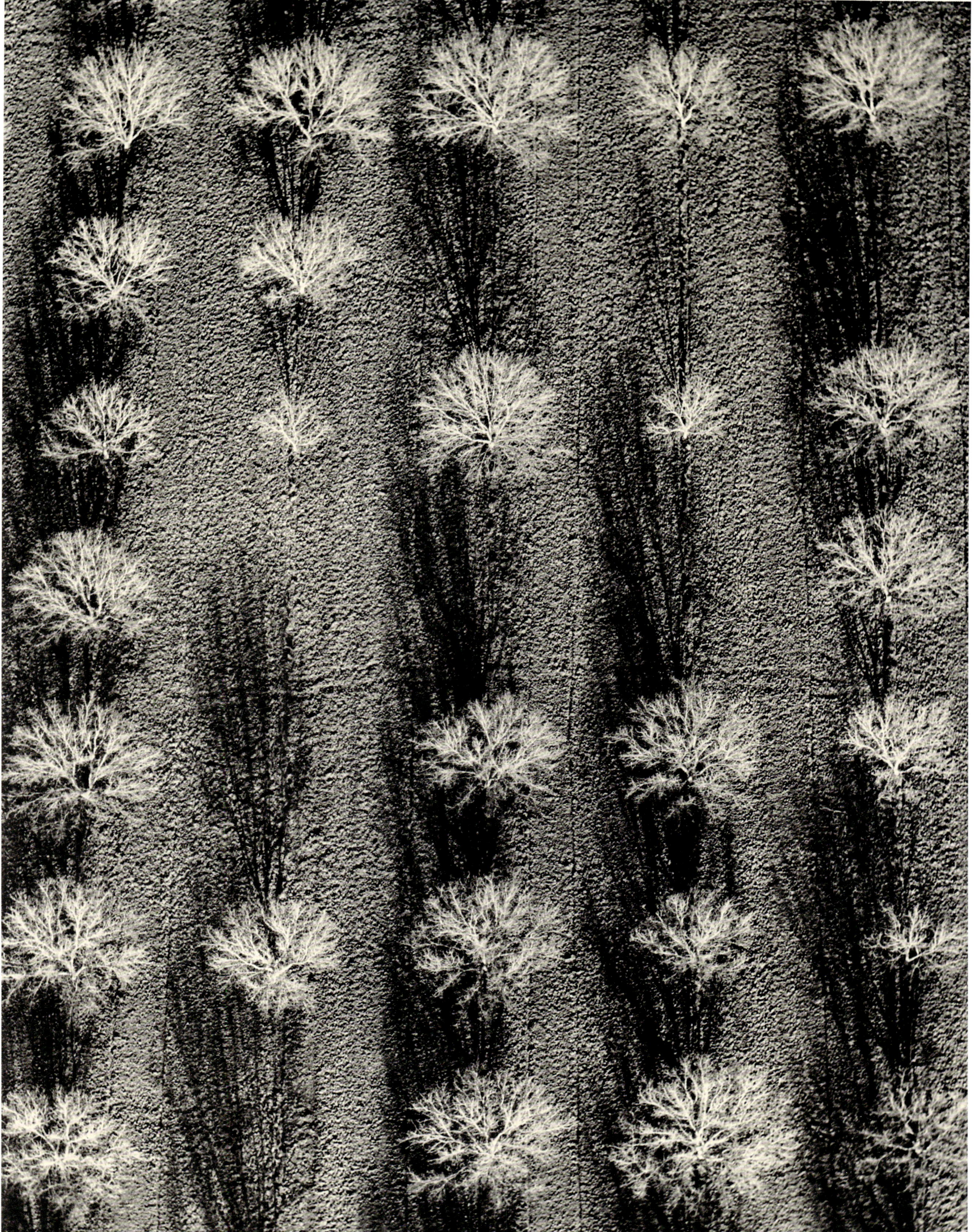

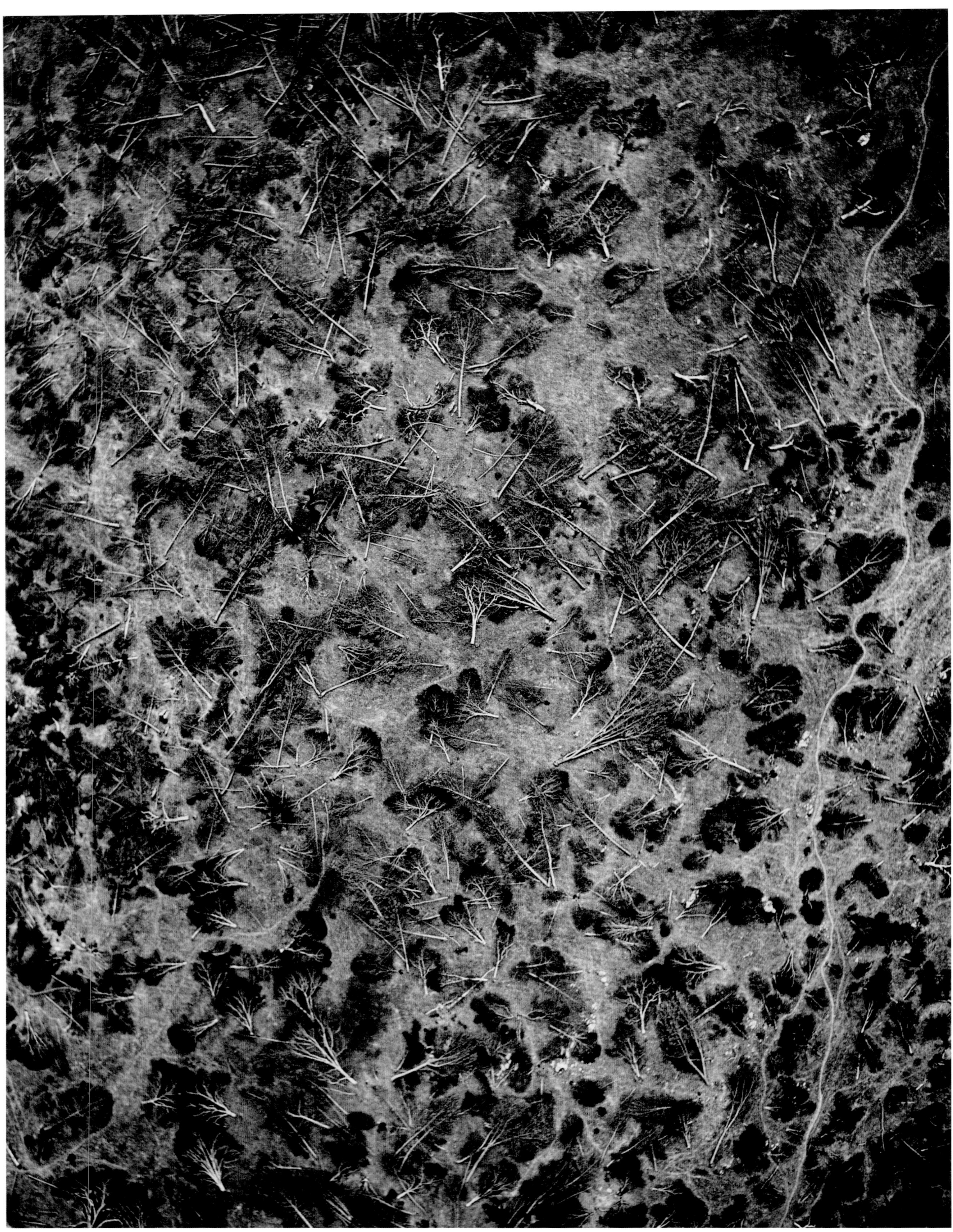

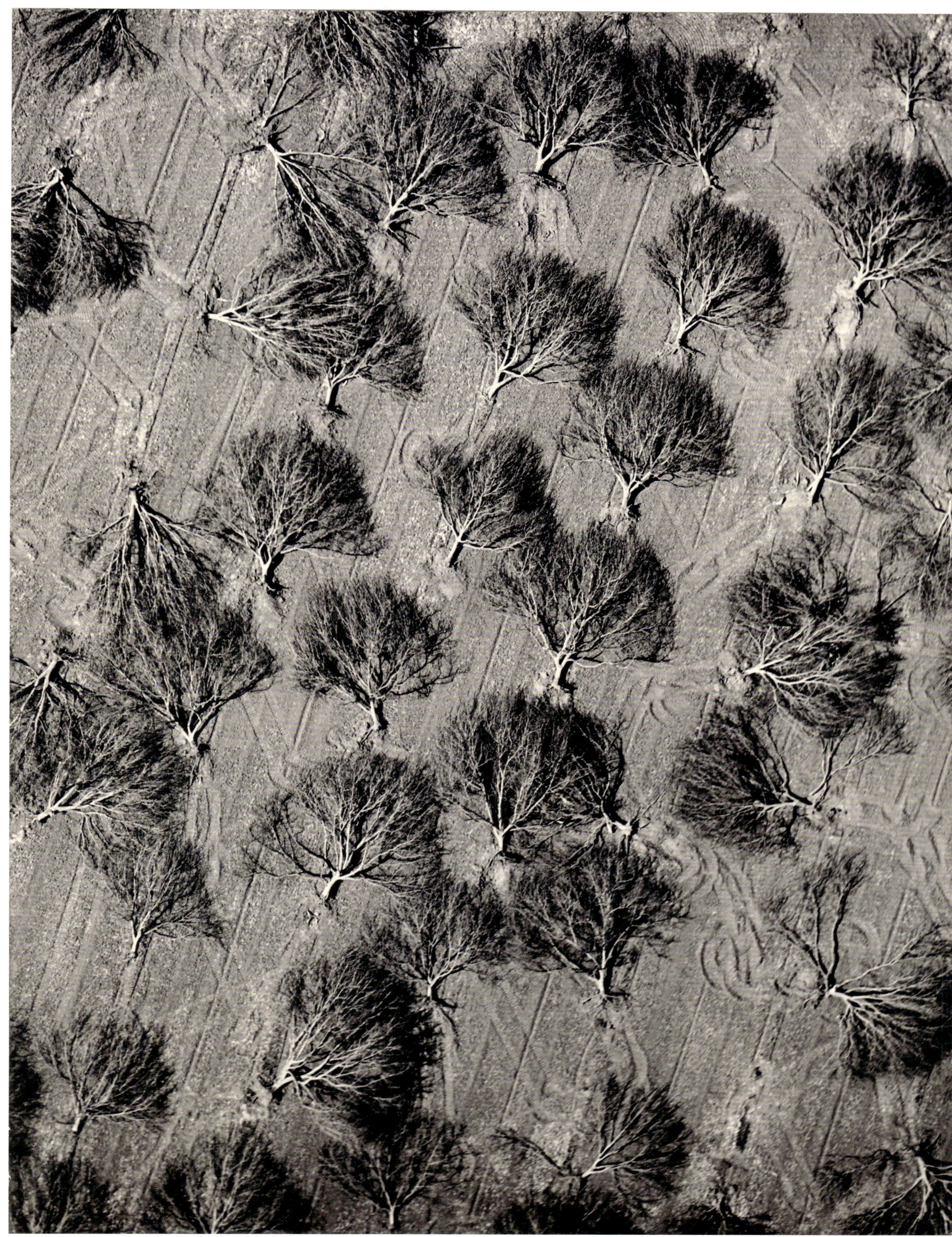

1950

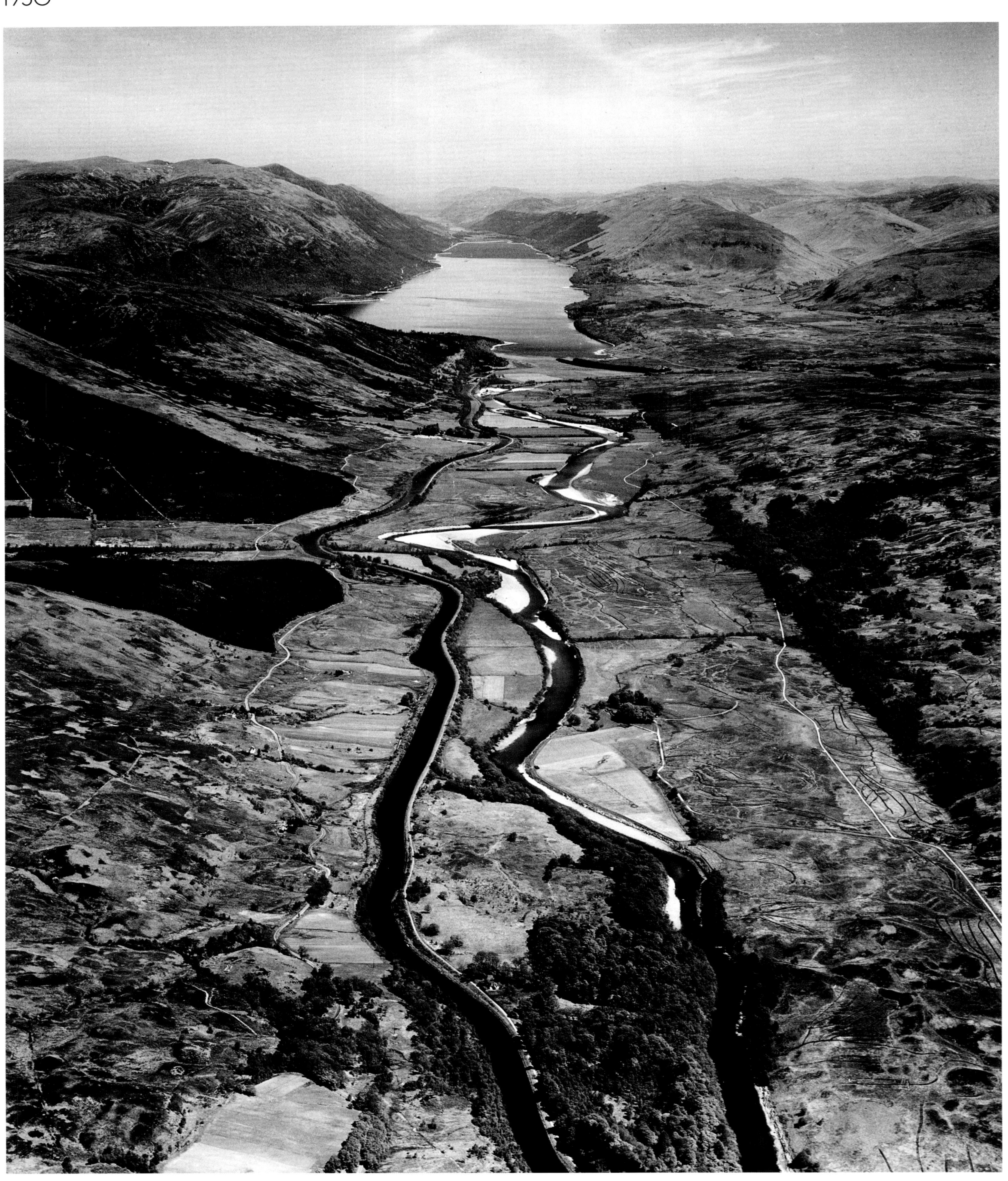

Opposite
Aerofilms Ltd
Caledonian Canal and River Lochy, Scotland, 1950.

Below
Fairchild Aerial Surveys, Inc.
Mid-town Manhattan, New York, USA, looking downtown, towards the Rockefeller Center and Empire State Building, *c.* 1950.

While leading air-survey company Aerofilms Ltd was busy recording aerial views of Great Britain (see pages 51, 52, 86–7 and opposite), Fairchild Aerial Surveys, Inc. continued to develop its aerial photographic work for commercial use in the United States. During World War II, the company had advised aerial photographic military departments, at home and abroad, and in the 1950s it produced low-altitude, oblique aerial views of New York (pictured below). Its history dated back to the early 1920s, when businessman and inventor Sherman Fairchild began a business that specialized in aerial photography and the production of aerial maps. The business provided aerial photography for city-planning purposes and for the mapping agency US Geological Survey. Fairchild Aerial Surveys, Inc. is also credited with playing a role in the creation of one of the first topographical maps to be compiled entirely from aerial photographs in the United States.

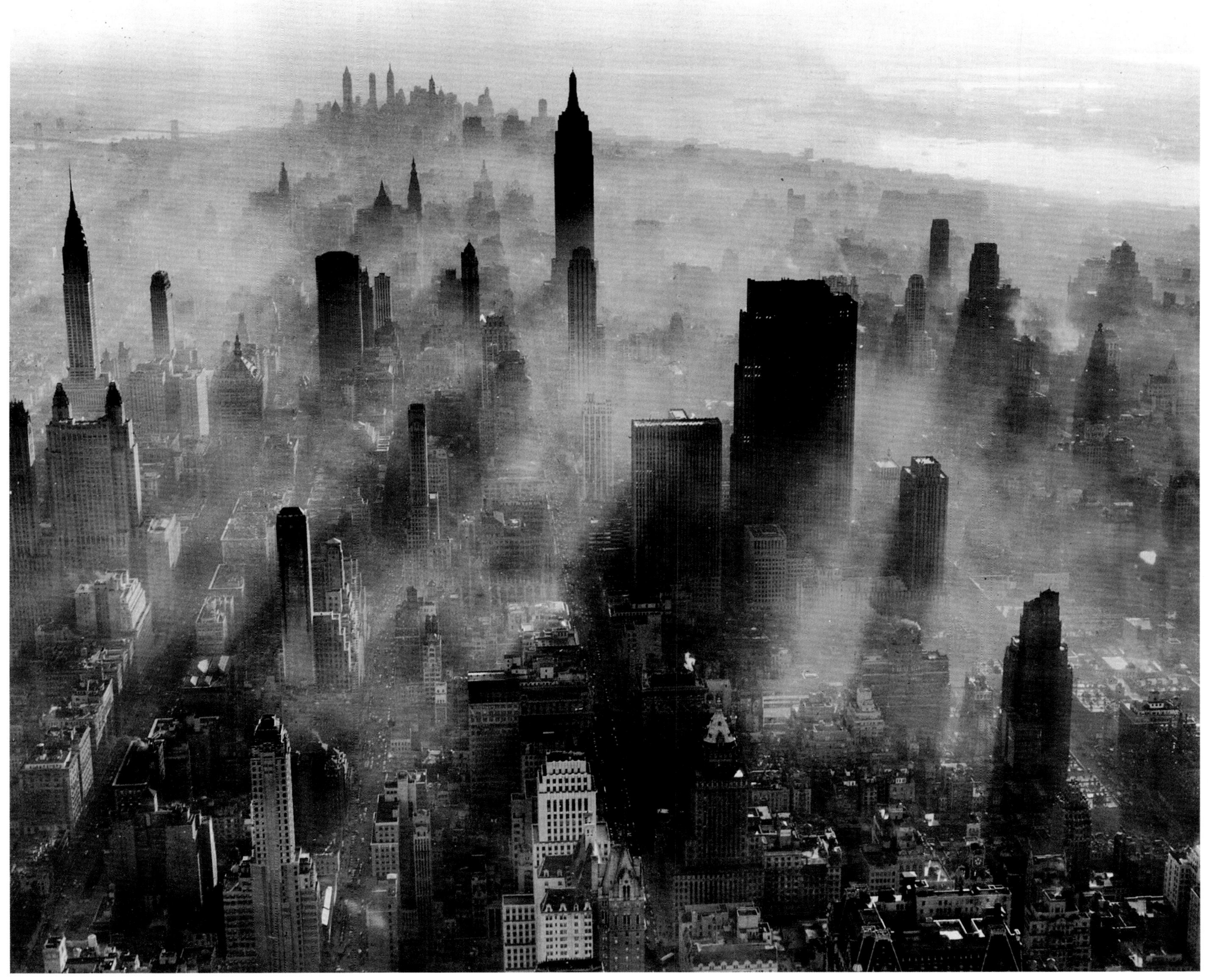

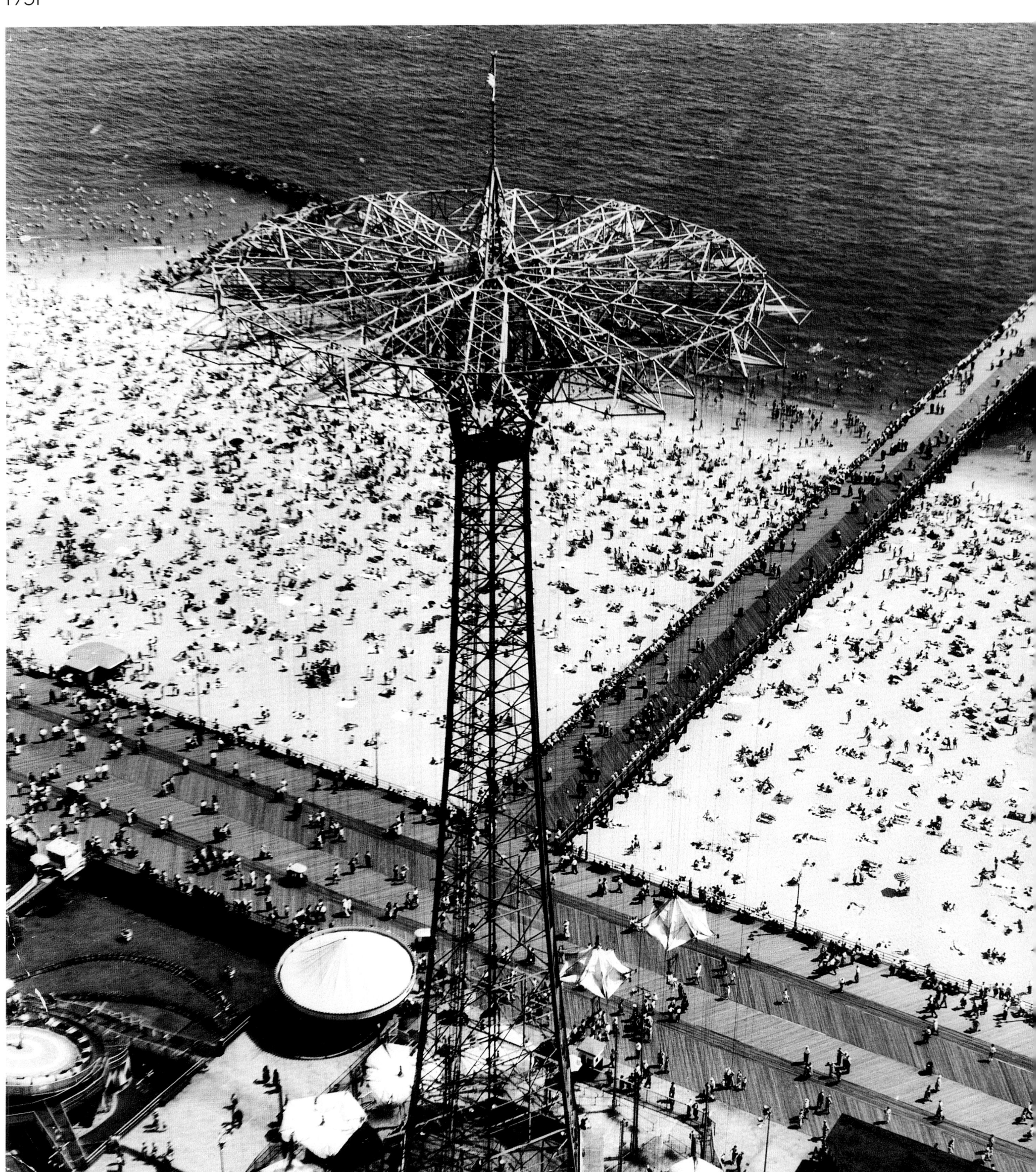

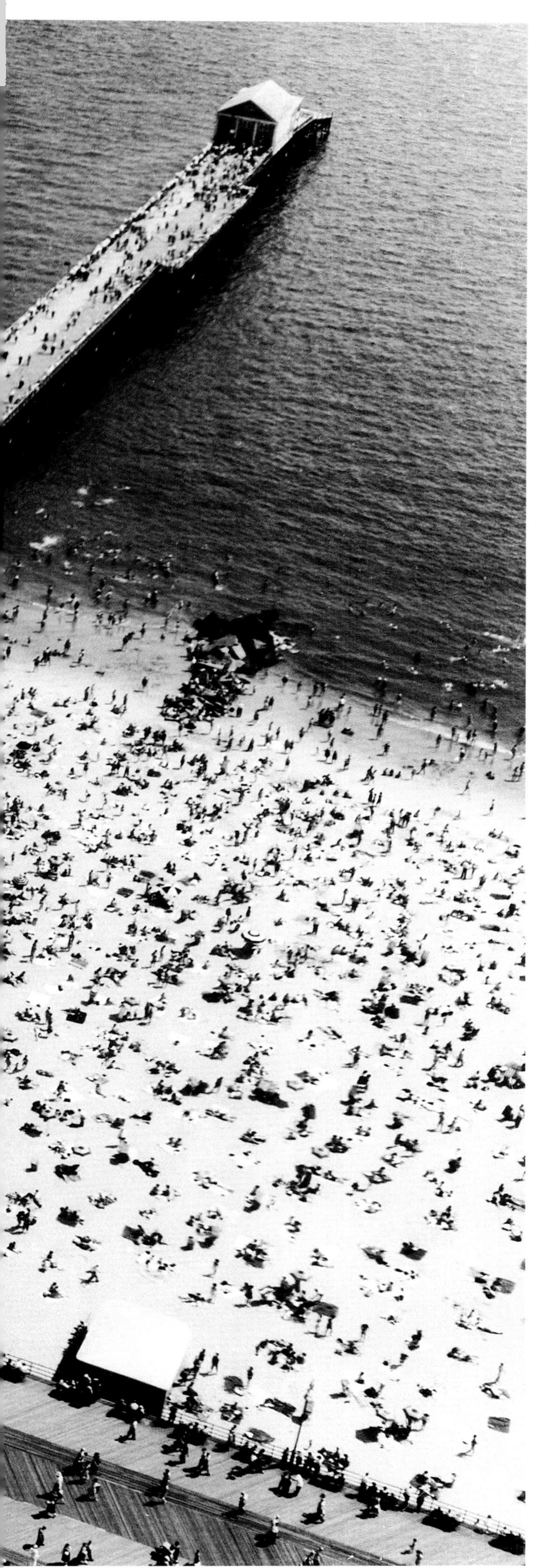

Margaret Bourke-White's early work during the 1930s for the magazines *Fortune* and *Life* had seen the photographer indulge her passion for machinery and industry whenever she had the chance, and, in the 1950s, Bourke-White returned to these subjects (after having been a prolific war photographer during World War II; see pages 68–9), photographing ports, bridges and steel mills across her native USA, sometimes from the air. Crowded beaches and sprawling landscapes were also Bourke-White's subjects, and her distinctive style, which often demonstrated a highly controlled handling of form, was apparent even in something as simple and ordinary as a photograph of a ploughed field (pictured overleaf) or a pier stretching out into the sea (pictured left).

Margaret Bourke-White
Crowded beach and pier at Coney Island, including the Parachute Jump amusement park ride, New York, USA, 1951.

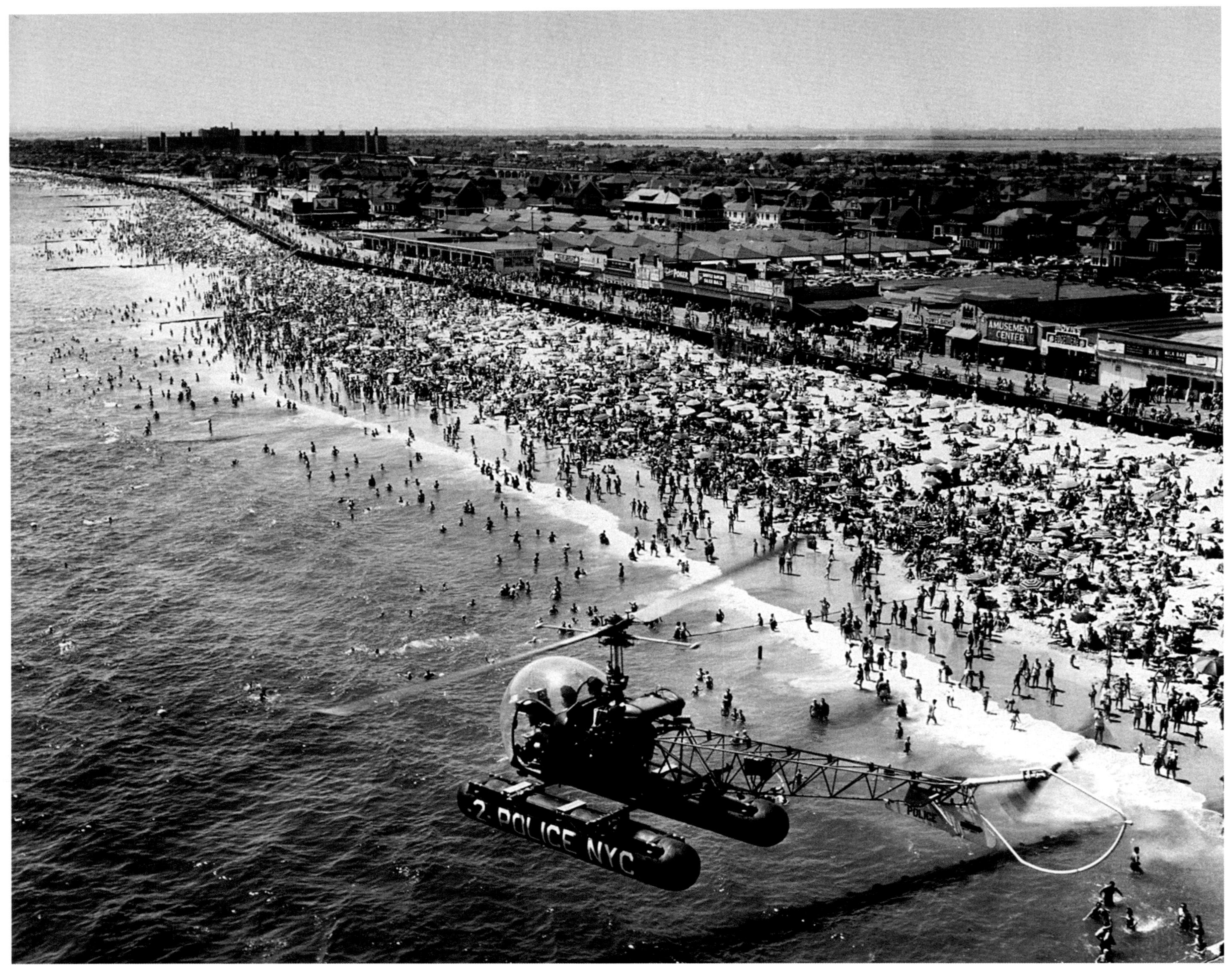

Above
Margaret Bourke-White
Police helicopter hovering over an Independence Day crowd at the beach at Far Rockaway, New York, USA, 1953.

Opposite
Margaret Bourke-White
Two tractors ploughing, Colorado, USA, 1954.

Overleaf
Margaret Bourke-White
Waterskiers and speedboats at Marine Stadium, Long Beach, California, USA, 1951.

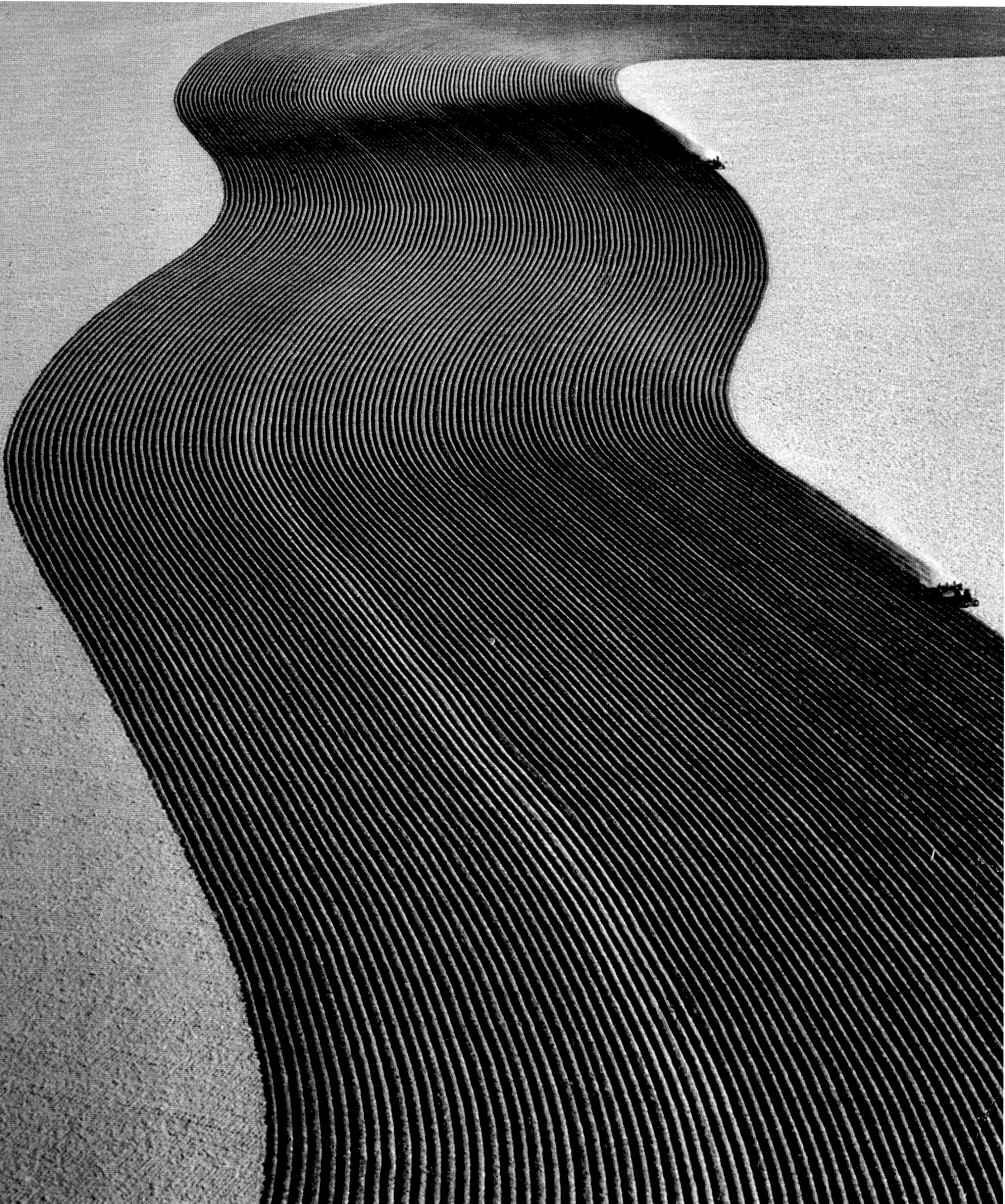

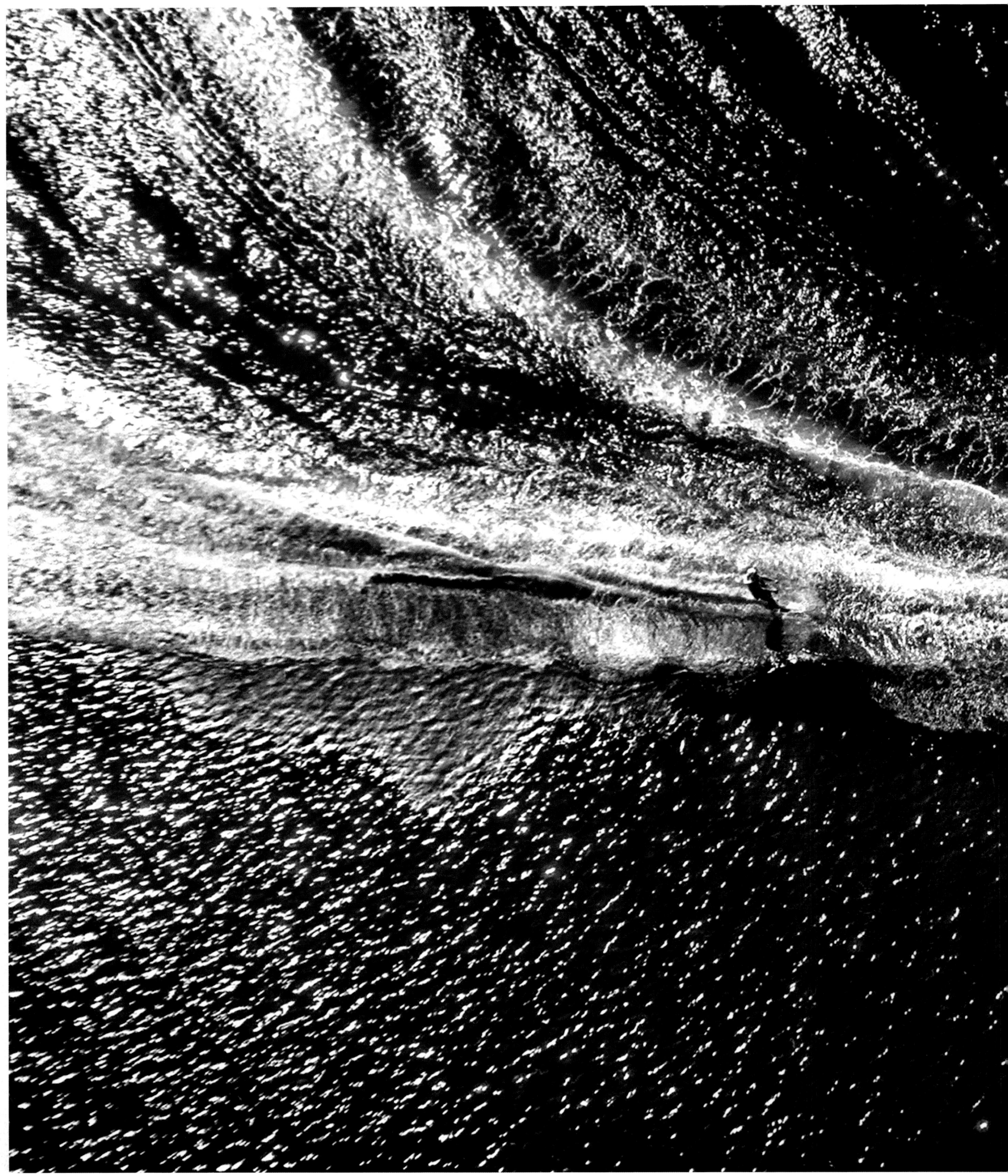

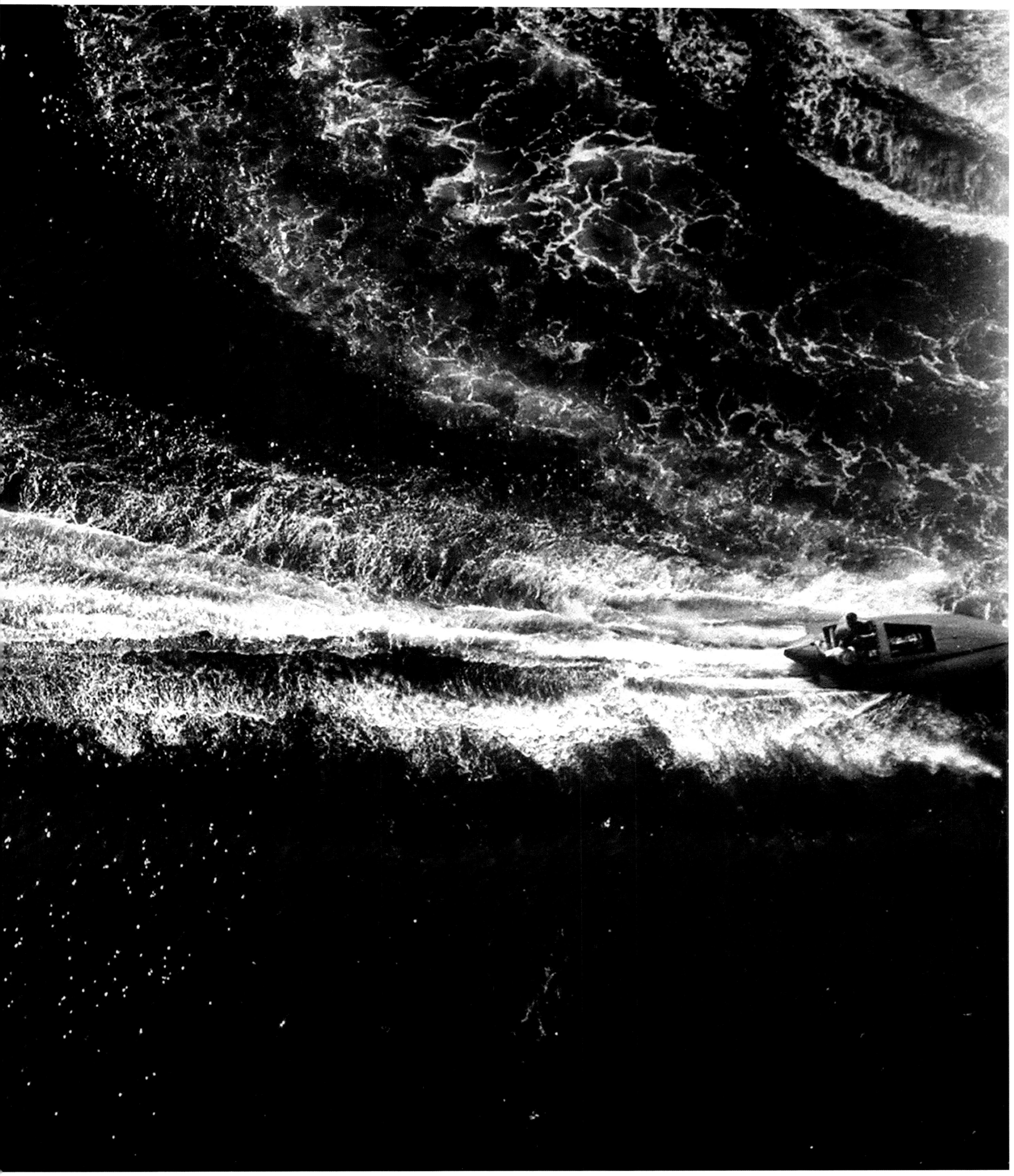

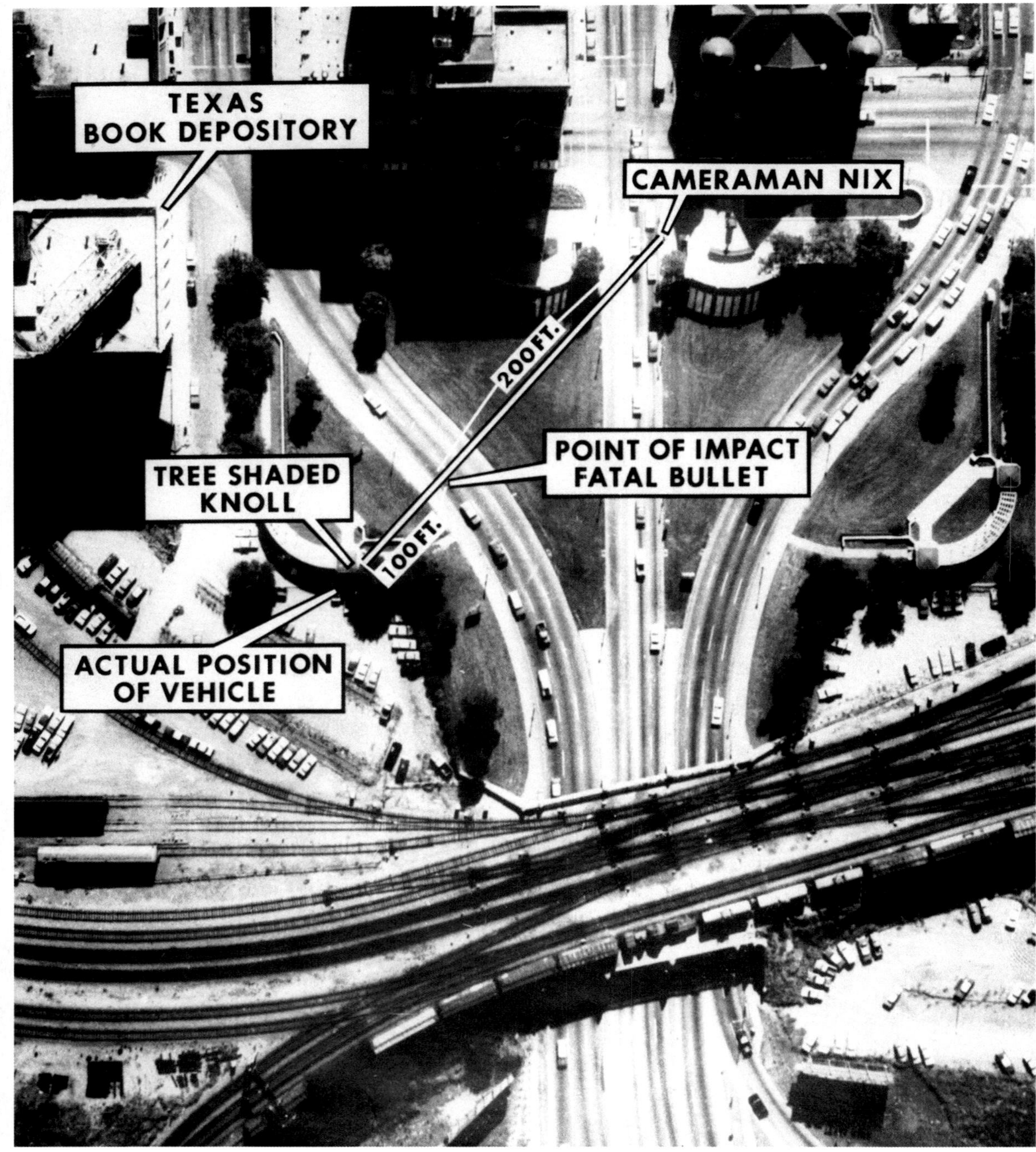

Photographer unknown
Study of the assassination of John F. Kennedy disproving the second-gunman theory, 1963.

On 22 November 1963, American president John F. Kennedy was shot dead in Dealey Plaza, Dallas, Texas. He had been travelling in a motorcade with his wife, Jackie. Former US Marine Lee Harvey Oswald is believed to have fired the fatal shot, although conspiracy theories suggesting the involvement of others abound. This aerial photograph serves as a map, and key points of reference have been added. For example, the Texas Book Depository, from where Oswald is thought to have assassinated the president through a sixth-floor window, is marked, as is the location of the cameraman who famously captured footage of the assassination. Despite the proliferation of conspiracy theories suggesting the involvement of a second gunman, a detailed scientific study of amateur video footage of the shooting carried out by Itek Corporation, a producer of aerial reconnaissance cameras, found no evidence of a rifleman on a grassy knoll (left of centre).

dropped from aircraft. Specifically, they are Vietnamese paratroopers during an aerial attack against Viet Cong guerrillas in Tây Ninh province, southern Vietnam. In March 1963, 16 United States Air Force C-123 aircraft dropped helicopters followed, deploying 1,500 additional troops. Airborne operations such as this were a vital part of the US and South Vietnam effort in the Vietnam War, since road convoys were vulnerable to ambush from the Viet Cong.

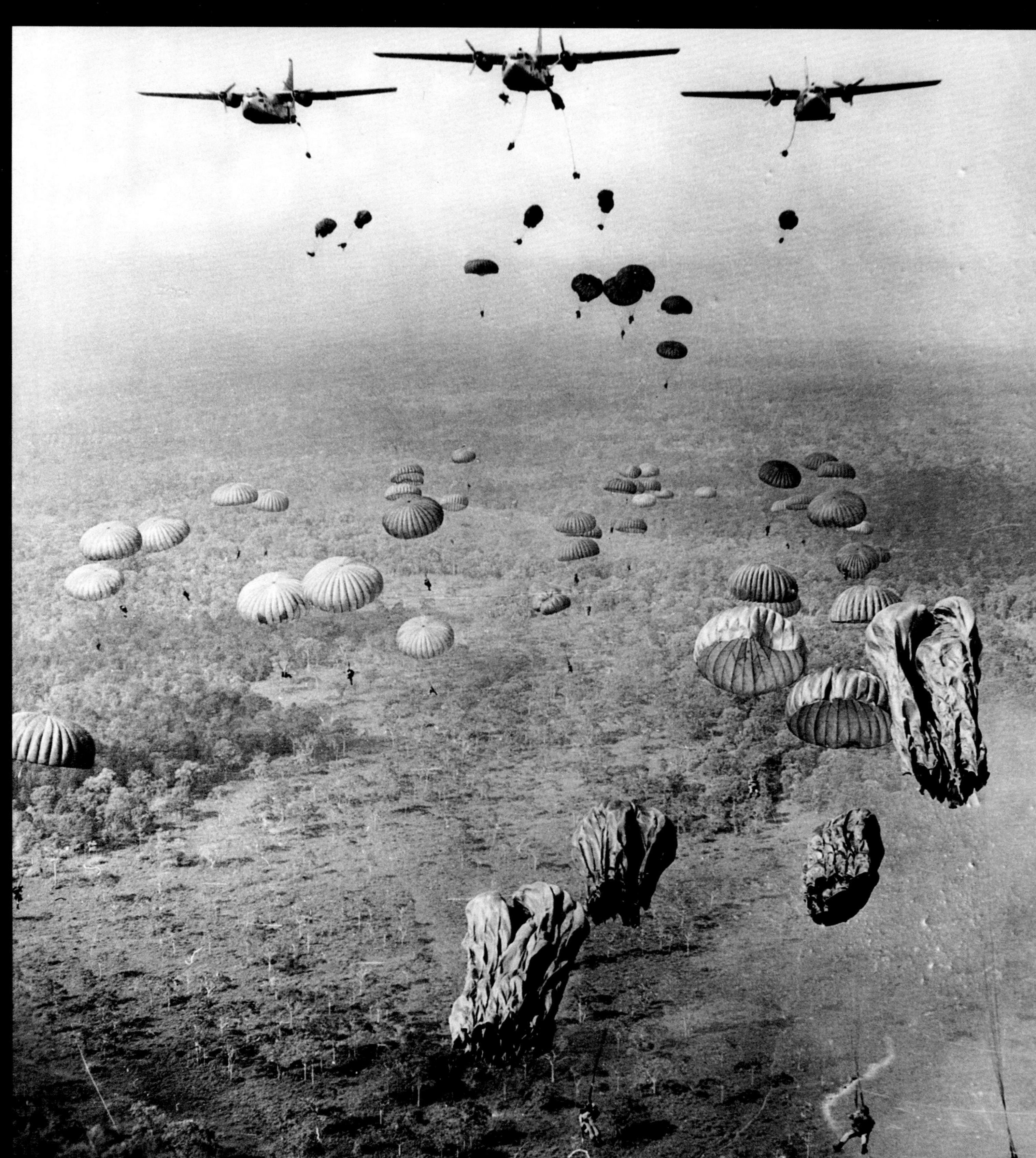

Photographer unknown
US Air force attack on Tây Ninh province, Vietnam, 1963.

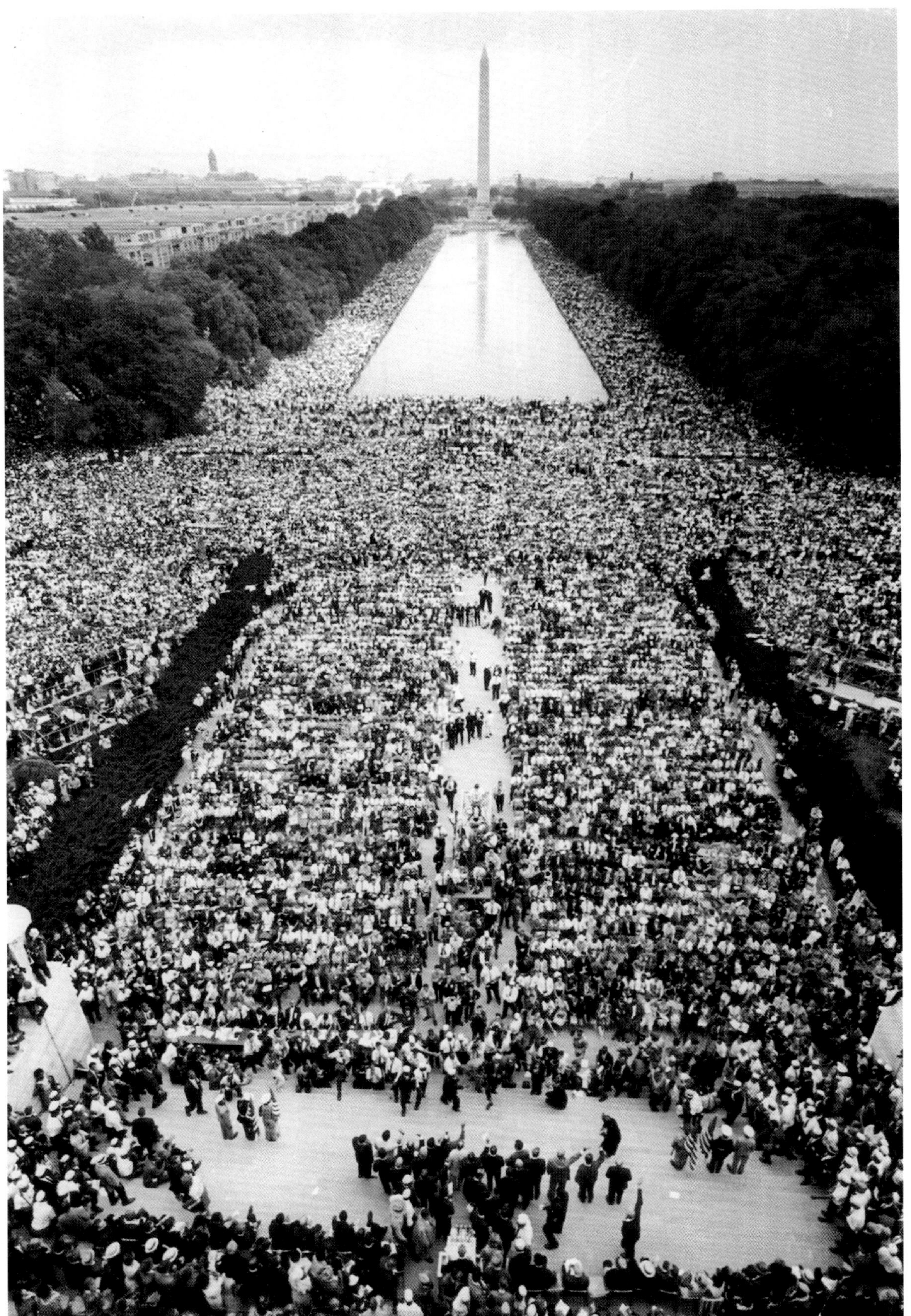

Photographer unknown
March on Washington for Jobs and Freedom, Washington, DC, USA, 1963.

On 28 August 1963, hundreds of thousands of people gathered in Washington DC, calling for civil and economic rights for African Americans. The March on Washington, as it is sometimes referred to, has been described as one of the largest political rallies for human rights in the history of the United States. It was an important part of the expanding Civil Rights Movement, which had been decades in the making but gained momentum in the 1950s and '60s. During the peaceful demonstration, Martin Luther King, Jr gave his famous 'I Have a Dream' speech from the steps in front of the Lincoln Memorial. All manner of images documenting the march exist, but aerial photographs such as this reveal the sheer scale of the protest, and serve as a reminder of aerial photography's unique ability to offer viewpoints impossible to achieve from the ground.

Photographer unknown
Marchers turning onto Charles Street from Boylston Street in this helicopter view of Dr Martin Luther King's Freedom March on Boston, 1965.

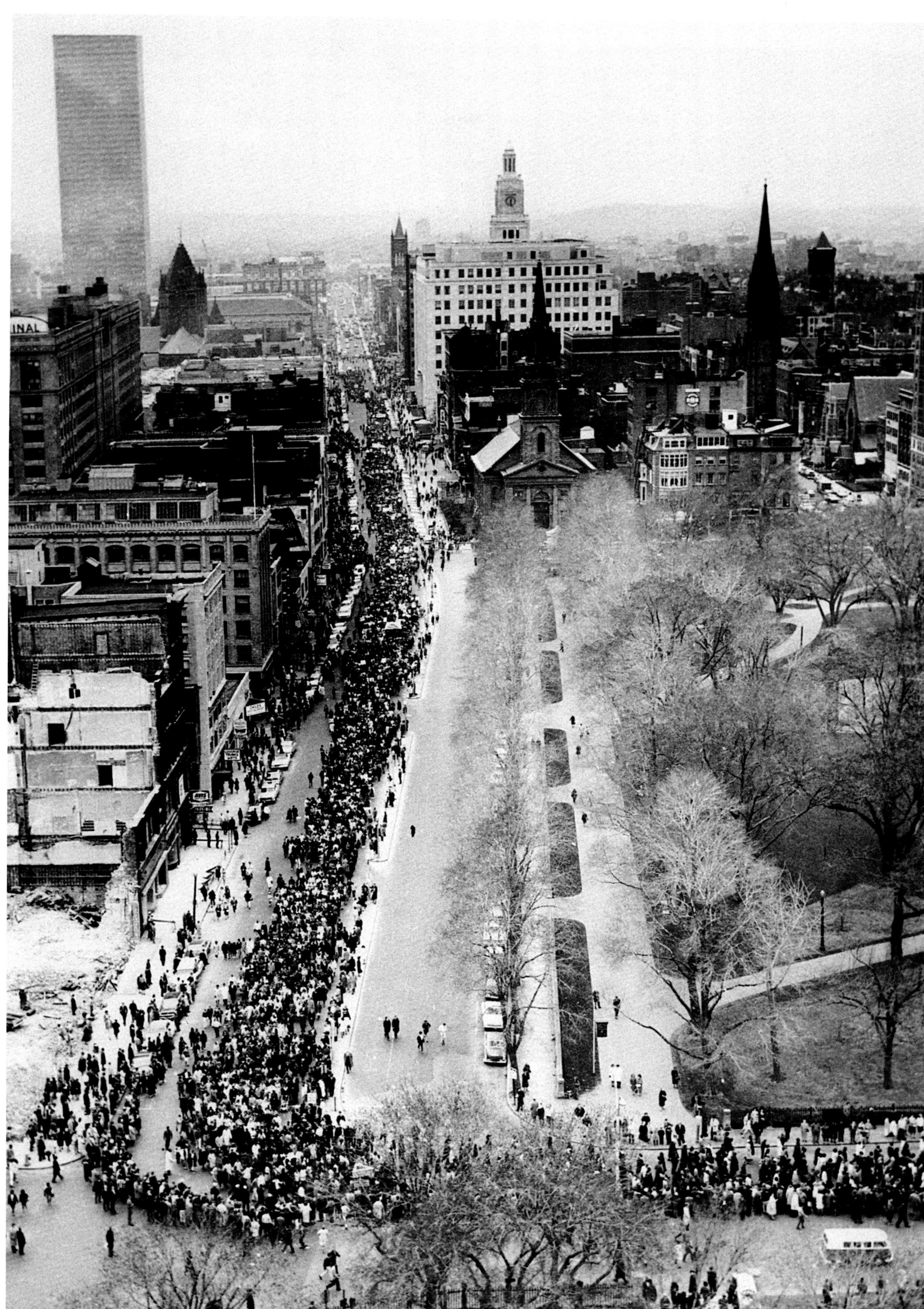

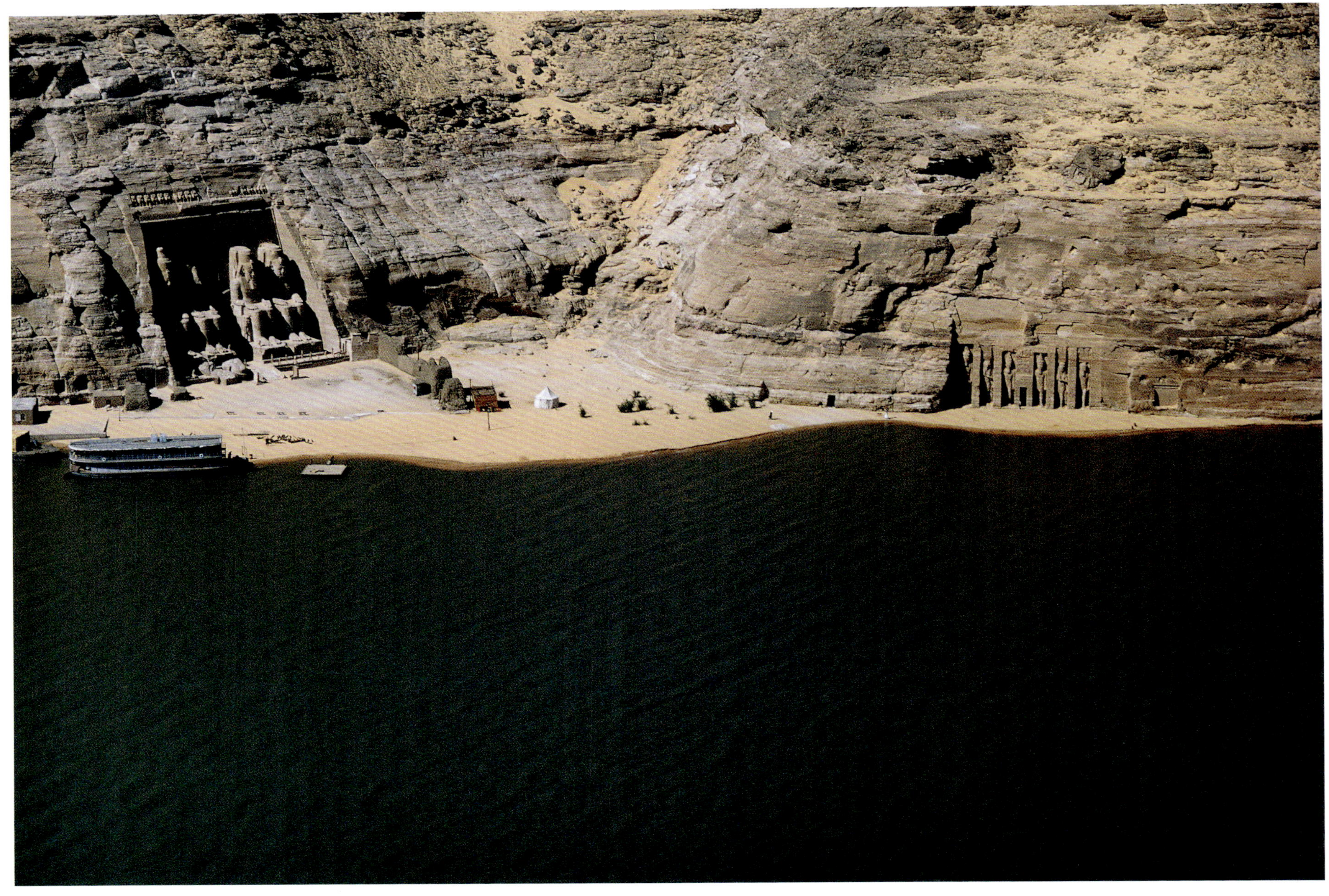

Georg Gerster
Abu Simbel Temple,
Nubia, Egypt, *c.* 1965.

From negotiating permission to enter airspace, to hanging precariously out of a small plane to make pictures, Georg Gerster did it all. The Swiss journalist and photographer, who was born in Winterthur in 1928, began shooting from the air in 1956, when he left his position as a magazine editor to become a freelance science reporter who also took aerial photographs. Over the ensuing 60-plus years, Gerster photographed every continent, and for two decades his aerial photographs were a mainstay on Swissair posters. If you're looking for the originator of aerial photography in the mid-twentieth century, Gerster, who spoke about his desire to turn the genre into something more 'reflective' and 'probing', is your man.

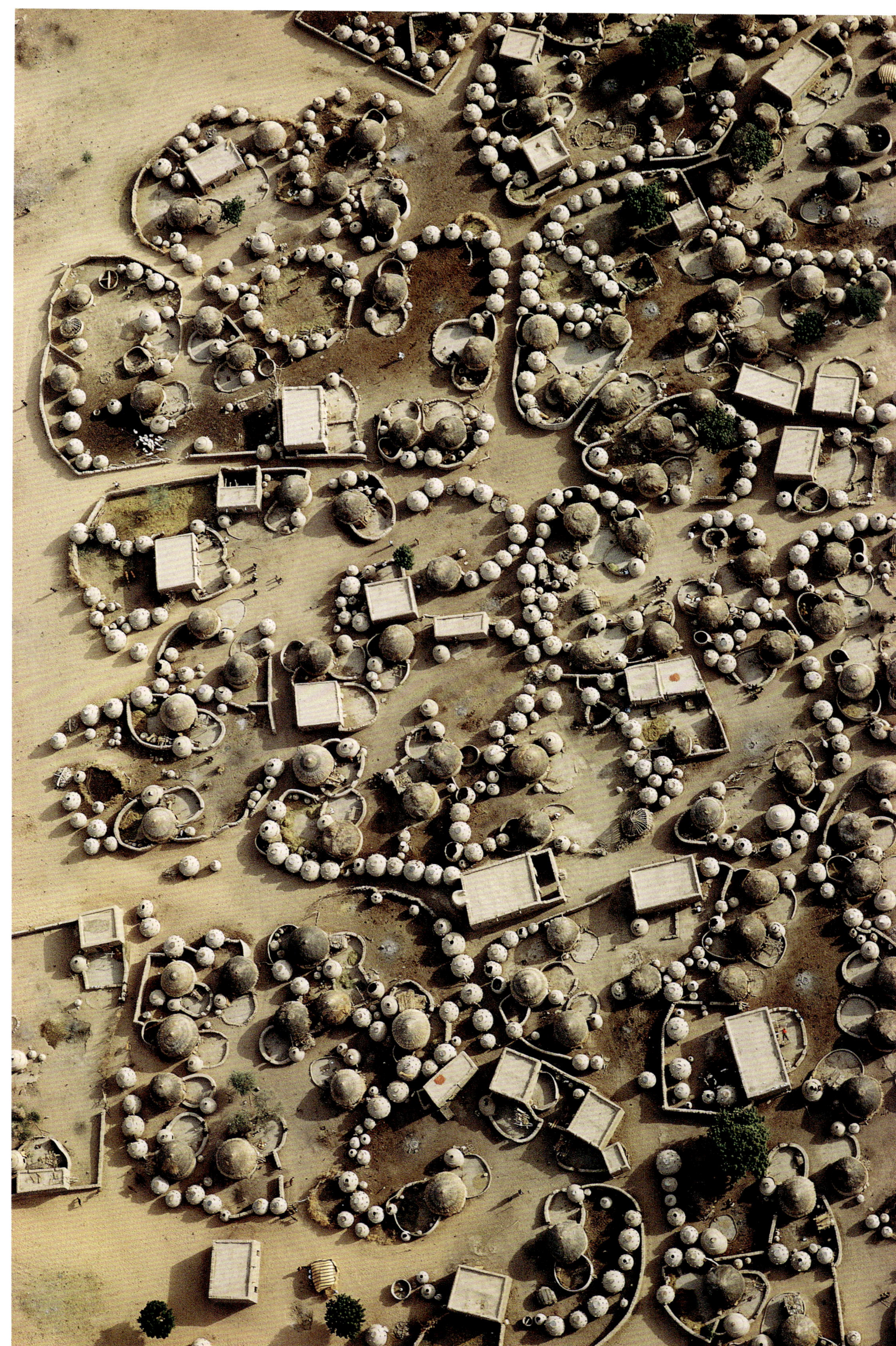

Georg Gerster
Labbezanga village, Mali,
West Africa, 1972.

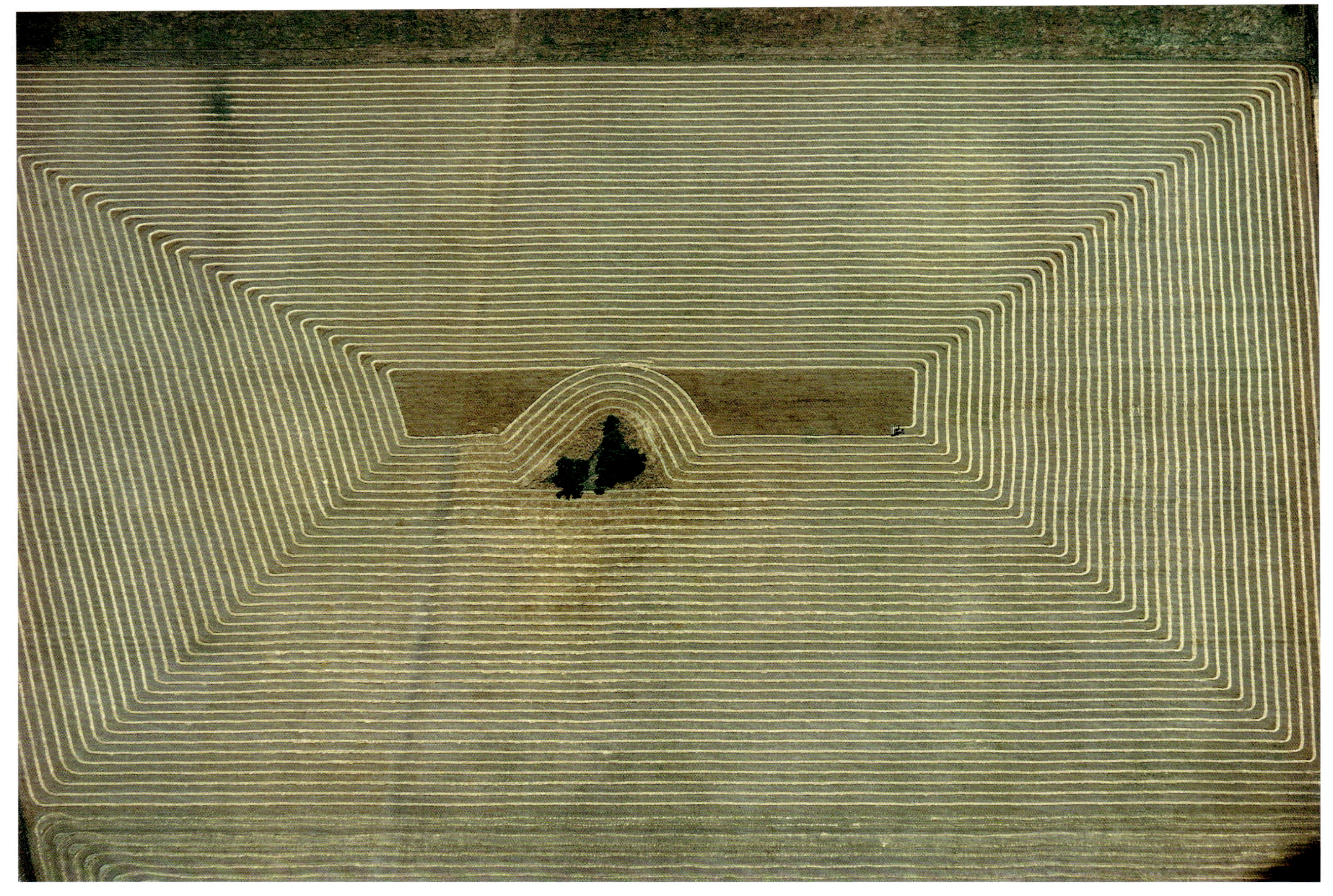

Georg Gerster
Harvest pattern, La
Pampa, Argentina, 1967.

Right
Georg Gerster
A camel caravan in the Soghun Valley, Iran, 1976.

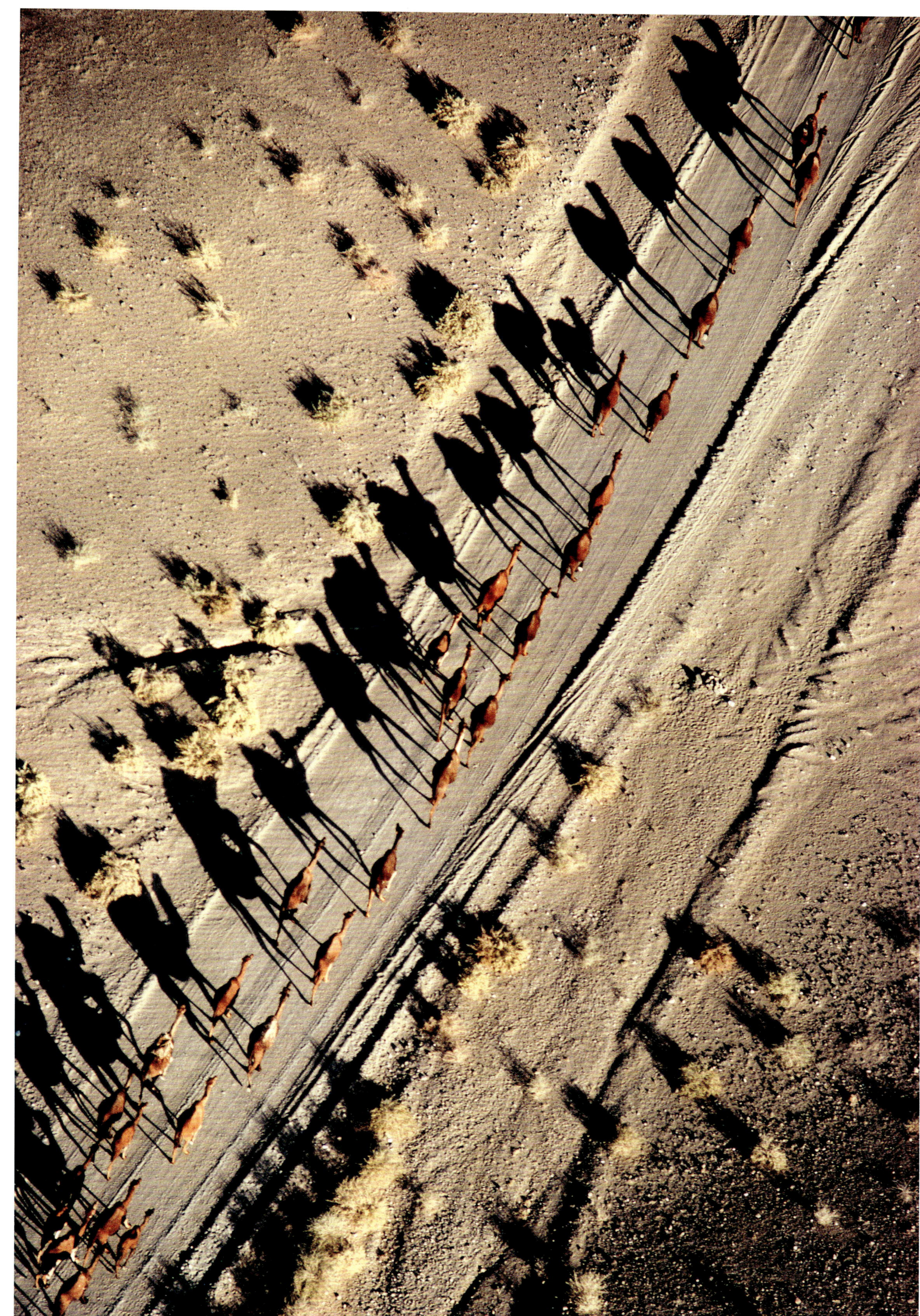

Overleaf
Georg Gerster
Peas and wheat in Washington, USA, 1979.

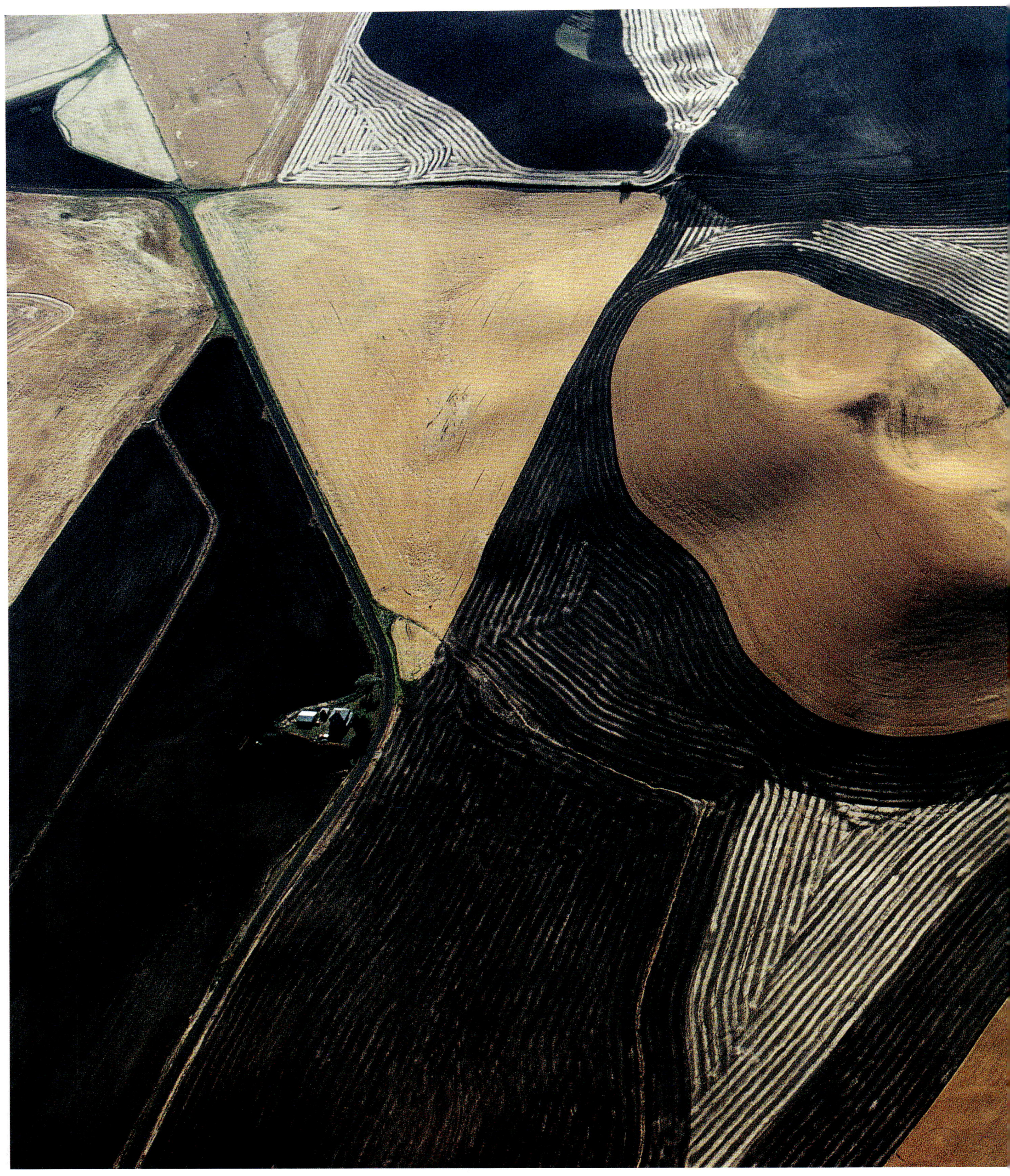

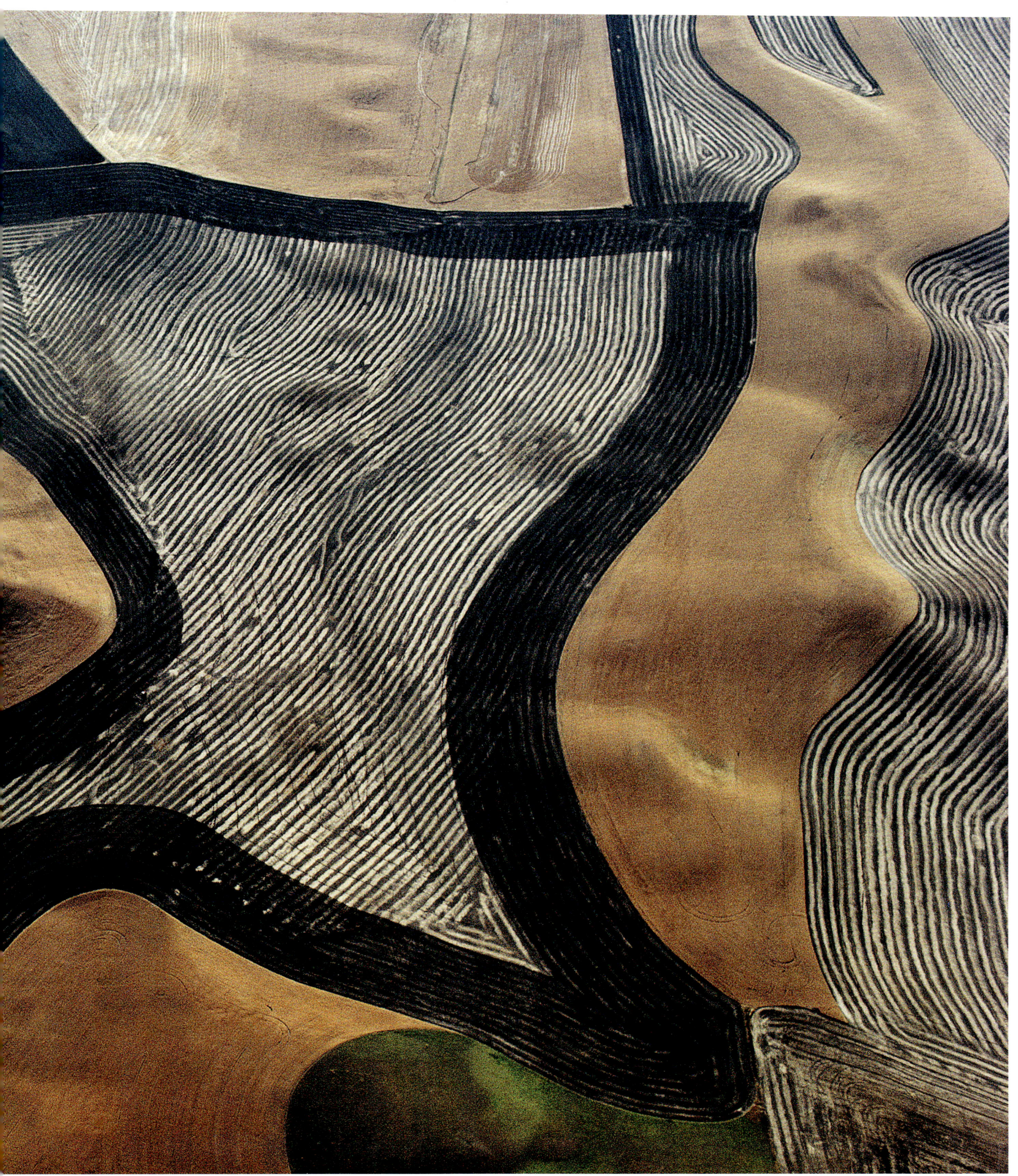

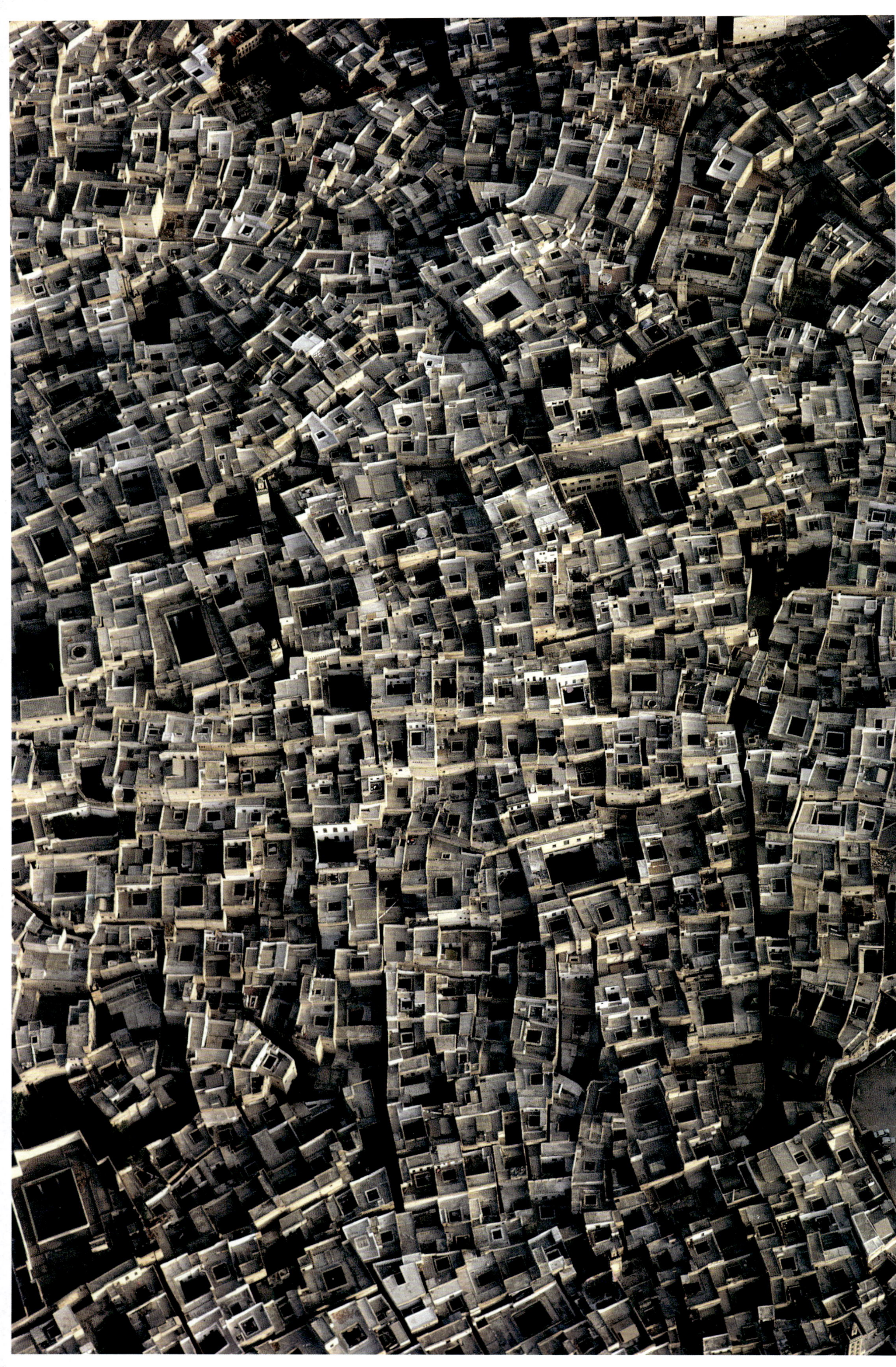

Georg Gerster
The medina (old city) of Fes el Bali, the larger of the two medinas of Fes, Morocco, 1982.

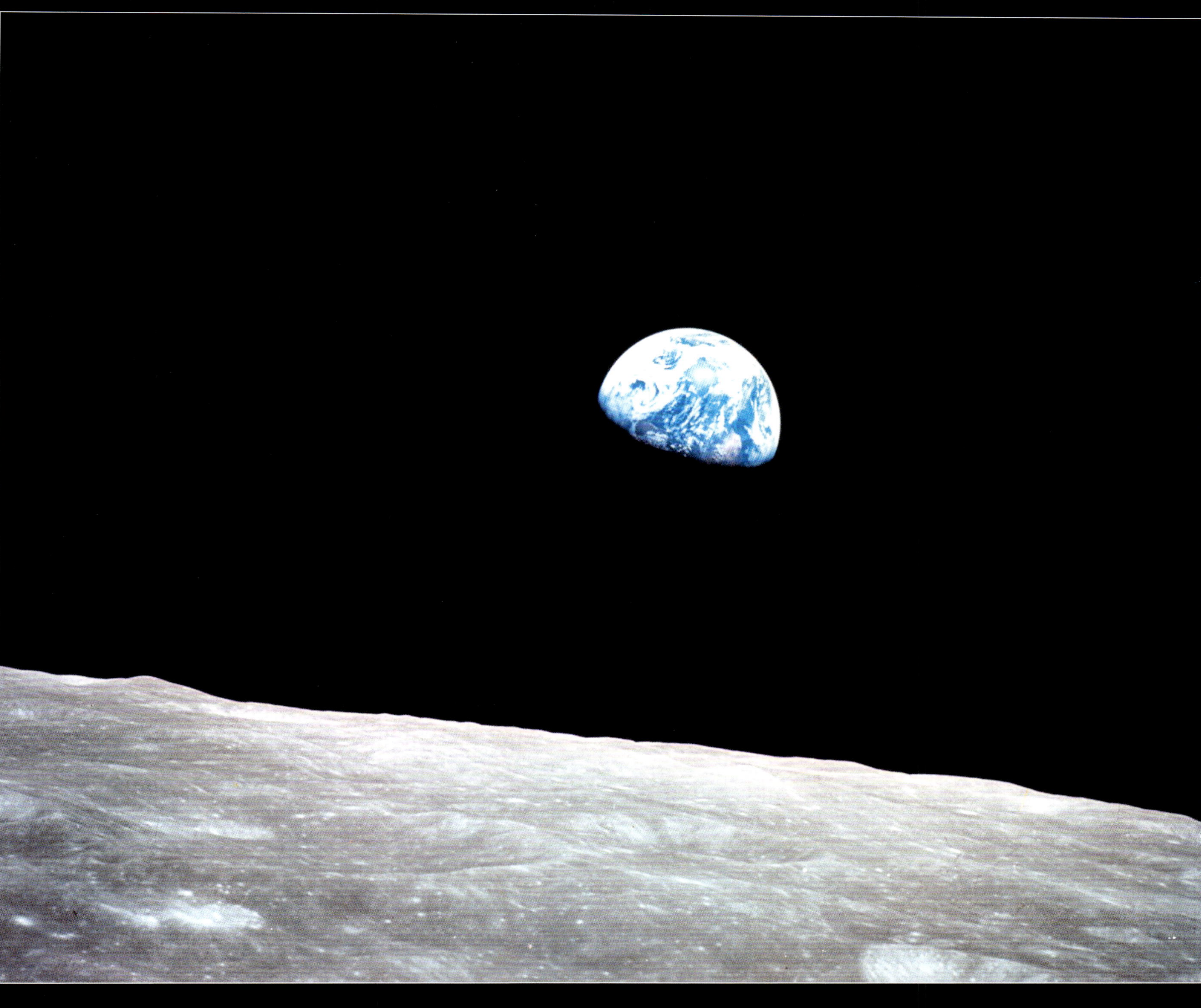

William Anders
Earthrise, as seen from NASA's *Apollo 8* spacecraft, 1968.

Possibly the most famous photograph of the Earth taken from the air, US astronaut William Anders's *Earthrise* is the first colour image of our planet from space. The story of how it came to be has been told many times, but the image remains as remarkable as ever. Anders was one of a three-person crew on *Apollo 8*, the first manned mission to the moon. It was Christmas Eve in 1968, and, as the spacecraft emerged from behind the moon, the crew saw the Earth appear right before their eyes. Anders took a shot in black and white before managing to capture the scene in colour.

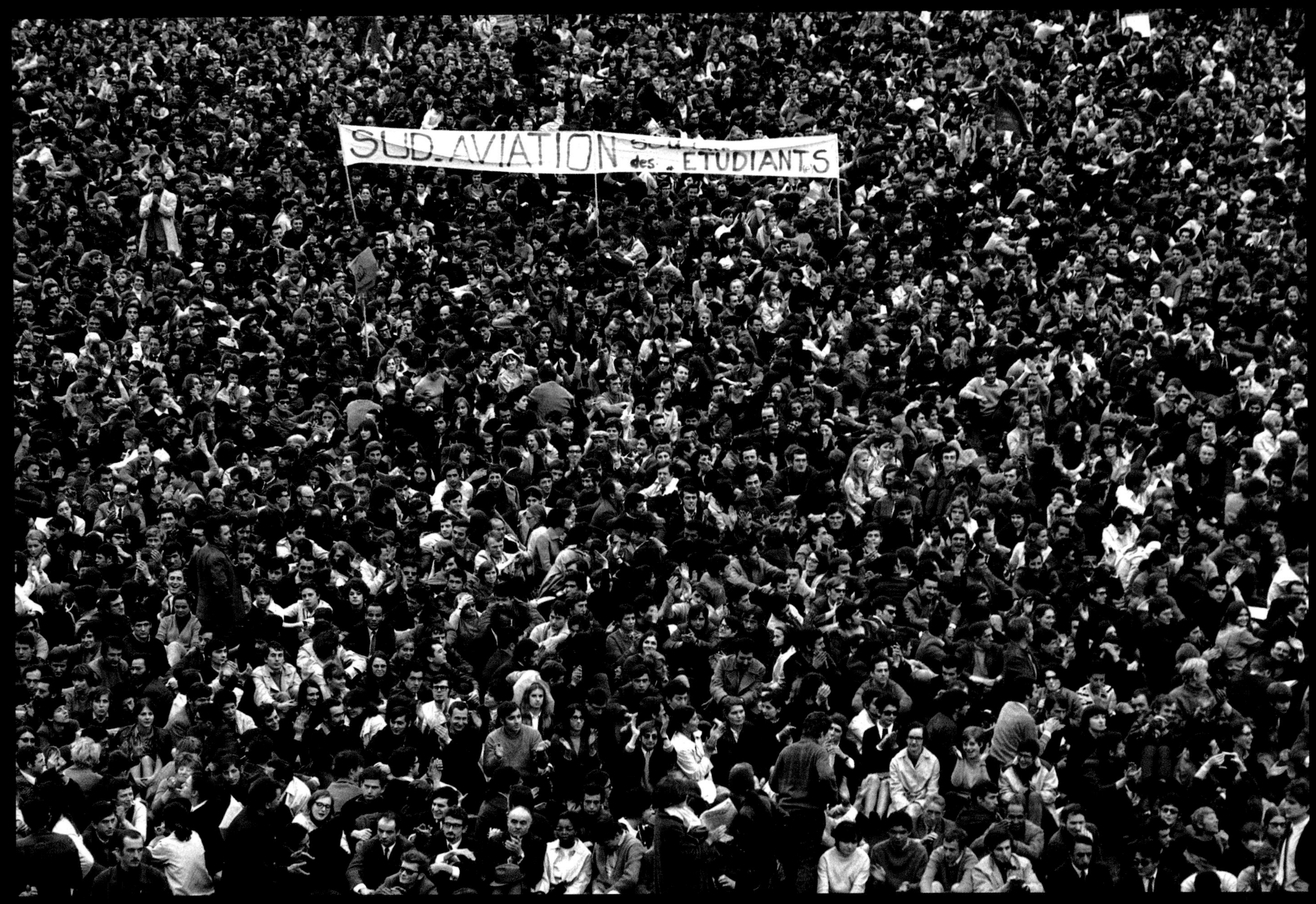

Photographer unknown
Demonstration of young students and workers for fair rights, Paris, France, 1968.

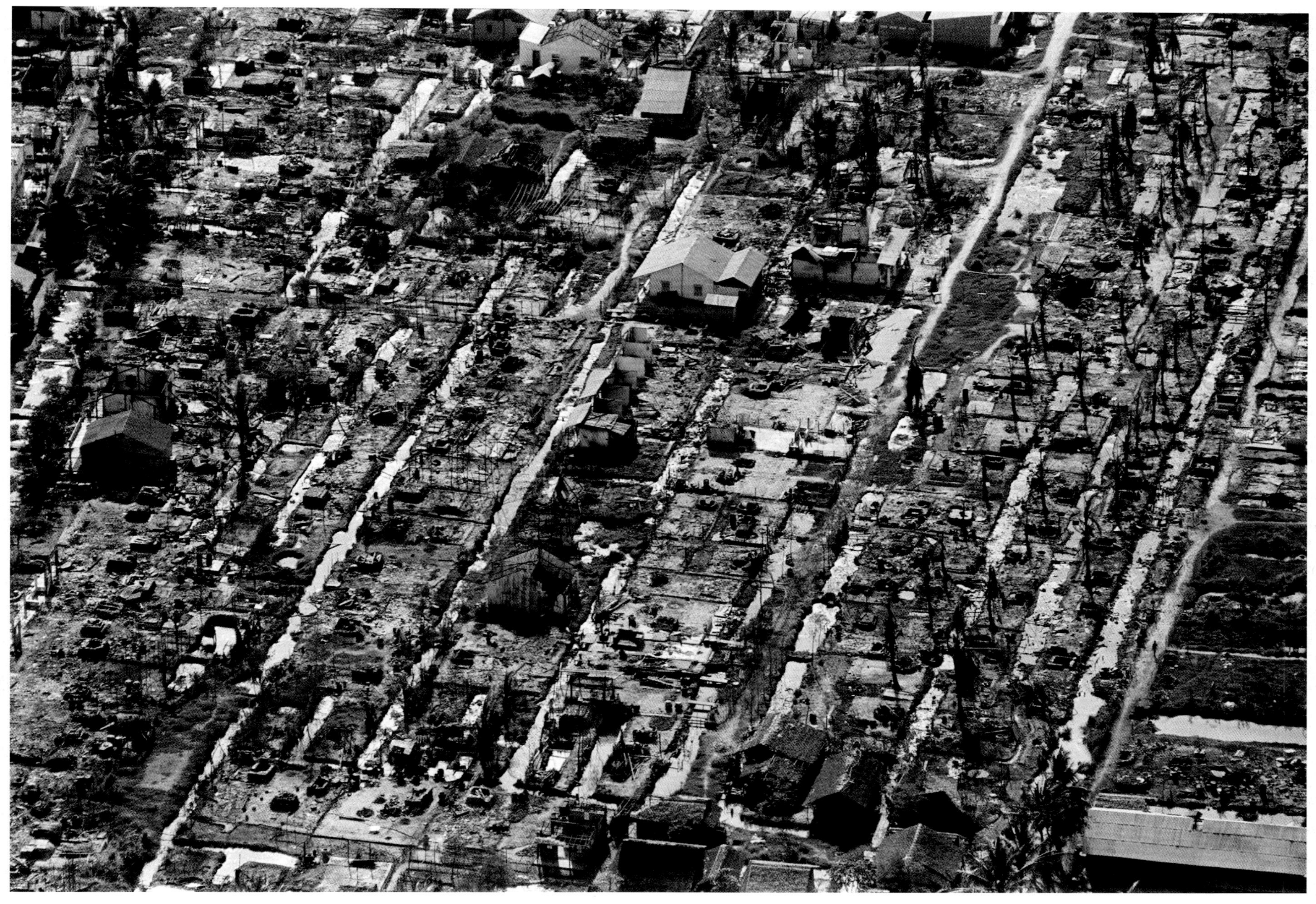

Philip Jones Griffiths
The levelled village of Ben Tre in the Mekong Delta, Vietnam, after the Tet Offensive, 1968.

On 31 January 1968, North Vietnamese communist forces attacked cities, towns and villages across South Vietnam in what has become known as the Tet Offensive – one of the largest military campaigns of the Vietnam War. Only from the air is it possible to take in the true scale of devastation caused, a view that photojournalist Philip Jones Griffiths presented among hundreds more in his seminal book *Vietnam, Inc.*, first published in 1971. In this work, Jones Griffiths famously showed what was really happening on the ground, and his aerial shots, including this one of Ben Tre village, are no exception – they confront the realities of war head-on. It has been said of Jones Griffiths that he came at the war from a different angle – a human angle in which he showed how ordinary people were caught up in the conflict – and in this photograph he, literally, presents a different perspective by flying above the obliterated village.

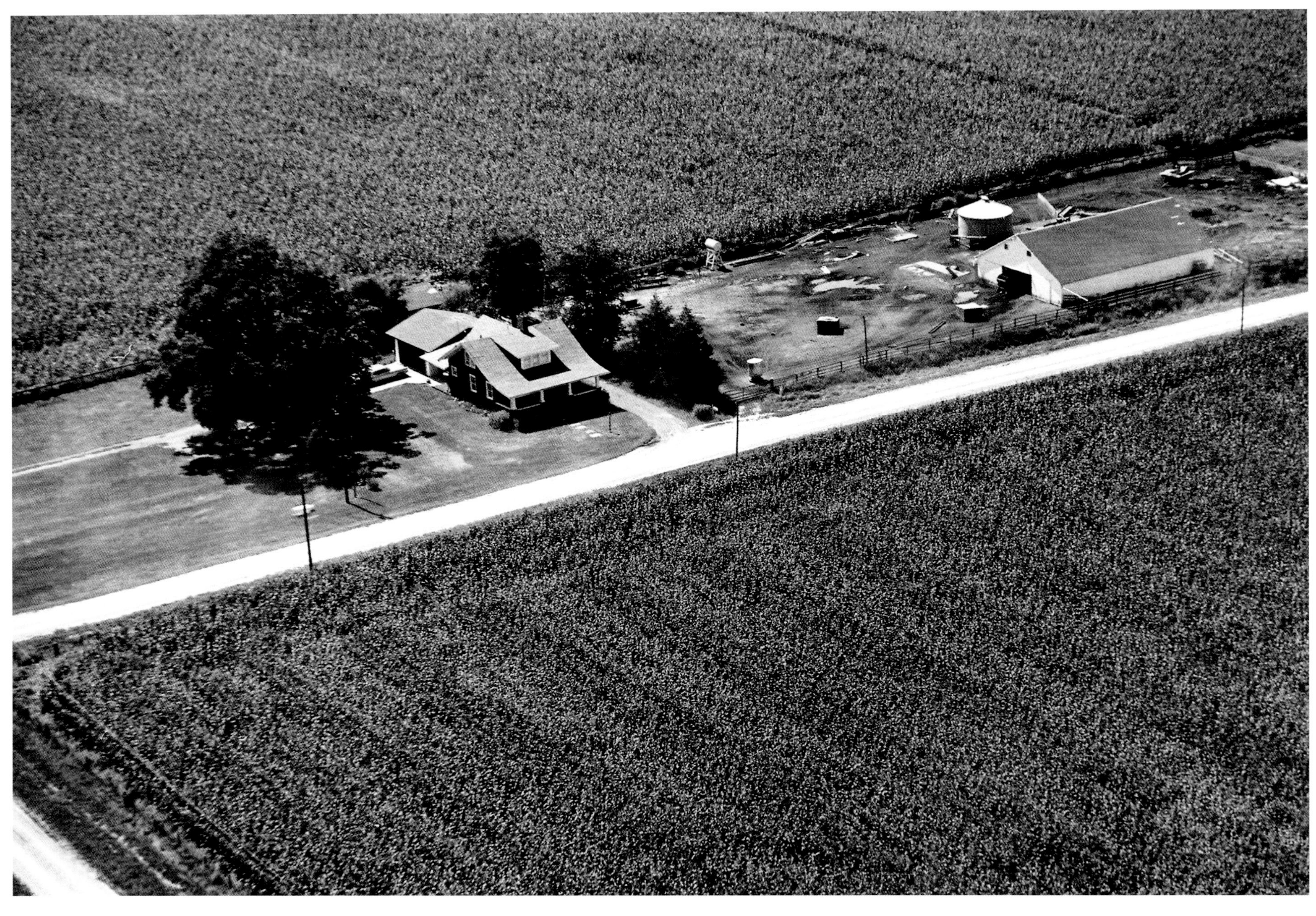

State Aerial was a prolific producer of aerial photographs of rural America from the 1960s onwards. The company would send out pilots with cameras fixed to their planes to take photographs across dozens of states, which it would then sell to farmers and landowners. Pilots captured aerial views across more than 40 states, creating an archive that comprises around 24 million images. The company licensed much of its material to Vintage Aerial, which sells the images and operates a web-based project that allows the public to access the digitized photographs for free and share their memories. The idea is to create an archive of images and stories that celebrates and preserves America's rural heritage. This 1969 aerial shot of a farm in Mercer County, Illinois, is a typical example of the type of image in the archive.

State Aerial, Inc.
A farm in Mercer County, Illinois, USA, 1969.

In August 1969, around 400,000 people flocked to Bethel, New York, for the famous Woodstock Festival. Rock photographer Barry Z. Levine was the stills photographer for a film being made about the festival and he took hundreds of photographs during the three-day music and arts event – from portraits of performers such as Jimi Hendrix to stage-side views and shots of festival-goers stripping off and soaking up the atmosphere. Levine also captured many images of the site from the air, which give a sense of the vast crowd. In this shot, a sea of people extends around the stage to the left of the frame.

Barry Z. Levine
Woodstock music festival,
New York, USA, 1969.

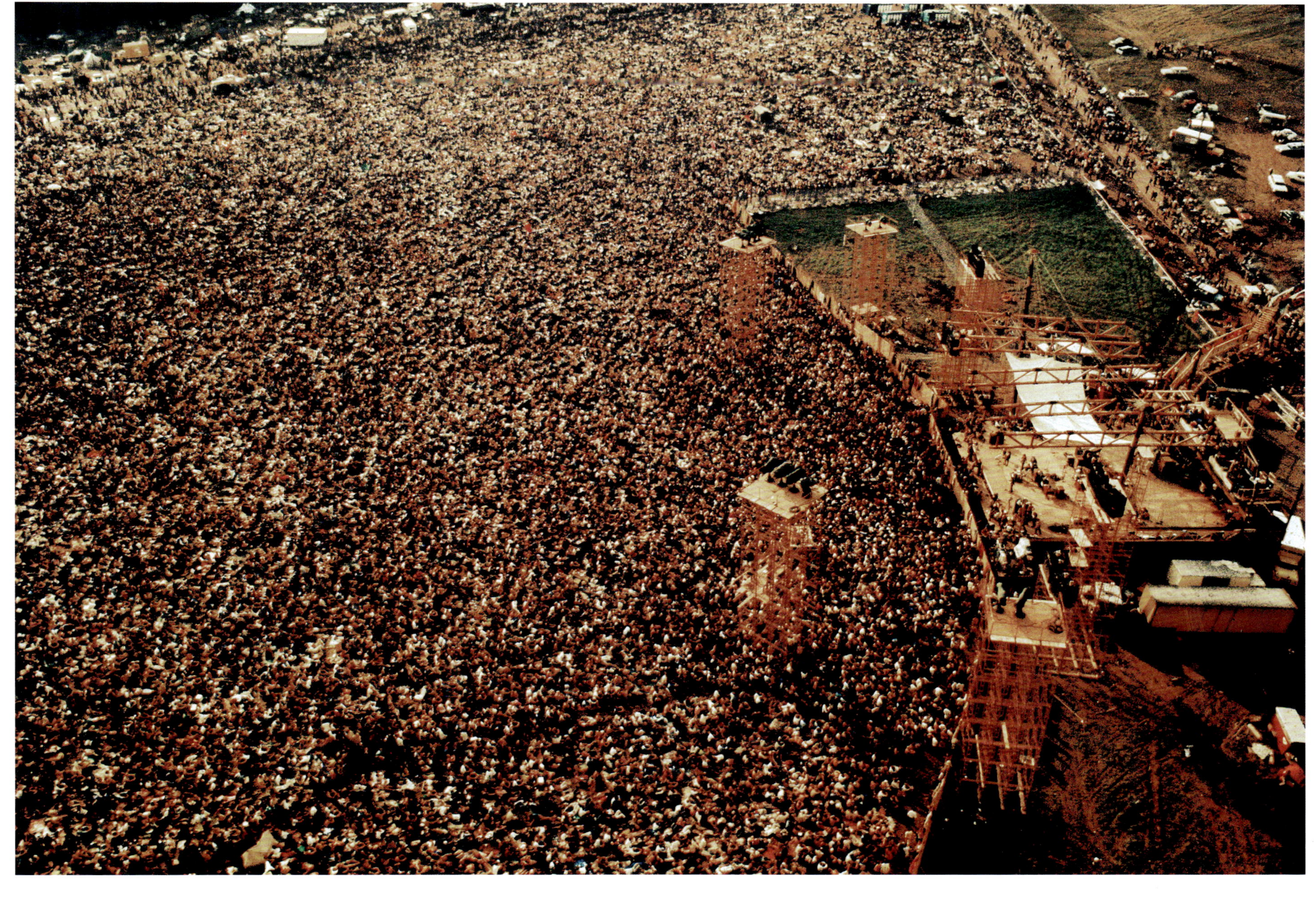

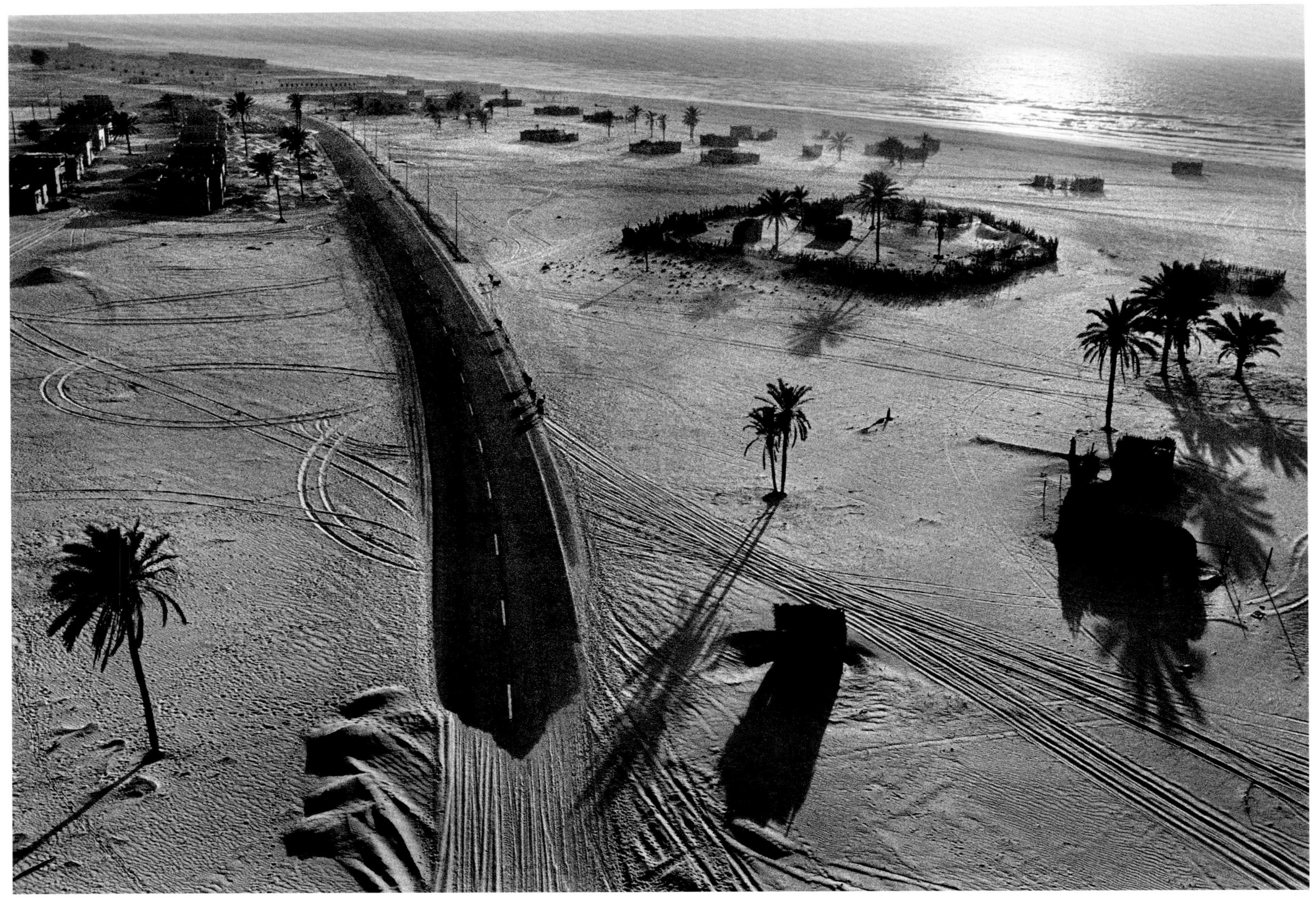

René Burri
Road from Abu Dhabi to Dubai, 1975.

It has been said that René Burri had a fascination with pyramids and pyramid motifs, and even in the Brazilian capital, Brasília, the Swiss photographer managed to find and photograph a pyramid-shaped building (pictured opposite). Burri, a photojournalist with Magnum Photos, returned to Brasília several times over the years, capturing its street life and architecture as well as views of the city from the sky. Although not strictly an aerial photographer, Burri also photographed South Vietnam from the air during the Vietnam War, and the United Arab Emirates in 1975 (pictured above).

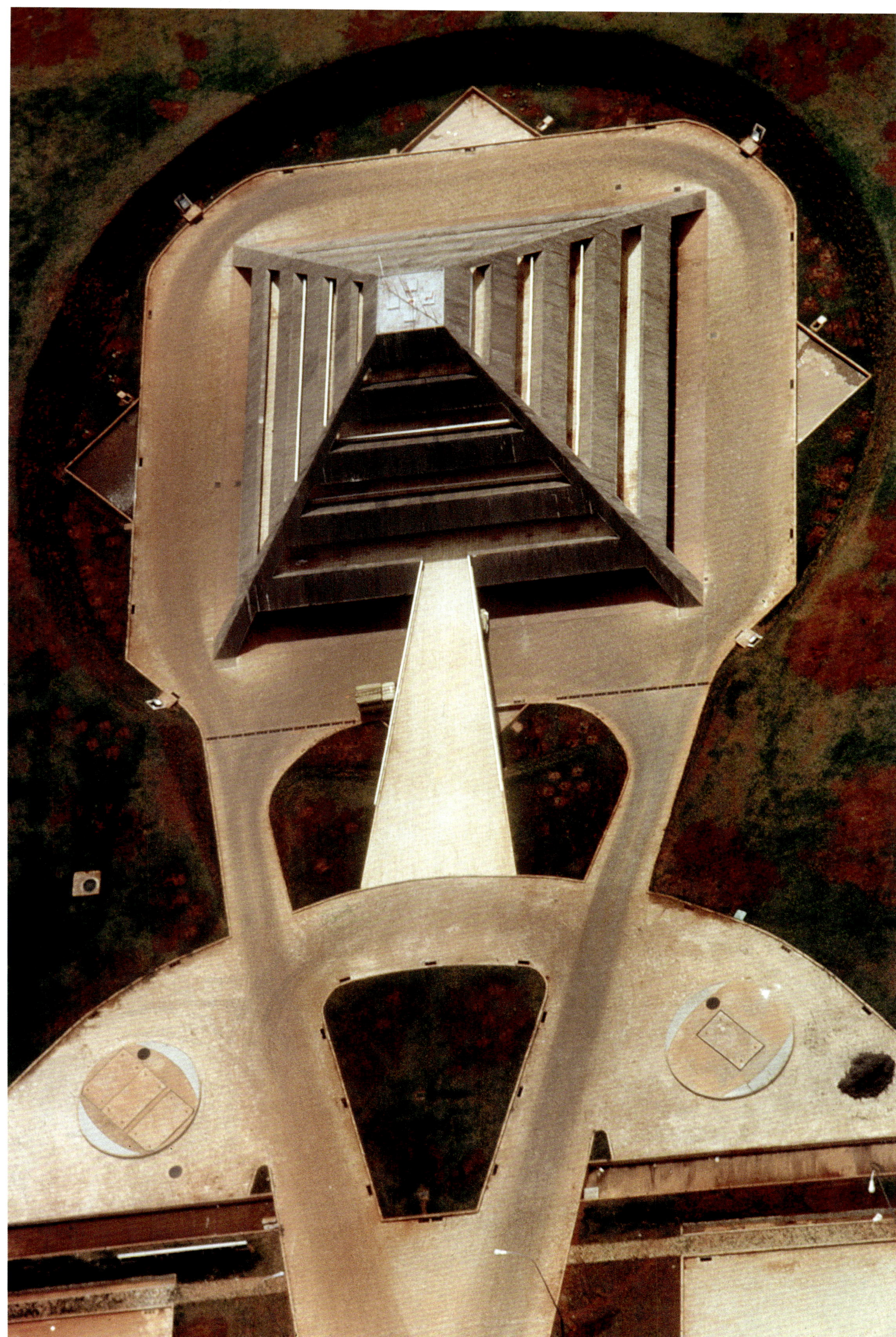

René Burri
Pyramid-shaped office building of the Electricity Company of Brasilía, Brazil, 1977.

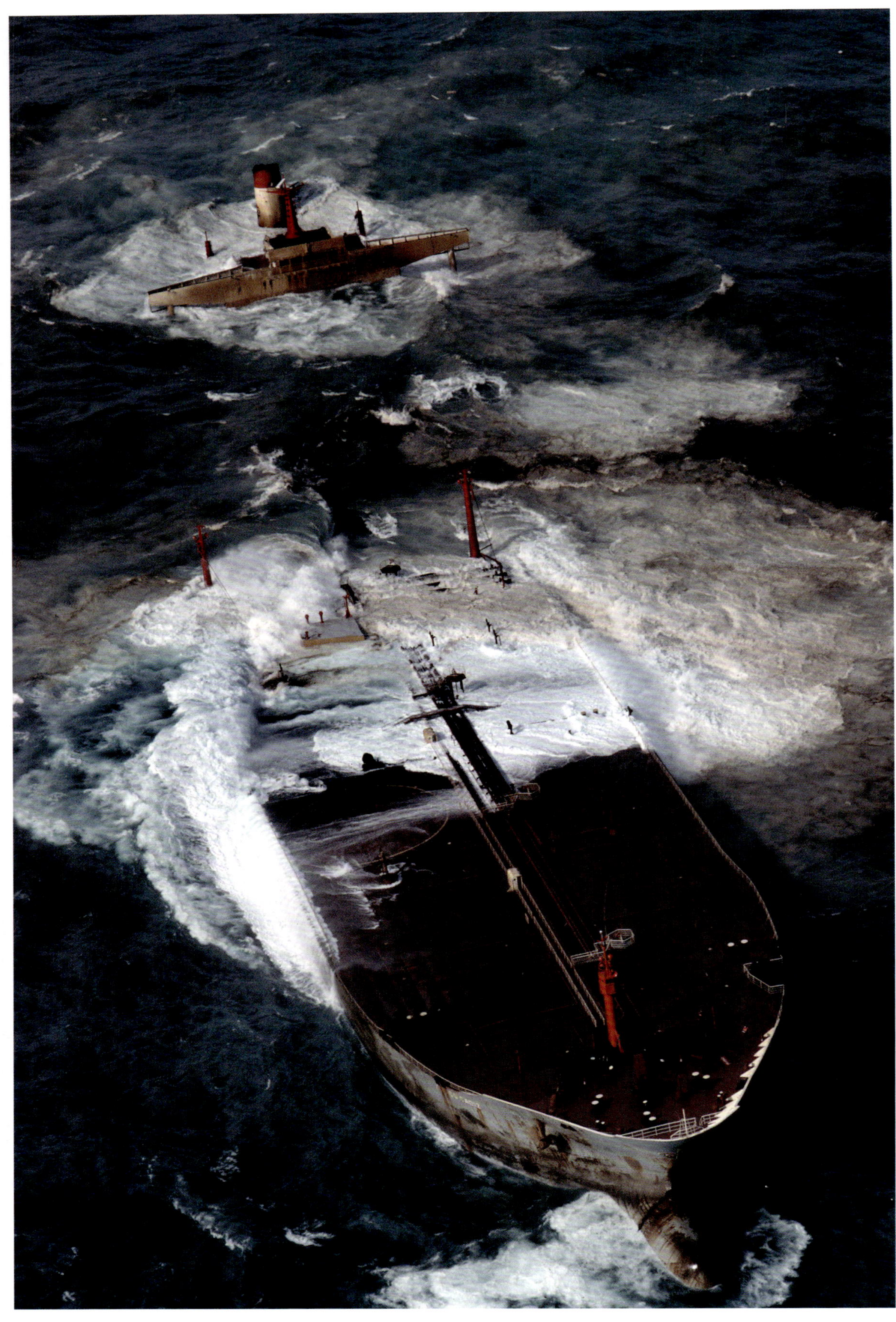

When the oil tanker *Amoco Cadiz* ran aground on the Portsall Rocks on 16 March 1978, 5 kilometres from the coast of Brittany, it was the world's worst-ever oil-tanker spill. The tanker had been en route from the Persian Gulf to Le Havre when the disaster occurred, spilling the entire cargo of more than 1.6 million barrels of oil into the sea. Jean Gaumy, a French photographer with Magnum Photos, was in a helicopter and captured images of the stricken vessel from above. He remembers being taken aback by the sight of the tanker so close to the shore and the huge volume of oil.

Jean Gaumy
Sinking of the *Amoco Cadiz*, Portsall Rocks, Brittany, France, 1978.

Marilyn Bridges's subjects include some of the greatest wonders of the world: Machu Picchu, the Pyramids of Giza and Uluru, Australia. Since the mid-1970s, the American photographer and pilot has been photographing the Earth from the air, creating images of ancient sites, in her signature black and white, that capitalize on stark shadows to emphasize the three-dimensionality of the landscape. Through her lens, familiar scenes are presented anew, with Bridges sometimes flying just 60 metres off the ground. 'I have to fly low to get the intimacy I need,' she told *The Independent* newspaper. 'But to get that close you have to slow the plane down to "stall speed", which means the plane almost stops flying.'

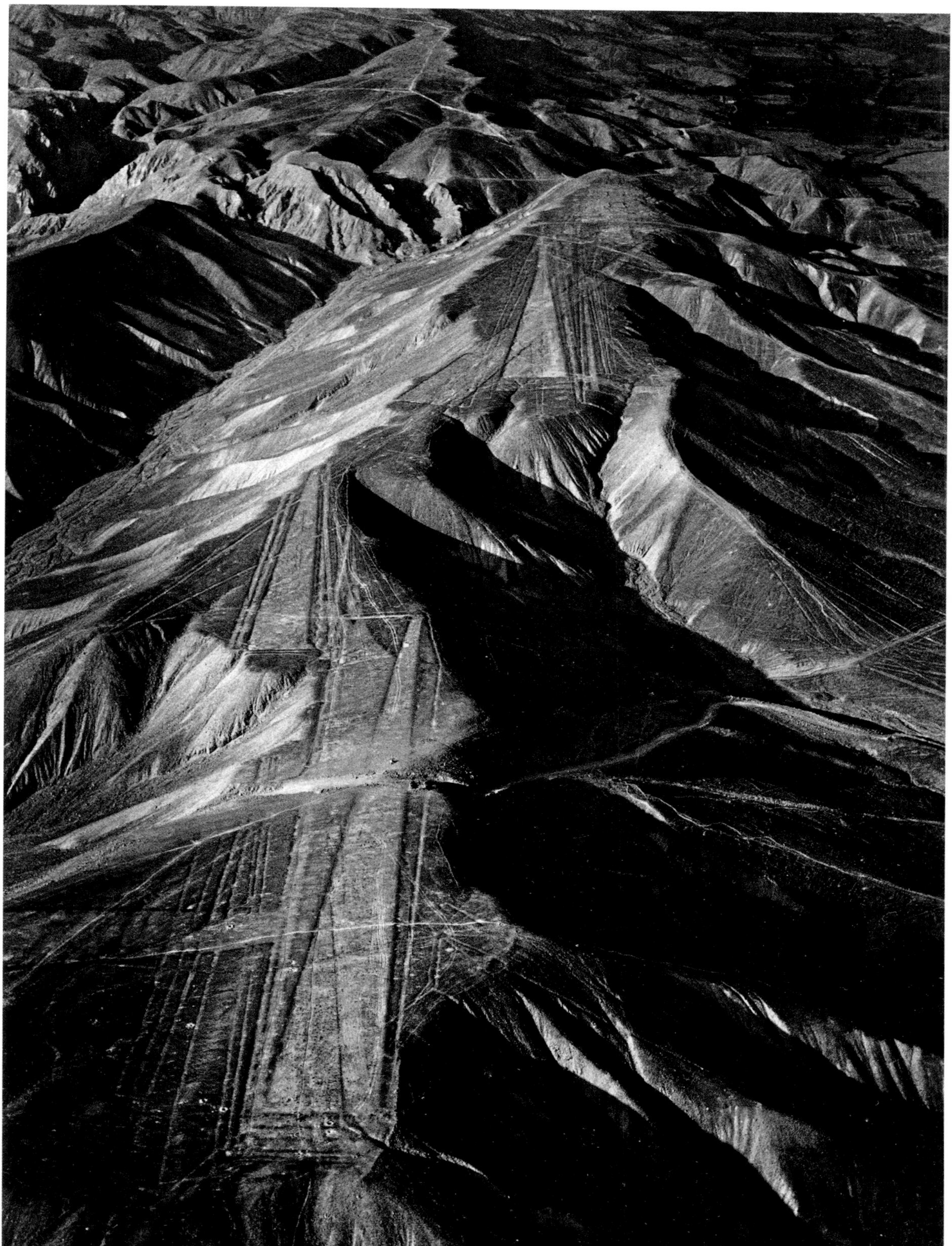

Marilyn Bridges
Nazca, Arrows over Rise,
Peru, 1979.

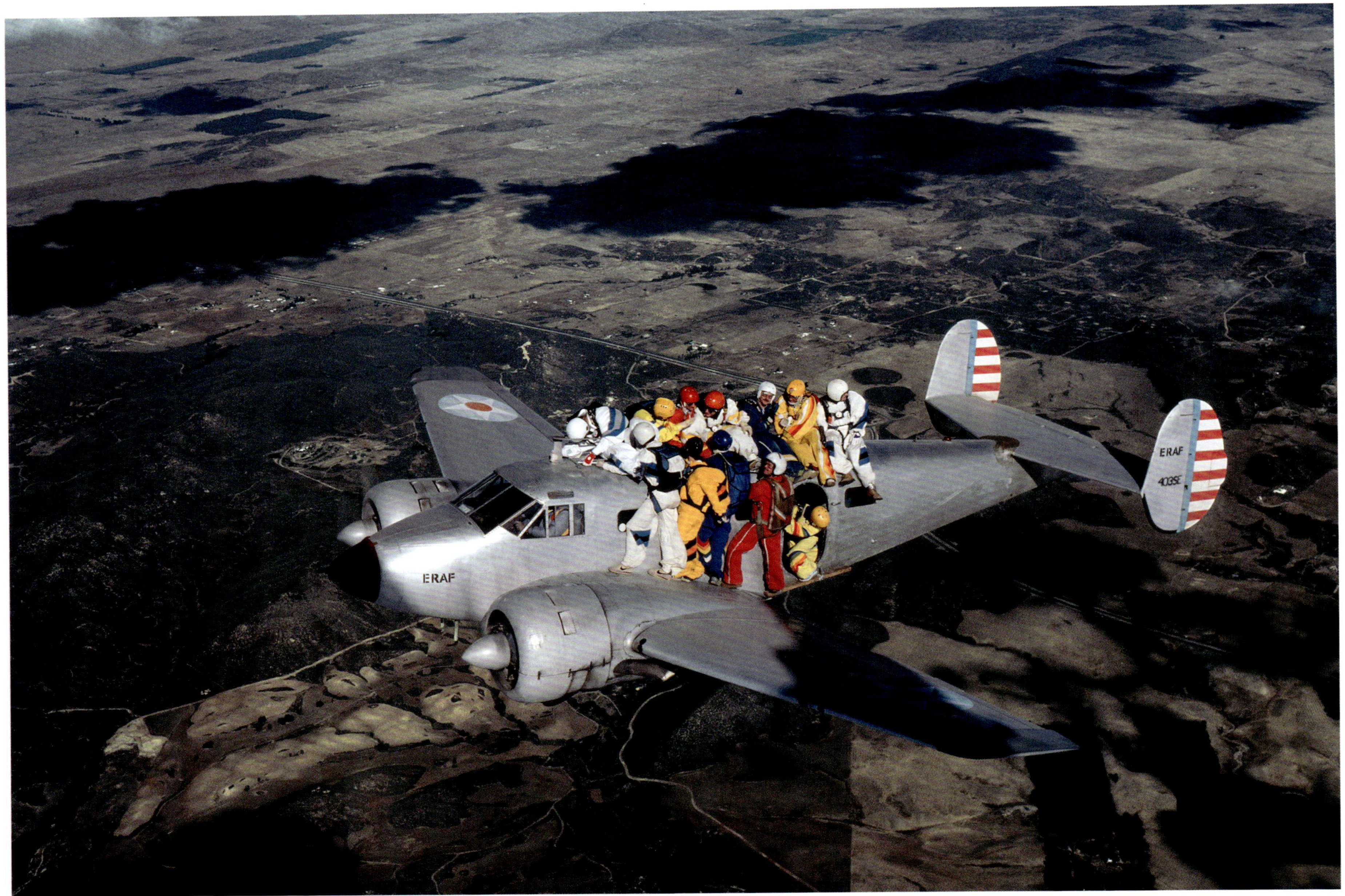

Sports and dance photographer Leo Mason has covered Summer and Winter Olympic Games, boxing championships and both football and rugby World Cups, to name just a few, but his career has also led him to photograph from the air, where he has captured some crazy antics. This is a group of skydivers preparing for a dive over Lake Elsinore in California, one of several images Mason took while on assignment for *Stern* magazine in 1980. Handles had been welded to the top of the fuselage so the skydivers could hold on once they had exited the aircraft. Mason flew alongside in a small Cessna plane with one of its doors removed.

Leo Mason
Skydivers preparing their dive over Lake Elsinore, California, USA, 1980.

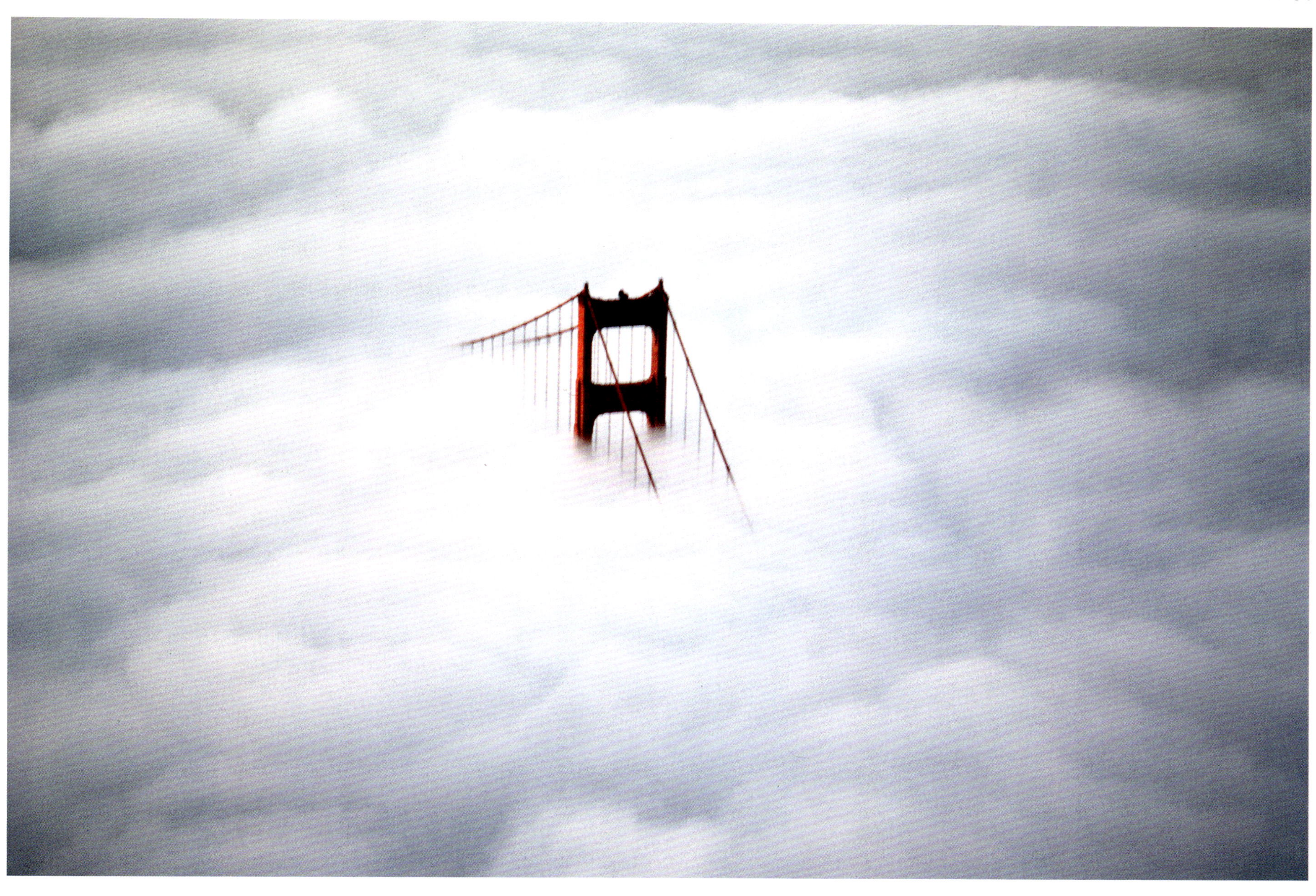

Baron Wolman
Golden Gate Bridge, San Francisco, USA, 1981.

In his role as chief photographer for *Rolling Stone* magazine, from 1967 until late 1970, Baron Wolman photographed Jimi Hendrix, Bob Dylan, The Rolling Stones, Pink Floyd and more. Keen to find a new subject, in the 1970s Wolman bought a small Cessna plane and began doing aerial photography, mostly over California where he lived, but also in Israel. Using a 35mm camera with lenses that included both 50mm and 105mm, Wolman eagerly embraced this new way of making pictures, capturing everything from housing developments to beaches and misty vistas. Among his most well-known aerial work is the series of images of San Francisco's Golden Gate Bridge, including this shot of the famous bridge in fog.

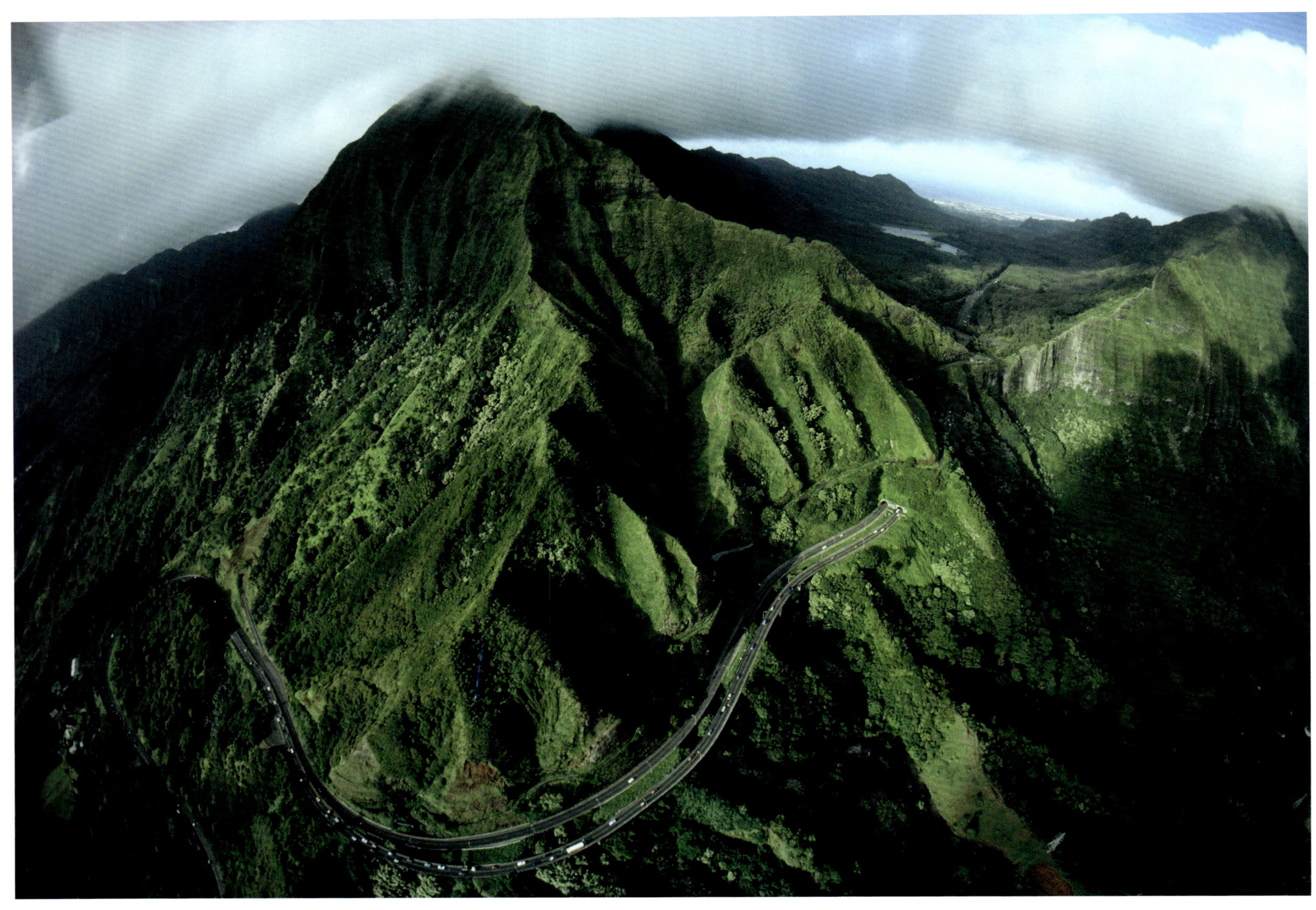

In his long career as a photojournalist, Steven L. Raymer shot countless stories for *National Geographic* magazine, with whom he worked for more than two decades. His assignments took him all over the world including to Hawaii (pictured above) where he embarked on a story about the history of the archipelago and its people. As Raymer explains in his autobiography, the story required that he took to the air, allowing him to show the full scale of the majestic vistas of Oahu.

Steven L. Raymer
Pali Highway sweeping up the Ko'olau Range, Oahu, Hawaii, 1982.

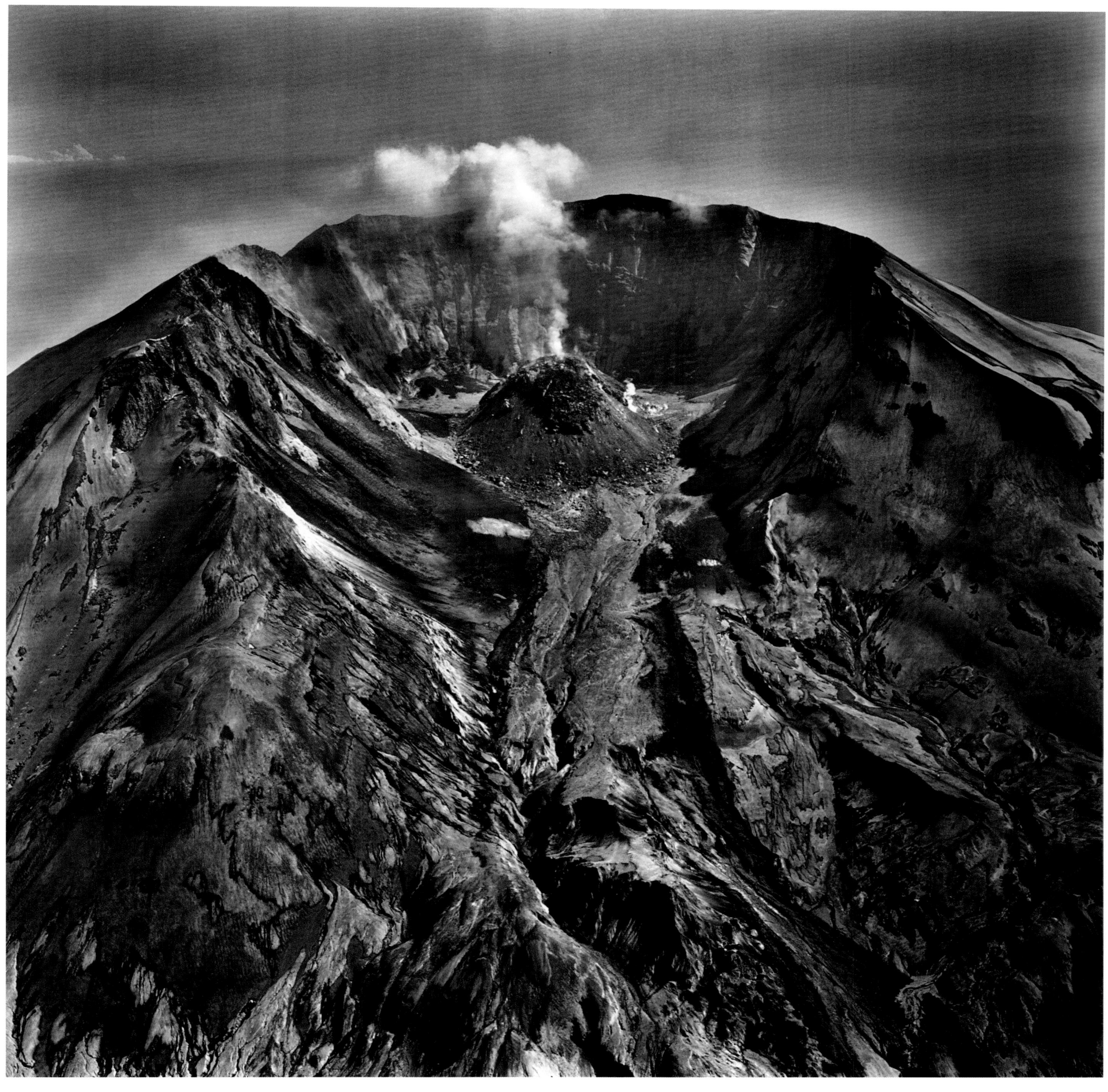

Above
Photographer unknown
Dome and crater of Mount St. Helens, Washington, USA, 1982.

Overleaf
Photographer unknown
Eruption of Mount St. Helens, Washington, USA, 1982.

Mount St. Helens has long been a source of fascination for both scientists and photographers alike, perhaps even more so after the catastrophic eruption on 18 May 1980 (pictured overleaf). Aerial photography came to the fore during and after the disaster, which killed approximately 57 people. Minor activity continued at the volcano for several years afterwards as the image above shows.

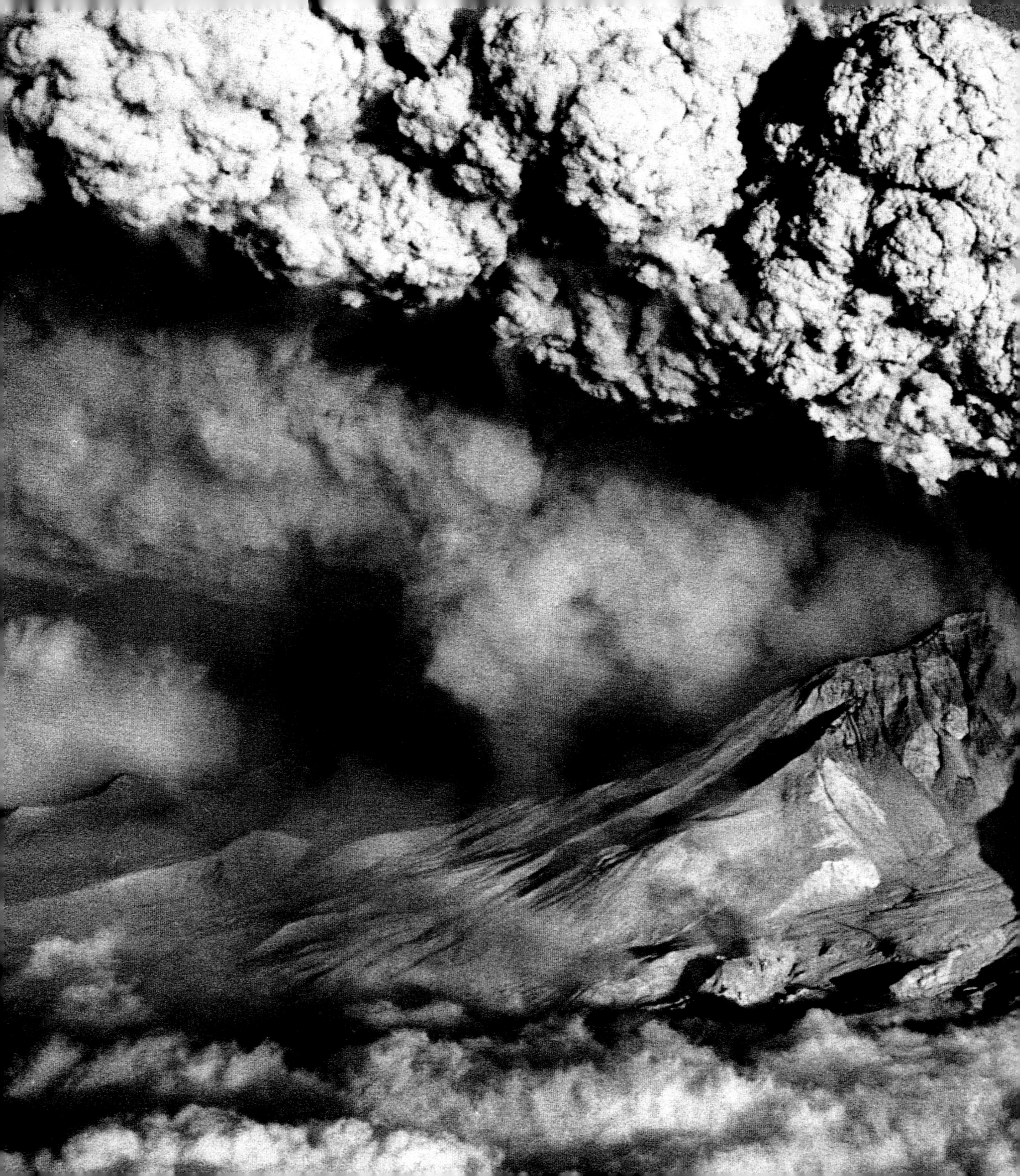

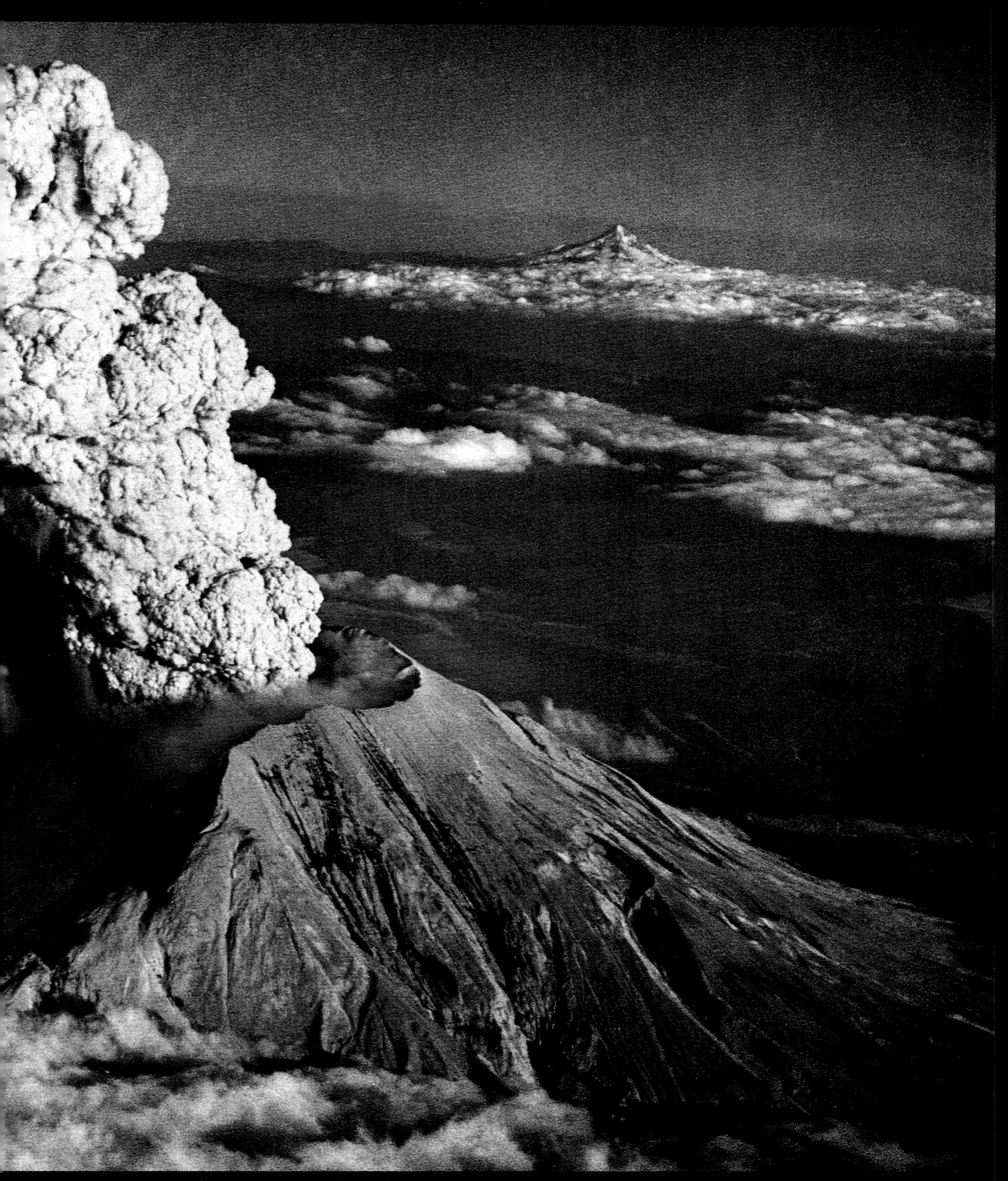

1983

Before turning his hand to photography, German photographer Thomas Hoepker studied art history and archaeology – training that clearly came in handy when photographing from the air, as he has done on occasion. Hoepker, a member and former president of photography collective Magnum Photos, may be best known for his colourful studies of everyday life in Valparaíso, Chile, and controversial photographs of 9/11, but his aerial photographs depicting scenes such as picnickers in New York's Central Park from 1983, or mountain ranges in Utah, clearly reflect his finely tuned appreciation of form, line, colour and shape. 'When there was a need and interest on a particular assignment I rented an airplane or a chopper, but I didn't do it very often,' he says.

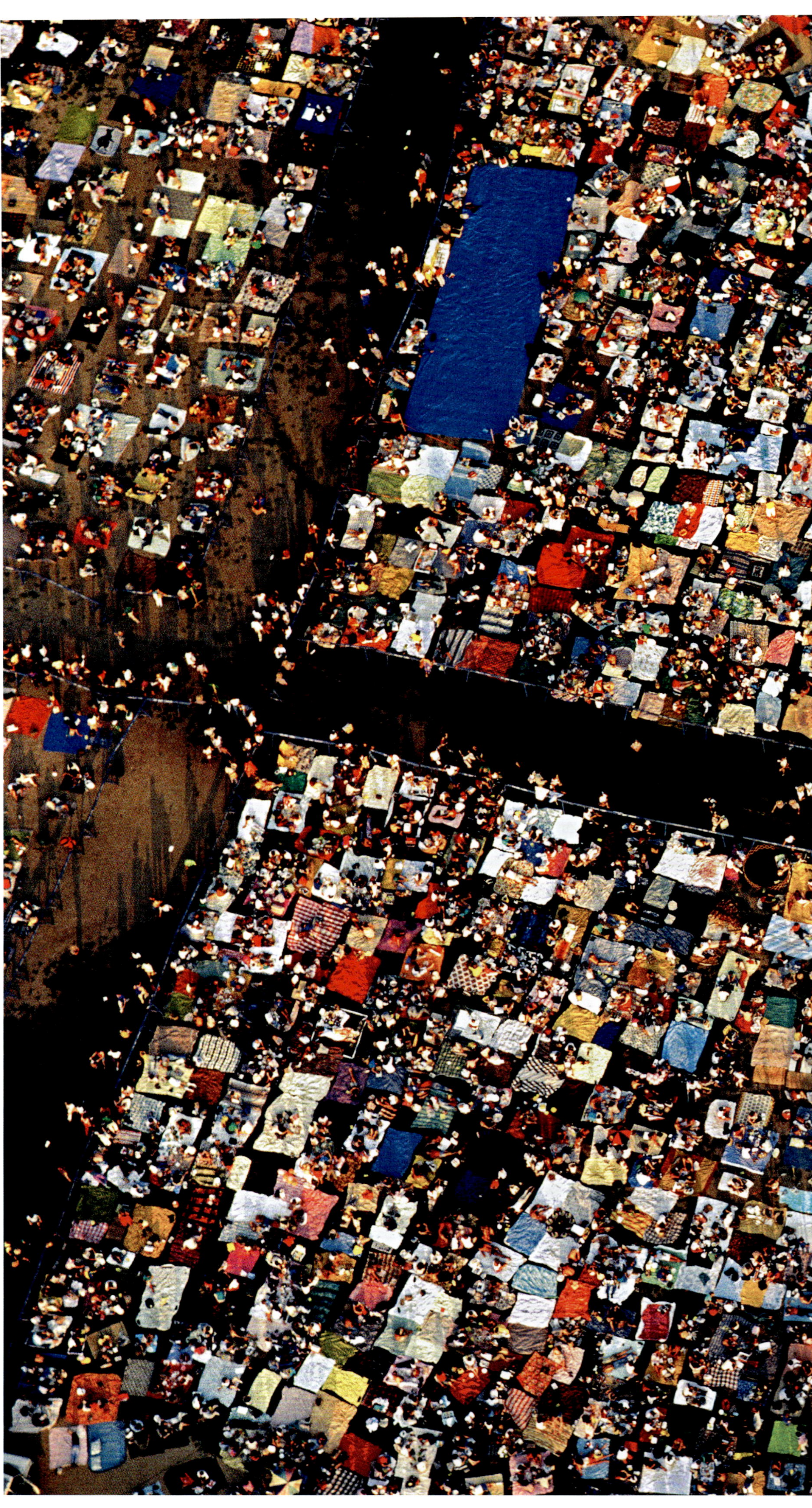

Thomas Hoepker
Picnickers in Central Park during a concert, New York, USA, 1983.

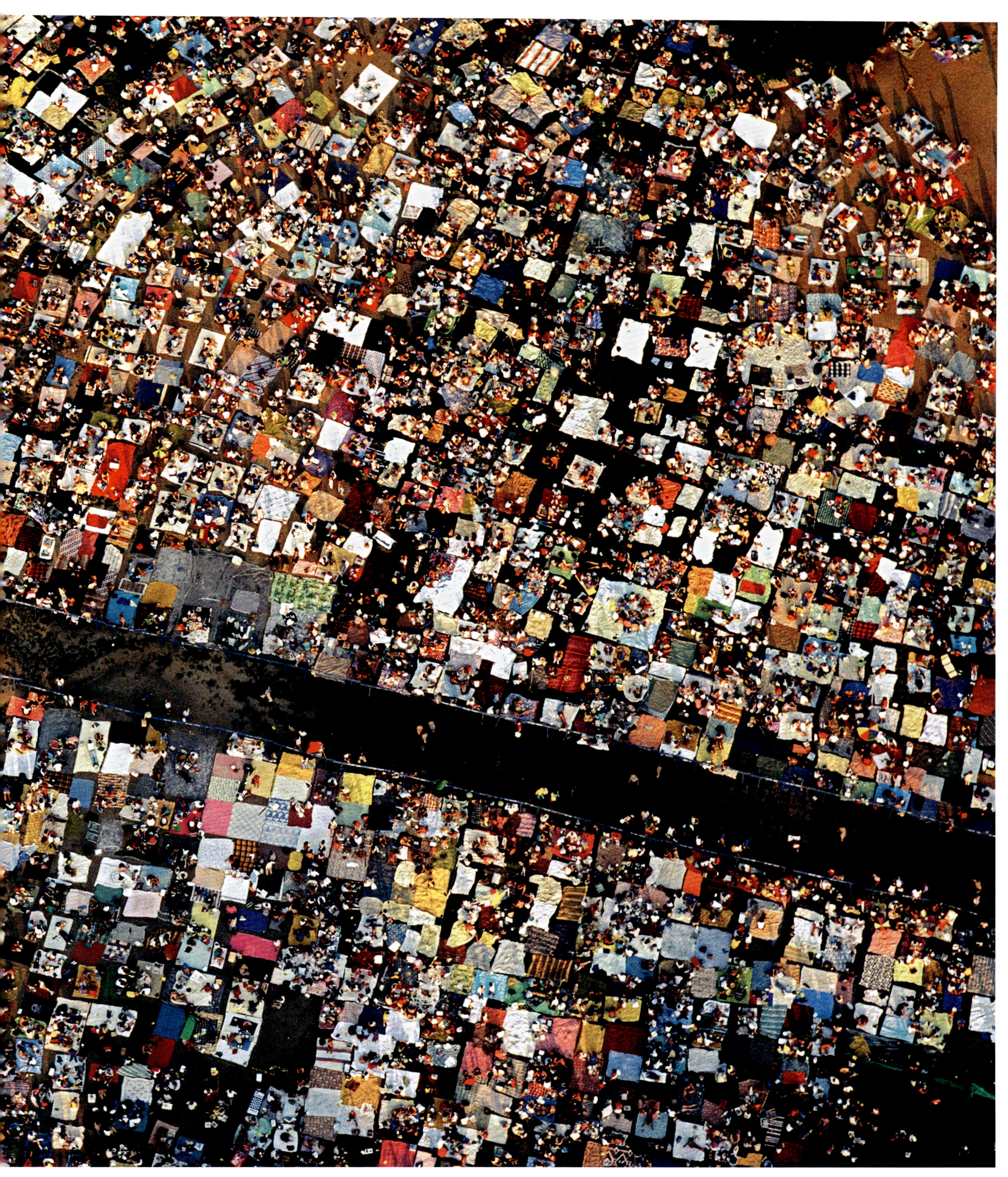

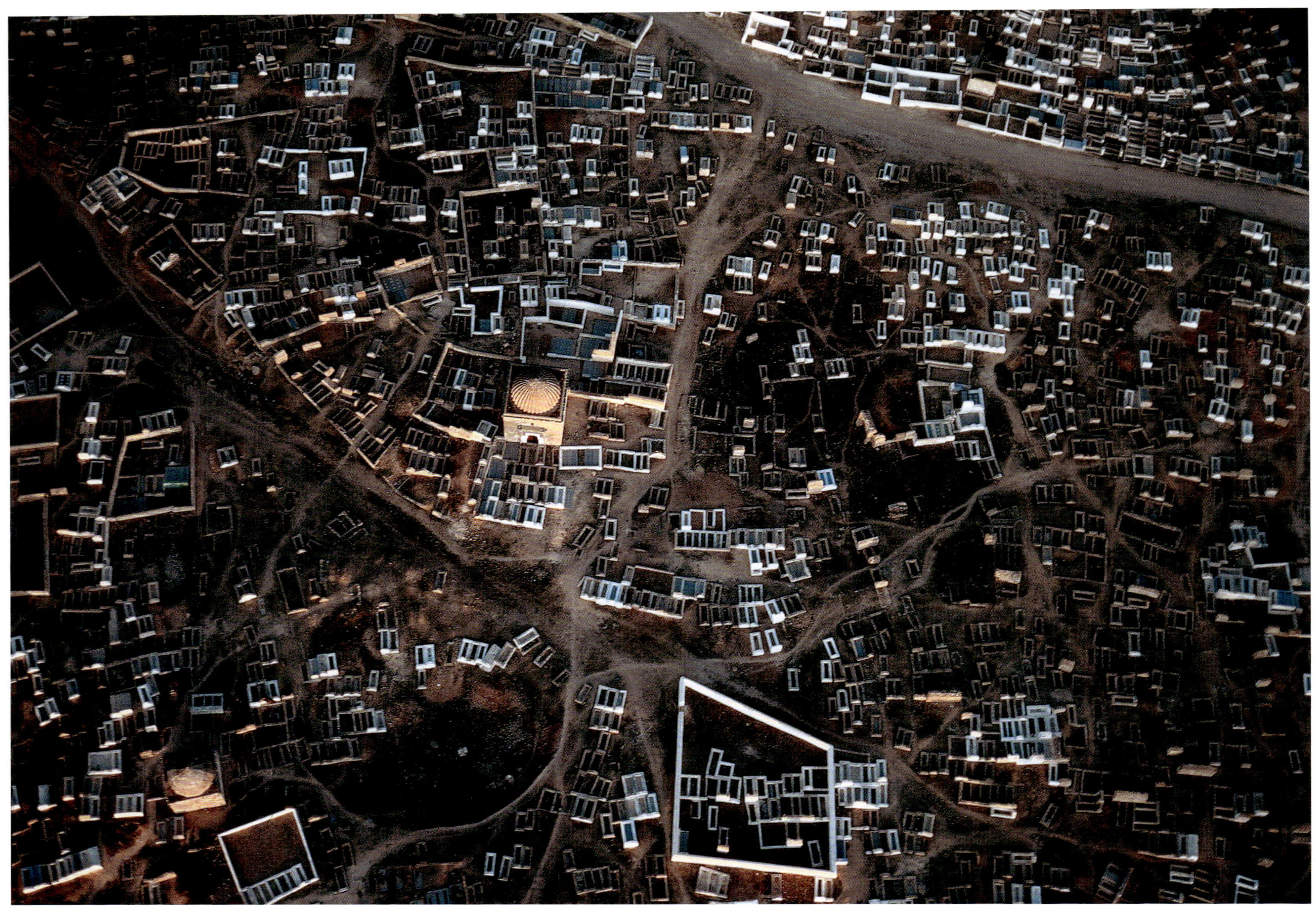

Bruno Barbey
Muslim cemetery in Fez, Morocco, 1985.

In his long career as a photographer, Moroccan-born Bruno Barbey has documented war and conflict the world over, from Nigeria to Vietnam, the Middle East, Northern Ireland to Iraq. He has also, on occasion, photographed from the air, driven not only by his interest in people, but also by a desire to 'describe' his surroundings. This curiosity propelled him to photograph in Marrakesh and Fez, where he was drawn to both cities' architecture and captured the buildings from a bird's-eye view. Barbey has said that his work is concerned with documenting situations that will one day disappear, and when you look at his images with this in mind, a sense of melancholy and nostalgia is palpable.

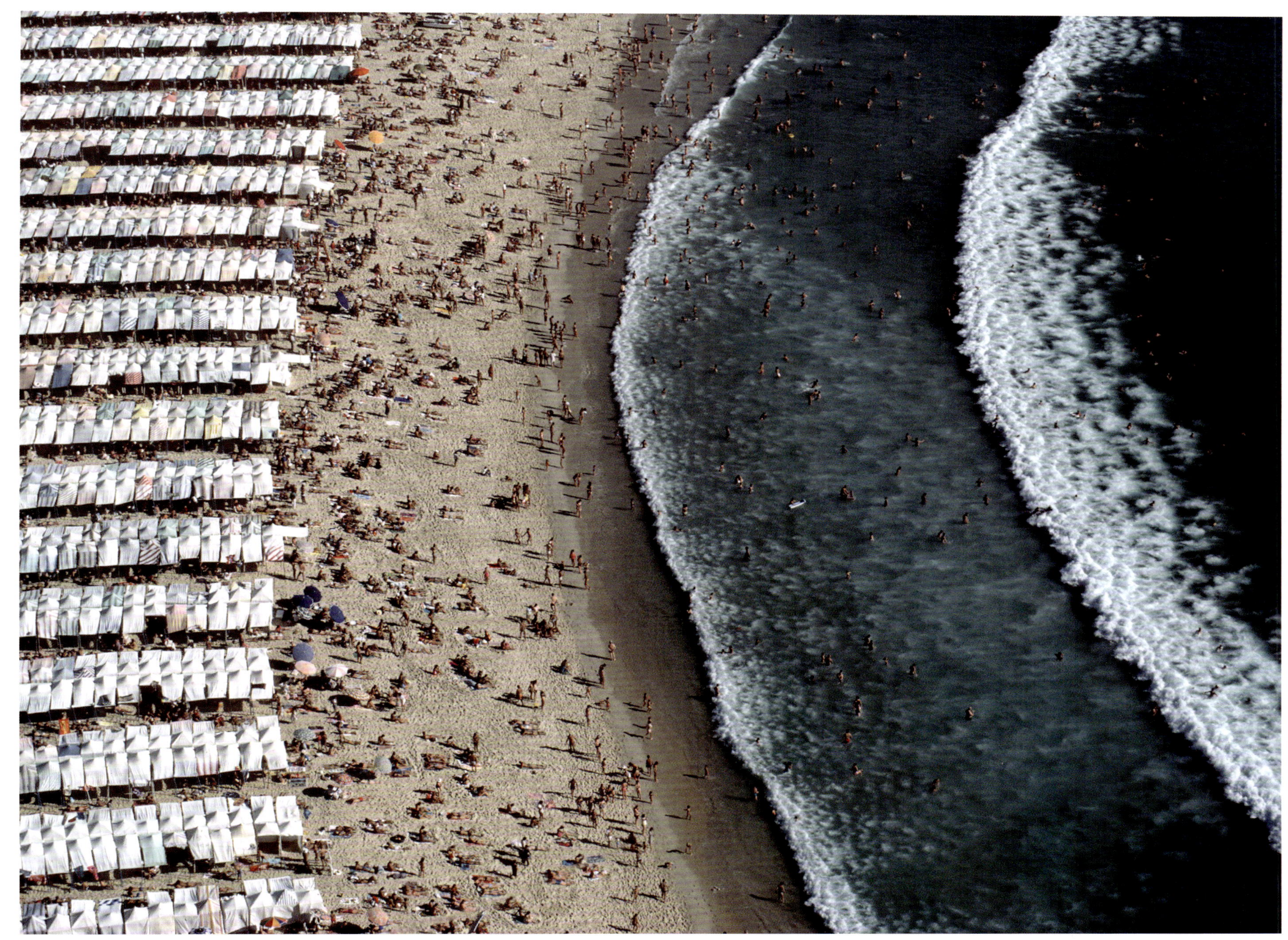

Bruno Barbey
A crowded beach at Nazaré,
Portugal, 1985.

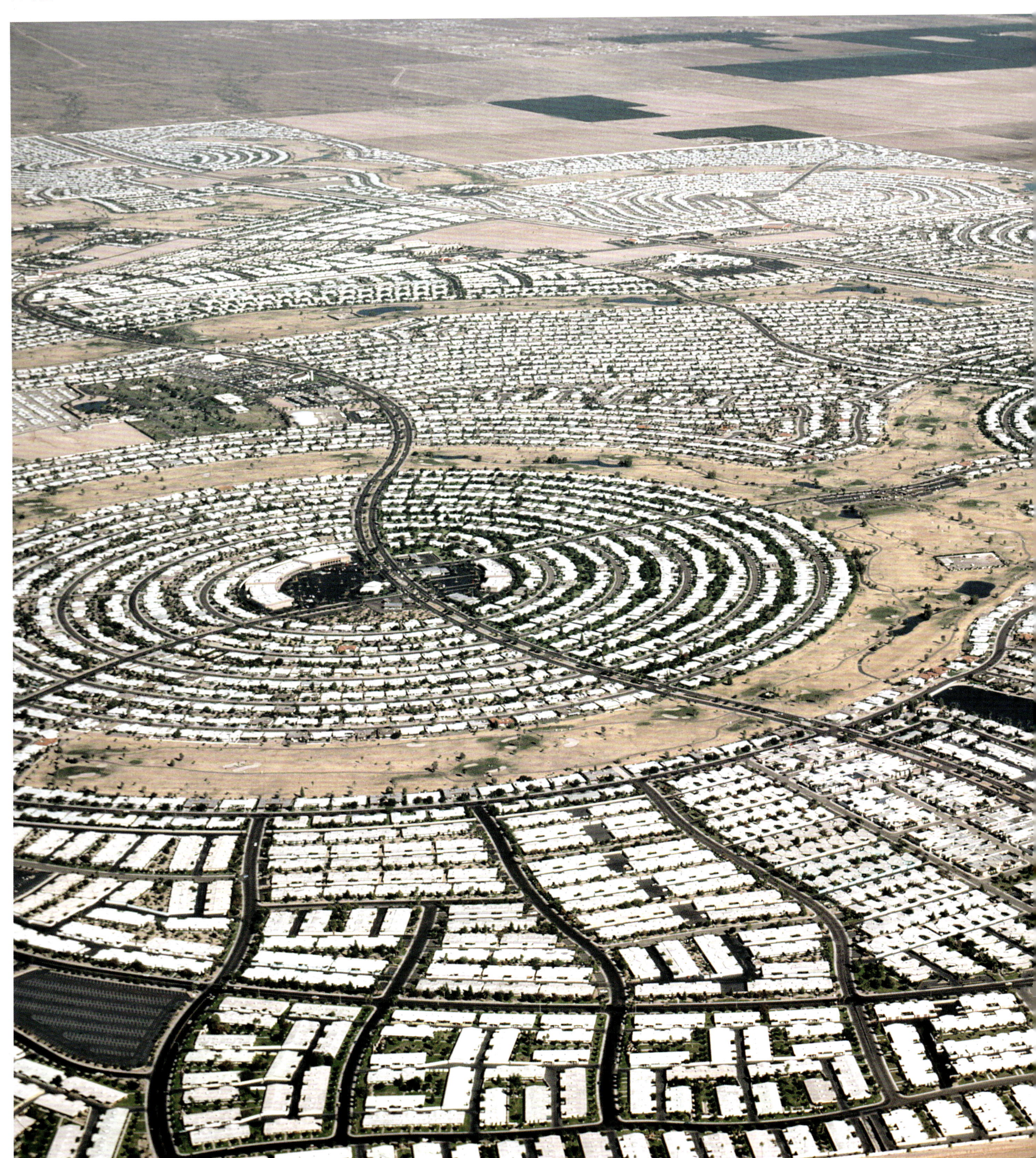

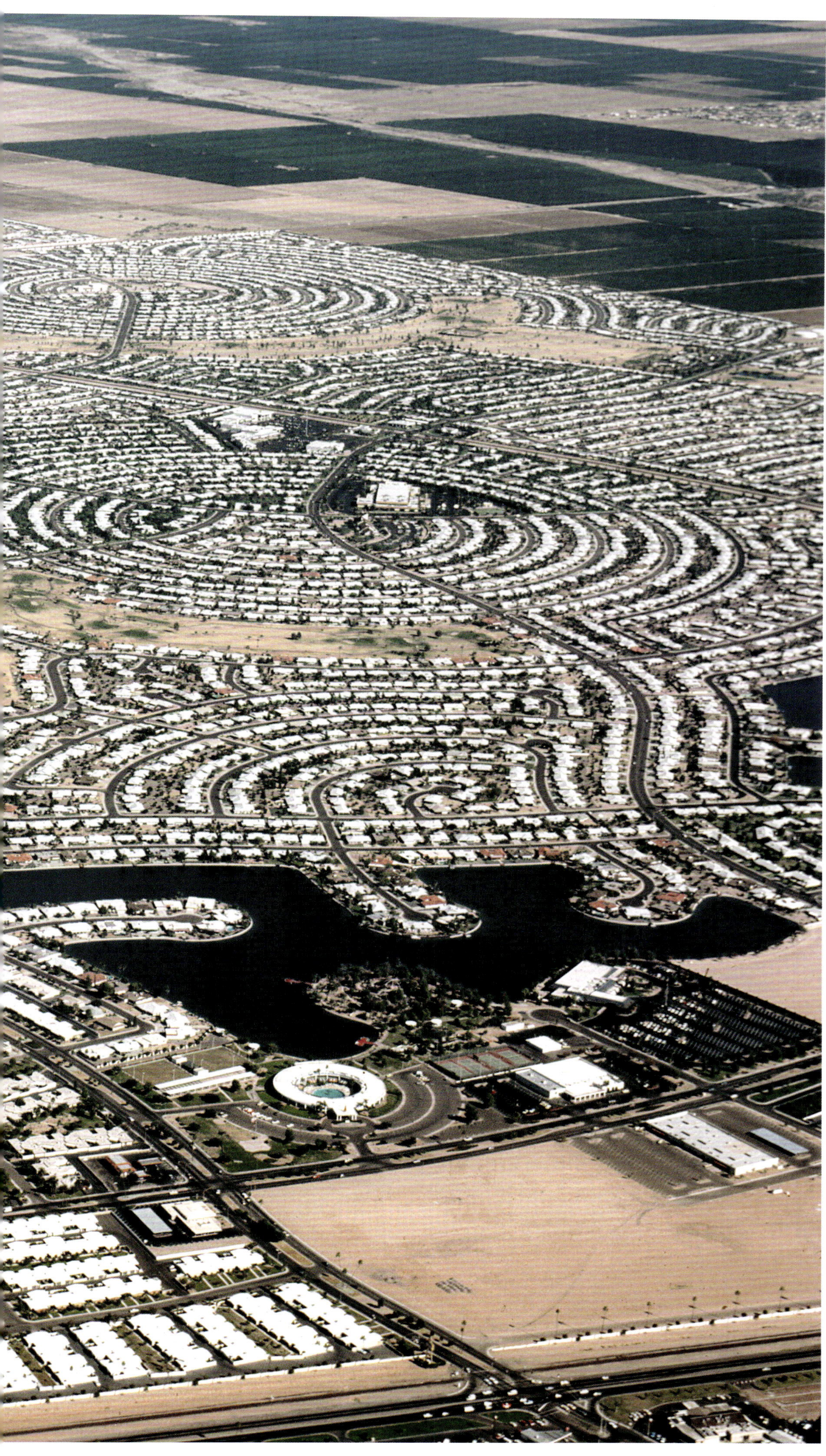

When David Hurn received a UK/ US Bicentennial Fellowship in 1979 to photograph the United States, the British photographer trained his lens on Arizona. The state, one of the driest in the US, must have made an impression on him as he visited several times over the years. A member of Magnum Photos, Hurn took this image of retirement community Sun City in Phoenix in 1992. The site, which had opened some 30 years earlier on 1 January 1960, boasted recreational facilities as well as model homes. The idea was to create a community for active retired people designed around leisure – a place that could meet residents' needs so they wouldn't ever have to leave. Hurn's aerial photograph gives a sense of the sheer scale of the site and its innovative design.

David Hurn
Sun City, Phoenix, Arizona, USA, 1992.

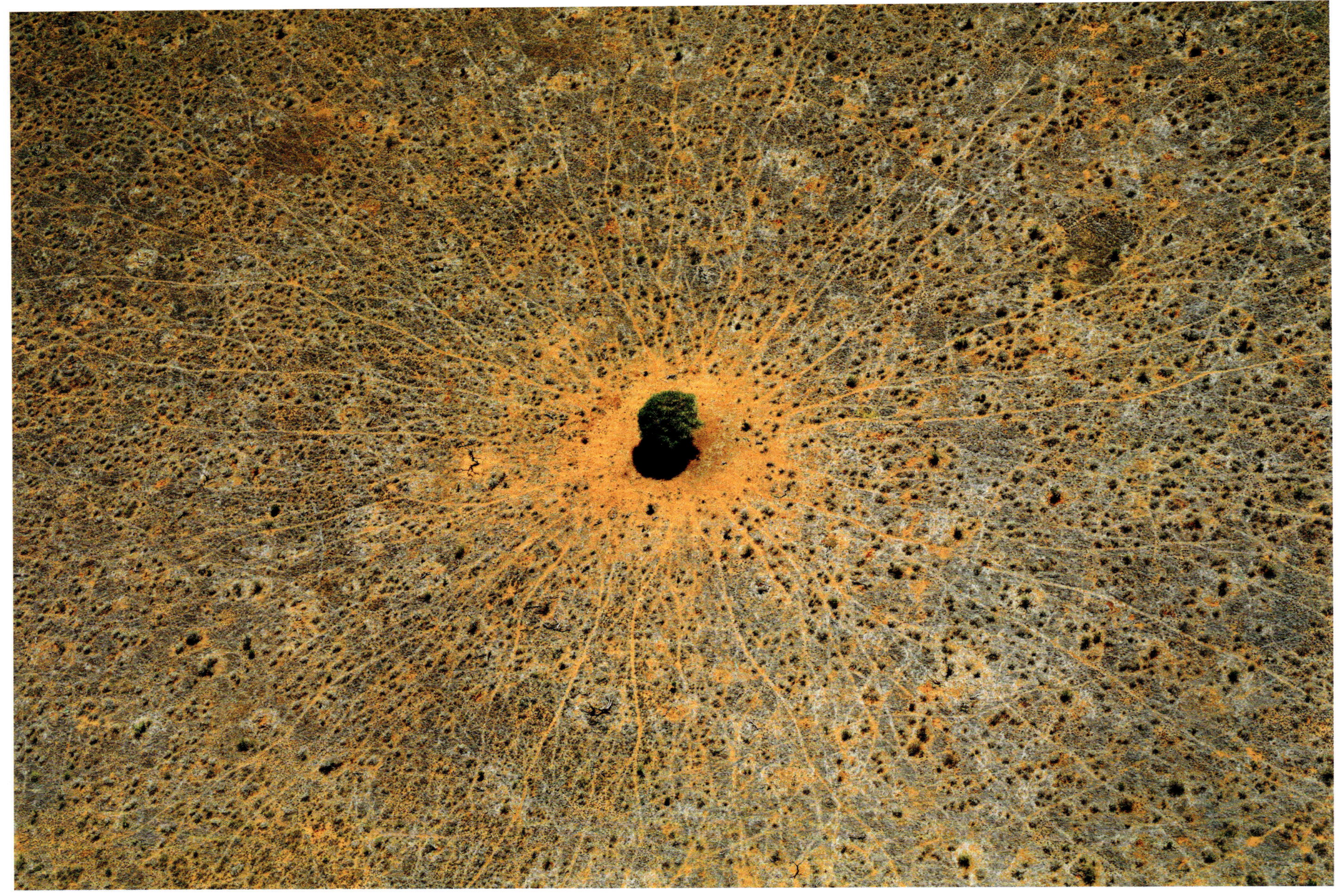

Yann Arthus-Bertrand
Animal tracks to the tree of life, Tsavo National Park, Kenya, 1993.

Photographer Yann Arthus-Bertrand is today known just as much for being an environmentalist and activist as he is an image-maker. But, really, these passions go hand in hand for the Frenchman, whose love for nature stretches back to childhood. Describing himself as a reporter focusing on environmental issues, Arthus-Bertrand, who was born in 1946, earned a living as a hot-air-balloon pilot in his early thirties while living in Kenya, where he was studying the behaviour of lions. He began using a camera to capture what he saw, and would go on to make his name as an aerial photographer. In 1991, Arthus-Bertrand founded the world's first aerial photography agency and his book *The Earth from the Air*, which was published in 2000, has sold millions of copies.

Below
Yann Arthus-Bertrand
Gardens at the Château de Vaux le Vicomte, Maincy, France, 2003.

Overleaf
Yann Arthus-Bertrand
Venice, Italy, 1993.

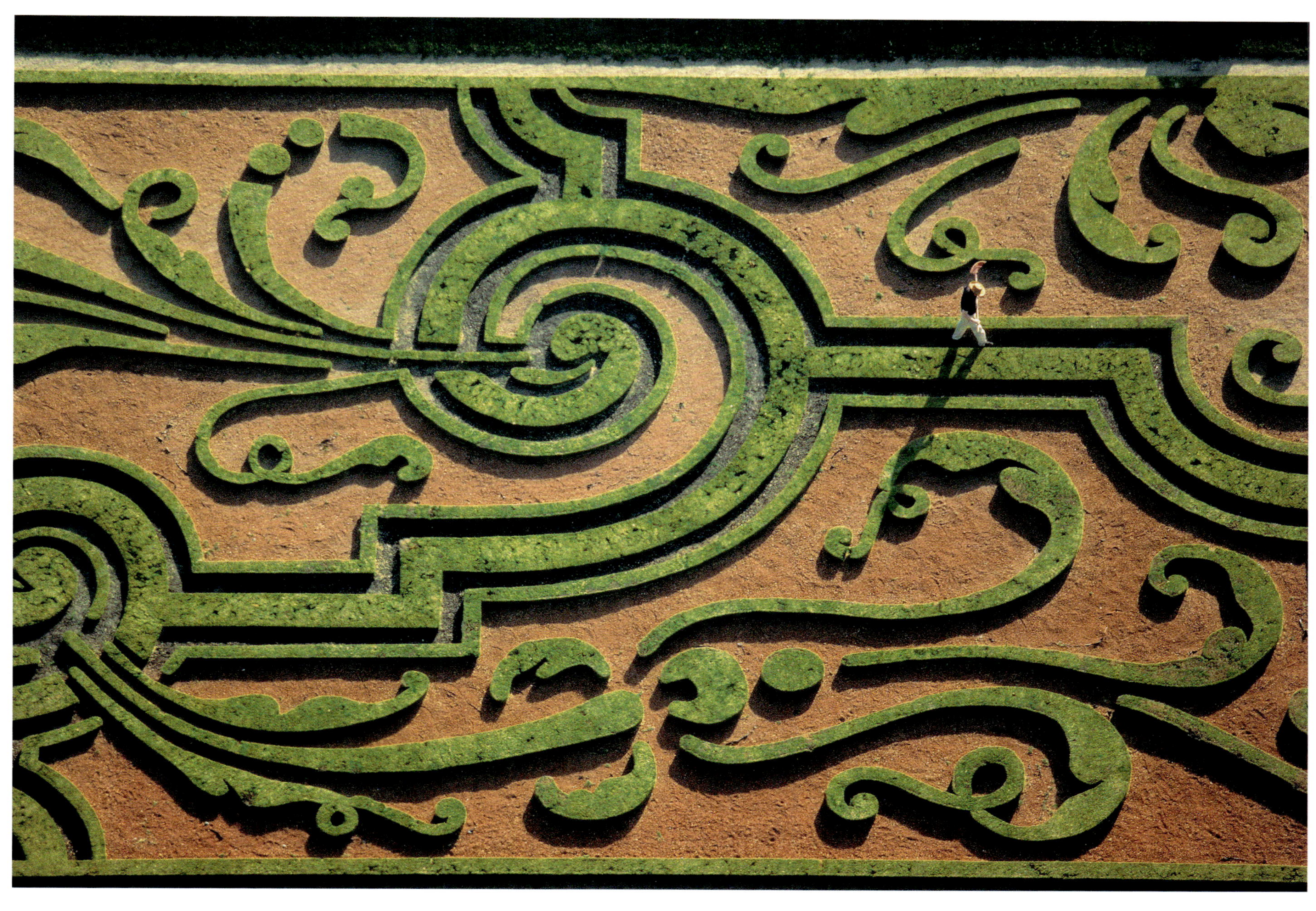

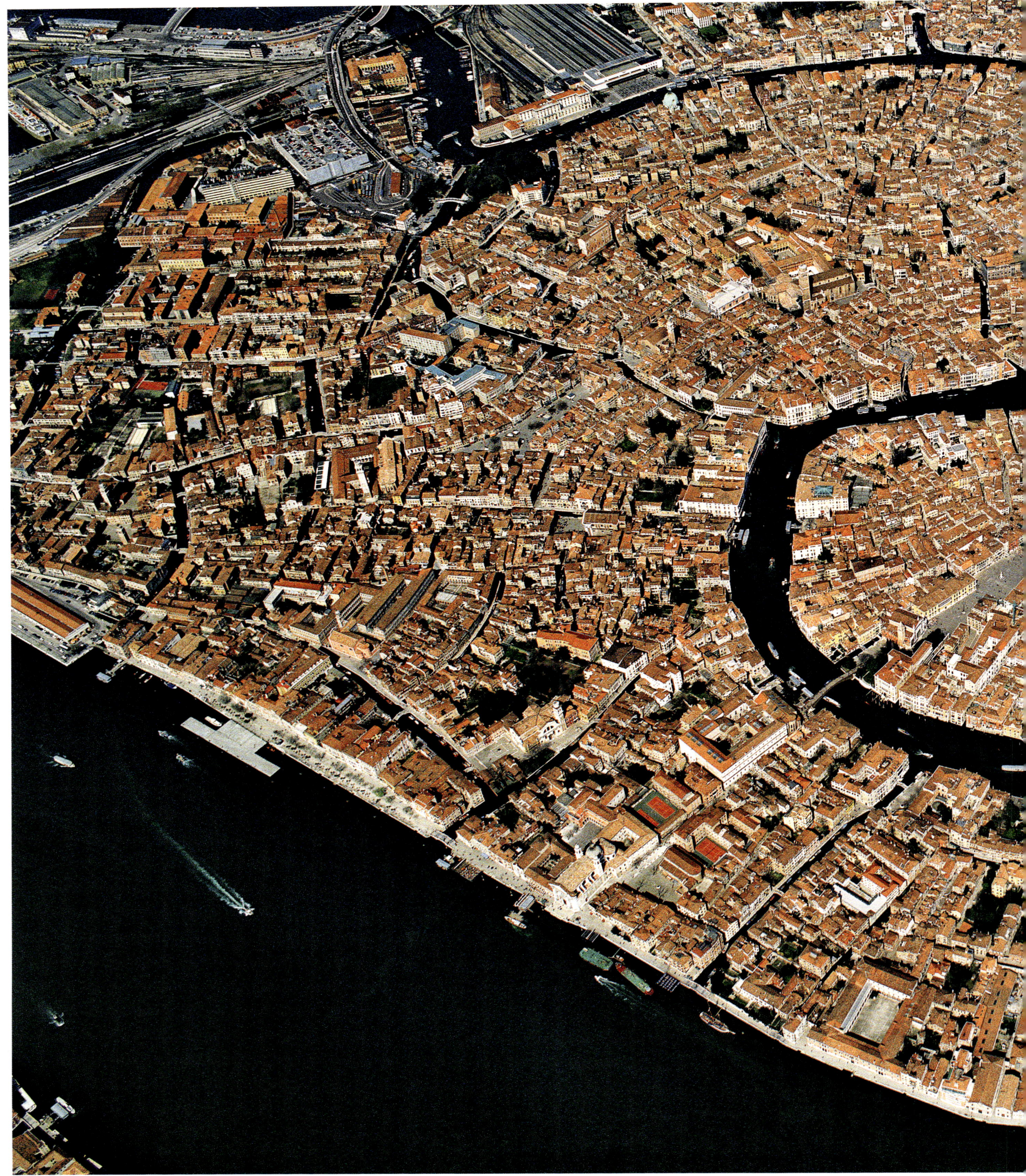

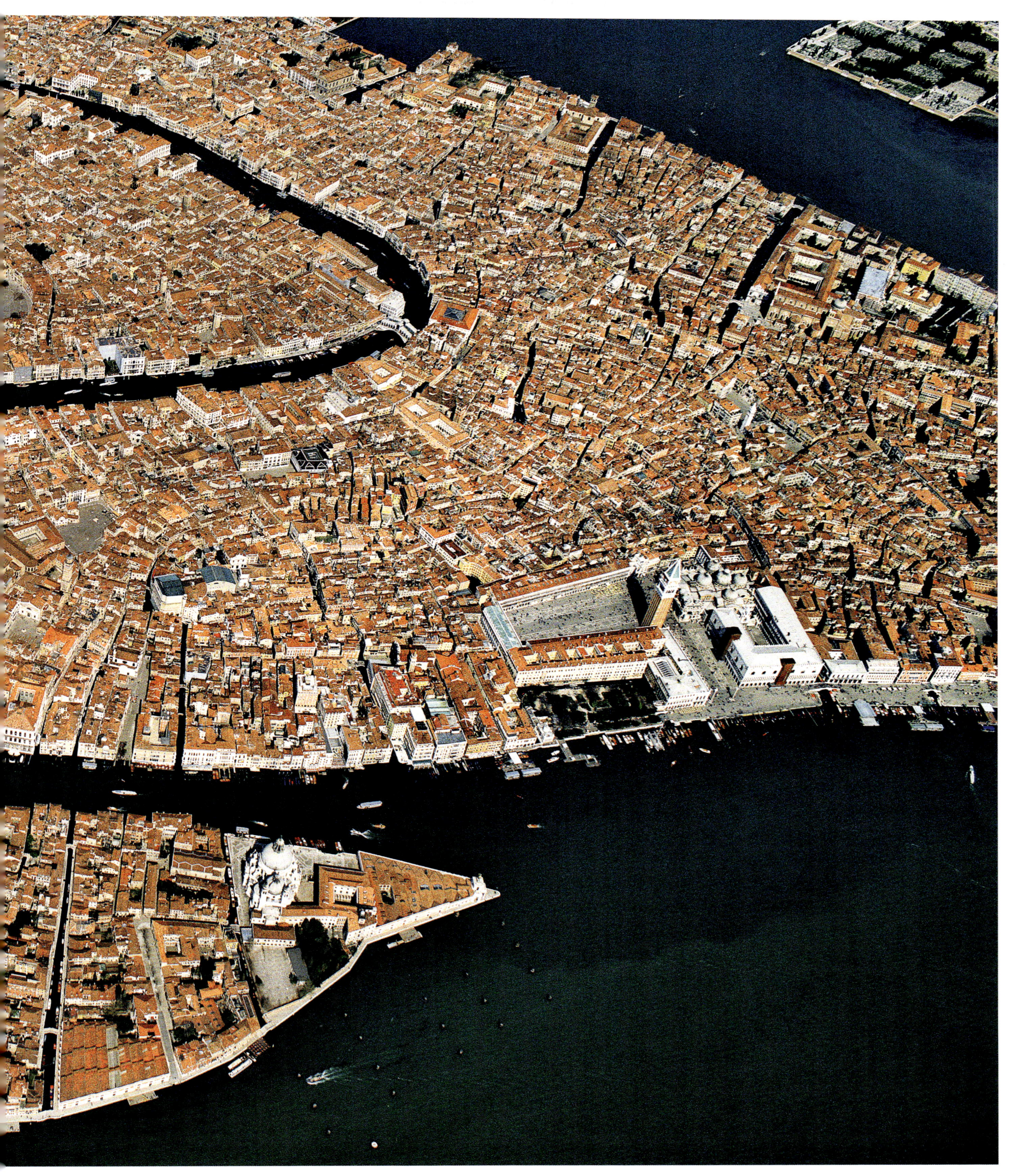

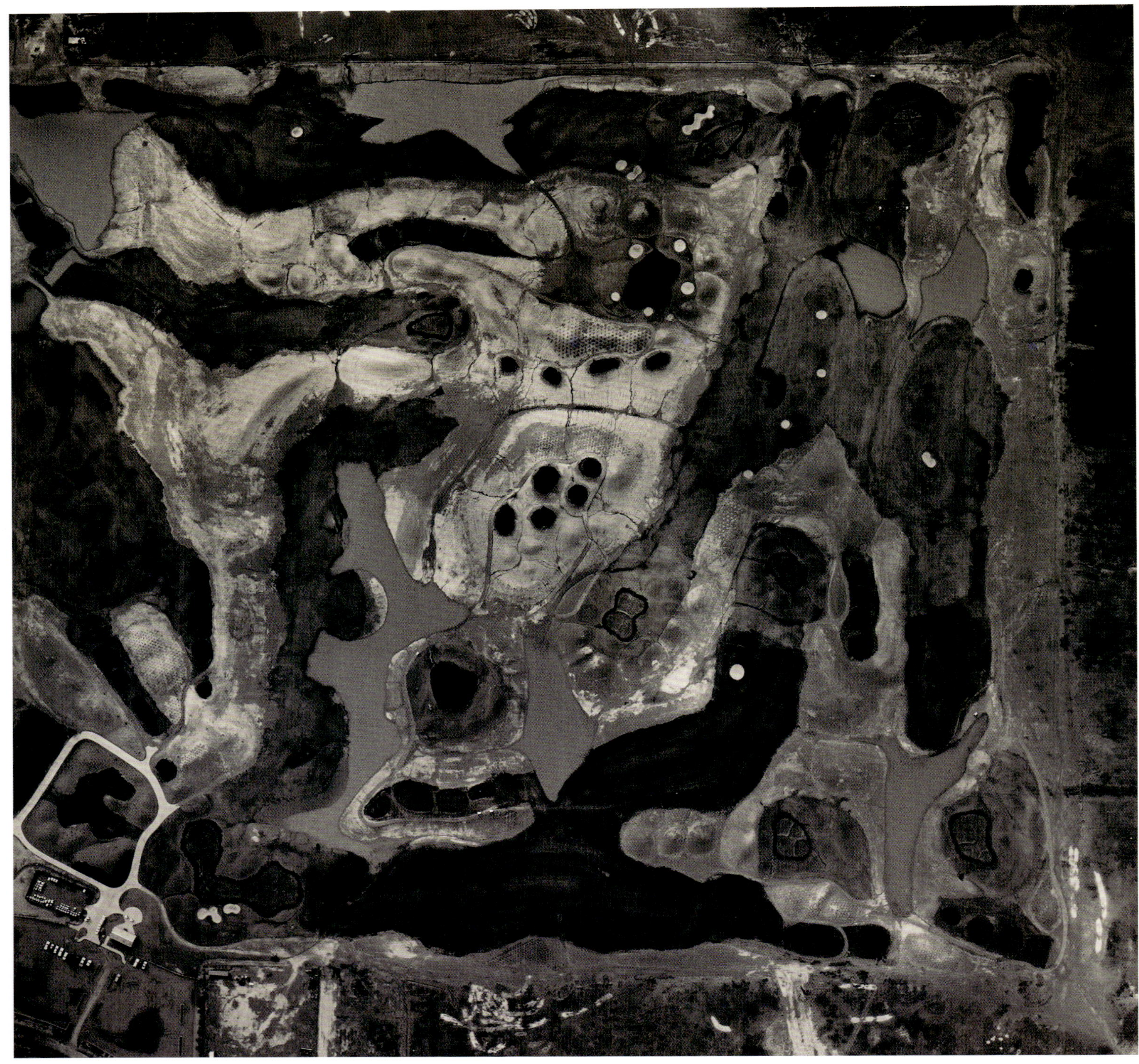

Emmet Gowin is known for his intimate images of his family, but the American photographer has also photographed from the sky, capturing everything from strip-mining sites to nuclear-testing grounds, agricultural fields and even a golf course under construction (pictured). In the 1980s, when he took up aerial photography, Gowin trained his lens on the American West, and in the years that followed he travelled to Mount St Helens in Washington and the Czech Republic, among other places. Gowin, who embraces the element of abstraction that comes with photographing from the air, focuses on landscapes altered by humans or nature. His images, not intended to be explicit calls to action, occupy the uncomfortable space between destruction and the sublime.

Emmet Gowin
Golf Course Under Construction, Arizona, USA, 1993.

This charming photograph, by the late Magnum photographer Peter Marlow, shows that even simple scenes can result in visually striking aerial photographs. It belongs to a series Marlow made in 1997 about cleaning up pollution in the Norfolk Broads. Marlow owned his own plane, a Piper Cherokee, but since there is no record in his flight log of any flights he made in the area in 1997, his widow Fiona Naylor believes that Marlow must not have been the captain on this occasion. Marlow was familiar with light aircraft and small flying clubs, Naylor recalls, so it's possible he got chatting to someone whom he asked to take him for a spin.

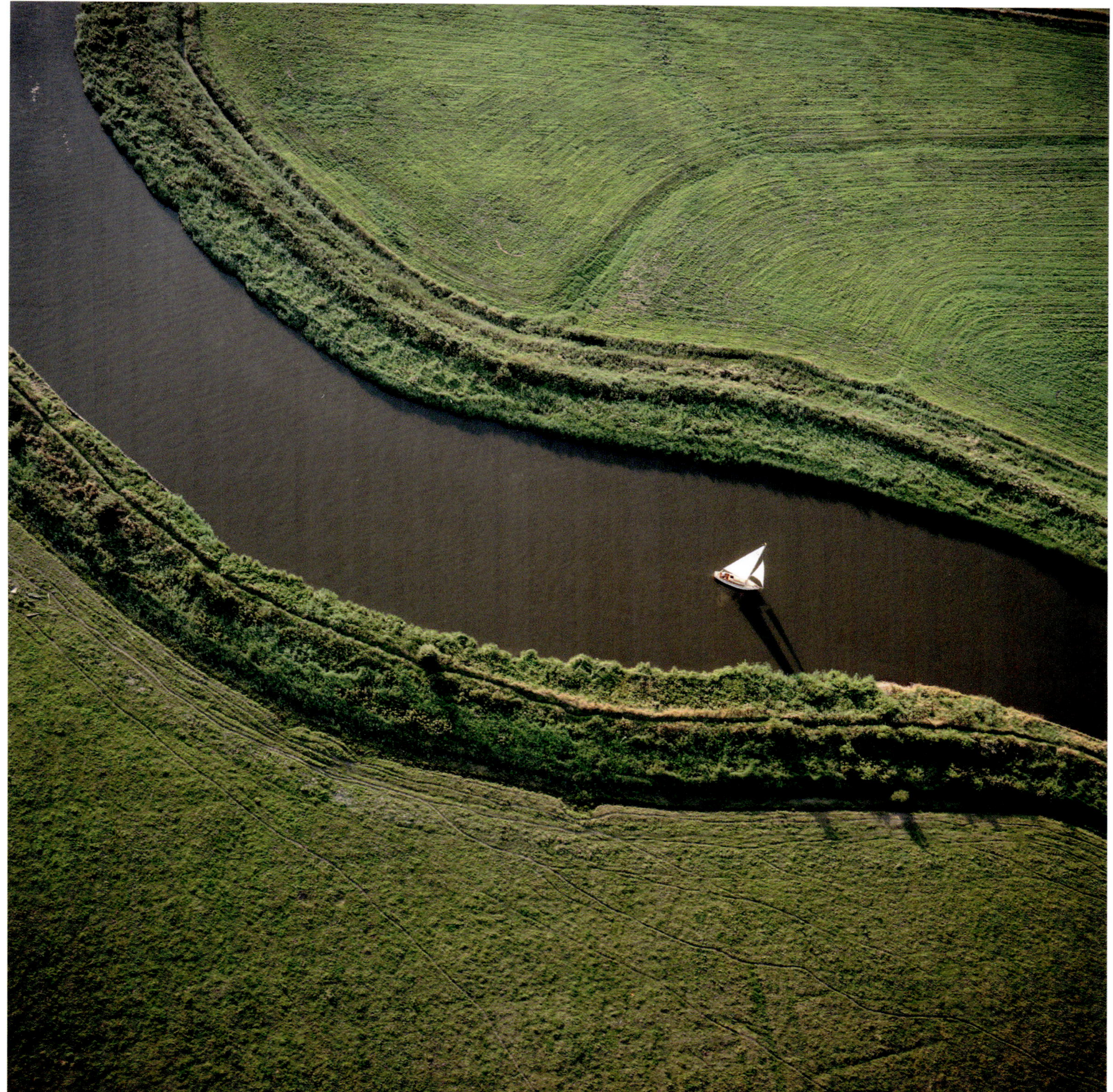

Peter Marlow
River Ant, Norfolk, England, 1997.

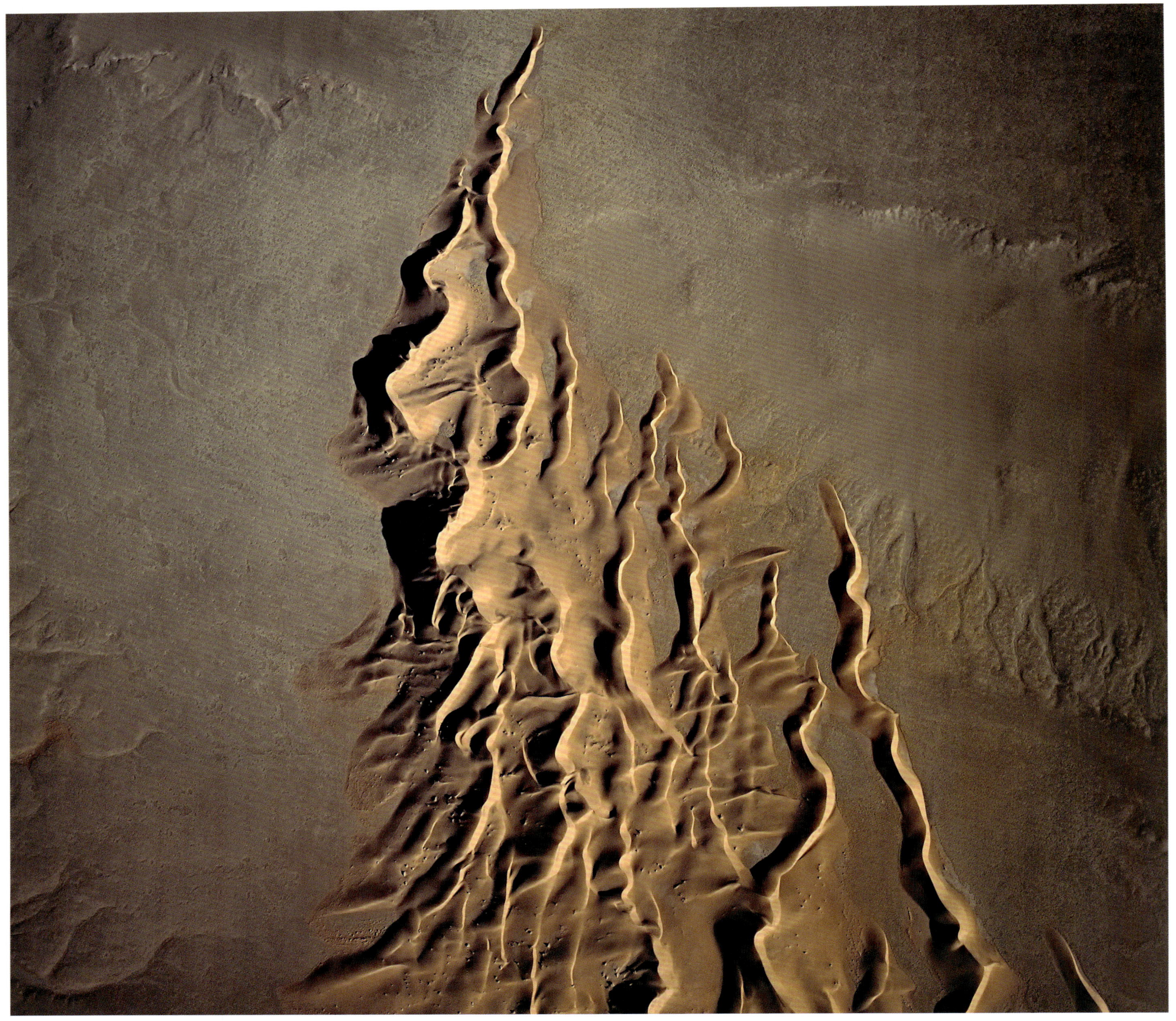

Driven by a desire to capture the natural world from the air, German photographer and geologist Bernhard Edmaier has dedicated the last 25 years to photographing the Earth's surface. He has travelled the world, from Hawaii to Namibia, Kenya, Russia and the United States, seeking out untouched places that are sometimes barely accessible. Hiring a plane locally, or getting a helicopter pilot to fly him where he wants to go, Edmaier has made it his life's mission to photograph naturally forming colours, patterns and structures in the landscape. As beautiful as they are informative, his images feature everything from bodies of water to volcanoes and lava, glaciers, rock formations and more. Most impressive of all, they reveal in startling detail what the areas of the world untouched by humankind really look like.

Bernhard Edmaier
Namib Desert, Namibia, 1997.

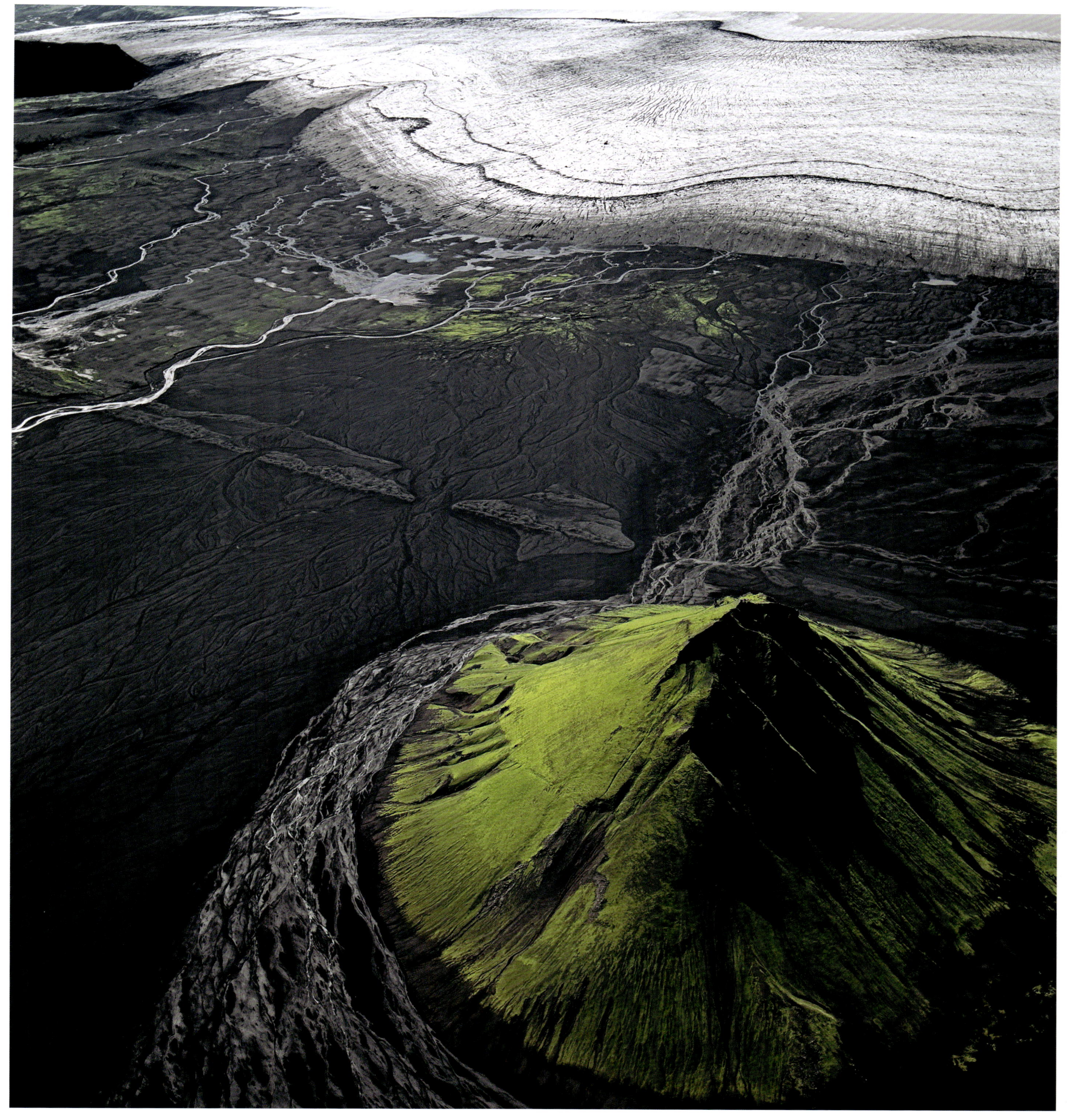

Bernhard Edmaier
Mælifell, Iceland, 2003.

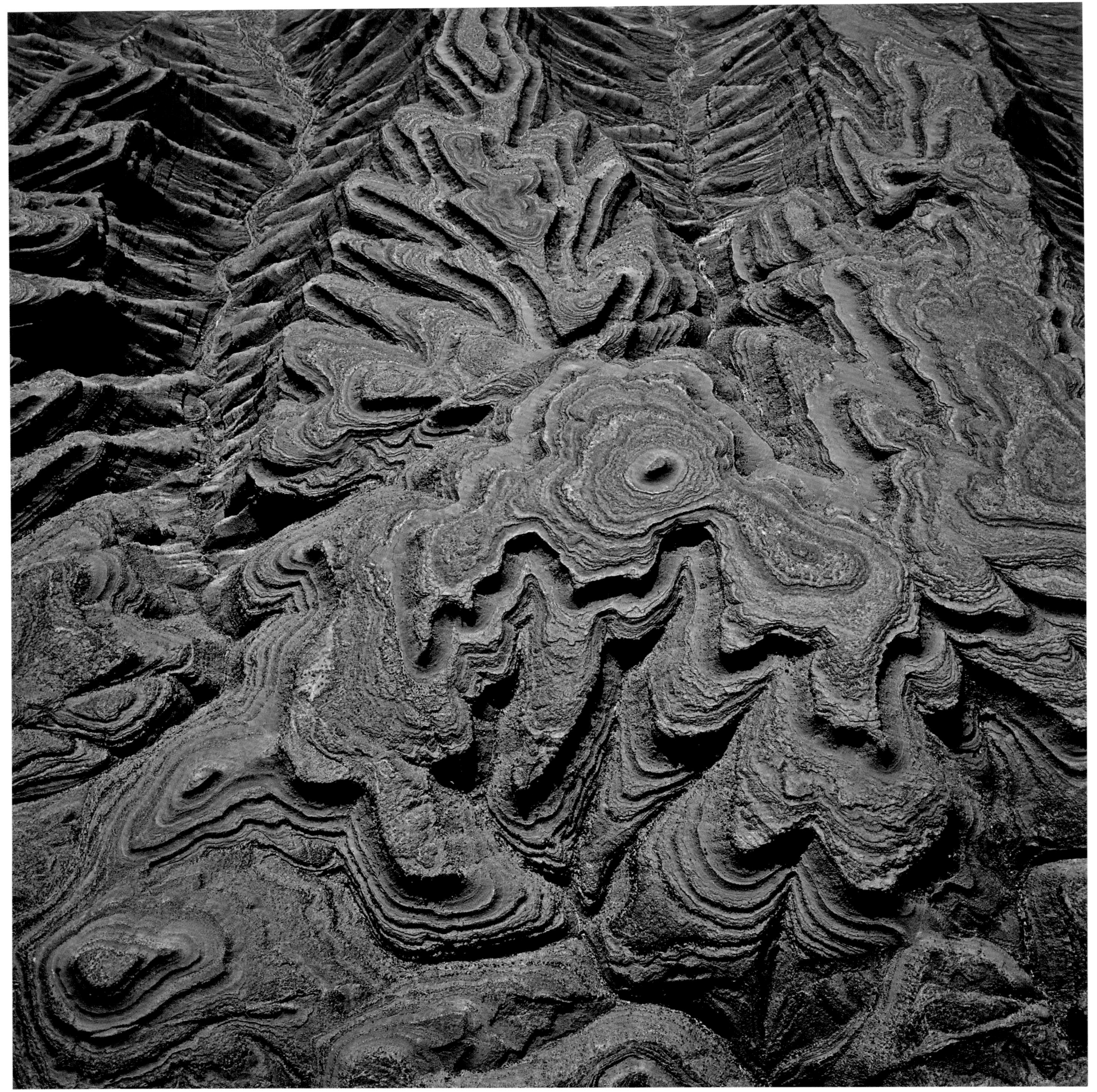

Bernhard Edmaier
Huns Mountains, Namibia,
1997.

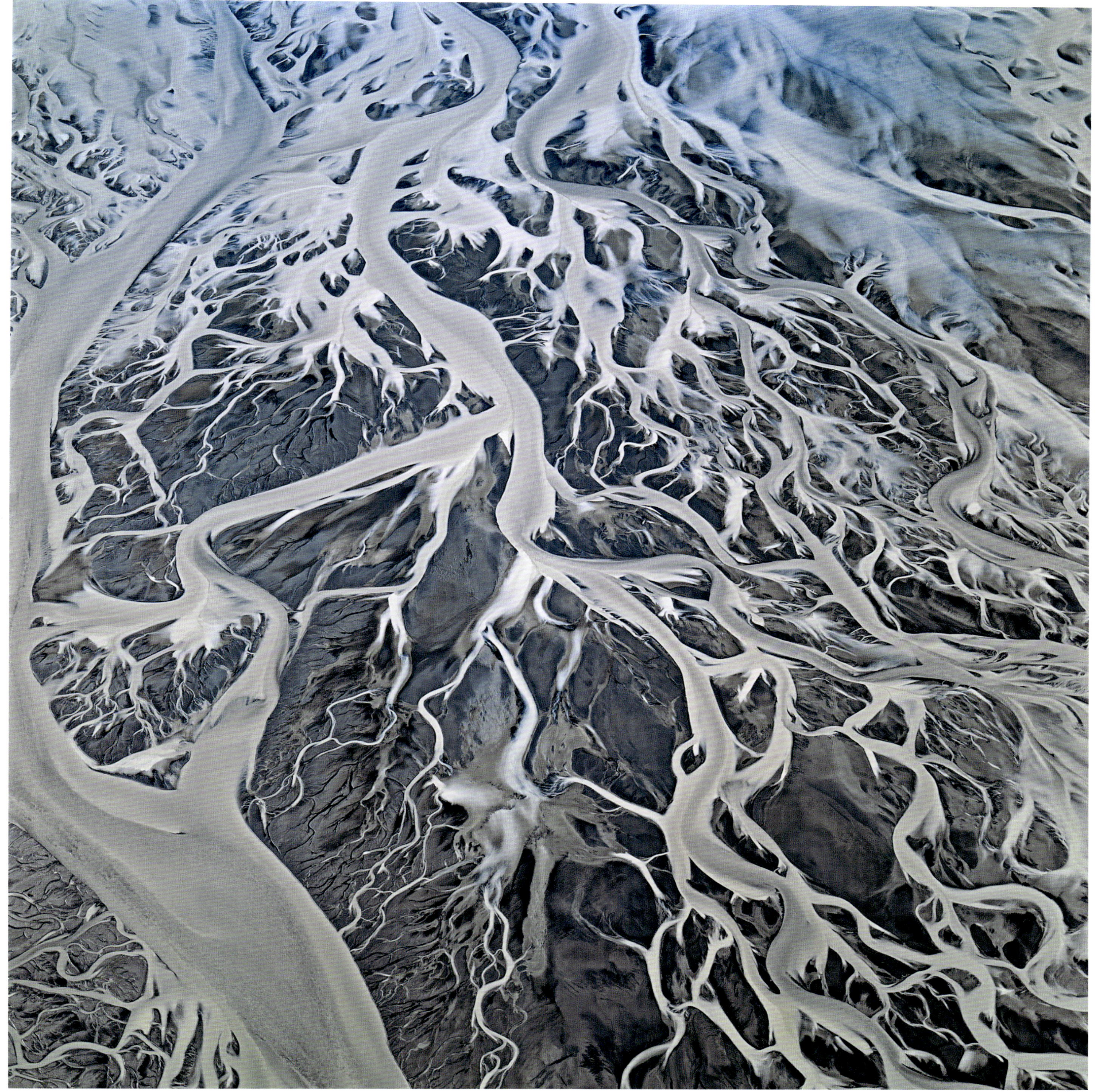

Bernhard Edmaier
Skeidararsandur, Iceland,
2003.

This image depicts the city of Brasília on 21 August 2001, during its dry season. It was created by scientific-software developer Jesse Allen, using Advanced Land Imager (ALI) technology on NASA's Earth Observing-1 (EO-1) satellite. The satellite was launched on 21 November 2000 as part of NASA's New Millennium Program, its principal goal being to facilitate and validate ALI technology, which was used to collect a range of data about the Earth, such as forest cover and crops. EO-1 was 'powered off' in March 2017 and is predicted to re-enter the Earth's atmosphere in 2056.

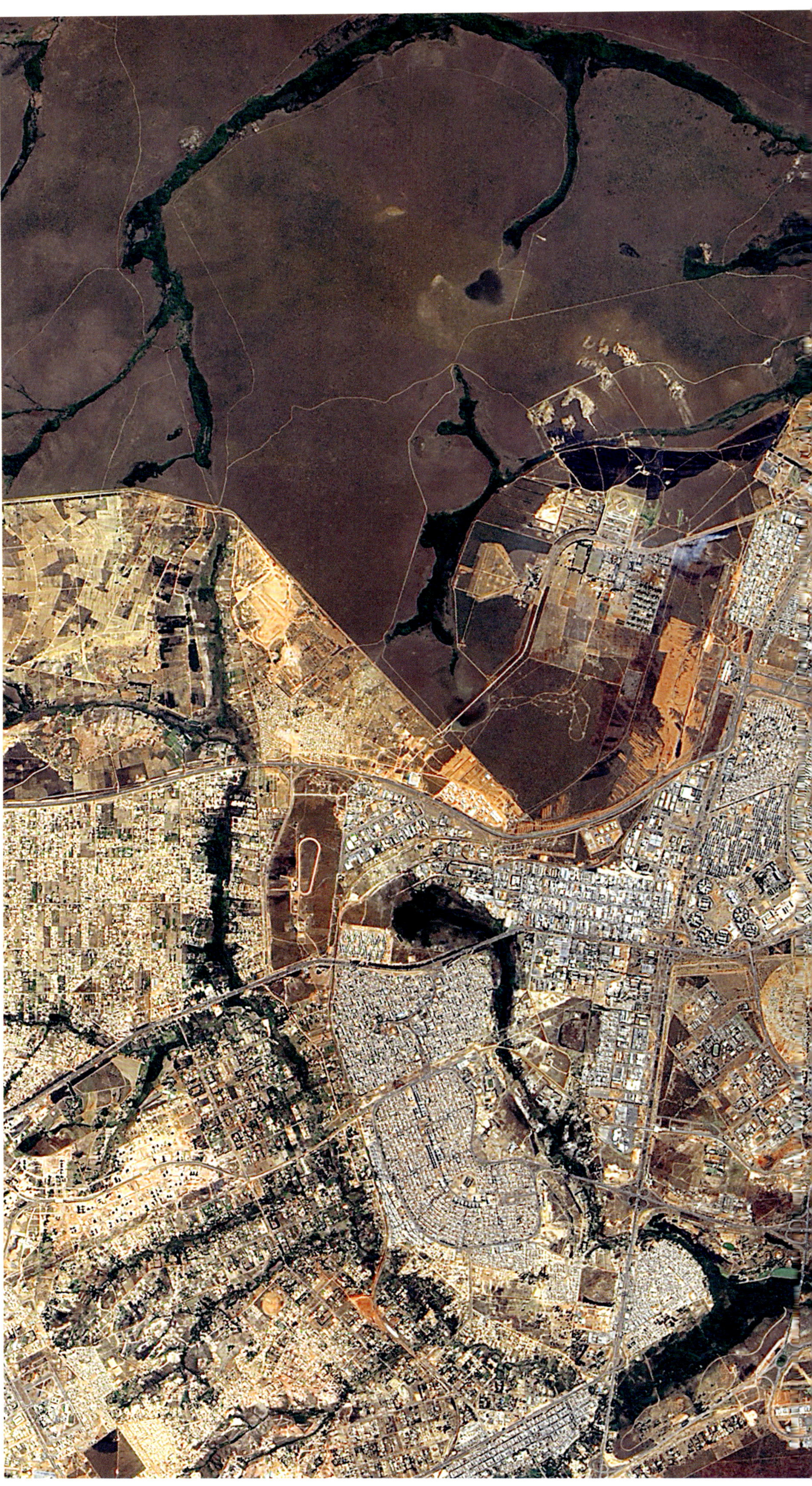

Jesse Allen
Brasília, Brazil, 2001.

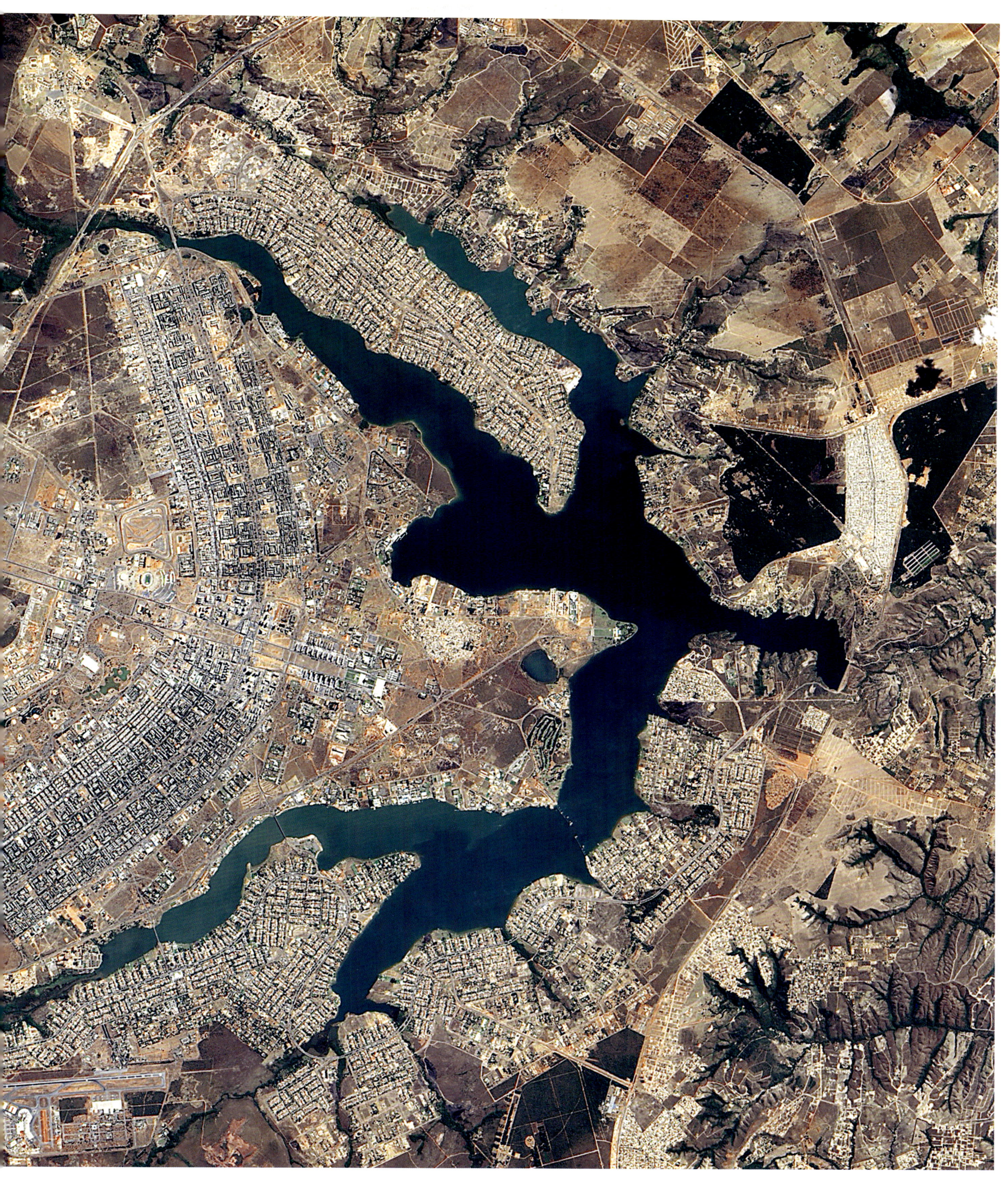

2001

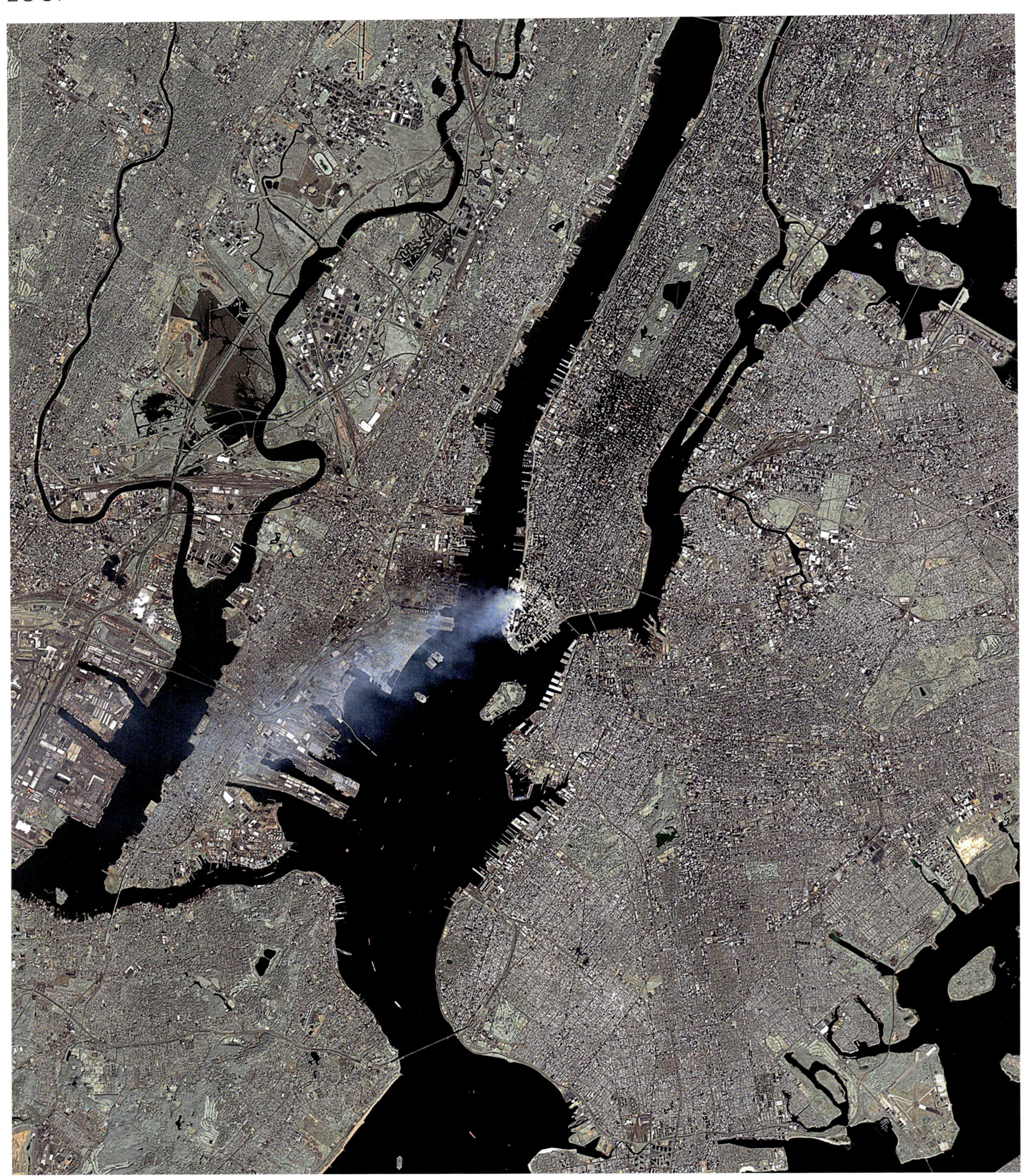

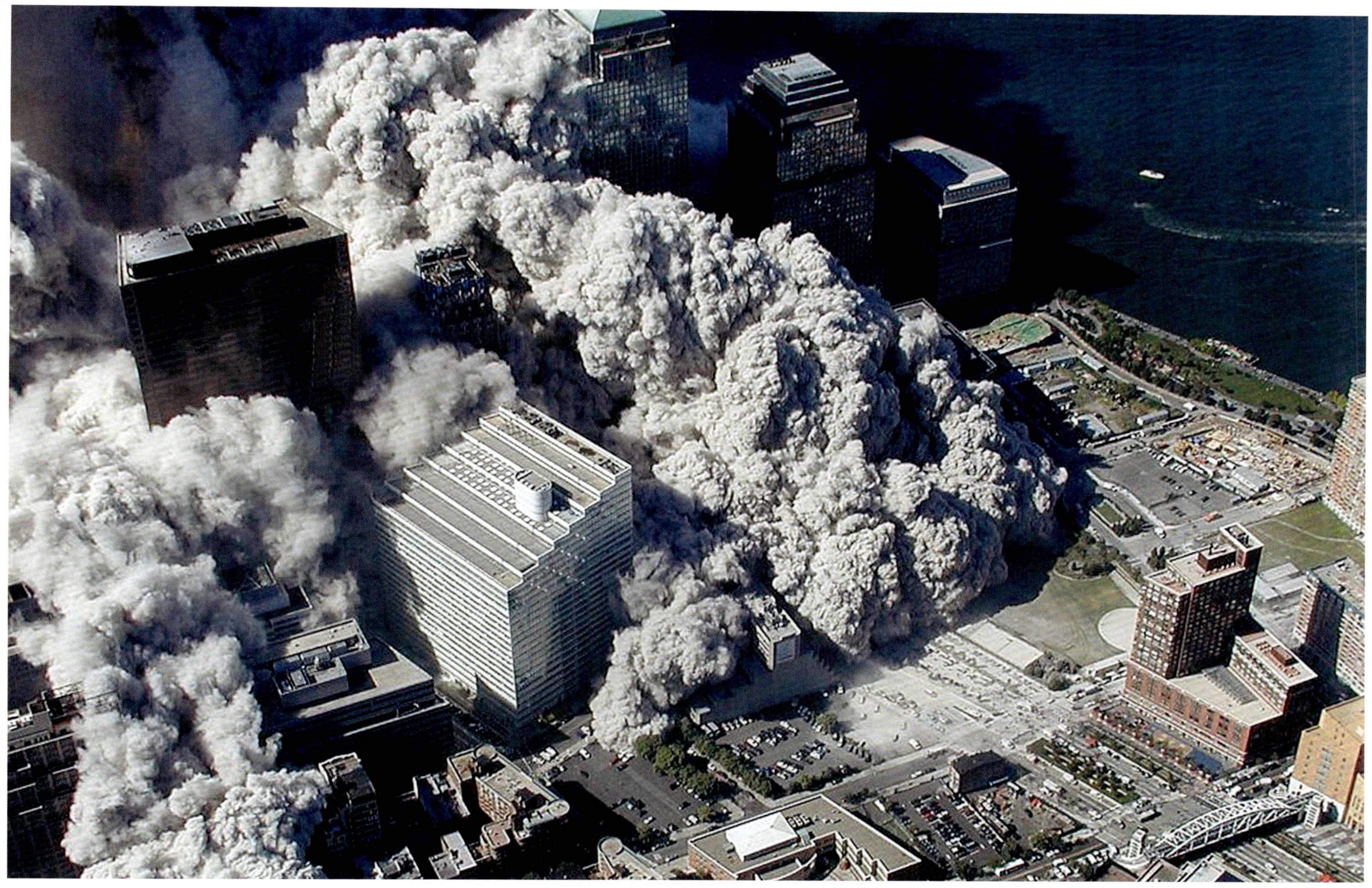

Opposite
NASA
Satellite image of the World Trade Center, New York, USA, 12 September 2001.

Above
New York Police Department
World Trade Center, New York, USA, 11 September 2001.

Overleaf
Photographer unknown
Remains of the World Trade Center, New York, USA, 19 September 2001.

On 11 September 2001, terrorists hijacked four aeroplanes, flying two into New York's Twin Towers and one into the Pentagon in Virginia. The fourth plane failed to reach its target and crashed in Pennsylvania. Almost 3,000 people were killed in the worst-ever terrorist attack on American soil. NASA's Landsat 7 satellite recorded the point of impact (pictured opposite). Many photographs of the aftermath exist, including a number that were taken from the air. In one image we see billowing smoke at Ground Zero (pictured above), while another, shot a few days after the attacks, when most of the smoke had cleared, reveals the extent of the devastation (pictured overleaf).

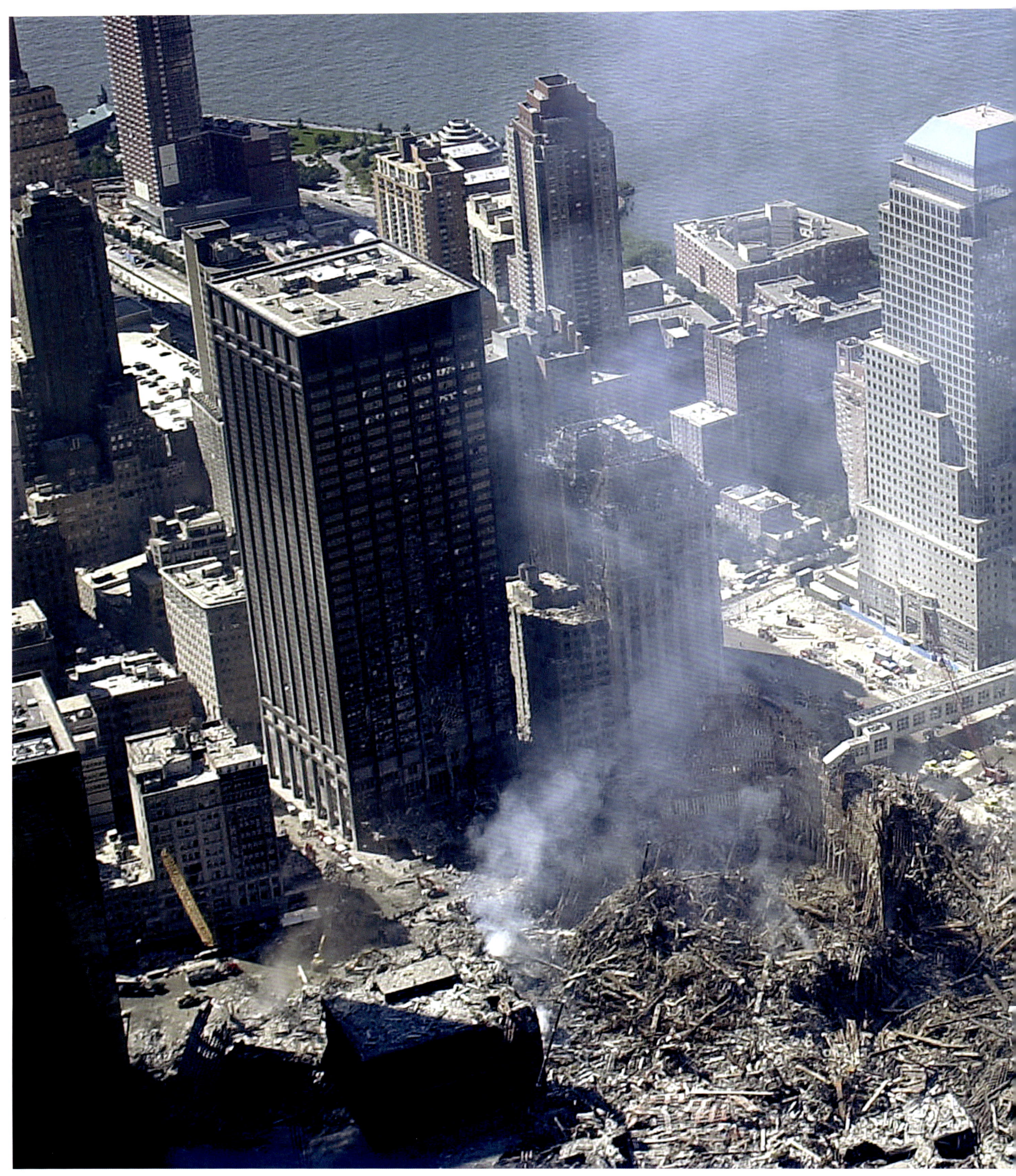

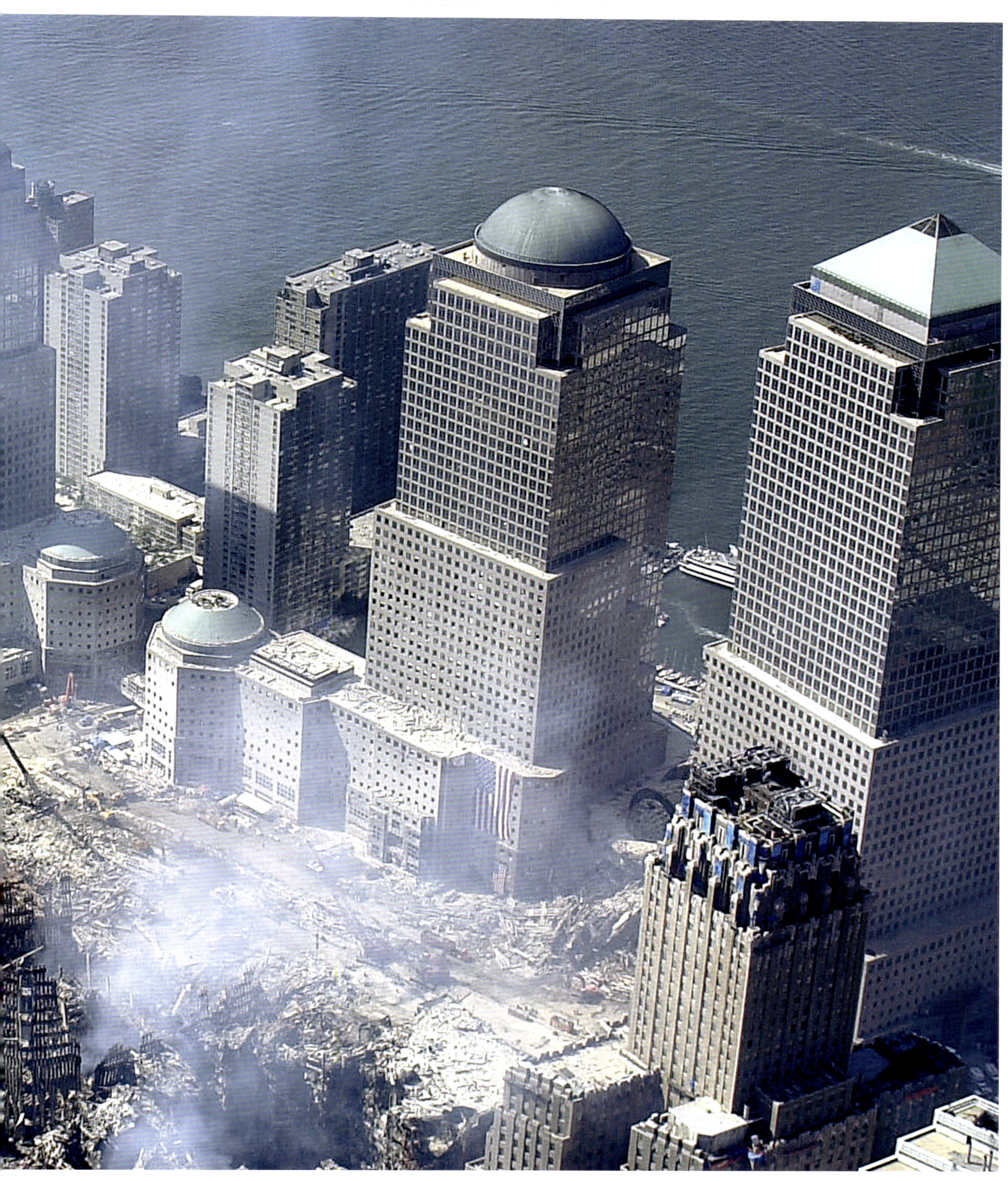

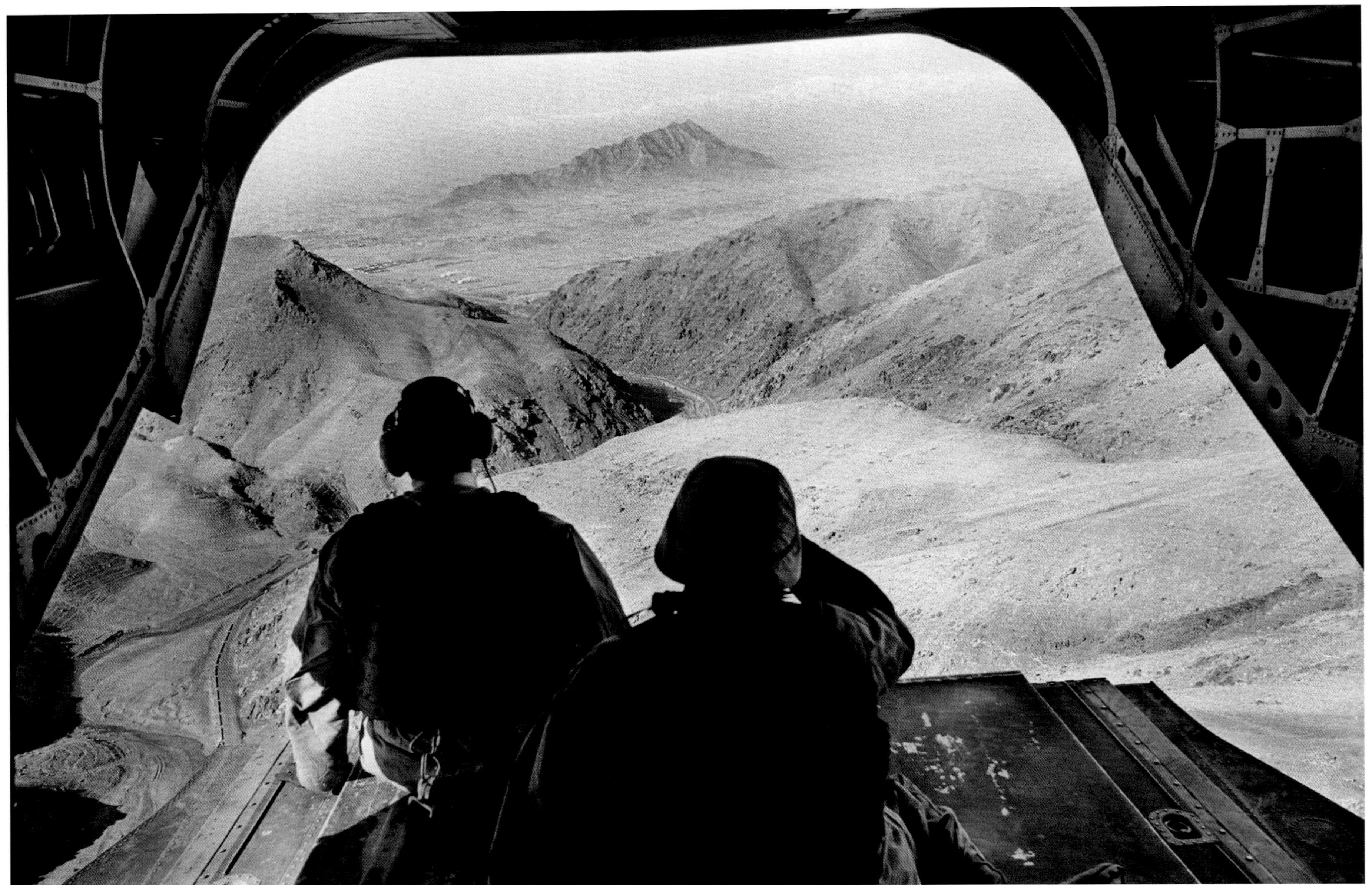

Irish photojournalist Seamus Murphy took this image while flying over the Kohi Safi District in Afghanistan's Parwan Province in 2002, a year after the fall of the Taliban regime in Kabul. Murphy had been travelling to Afghanistan since 1994, but this was the first time he'd been embedded with US forces. He spent a couple of days with the US 82nd Airborne Division, who were carrying out missions to find arms caches and gather intelligence on Taliban activities. He remembers: 'It was a joy to get into an aircraft and fly over the extraordinary landscape of Afghanistan with its high mountains, deep valleys and vast plains. The US personnel I flew with on this mission were overawed by Afghanistan, with its physical beauty and mysterious people.'

Seamus Murphy
Kohi Safi District, Afghanistan, 2002.

To create his distinctive, if disorientating, photographs, shot from the sky, Olivo Barbieri, who was born and is based in Italy, uses a large-format camera with a tilt-shift lens. Shooting from a helicopter, Barbieri homes in on the hustle and bustle of everyday life in some of the world's most famous cities, including Rome, Las Vegas, New York and Shanghai. His series 'Site Specific', which he began in 2003, offers a startling view of these well-known places, where people look like ants and the streets and buildings are model-like. Nature – in particular waterfalls and mountains – is also the subject of his playful gaze.

Olivo Barbieri
site specific_ROMA 04, Italy, from the series 'Site Specific', 2003.

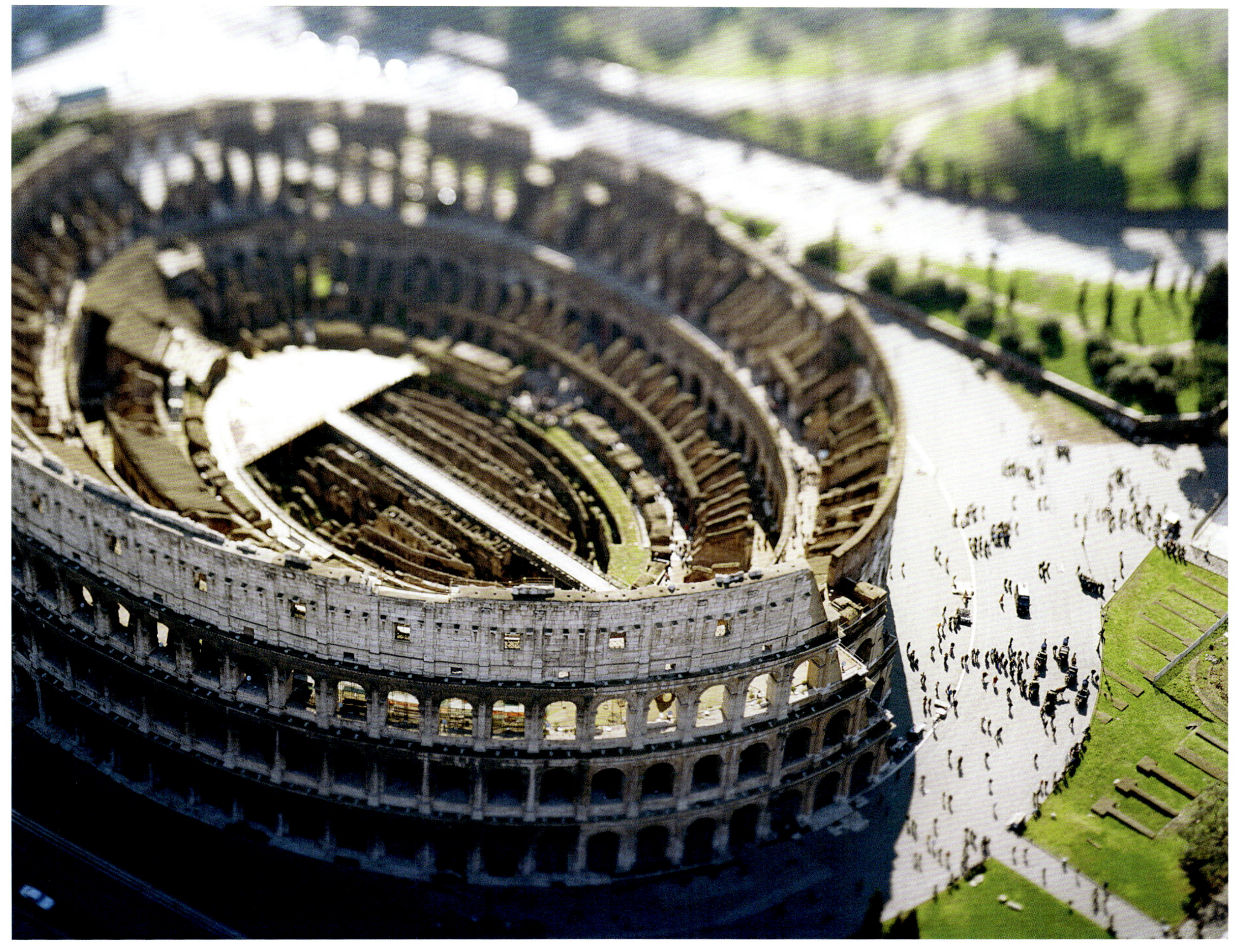

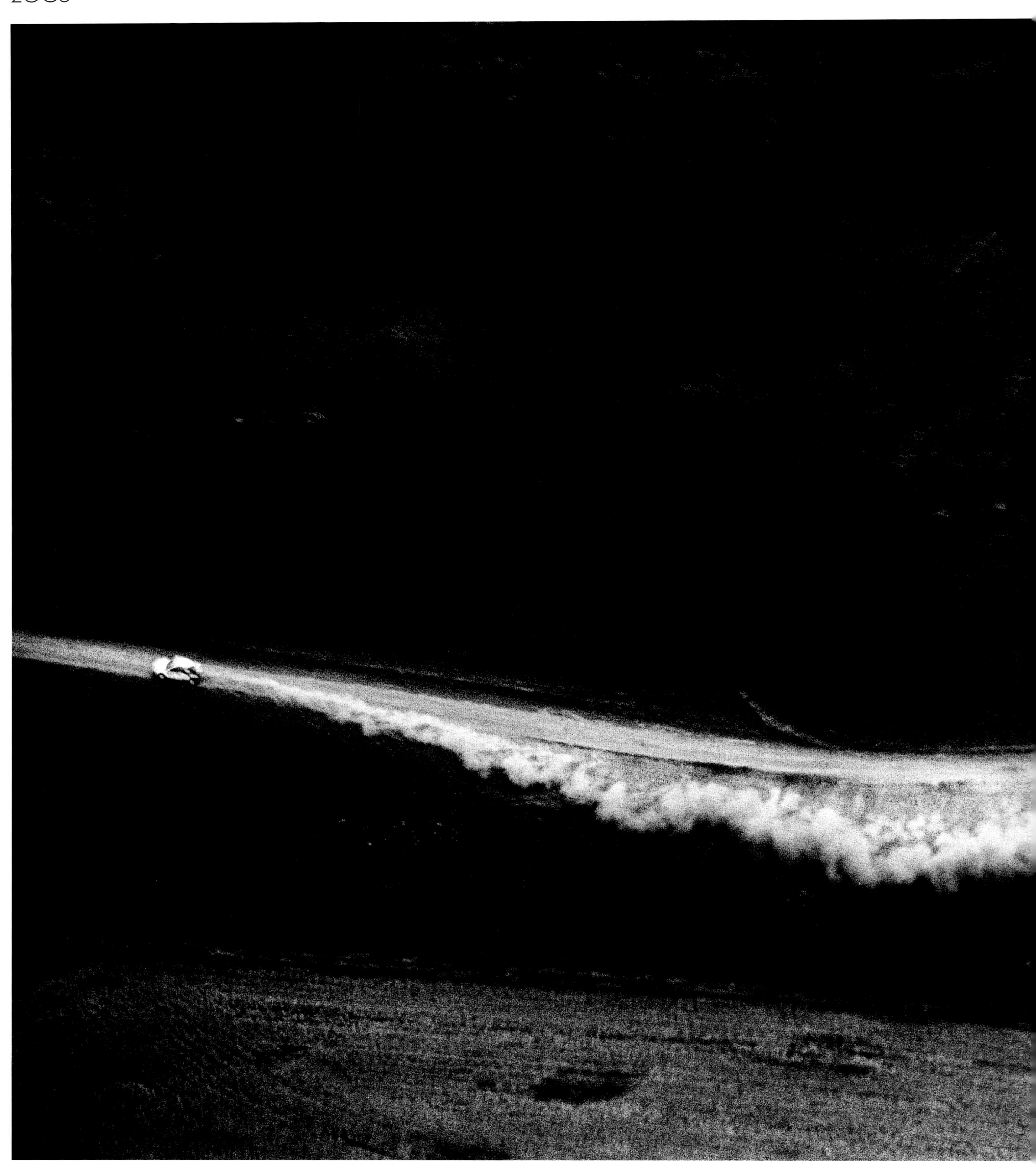

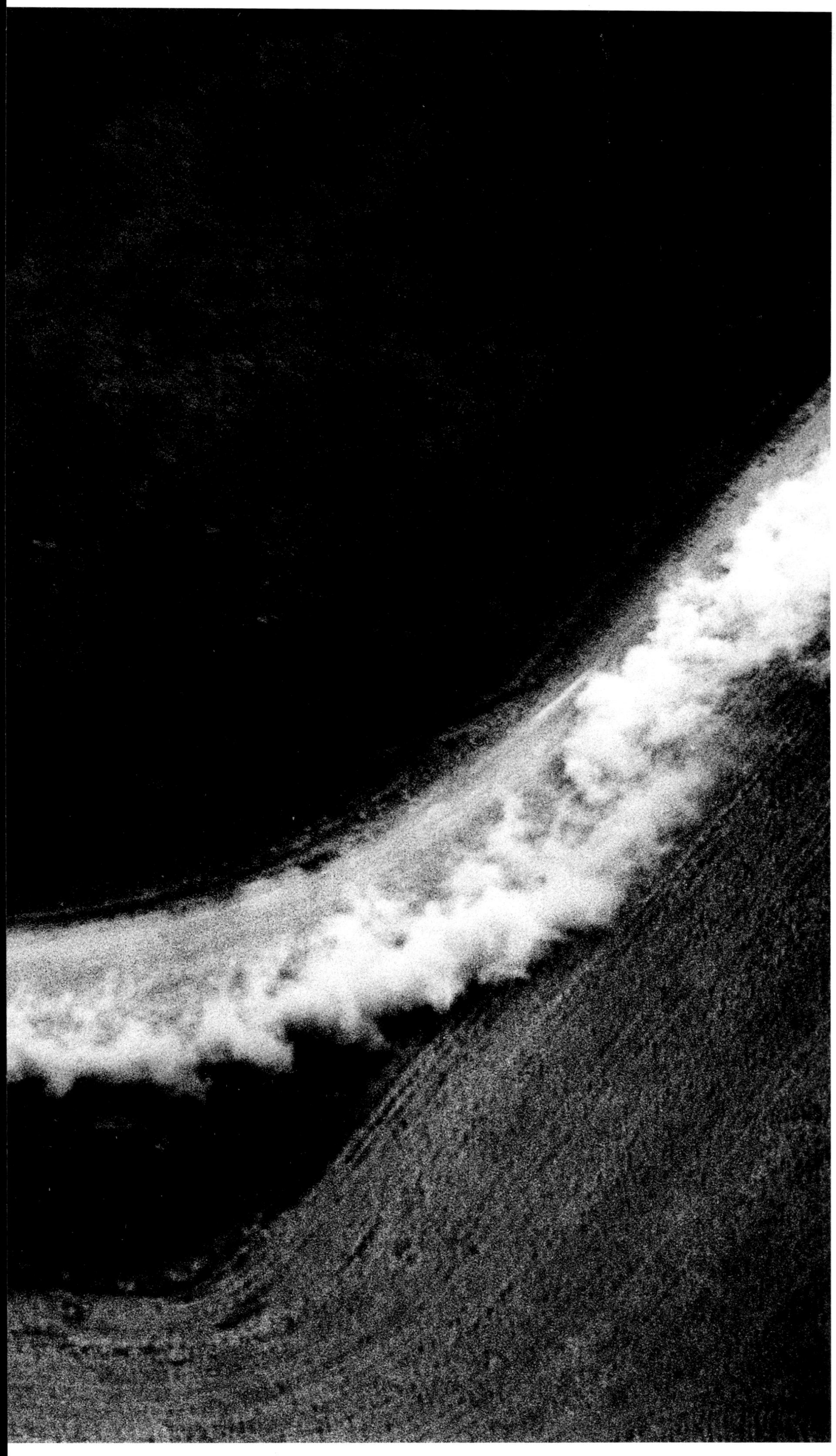

Australian photographer Trent Parke was covering the World Rally Championship in Western Australia when he took this dramatic shot. He remembers the spectacular sight of the dust coming off the cars, and recalls thinking how much more dramatic it would be if he could photograph the scene from the air. Fortunately, a small helicopter was carrying out flights for spectators and Parke seized his chance. The curved viewing glass made it difficult to get shots that were in focus, but one image – this one – came out perfectly 'and just so happened to be one of the best moments on the roll'.

Trent Parke
World Rally Championships, Muresk, Western Australia, 2003.

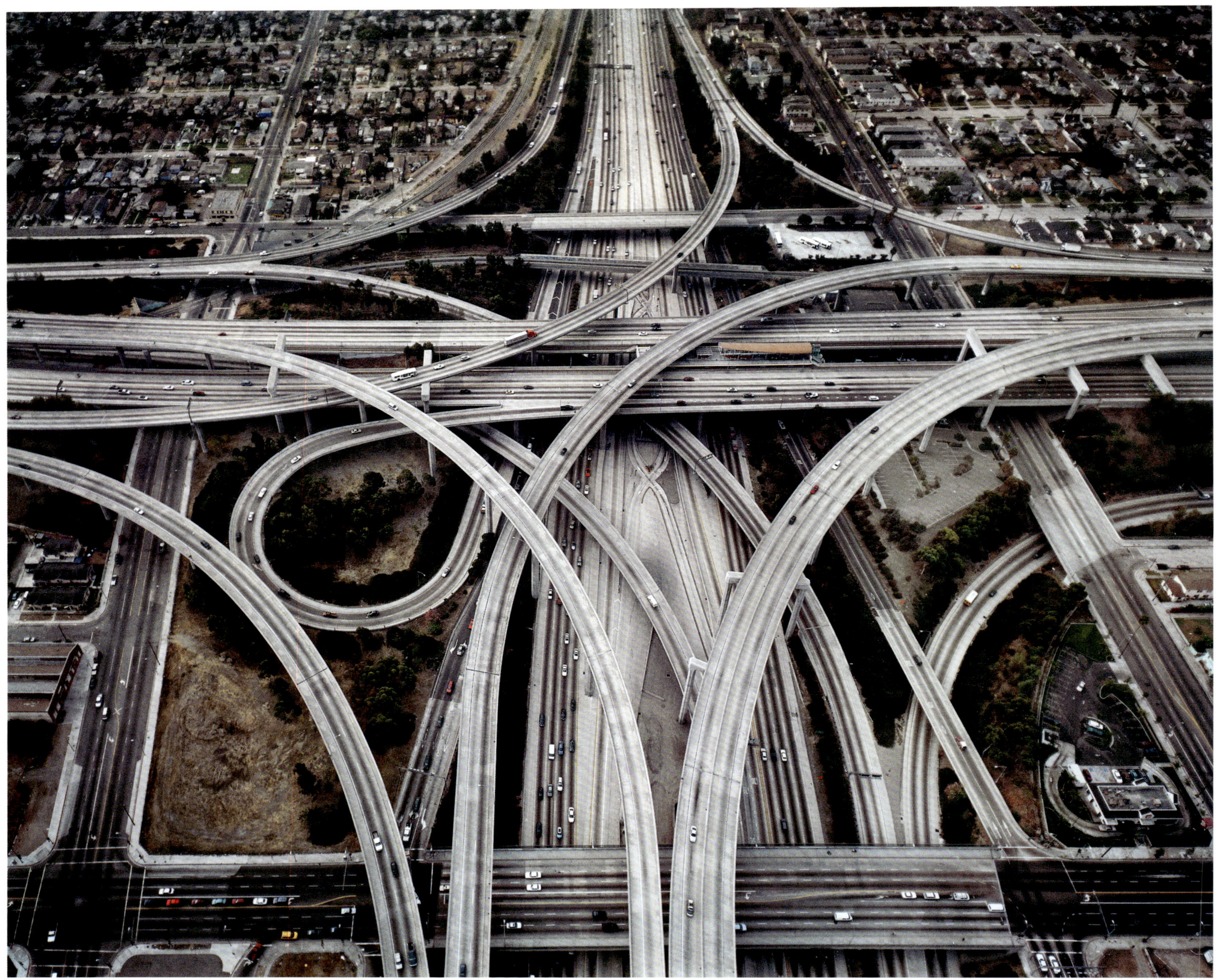

Detecting and photographing the traces of human impact on the environment has become Edward Burtynsky's life's work. Everything from oil fields to open-cast mines, reservoirs and, more recently, salt pans in northern India, feature in the Canadian's beautiful, if disturbing, aerial photographs. His subject matter is the world's industrial landscapes – those transformed by human activity – and he has produced bodies of work that take a questioning look at many of our key industries, among them mining, quarrying and the oil industry. Burtynsky's arsenal for capturing these views from the air now includes GPS technology and cameras mounted on drones, but he made his name creating large-format photographs from planes.

Edward Burtynsky
Highway #1, Intersection 105 & 110, Los Angeles, California, USA, 2003.

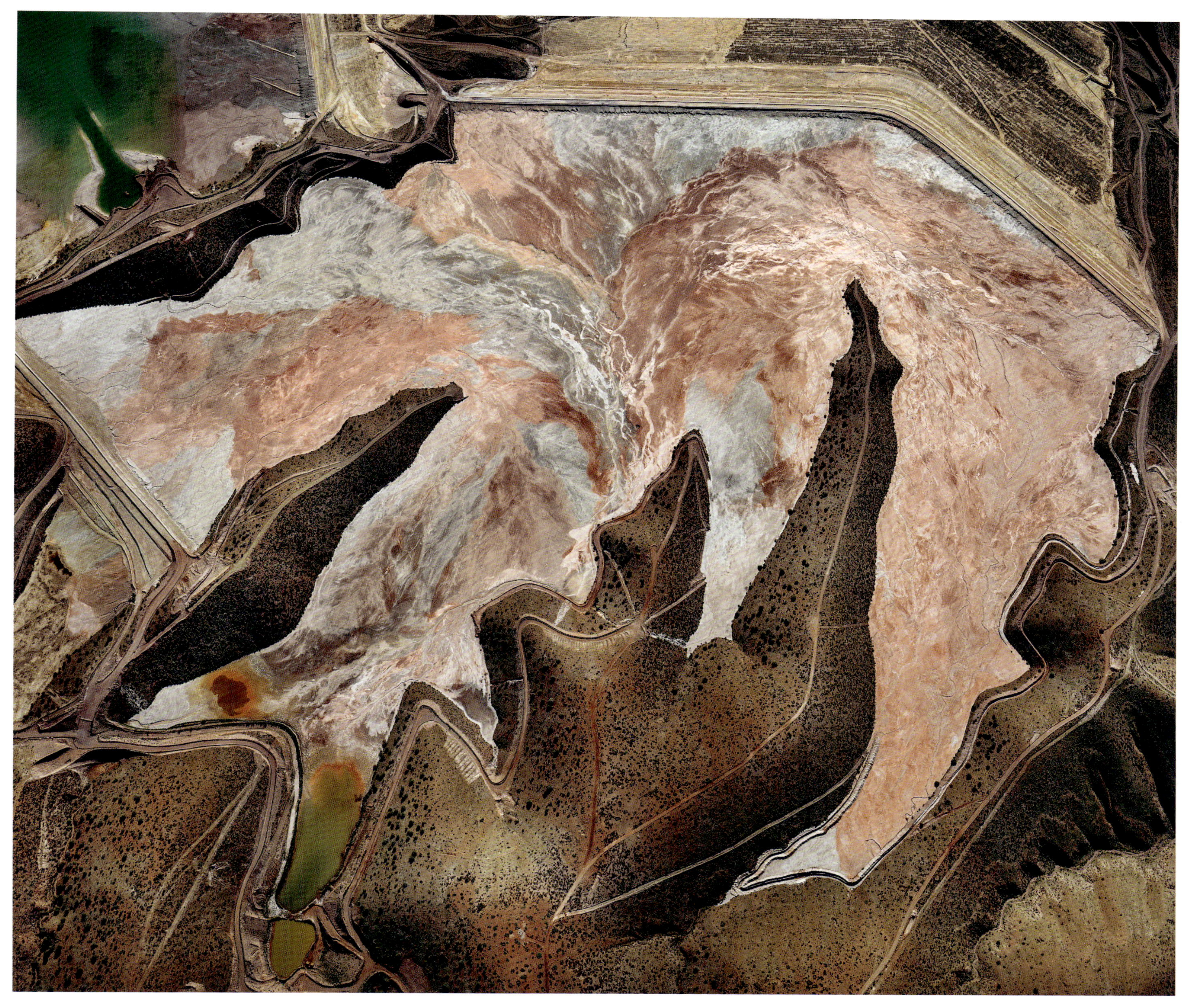

Edward Burtynsky
Morenci Mine #1, Clifton, Arizona, USA, 2012.

Edward Burtynsky
Salinas #2, Cadiz, Spain,
2013.

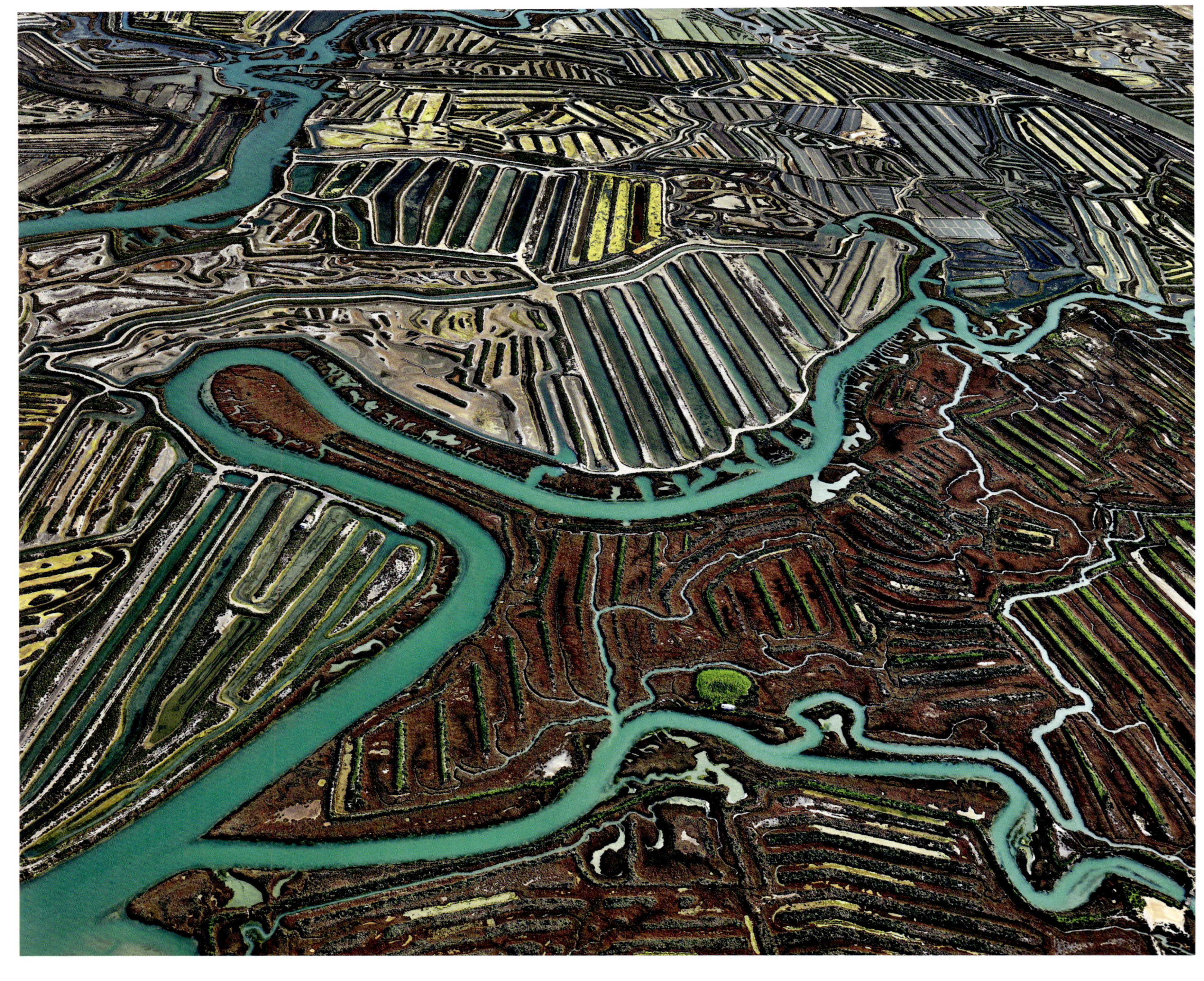

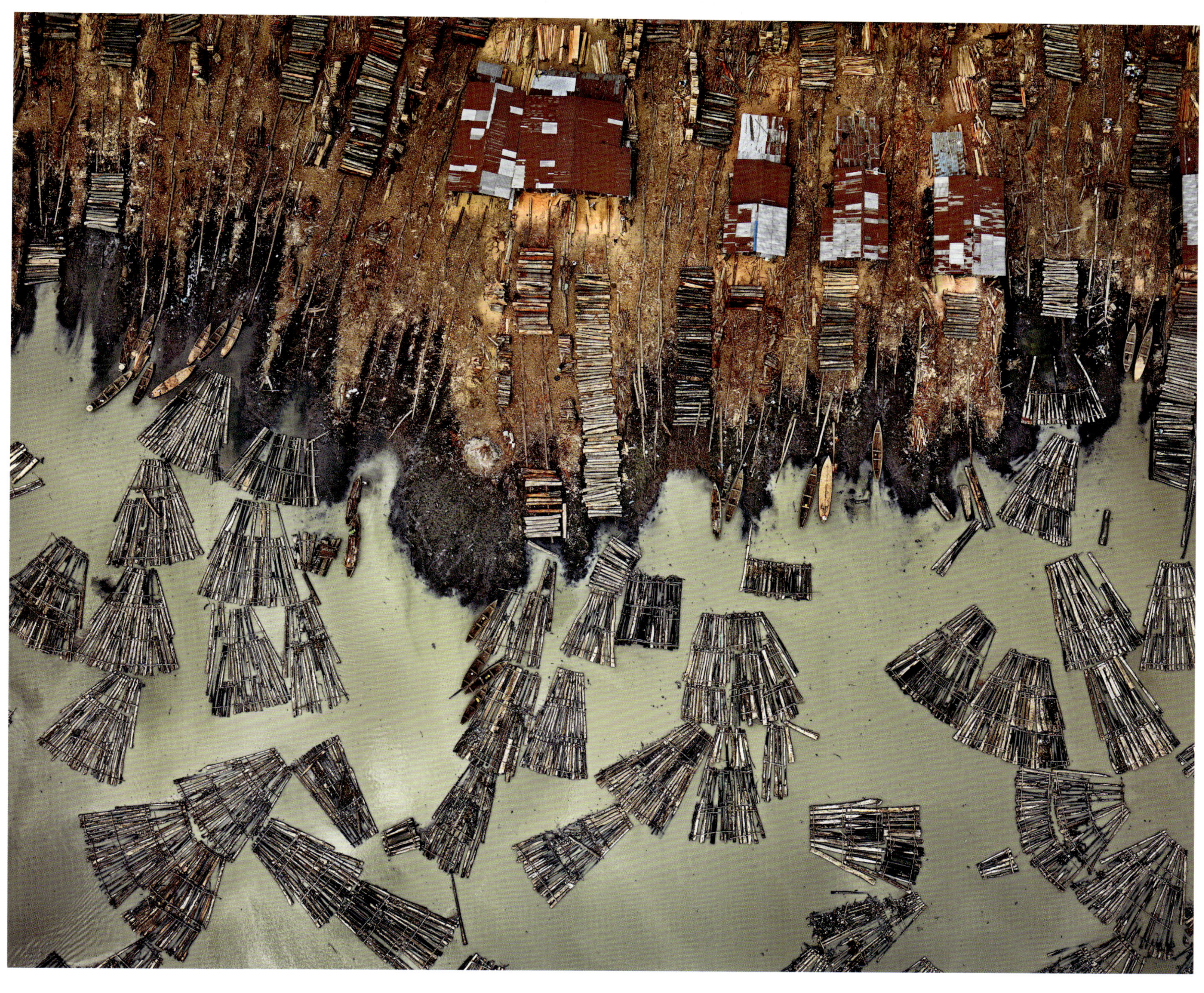

Edward Burtynsky
Saw Mills #1, Lagos, Nigeria, 2016.

Describing himself as a 'photographer who flies, not a pilot who take pictures', George Steinmetz has photographed all over the world – across deserts, valleys, farmland and plains – from a motorized paraglider. The aircraft allows an unrestricted 180-degree view horizontally and vertically, explains the American, who can fly as high as 1,800 metres, but says he prefers to be between 30 and 150 metres off the ground as it enables him to take more intimate views of the landscape below. Using one camera body and a couple of (usually zoom) lenses, Steinmetz can be in the air for two to three hours at a time, and tends to fly early in the morning or late afternoon, when the light is best.

In June 2013, Steinmetz was arrested and briefly detained by authorities in Kansas while shooting aerial photographs for *National Geographic* magazine. He was working on a story about the growing demand for food worldwide and had been making pictures of cropland and cattle feedlots from the air. Steinmetz and an assistant were to be prosecuted on criminal trespassing charges, but the case was dismissed.

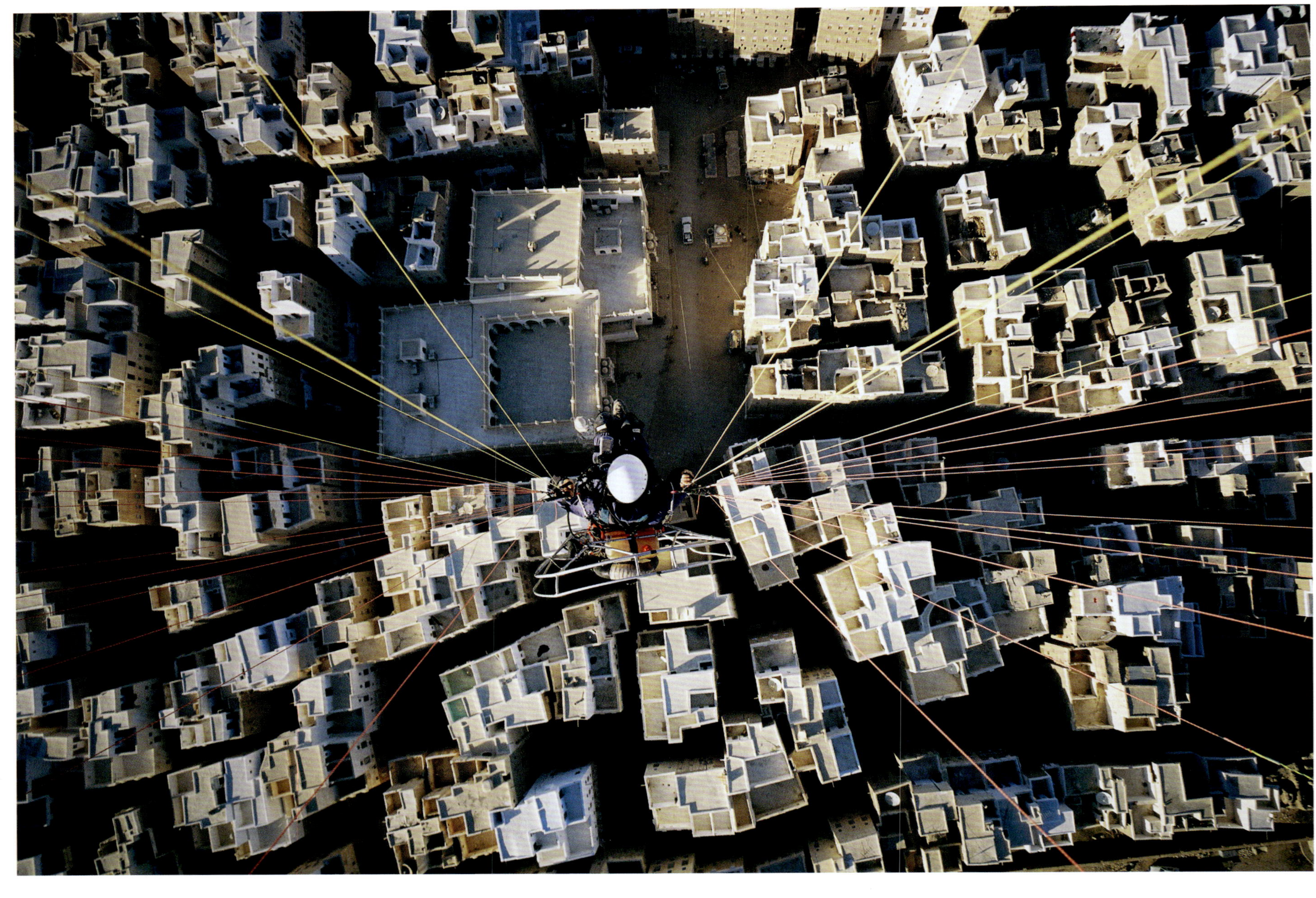

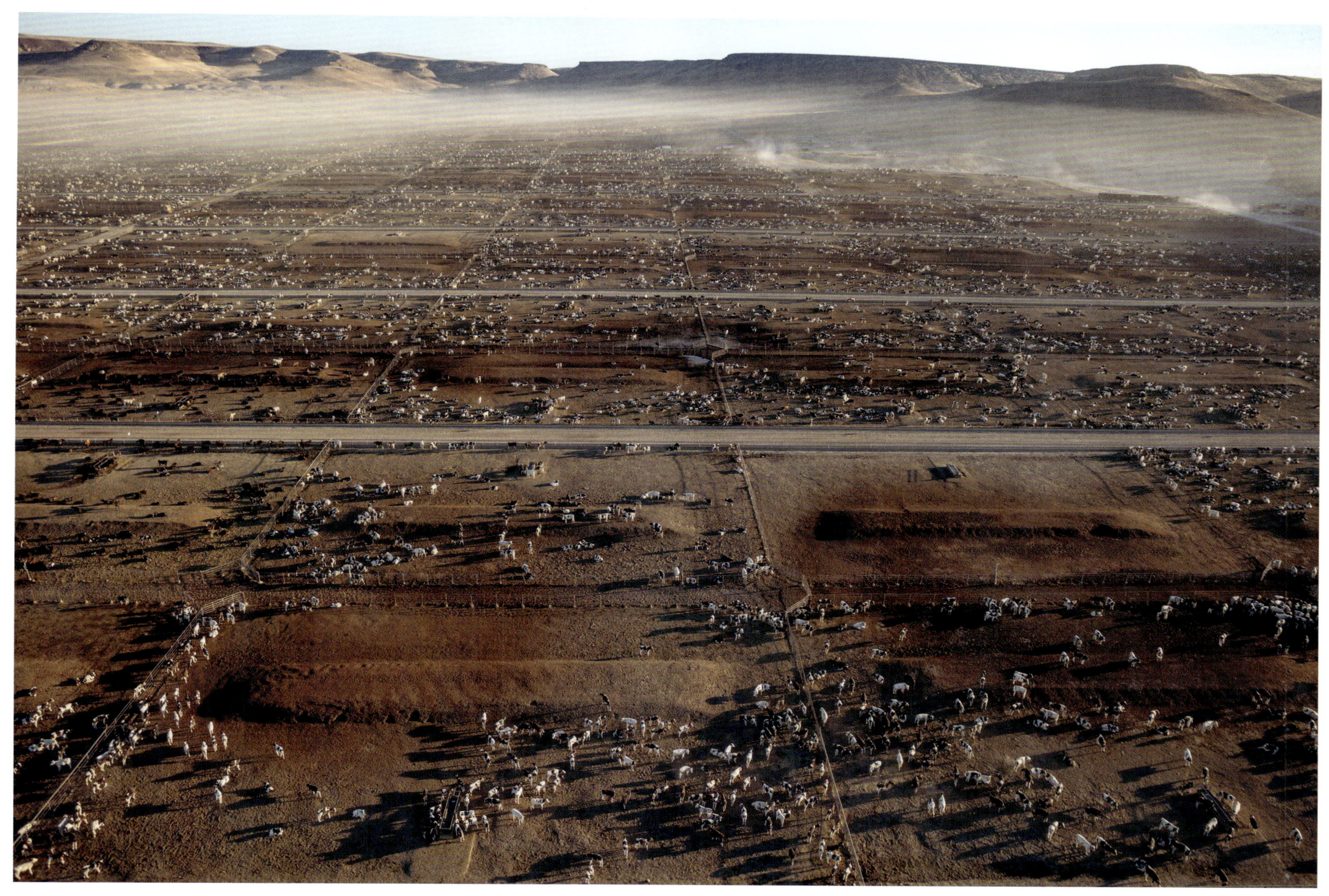

Opposite
George Steinmetz
The photographer piloting a motorized paraglider over Shibam, Yemen, 2004.

Above
George Steinmetz
Cattle feedlot, Idaho, USA, 2016.

Overleaf
George Steinmetz
Beni Isguen, Ghardaïa, Algeria, 2009.

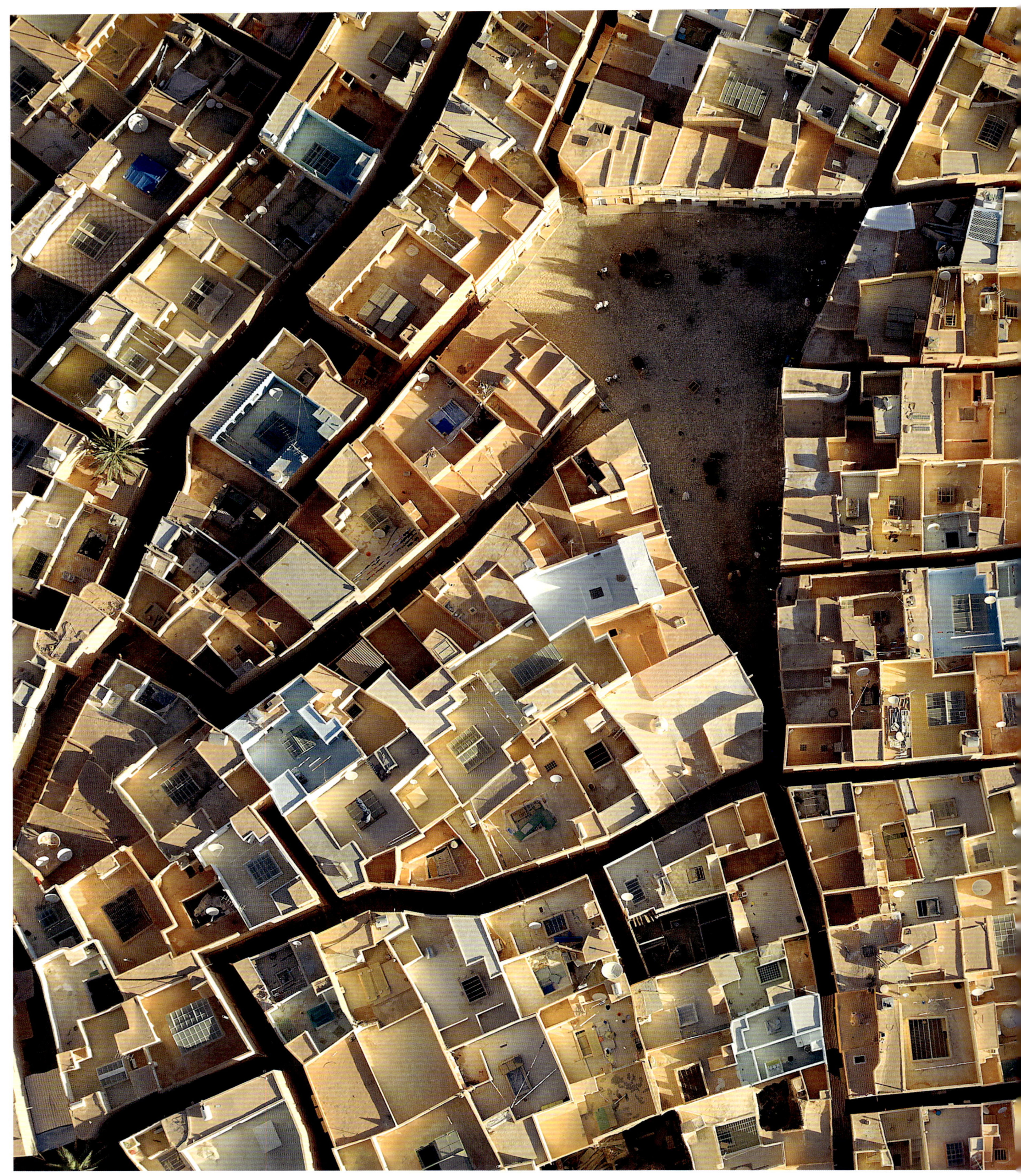

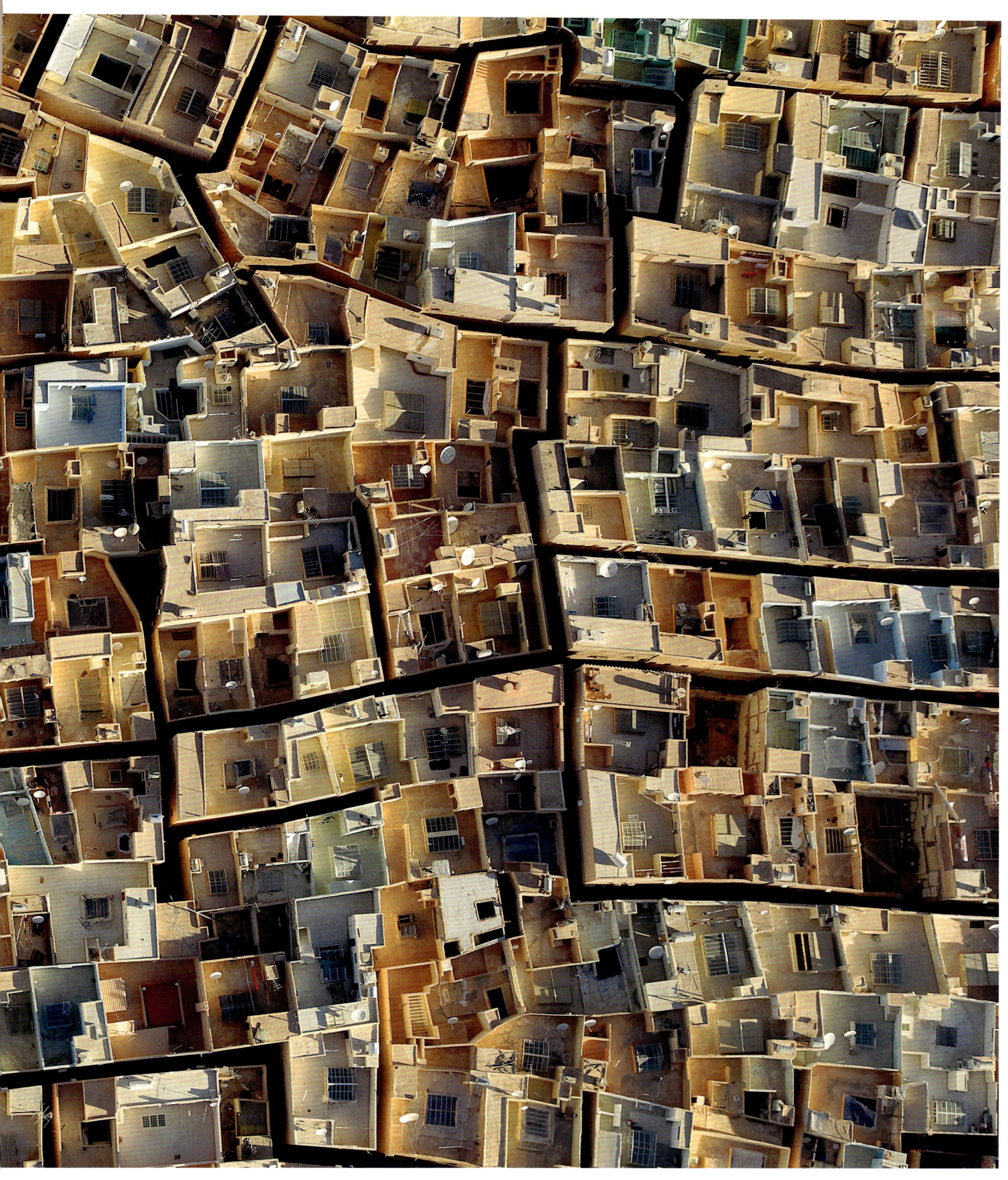

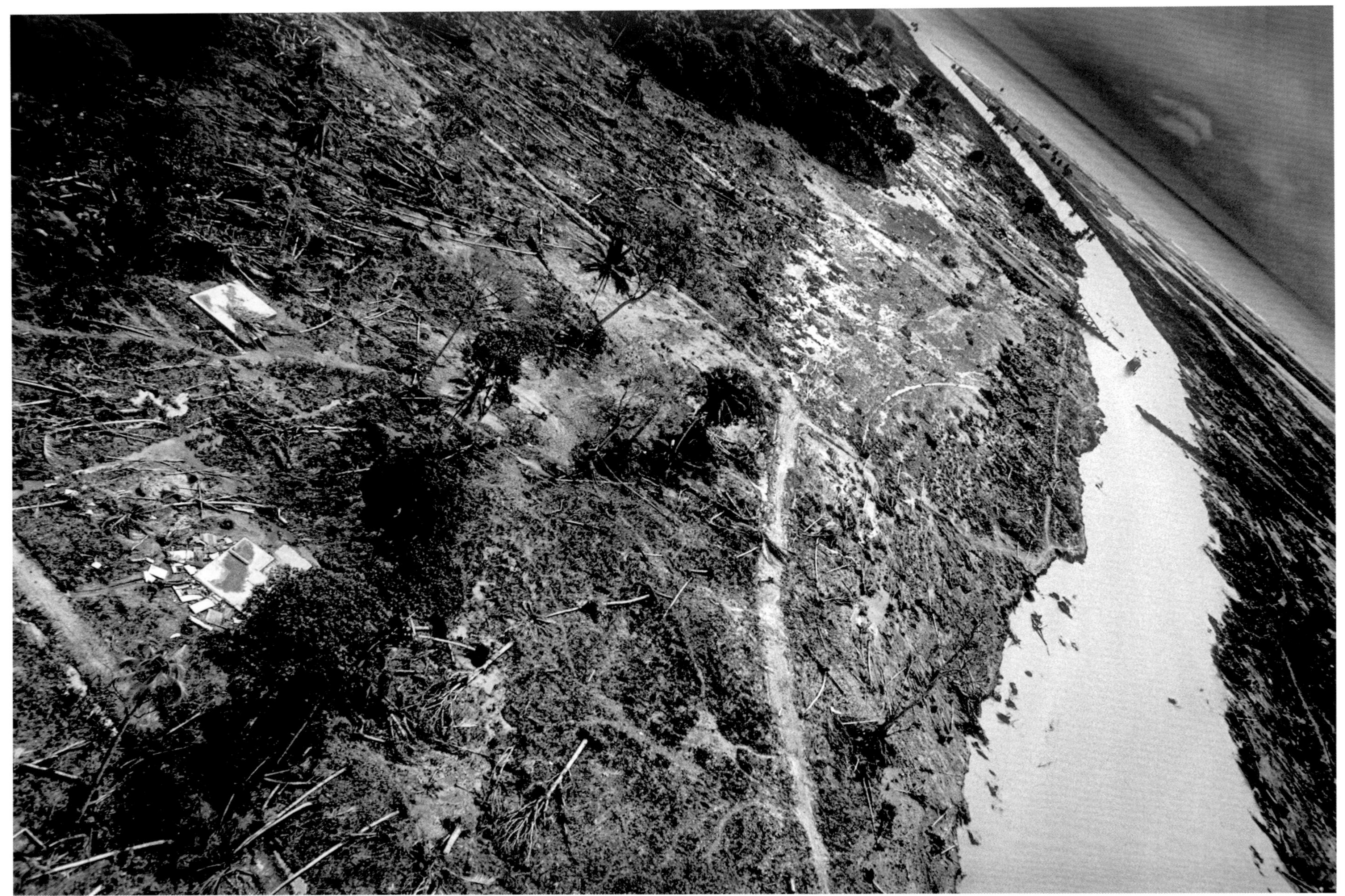

Paolo Pellegrin
After the tsunami, Banda Aceh, Sumatra, Indonesia, 2005.

When Italian photojournalist Paolo Pellegrin covered the aftermath of the Boxing Day 2004 Indian Ocean earthquake and tsunami, he created a body of work that points, with brutal and unflinching honesty, towards the true horror and sheer scale of the disaster that claimed the lives of around 230,000 people across 14 countries. Focusing on the Indonesian island of Sumatra, which was the most badly affected location, Pellegrin photographed everything from bodies in mass graves to washed-up photo albums. He also made aerial photographs like this one, which offers a glimpse of the post-apocalyptic reality into which so many people were thrust.

Jeff Williams
Cleveland Volcano,
Alaska, USA, 2006.

Jeff Williams, flight engineer with the International Space Station (ISS) Expedition 13, took this image of Cleveland Volcano on 23 May 2006, shortly after a plume of ash was sighted. The volcano is located on the western side of uninhabited Chuginadak Island in the Aleutian archipelago and is one of the region's most active. To capture this 'astronaut photograph', Williams used a Kodak 760C digital camera with an 800mm lens. It was created with support from the ISS Program, which helps astronauts take pictures of the Earth that can then be used by scientists for research purposes. Images are free to view at Gateway to Astronaut Photography of Earth.

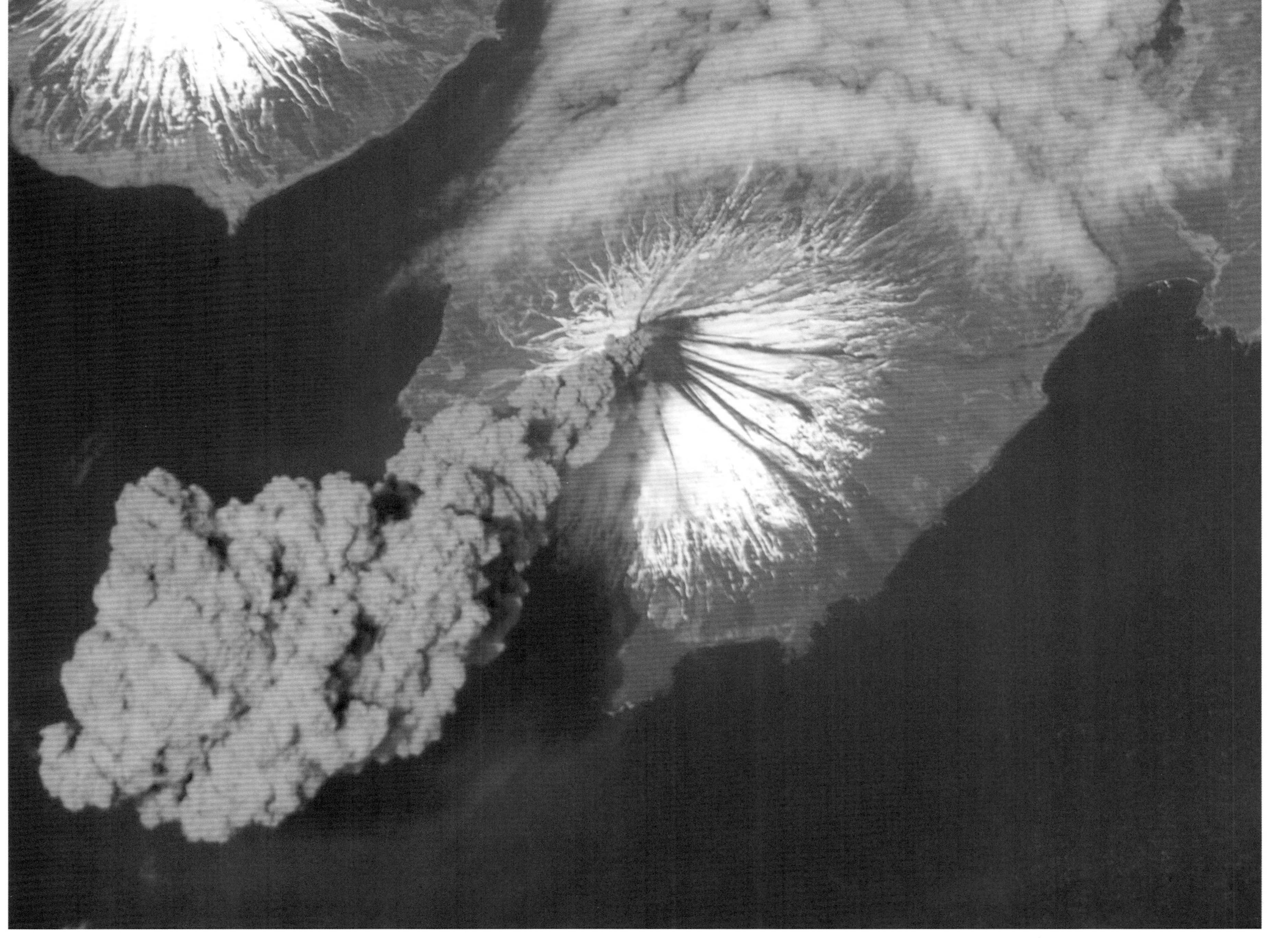

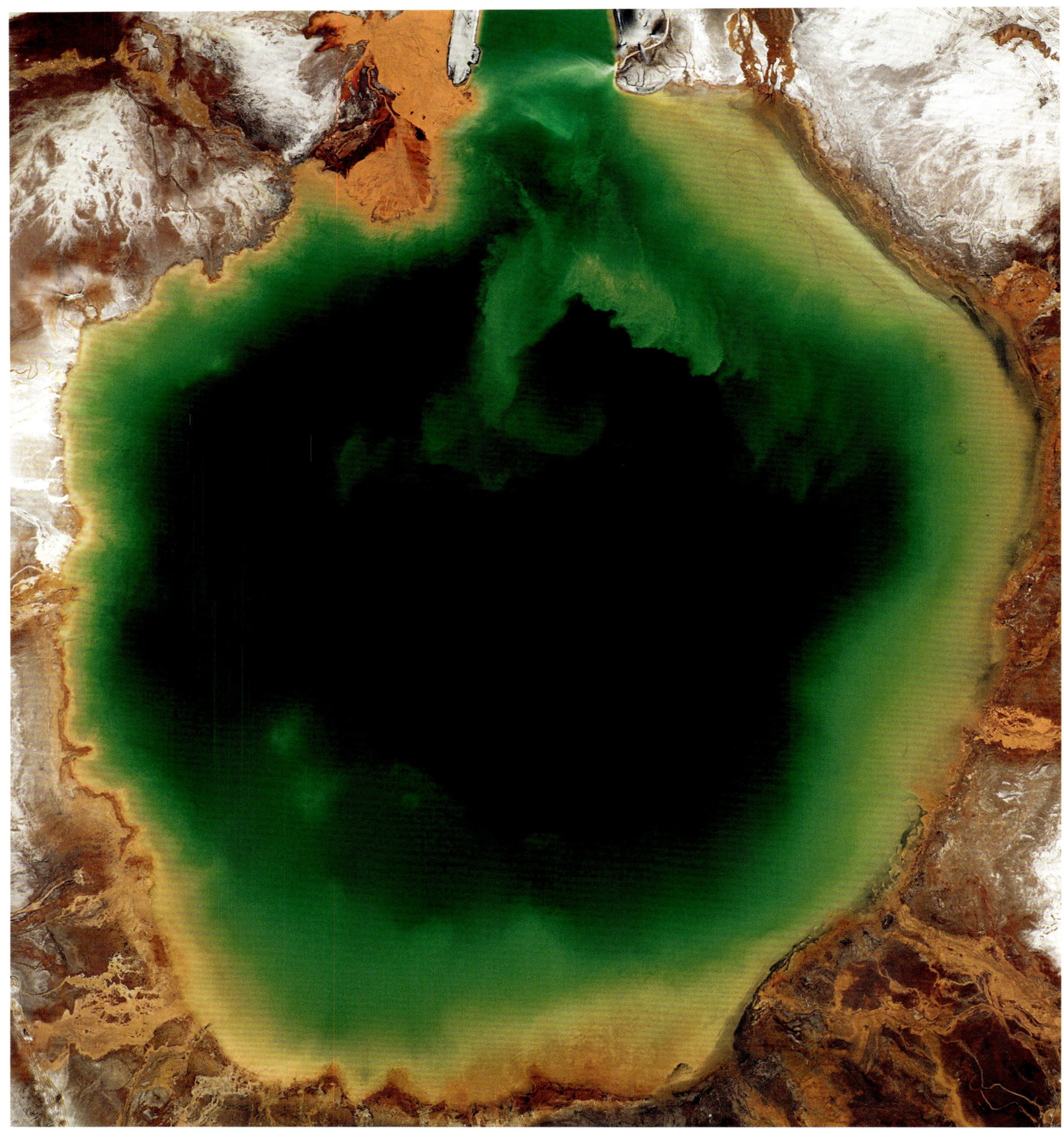

For more than 30 years, American artist David Maisel has been making aerial photographs of human-altered landscapes, cataloguing his finds in (sometimes interconnected) series that explore our complex and multi-faceted relationship with nature. Much of his work has been focused on the extraction of natural resources and its consequences – in particular, open-pit mining across the United States, a theme that runs through Maisel's series 'Black Maps', 'The Mining Project' and 'American Mine', which are shot from the air. On one level, his images are visual records of the destruction to the planet caused by people, and on another, they serve as abstract and almost surreal, or hyper-real, meditations on the environmental sublime.

David Maisel
Carlin, Nevada 1, USA, from the series 'American Mine', 2007.

If there is one thing photographers who have photographed from the air have in common it is a fascination with the way the Earth looks from above – the patterns and shapes that become apparent, appearing as if from nowhere. In recent years, it has often been the loud and colourful compositions that are the most talked about and shared, especially on Instagram, so the minimalism of an image like Ferdinando Scianna's aerial photograph shot over northern Italy's Po Plain is a breath of fresh air. The perfectly positioned lone tree simply but powerfully brings together all the elements of the picture, proving that when it comes to aerial photography, less really can be more.

Ferdinando Scianna
River Po Plain, Italy, 2008.

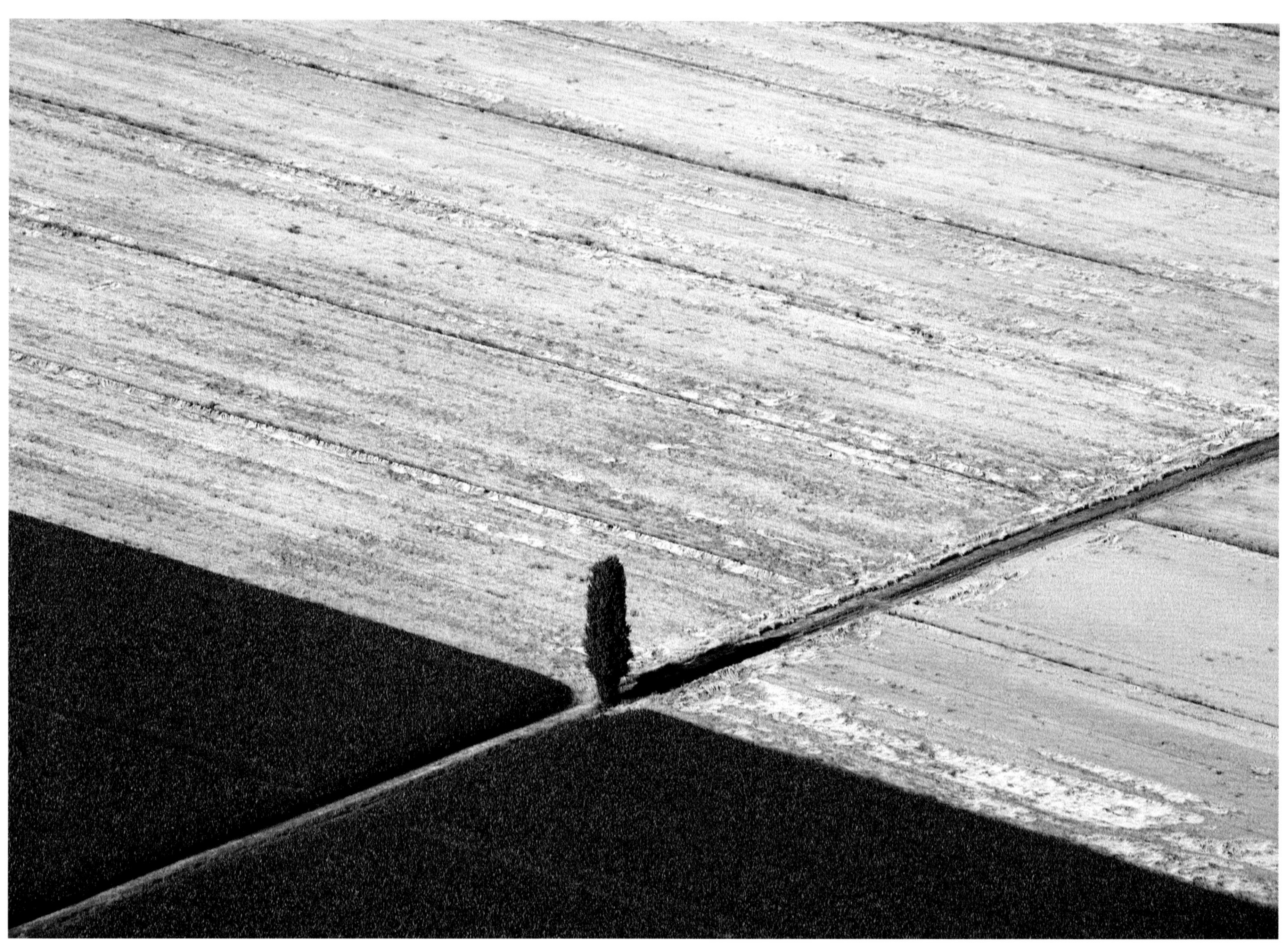

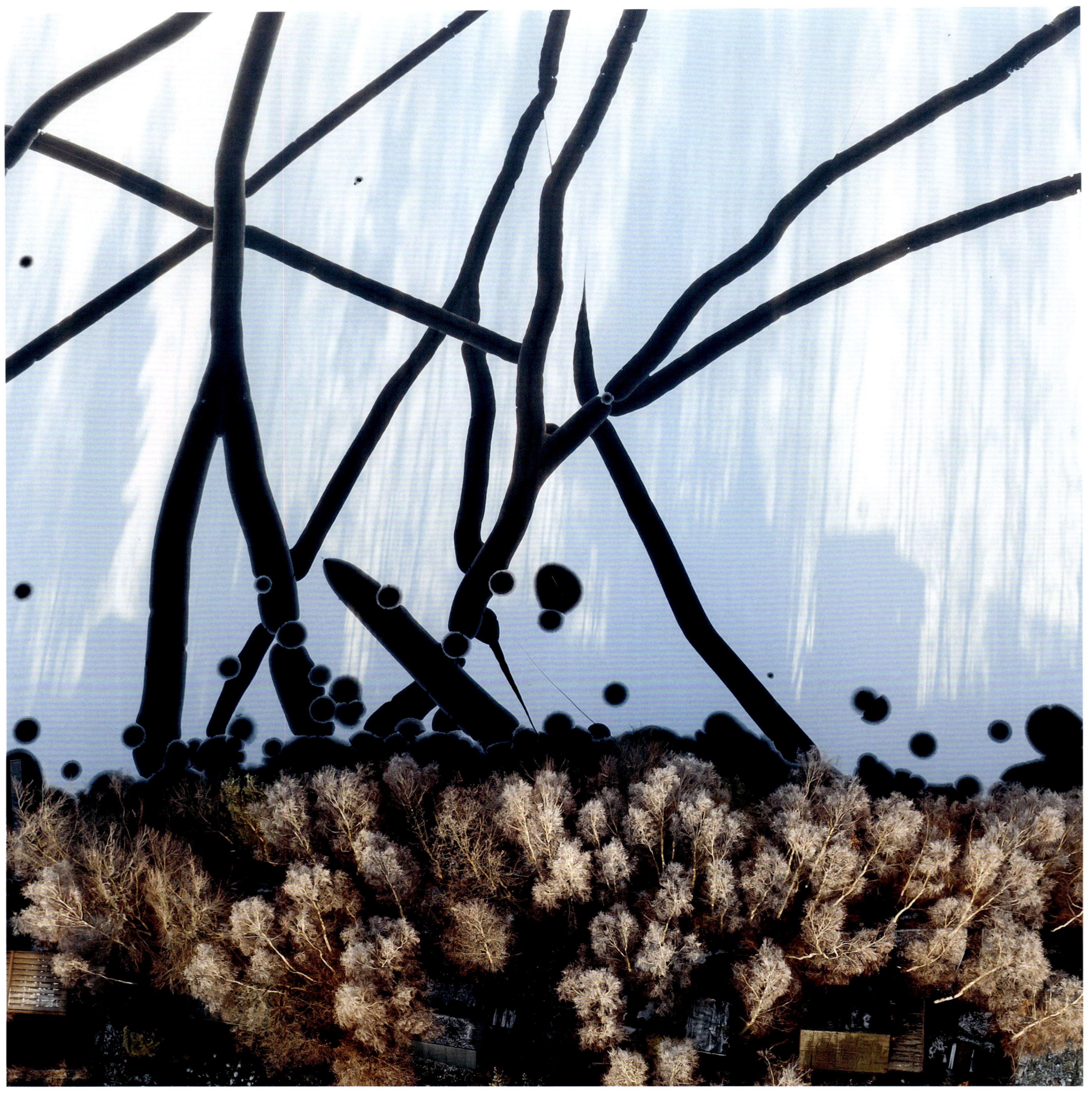

Kacper Kowalski
Kashubia region,
Pomerania, Poland, 2008.

He qualified and worked for a time as an architect, but in the mid-90s, Polish photographer Kacper Kowalski realized that flying was his true passion. In 2006, he began to work as an aerial photographer full-time. A qualified pilot and paraglider, Kowalski captures meticulous images of the Earth, which he collates into documentary series that grapple with environmental and ecological issues. His passion for flying has taken him to India, Mongolia and China, but most of his time is spent working within an 80-kilometre radius of Gdynia, his home town. When flying a paramotor, Kowalski may be as little as 150 metres above the ground, enabling him to record everything from the natural world to the built environment, industrial scenes and human activity with crystal clarity.

Kacper Kowalski
A snow-covered depot in Żarnowiec, Poland, 2013.

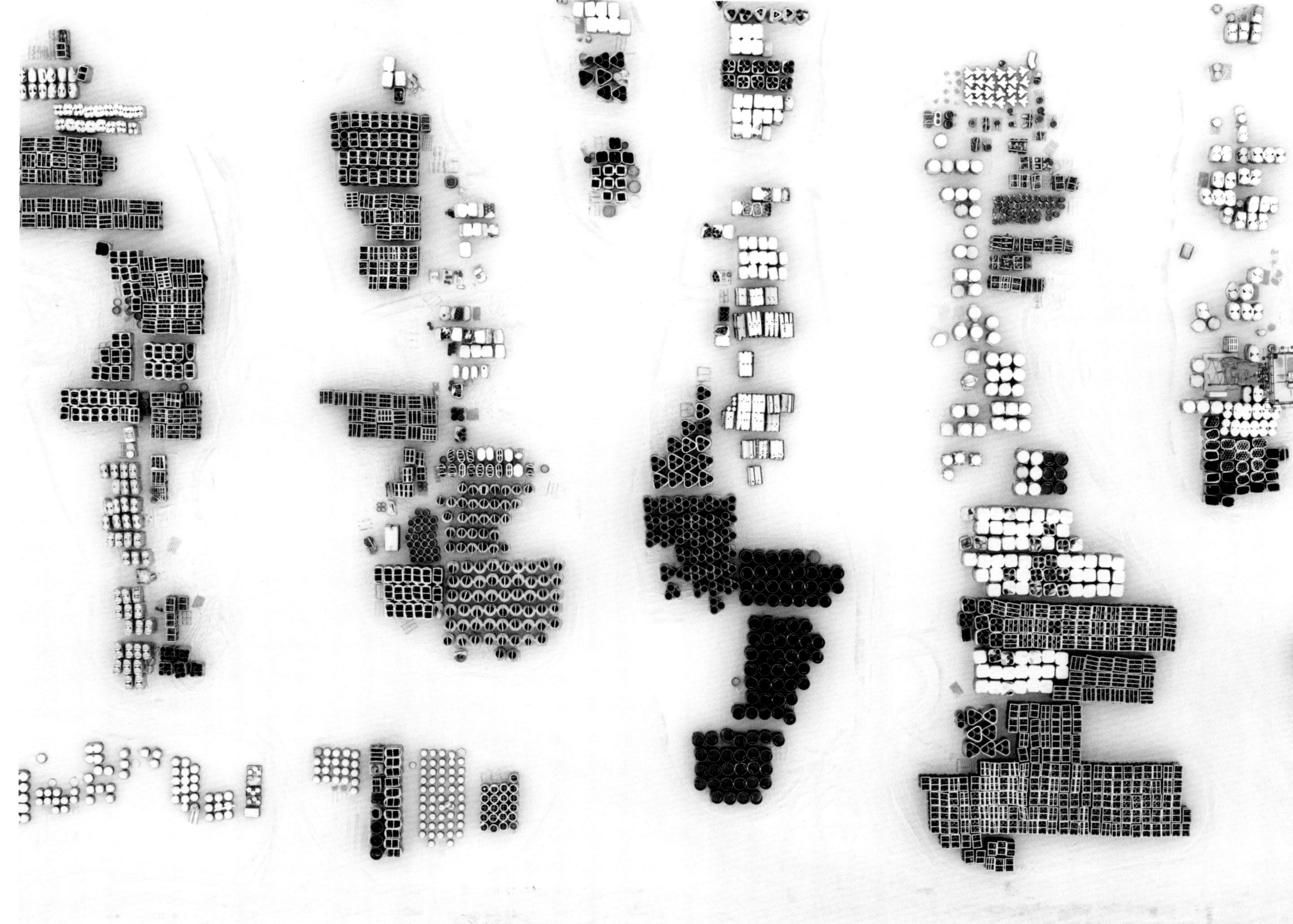

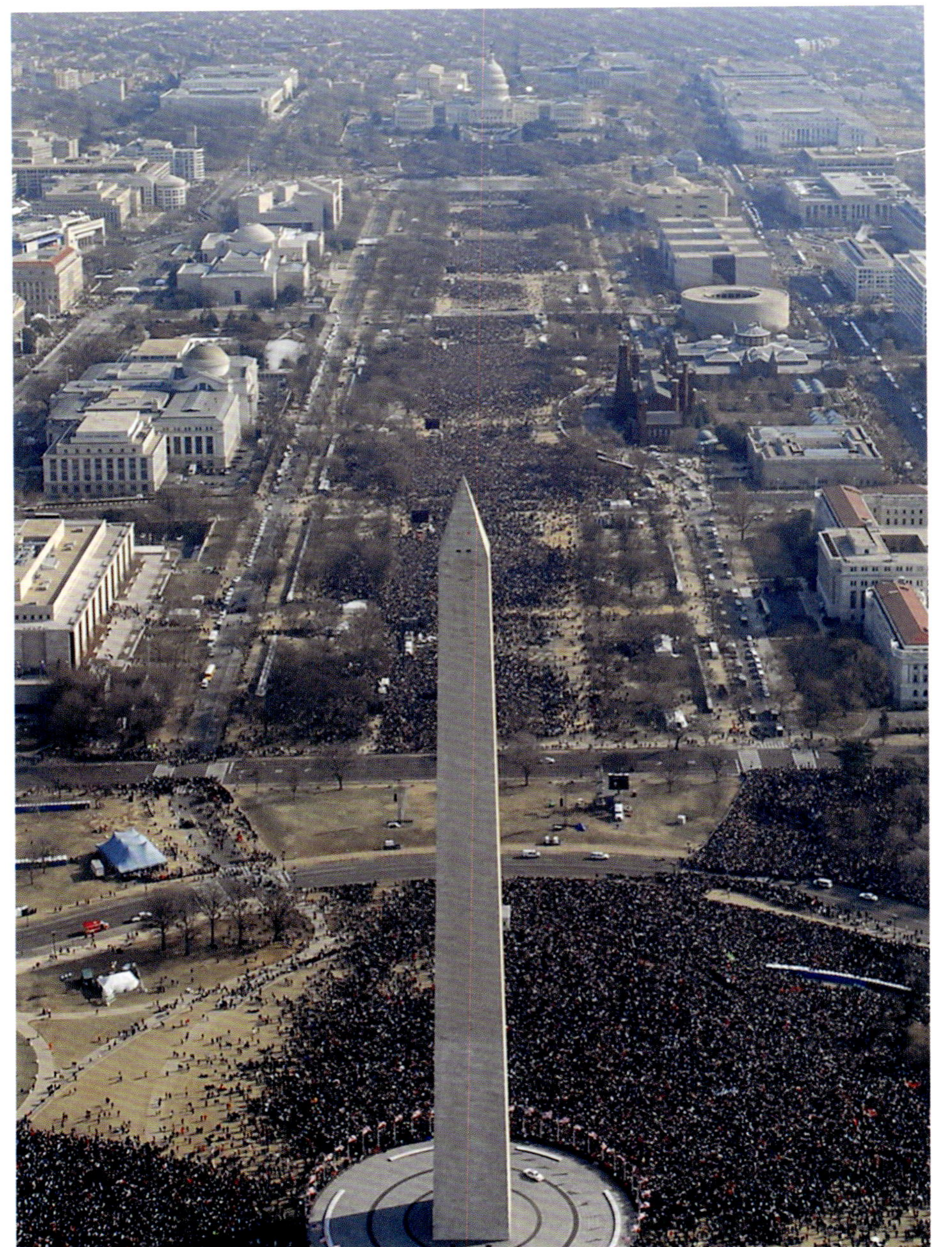

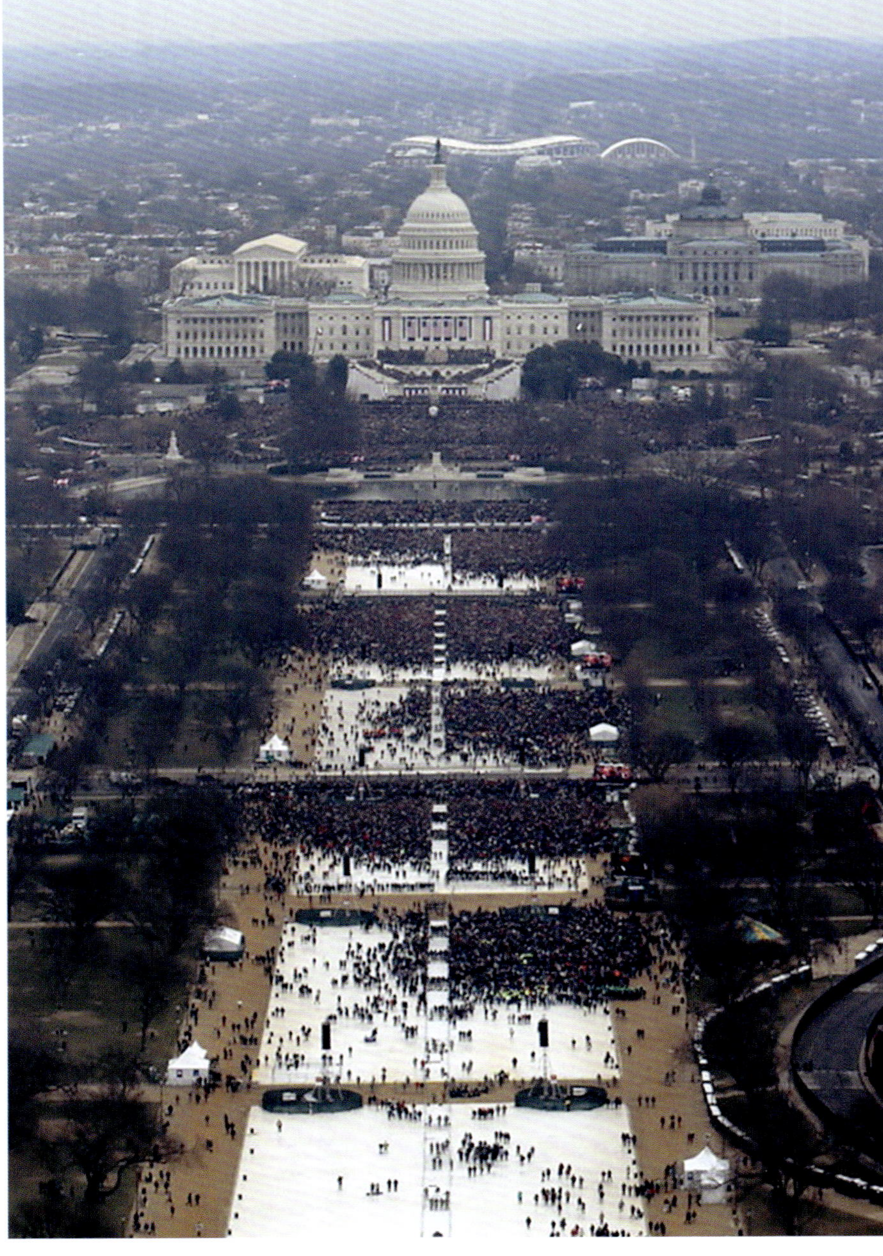

Sometimes, aerial photography can play a role in politics, or at least reflect the mood of a nation with regard to political goings-on. In early 2017, aerial photographs comparing the crowd sizes at the inaugurations of Presidents Obama and Trump went viral. Various versions and combinations of the images appeared in international media reports, all of which appeared to make the same point: the number of people who attended Obama's inauguration in 2009 far exceeded the turnout for Trump's. Some estimates suggested that the number was twice as high.

Above left
Photographer unknown
The inauguration of Barack Obama, 2009.

Above right
Photographer unknown
The inauguration of Donald Trump, 2017.

In her work, Irish-Iraqi artist Jananne Al-Ani uses photography and film to explore themes such as absence, loss and memory. The images shown here are still photographs from her film *Shadow Sites II*, in which Al-Ani takes viewers on an aerial journey across Middle Eastern landscapes, where archaeological sites and settlements reveal themselves when the sun is at its lowest. Traces of natural and man-made activity within the landscape also come to light when the sun passes over them, taking the form of what are commonly referred to as 'shadow sites'.

Below and overleaf
Jananne Al-Ani
'Aerial IV', 'Aerial III' and 'Aerial I' from *Shadow Sites II*, 2011.

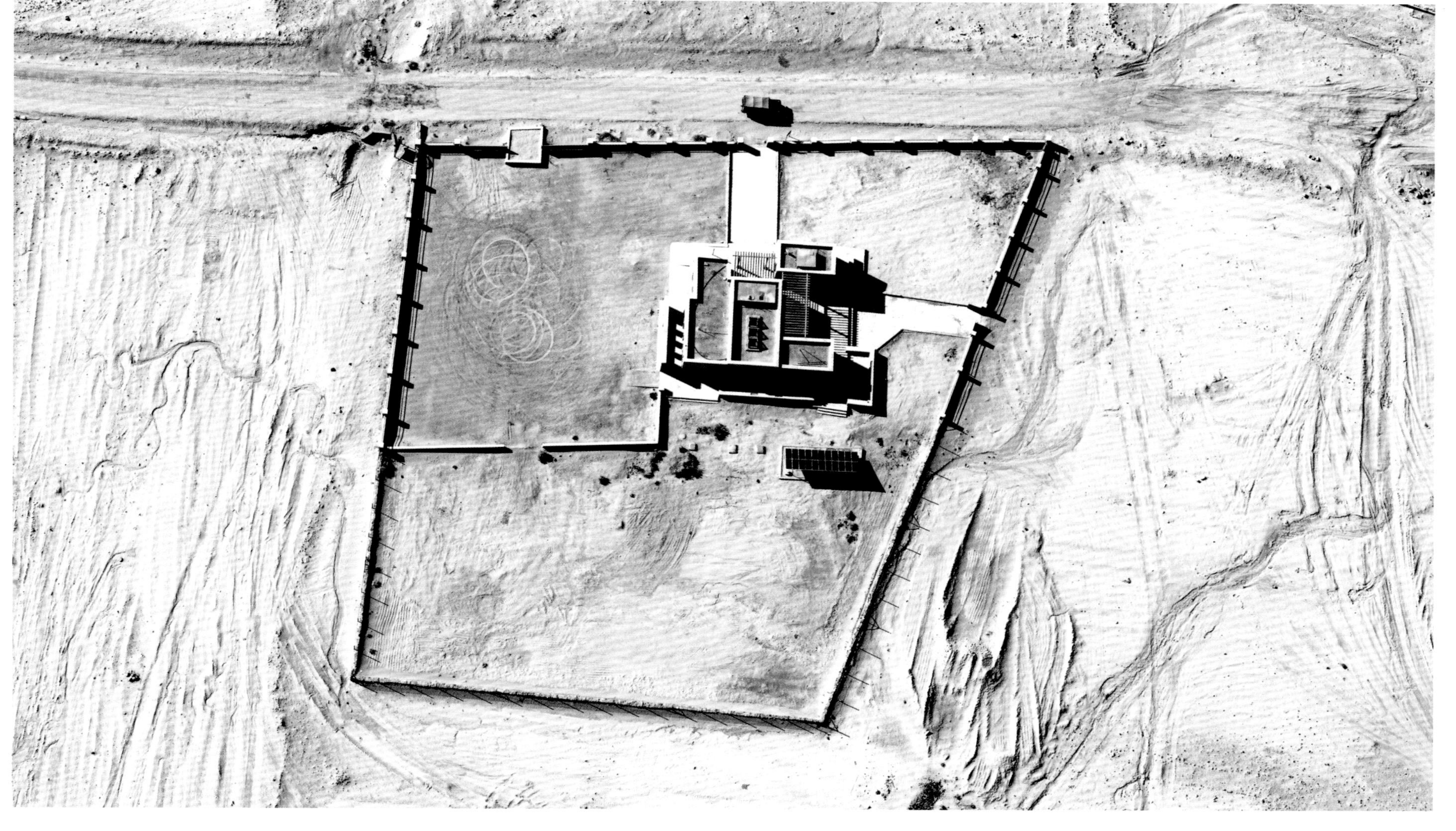

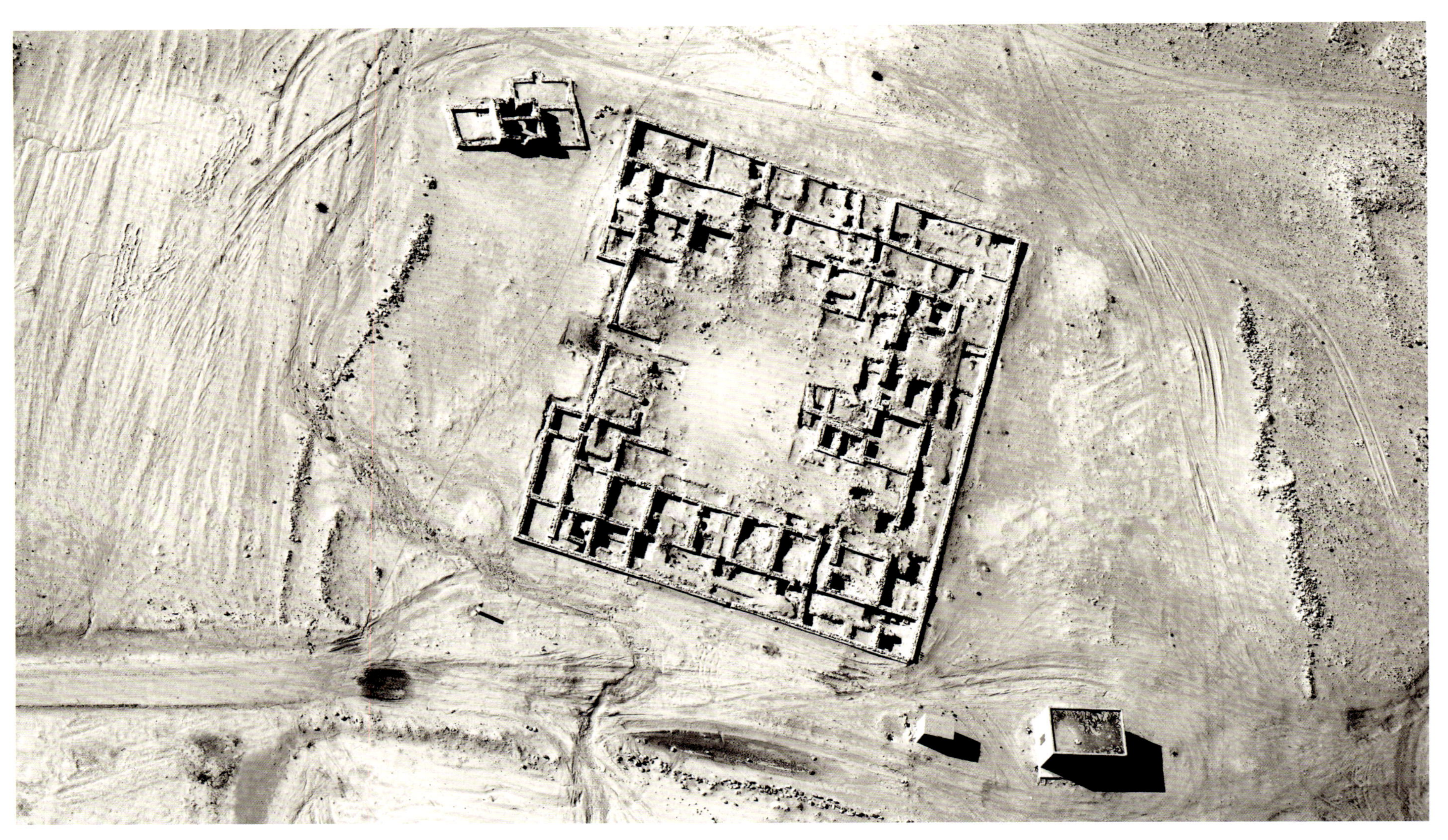

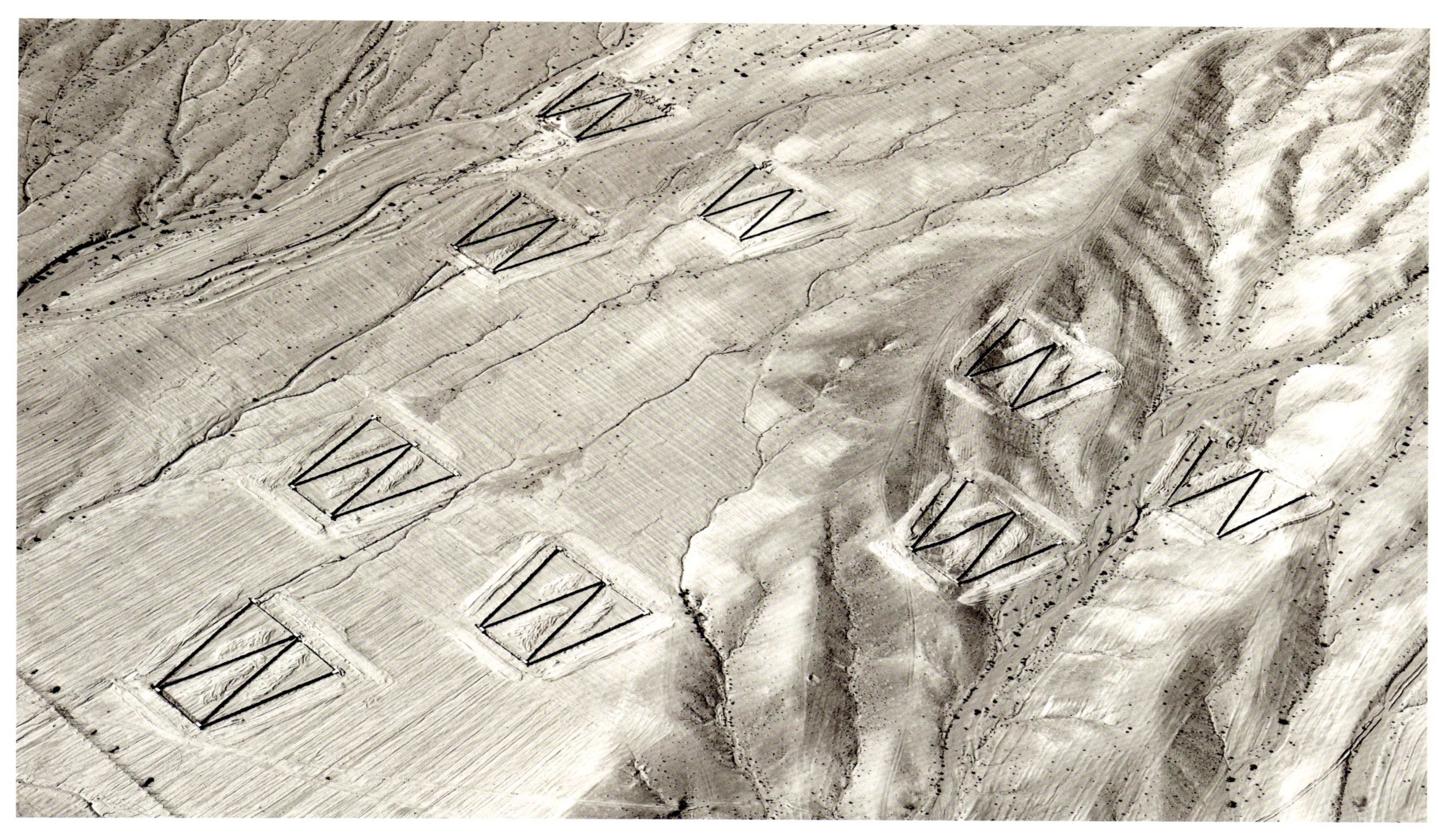

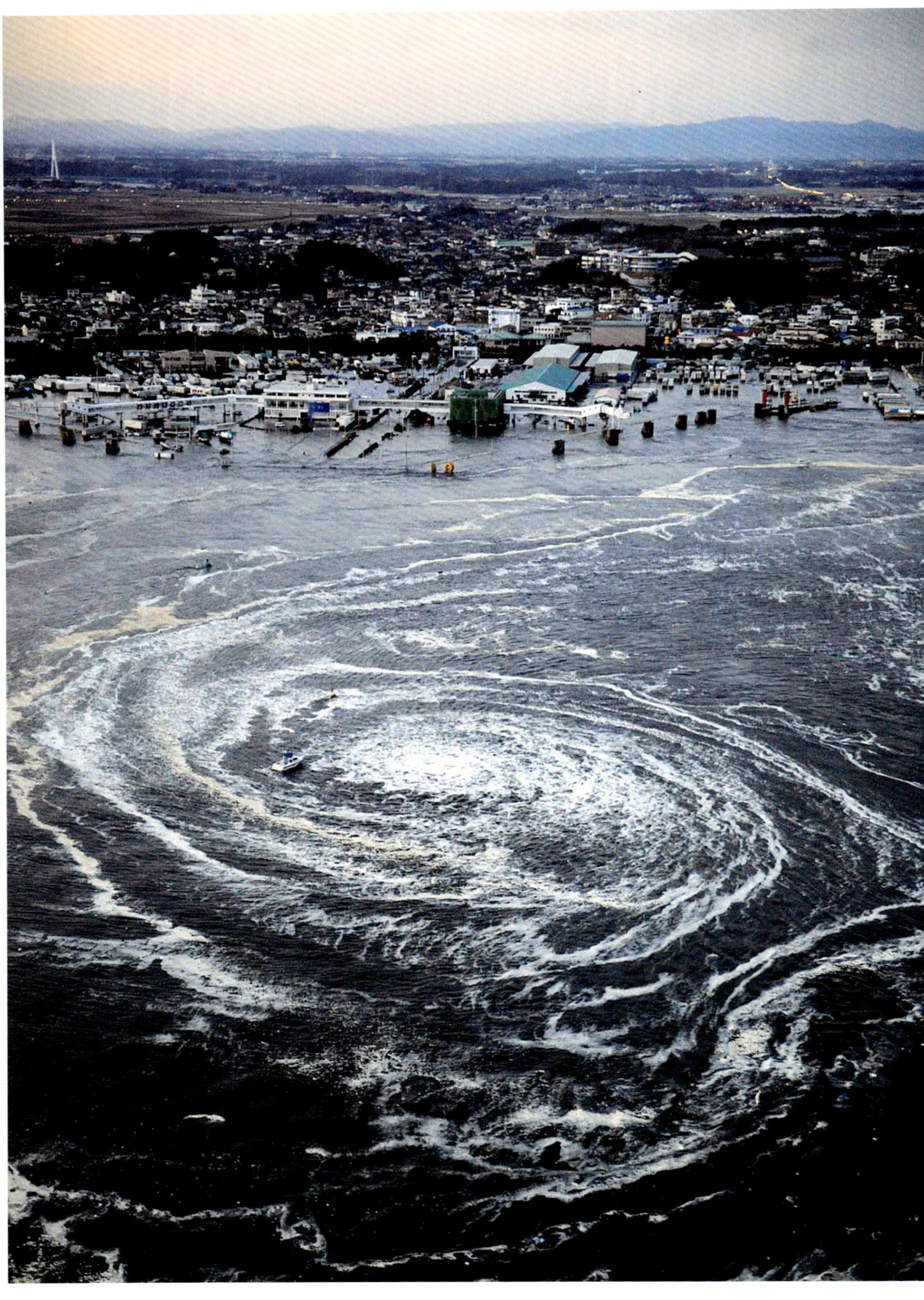

It is from the air that the devastation in Japan after the tsunami of 2011 was most apparent. On 11 March at 2.46pm, a magnitude-9 earthquake struck off the northeastern coast of Honshu, Japan's main island. More than 120,000 buildings were destroyed outright. The quake, believed to be one of the most powerful ever recorded, triggered tsunami waves that ravaged many coastal regions and caused a disastrous accident at the Fukushima Daiichi nuclear-power plant. Houses, debris and people were swept out to sea and swathes of land were left submerged. Some reports suggest the death toll reached 20,000.

Above
Photographer unknown
Photograph taken from a Kyodo News helicopter showing a whirlpool caused by a tsunami near a port in Oarai, Ibaraki Prefecture, Japan, 2011.

Below
Photographer unknown
Houses burn after being swept out to sea by the tsunami in Natori, Miyagi Prefecture, Japan, 2011.

Overleaf
Photographer unknown
A tsunami hits the coastal area of Iwanuma, Miyagi Prefecture, northeastern Japan, 2011.

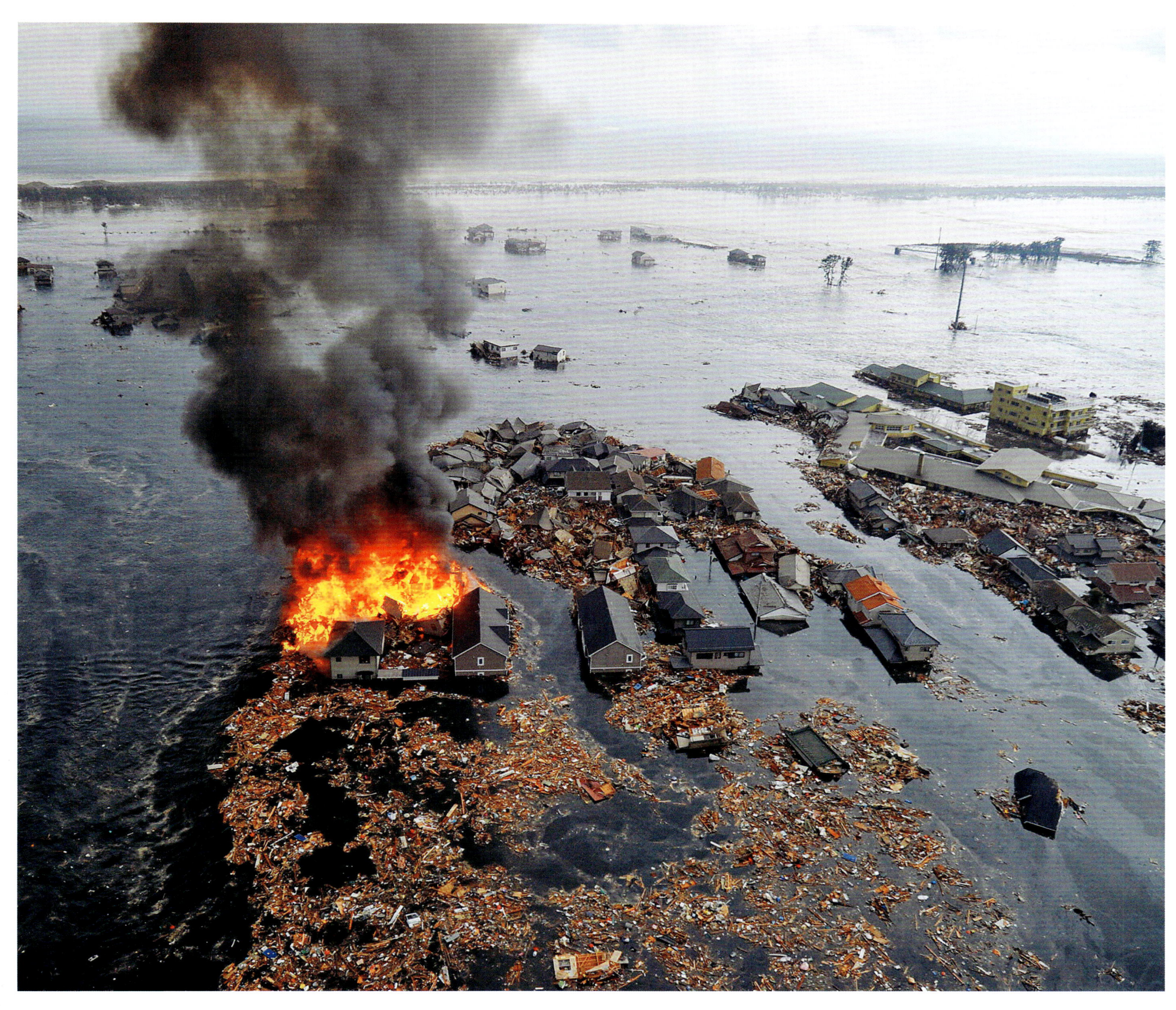

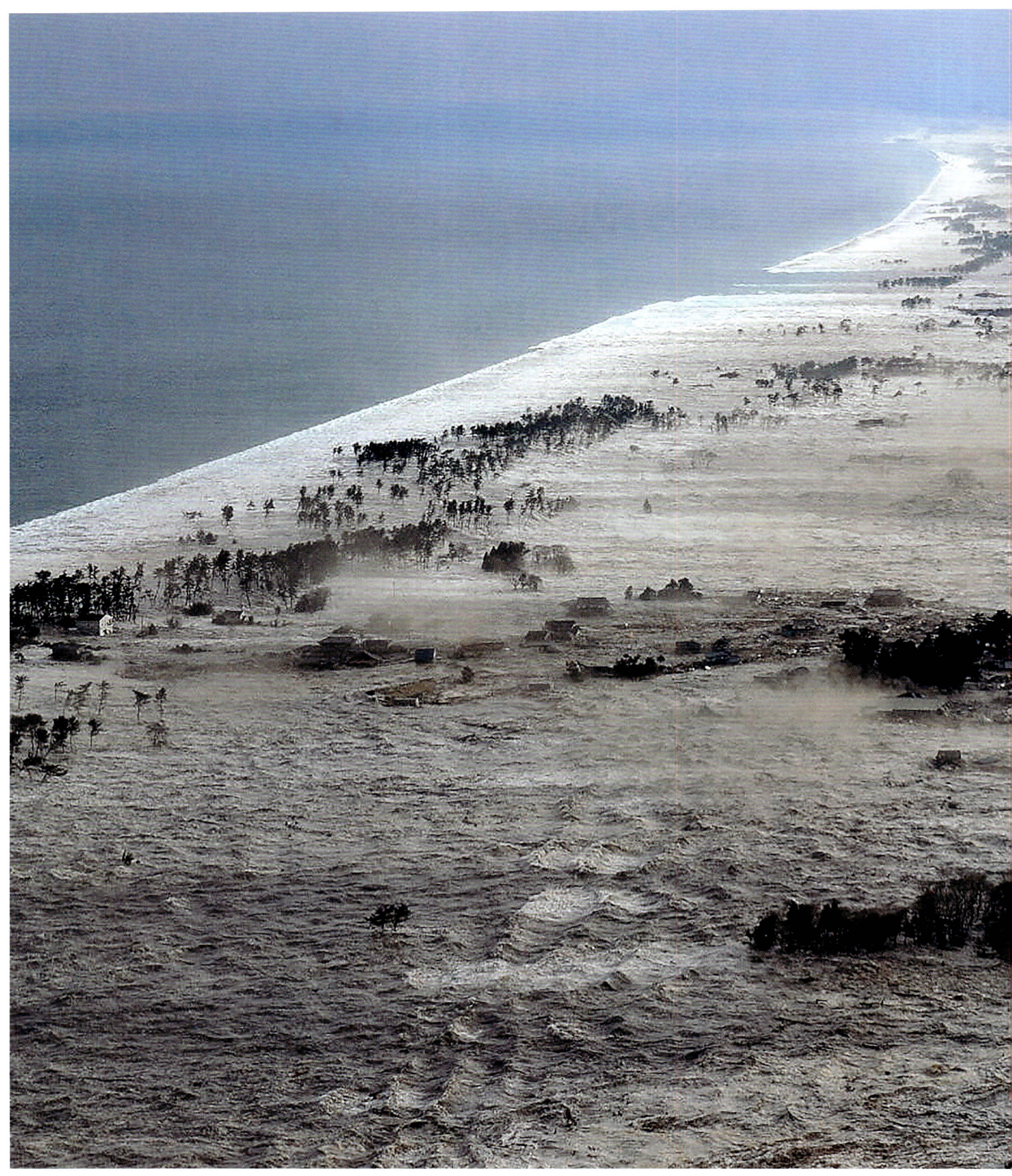

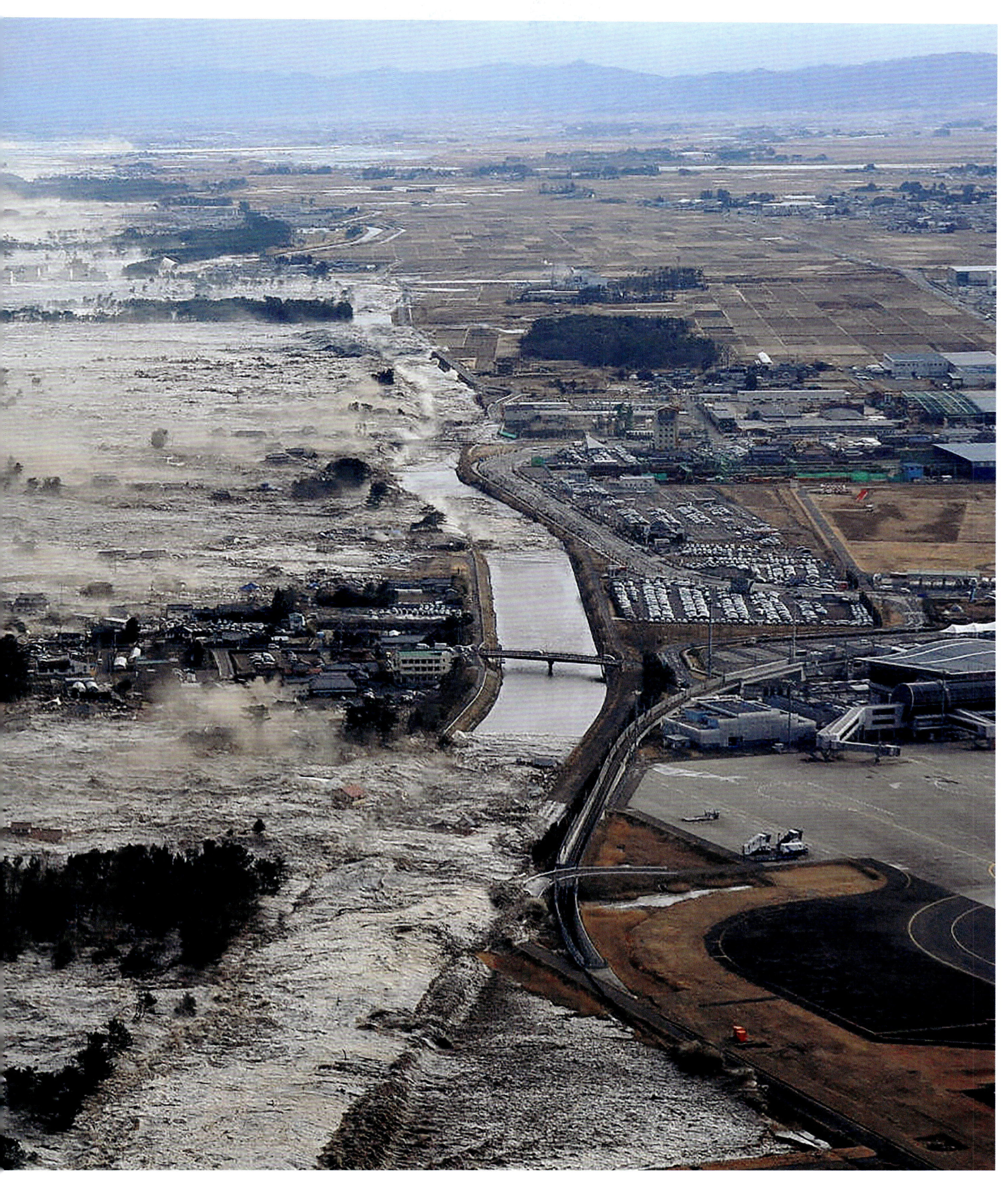

Soft raking sunlight illuminates areas of Petare shantytown to the east of Caracas, Venezuela. This photograph taken by Leo Ramírez shows just how dense the population is in this corner of the country's largest city. The image records in sharp relief some of the hundreds of shanties that cling to the mountainside, hinting at the lives contained within, but leaving us to imagine what life is like for the people who call these slums home. Gang violence and poverty in Petare is rife, and the threat of mudslides hangs over residents.

Leo Ramírez
Petare favela in Caracas, Venezuela, 2012.

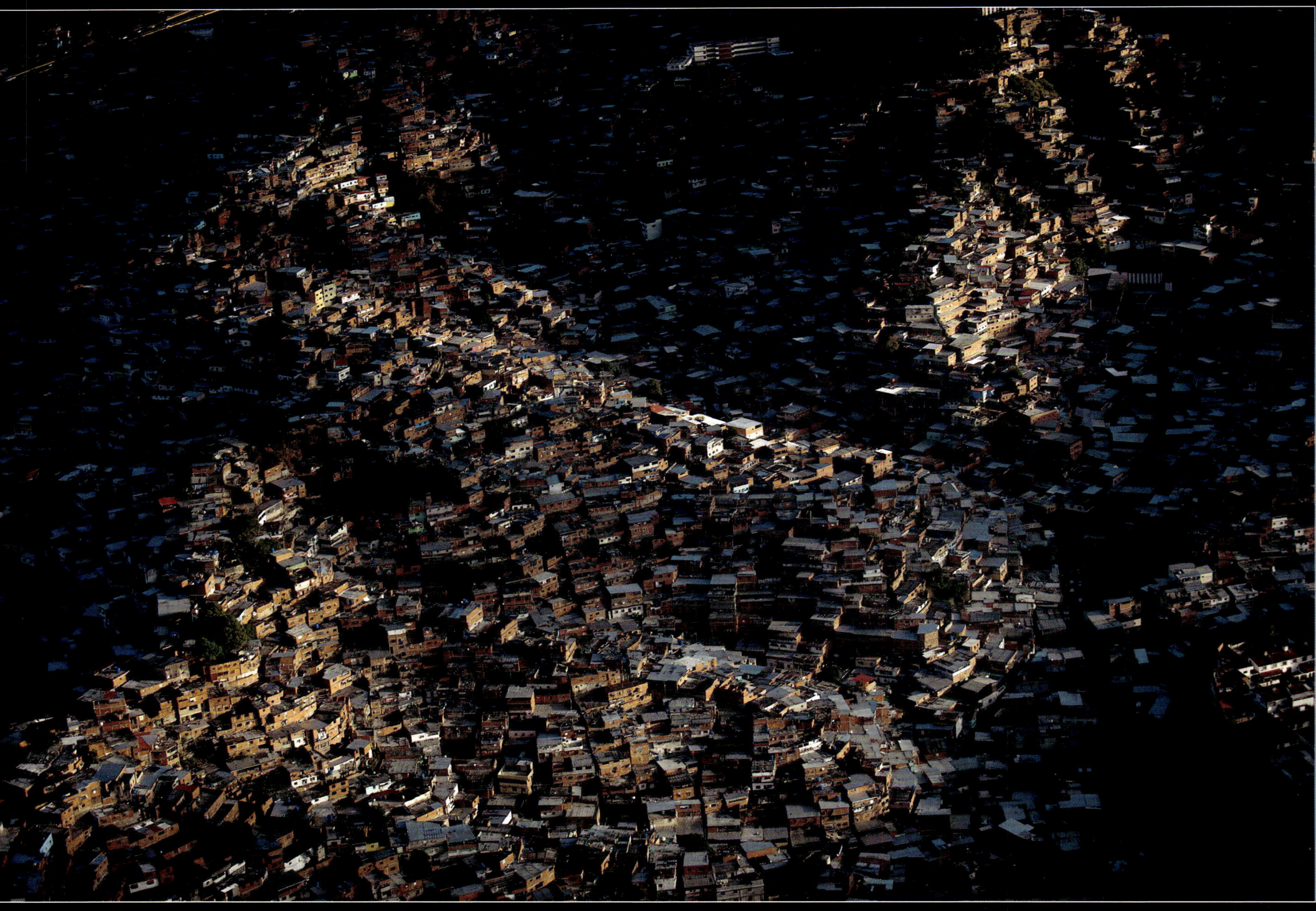

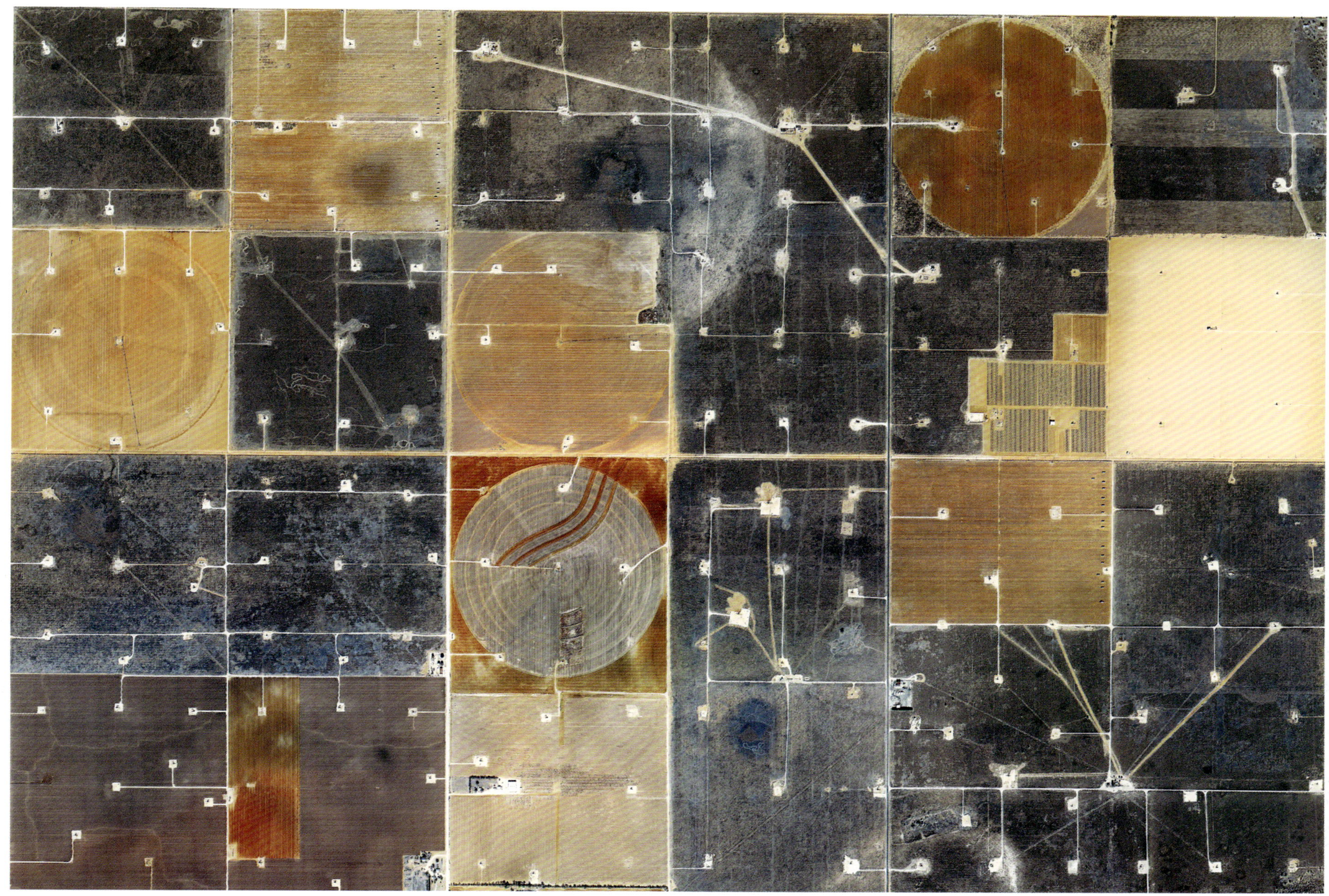

Mishka Henner
Levelland Oil Field #1, Hockley County, Texas, USA, 2013.

Belgian-born artist Mishka Henner, who is based in England, uses freely available imagery from Google Earth to create his dramatic, and at times painterly, works. Made by stitching together screenshots using digital-imaging software, the images not only offer an alternative view of the world, but also call into question the role of photography in the Internet age, highlighting issues around surveillance, censorship and privacy. From US military outposts to Dutch landscapes, and Libyan and American oil fields, Henner pictures the Earth in ways not possible from the ground.

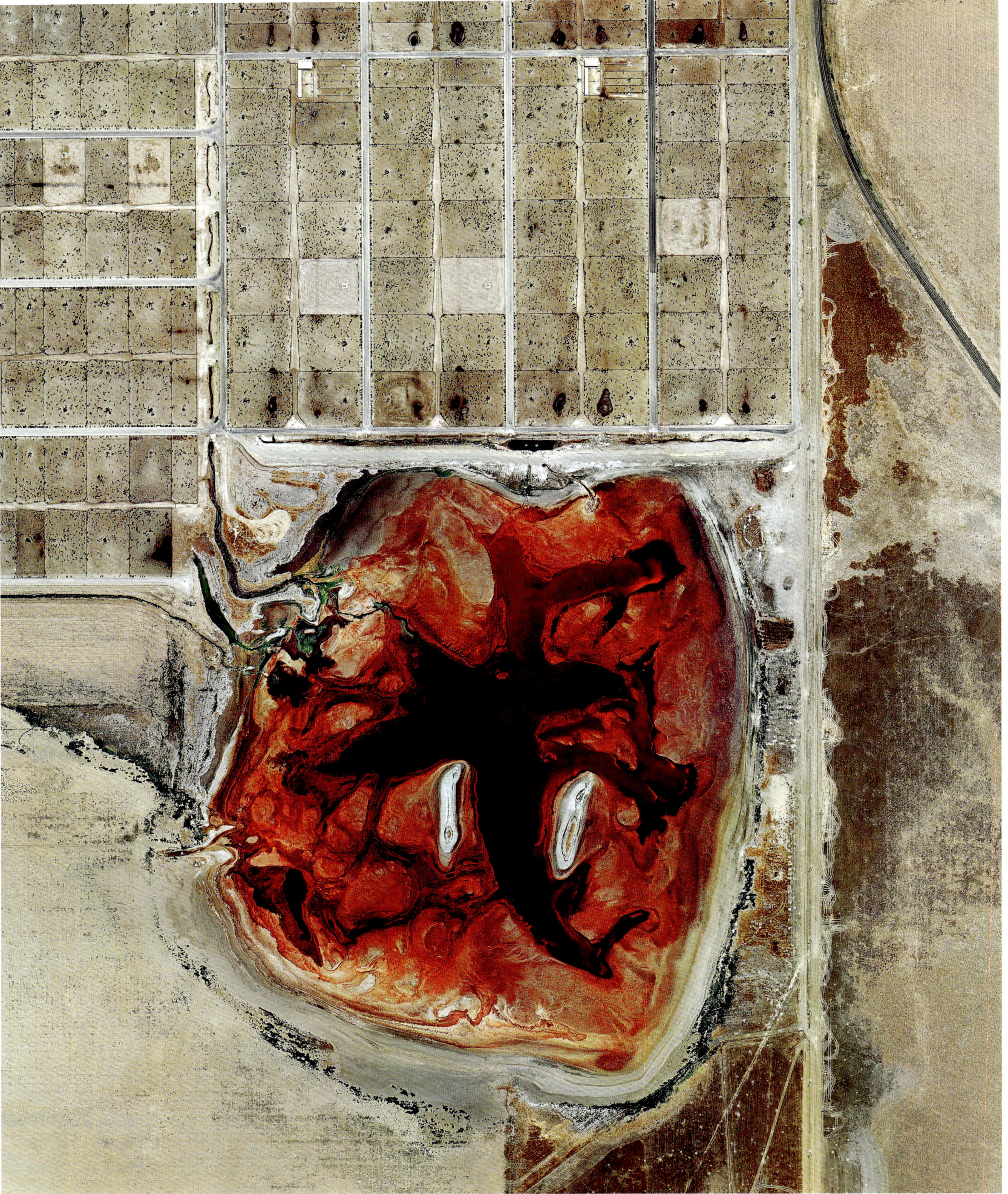

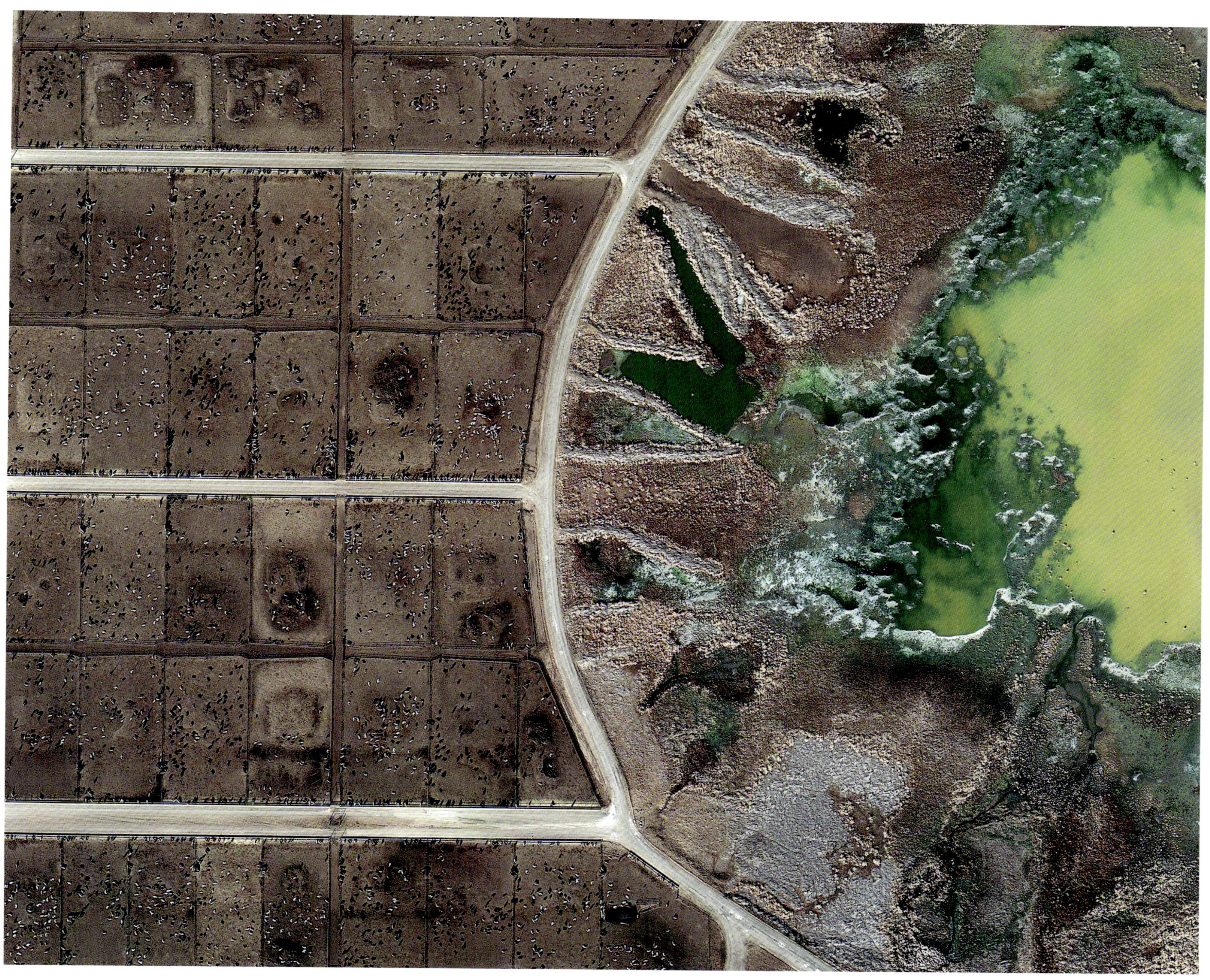

Opposite
Mishka Henner
Coronado Feeders, Dalhart, Texas, USA, 2012.

Above
Mishka Henner
Tascosa Feedyard, Bushland, Texas, USA (detail), 2013.

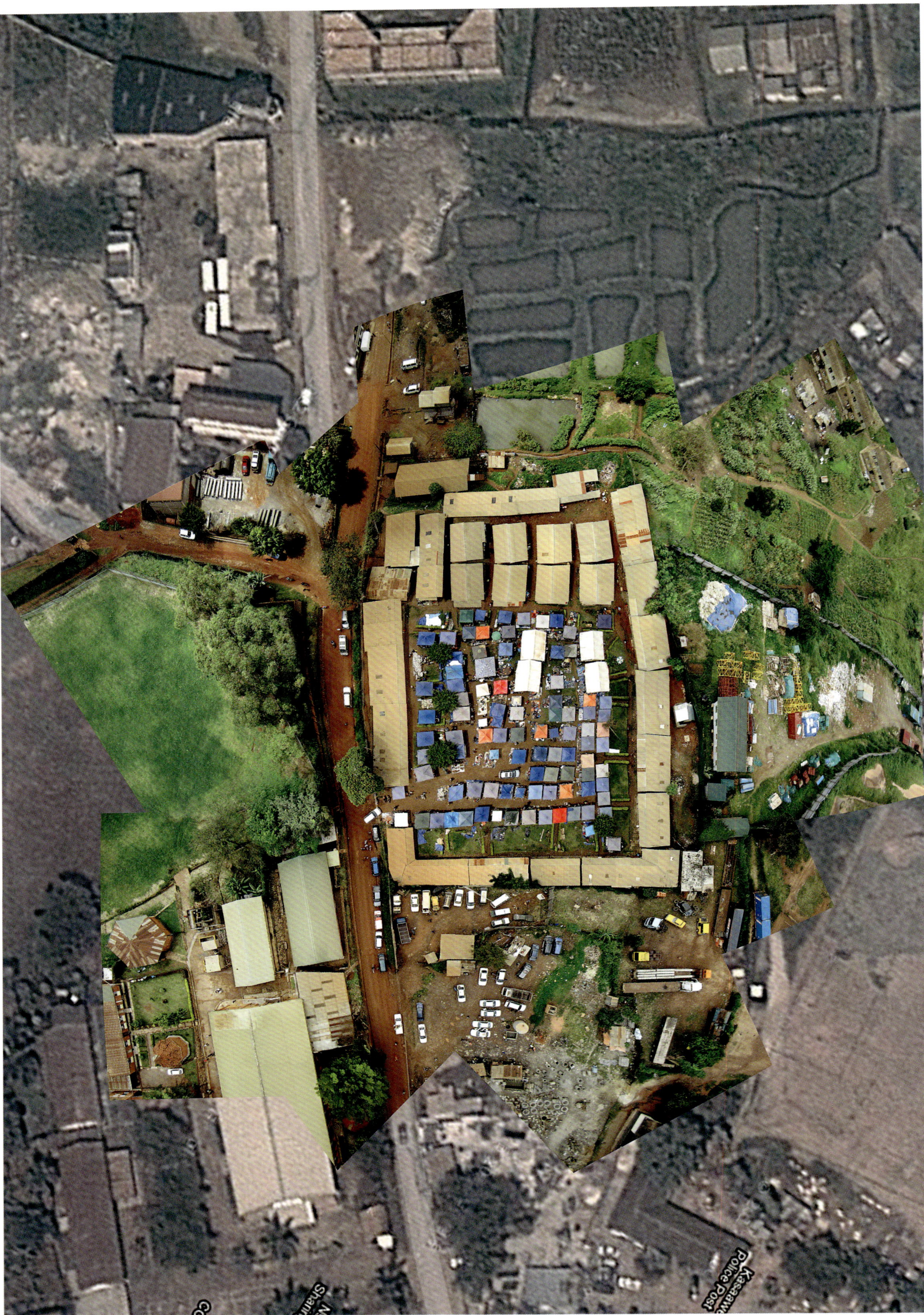

Public Lab
Balloon mapping to temporarily stall eviction proceedings, Kampala, Uganda, 2013.

Although many images shot from the air are created to entertain, to look pretty or purely for the thrill of it, there are people eager to use DIY aerial photography techniques to inform. Public Lab is a community of people who develop and utilize open-source technology to raise awareness around environmental issues. In the organization's early days, founding members used helium balloons, kites and inexpensive digital cameras to create their own 'community satellites' in response to the 2010 BP Deepwater Horizon oil spill in the Gulf of Mexico and the lack of information that was available at the time. Since then, projects that employ techniques such as balloon mapping and 'DIY multispectral kite photography' (imagery that captures more than one frequency or wavelength in the electromagnetic spectrum) have been carried out to monitor wetlands, investigate potential water contamination, and even to stall eviction proceedings in Kampala, Uganda (pictured opposite).

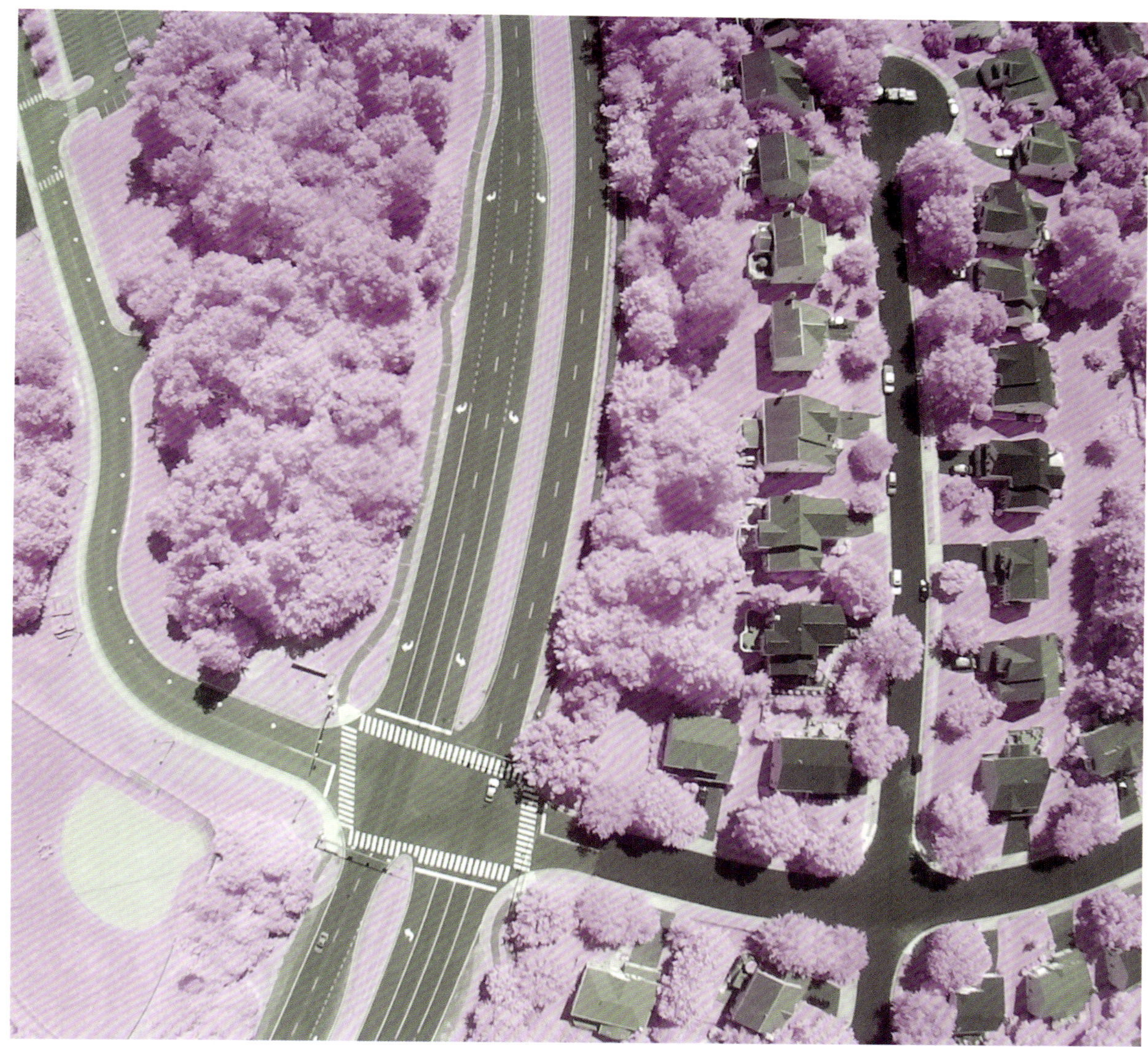

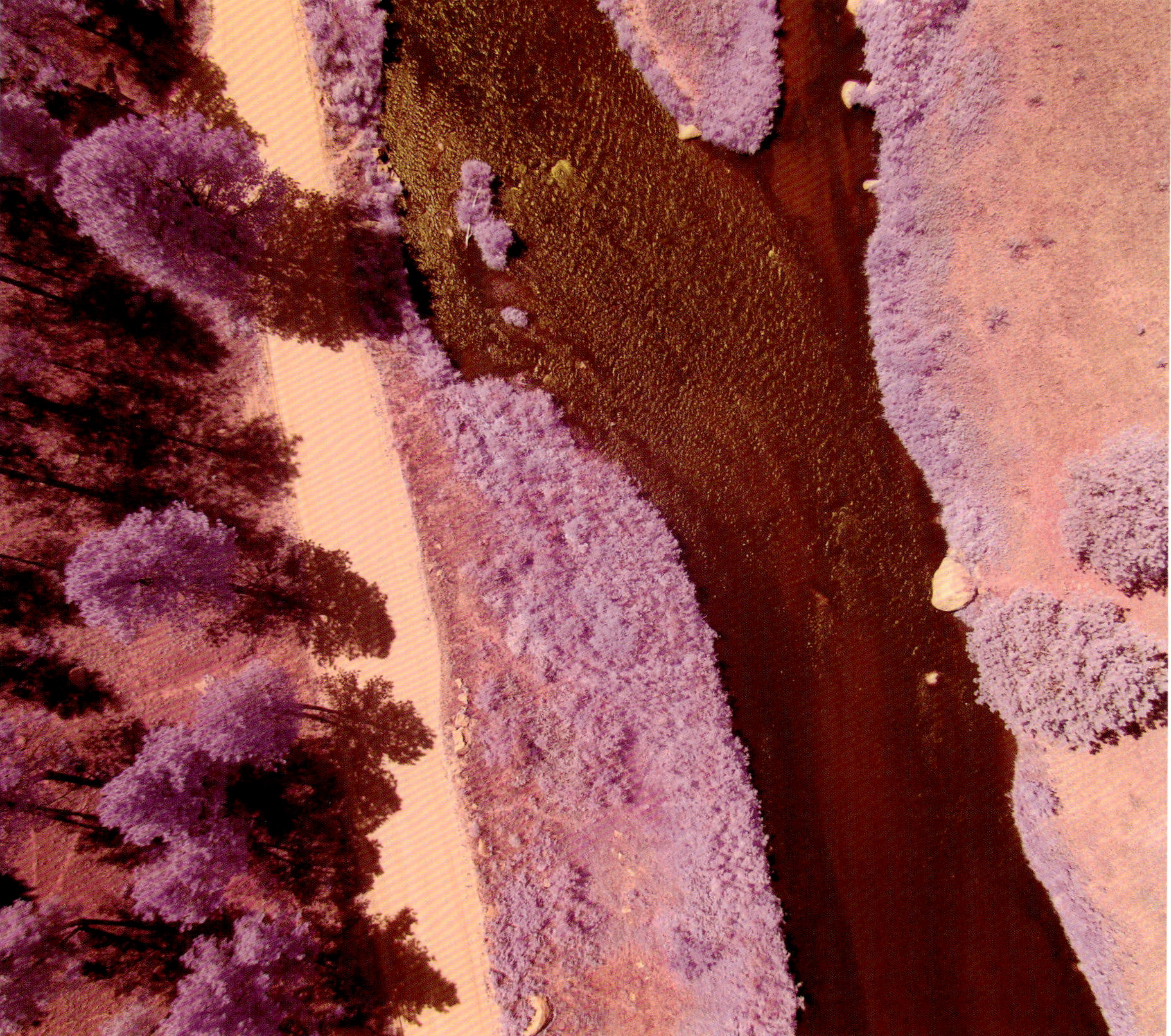

Right
Public Lab
An Infragram plant-health project view of Potomac Falls, USA, 2018.

Above
Public Lab
An Infragram plant-health project view, location unknown, 2018.

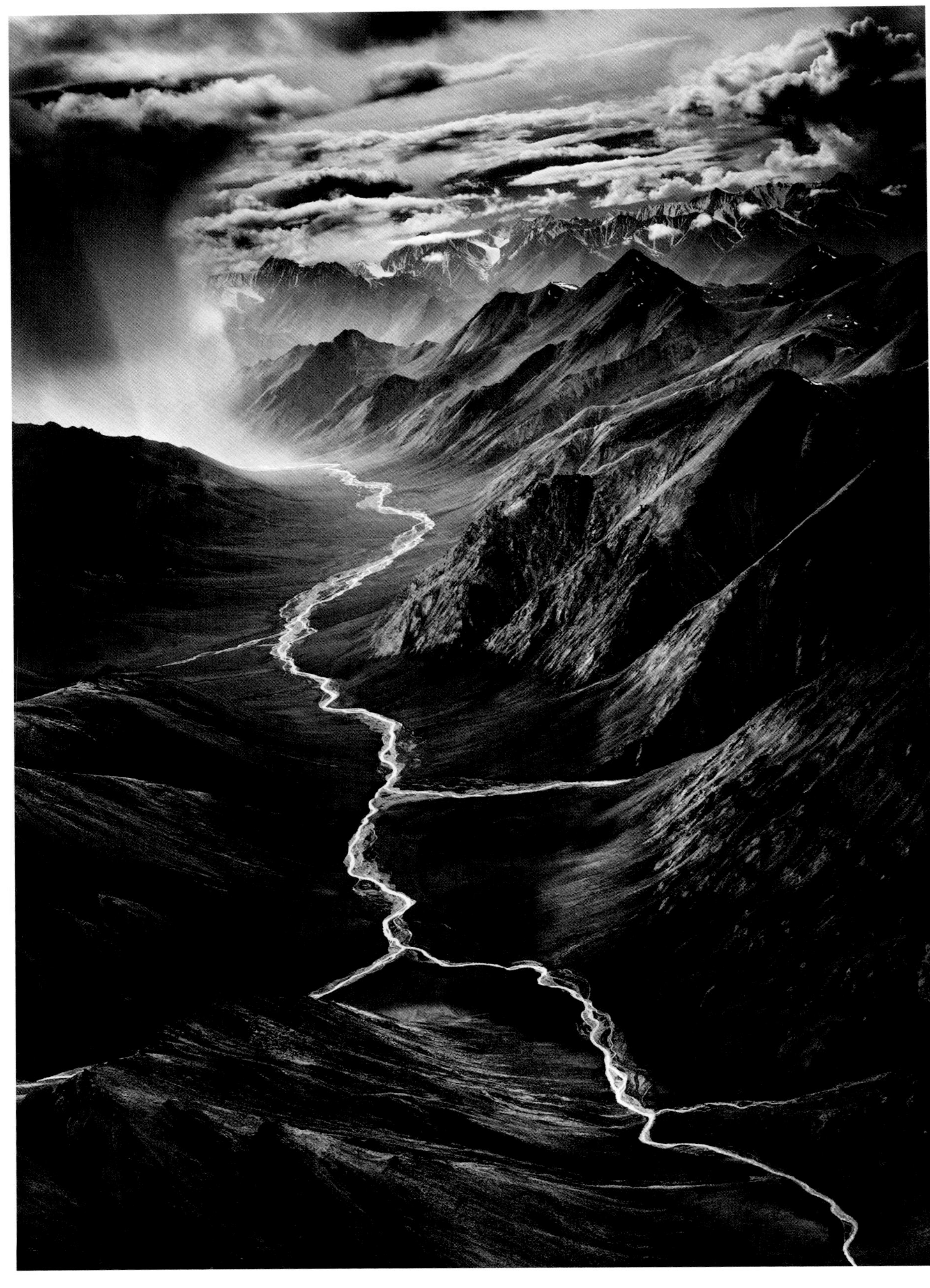

Sebastião Salgado
Arctic National Wildlife Refuge, Alaska, USA, from the series 'Genesis', 2013.

Having trained as an economist, in the early 1970s Brazilian Sebastião Salgado discovered the camera and he is now one of the world's most famous living photographers. His work, captured in black and white, focuses on the natural world and its elemental beauty. In the epic series 'Genesis', made over eight years during 32 trips to far-flung parts of the world, vast landscapes drenched in almost heavenly light stretch out before us as planet Earth opens up before Salgado's lens. He used a light aircraft and even a hot-air balloon to reach some of the remotest destinations in what he referred to as his 'love letter to the planet'.

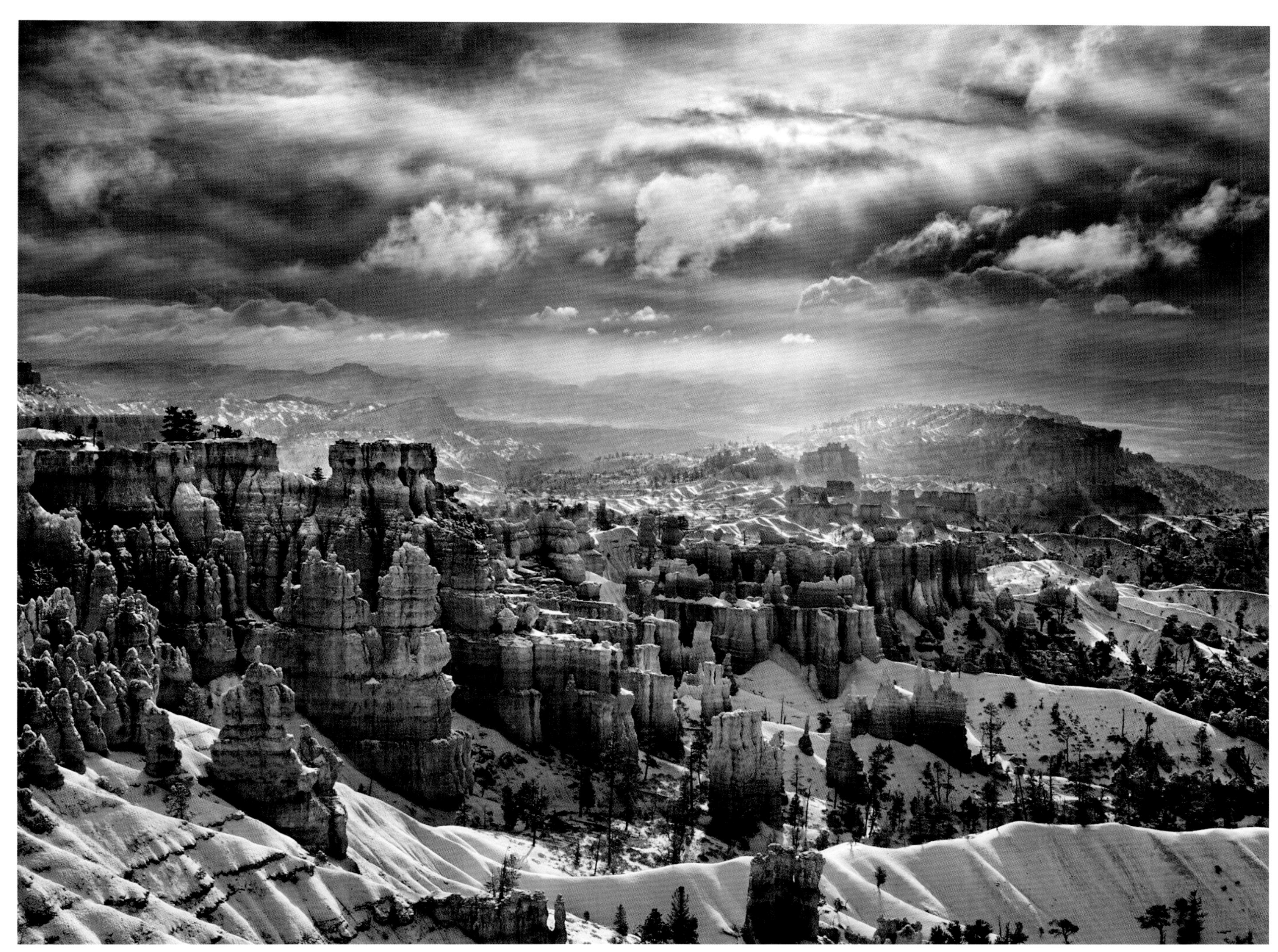

Sebastião Salgado
Hoodoos, Bryce Canyon National Park, Utah, USA, from the series 'Genesis', 2013.

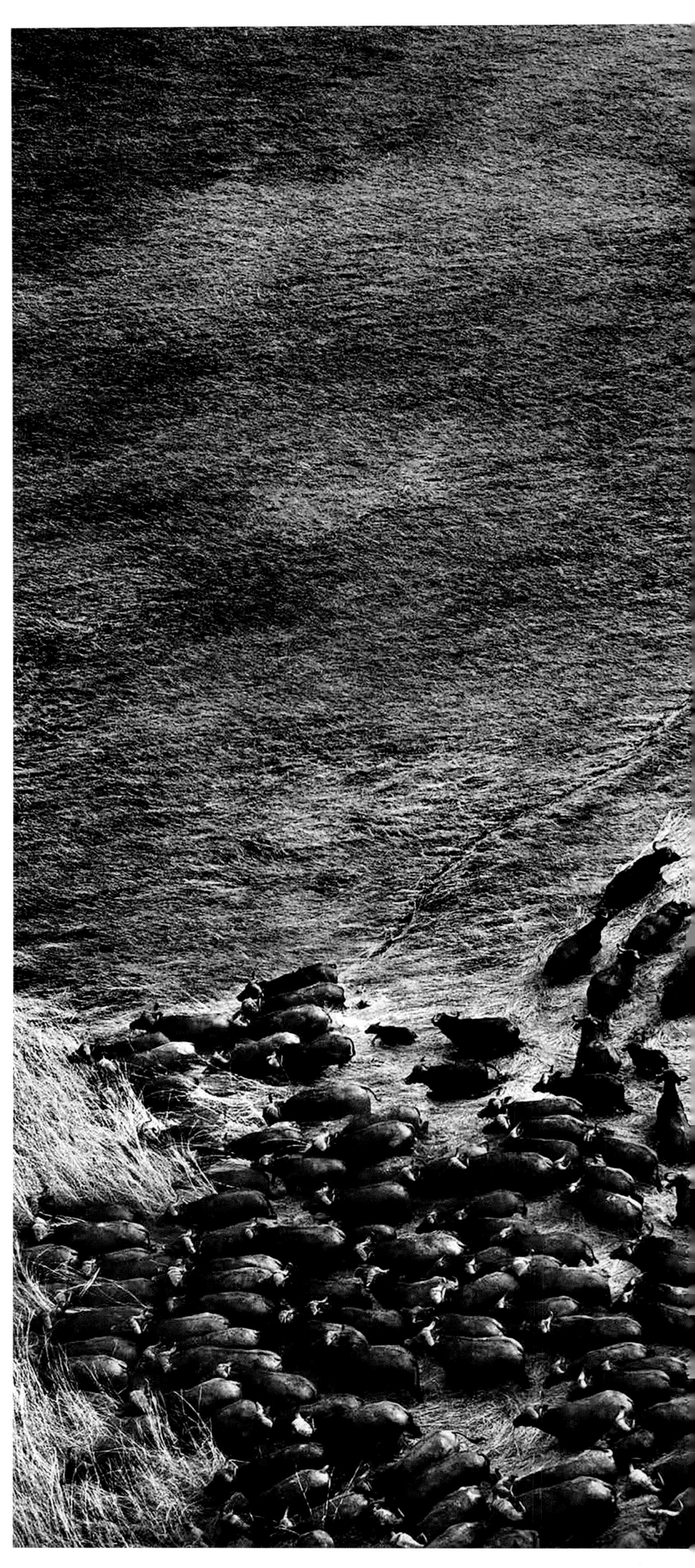

Sebastião Salgado
Buffalo at Kafue National Park, Zambia, from the series 'Genesis', 2018.

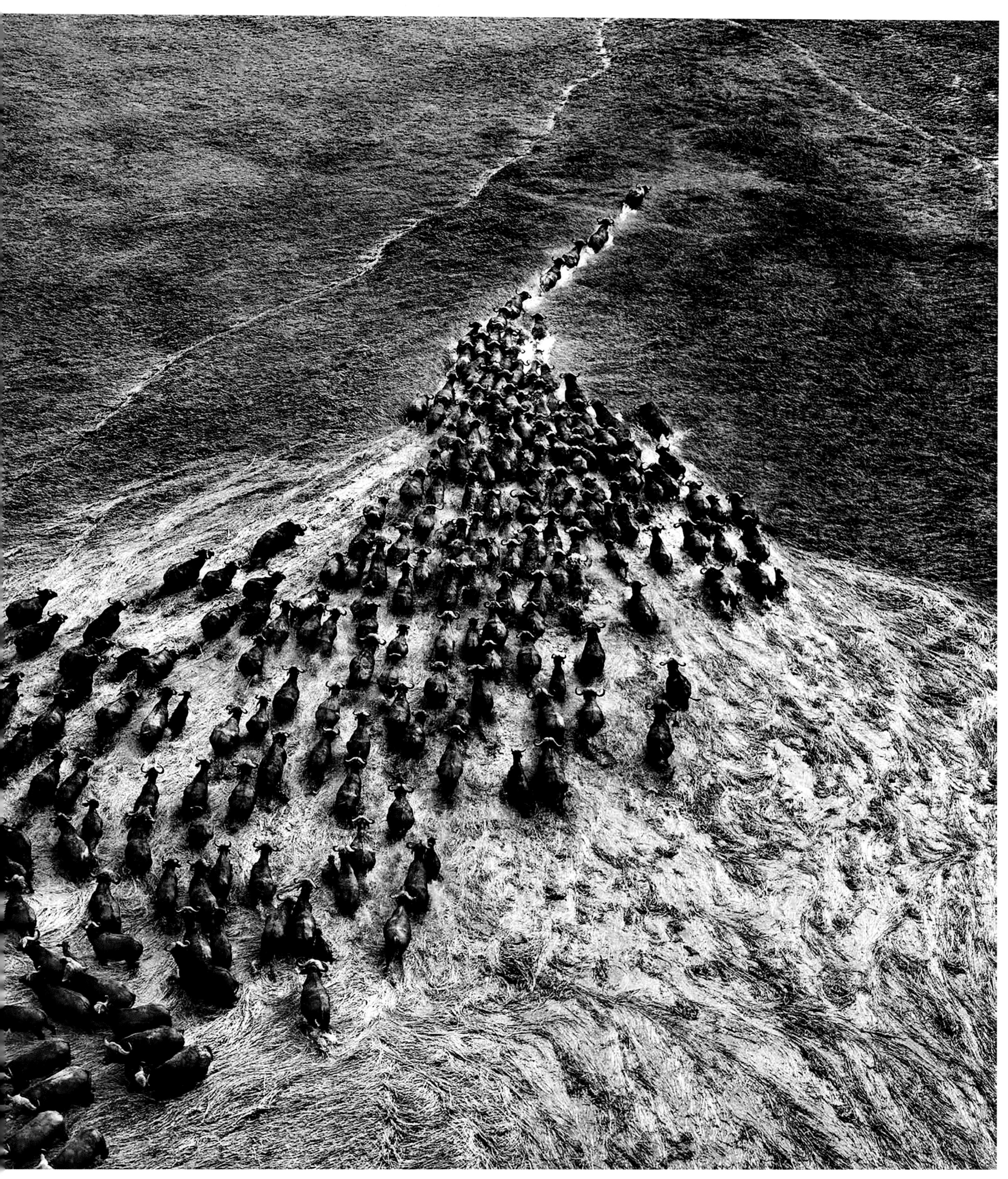

Alex MacLean
Ore runoff, Duluth, Minnesota, USA, 2014.

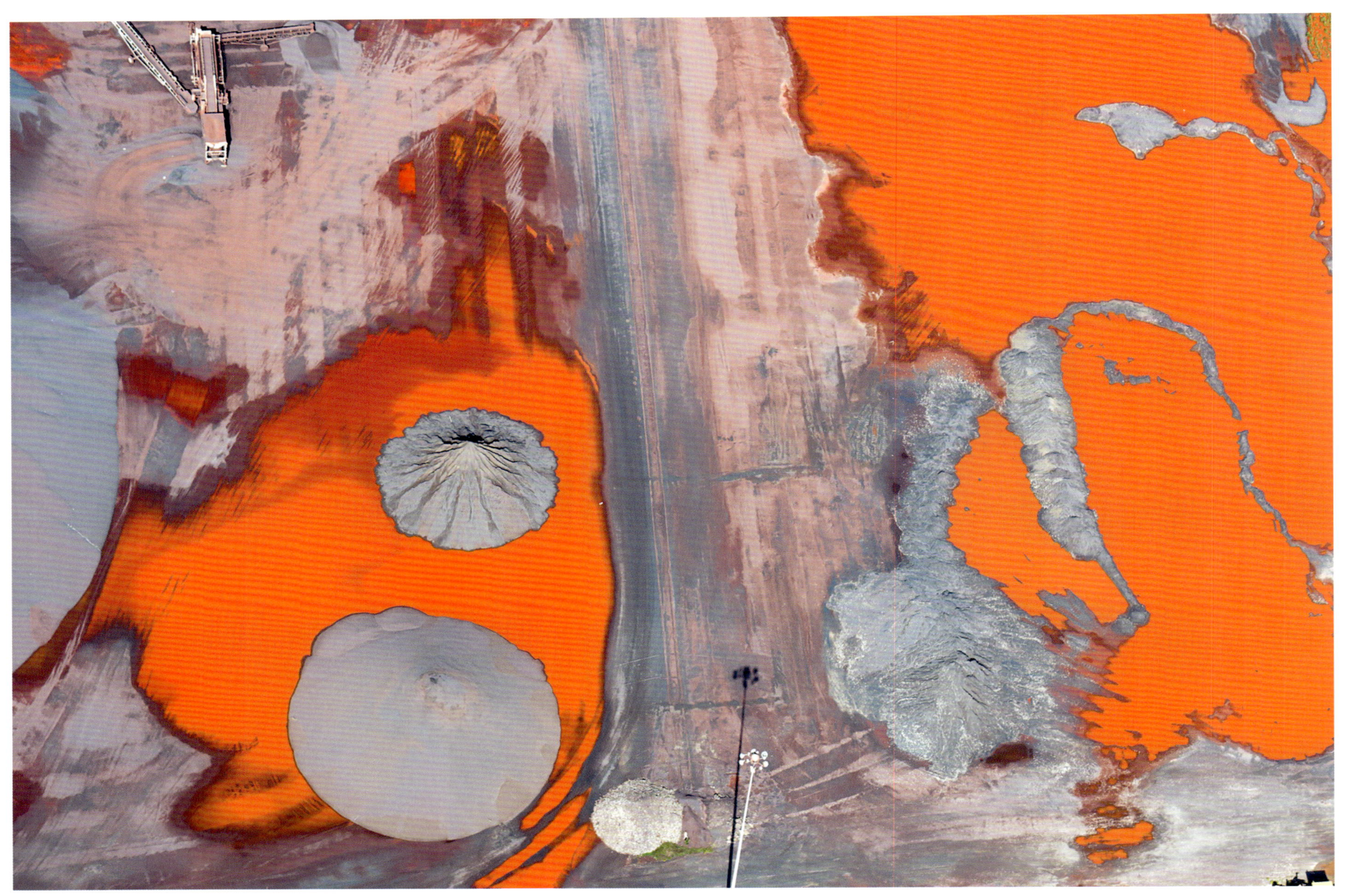

For 40 years, photographer and pilot Alex MacLean, who trained as an architect, has photographed everything from agricultural patterns to city grids, highways, boats, bombers and more across the United States. He began his career making aerial photographs for architects and urban planners, but was compelled to create more aesthetically pleasing shots that could also inform. MacLean, who shoots from a Cessna 182 plane, 150 metres in the air, has expressed the hope that his images will encourage people to think about the impact of pollution and the extraction of resources on our planet.

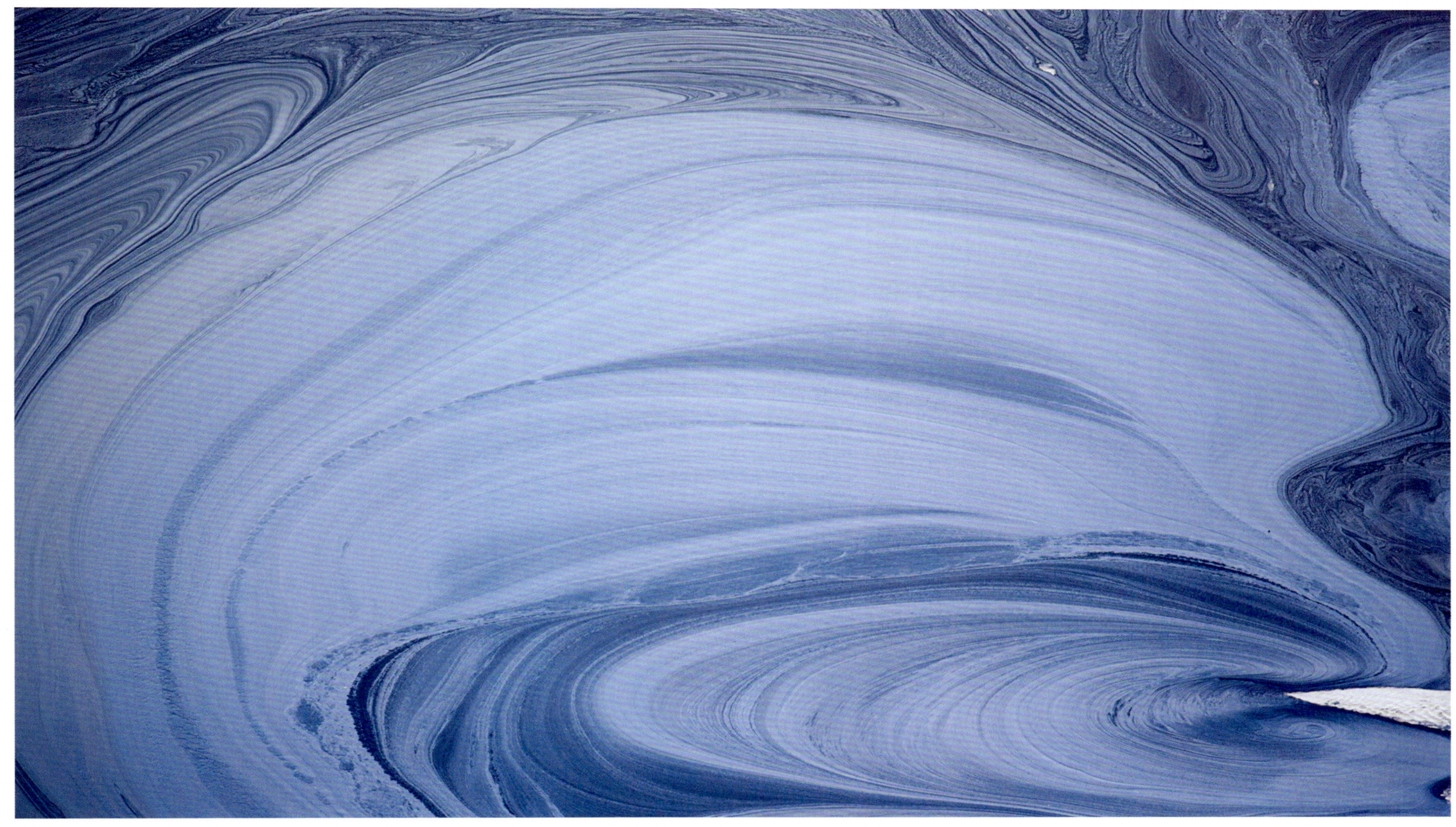

Above
Alex MacLean
Surface oil on tailing pond, Alberta, Canada, 2014.

Overleaf
Alex MacLean
Oil Swirls Among Wastewater, Alberta, Canada, 2014.

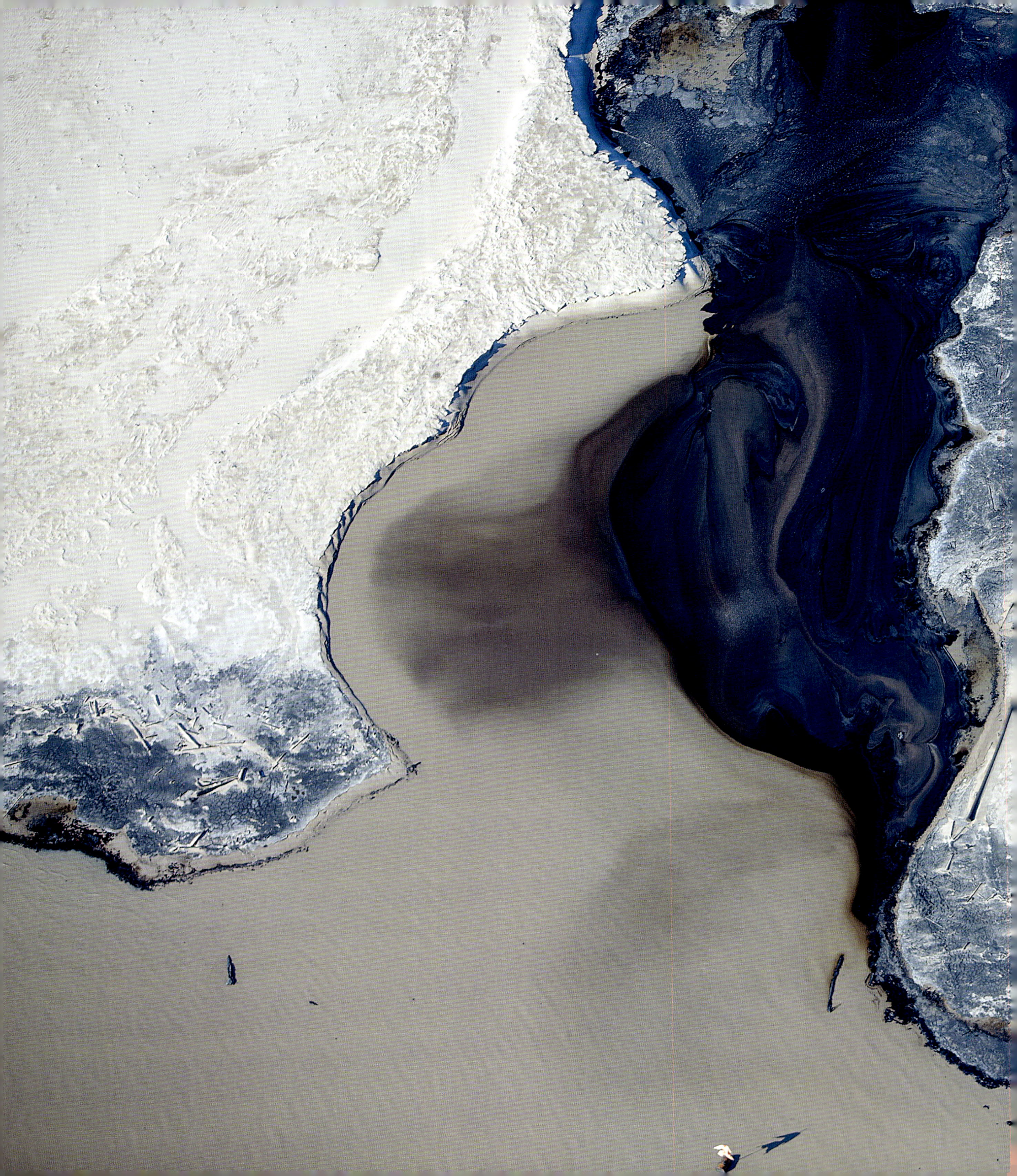

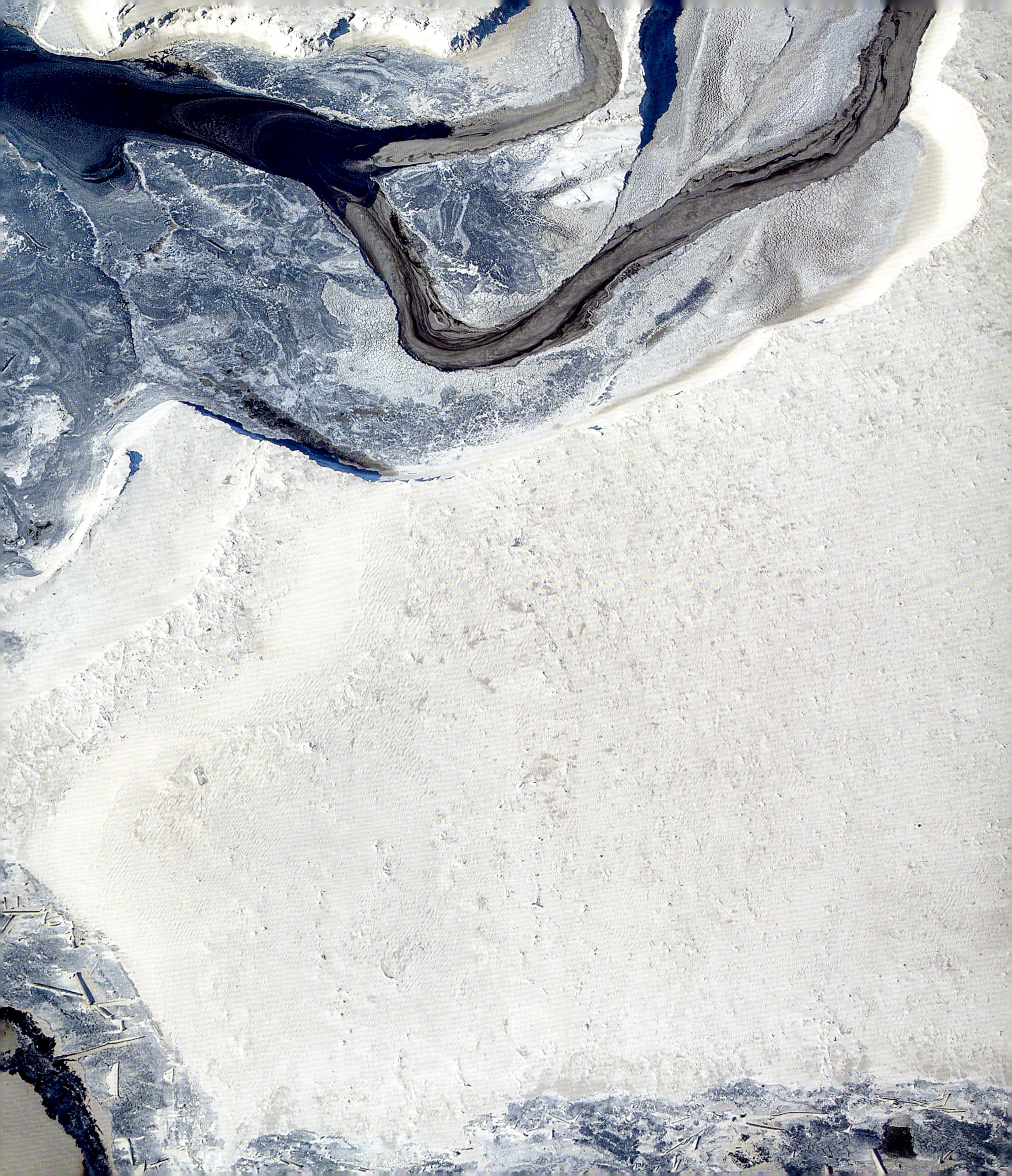

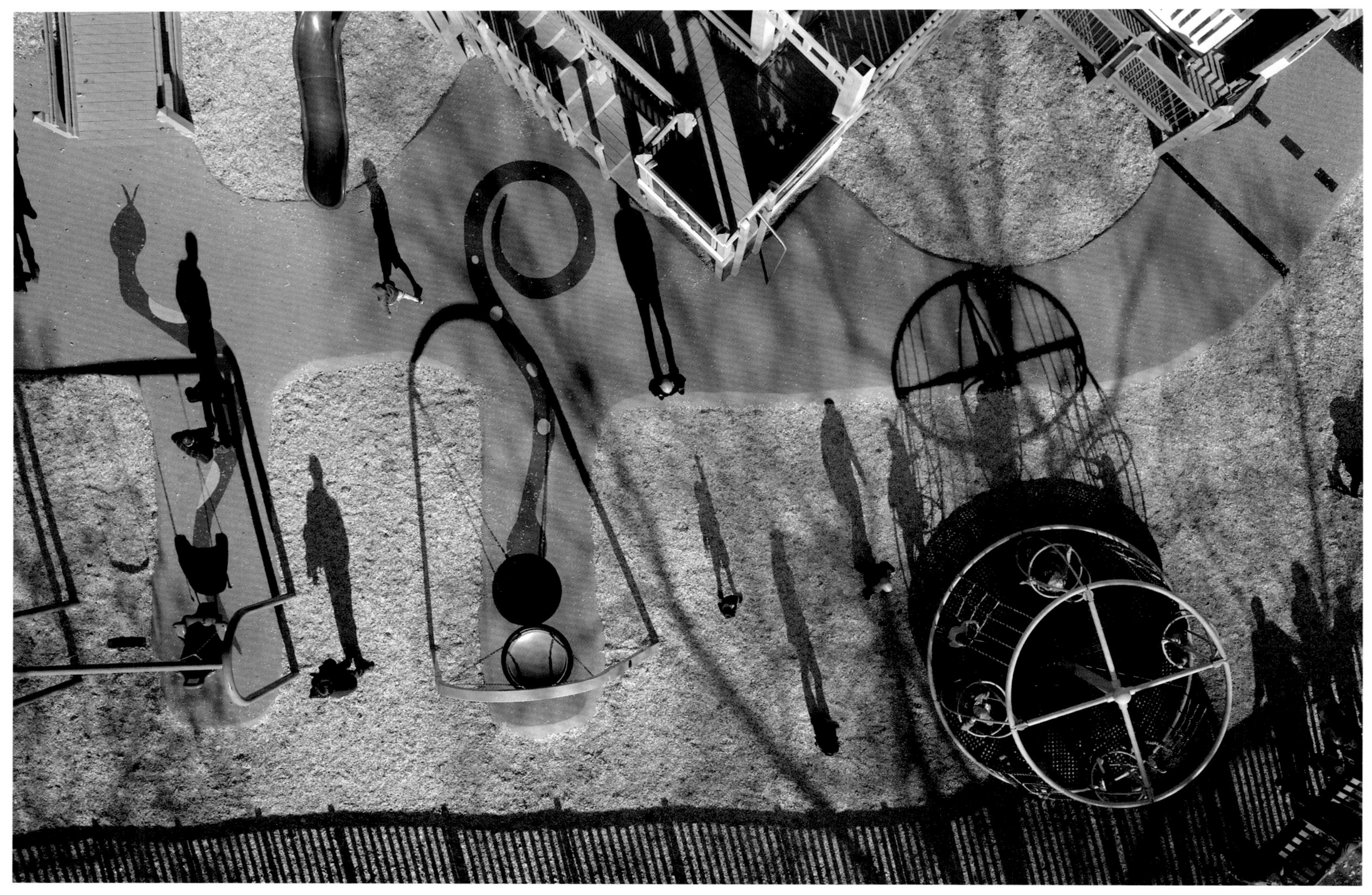

Photographer Tomas van Houtryve's work is concerned with themes such as identity, borders, privacy, power and surveillance, and in his series 'Blue Sky Days', he explores some of these ideas through powerful aerial photographs. The images, taken by a camera attached to a drone, show everyday scenes across America: weddings, playgrounds and people exercising, for example – events that have been associated with targeted or mistaken air strikes elsewhere in the world. The stark downward perspective creates sharp shadows, giving the photographs a unique look that is both abstract and absurd, yet oddly familiar. Van Houtryve makes the point that the people killed by American drone strikes are just like Americans.

Tomas van Houtryve
A playground in Sacramento County, USA, 2014.

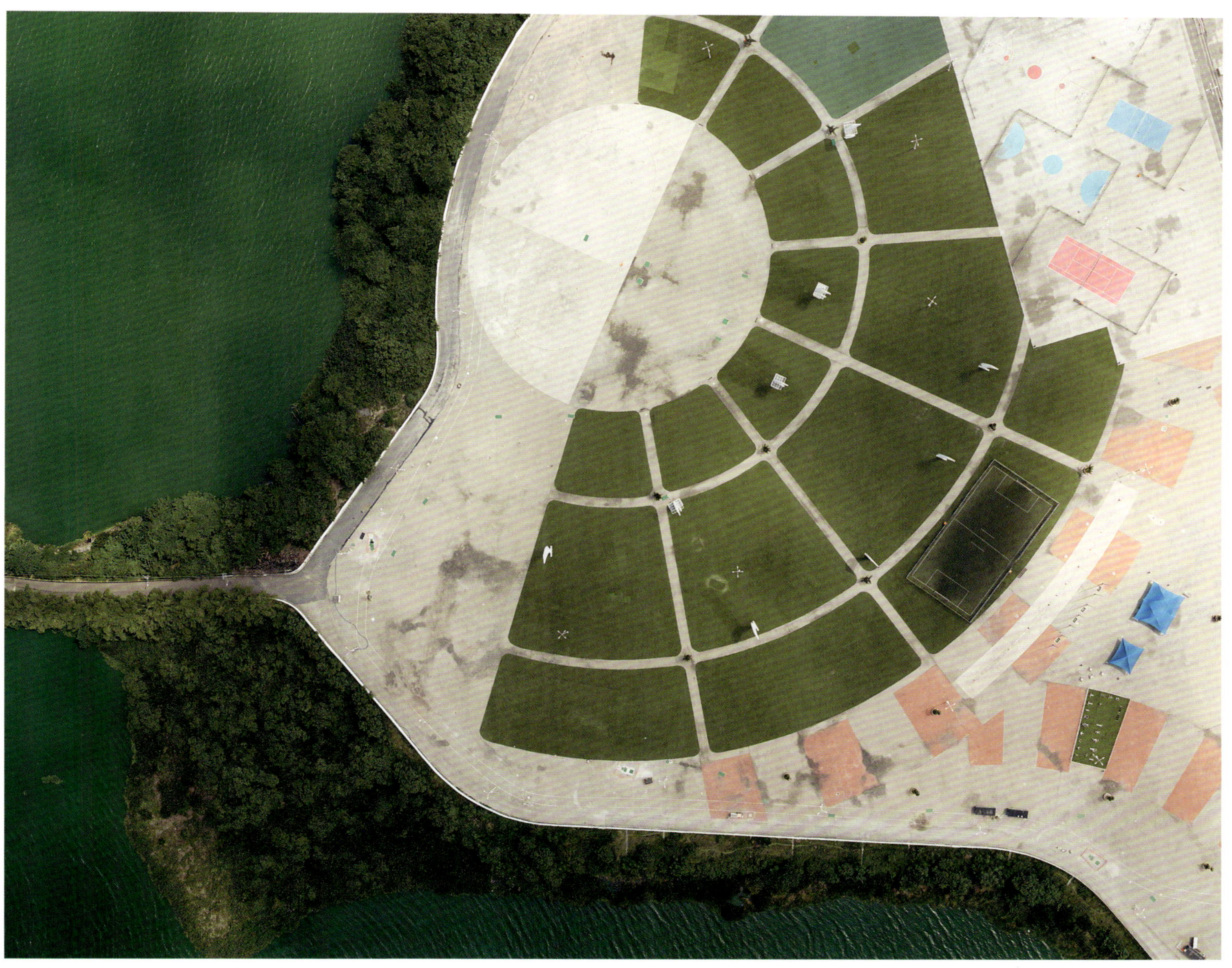

Giles Price
The athletes' park,
Barra da Tijuca,
Rio de Janeiro, from the
series '*Morar Olimpíadas*',
2015.

English photographer Giles Price had his first taste of aerial photography in 1990 while serving with the Royal Marine Commandos in northern Iraq and Kurdistan at the end of the first Gulf War. He took pictures from a helicopter, which came in handy when later forging a career in photography. Having photographed London from the air in the run-up to the 2012 Summer Olympics, Price then turned his attentions to Rio de Janeiro, where he made the series '*Morar Olimpíadas*' (meaning 'Olympics live', pictured above and overleaf) between 2014 and 2016. In this work, Price depicted the rapid urban transformation of Rio as the state prepared to host the 2016 Summer Olympics. He offered a new perspective on the scale of the construction, while conveying a sense of the social inequality and environmental consequences brought about by the games – favelas were bulldozed to make way for new infrastructures, and developments were built in protected areas.

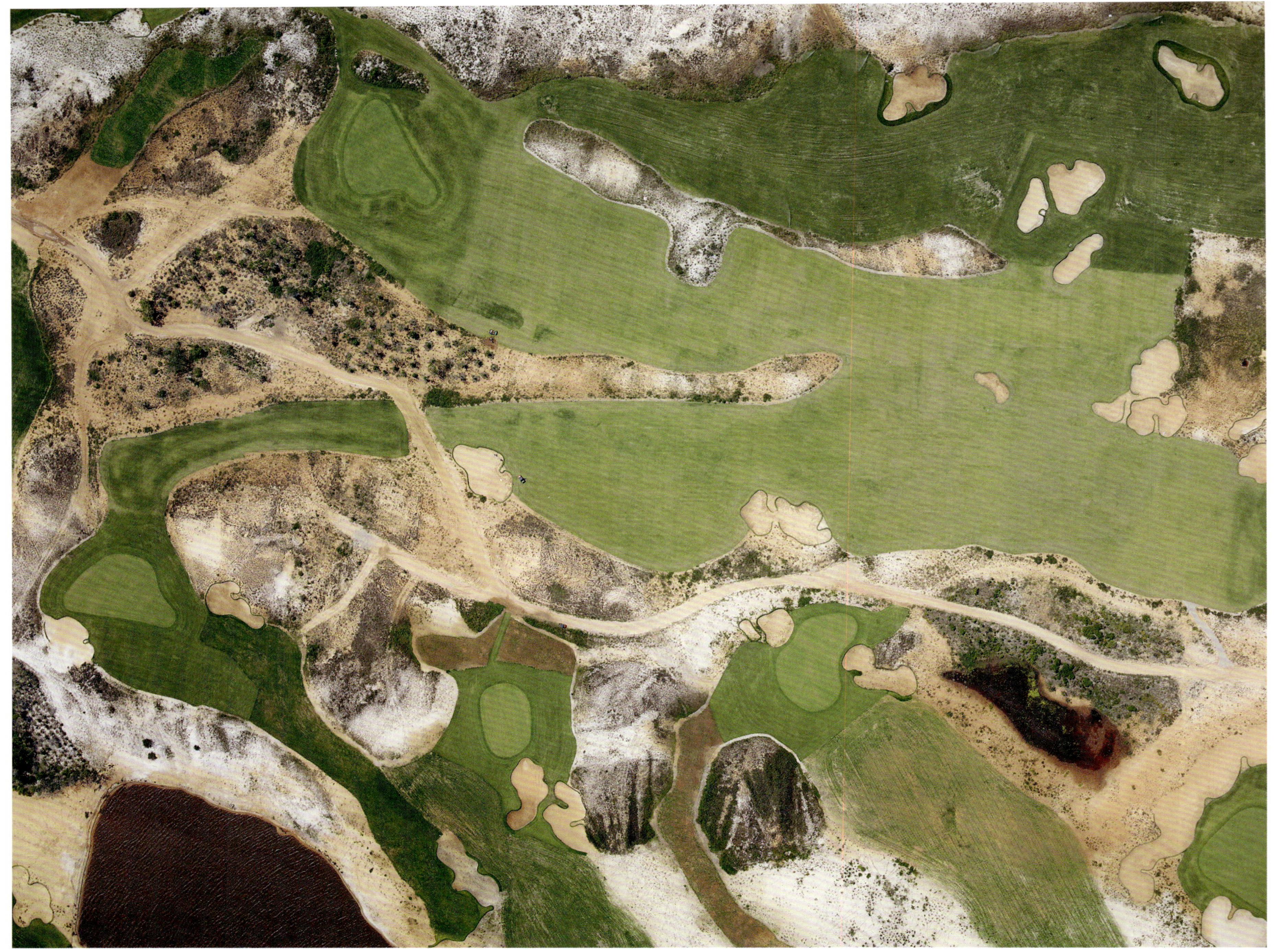

Giles Price
Olympic golf course, Barra da Tijuca, Rio de Janeiro, from the series '*Morar Olimpíadas*', 2015.

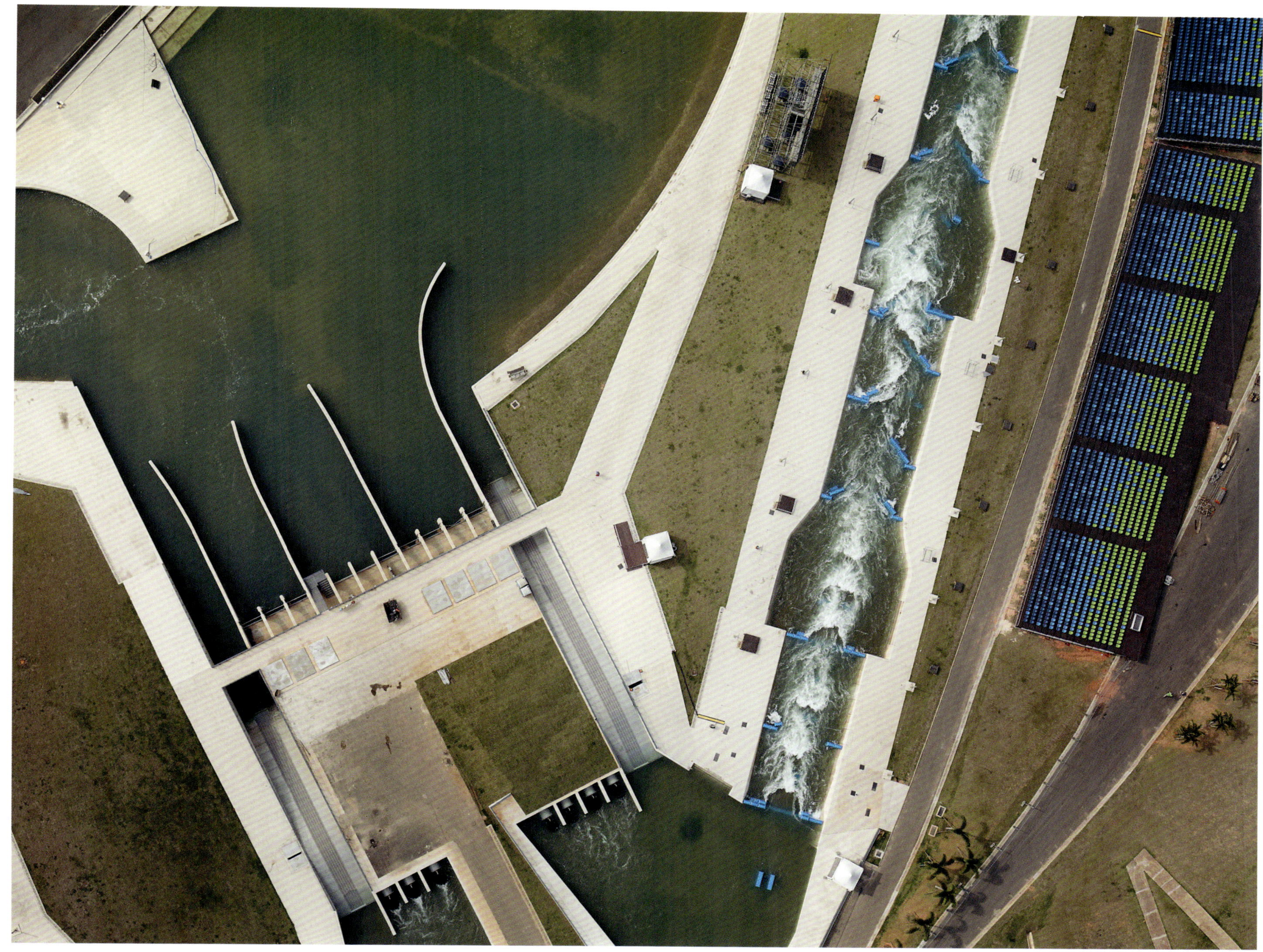

Giles Price
The Whitewater Stadium, Deodoro, Rio de Janeiro, from the series '*Morar Olimpíadas*', 2016.

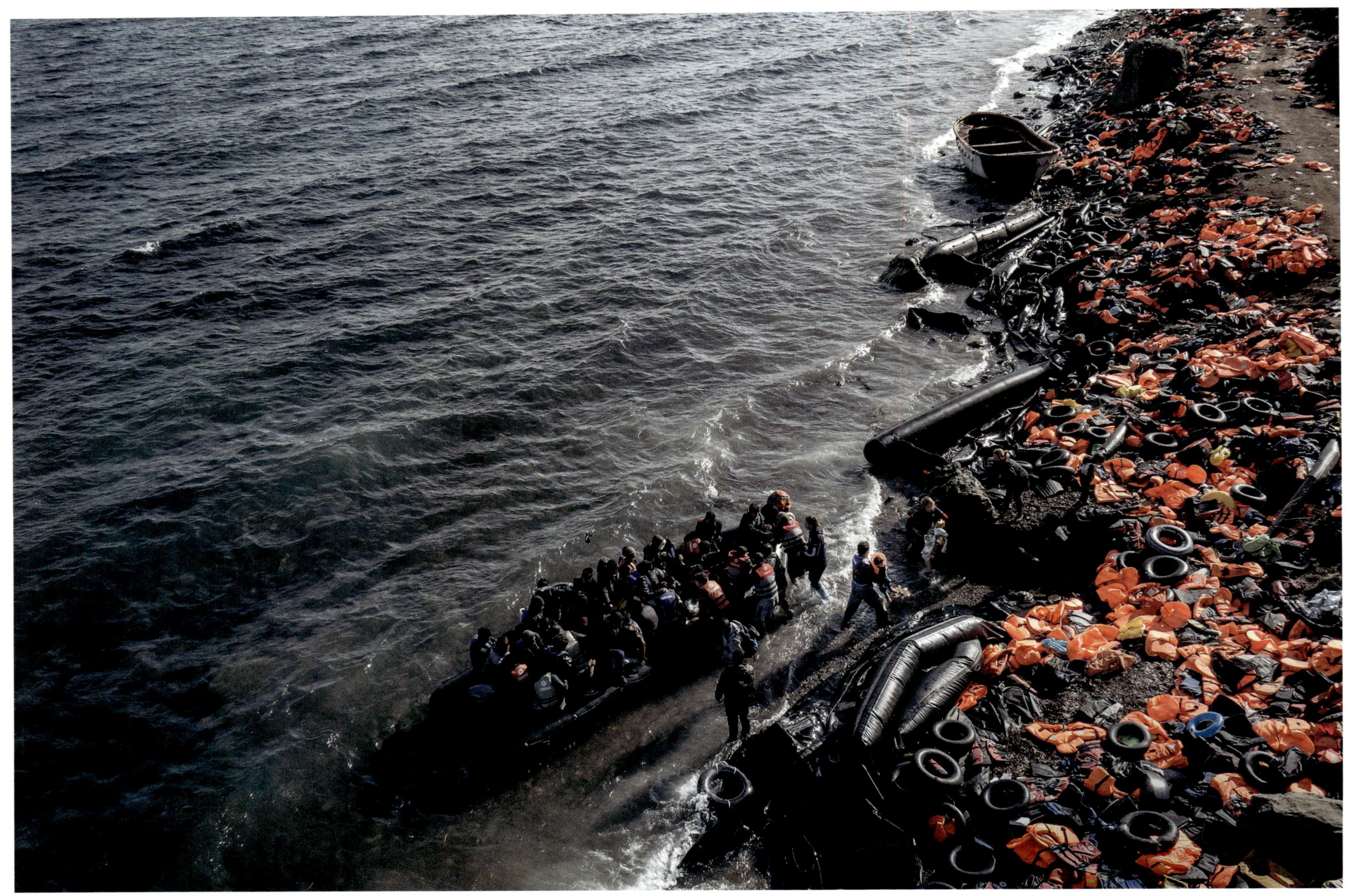

In early summer 2015, Danish photographer Rasmus Degnbol began a documentary project about Europe's borders – namely the changes taking place and their impact on migrants and refugees. Using a drone that he had built, which had a camera attached to it, Degnbol photographed in countries such as Bulgaria, Hungary, Macedonia and Serbia, recording troubling scenes that include people crammed into boats, and what appear to be lifejackets discarded or washed up on the shore. Flying his drone just 25 or 30 metres up in the air enabled Degnbol to capture what he witnessed at close range. His images present a startlingly intimate and, one could argue, politically charged, view of the European migrant crisis.

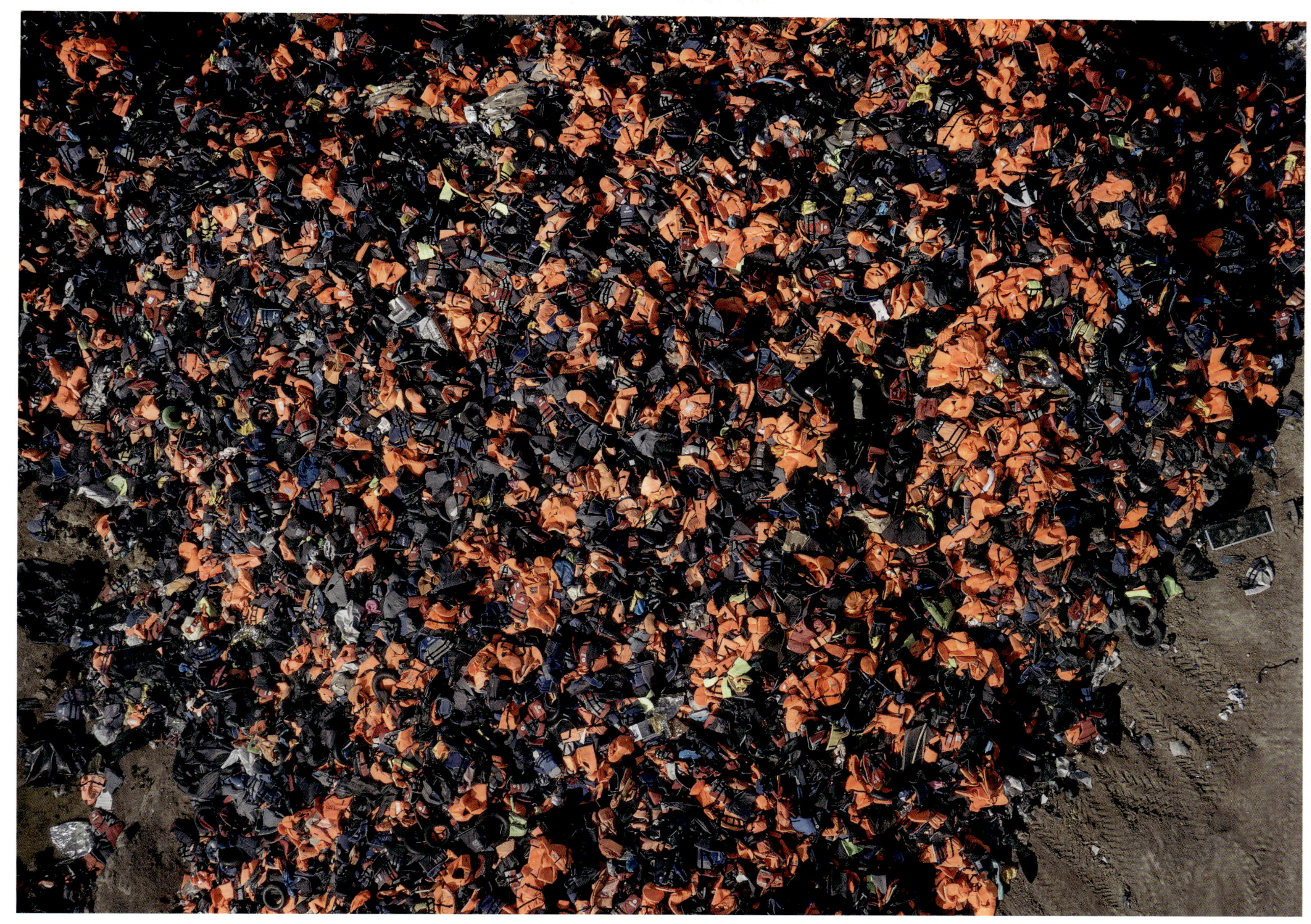

Rasmus Degnbol
From the series
'Europe's New Borders',
2015.

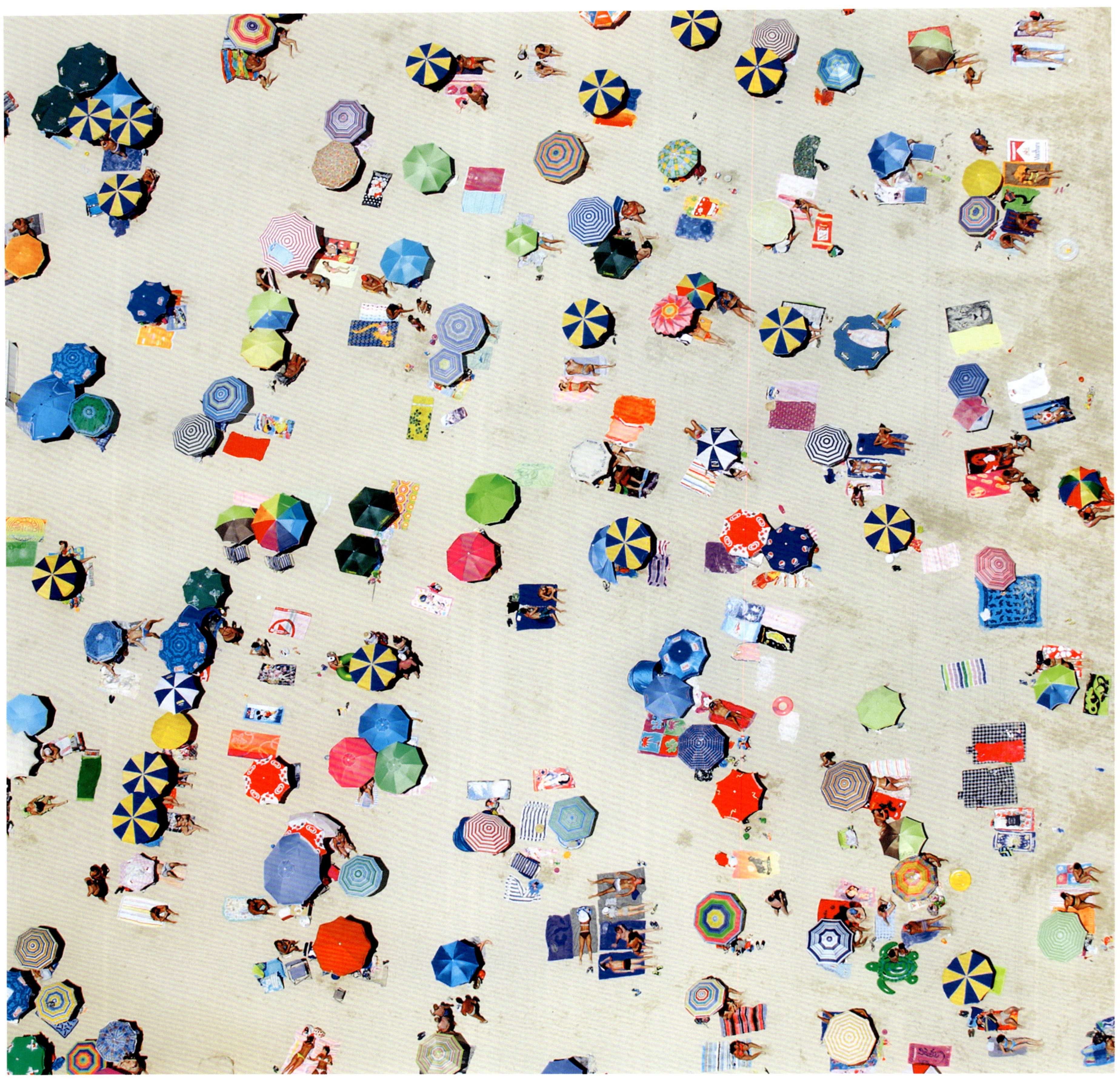

Tommy Clarke's professional life changed in 2011 when he chartered a plane at Bondi Beach, Sydney, to photograph a swimming contest. The images were a hit and they set the young photographer on course to become one of the world's most in-demand aerial photographers. Clarke's current portfolio of meticulously executed images – from glaciers in Iceland to a salt mine in Australia – is a wonderful celebration of the diversity of planet Earth. Inevitably, perhaps, Clarke, who shoots from a helicopter or small plane, is beginning to turn his attention towards environmental concerns such as the issue of floating plastic in the Pacific.

Opposite
Tommy Clarke
North Amadores, from the series 'Gran Canaria', 2015.

Right
Tommy Clarke
Lagoon Fence, from the series 'Shark Bay', Western Austalia, 2016.

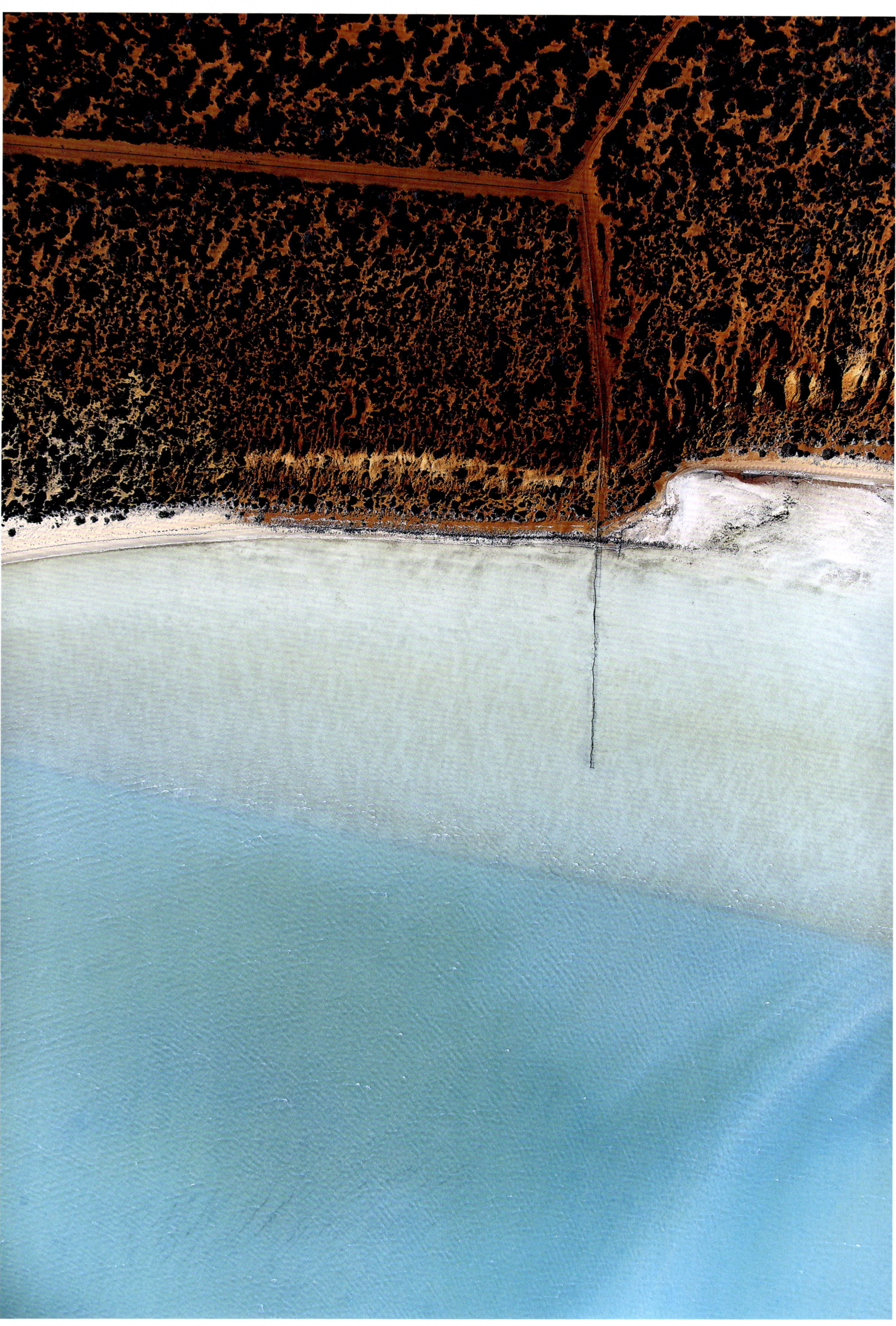

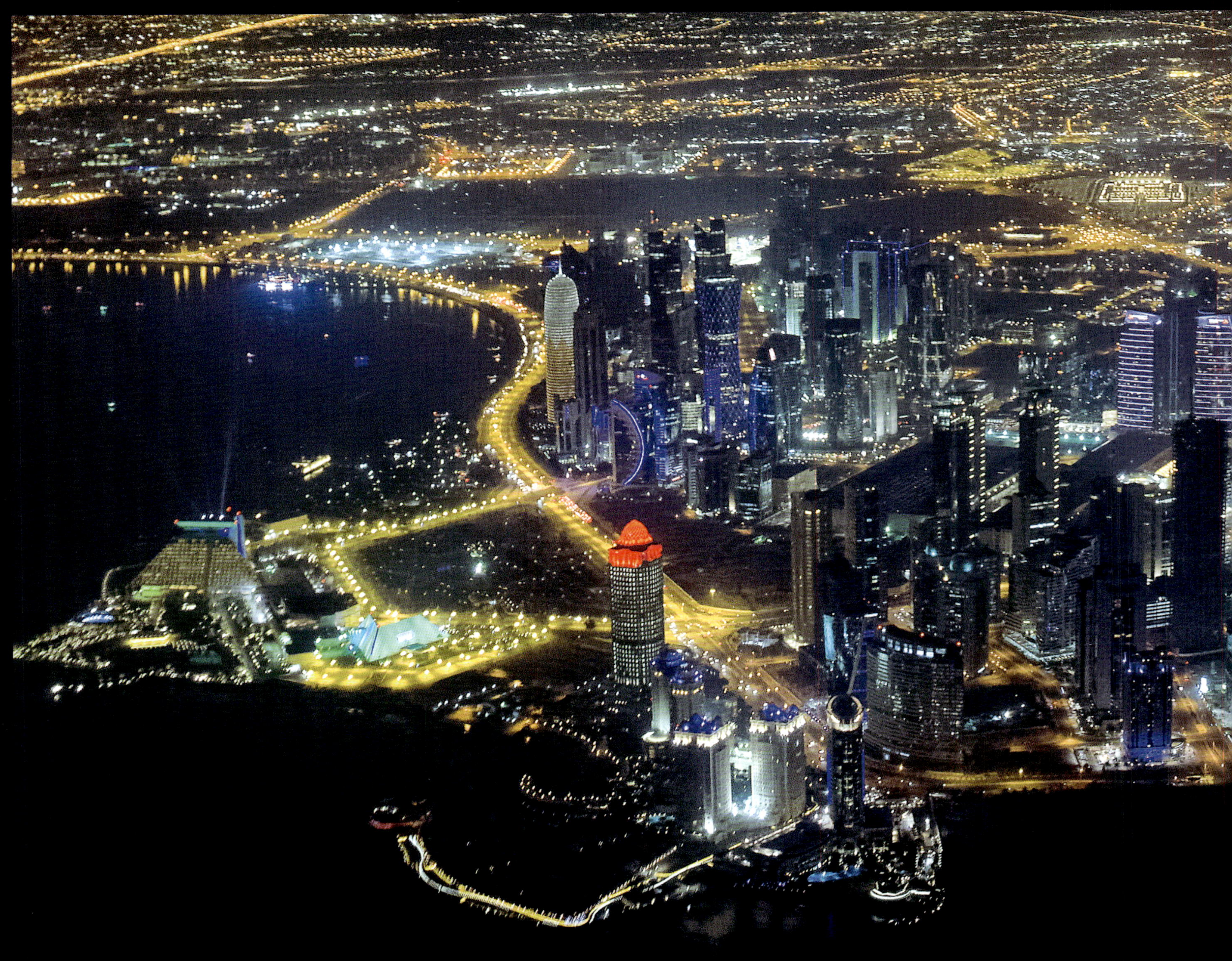

Jon Bowles
West Bay in Doha,
Qatar, 2016.

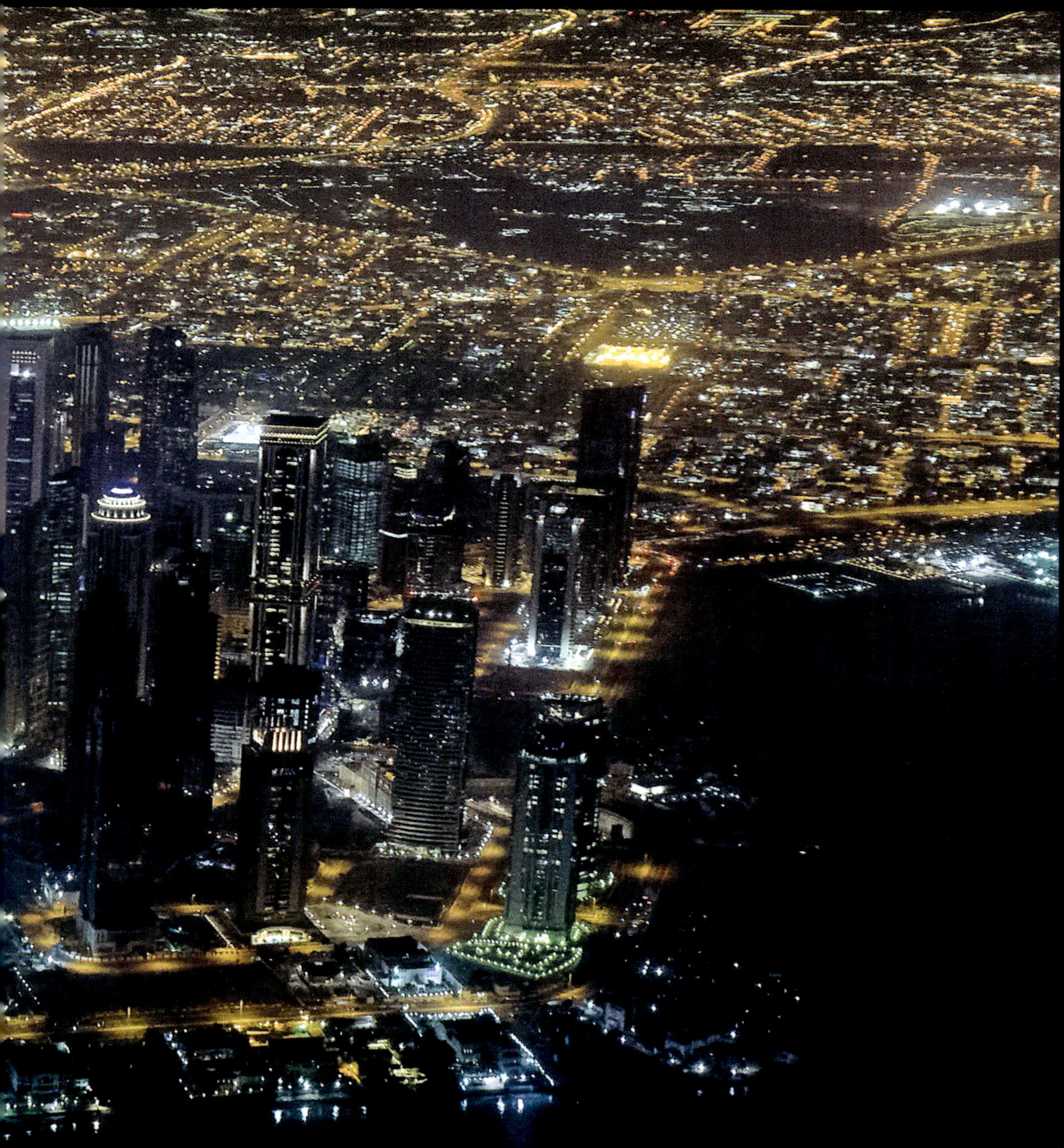

For 40 years, British pilot Captain Jon Bowles has been transporting passengers across the world, flying over everywhere from West Bay in Qatar to Kuwait, Budapest, Cairo, Buenos Aires and southern China. In 2011, Bowles began making photographs from the cockpit of his Boeing 777, capturing magnificent illuminated cityscapes at night, such as these *Blade Runner*-esque shots of Qatar. He looks for interesting shapes and patterns in the way a city is laid out, and keeps an eye out for light and dark areas that might make for a good composition. His hope is that such images will convey a sense of the impact of urbanization on the planet.

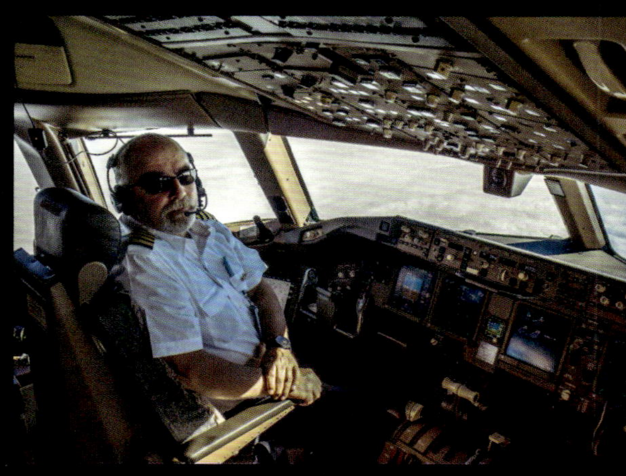

John Bowles in his Boeing 777, 2016.

2016

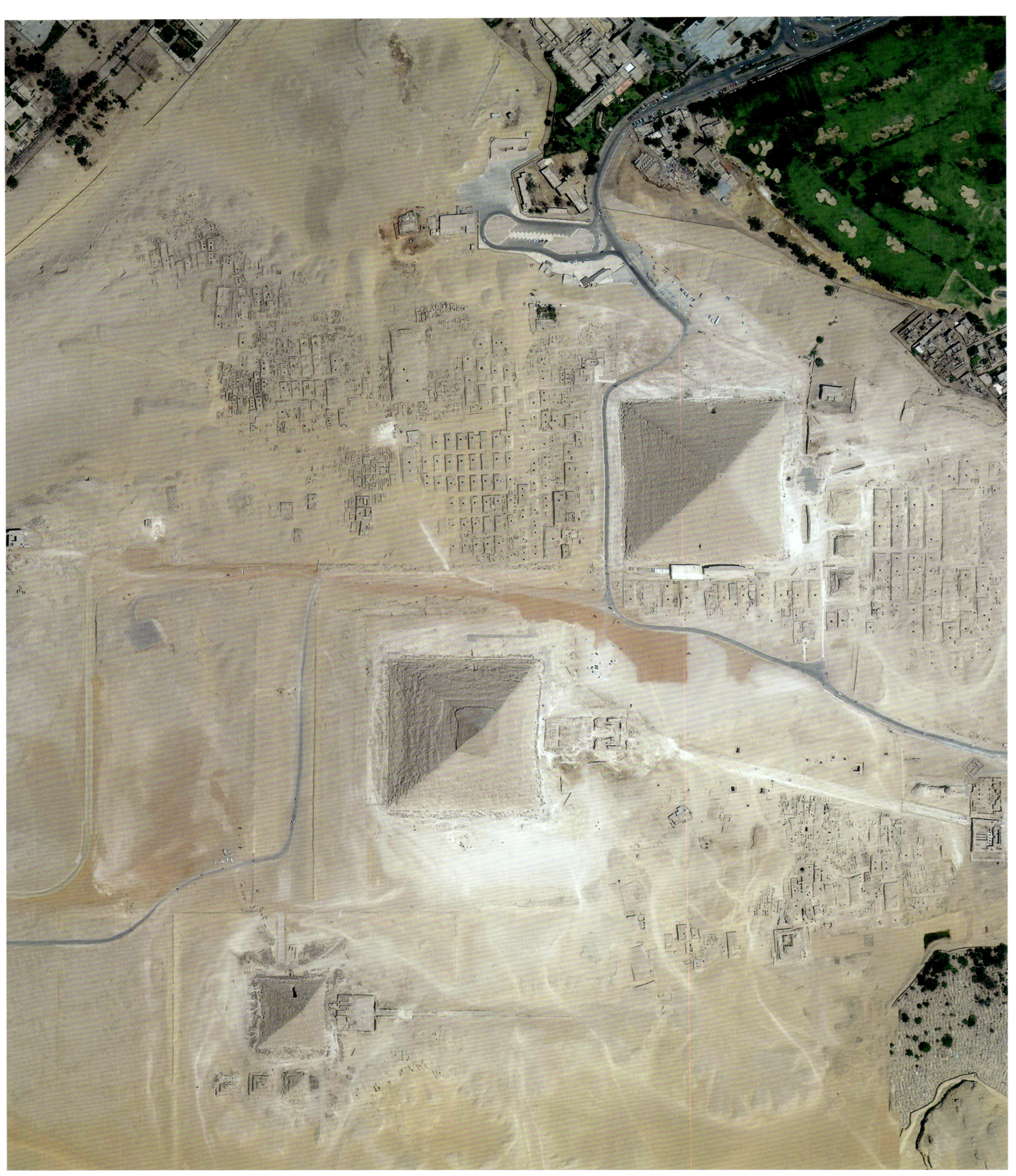

American Benjamin Grant works with satellite imagery to create highly detailed, yet disorientating, composite aerial images. In 2013, he began posting views he had collected from Apple Maps and Google Earth on a blog called the Daily Overview. His blog and the images he shared on social media became so popular that Grant sought permission from the operator DigitalGlobe to use the original high-res satellite image files to create his own composites. Each image comprises between 6 and 20 satellite images, which Grant edits together in Photoshop. Places he has depicted in this way include the pyramids of Giza, in Egypt, and residential developments in Barcelona, whose intricate designs become apparent from above.

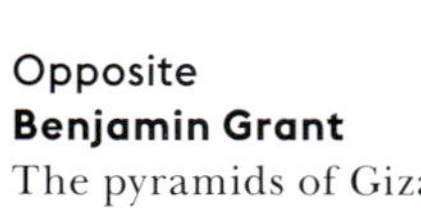

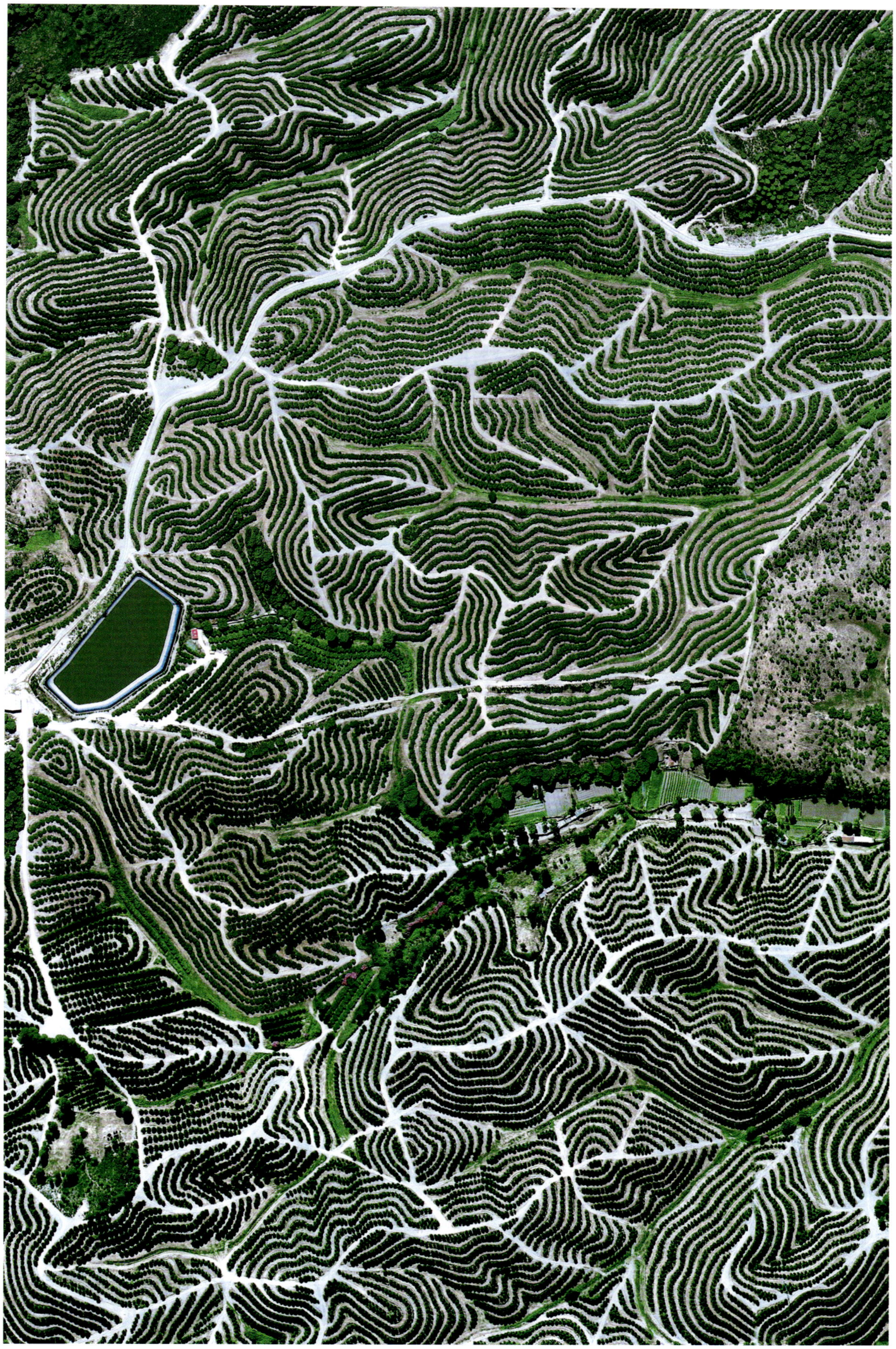

Opposite
Benjamin Grant
The pyramids of Giza, Cairo, Egypt, 2016.

Right
Benjamin Grant
Fruit-tree orchards, Huelva, Spain, 2016.

Overleaf
Benjamin Grant
The Eixample district, Barcelona, Spain, 2016.

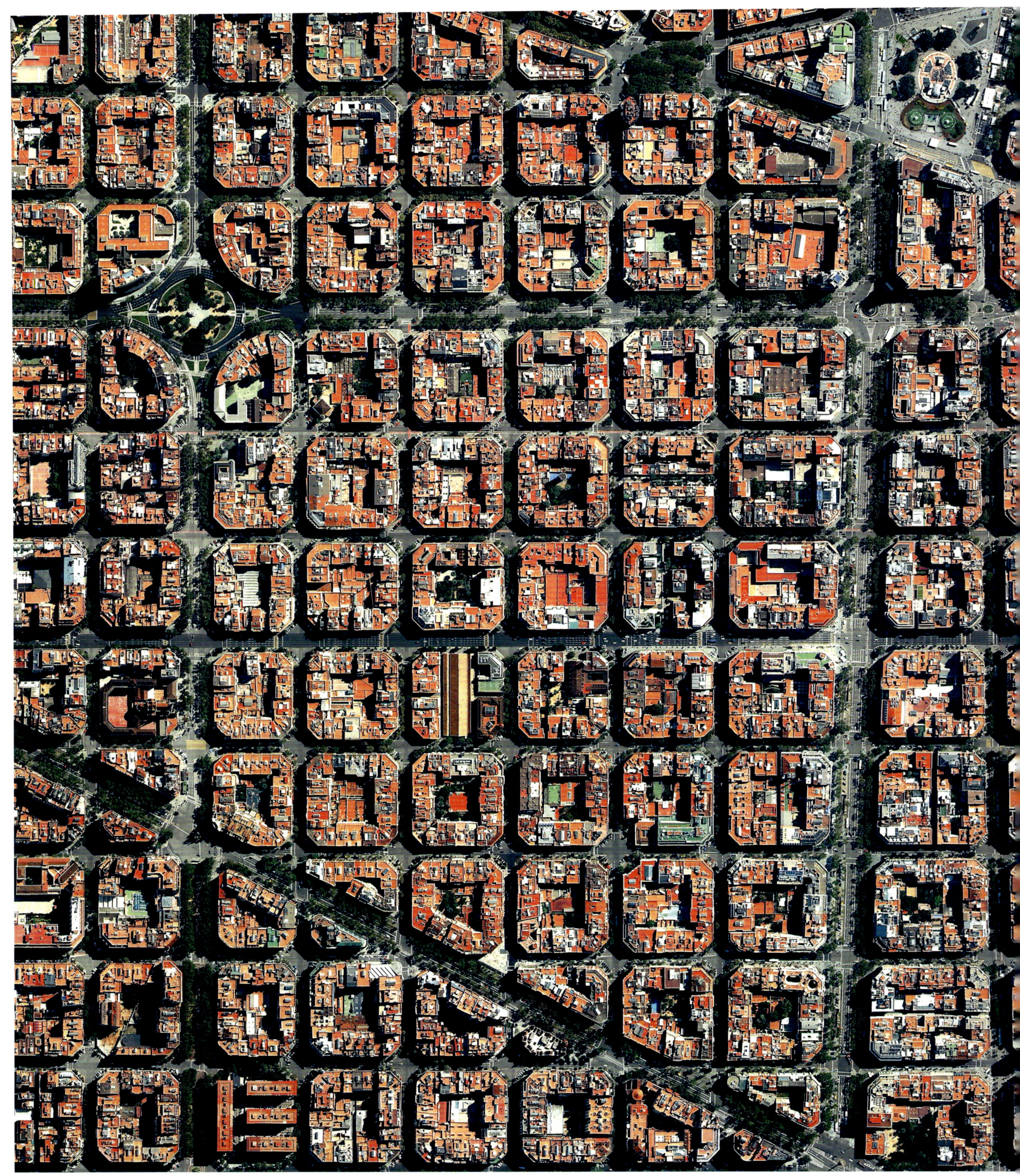

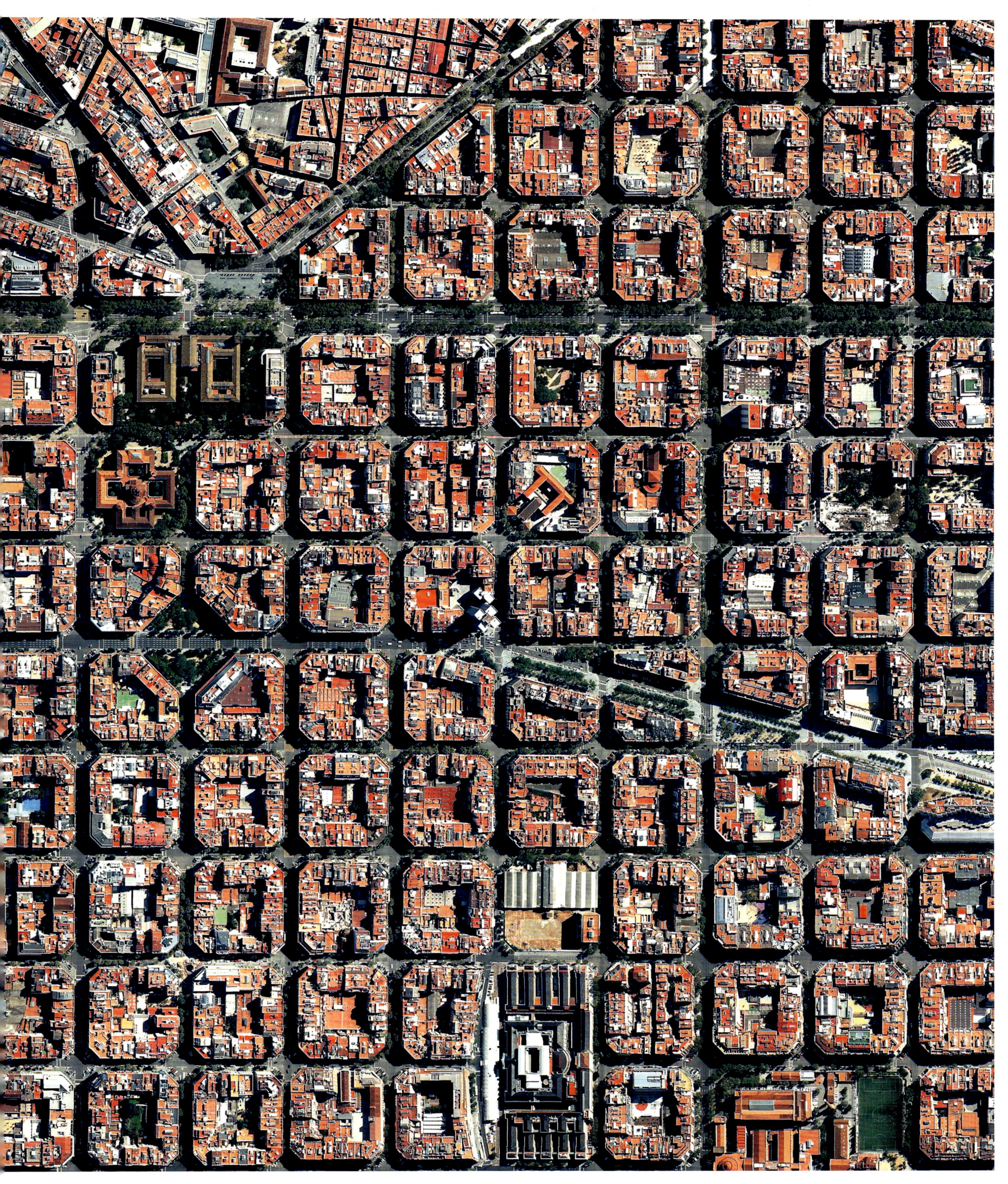

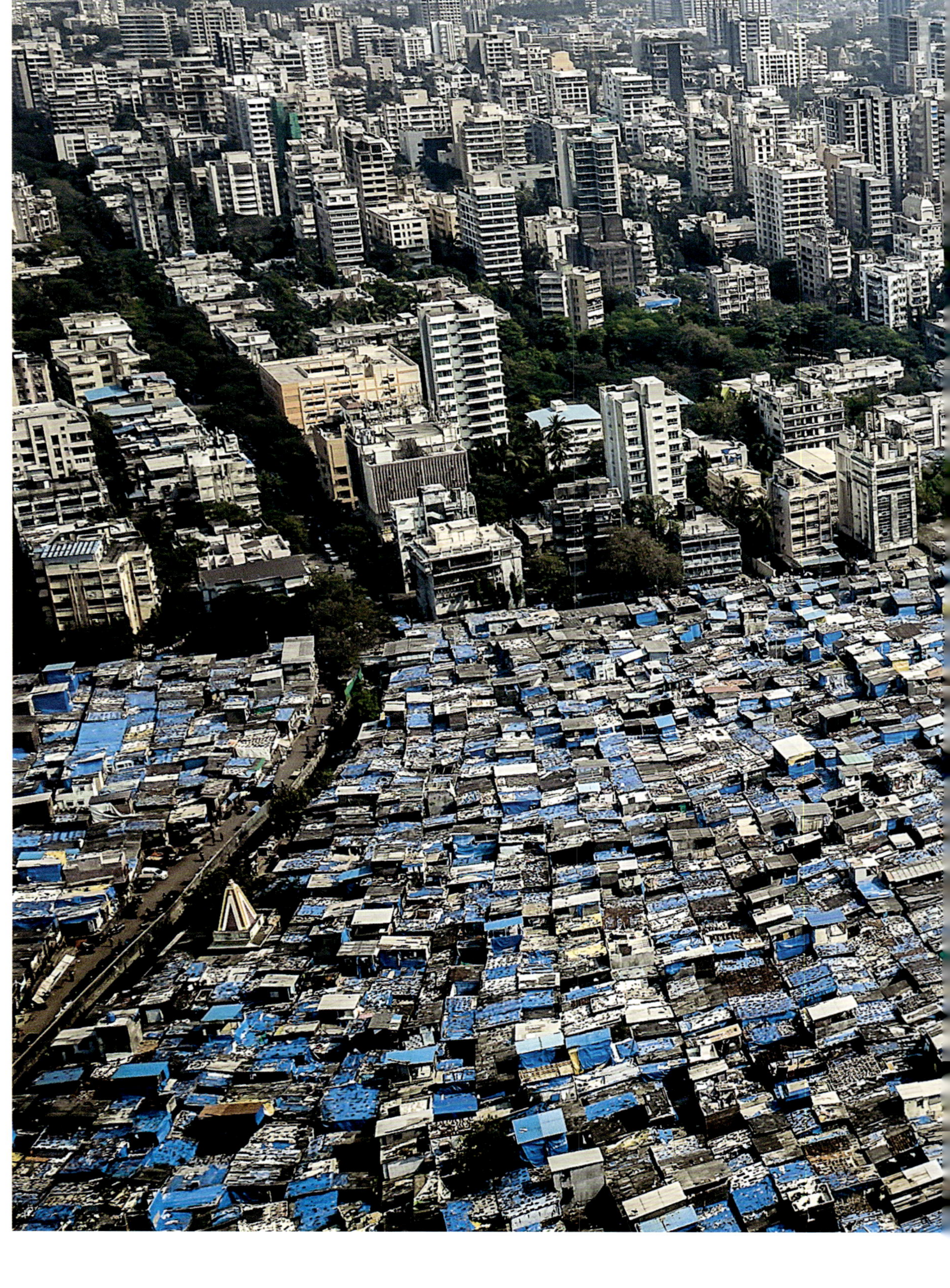

In 2016, Johnny Miller began a project that shone a light on South Africa in a way that hadn't been done before. Using a drone, which he flew over the country's townships and gated communities, Miller captured striking aerial views that document the stark differences between the way rich and poor people live. The series 'Unequal Scenes' was born, but Miller didn't stop there; he has since taken his project to places that include Mexico City, Nairobi and Mumbai (pictured), where skyscrapers dwarf vast slums. Miller has encountered inequality and unequal scenes in many countries, but his images are intended to provoke conversations that may result in real change.

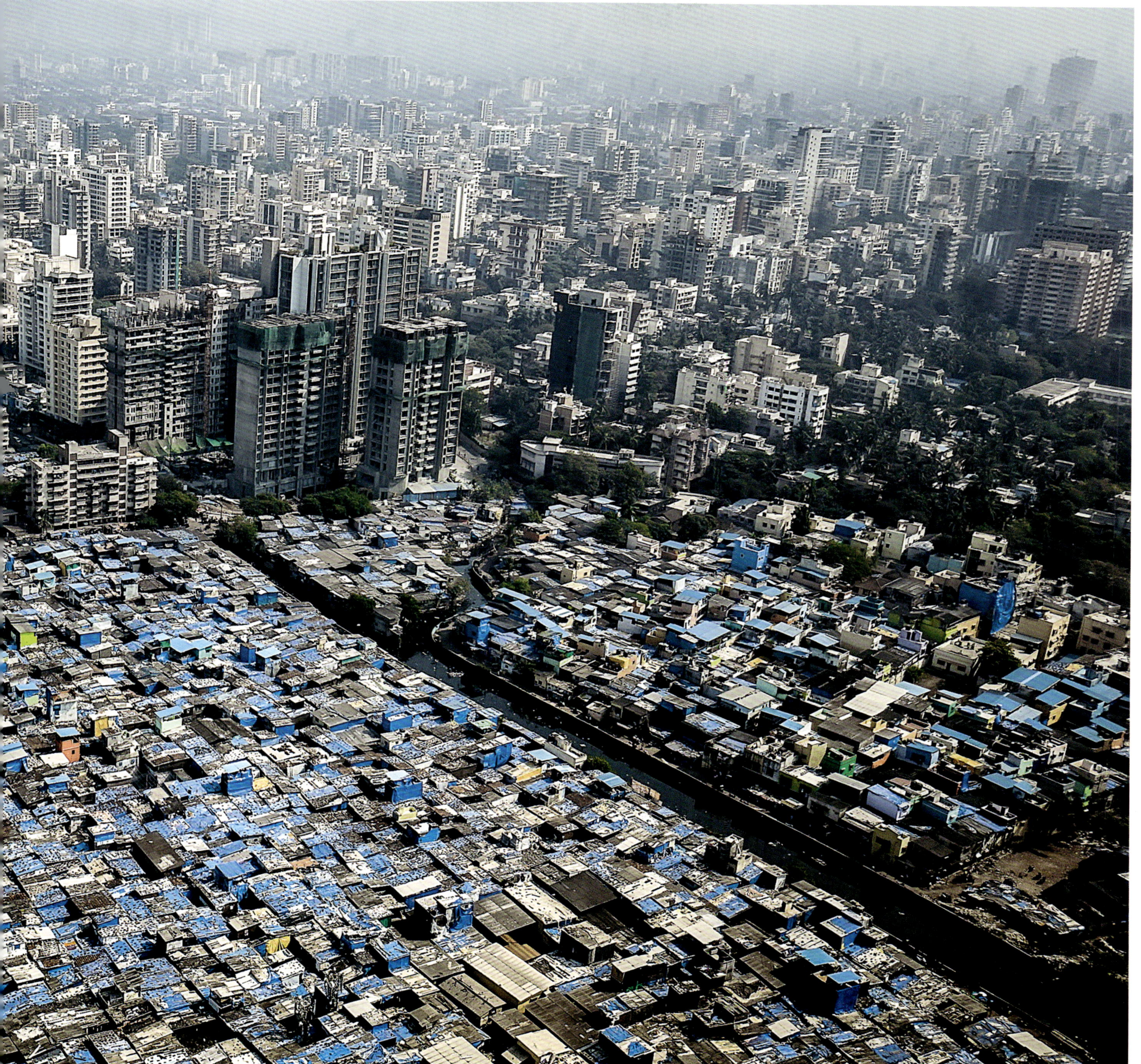

Johnny Miller
Mumbai, India, from the series 'Unequal Scenes', 2016.

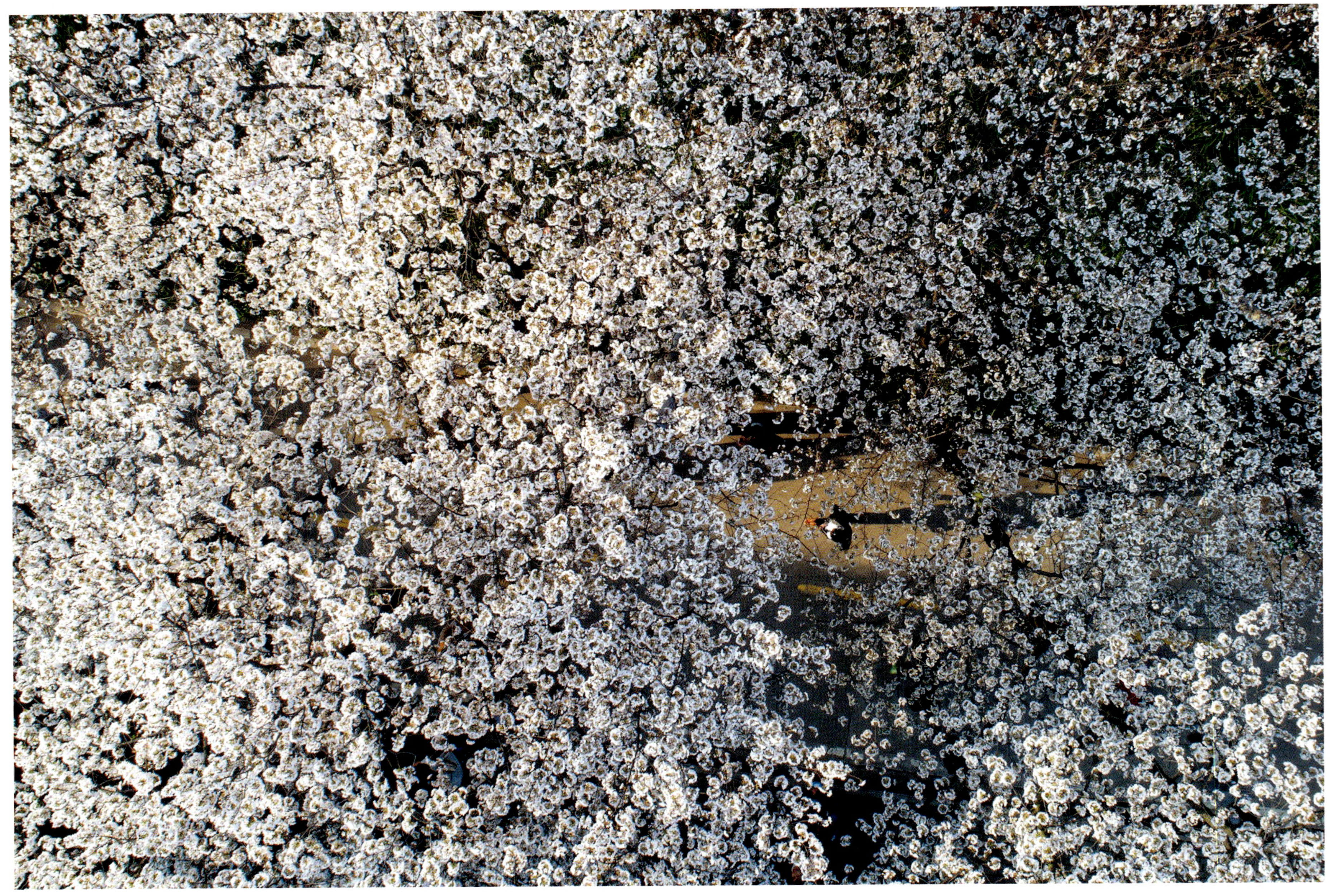

When you think of cherry blossom season, it is usually Japan that springs to mind, but from late March to early April, many provinces across China are also awash with springtime blossom. Every year, Shanghai holds its Cherry Blossom Festival and, in 2017, the public was invited to submit images of the blooms. Submissions included: drone-camera shots of flowers in Gucun Pak, Shanghai's largest suburban park and the main site of the festival; an aerial image of a visitor walking beneath cherry blossom in Wuhan University, in central China's Hubei province (pictured above); and blossoms in Guizhou province, south-western China (pictured opposite).

Photographer unknown
Cherry blossoms in the grounds of Wuhan University, Hubei province, China, 2017.

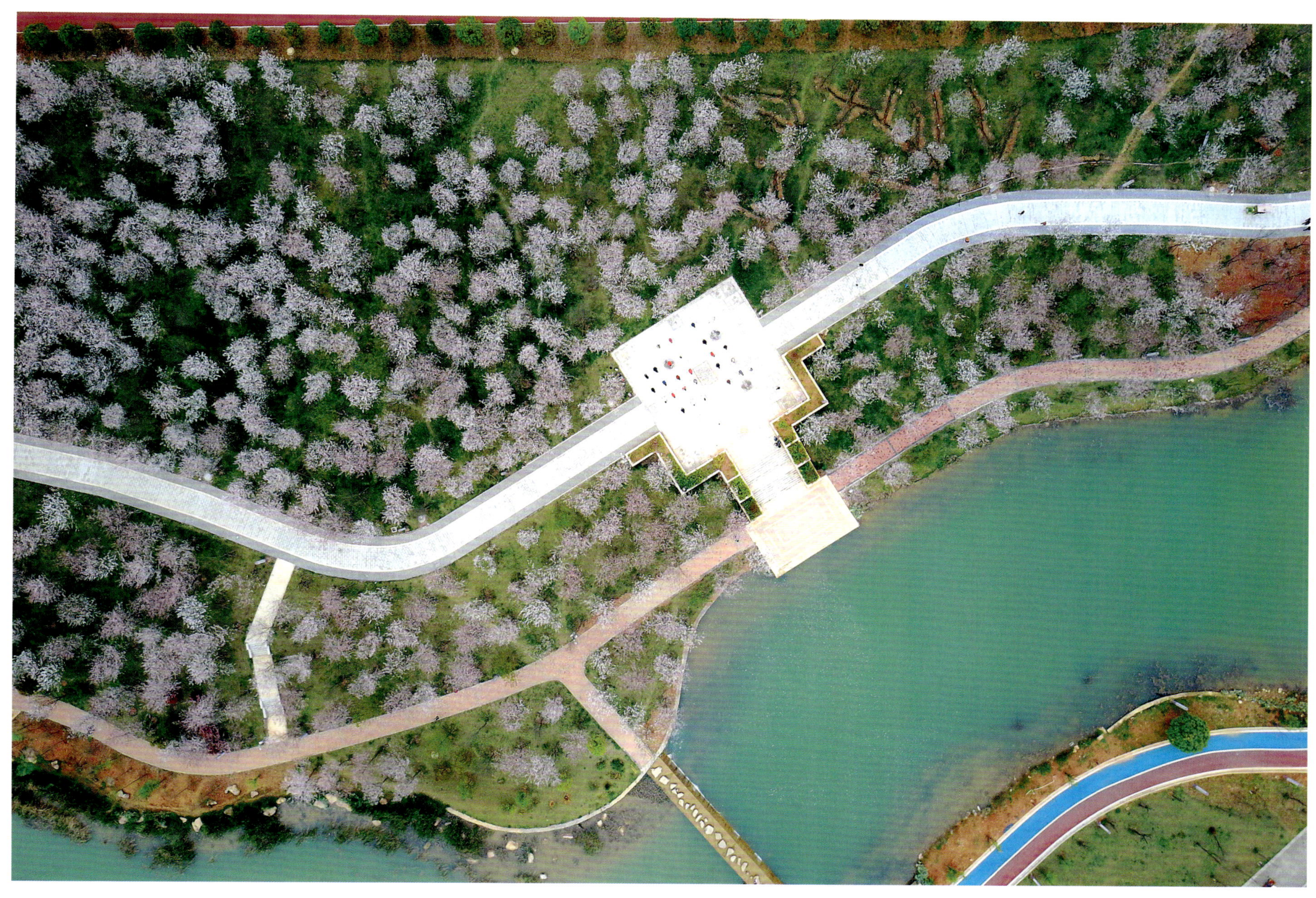

Photographer unknown
Cherry blossoms in Yilong, Guizhou province, China, 2017.

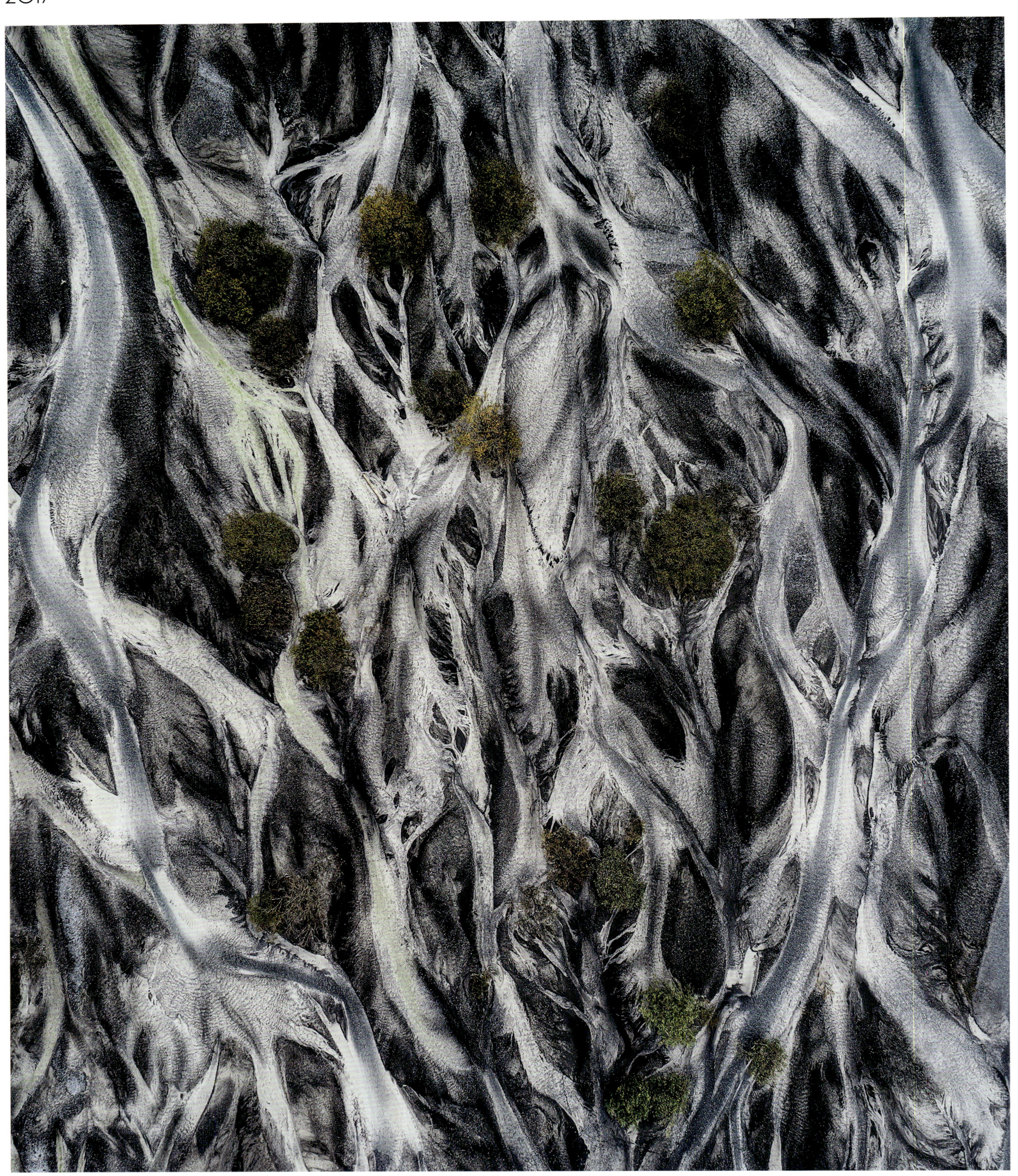

When brothers Mike and J. P. Andrews set off for Australia with a drone and a camera, their intention was to photograph the Earth from above. But as they looked at their images, they were at a loss to know how to describe what they were seeing. It was then that an idea came to them – to launch Abstract Aerial Art and embrace the artistic abstractions. Over the next four months, the brothers travelled 50,000 kilometres around the continent, photographing with their camera facing directly down to show 'how weird and wonderful the world can look from above'. Since returning to the UK, the brothers have continued their drone photography adventure at home and in Europe (pictured here and overleaf).

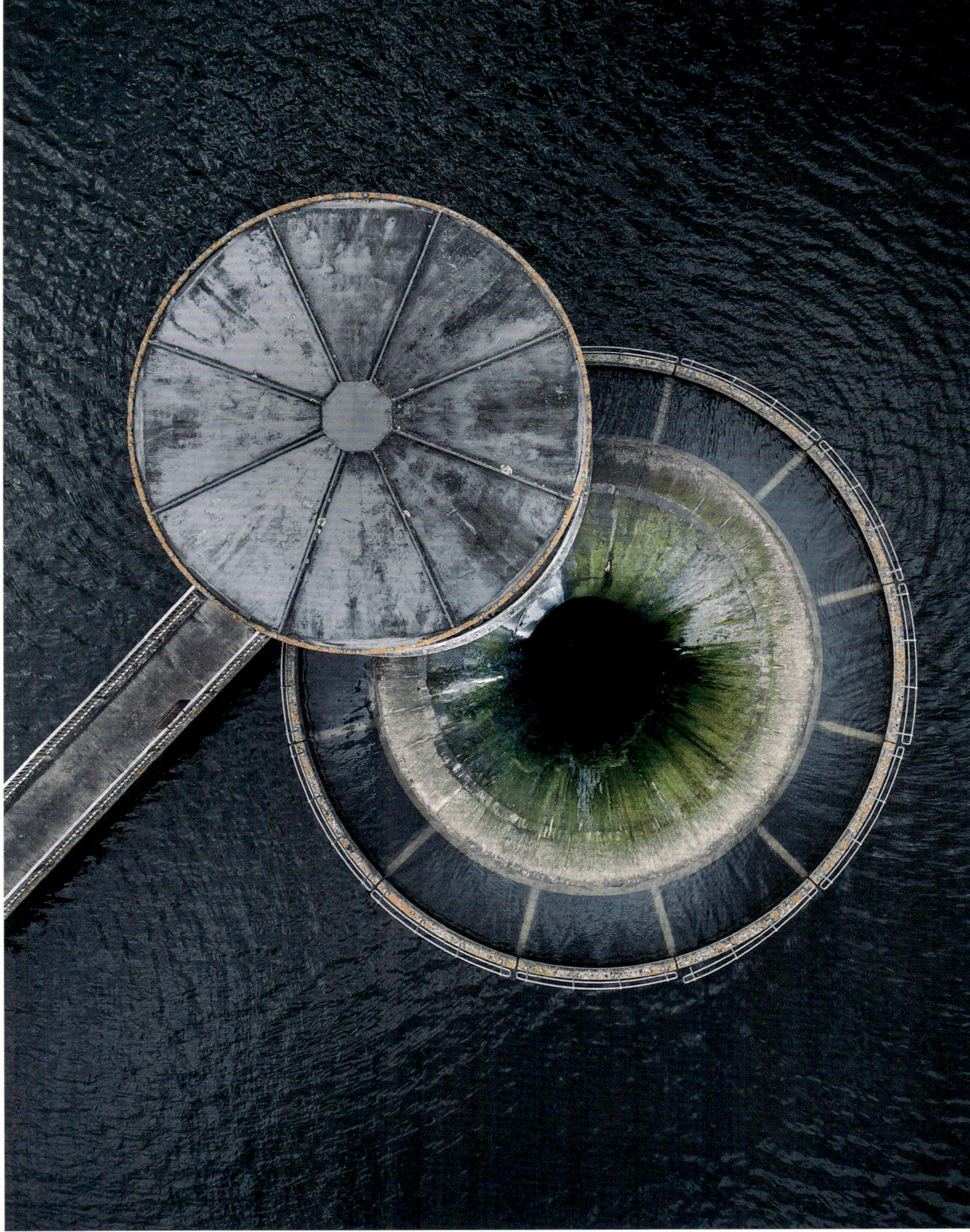

Opposite
Mike and J. P. Andrews
Interweave, Switzerland, 2017.

Right
Mike and J. P. Andrews
Event Horizon, East Sussex, England, 2017.

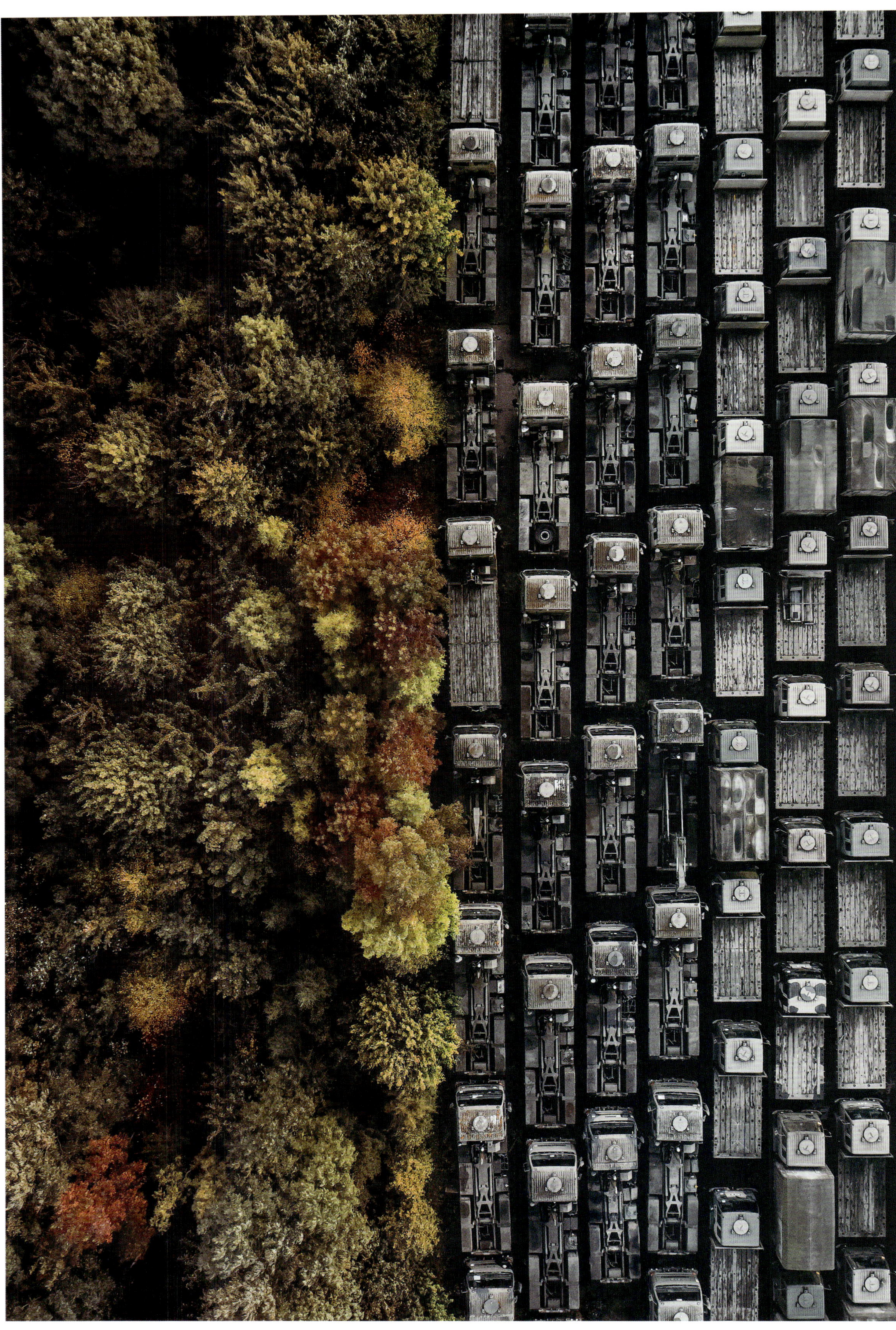

Mike and J. P. Andrews
Man Vs Wild, Nottingham, England, 2017.

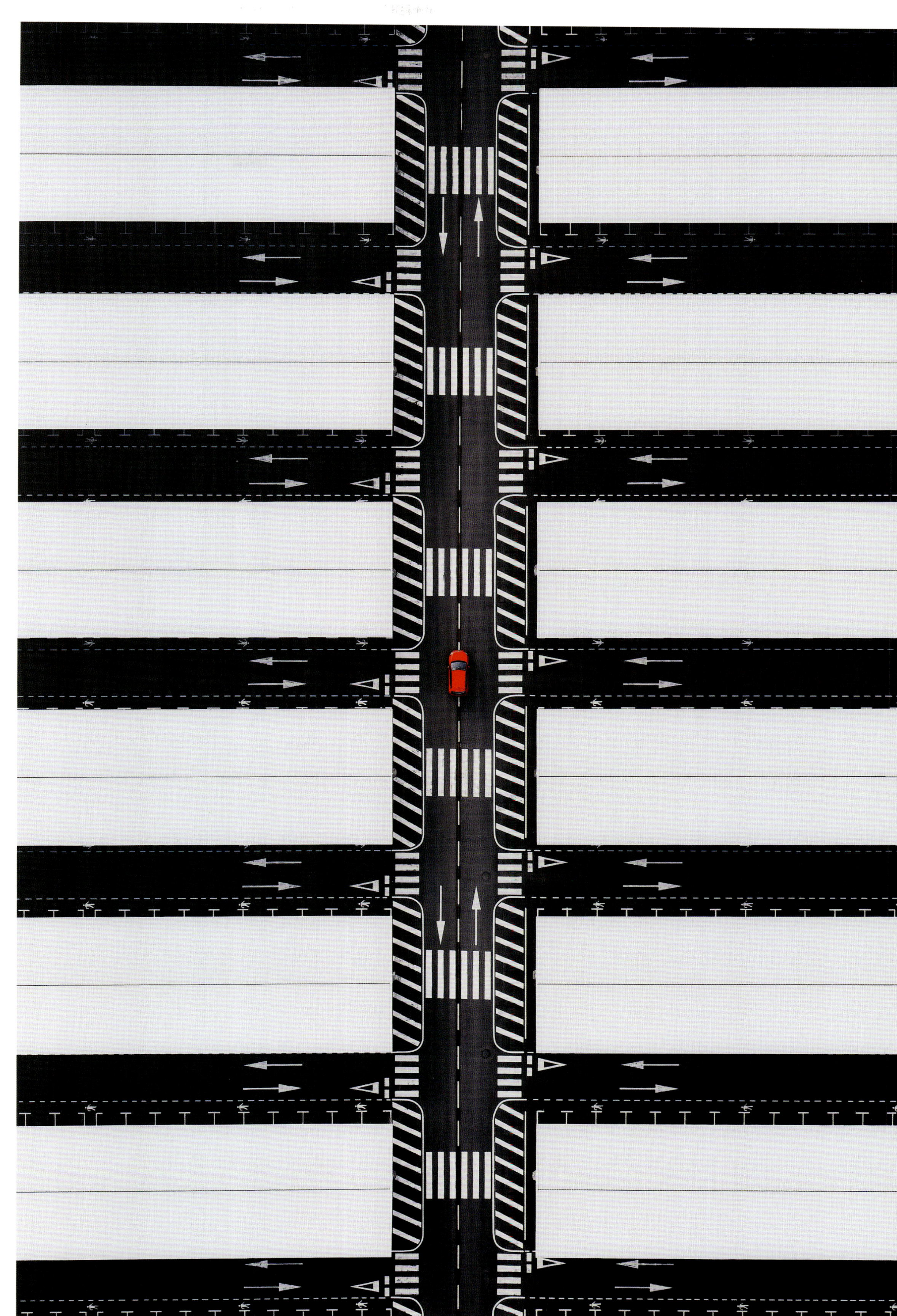

Mike and J. P. Andrews
The Terminal, Ciudad Real, Spain, 2017.

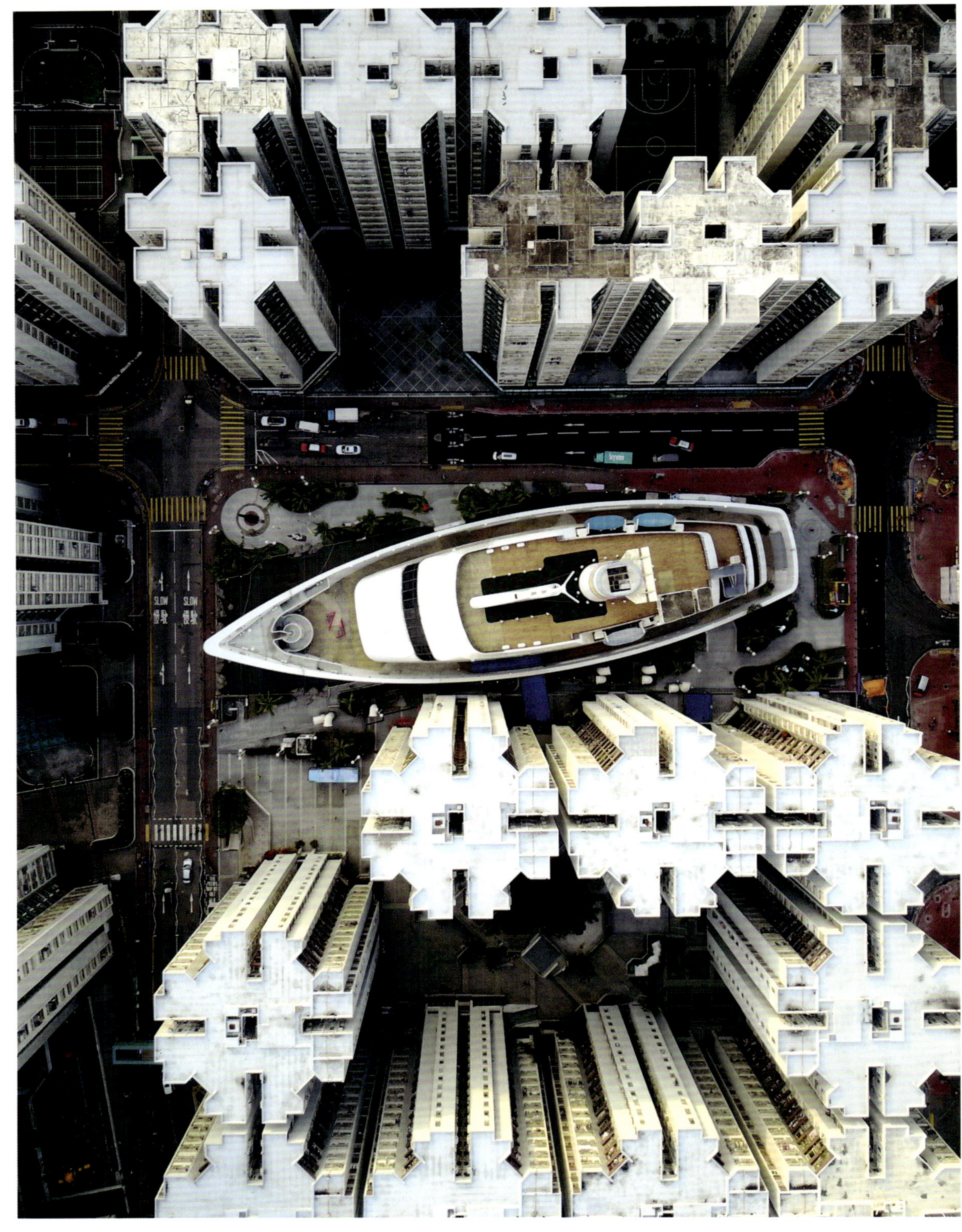

How strange it is to see a huge ship in the centre of a metropolis, surrounded by skyscrapers. This, however, is no ordinary boat. The Whampoa is a shopping mall in Hong Kong that has been made to look like a luxury liner. Situated in Hung Hom, Kowloon, the building belongs to the Wonderful Worlds of Whampoa shopping complex. It was photographed by Bernie Ng, who belongs to a pioneering new breed of photographers who are marrying drone technology with Instagram. As is the case in many countries, Hong Kong has strict laws governing drone use. For example, drones must be flown below 90 metres, and a permit is required for unmanned aerial vehicles that weigh over 7 kilograms. But, despite restrictions, drone enthusiasts around the world continue to use the technology to search for the perfect picture.

Bernie Ng
The Whampoa shopping centre, Hong Kong, 2017.

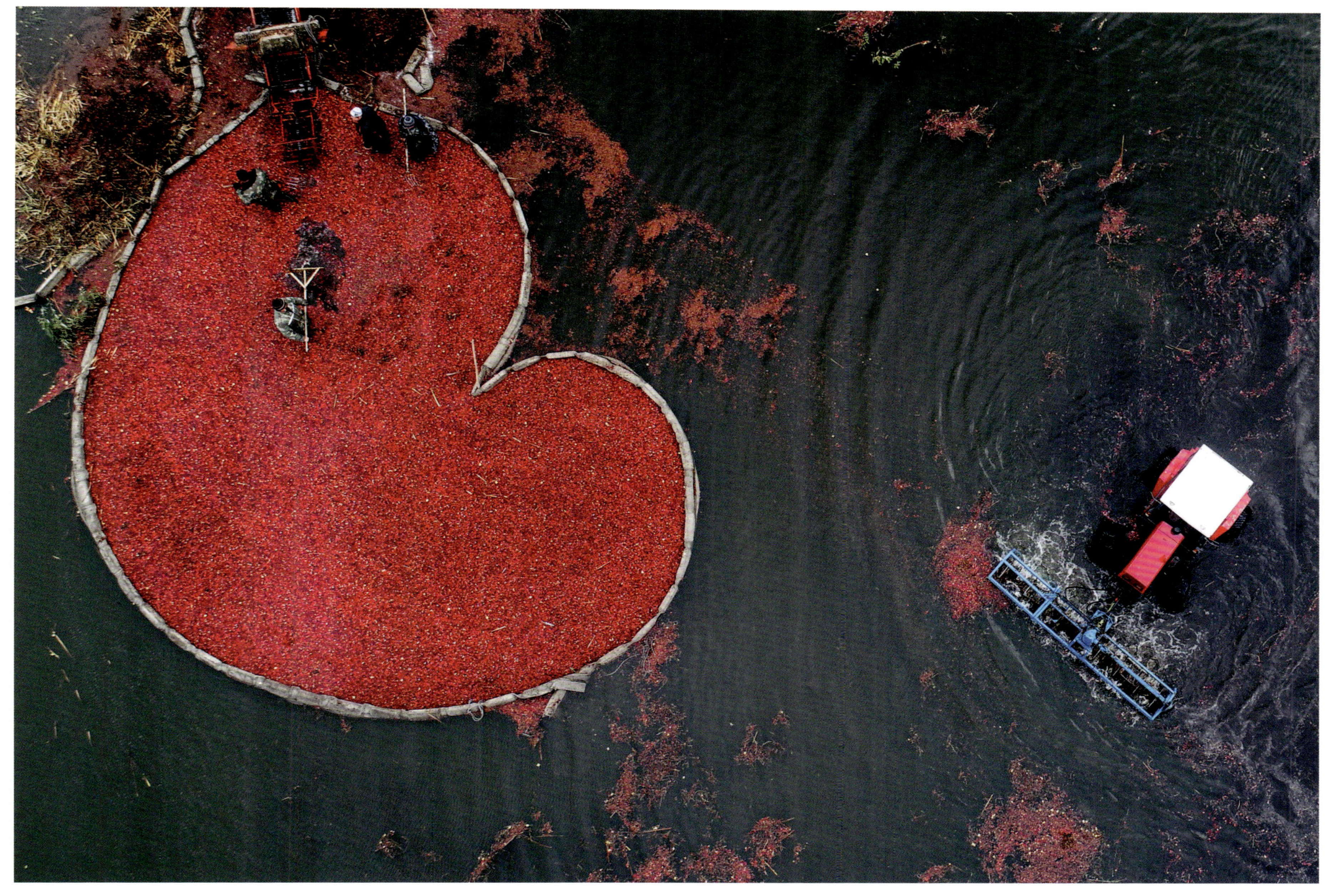

Sergei Gapon
Harvesting cranberries at a farm in the village of Selishche, Belarus, 2017.

As the technology has become more affordable and therefore accessible, DIY drone culture has continued to gather momentum. No longer the pursuit of a small number of dedicated hobbyists, aerial photography is available to more people than ever before. Photojournalists, such as Agence France-Presse photographer Sergei Gapon, are also embracing the technology. Using a drone, Gapon captured the rich reds of the cranberry harvest in Belarus's Pinsk District. In a region where unemployment is high, locals rely on the harvest to make ends meet. Gapon's image is not just pleasing to look at, it conveys an important message too: the harvest is the community's beating heart.

During an assignment to tell the story of sardine fishermen in Dhofar, southern Oman, photographer Ahmed Mohammed Hamdoon Al Toqi photographed the activity on the ground, but also from above using a drone. The fisherman use huge nets to haul in their catch. The sardines, which pass by the coast of Dhofar as they migrate to warmer waters, are sold to local markets and abroad.

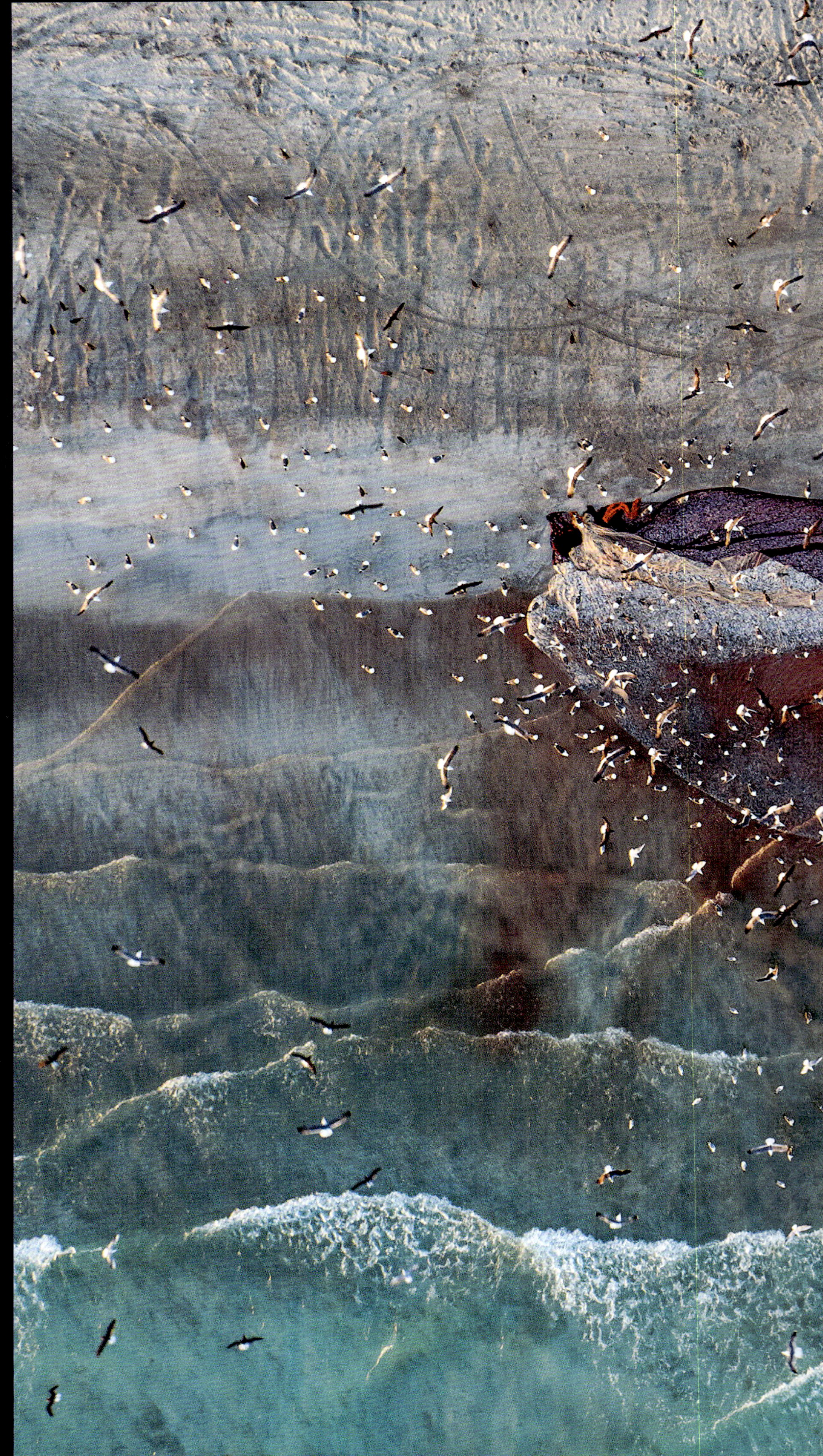

Ahmed Mohamed Al Toqi
Fishing for sardines,
Dhofar, Oman, 2017.

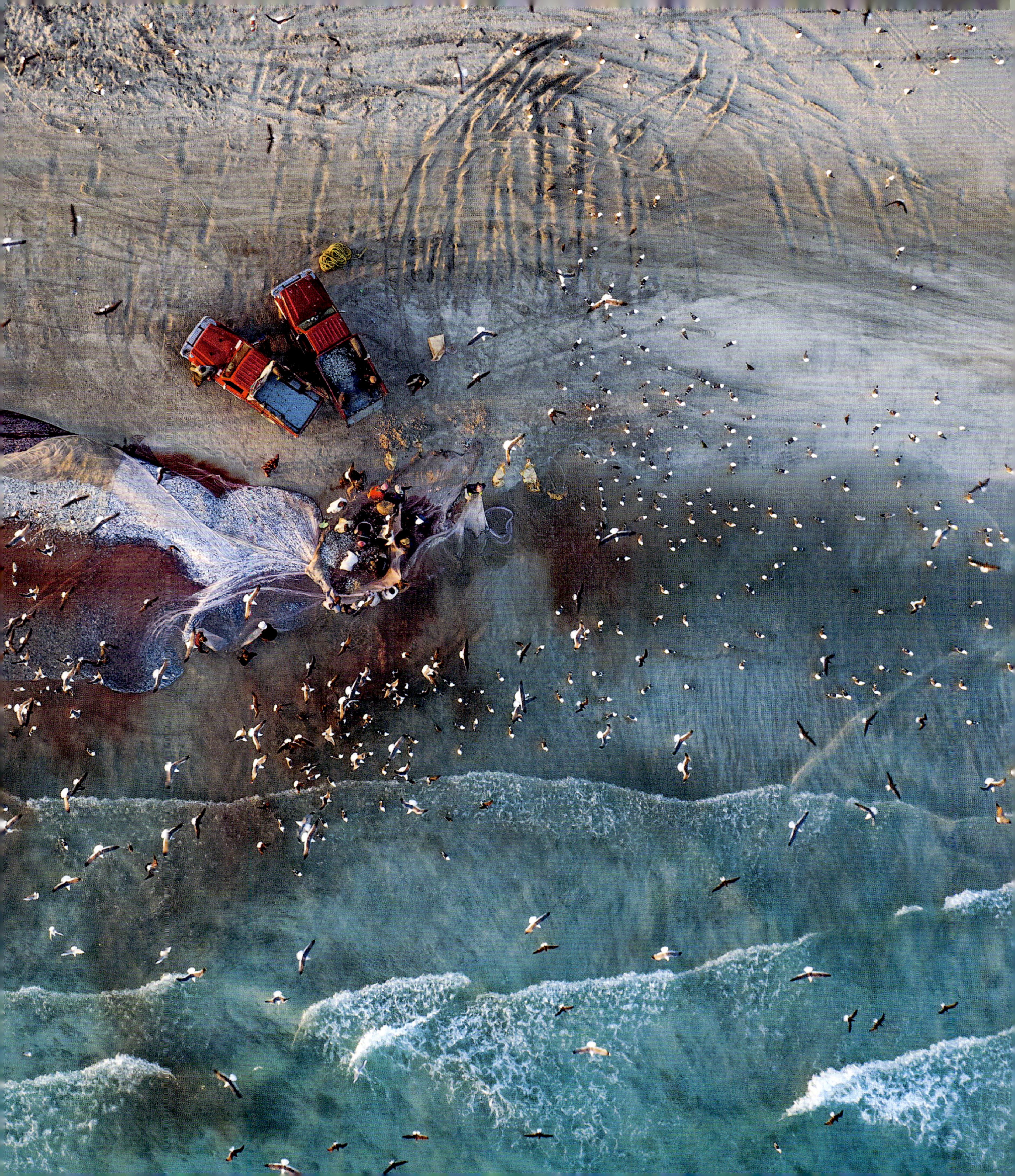

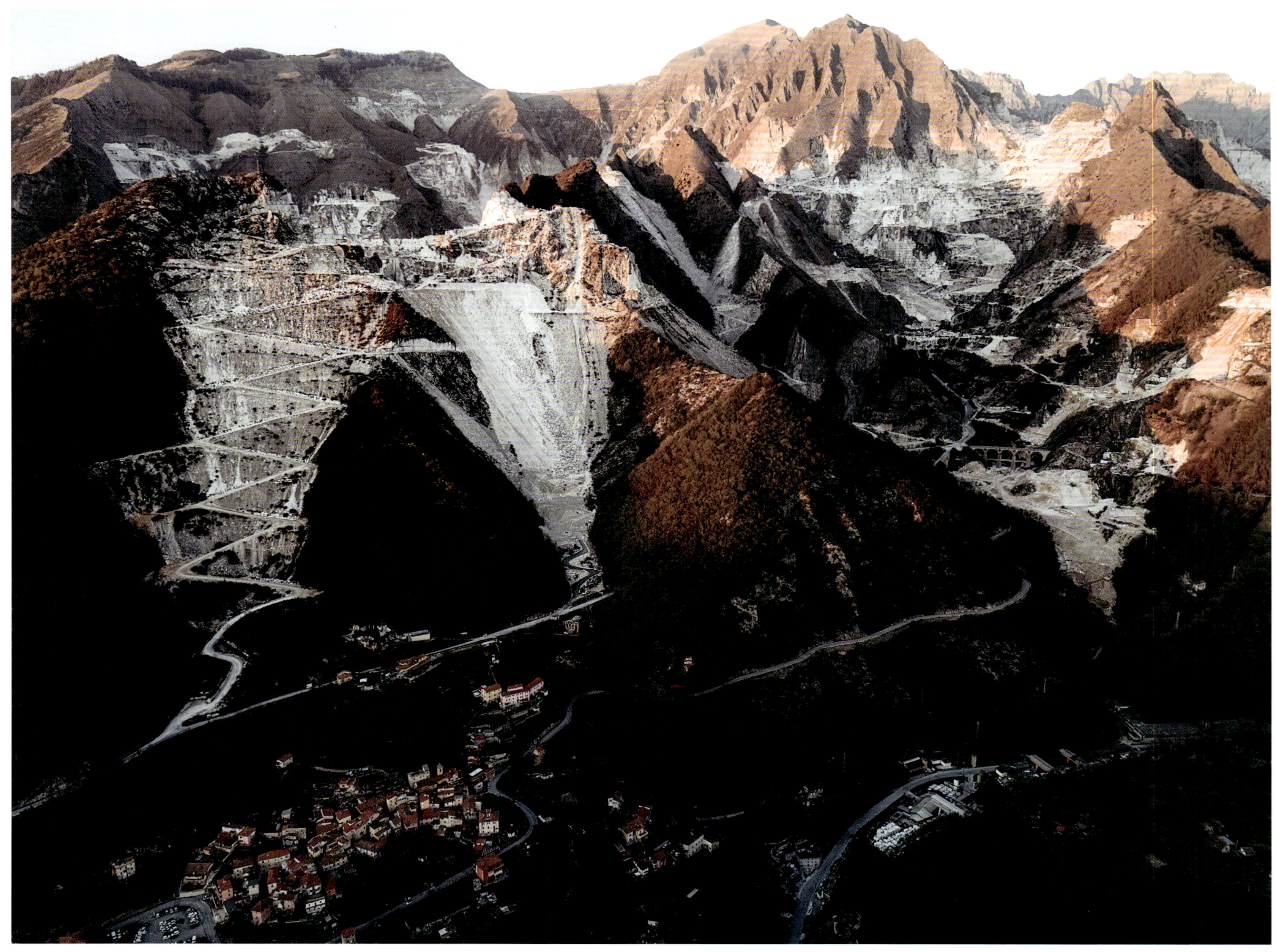

Italian photographer Luca Locatelli is no stranger to creating photographs that draw attention to the ways in which humans and technology are changing the world. For this series about northern Italy's majestic marble quarries, he took to the air to document humankind's literal impact on the Earth. Many of its images were shot using a drone camera while Locatelli was on assignment for the *New York Times Magazine* in 2017, and in them we can begin to appreciate the staggering size of these ancient quarries in the Apuan Alps, an area rich in marble. Man has been ripping the valuable white stone from the ground here since Roman times, and demand is as high as ever.

Luca Locatelli
Quarry in the Apuan Alps, Tuscany, Italy, 2017.

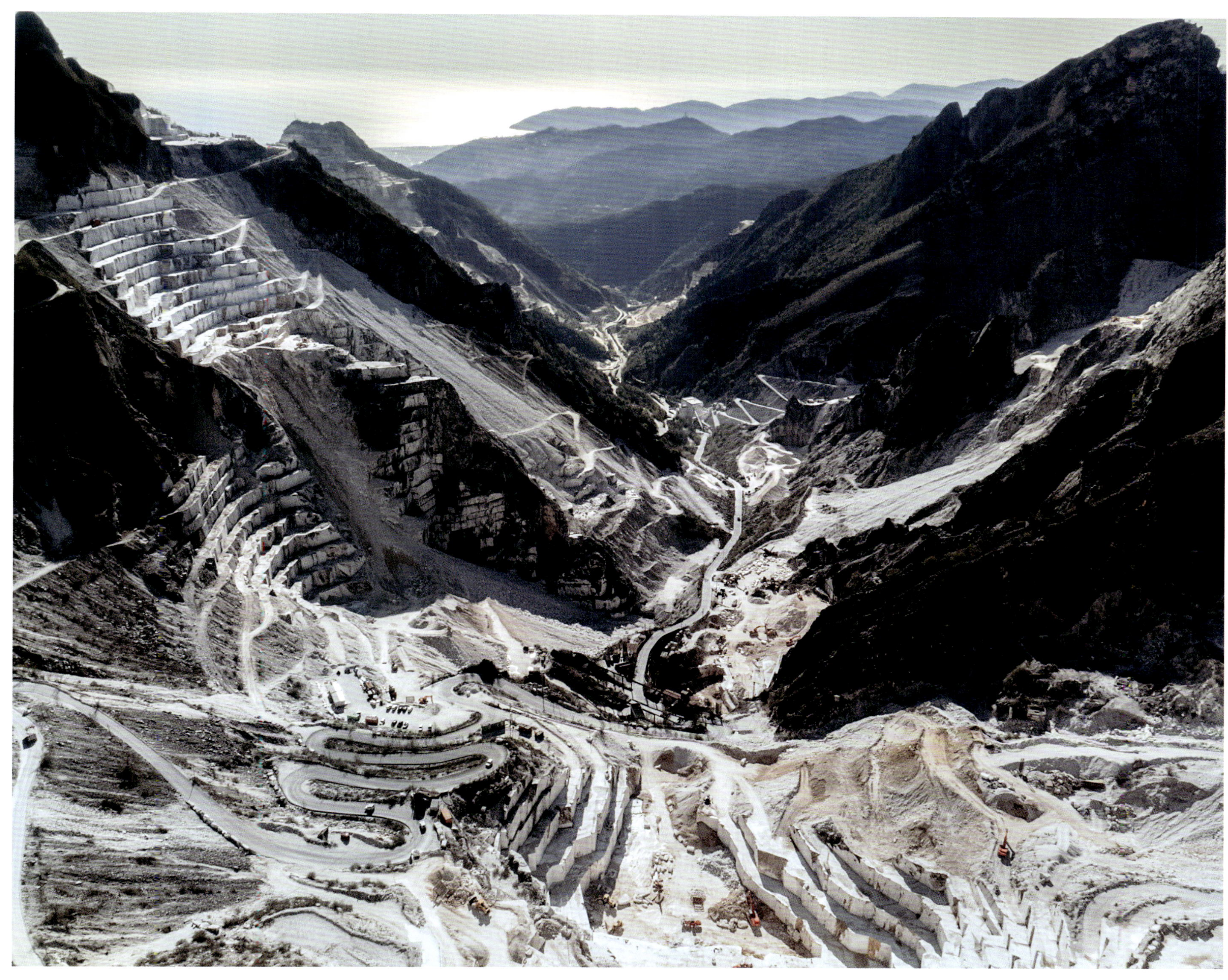

Luca Locatelli
Torano's 'marble valley', Tuscany, Italy, 2017.

Architect and graphic designer Jeffrey Milstein took up photography professionally in 2000, but his interest in flying goes back much further. Growing up in Los Angeles, Milstein had a passion for planes, which he indulged as a teenager by sweeping out hangars in an airport in return for flying lessons. He also shot 8mm films from the air, having obtained a private pilot's licence in 1961 at the age of 17. Now based in New York, Milstein makes pictures by hanging out of a helicopter. As well as capturing views over his adopted city, Milstein has photographed extensively in Los Angeles, recording the grids and geometry of the neigbourhoods and rooftops below.

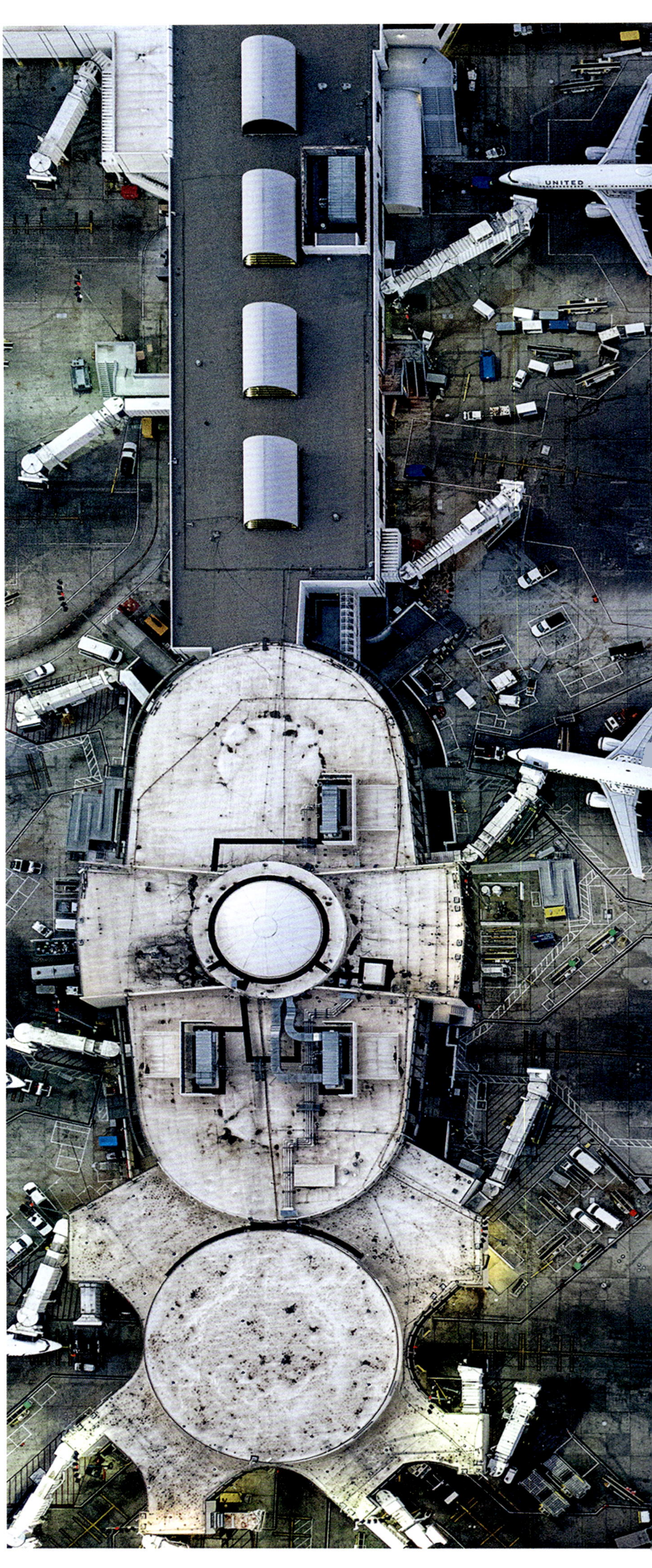

Jeffrey Milstein
Los Angeles International Airport, USA, 2017.

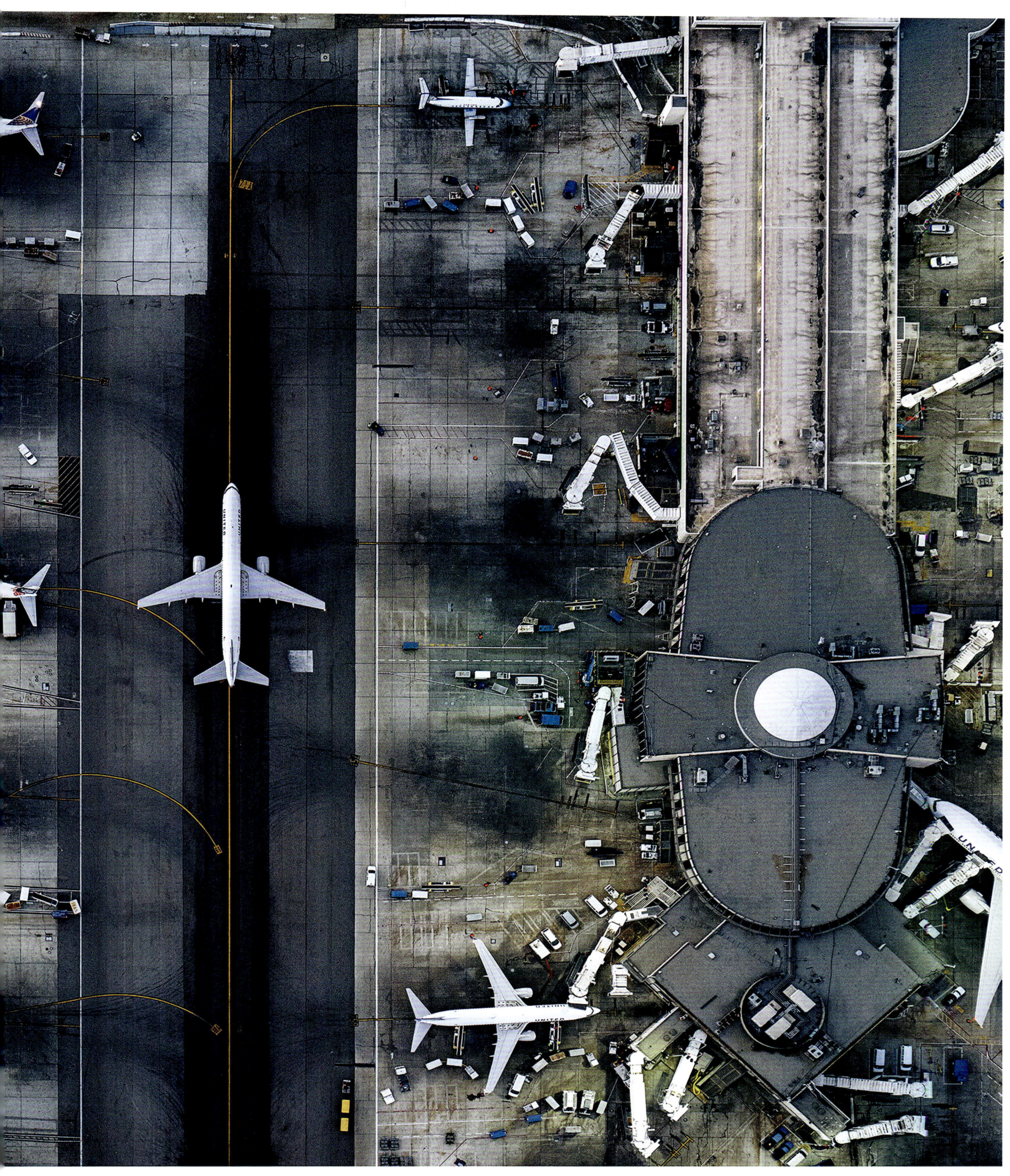

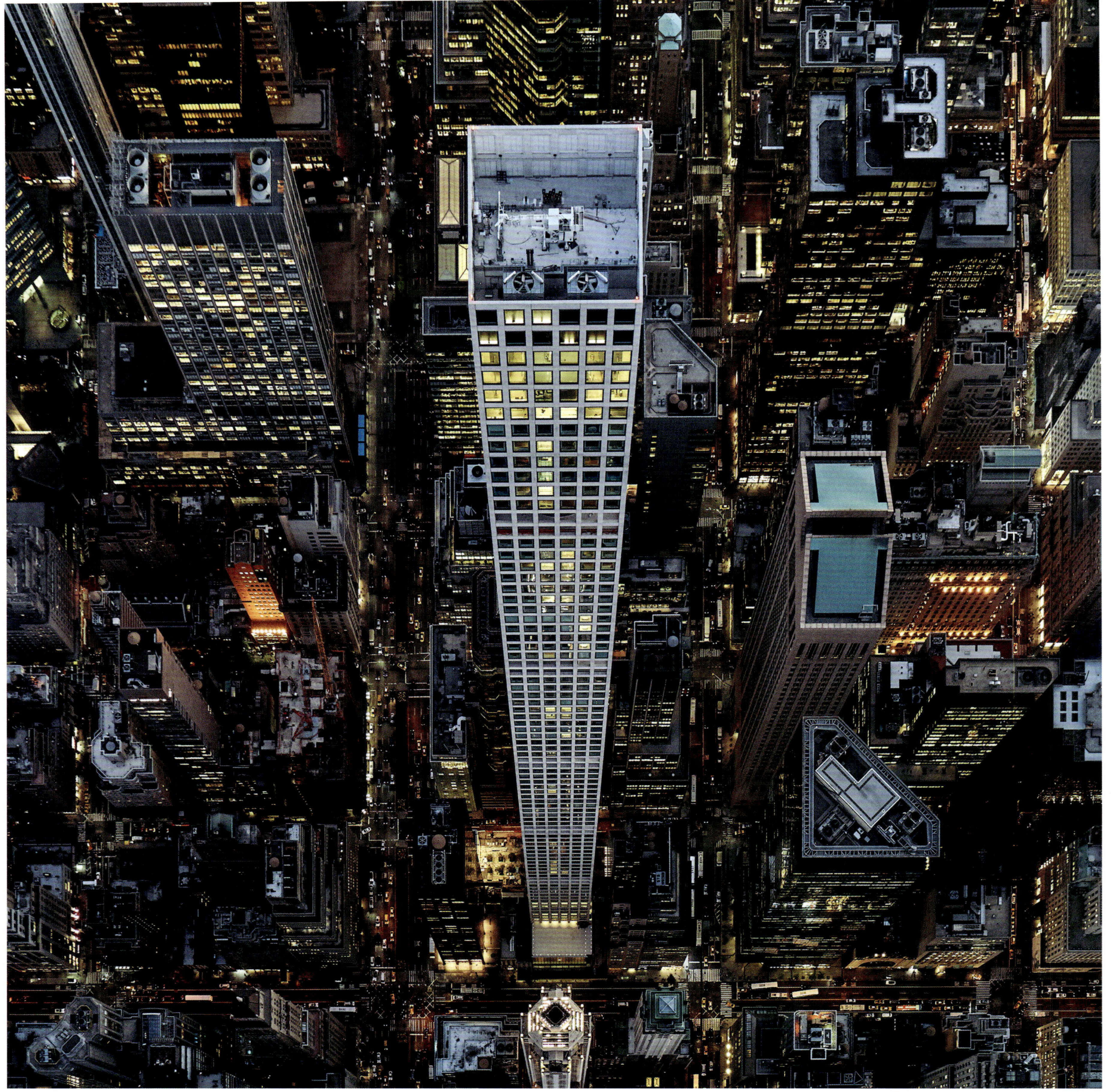

Above
Jeffrey Milstein
432 Park Ave, New York, USA, 2017.

Opposite
Jeffrey Milstein
Statue of Liberty, New York, USA, 2017.

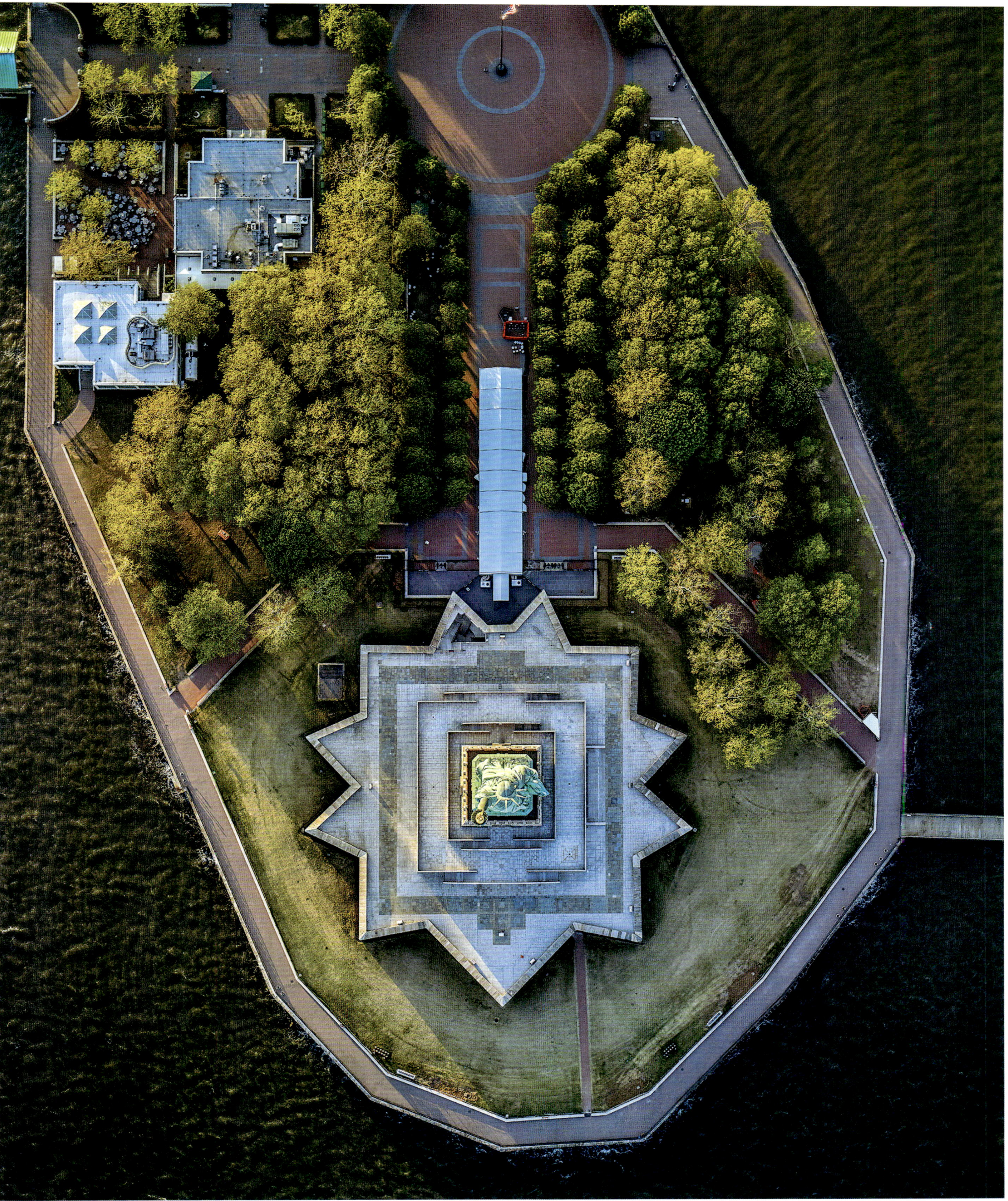

017

In October 2017, Canadian photojournalist Kevin Frayer spent time photographing the plight of Rohingya refugees. More than half a million people fled to Bangladesh following a bloody crackdown in Myanmar by the military, which started in late 2016. As well as revealing the horrors on the ground, Frayer photographed from the air, capturing images such as this (pictured right), depicting the sprawling Balukhali refugee camp at Cox's Bazar. Frayer is no stranger to shooting from the air. In 2011, he flew in a US Army 'medevac' helicopter from which he photographed Helmand Province in Afghanistan. Frayer's work in the sky, and that of photojournalists like him, proves just how much aerial photographs can add to a photo essay; by shooting from further away, such images, paradoxically, bring us closer to a story, adding to our understanding of humanity.

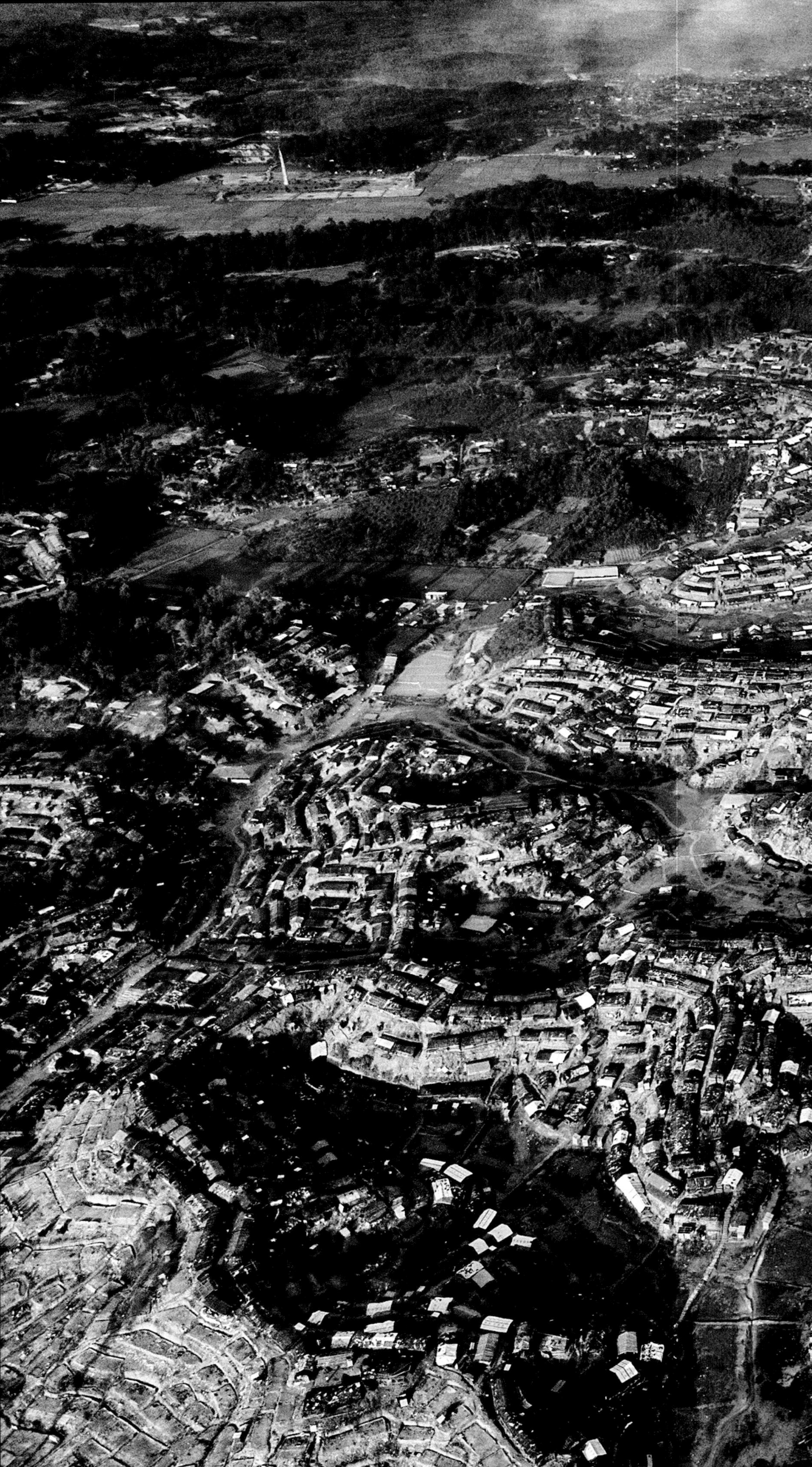

Kevin Frayer
Balukali Rohingya refugee camp, Cox's Bazar, Bangladesh, 2017.

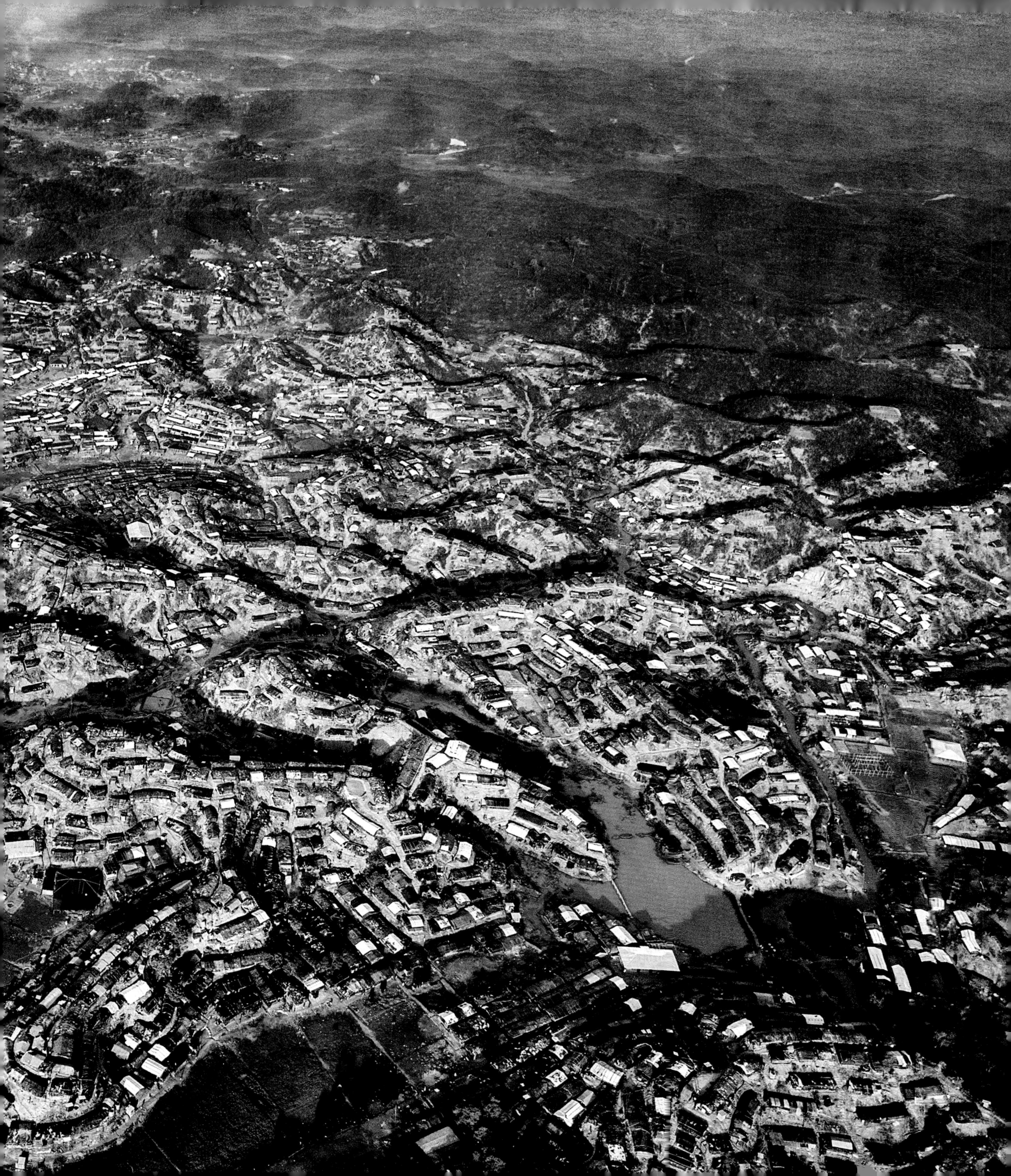

A drone camera captures the refugee camp Vagiohori in thick snow and sub-zero temperatures. Situated near the port city of Thessaloniki in northern Greece, the camp, run by the Greek military and the UN Refugee Agency (UNHCR), was made up of tents that did not have adequate insulation because they were designed to be used in the summer. Most of the inhabitants were eventually moved into hotels, but 19 people stayed behind because they were afraid they might be deported. Greece has long been a 'corridor' into Europe for refugees and migrants fleeing the war in Syria and conflict and poverty in the Middle East and Africa.

Nicolas Economou
Vagiohori refugee camp, Greece, 2017.

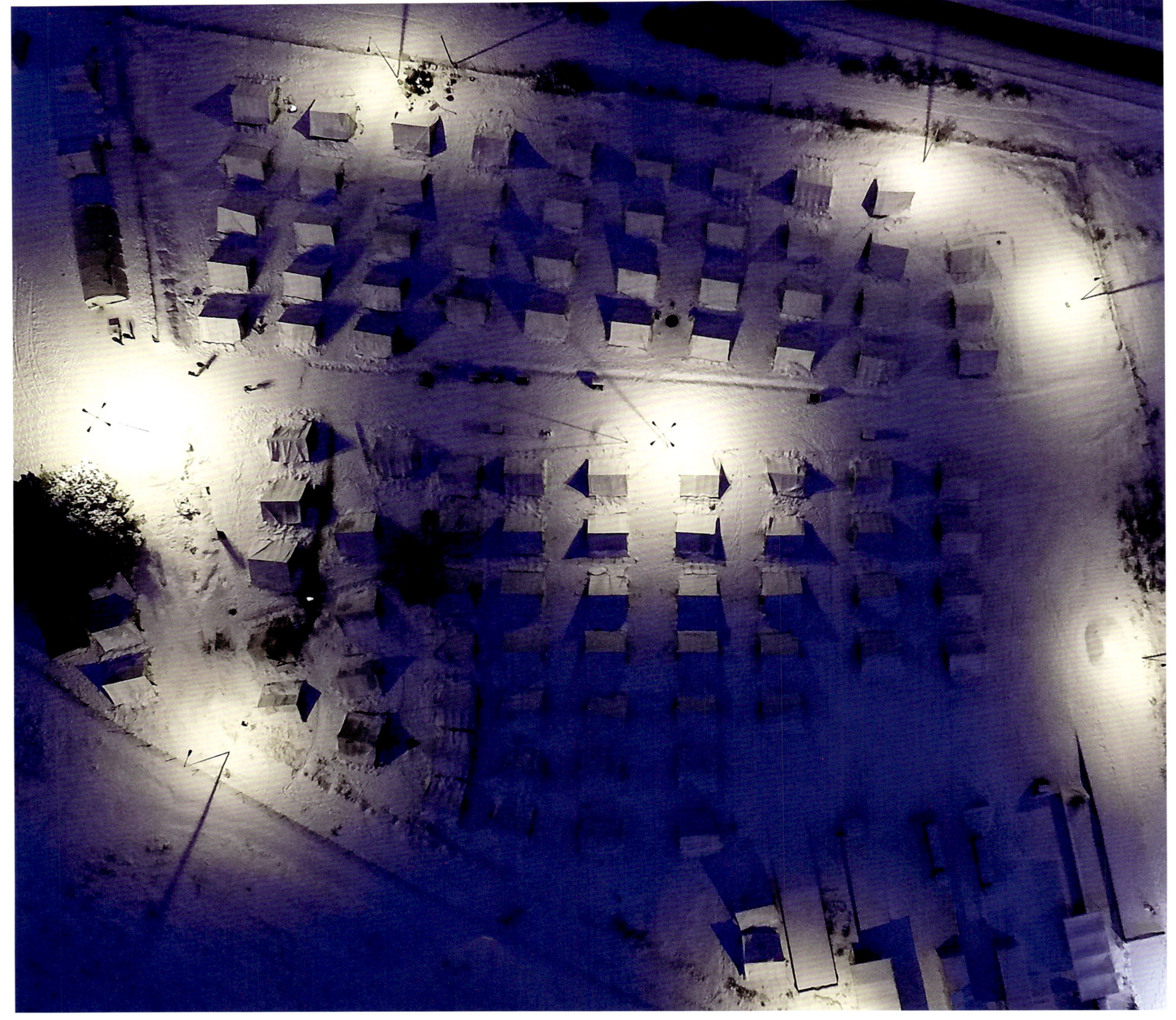

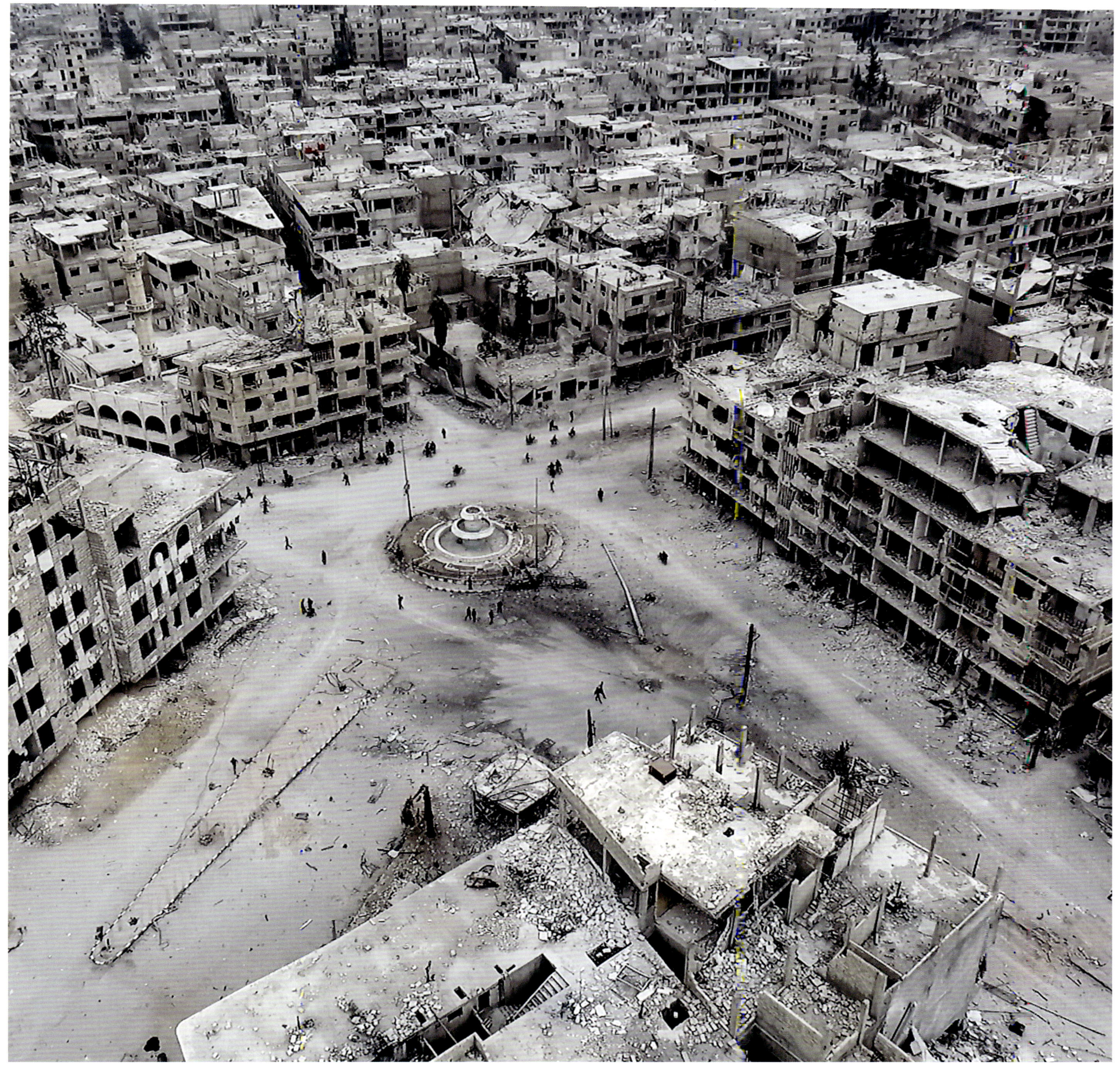

Ammar Al Bushy
Arbin town, Eastern Ghouta region, Damascus, Syria, 2018.

If modern drone-camera technology provides the means to show and celebrate the Earth's beauty, it follows that it can, and arguably should, be used to gain insight into and record a darker side of life, as the image (pictured above) starkly demonstrates. Attributed to Ammar Al Bushy, a photojournalist with the Anadolu Agency, the picture was taken by an unmanned aerial vehicle (UAV) in March 2018. It depicts the wreckages of buildings in Arbin in the eastern Ghouta region, which was targeted in brutal air strikes carried out by the Assad regime.

New South Wales in Australia hit the headlines in August 2018 when news agencies reported that parts of the country were experiencing the worst drought in decades. Australia as a whole recorded its driest July since 2002, with New South Wales and neighbouring Queensland especially affected by the lack of rainfall. Farmers felt the impact most acutely, with many forced to buy in food for their livestock. Chief photographer at Reuters Australia, David Gray covered the story, choosing to photograph the outback from above. As he explained to Reuters TV, 'I used a drone because I felt that seeing the conditions of the landscape from the air shows just how severe this drought has become.'

Below
David Gray
A lone tree stands near a water trough in a drought-affected paddock on the outskirts of Walgett, New South Wales, Australia, 2018.

Opposite top
David Gray
A road next to tracks leading to a water tank in a drought-affected paddock west of Gunnedah, New South Wales, Australia, 2018.

Opposite bottom
David Gray
Sheep eating grain in a drought-affected paddock on the outskirts of Tamworth, New South Wales, Australia, 2018.

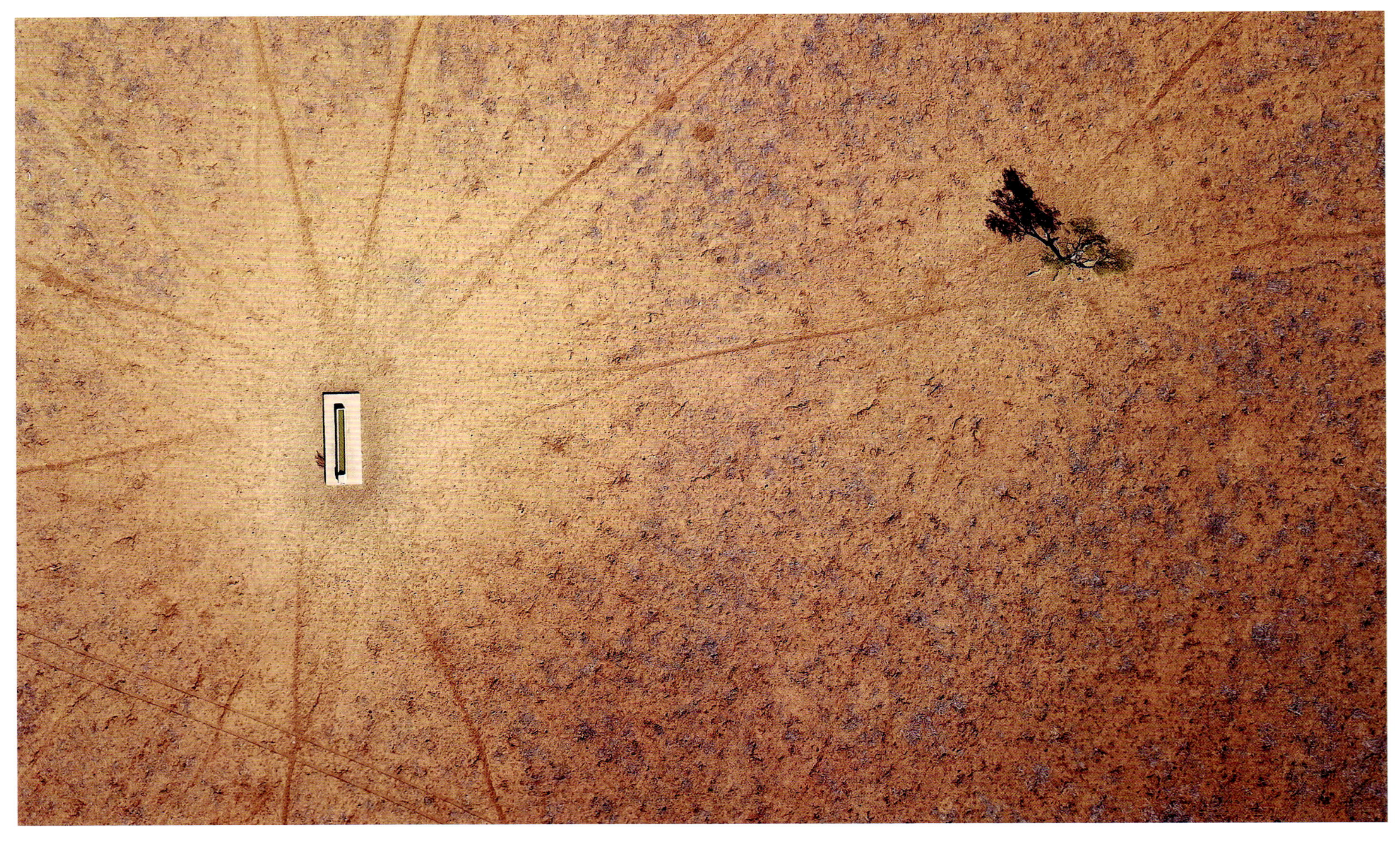

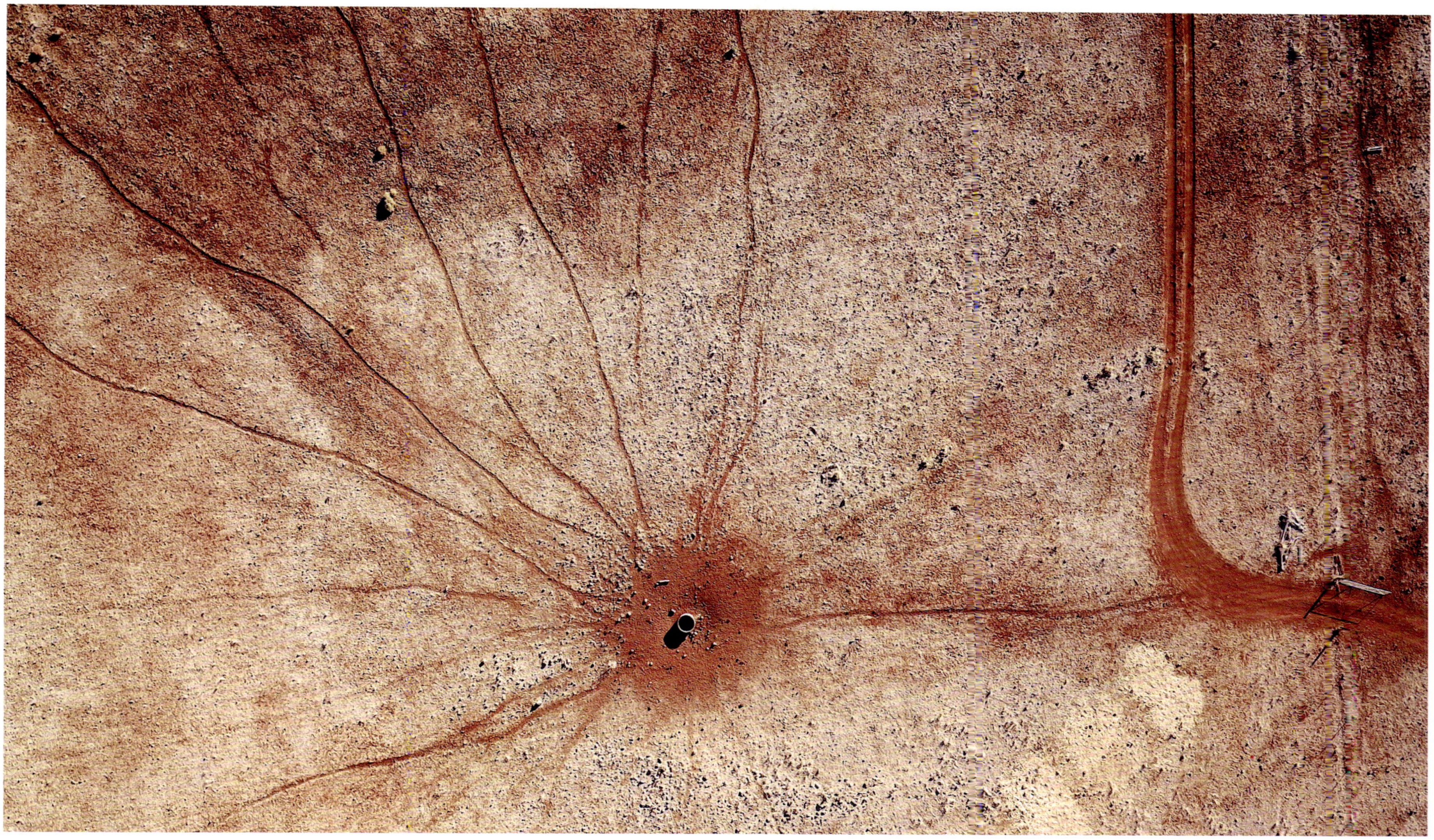

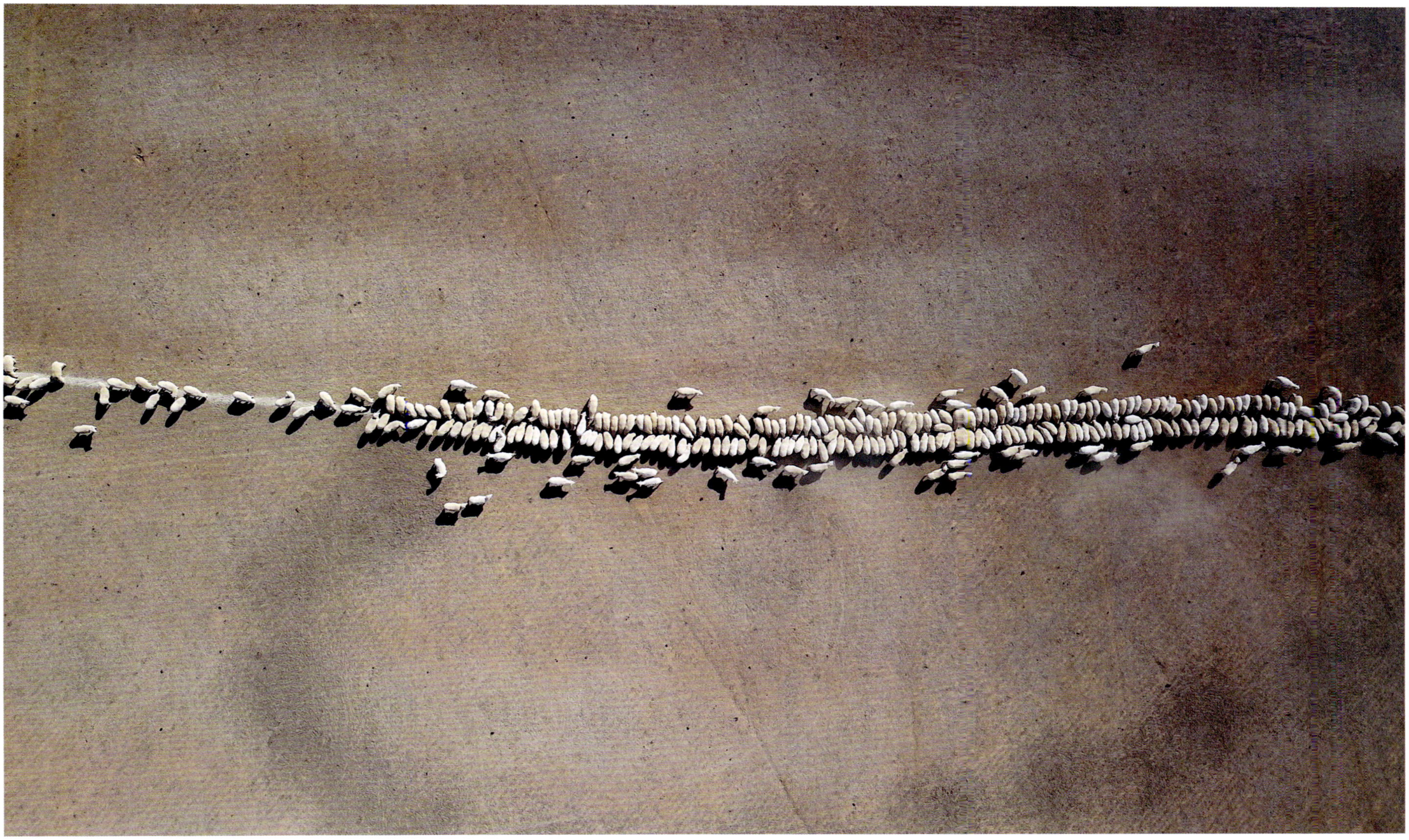

In 2010, Spanish photographer Markel Redondo photographed some of the many housing developments in his home country that had been abandoned in the wake of the 2008 global financial crash. Eight years later, he returned to a number of the sites, this time using a drone camera to capture a new perspective. Over a fortnight in early 2018, he travelled across southern Spain, making dramatic shots of the unfinished developments from directly above. Although often shot in nice light and pleasing to look at, the images possess an almost apocalyptic feel, and a palpable sense of unrealized ambition.

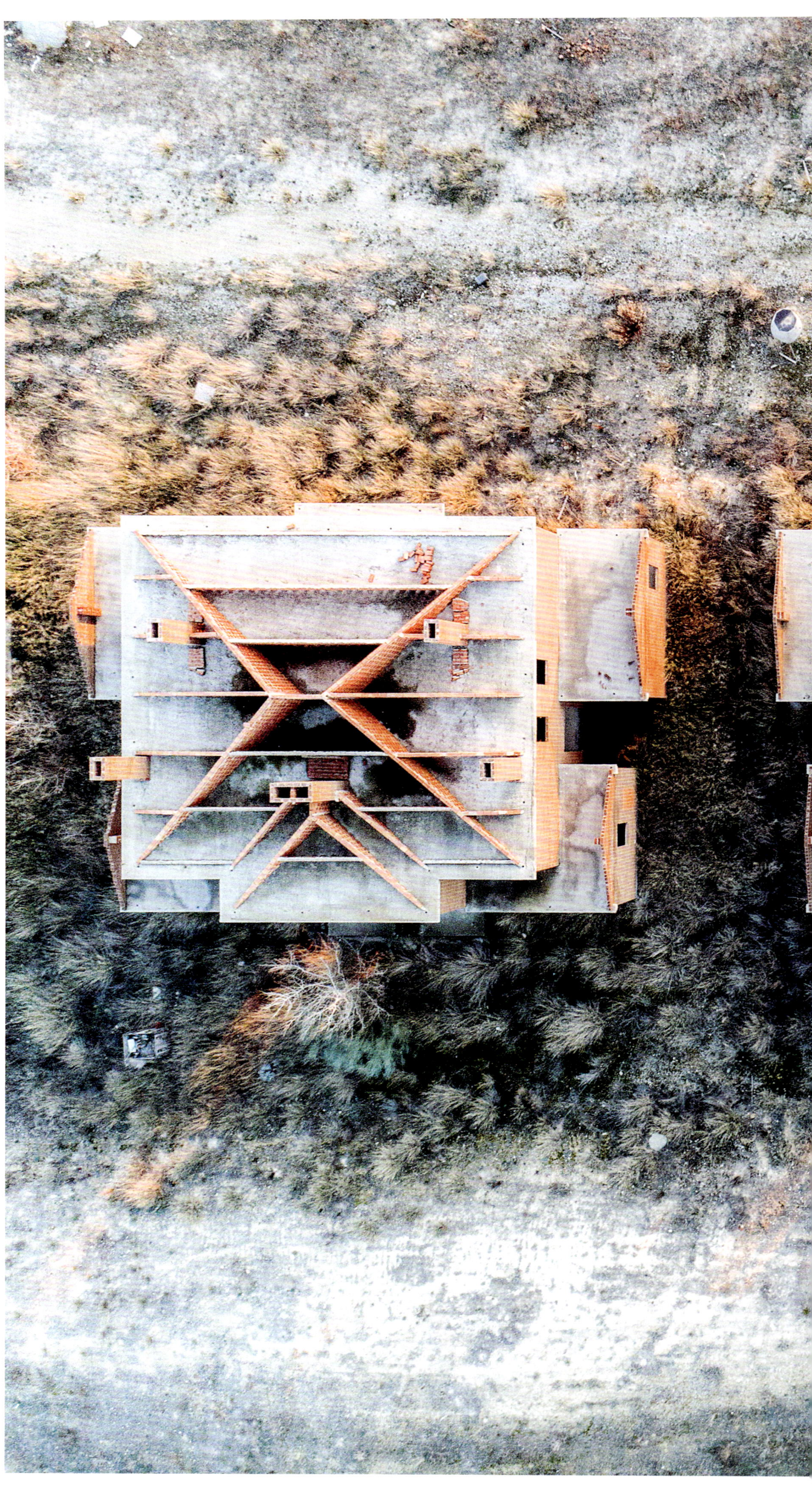

Markel Redondo
San Mateo de Gallego, Spain, 2018.

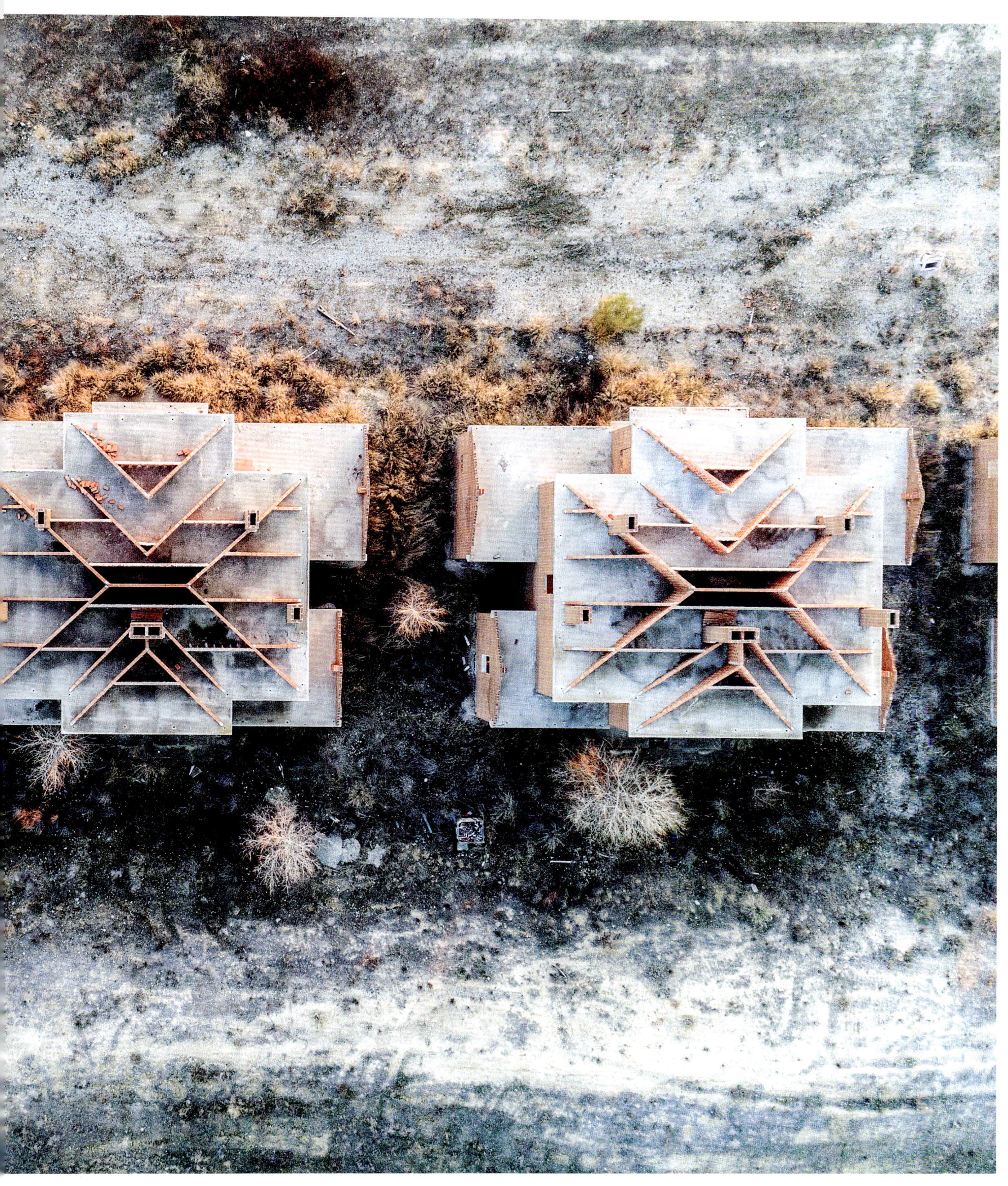

2018

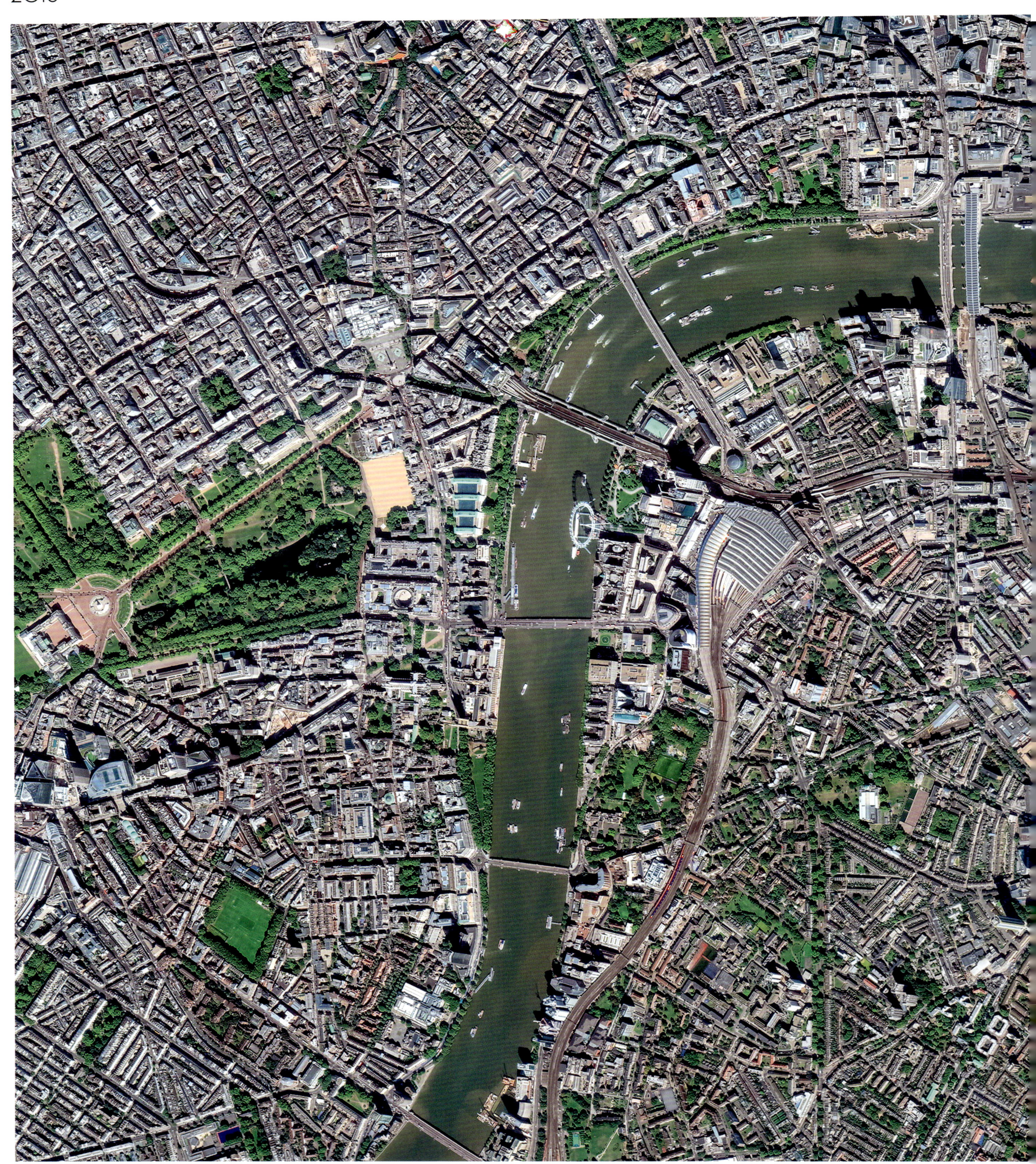

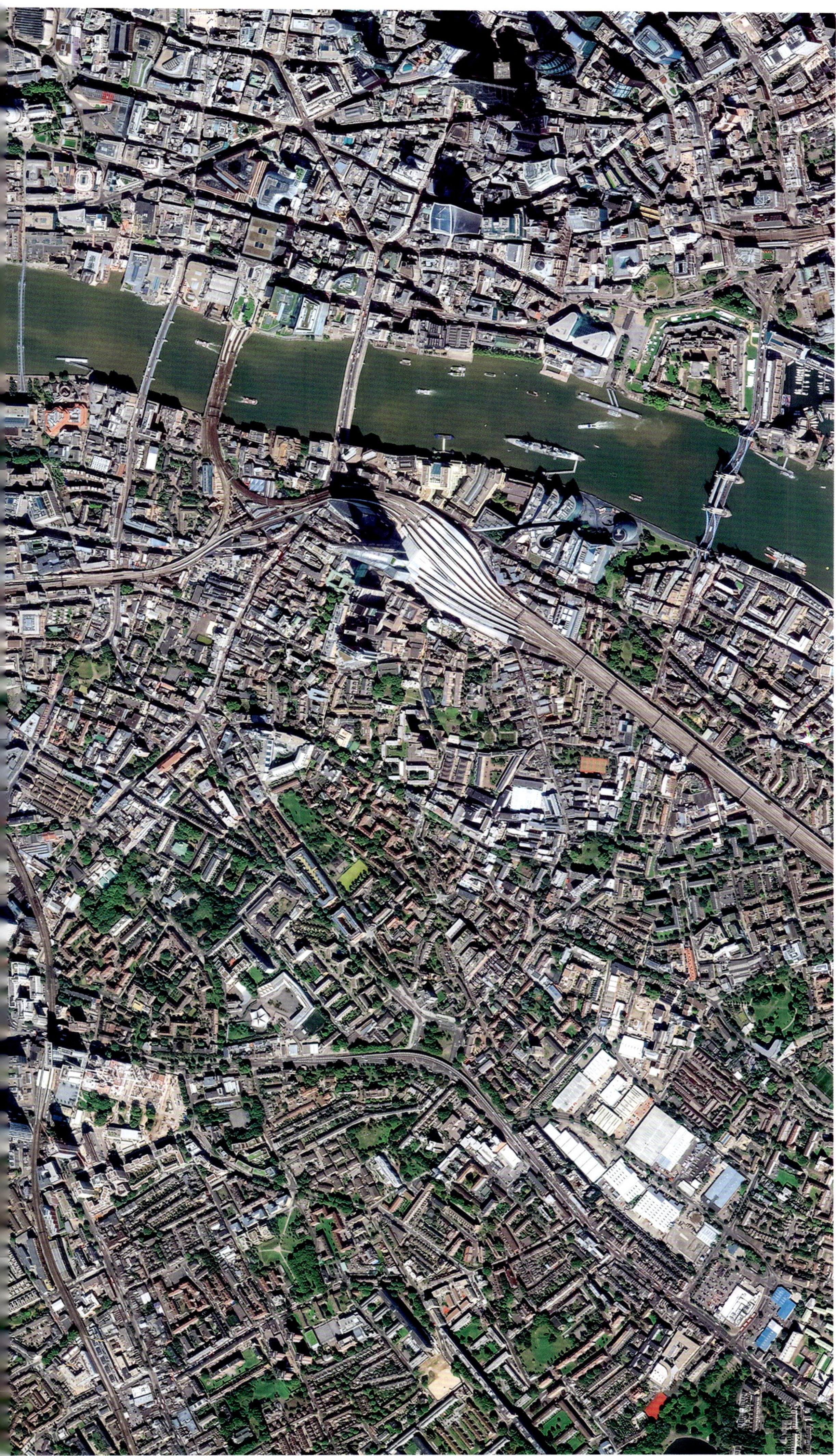

Whether we like it or not, satellite photography is an everyday part of life. It takes many forms and has many uses. For example, when it comes to volcano eruptions, wildfires and floods, first responders and government agencies might turn to satellite imagery to monitor what's going on and use the information gathered to plan an appropriate response. Scientists also use data obtained from satellite imagery to monitor changes to glaciers and rising sea levels, while companies license such imagery for commercial use. Meteorologists rely on satellite images to forecast weather systems. And who doesn't enjoy taking in views over London (pictured left) or seeing Glastonbury Festival (pictured overleaf) from the air?

Left
Satellite photograph
Central London, England, 2018.

Overleaf
Satellite photograph
Glastonbury Festival, Somerset, England, 2018.

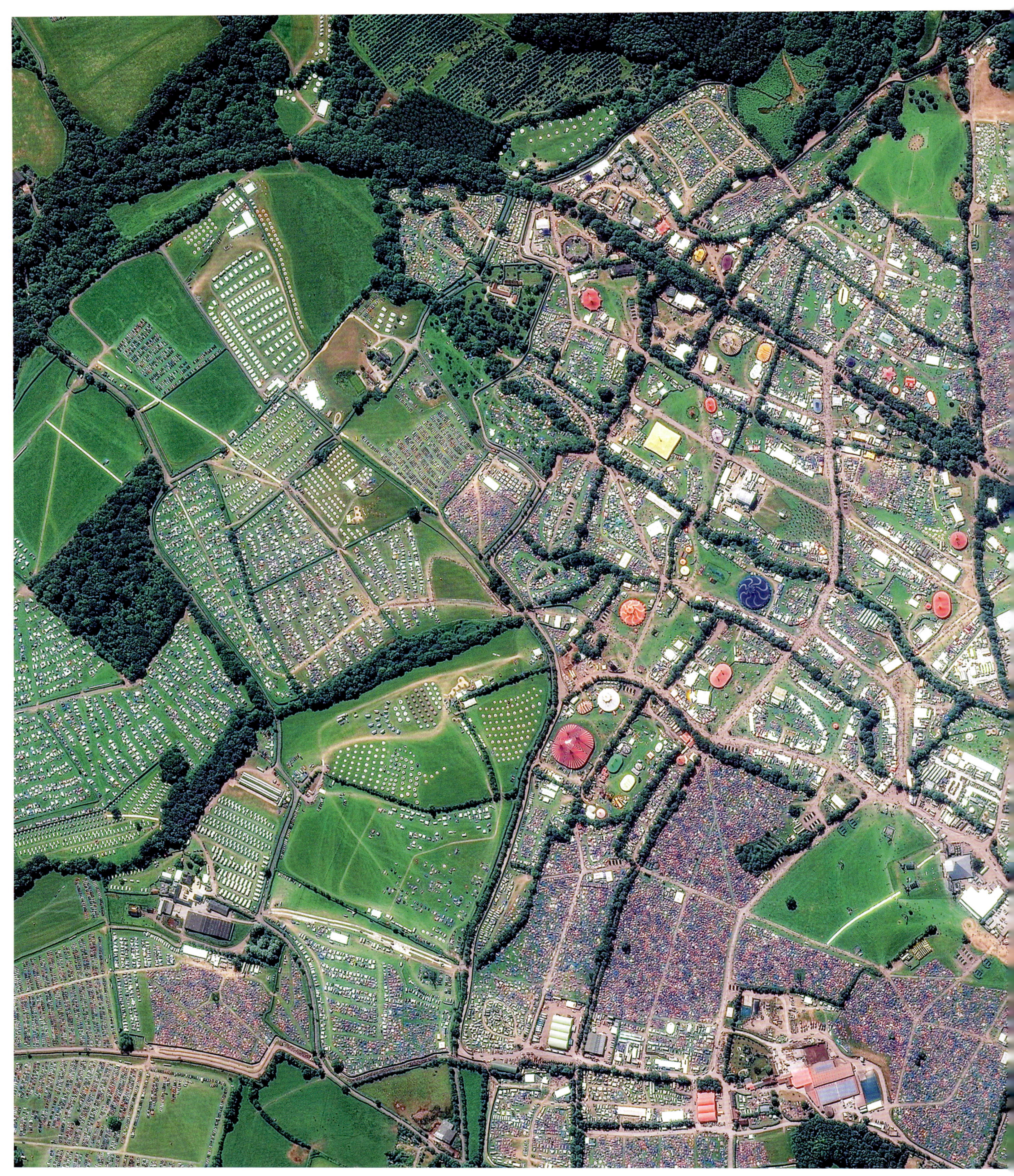

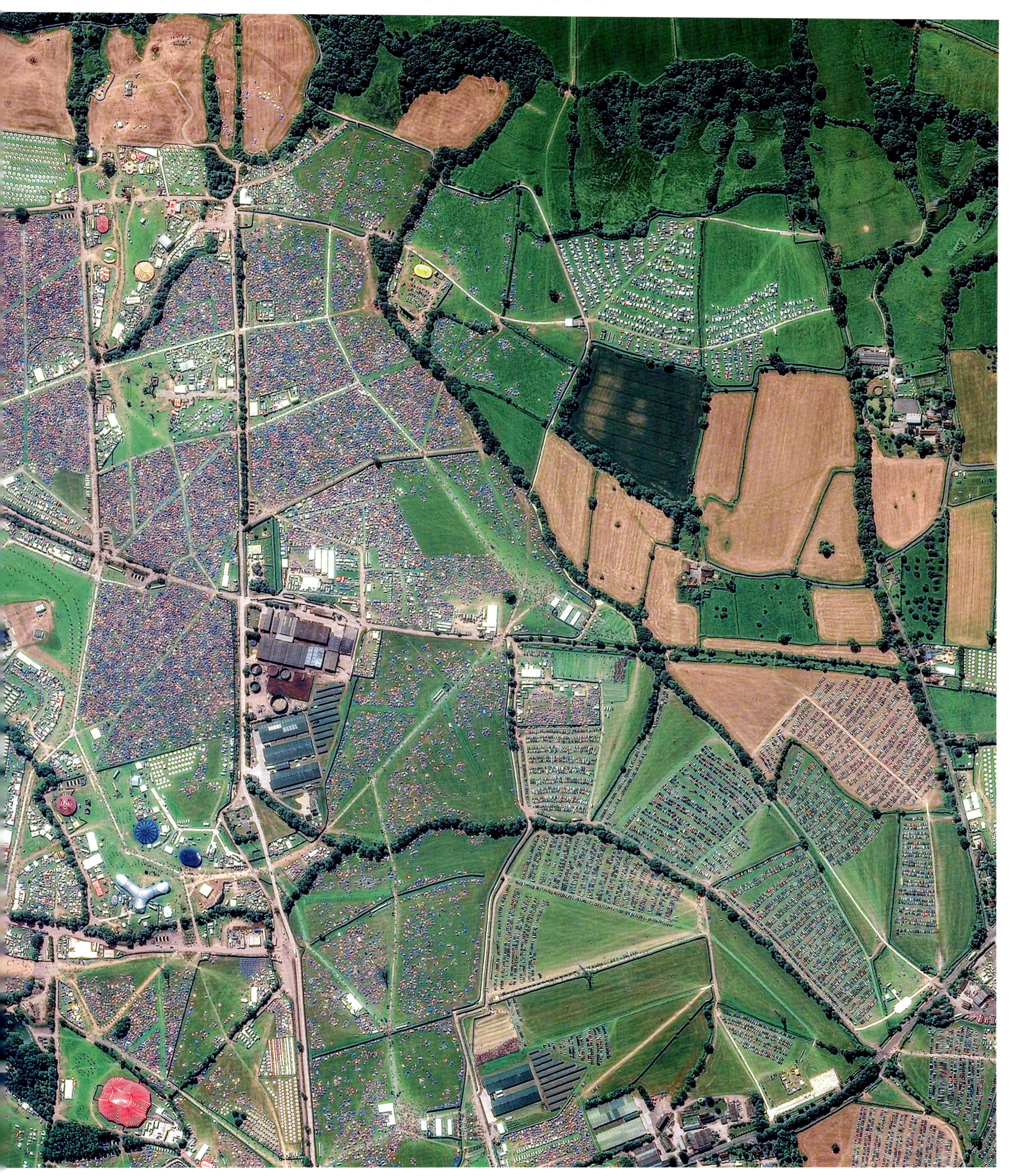

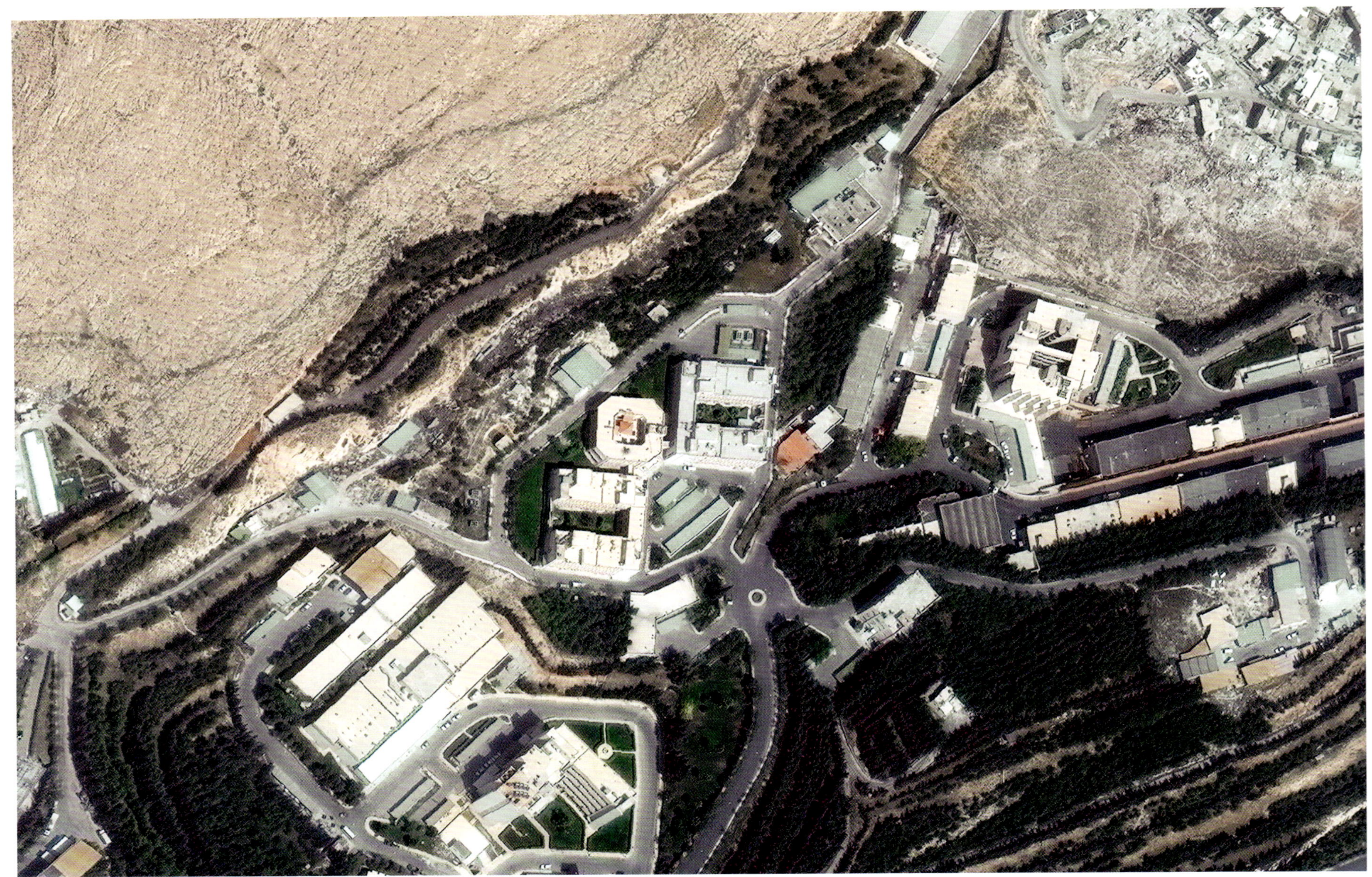

These stark 'before and after' satellite images of Syria give an idea of the terrible impact drone strikes have on their targets. On 14 April 2018, the United States, Britain and France carried out a series of coordinated air strikes on specific sites in Syria. The strikes were made in response to a suspected chemical weapons attack in the town of Douma, which is believed to have killed dozens of people. Three sites said to have been involved in the creation of chemical weapons were targeted, including the Barzah Research and Development Center near Damascus.

Satellite photograph
Syria before drone strike, 2018.

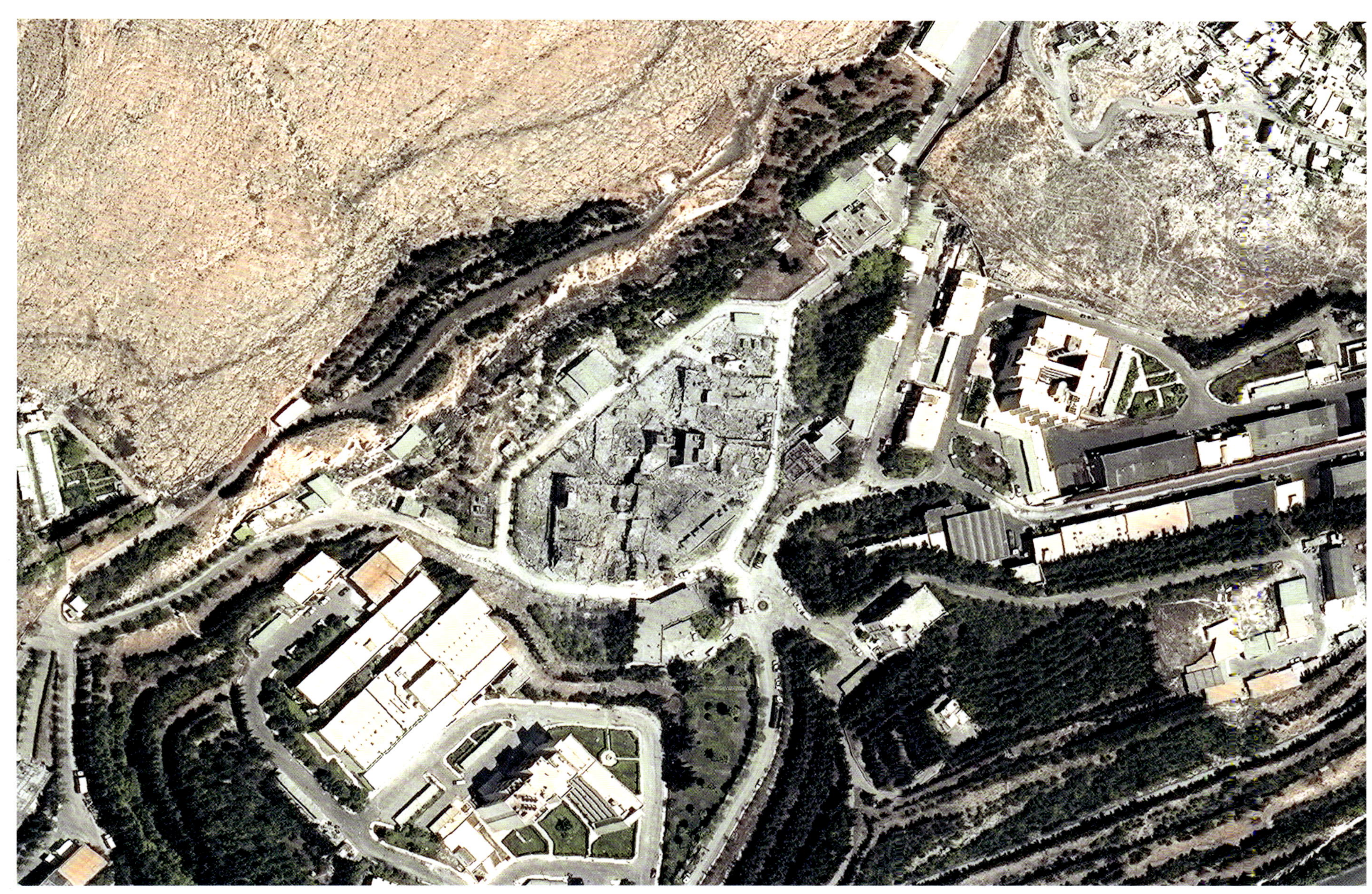

Satellite photograph
Syria after drone strike,
2018.

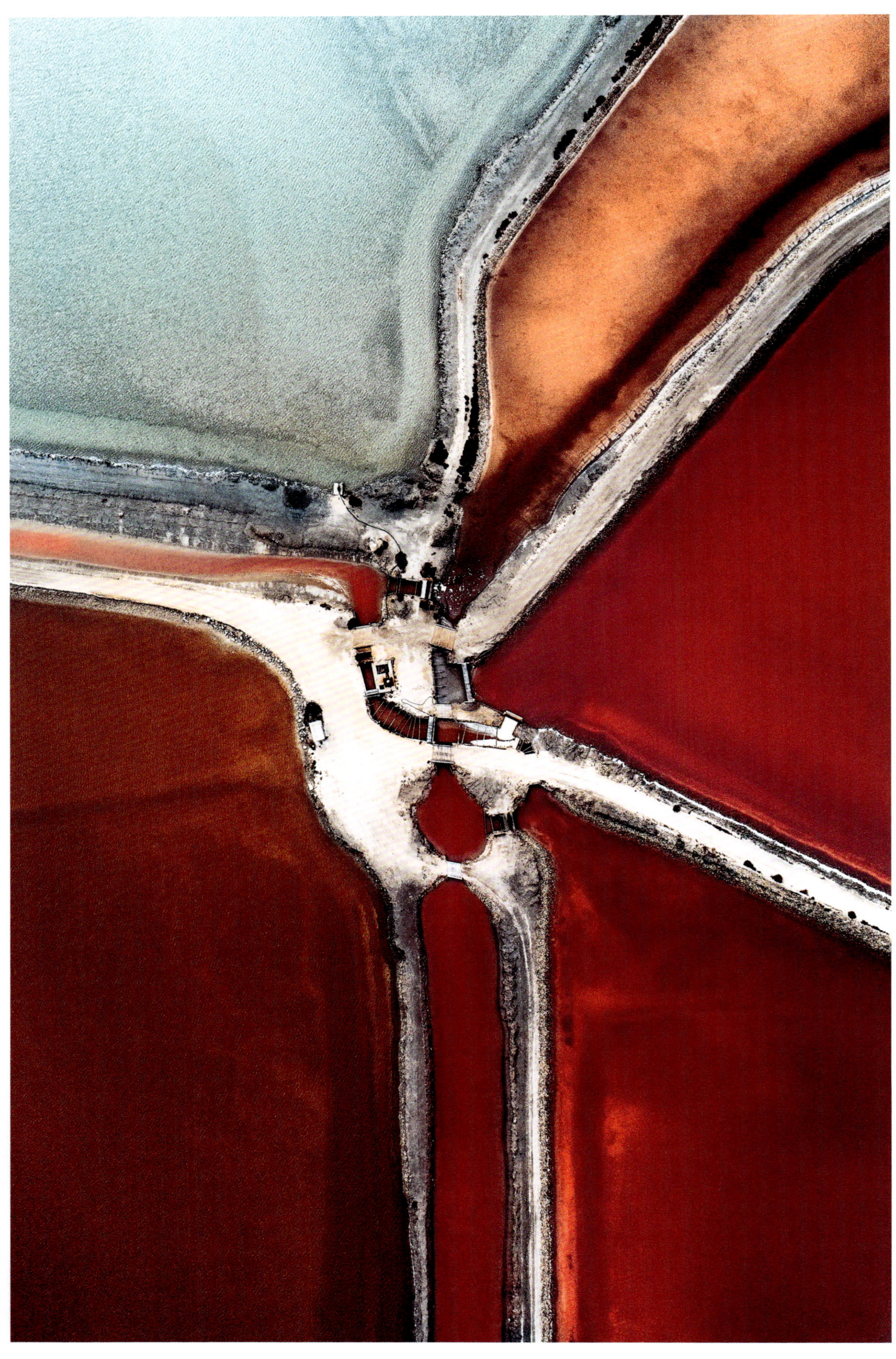

Tom Hegen
Untitled, near Montpellier, France, from the series 'Salt', 2018.

In his aerial photography, German photographer and designer Tom Hegen captures landscapes that have been heavily altered by humans. This striking image is from a series about the production of salt in Europe. Using a DJI Phantom 4 Pro drone to make the work, Hegen was attracted to the strong contrasts, vivid colours and geometric shapes of the salt ponds he saw in Spain and southern France, which reminded him of abstract paintings. Hegen has been photographing the Earth from above for more than four years and uses hot-air balloons, helicopters and planes as well as drones to achieve his vantage points.

Tom Hegen
Untitled, near Montpellier, France, from the series 'Salt', 2018.

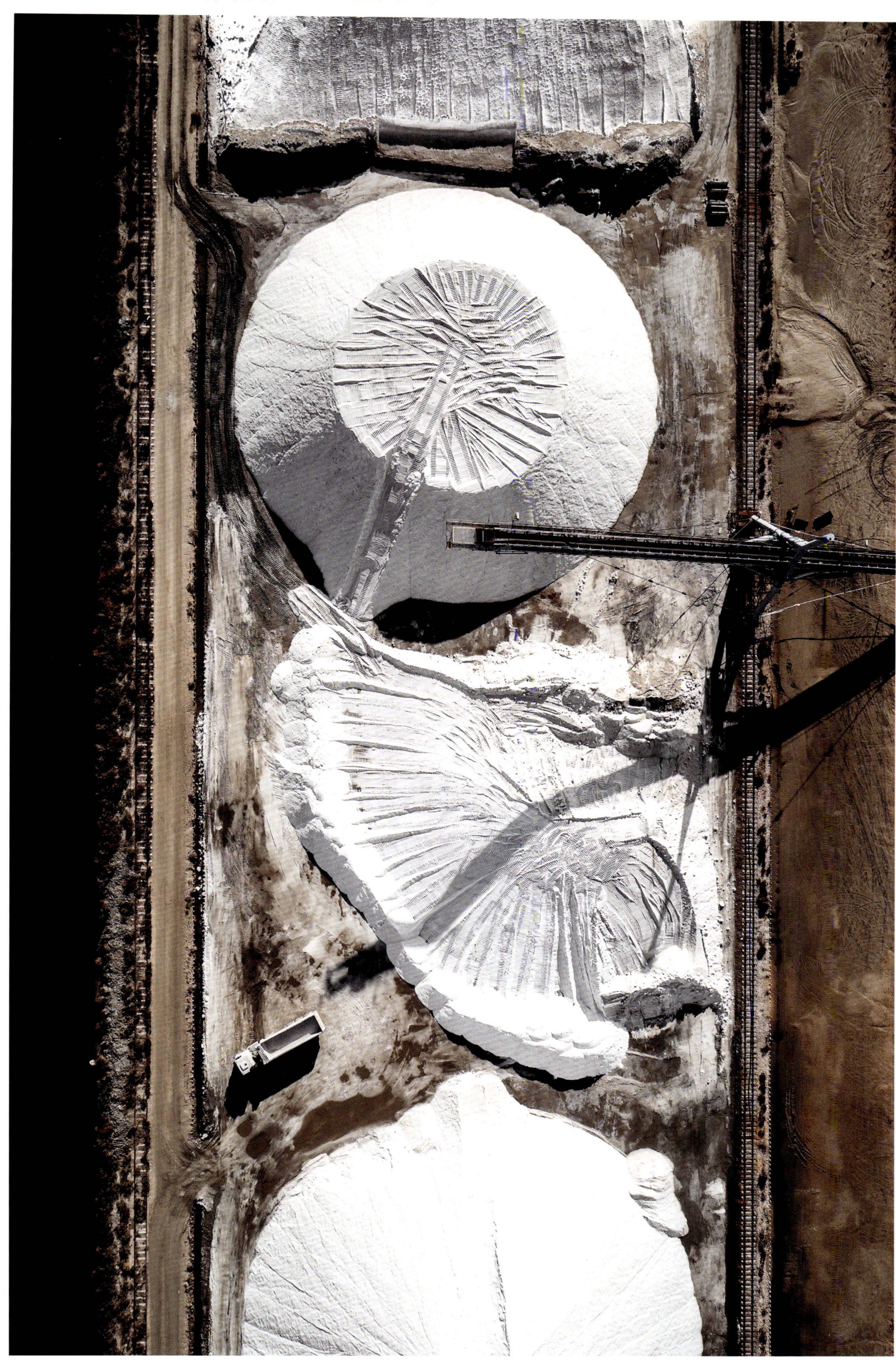

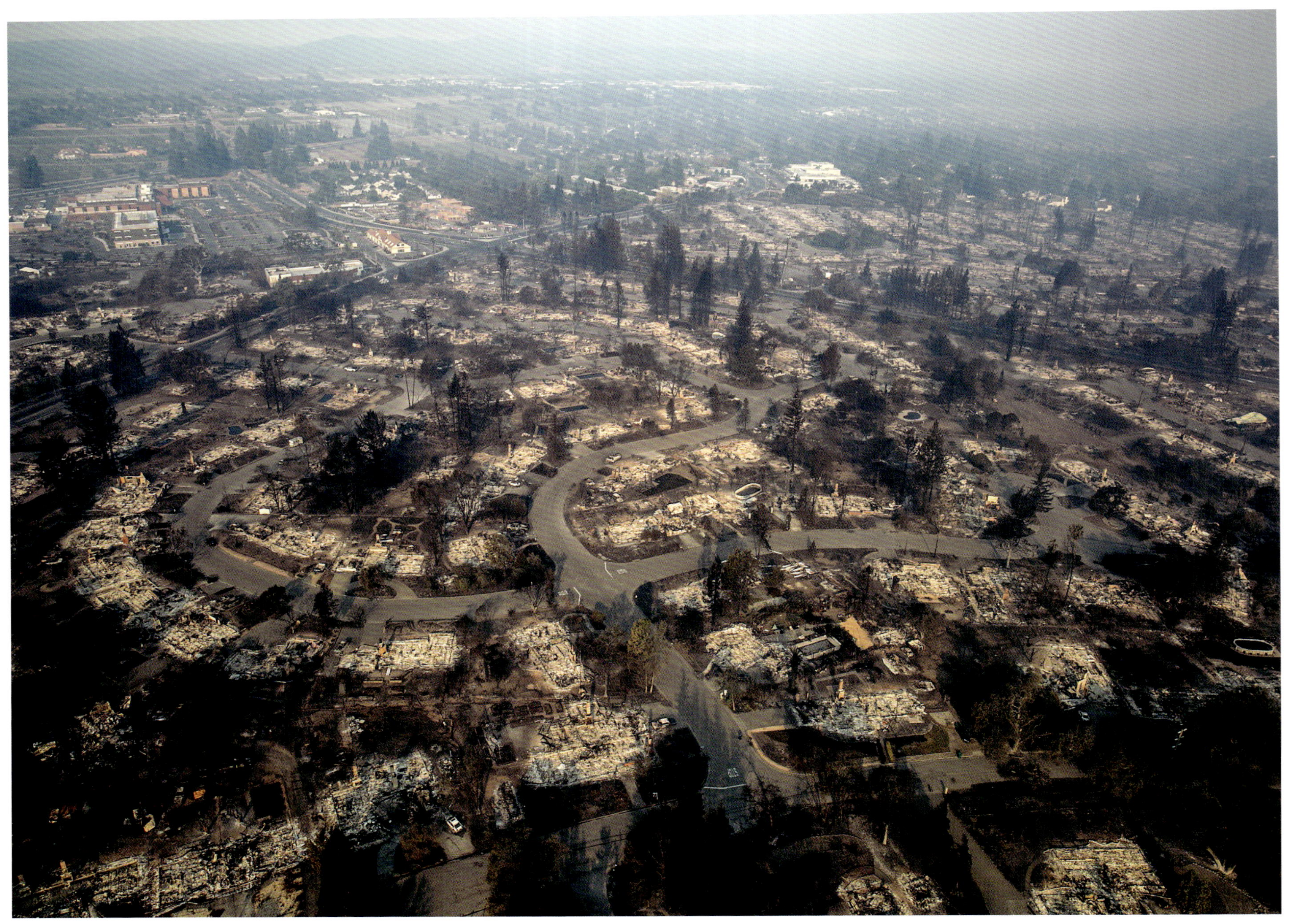

Until 2018's Camp Fire (opposite and overleaf), the wildfire that ravaged northern California's wine country in October 2017 was widely cited as the most destructive in the state's history. Tubbs Fire, as it is known, destroyed thousands of houses and structures and killed at least 23 people as it burned through the counties of Napa and Sonoma. Photojournalist, and former staff photographer for the *Los Angeles Times*, George Rose captured this desolate aerial view (pictured above) across the Mark West Estates neighbourhood in Santa Rosa from a helicopter. Rose uses helicopters exclusively, as opposed to drones, because of the ability to move back and forth with two cameras and two lenses.

Above
George Rose
Mark West Estates neighbourhood, Santa Rosa, California, USA, 2017.

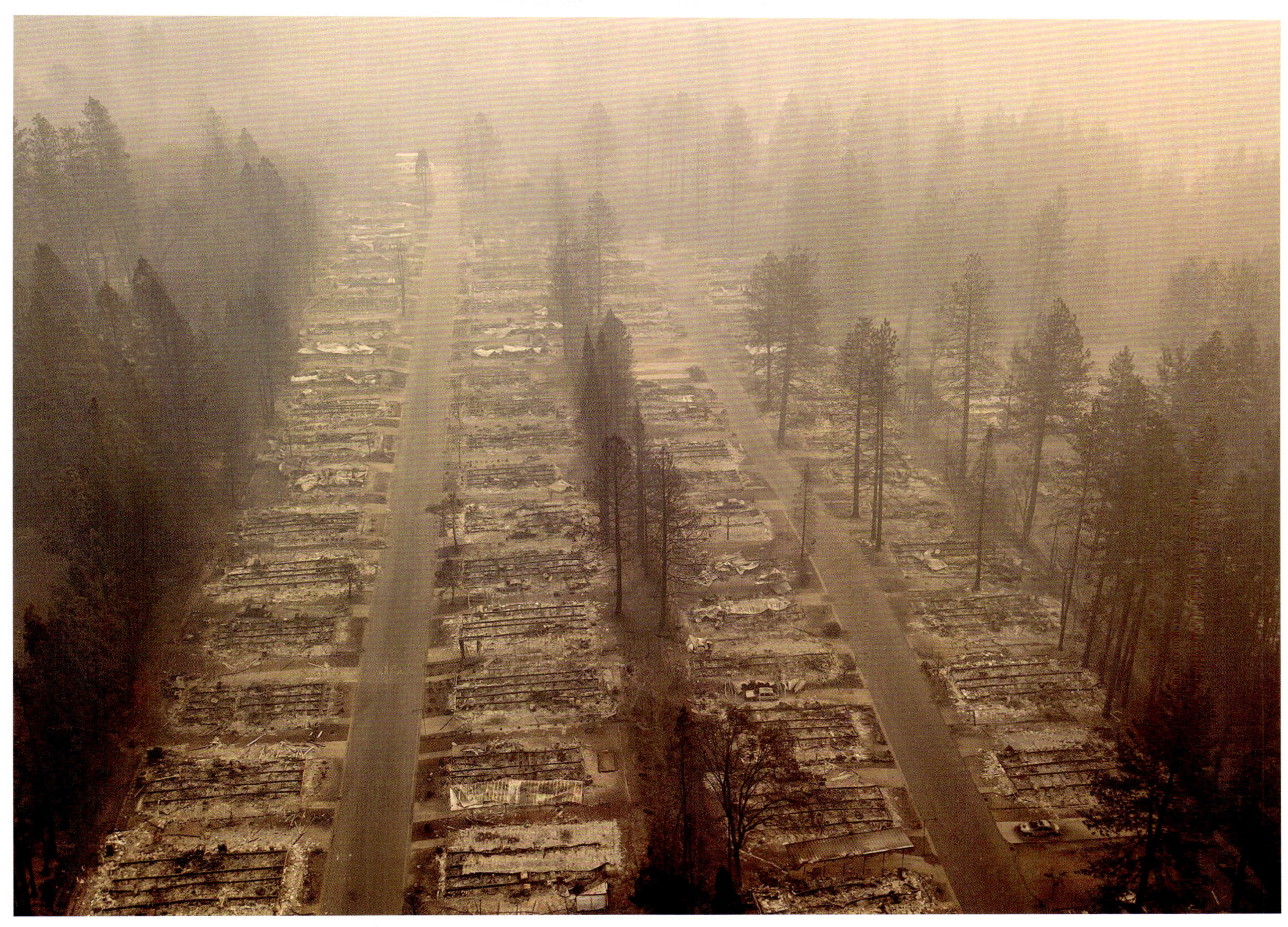

Above and overleaf
Josh Edelson
Burned-out neighbourhood after camp fire, Paradise, California, USA, 2018.

On 8 November 2018, a fire broke out that would prove to be the deadliest in California's history. Aided by strong winds, camp fire spread rapidly, wiping out the entire town of Paradise in northern California and claiming the lives of at least 86 people. When he heard about the blaze, San Francisco-based freelance photographer Josh Edelson, who has many years' experience of photographing wildfires, rushed to the region where he captured the devastation wrought by the fire, both from the ground and the air. Edelson took this shot using a drone during a brief opening up of the TFL (temporary flight restriction) by Cal Fire, California's Department of Forestry and Fire Protection.

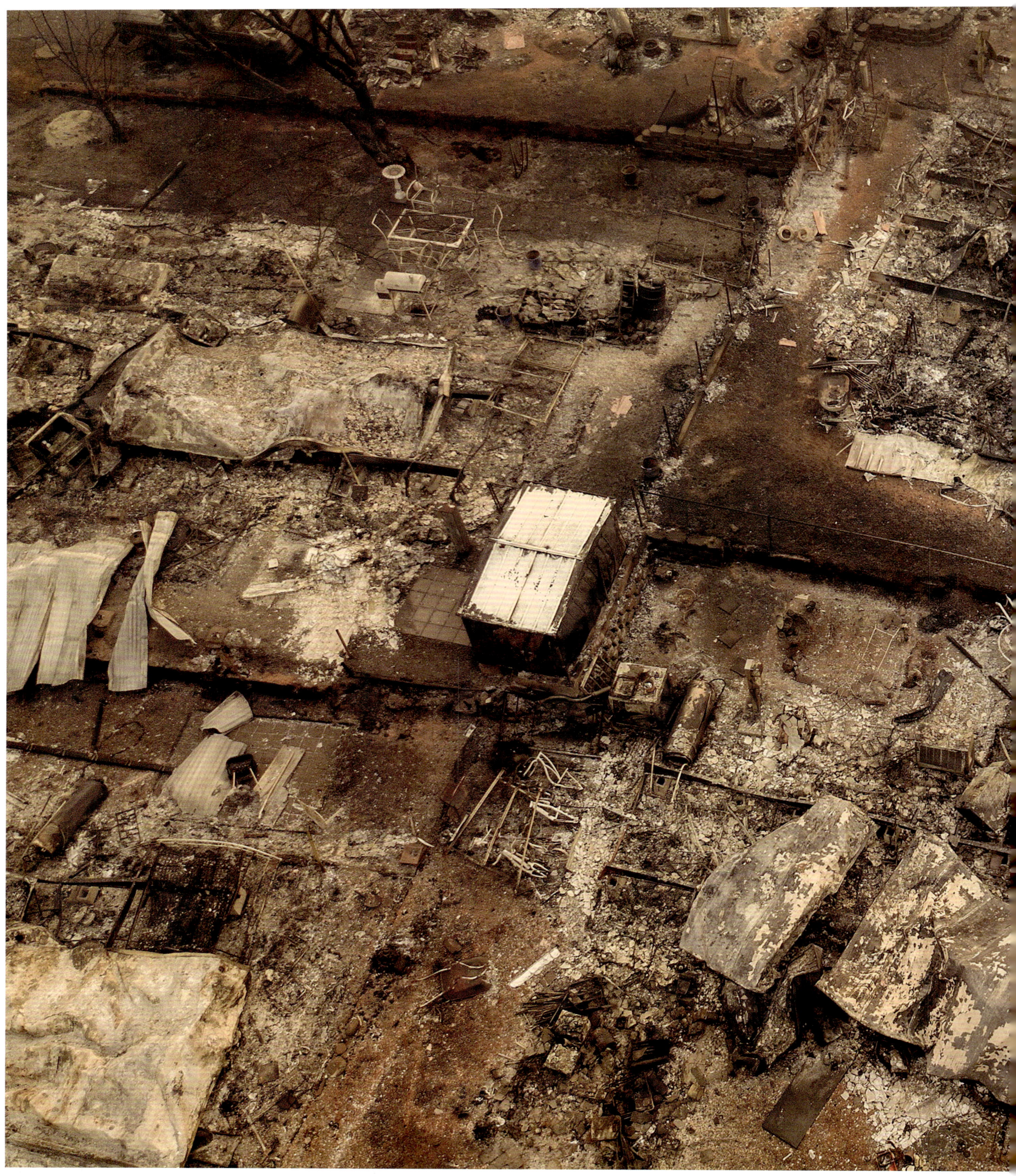

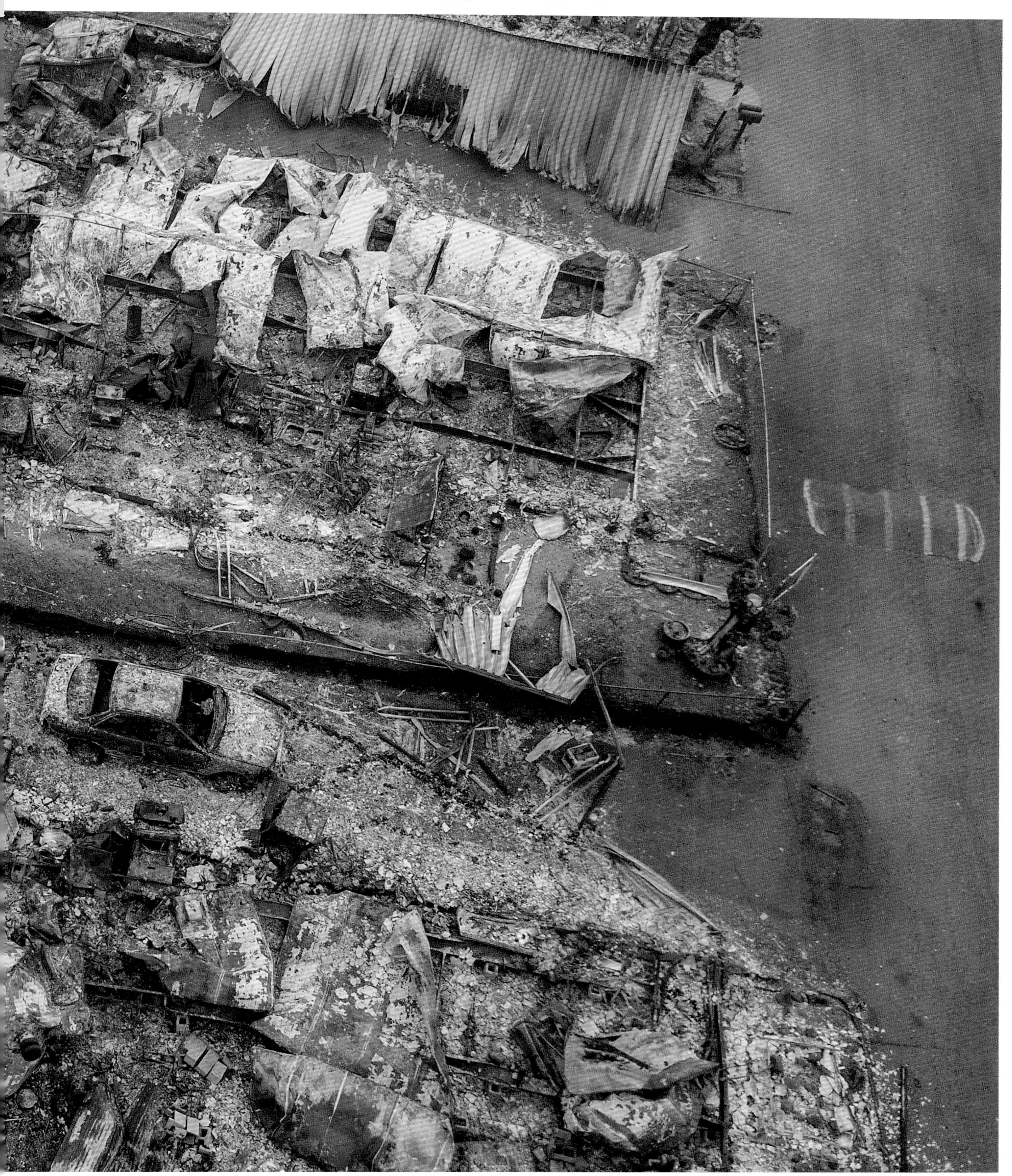

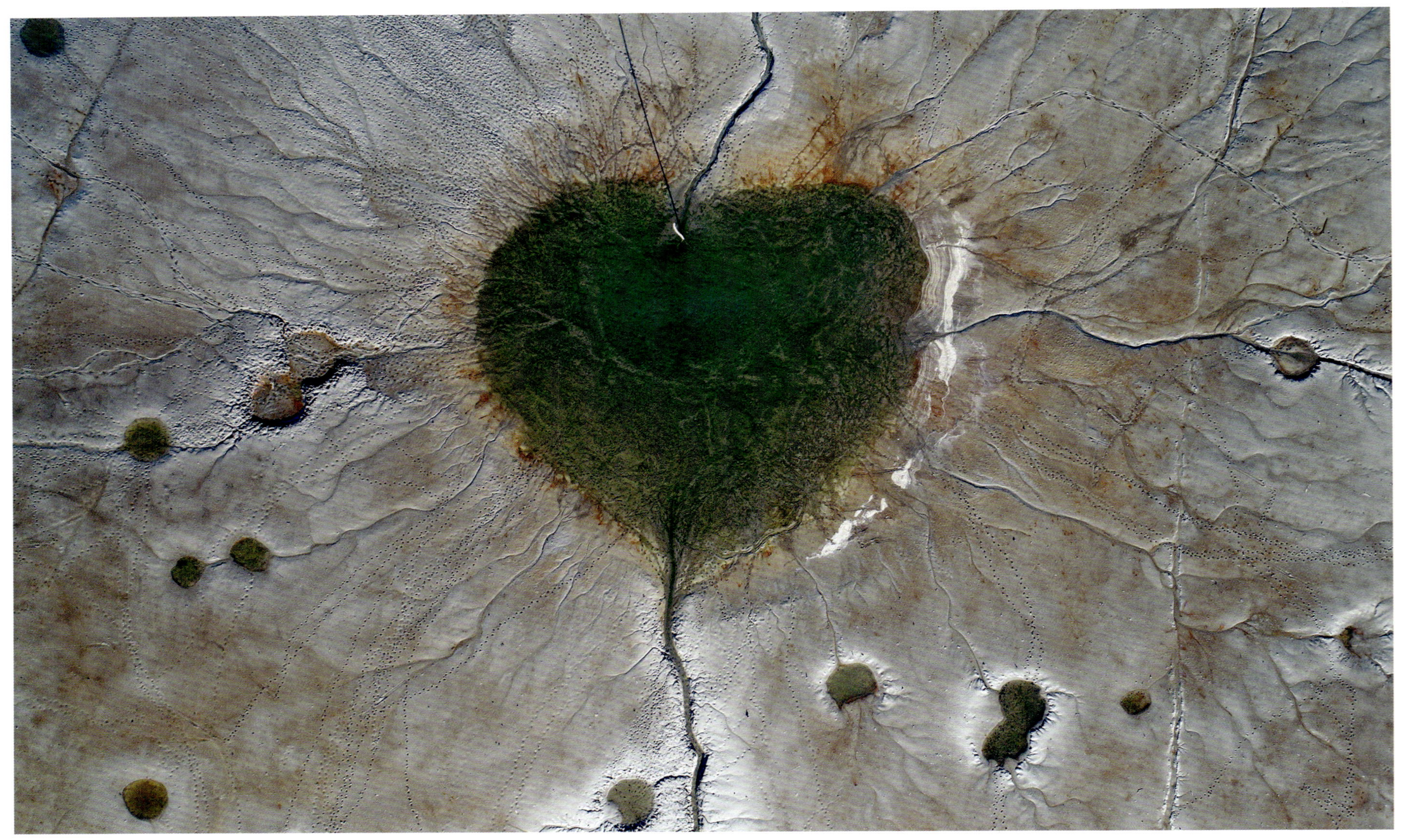

The popularity of drone photography among professionals and enthusiasts has given rise to platforms such as Dronestagram and competitions including the Drone Awards, organized by the Art Photo Travel Association. In July 2018, the organization announced the winners and runners-up of its first contest, in six categories: abstract, nature, people, urban, sport and wildlife. The competition, which is open to everyone and free to enter, received 4,400 entries from more than 100 countries, underlining the popularity and global reach of drone photography. Entrants could submit images taken anywhere, at any time, as long as the photographs were shot from the air. The work of nature photographer Milan Radisics, whose image (pictured above) was shortlisted in the competition, is an example of how photographers are creating aerial images of the natural world that are at once beautiful and have the potential to tell us more about the changing face of our planet. Recently, Radisics, who has had images published in the Hungarian edition of *National Geographic*, has been using an aerial perspective to show how water shapes our planet in a bid to convey just how precious a resource it is.

Milan Radisics
Heart in lakebed, Hács, Hungary, 2018.

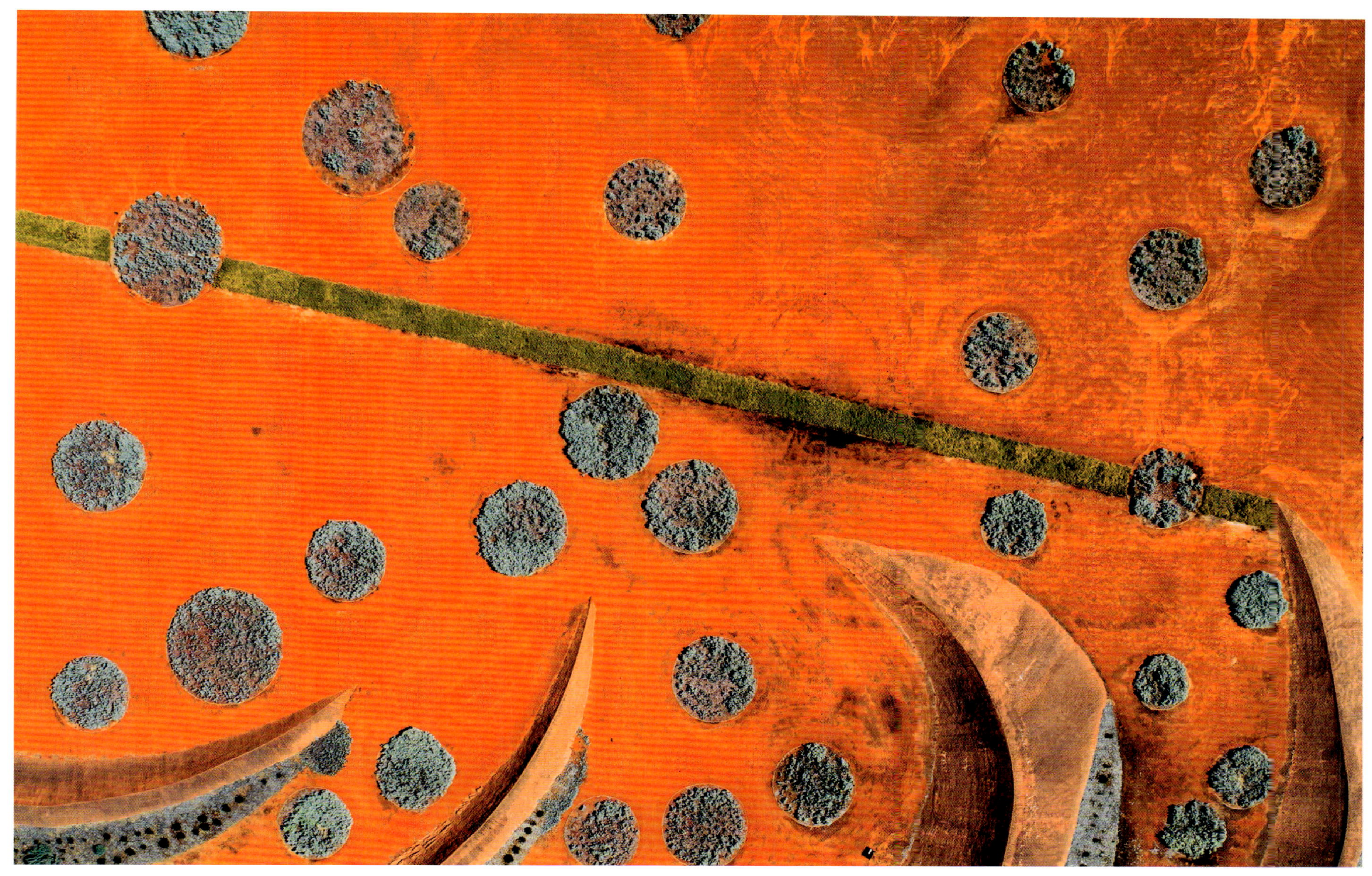

Peter Virag
Red Sand Garden at the Royal Botanic Gardens Victoria (Cranbourne site), Australia, 2018.

There is no doubt that the enormous technological strides in drone photography in recent years have allowed humans to view and record the Earth in new ways and with ever-improving accuracy and detail. Drone cameras have opened up aerial photography by making it available to anyone and, consequently, access to such views is no longer the sole preserve of professional photographers. Numerous self-taught photographers have seized the opportunity to take incredible images from the air, some of which are reminiscent of those by the giants of aerial photography. Peter Virag is one such photographer who has mastered the art of combining vivid colours and abstract forms in dazzling ways. Virag, who is originally from Hungary but has been living in Melbourne since 2007, took this shot of the Red Sand Garden at the Royal Botanic Gardens in Cranbourne using a DJI Phantom 4 Pro drone at an altitude of 120 metres. Areas of grey foliage are dotted across the expanse of red sand, creating an aerial image that could be mistaken for a micrograph.

Rodrigo Kugnharski is typical of a new breed of creative professionals who are using drone photography to complement their day job. The designer and art director, who has made aerial views over the city and river port of Tefé in Brazil and Cascais in Portugal, flew his drone over the Arc de Triomphe in Paris where he captured the surrounding roads that converge in the centre like the spokes of a wheel.

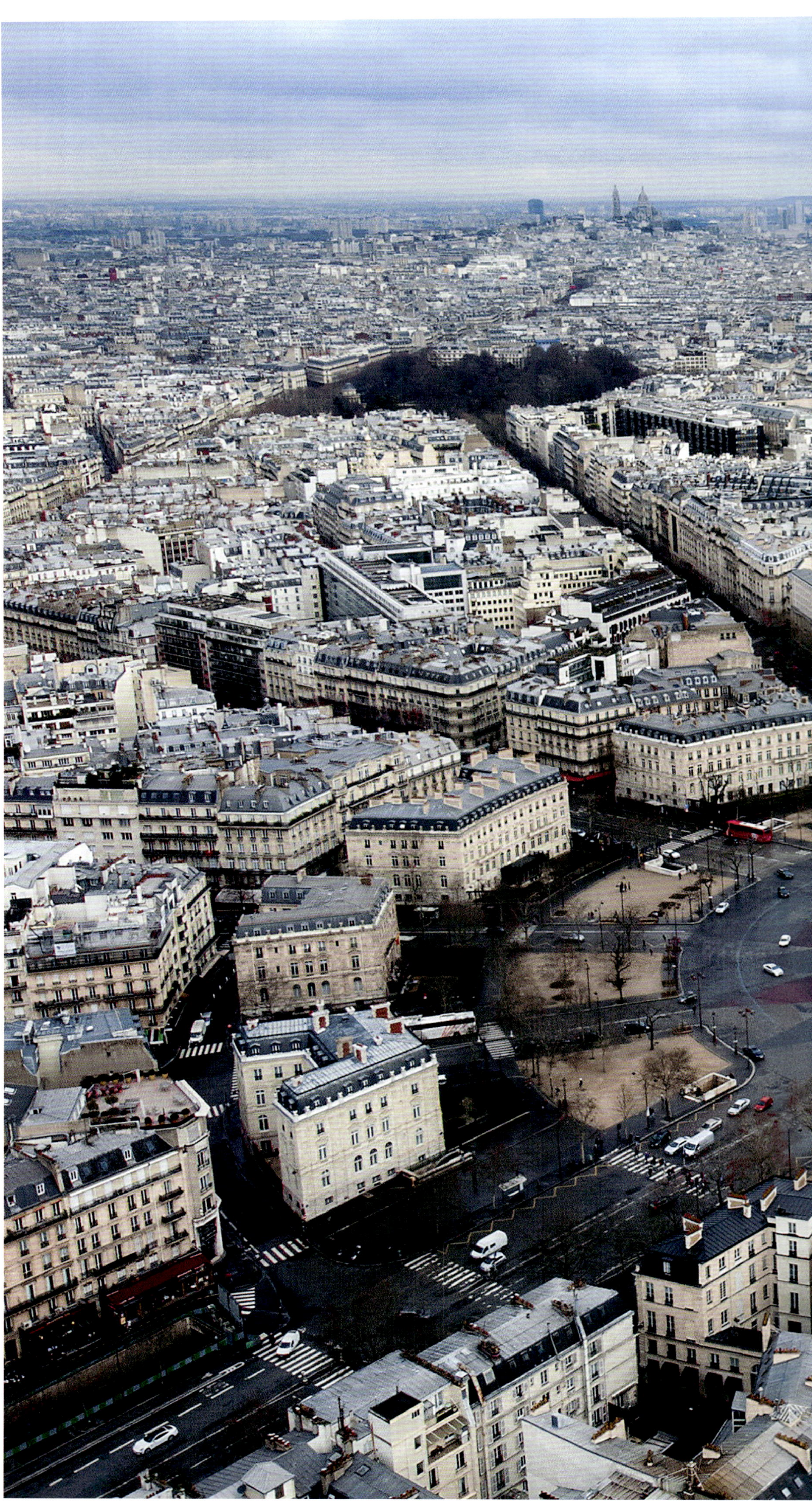

Rodrigo Kugnharski
Arc de Triomphe,
Paris, France, *c.* 2018.

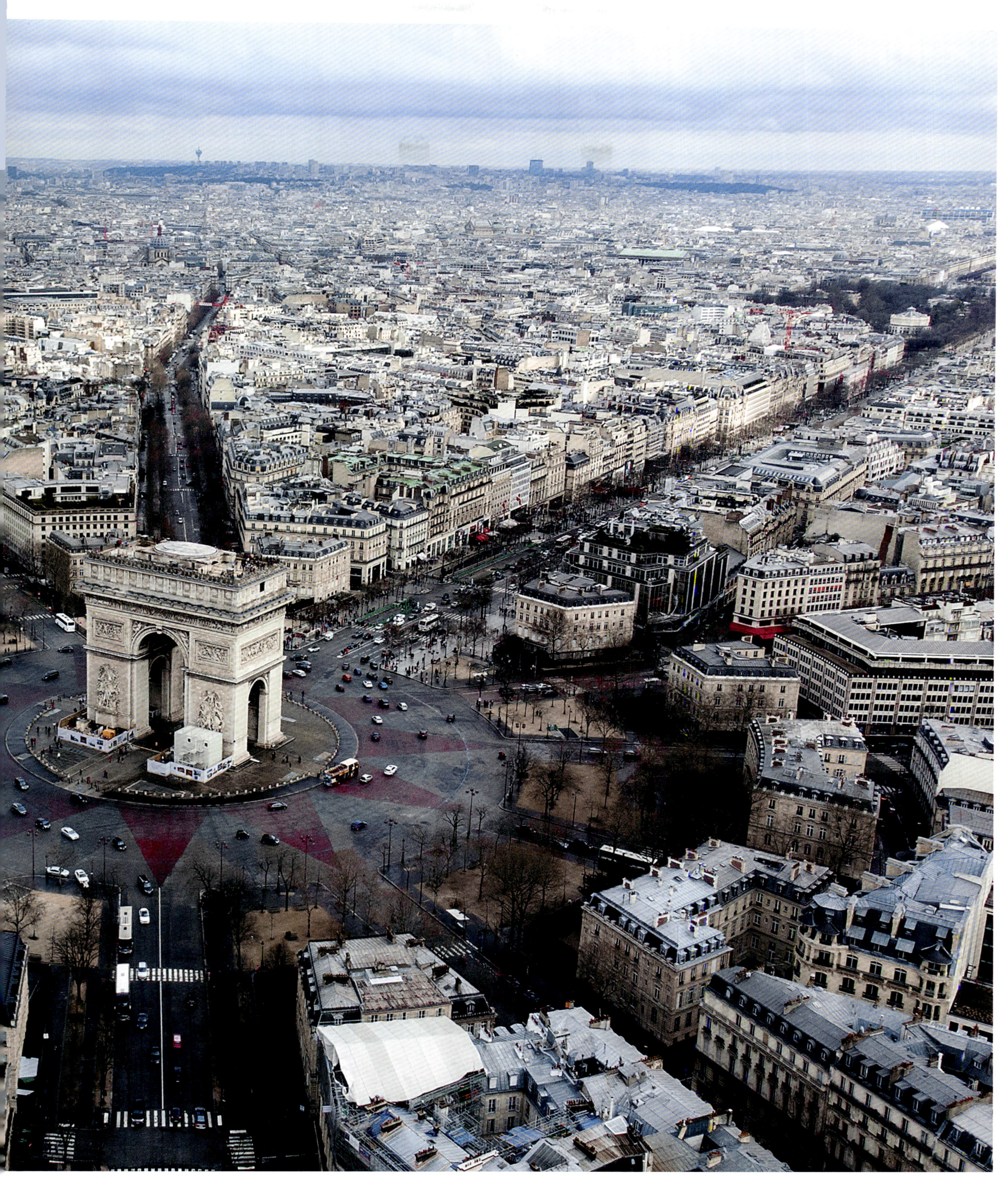

FURTHER READING

Above the World: Earth Through a Drone's Eye (teNeues, Kempen, 2016)

Martin Barber, *A History of Aerial Photography and Archaeology* (Historic England, Swindon, 2011)

Adam Begle, *The Great Nadar: The Man Behind the Camera* (Tim Duggan Books, London, 2017)

Yann Arthus-Bertrand, *The Earth from the Air* (Thames & Hudson, London, 2017)

Margaret Bourke-White, *Portrait of Myself* (Franklin Classics Trade Press, Emeryville, CA, 2018)

Marilyn Bridges, *Markings: Aerial Views of Sacred Landscapes* (Aperture, New York, 1996)

Piet Chielens and Birger Stichelbaut, *The Great War Seen from the Air: In Flanders Fields, 1914–1918* (Yale University Press, New Haven, CT, 2014)

Noam Chomsky, *Vietnam Inc: Philip Jones Griffiths* (Phaidon Press, London, 2006)

Denis Cosgrove and William L. Fox, *Photography and Flight* (Reaktion, London, 2010)

Julian Cox (ed.), *David Maisel: Black Maps: American Landscape and the Apocalyptic Sublime* (Steidl, Göttingen, 2013)

James Crawford, Katy Whitaker and Allan Williams, *Aerofilms: A History of Britain From Above* (Historic England, Swindon, 2014)

Nicoló Degiorgis and Audrey Solomon (eds), *The Pigeon Photographer* (Rohof, Bolzano, 2019)

Bernhard Edmaier, *Earthsong* (Phaidon Press, London, 2008)

William A. Ewing (ed.) *Edward Burtynsky: Essential Elements* (Thames & Hudson, London, 2016)

Terence J. Finnegan, *Shooting the Front* (Spellmount Ltd, Staplehurst, Kent, 2014)

Benjamin Grant, *Overview: A New Perspective of Earth* (Preface Publishing, London, 2016)

Tom Hegen, *Habitat* (Kerber Verlag, Bielefeld, 2019)

Alex Maclean, *Over: The American Landscape at the Tipping Point* (Abrams, New York, 2008)

Manufactured Landscapes: The Photographs of Edward Burtynsky (Yale University Press, New Haven, CT, 2009)

Jeffrey Milstein, *LA NY: Aerial Photographs of Los Angeles and New York* (Thames & Hudson, London, 2017)

Christopher Phillips (ed.), *Olivo Barbieri: Site Specific* (Aperture, New York, 2013)

Jock Reynolds, *Emmet Gowin: Changing the Earth* (Yale University Press, New Haven, CT, 2002)

Sebastião Salgado, *Genesis* (Taschen, Cologne, 2013)

Hilar Stadler (ed.), *Eduard Spelterini and the Spectacle of Images* (University of Chicago Press, Chicago, 2010)

George Steinmetz, *African Air* (Abrams, New York, 2008)

___, *Desert Air* (Abrams, New York, 2012)

Charlotte Trümpler, *The Past from Above: Photographs by Georg Gerster* (Frances Lincoln, London, 2006)

Ruedi Weidmann, *Swissair: Aerial Photography* (Scheidegger und Spiess AG, Verlag, Zurich, 2014)

KEY:

a = above; **b** = below; **l** = left; **r** = right, **c** = centre

Cover: Photo © Edward Burtynsky, courtesy Flowers Gallery, London/Metivier Gallery, Toronto; **front jacket l:** © Jean Gaumy/Magnum Photos; **front jacket c:** © Georg Gerster/Panos Pictures; **front jacket tr, br:** Margaret Bourke-White/The LIFE Picture Collection/Getty Images; **back jacket l:** © Jeffrey Milstein; **back jacket c:** Universal History Archive/UIG/akg-images; **back jacket r:** WENN UK/Alamy; **5:** Margaret Bourke-White/The LIFE Picture Collection/Getty Images; **6:** © Eamonn McCabe; **10:** SSPL/Getty Images; **11a:** Nadar/Hulton Archive/Getty Images; **11bl:** Courtesy National Gallery of Art, Washington, D.C. Rosenwald Collection (1954.12.22); **11br:** Courtesy The Metropolitan Museum of Art, New York. Gilman Collection, Museum Purchase, 2005 (2005.100.313); **12:** Courtesy The Metropolitan Museum of Art, New York. Gilman Collection, Purchase, Ann Tenenbaum and Thomas H. Lee Gift, 2005 (2005.100.87); **13a, 13bl, 13br:** © Historic England Archive; **14, 15a, 15b:** Collection Espace photographique Arthur Batut/Archives départementales du Tarn; **16:** E. Neurdein, Library of Congress, Washington, D.C.; **17, 18–19:** Geo. R. Lawrence Co., Library of Congress, Washington, D.C.; **20:** © Historic England Archive; **21a:** Rorhof, Stadarchiv Kronberg, Deutsches Technikmuseum, Berlin; **21b:** Universal History Archive/UIG/akg-images; **22–3:** Rorhof, Stadarchiv Kronberg, Deutsches Technikmuseum, Berlin; **24, 25, 26–7:** Helvetic Archives/Swiss National Library, Bern; **28l, 28r:** Mirrorpix; **29:** Colin Waters/Alamy; **30:** adoc-photos/Corbis/Getty Images; **31:** N.E. Brown; **32a, 32b, 33, 34–5:** Wellcome Collection. Photo Wellcome Images; **36:** Photo 12/Alamy; **37:** Military History Collection/Alamy; **38:** © Imperial War Museum, London; **39:** Central News Photo Service, Library of Congress, Washington, D.C.; **40–41:** © SZ Photo/Scherl/Bridgeman Images; **42:** Library of Congress, Washington, D.C./Science Photo Library; **43a:** Shotshop GmbH/Alamy; **43b:** Chronicle/Alamy; **44, 45a:** from an untitled album of World War I photographs, 1918/19. All photographs taken by the Photographic Section, U.S. Air Service, American Expeditionary Forces (AEF), 1918/19. Album assembled by Major Edward J. Steichen, A.S.A. in 1919. Art Institute of Chicago. Gift of William Kistler (1977.678-760) **45b** U.S. National Archives, Library of Congress, Washington, D.C.; **46, 47, 48–9:** © Richard and John Buckham; **50:** Smith Collection/Gado/Getty Images; **51:** Photo 12/Alamy; **52:** © Historic England Archive, Aerofilms Collection; **53:** Library of Congress, Washington, D.C.; **54:** Bettmann/Getty Images; **55:** ETH-Bibliothek Zürich, Bildarchiv/Stiftung Luftbild Schweiz/Photo Walter Mittelholzer (LBS_MH02-08-0289); **56–7:** ETH-Bibliothek Zürich, Bildarchiv/Stiftung Luftbild Schweiz/Photo Walter Mittelholzer (LBS_MH02-08-0082); **58:** Heritage Image Partnership Ltd/Alamy; **59:** Photo 12/Alamy; **60l:** Bettmann/Getty Images; **60–61:** TopFoto; **62:** Photo Edgar Orr; **63a:** Prisma by Dukas Presseagentur GmbH/Alamy; **63b:** Nigel J. Clarke/Alamy; **64:** De Agostini Picture Library/Getty Images; **65:** Military History Collection/Alamy; **66, 67:** © Imperial War Museum, London; **68, 69:** Margaret Bourke-White/The LIFE Picture Collection/Getty Images; **70:** U.S. Air Force; **71:** U.S. National Archives; **72, 73:** © Historic Environment Scotland; **74–5:** Keystone-France/Gamma-Rapho/Getty Images; **76:** W. Eugene Smith/The LIFE Picture Collection/Getty Images; **77:** William Vandivert/The LIFE Picture Collection/Getty Images; **78:** Fritz Goro/The LIFE Picture Collection/Getty Images; **79:** Prisma by Dukas Presseagentur GmbH/Alamy; **80l:** U.S. Army, Library of Congress, Washington, D.C.; **80–81:** John van Hasselt/Sygma/Getty Images; **82–3:** Bettmann/Getty Images; **84:** Wallace Kirkland/The LIFE Picture Collection/Getty Images; **85:** U.S. Air Force, Library of Congress, Washington, D.C.; **86, 87:** © Historic England Archive, Aerofilms Collection; **88, 89:** New York State Archives; **90–91:** Denver Post/Getty Images; **92:** © Estate of William A. Garnett. Photo The J. Paul Getty Museum, Los Angeles (2000.32.29); **93:** © Estate of William A. Garnett. Photo The J. Paul Getty Museum, Los Angeles (2000.32.22); **94:** © Estate of William A. Garnett. Photo The J. Paul Getty Museum, Los Angeles (2000.32.21); **95:** © Estate of William A. Garnett. Photo The J. Paul Getty Museum, Los Angeles (2000.32.33); **96:** © Historic Environment Scotland; **97:** Hulton Archive/Getty Images; **98–9, 100, 101, 102–3:** Margaret Bourke-White/The LIFE Picture Collection/Getty Images; **104:** Bettmann/Getty Images; **105:** Hulton-Deutsch Collection/Corbis/Getty Images; **106:** Hulton Archive/Getty Images; **107:** Bettmann/Getty Images; **108, 109, 110, 111, 112–13, 114:** © Georg Gerster/Panos Pictures; **115:** NASA; **116:** Mario de Biasi, Sergio Del Grande/Mondadori Portfolio/Getty Images; **117:** © Philip Jones Griffiths/Magnum Photos; **118:** © Vintage Aerial; **119:** Barry Z. Levine/Getty Images; **120, 121:** © René Burri/Magnum Photos; **122:** © Jean Gaumy/Magnum Photos; **123:** © Marilyn Bridges, 1979; **124:** Leo Mason/Popperfoto/Getty Images; **125:** Baron Wolman/Getty Images; **126:** Steven L. Raymer/National Geographic/Getty Images **127:** Corbis/Getty Images; **128–9:** Bettmann/Getty Images; **130–3:l** © Thomas Hoepker/Magnum Photos; **132, 133:** © Bruno Barbey/Magnum Photos; **134–5:** © David Hurn/Magnum Photos; **136, 137, 138–9:** © Yann Arthus-Bertrand; **140:** © Emmet and Edith Gowin, courtesy Pace/MacGill Gallery, New York; **141:** © Peter Marlow/Magnum Photos; **142, 143, 144, 145:** © Bernard Edmaier; **146–7:** NASA Earth Observatory image created by Jesse Allen, using EO-1 ALI data provided courtesy of the NASA EO-1 team and the United States Geological Survey; **148:** USGS Landsat 7 Team, at the EROS Data Center; **149:** Greg Semendinger/NYPD/REX/Shutterstock; **150–51:** Pool photo courtesy of NYC Office of Emergency Management/Getty Images; **152:** © Seamus Murphy/Panos Pictures; **153:** © Olivo Barbieri, Site Specific (ROMA 04). Courtesy Yancey Richardson Gallery, New York; **154–5:** © Trent Parke/Magnum Photos; **156, 157, 158, 159:** Photo © Edward Burtynsky, courtesy Flowers Gallery, London/Metivier Gallery, Toronto **160, 161, 162–3:** © George Steinmetz; **164:** © Paolo Pellegrin/Magnum Photos; **165:** Photo Flight Engineer Jeff Williams from the International Space Station (ISS) Expedition 13/Image Science & Analysis Group, Johnson Space Center/NASA; **166:** © David Maisel/INSTITUTE; **167:** © Ferdinando Scianna/Magnum Photos; **168, 169:** © Kacper Kowalski/Panos Pictures; **170:** National Park Service; **171, 172, 173:** © Jananne Al-Ani. Production still from the film *Shadow Sites II*, 2011. Courtesy the Artist and Abraaj Capital Art Prize. Photography Adrian Warren; **174:** WENN UK/Alamy; **175, 176–7:** Newscon/Alamy; **178:** Leo Ramirez/AFP/Getty Images; **179, 180, 181:** © Mishka Henner; **182, 183a, 183b:** © Public Lab; **184, 185, 186–7:** © Sebastião Salgado/*nb pictures; **188, 189, 190–91:** © Alex S. MacLean; **192:** © Tomas van Houtryve/VII/Redux/eyevine; **193, 194, 195:** © Giles Price/INSTITUTE; **196, 197:** © Rasmus Degnbol/Redux/eyevine **198, 199:** © Tommy Clarke; **200–201, 201r:** © Jon Bowles Photography (www.jonbowlesphotography.co.uk); **202, 203, 204–5:** © Daily Overview; **206–7:** Johnny Miller/Unequal Scenes; **208:** STR/AFP/Getty Images; **209:** Xinhua/Liu Chaofu/Sipa USA/PA Images; **210, 211, 212, 213:** © Mike and J.P. Andrews/Abstract Aerial Art Ltd; **214:** © Bernie Ng (@itsbernie81); **215:** Sergei Gapon/AFP/Getty Images; **216–17:** Ahmed Mohamed Al Toqi/Barcroft Media/Getty Images; **218, 219:** © Luca Locatelli/INSTITUTE; **220–21, 222, 223:** © Jeffrey Milstein; **224–5:** Kevin Frayer/Getty Images; **226:** Nicolas Economou/NurPhoto/Getty Images; **227** Asmar Al Bushy/Anadolu Agency/Getty Images **228, 229a, 229b:** © David Gray/Reuters; **230–31:** © Markel Redondo/Panos Pictures; **232–3, 234–5:** DigitalGlobe/ScapeWare3d/Getty Images; **236, 237:** DigitalGlobe/Getty Images; **238, 239:** © Tom Hegen; **240** George Rose/Getty Images; **241, 242–3:** Josh Edelson/AFP/Getty Images; **244:** © Milan Radisics; **245:** © Peter Virag; **246–7:** © Rodrigo Kugnharski on Unsplash.

INDEX

Page numbers in *italics* indicate illustrations

INDEX

O

P

Q

R

S

T

Eamonn McCabe is an award-winning photographer, picture editor and TV presenter whose career has spanned many forms of photography.

While working for *The Observer* in the 1970s and '80s he won Sports Photographer of the Year four times and in 1985 was named News Photographer of the Year for his his documentation of the Heysel Stadium disaster in Brussels. In the late 1980s he joined *The Guardian* as picture editor, where he won Picture Editor of the Year a record six times. McCabe now works as a freelance photographer, making portraits of artists, writers, poets and musicians for *The Guardian* as well as other newspapers and magazines.

McCabe's publications include *The Making of Great Photographs* (David & Charles, New York, 2005), *Artists and their Studios* (Angela Patchell Books, Hove, 2008) and *DECADE* (Phaidon, London, 2010). He has exhibited widely in Britain and has several pieces of work in The National Portrait Gallery collection, London. In 2017 he presented BBC4's *Britain in Focus: A Photographic History*.

Gemma Padley is a writer and editor on photography. Her writing has been published by *Foam*, *Photomonitor*, *AnOther*, *The Telegraph*, *Elephant*, *British Journal of Photography*, *RPS Journal* and *1000 Words* magazine.

I would like to give great thanks for all their help and advice to Ian Carter and Geoffrey Spender, photographic curators at the Imperial War Museum, London.

—*Eamonn McCabe*

A huge thank you to Laurence King, especially to John Parton and Blanche Craig, thank you to Eamonn McCabe, and to Tom and my family for their unwavering support.

—*Gemma Padley*